Herausforderungen an das Management

Schriftenreihe der
Graduate School of Business Administration
Zürich

Herausgegeben von

Prof. Dr. Ralph Berndt, Tübingen
(Geschäftsführender Herausgeber)
Prof. Dr. Salvatore Belardo, New York
Prof. Dr. Udo Koppelmann, Köln
Prof. Dr. Reinhart Schmidt, Halle-Wittenberg
Dr. Albert Stähli, Zürich
Prof. Dr. Godwin Wong, Berkeley

Band 5:
Unternehmen im Wandel –
Change Management

Jubiläumsausgabe zum 30jährigen Bestehen der Oekreal

Springer

Berlin
Heidelberg
New York
Barcelona
Budapest
Hongkong
London
Mailand
Paris
Santa Clara
Singapur
Tokio

Ralph Berndt (Hrsg.)

Unternehmen im Wandel – Change Management

Mit 109 Abbildungen
und 11 Tabellen

Springer

Professor Dr. Ralph Berndt
c/o
Graduate School of Business
Administration Zürich
Bahnhofstraße/Schützengasse 4
CH-8023 Zürich, Schweiz

ISBN 3-540-64072-X Springer-Verlag Berlin Heidelberg New York

Die Deutsche Bibliothek - CIP-Einheitsaufnahme
Unternehmen im Wandel - Change Management: mit 11 Tabellen /
Ralph Berndt (Hrsg.). -
Berlin; Heidelberg; New York; Barcelona; Budapest; Hongkong,
London; Mailand; Paris; Santa Clara; Singapur; Tokio : Springer, 1998
(Herausforderungen an das Management; Band 5)
ISBN 3-540-64072-X
NE: Berndt, Ralph [Hrsg.]; GT

Die Wiedergabe von Gebrauchsnamen, Handelsnamen, Warenbezeichnungen usw. in
diesem Werk berechtigt auch ohne besondere Kennzeichnung nicht zu der Annahme,
daß solche Namen im Sinne der Warenzeichen- und Markenschutz-Gesetzgebung als
frei zu betrachten wären und daher von jedermann benutzt werden dürften.

Einbandgestaltung: Erich Kirchner, Heidelberg
SPIN 10656390   43/2202-5 4 3 2 1 0 - Gedruckt auf säurefreiem Papier

Geleitwort

In Chinese, the word ji when combined with hui means opportunity and when combined with wei means crisis. Similarly the English word change evokes the notion of something beneficial as well as something humans try to resist. Ben Okri, an award winning Nigerian poet describes both feelings in his poem entitled „Dancing with Change".

„Change is good, but no change is better.
It rang the great hall as it has resounded silently throughout the ages.
It rang past the faces of stern masters and poets and lords of learning asleep in their hidden academies."

„But the river flows, and so must we,
Change is the happy god that Heraclitus saw in the golden river
Spread illumination through the darkening world
Spread illumination through the darkening world
No change is good
But dancing with change is better."

Change is occurring at an increasing rate, and in proportion to the increase in knowledge available. Barbara Sizemore, a professor at the University of Pittsburgh and a researcher at the Digital Corporation, estimates that knowledge has been increasing at a rate such that by the year 2020, knowledge will double every 73 days. Information technology and information processing capabilities are at the heart of this phenomenon. To get a sense of the power of today's computers, just look at your thumbnail. A current state of the art silicon chip that size contains the complexity of a complete road map of the United States with every Interstate, street, and alley in every city. Gordon Moore co-founder of Intel proposed Moore's law which states that the raw power of silicon technology doubles every eighteen months. Coupled with Metcalfe's law which states that the power of the computer network increases by the square of the number of users, we can get some idea as to what is causing this increase in knowledge and the driving force behind the unbridled change we are experiencing. Peter Drucker noted that the Industrial Revolution increased productivity 50 fold. In the last 25 years since the microprocessor was invented, computer power has increased 1000 fold. This is equivalent to an industrials revolution every year. Terry Neill, the Worldwide Managing Partner of Andersen Consulting's Change Management Practice, describes change as a permanent condition and concludes that managers must settle in for the „long haul." He concludes that in the past, Change Management was a novel service offered by consultants, but today it has become a „management discipline with legs."

This book presents a number of papers that discuss the inevitability of change, and the ways various functional strategies have been developed to help better manage what has become the permanent condition.

Prof. Dr. Don Bourque
Dean
State University of New York
at Albany

Editorial

Der jetzt vorliegende Sammelband „**Unternehmen im Wandel - Change Management**" ist der fünfte Band der Schriftenreihe der Graduate School of Business Administration Zürich. Gegenstand des ersten Teils ist das Konzept des Change Management, das in vier Beiträgen vorgestellt wird. Die typische heutige Wettbewerbssituation ist Gegenstand des Beitrages von *Hans H. Hinterhuber* und *Enrico Valdani* (Innsbruck und Mailand); angemessene Verhaltensstrategien werden herausgearbeitet. *Jan S. Krulis-Randa* und *Rudolf Ergenziger* (Zürich) machen deutlich, daß eine marktliche Wertschöpfung im Vergleich zu einem Kostenabbau in operativen Prozessen vorzuziehen ist. Veränderungsprozesse in dem sehr interessanten Konzept einer lernenden Organisation werden von *Salvatore Balardo* und *Jackov Crukovic* (Albany) untersucht. *Douglas K. Macbeth* und seine Mitarbeiter (Glasgow) erarbeiten ein Konzept zur partnerschaftlichen Zusammenarbeit, welches den Bedingungen des Wandels entspricht.

Die Bedeutung des Change Management im Bereich der **Management Education** wird im zweiten Teil untersucht. In welcher Weise auf die heutigen Bedingungen im Bereich der Management-Weiterbildung zu reagieren ist, wird von *Albert Stähli* (Zürich) herausgearbeitet; die besondere Bedeutung von MBA-Programmen für Führungskräfte, die im Rahmen internationaler Kooperationen realisiert werden, wird offensichtlich. *Daniel J. McCarthy* und *Sheila M. Puffer* (Boston) legen dar, welche Weiterbildungsprogramme für Führungskräfte in Rußland besonders geeignet sind.

Gegenstand des dritten Teils ist das Change Management im Bereich der **Corporate Strategy**. *Reinhart Schmidt* (Halle) analysiert, wie sich die Unternehmensziele im Zeitablauf gewandelt haben. Der Beitrag von *Jean Claude Som* (Genf) hat virtuelle Unternehmen zum Gegenstand; insbes. Beschaffungsstrategien werden erörtert. Zwei Beispiele für erfolgreiche Unternehmensstrategien folgen. *Godwin Wong* und *Peter Oswald* (San Franzisko/Hongkong) stellen eine erfolgreiche Bearbeitung des chinesischen Marktes durch ein deutsches Unternehmen dar; *Welch* (Boston) beschreibt eine gewagte, aber erfolgreiche Unternehmens-Akquisition in der US-Rüstungsindustrie.

Das Change Management im Bereich des **Marketing** wird im vierten Teil intensiv untersucht; in fünf Beiträgen wird insbes. die Führung von Markenartikeln in der jetzigen Zeit betrachtet. *Ralph Berndt* (Tübingen) zeigt die typischen Trends beim Konsumentenverhalten, beim Handel und bei den Markenartikelproduzenten auf und arbeitet angemessene einzelwirtschaftliche sowie kooperative Systeme des Markenmanagement heraus. *Matthias Sander* (Tübingen) erörtert die Konsequenzen für die Führung von Markenartikeln unter den heutigen Kommunikationsbedingungen. Gegenstand des Beitrages von *Orville C. Walker* und *Linda M. Keefe* (Minnesota) ist der Bezug zwischen Corporate Identity und denkbaren

Markenstrategien. *Claudia Fantapié Altobelli* und *Stefan Hoffmann* (Hamburg) legen dar, welche innovativen Marketing-Konzepte im interaktiven Zeitalter möglich sind. *Udo Koppelmann* (Köln) schließlich setzt sich mit dem strategischen Beschaffungsmarketing auseinander; ein angemessenes Konzept wird erarbeitet.

Die Schnittstelle Change Management und **Operations Management** ist Gegenstand des fünften Teils. In welcher Weise Effektivität und Effizienz von Geschäftsprozessen gesteigert werden können, wird von *Claus W. Gerberich* (Worms) untersucht; die besondere Bedeutung cross-funktionaler Teams, die Nachteile traditioneller funktionaler und hierarchisch geprägter Organisationsstrukturen unter heutigen Bedingungen werden offensichtlich.

Welche Bedeutung das Change Management im Bereich des **Finance Management hat,** wird im sechsten Teil hinterfragt. *Manfred Steiner* und *Hermann-Josef Tebroke* (Augsburg) setzten sich mit der besonderen Relevanz des Shareholder-Value-Konzeptes für das Management von Unternehmen in einem dynamischen Umfeld auseinander. *Jens Jokisch* (Braunschweig) behandelt das Problem des Management von Zinsrisiken; die Eignung originärer und derivativer Finanzinnovationen wird herausgearbeitet.

Schwerpunkt des siebten Teils sind die **Management Information Systems**. *Urs E. Gattiker* (Aarhus) arbeitet die relevanten Trends im Kommunikations- und Informationsbereich heraus; angemessene Unternehmensstrategien als Antwort auf diese Trends werden dargestellt. *William K. Holstein* (Albany) setzt sich kritisch mit Entscheidungs-Unterstützungs-Systemen auseinander, deren Eignung für das Strategische Management unter heutigen Bedingungen wird erörtert.

Die Implikationen des Change Management für das **Human Resources Management** werden im achten Teil herausgearbeitet. Für verschiedene Beispiele des organisatorischen Wandels werden von *Randall S. Schuler* und *Susan E. Jackson* (New York) die Konsequenzen im Bereich des Human Resource Management aufgezeigt.

Die Gliederung des Sammelbandes entspricht im wesentlichen dem Aufbau des **MBA-Studiums an der Graduate School of Business Administration** Zürich, welches in den sechs Blöcken

- Corporate Strategy,
- Marketing Management,
- Operations Management,
- Finance Management,
- Controlling/Management Informations Systems,
- Human Resources Management

durchlaufen wird. Jeder Unterrichtsblock wird zweisprachig durchgeführt und von einem deutsch- und einem englischsprachigen Professor geleitet; dies drückt sich auch in der Zweisprachigkeit des vorliegenden Sammelbandes aus.

Viele Autoren des Sammelbandes sind Professoren, die an der GSBA Zürich lehren; sie stammen aus anerkannten bundesdeutschen und amerikanischen Universitäten und bürgen für die hohe Ausbildungsqualität der GSBA Zürich. Einige Autoren sind regelmäßige Hearing-Gäste der GSBA Zürich bzw. Absolventen des MBA-Studienganges an der GSBA Zürich. Wir würden uns im Namen aller Autoren sehr freuen, wenn auch dieser Sammelband eine gute Aufnahme und eine erfolgreiche Umsetzung in der Praxis fände.

Zürich, im März 1998   Die Herausgeber

Inhaltsverzeichnis

Erster Teil

Change Management

Hans H. Hinterhuber/Enrico Valdani

Die neuen Spielregeln des Wettbewerbs

- Von der Evolution zur Ko-Evolution... 3

Jan S. Krulis-Randa/Rudolf Ergenzinger

Strategic Change Management - Marktliche Wertschöpfung

als Gegensatz zum Kostenabbau in operativen Prozessen............................. 19

Salvatore Belardo/Jackov Crnkovic

Change and the Learning Organization 41

Douglas K. Macbeth/David Boddy/Beverly Wagner/
Marilyn Charles

Implementing Partnering Relationships: A Change Process Model 59

Zweiter Teil

Change Management und Management Education

Albert Stähli

Change Management in der Management Andragogik...................................... 77

Daniel J. McCarthy/Sheila M. Puffer

Changes Ahead for Russian Management Education

- Reflections From the American Experience 101

Dritter Teil

Change Management und Corporate Strategy

Reinhart Schmidt

Wandel von Unternehmensleitbild und Unternehmenszielen:

Eine Analyse anhand der Geschäftsberichte der größten Aktiengesell-

schaften aus vier europäischen Ländern 119

Jean Claude Som

The Key Role of Purchasing within

Virtualizing Organizations 139

Godwin Wong/Peter Oswald

Implementation of a Tactical Strategy in China

by a German Company 173

Jonathan B. Welch

Managing Change in the US Defense Industry

- The Case of Lockheed Martin's Acquisition of Loral 191

Vierter Teil

Change Management im Marketing

Ralph Berndt

Markenmanagement im Zeitalter von Konzentrationsprozessen und
Machtverschiebungen auf mehrstufigen Märkten 199

Matthias Sander

Markenführung unter geänderten Kommunikationsbedingungen 223

Orville C. Walker Jr./Linda M. Keefe

Corporate Identity and International Branding Strategies 239

Claudia Fantapié Altobelli/Stefan Hoffmann

Marketing im interaktiven Zeitalter 261

Udo Koppelmann

Einkauf im Wandel - von der Versorgungserfüllung zum
Strategischen Beschaffungsmarketing 277

Fünfter Teil

Change Management und Operations-Management

Claus W. Gerberich

Die Praxis der Steuerung cross-funktionaler Teams zur Steigerung
von Effektivität und Effizienz von Geschäftsprozessen 303

Sechster Teil

Change Management und Finance Management

Manfred Steiner/Hermann-Josef Tebroke

Shareholder-Value-Konzepte für das Management von

Unternehmen im dynamischen Umfeld 319

Jens Jokisch

Originäre und derivative Finanzinnovationen als Instrumente

zum Management von Zinsrisiken 333

Siebter Teil

Change Management und Management Information Systems

Urs E. Gattiker

Benchmarking, Innovation and Reengineering: Should we Pull

the Plug on the Internet or Make it Serve us Better? 351

William K. Holstein

Decision Support Systems for Strategic Management

- What Will DSS Systems Do to Help Senior Managers with

Strategic Management Tasks? 379

Achter Teil

Change Management und Human Resources Management

Randall S. Schuler/Susan E. Jackson

Managing Organizational Changes and the Role of
Human Resource Management 395

Sachverzeichnis 419

Autorenverzeichnis

Prof. Dr. Salvatore Belardo

Professor of Management Science and Information Systems at the State University of New York at Albany; Präsident des Joint Committee of Management Education der GSBA, Zürich

Prof. Dr. Ralph Berndt

Inhaber des Lehrstuhls für Betriebswirtschaftslehre, insb. Absatzwirtschaft der Eberhard-Karls-Universität Tübingen; Mitglied des Stiftungsrates der GSBA Zürich

David Boddy

Reader in Organizational Behaviour at the University of Glasgow

Prof. Dr. Don Bourque

Dean, State University of New York at Albany

Marilyn Charles

Research Assistant at the University of Glasgow

Prof. Dr. Jackov Crnkovic

Professor at Saint Rose College at Albany, New York

Dr. Rudolf Ergenzinger

Oberassistent am betriebswirtschaftlichen Institut der Universität Zürich; Lehrbeauftragter der Universität Zürich

Prof. Dr. Claudia Fantapié Altobelli

Inhaberin des Lehrstuhls für Betriebswirtschaftslehre, insb. Marketing an der Universität der Bundeswehr Hamburg; Hearing-Gast bei der GSBA Zürich

Prof. Dr. Urs E. Gattiker

Director of the Centre for Technology and Innovation Management and holds the Obel Foundation Chair for Innovation and Technology Management (Entrepreneurship) in the Faculty of Engineering and Science at the University of Aalborg, Denmark and Research Professor at the Aarhus School of Business, Aarhus, Denmark; Hearing-Gast bei der GSBA Zürich

Prof. Dr. Claus W. Gerberich	Professor für Internationale Unternehmensführung und Controlling an der Hochschule Rheinland-Pfalz, Worms; Gerberich & Partner, Internationale Unternehmensberatung, Mannheim, Düsseldorf, Zürich, Wien; Hearing-Gast bei der GSBA Zürich
Prof. Dipl.-Ing. Hans H. Hinterhuber	Vorstand des Instituts für Unternehmensführung der Universität Innsbruck; Professor für Internationales Management an der Wirtschaftsuniversität Bocconi in Mailand; Mitglied des JCME der GSBA Zürich
Dipl.-Kfm. Stefan Hoffmann	Doktorand am Institut für Marketing der Universität der Bundeswehr Hamburg
Prof. Dr. William K. Holstein	Distinguished Service Professor at the State University of New York at Albany; Mitglied des JCME der GSBA Zürich
Prof. Dr. Susan E. Jackson	Professor at Stern School of Business, New York University
Prof. Dr. Jens Jokisch	Inhaber des Lehrstuhls für Finanzwirtschaft an der Technischen Universität Braunschweig
Linda M. Keefe	Vice President Strategic Marketing and Design, Yamamoto Moss, Mineapolis
Prof. Dr. Udo Koppelmann	Direktor des Seminars für Allgemeine Betriebswirtschaftslehre, Beschaffung und Produktpolitik der Universität zu Köln; Mitglied des Stifungsrates der GSBA Zürich
Prof. Dr. h.c. Jan S. Krulis-Randa	em. Ordinarius für Betriebswirtschaftslehre, insbes. Marketing und Personalwirtschaft; Präsident der Prüfungskommission und Mitglied des Advisory Board der GSBA Zürich

Prof. Dr. Douglas K. Macbeth	Professor of Management at the University of Glasgow Business School; Mitglied des JCME der GSBA Zürich
Prof. Dr. Daniel J. McCarthy	The Philip R. McDonald Professor of Business Administration at the Northeastern Univesity at Boston (Massachusetts); Mitglied des JCME der GSBA Zürich
Dipl.Ing. Peter Oswald	Managing Director of Brückner Far East Ltd. Honkong; Absolvent des MBA-Studienganges der GSBA Zürich
Prof. Dr. Sheily Puffer	Associate Professor of Human Resources and International Management at the Northeastern University, Boston (Massachusetts)
Privatdozent Dr. Matthias Sander	Privatdozent an der Wirtschaftswissenschaftlichen Fakultät der Eberhard-Karls-Universität Tübingen
Prof. Dr. Reinhart Schmidt	Inhaber des Lehrstuhls für Finanzwirtschaft und Bankbetriebslehre an der Universität Halle-Wittenberg; Präsident des Stiftungsrates der GSBA Zürich
Prof. Dr. Randell Schuler	Professor of Human Resources Management, Leonard Stern School of Business at New York; Mitglied des JCME der GSBA Zürich
Jean-Claude Som	Account Manager der DEC Digital Equipment Corporation, Genf
Dr. Albert Stähli	Dean der GSBA Zürich; Rektor der Oekreal Schools of Business, Zürich; Präsident des Instituts für Management-Andragoik, Zürich
Prof. Dr. Manfred Steiner	Inhaber des Lehrstuhls für Betriebswirtschaftslehre insb. Bank- und Finanzwirtschaft der Universität Augsburg; Mitglied des JCME der GSBA Zürich

Dr. Hermann-Josef Tebroke	Hochschulassistent am Lehrstuhl für Betriebswirtschaftslehre, insb. Bank- und Finanzwirtschaft der Universität Augsburg
Prof. Dr. Enrico Valdani	Professor für Marketing an der Wirtschaftsuniversität Bocconi in Mailand
Beverley Wagner	Research Assistant at the University of Glasgow
Prof. Dr. Orville C. Walker, Jr.	The James D. Watkins Professor of Marketing, University of Minnesota; Mitglied des JCME der GSBA Zürich
Prof. Dr. Jonathan B. Welch	Professor of Finance at Northeastern University, Boston; Mitglied des JCME der GSBA Zürich
Prof. Dr. Godwin Wong	Professor of Management Information at the University of California at Berkeley (CA); Mitglied des JCME der GSBA Zürich

Erster Teil

Change Management

Die neuen Spielregeln des Wettbewerbs
- Von der Evolution zur Ko-Evolution

Hans H. Hinterhuber
Enrico Valdani

Summary:

This paper addresses the issue of how to develop and implement strategies for firms which are in a hypercompetitive and turbulent environment. Referring to a military metaphor, hypercompetition in a turbulent environment is compared to a position war, with detrimental effects for all competitors. Incremental change does not work for breaking out from a position war and transforming it into a movement war. Leadership is needed. Leadership means discovering new opportunities and changing the rules of the game. Leadership, however, needs to be supplemented with a new approach which enables firms, operating in different industries, to share their core competencies and to form a co-evolving new system that learns its way into the future. The paper shows that co-evolution is a new way for both survival and value creation in a hypercompetitive and turbulent environment.

1. Einleitung

> Ahead of us are Darwinian shakeouts in every major market place with no consolation prizes for losing companies and nations
>
> Jack Welch

Gesundschrumpfen durch Konzentration auf die Kernkompetenzen und Outsourcing nicht-kompetitiver Tätigkeiten zeichnet keinen Unternehmer und keine Führungskraft auf Dauer aus. In der Industriegeschichte gibt es keine Beispiele für Unternehmungen, die durch Gesundschrumpfen groß geworden sind. Auch die evolutionäre Anpassung der Unternehmung an das sich wandelnde Umfeld reicht in turbulenten Zeiten nicht aus, um ihr Überleben und ihre Wertsteigerung zu gewährleisten. Je mehr wir uns vom Zeitalter der Maschine in das Informationszeitalter bewegen, desto fragwürdiger werden traditionelle Führungsansätze. Führungsansätze die im Zeitalter der Maschine ihre Berechtigung hatten, können

4

sich im Informationszeitalter als irrelevant erweisen (Hamel/Prahalad, 1996, S. 237). Die Hauptverantwortung der Führenden in turbulenten Zeiten besteht darin, die Führungskräfte und Mitarbeiter anzuregen, zu inspirieren, **neue Möglichkeiten** zu entdecken und umzusetzen, die Werte für die Kunden, aber auch für die anderen "Stakeholder" der Unternehmung - die Mitarbeiter, die Anteilseigner, die Gesellschaft, die Lieferanten und die Partner in strategischen Netzwerken - schaffen. Neue Möglichkeiten entstehen auf dreifache Weise:

(1) durch das "Erfinden" neuer Märkte,
(2) durch die Änderung der Spielregeln in bestehenden Märkten und im Umfeld der Unternehmung und
(3) durch die Änderung der Struktur der Branche (z.B. durch Akquisitionen und Fusionen).

Die turbulenten kompetitiven Bedingungen unserer Zeit rechtfertigen es, die Spielregeln des Wettbewerbs sorgfältig zu analysieren und nach neuen Führungsansätzen zu suchen.. Dies soll hier in drei Abschnitten geschehen. Erstens wird gezeigt, daß der Hyperwettbewerb in vielen Sektoren mit einem Stellungskrieg verglichen werden kann. Die Aufgabe der Führenden besteht darin, aus einem Stellungskrieg auszubrechen und einen Bewegungskrieg einzuleiten. Wie dies mit Hilfe von Leadership geschehen kann, wird im zweiten Abschnitt dargelegt. Im dritten Abschnitt wird die These entwickelt, daß in einem turbulenten Umfeld nur die Unternehmungen überleben und ihren Wert steigern, die:

(1) mit ihren Mitarbeitern eine gemeinsame Sicht der Zukunft aufbauen,
(2) das Beharrungsvermögen der Unternehmung schneller und wirksamer abbauen als dies die Konkurrenten zu tun in der Lage sind, und
(3) die Kernkompetenzen der Unternehmung mit denen erfolgreicher Unternehmungen in anderen Branchen zum Zwecke einer "symbiotischen Partnerschaft" bündeln.

Die Ko-Evolution ist eine indirekte Strategie (Hinterhuber 1990, S. 68), mit der Unternehmungen aus unterschiedlichen Branchen ihre Kernkompetenzen bündeln und damit gleichsam eine Art "Meta-System" aufbauen, das seinen eigenen Weg in die Zukunft findet. In diesem neuen, ko-evolvierenden System lernen die beteiligten Unternehmungen und verändern ihr Verhalten (Stacey, 1996, S. 335).

2. Führung in turbulenten Zeiten

> Ich habe nie Probleme, ich habe nur Möglichkeiten
>
> K. Fredheim

Die Globalisierung der Märkte, die neuen Informationstechnologien, die günstigen Transportmöglichkeiten und der Rückzug des Staates aus der Wirtschaft haben zu einem noch nie dagewesenen Wettbewerb geführt. In keinem Geschäftsfeld ist die Position des Marktführers gesichert; führende Konkurrenten werden von innovativen Unternehmungen aus den entferntesten Regionen der Welt angegriffen, etablierte Spielregeln des Wettbewerbs werden laufend verletzt oder umgangen, um bestehende Marktverhältnisse aufzubrechen und Marktgleichgewichte zum eigenen Vorteil zu verändern (Rühli 1996, S. 115).

Lester Thurow sieht insgesamt fünf systemformende Bewegungen, die wie "Tektonikplatten", den Bewegungen der Erdkruste gleich, auf einem imaginären Magma schwimmen. Sie driften auseinander, treiben aufeinander zu, überlagern sich, kollidieren und formen so eine neue weltwirtschaftliche Basis. Die fünf Tektonikplatten sind (Thurow 1996, S. 19ff.):

(1) das **"Ende des Kommunismus"** mit seinen Konsequenzen:
- Überflutung der Welt mit früher schlecht genutzten Energievorräten wie z.B. Erdöl und Erdgas, Aluminium, Nickel, Titan und dgl. mehr,
- "Billigangebote" an russischen Wissenschaftlern,
- Verlagerung von Investitionen in die Transformationsländer mit ihrem niedrigen Lohnniveau,
- Überschwemmung des Westens mit Agrarprodukten.

(2) **Wissen und Ausbildung als entscheidende Standortvorteile**:
- in der Vergangenheit richteten sich die Standorte nach den Rohstoffvorkommen, später nach der Verfügbarkeit von Kapital und Arbeit, heute ist die Ausbildung entscheidend;
- in einer globalisierten Wirtschaft läßt sich praktisch alles überall herstellen;
- der "Lohnbonus" für amerikanische und europäische Arbeitnehmer ist überholt und baut sich ab;
- das Lohnniveau für unqualifizierte Arbeit in den Industrieländern wird auf jenes der Entwicklungsländer zurücksinken.

(3) die **Bevölkerungsdynamik**:
- in 30 Jahren wird sich die Weltbevölkerung um 50%, von gegenwärtig 5,7 Milliarden auf 8,5 Milliarden Menschen, vergrößern;
- das Bevölkerungswachstum ist größer als das Wirtschaftswachstum;
- der Immigrationsdruck vom Süden in den Norden wird zunehmen;
- die Überalterung und die Pensionen ruinieren den Wohlfahrtsstaat, zerstören die Staatsfinanzen und verhindern die dringend benötigten Investitionen zur Sicherung der gesellschaftlichen und volkswirtschaftlichen Zukunft;
- ein "unglaublicher" Ressourcentransfer zu den nichtproduktiven Bevölkerungsteilen steht bevor;
- der Bevölkerungsanteil der über Fünfundsechzigjährigen wird sich in den nächsten dreißig Jahren verdoppeln;
- da diese auch Wähler sind, werden sie nicht davor zurückscheuen, den sozialen Wohlfartsstaat in den Ruin zu treiben;
- alle Industrieländer zusammen geben heute bereits pro Kopf fünfmal größere Sozialbeiträge für "unproduktive" Menschen über 65 als für die Gruppe der Produktiven zwischen 14 und 65 Jahren aus.

(4) die **Globalisierungsprobleme**:
- die großen Handelsblöcke wie z.B. Nafta, Mercosur und Apec werden mangels einer Vision nicht von Dauer sein;
- der allzu starre Arbeitsplatzschutz in der EU führt zu großen Abwanderungen von Unternehmungen in Länder mit geringeren Steuern und Sozialabgaben;
- die Produktionsstandorte von Mercedes Benz und BMW in Alabama und South Carolina wurden deshalb gewählt, weil beide Staaten die geringste Regelungsdichte aufweisen, die Sozialleistungen am niedrigsten sind und das "Hire and Fire" am einfachsten ist;
- die schwindenden Steueraufkommen werden überall Haushaltskürzungen erzwingen und die Aufwendungen für Ausbildung, Infrastrukturen und Alterssicherung weiter schrumpfen lassen.

(5) die **Machtverteilung in der Welt**:
- die europäischen Probleme und Perspektiven decken sich nach dem Zusammenbruch des Kommunismus nicht mehr mit denen der USA;
- die USA werden in den Isolationismus der dreißiger Jahre zurücksinken;
- Europa ist noch nicht reif und wird sich noch fünfzig Jahre mit seiner Vereinigung beschäftigen müssen;
- Japan kommt mangels politischem Interesse am Rest der Welt und mangels militärischer Kapazität für eine Führungsrolle nicht in Frage;
- die Zukunft wird durch eine multipolare Welt ohne dominante Macht und ohne einen zentralen Schwerpunkt geprägt sein;
- auf einen Kapitalismus, der keine ethischen Werte mehr ausstrahlt und dessen Ziel nur die persönliche Bedürfnisbefriedigung ist, läßt sich keine Gesellschaft aufbauen.

Nach K. Mahbubani, dem Generalsekretär im Ministerium für Auswärtige Angelegenheiten Singapurs, ist die wichtigste Kraft im weltweiten Wettbewerb "das zunehmende Bewußtsein der Ostasiaten, daß ihr Augenblick in der Geschichte gekommen ist, daß sie sich endlich in die Gruppe der entwickelten Gesellschaften einreihen können ... Ein Europäer oder Nordamerikaner wird nur schwer die Bedeutung der psychologischen Revolution verstehen, die sich zur Zeit in Ostasien abspielt, da sie nicht in die asiatische Mentalität eindringen können. Ihr Verstand war nie durch den Kolonialismus gebunden. Sie haben nie gegen die unbewußte Überzeugung gekämpft, Menschen zweiter Klasse zu sein, die niemals tüchtig genug sind, die Nummer Eins zu werden. Die zunehmende Bewußtheit, daß die Ostasiaten jede Sache genauso gut, wenn nicht besser machen können als andere Kulturen, hat zu einer Vertrauensexplosion geführt. Dieses Vertrauen wird durch die Feststellung gestärkt, daß die Zeit bis zum Einholen der entwickelten Welt immer kürzer wird" (Mahbubani 1995, S. 105).

Die beiden Erklärungsmodelle, die stellvertretend für viele andere ausgewählt werden, veranschaulichen, daß sich unser Wirtschaftssystem in Richtungen

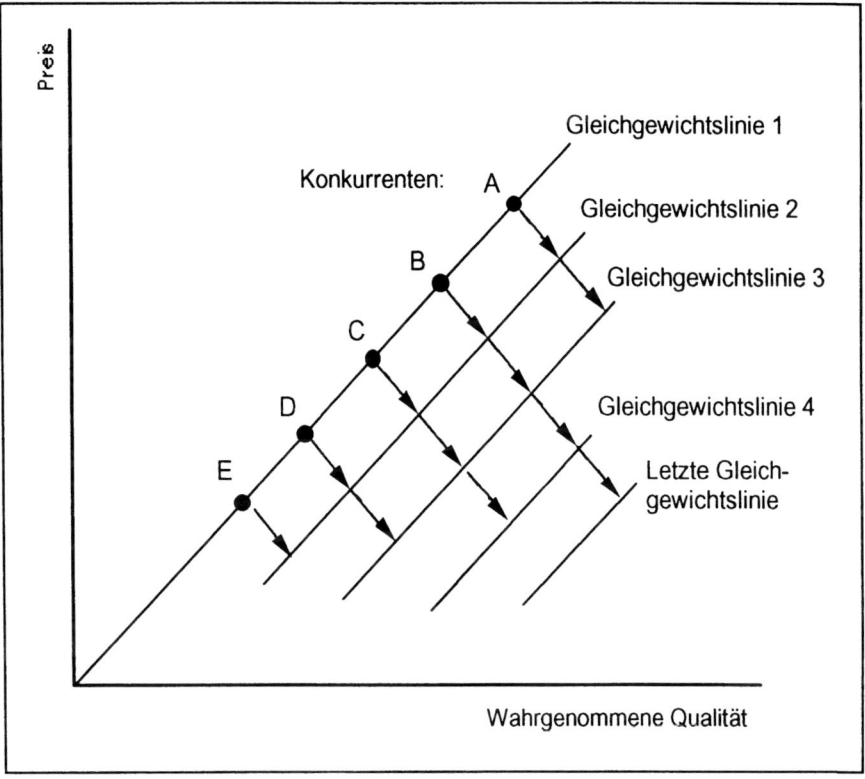

Quelle: In Anlehnung an D´Aveni 1994.

Abb. 1: Das Grundschema des Hyperwettbewerbs

bewegt, die nicht vorhersehbar sind. Die einzigen Sicherheiten sind, daß es keine Sicherheit gibt und daß die Komplexität und die Geschwindigkeit des Wandels zunehmen. In dieser Situation müssen die Unternehmungen immer vorbereitet sein, neue Möglichkeiten zu nutzen und schlecht kalkulierte Risiken abzuwenden.

Trägt man in einem Koordinatensystem auf der Senkrechten den Preis und auf der Waagrechten die wahrgenommene Qualität auf, lassen sich auf der Diagonale die Konkurrenten reihen: Konkurrenten, die eine hohe Qualität zu einem hohen Preis anbieten bis zu Konkurrenten, die Billiganbieter von Produkten/Dienstleistungen geringer Qualität sind (Abb. 1). Die Situation ist so lange im Gleichgewicht, bis irgendwo ein Konkurrent "more value for money" anbietet oder "you get more than what you pay for" oder den Preis senkt (D'Aveni 1994, S. 90). Die Konkurrenten sind gezwungen, sich anzupassen, so daß sich die Wert- oder Gleichgewichtskurve nach rechts verschiebt. Senkt wieder ein Konkurrent den Preis oder bietet er zusätzliche Leistungen an, sind die Wettbewerber gezwungen, sich auf der neuen, noch weiter rechtsliegenden Gleichgewichtslinie anzupassen. Im Laufe

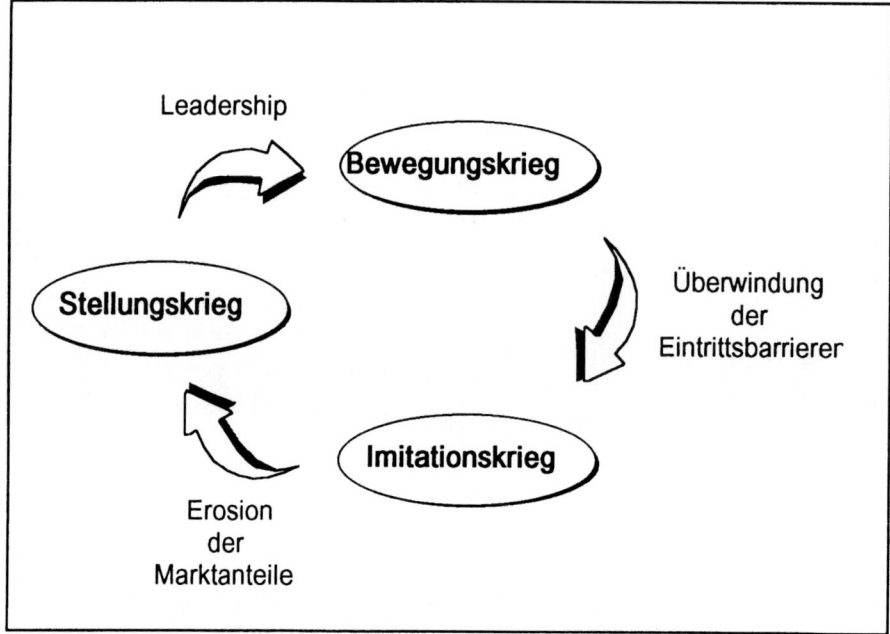

Abb. 2: Die drei Arenen des Wettbewerbs

dieses eskalierenden Wettbewerbs scheiden Konkurrenten aus dem Markt aus; die Erfahrung zeigt, daß in der Regel die Unternehmungen, die Produkte mit hoher Qualität zu hohen Preisen anbieten, die besten Überlebenschancen haben. Das Spiel kann so lange fortgesetzt werden, bis die im Markt verbliebenen Konkurrenten die letzte Gleichgewichtsgrenze erreicht haben.

Nicht in allen Branchen eskaliert der Wettbewerb zu dieser letzten Gleichgewichtsgrenze, auf der die Konkurrenten austauschbare Produkte in bezug auf Preis und Qualität anbieten und somit über keine Wettbewerbsvorteile mehr verfügen. Die vier eingangs erwähnten Faktoren zwingen jedoch die Unternehmungen in einer zunehmenden Anzahl von Branchen zu einem Wettbewerb, der für alle Konkurrenten einen Kampf auf Überleben oder Tod bedeutet. Die Situation ist mit einem **Stellungskrieg** im militärischen Sinn vergleichbar. Die Kunst der Führung besteht darin, den Stellungskrieg in einen **Bewegungskrieg** zu verwandeln (Abb. 2). Dies gelingt nur, wenn die Führenden **Leadership** beweisen.

3. Die drei Arenen des Wettbewerbs

Always fight fairly, but avoid fair fights

Maxime der strategischen Führung
Autor unbekannt

Der wichtigste Aspekt bei der Formulierung der Strategie im Hyperwettbewerb unserer Zeit besteht drin:
(1) die Grenzen und Barrieren zu überwinden, die Tradition, Erbe der Vergangenheit, Kultur und Gewohnheiten in jeder Unternehmung errichtet haben,
(2) mit Kreativität und Phantasie einen Handlungsspielraum zu schaffen, der über die angesammelten Erfahrungen hinausgeht,
(3) Kompetenzenkorridore zu schaffen, die mehr Optionen bieten als heute bestehen (Hinterhuber 1997, S. 145).
Der Hyperwettbewerb findet in drei Arenen statt und kann als Stellungskrieg, Bewegungskrieg oder Imitationskrieg in Erscheinung treten (Abb. 2). Der Gebrauch einer Methapher aus dem Bereich der Militärstrategie ist die natürliche Folge der zunehmend stärkeren Aufmerksamkeit, die der Beurteilung des Verhaltens der Konkurrenten und der Entwicklung von Wettbewerbsstrategien gewidmet wird. Der Wettbewerb kann als zivilisierte Form des Krieges betrachtet werden, in dem viele Schlachten mit der Kraft der Ideen und der Disziplin des Denkens und Handelns gewonnen werden.

"Mit dem Blick in den Abgrund kann man keine Unternehmung leiten". Mit dieser Aussage des Generaldirektors einer großen, weltweit tätigen Maschinenbauunternehmung ist das Hauptproblem der Führenden in einem **Stellungskrieg** angesprochen. Für die Einnahmen gibt es keine Sicherheit, außer denen, daß sie aufgrund der Wettbewerbsdynamik zurückgehen werden. Die Ausgaben werden jedoch unter strengen Haftungsbedingungen festgeschrieben: Menschen mit Abfertigungsansprüchen werden eingestellt, Gebäude errichtet, Maschinen gekauft und Kredite aufgenommen. Das Anbieten von zusätzlichen Leistungen, das Erfüllen von schwierigen Aufträgen, das Ertragen von Widersprüchlichkeiten und Zwielichtigkeiten gehören zu den Rahmenbedingungen im Stellungskrieg.

Führende müssen ihre eigene Bedrohtheit und Unsicherheit in Zuversicht und Vertrauen ihrer Mitarbeiter umwandeln. Der erwähnte Generaldirektor sagte: "Wenn man unter dem Eindruck einer gefährlichen Situation steht, unter einer besonders schlechten Nachricht, darf man diese nicht an Mitarbeiter weitersagen, die man erst wieder in einigen Wochen zu sehen und zu sprechen bekommt. Denn diese behalten den momentanen Eindruck ungetröstet im Gedächtnis, während man selbst vielleicht schon am nächsten Tag eine Lösung gefunden hat, worüber der gestrige Gesprächspartner nichts weiß" (Mandl 1994, S. 11).

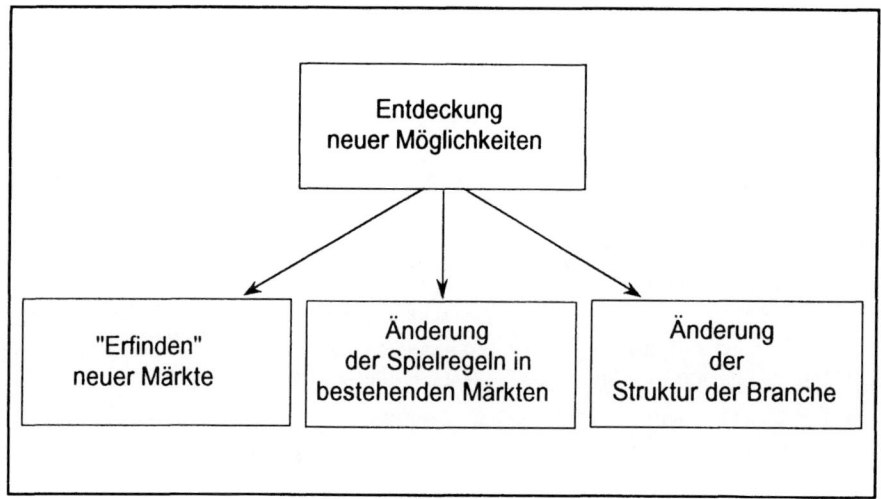

Abb. 3: Leadership heißt, neue Möglichkeiten entdecken und umsetzen oder umsetzen lassen

Der Stellungskrieg geht in einen **Bewegungskrieg** über, wenn: (1) eine im Markt etablierte Unternehmung durch eine Innovation oder durch ein innovatives Konzept die Spielregeln des Wettbewerbs verändert oder ein neuer Konkurrent mit einem innovativen Produkt oder Verfahren in diesen Markt eindringt, oder (2) eine Unternehmung mit Hilfe einer Innovation oder eines revolutionären unternehmerischen Konzeptes aus dem mörderischen Wettbewerb ausbricht und einen neuen Markt schafft. Abb. 3 zeigt die drei Möglichkeiten, mit denen aus einem Stellungskrieg ausgebrochen werden kann.

Die Innovation, mit der ein neuer Markt geschaffen, die Spielregeln im bestehenden Markt und im Umfeld der Unternehmung verändert oder etablierte Marktstrukturen aufgebrochen werden, führt zu einem Bewegungskrieg, der die Gewinnaussichten der Unternehmung in dem Maße verbessert, wie die Unternehmung sich von der Konkurrenz unterscheidet und Werte für die Kunden schafft. Früher oder später geht der Bewegungskrieg allerdings in einen **Imitationskrieg** über, der umso härter ist, je niedriger die Eintrittsbarrieren sind oder je leichter diese umgangen werden können. Der Imitationskrieg führt in der Folge wieder zum Stellungskrieg. Der Stellungskrieg verschafft den Kunden Vorteile, senkt aber dramatisch die Attraktivität der Branche.

Im harten Wettbewerb muß eine Unternehmung über Ressourcen und Kompetenzen verfügen, die es ermöglichen, **gleichzeitig** drei Arten von Kriegen zu führen: den Stellungskrieg, den Bewegungskrieg und den Imitationskrieg. Befindet sich die Unternehmung in einem Stellungskrieg, muß sie vor allem versuchen, mit neuen, beschleunigenden Momenten aus diesem auszubrechen.

4. Mit Leadership zu neuen Ufern

Leadership ist Charakter und Urteilsfähigkeit

W. Bennis

In allen Unternehmungen lassen sich drei Arten von Führungskräften unterscheiden (Hinterhuber/Krauthammer, 1997, S. 6): Verwalter, Veränderer und Führende. **Verwaltungsmanager** "verwalten" nur und passen sich nicht an geänderte Situationen an; im Grunde sind sie geistig tot. **Veränderungsmanager** versuchen, vereinbarte Ziele kreativ und innovativ zu erreichen. Unternehmungen brauchen Veränderungsmanager, wenn sie im Stellungskrieg überleben wollen. Ein **Führender** hat eine Vision, entdeckt neue Möglichkeiten, erfindet die Zukunft und vereinbart mit dem Veränderungsmanager attraktive Ziele. Er ist Vorbild und schafft Werte für die Kunden, die Mitarbeiter, die Anteilseigner und die anderen "Stakeholder" der Unternehmung (Abb. 4). G. Lindahl, Executive Vice President von ABB, sagt in diesem Zusammenhang: "Meine erste Aufgabe ist, die Strukturen zu liefern, die es ermöglichen, daß Ingenieure und andere Experten sich als Führungskräfte ('Manager') entwicklen können; die nächste Herausforderung besteht darin, die Strukturen zu lockern, damit diejenigen Führende ('Leader') werden können, die bereit sind, die Verantwortung für die Festsetzung der eigenen Ziele und Standards zu übernehmen. Wenn ich das Umfeld geschaffen habe, das es allen Führungskräften ermöglicht, Führende zu werden, dann werden wir eine Organisation haben, die sich selbst regelt und erneuert. In dieser Perspektive verschwinden die strategischen Planungssysteme, die Controlling- und

Leadership		
Visionär sein:	**Vorbild sein - vorleben:**	**Den Unternehmungswert steigern:**
"Die Richtung angeben und Sinn vermitteln"	"Engagement zeigen, Energien freisetzen und Talente fördern"	"Wohlstand für alle 'Stakeholder' schaffen"
· Einen Kernauftrag entwickeln	· Durch das Wellbeing	· Mit der Organisation/mit den Führungskräften und Mitarbeitern
· Die Kernkompetenzen bestimmen/festhalten	· Durch die Kultur	· Mit den Strategien
· Die Kernprodukte und -dienstleistungen ableiten	· Durch das Jahresleitbild - Verhaltensauftrag	· Mit dem Firmenbild/CI
· Die Kerndifferenzierungen zur Konkurrenz ausbauen - die Wettbewerbsvorteile		
Kunden		

Quelle: Hinterhuber/Krauthammer 1997.

Abb. 4: Das Konzept „Leadership-Haus" für erfolgreiches Führen

12

Informationssysteme nicht, sie werden jedoch von Machtinstrumenten in Instrumente umgewandelt, die die Entwicklung und Ausbreitung des Wissens unterstützen" (zitiert in Bartlett/Goshal 1995, S. 815). Das Ausbrechen aus dem Stellungskrieg ist eine Leadership-Aufgabe.

Leadership heißt, neue Möglichkeiten entdecken und umsetzen oder umsetzen lassen sowie die unternehmerischen Veränderungsprozesse so gestalten, daß Werte für alle "Stakeholder" - die Kunden, die Mitarbeiter, die Anteilseigner und die "financial community", die Gesellschaft, die Lieferanten und Partnerunternehmungen - geschaffen und gleichzeitig auch der Wert der Unternehmung erhöht werden. **Management** heißt, Probleme auf eine kreative Weise lösen. Dafür gibt es eine Vielzahl von Instrumenten, Methoden und Einstellungen, mit denen die Unternehmung Wettbewerbsvorteile erzielen kann. Management läßt sich leichter erlernen als Leadership; in turbulenten Zeiten ist jedoch Leadership wichtiger als Management, wenn es darum geht, radikale Veränderungen durchzusetzen, um kreative und nachhaltige Leistungsverbesserungen zu erzielen. Die Unternehmung braucht beides, Leadership und Management, um in turbulenten Zeiten neue Möglichkeiten zu entdecken und die "Stakeholder" besser und schneller zufriedenzustellen als dies die Konkurrenten oder andere Referenzunternehmungen tun können (Abb. 5) (Hinterhuber/Krauthammer 1997, S. 5). Leadership ist mit dem Beruf eines hochqualifizierten Dirigenten oder Bauherrn, Management mit dem eines Kapellmeisters oder eines Baumeisters vergleichbar.

Leadership ist die natürliche und spontane Fähigkeit, Mitarbeiter zu inspirieren und sie in die Lage zu versetzen, sich freiwillig und begeistert für die Verwirklichung gemeinsamer Ziele einzusetzen. Dazu bedarf es einer großen Energie seitens des Unternehmers oder der obersten Führungskräfte, aber auch Respekt und Ehrfurcht vor den Menschen. Leadership-Verhalten und aufrichtiges Interesse für die Menschen gehören zusammen. Die natürliche Autorität und Glaubwürdigkeit der Unternehmer und Führungskräfte hängt davon ab, ob ihre vorgelebte Vision, ihre Strategien und Einstellungen von den Mitarbeitern akzeptiert werden oder nicht. Die wirklichen Wurzeln von Leadership liegen in Idealen und Werten sowie im selbstlosen Dienen und in einem Einsatz, der über den persönlichen Bereich hinausgeht (Donnithorne 1994, S. 126).

5. Von der Evolution zur Ko-Evolution

> Wer kreative Arbeit macht, darf die Phantasie seiner Kinderjahre nicht verlieren
>
> Nicolas G. Hayek

Evolution ist Anpassung an die Bedürfnisse und Erwartungen der Stakeholder der Unternehmung. Nicht alle Kunden, Mitarbeiter, Lieferanten, Anteilseigner,

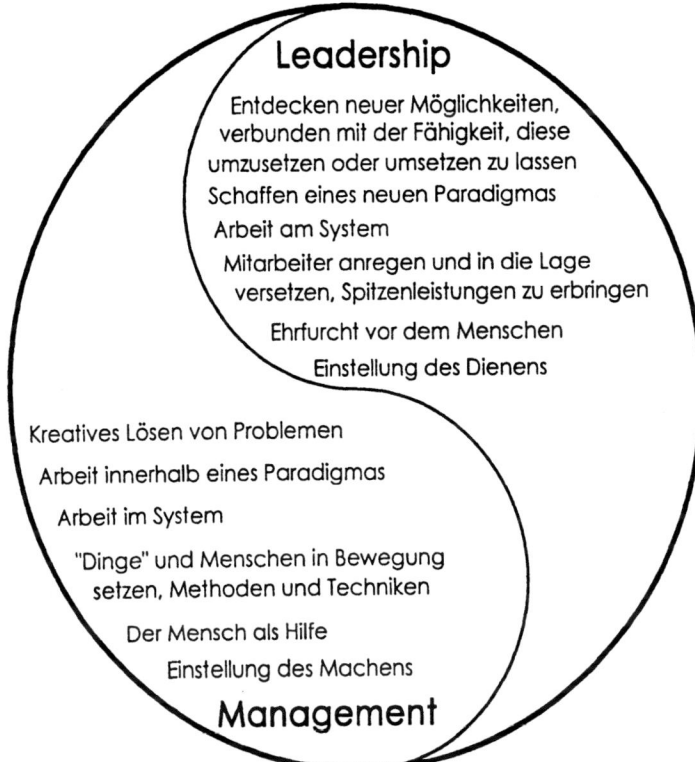

Abb. 5: Management versus Leadership

gesellschaftliche Interessenträger oder Partner-Unternehmungen sind jedoch Stakeholder. Stakeholder sind die Interessengruppen, die Schaden leiden, wenn die Unternehmung vom Markt verschwinden würde. Die Kunden sind nur dann Stakeholder, wenn sie für wichtige Problemlösungsangebote von einer Unternehmung abhängen und über keine Alternativen verfügen für den Fall, daß es diese Unternehmung nicht mehr geben sollte. Mitarbeiter werden nur dann zu Stakeholdern, wenn sie Zeit und Energie für den Aufbau eines firmenspezifischen Wissens aufgewendet haben, das außerhalb der Unternehmung keinen Marktwert besitzt. Stakeholder sind nur die Mitarbeiter, die ein für die Kernkompetenzen der Unternehmung wichtiges Wissen verkörpern und in unternehmungsinterne und -externe Beziehungsnetzwerke eingebunden sind. Ähnliches gilt für die übrigen Stakeholder der Unternehmung. So sind z.B. nur die Anteilseigner Stakeholder, die ihr Schicksal mit dem der Unternehmung verbunden haben oder die Lieferanten, für die die Unternehmung der Hauptabnehmer ihrer Produkte oder Dienstleistungen ist.

"Es gibt etwas, das sogar Gott nicht kann", sagte einmal Nasreddin zu seinem Schüler, der fürchtete, jemanden zu kränken. "Was ist das?", fragte der Schüler.

14

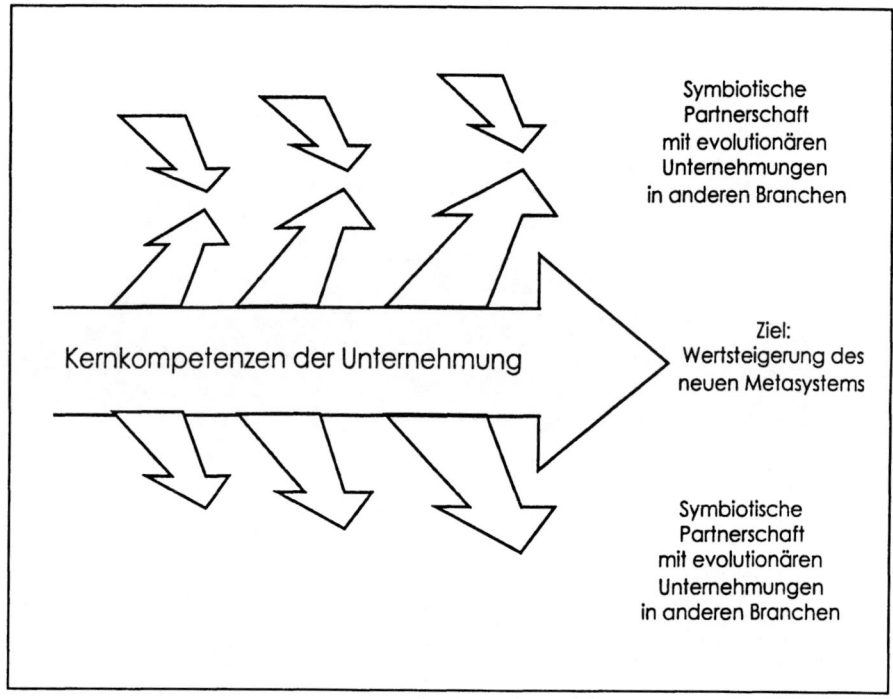

Symbiotische
Partnerschaft
mit evolutionären
Unternehmungen
in anderen Branchen

Kernkompetenzen der Unternehmung

Ziel:
Wertsteigerung des
neuen Metasystems

Symbiotische
Partnerschaft
mit evolutionären
Unternehmungen
in anderen Branchen

Abb. 6: Von der Evolution zur Ko-Evolution

"Er kann nicht jeden zufriedenstellen", antwortete Nasreddin. In der Zufriedenstellung der Stakeholder muß deshalb jede Unternehmung **Prioritäten** setzen (Hinterhuber 1996, S. 27).

Ko-Evolution ist Anpassung an die Bedürfnisse und Erwartungen der "Stakeholder" des neuen oder Meta-Systems, das entsteht, wenn Unternehmungen aus unterschiedlichen Branchen ihre Kernkompetenzen bündeln (Abb. 6). Ko-Evolution ist wechselseitiger evolutionärer Wandel in interagierenden Systemen oder, mit anderen Worten, Anpassung deren jeweiligen Bedürfnisse und Erwartungen. Die beteiligten Unternehmungen bilden gemeinsam mit ihrer neuen Umwelt ein ko-evolvierendes Meta-System, "that learns its way into the future" (Stacey 1996, S. 335). In diesem ko-evolvierenden Meta-System findet ein neuer Lernprozeß auch für die beteiligten Unternehmungen statt, die ihr Verhalten in dem Maße ändern, wie sie Impulse und Rückkoppelungen aus dem Meta-System deuten (Hinterhuber/ Stahl, 1996). Im neuen System tritt, häufig ungeplant, eine neue Qualität auf, die aus den Eigenschaften und Beziehungen seiner Mitglieder nicht erklärt werden kann; das neue System ist somit ein "emergentes System" (Stahl 1996, S. 360).

Ko-Evolution ist somit Anpassung an die Bedürfnisse und Erwartungen nicht nur der "Stakeholder" der Unternehmung, sondern auch der Partner-Unternehmungen und deren Stakeholder in anderen Märkten. Ein Beispiel für Ko-Evolution ist die Zusammenarbeit zwischen SWATCH und Mercedes-Benz. Die Verknüpfung der Kernkompetenzen zweier Unternehmungen in jeweils evolvierenden Branchen führt zu einem innovativen Produkt, das einen neuen Markt schaffen oder die Spielregeln in einem bestehenden Marktsegment radikal verändern kann. Beide Unternehmungen operieren in attraktiven Märkten; mit der Entwicklung, Herstellung und Distribution des SMART gehen sie eine symbiotische Partnerschaft in einem für beide Partner neuen und attraktiven Markt ein. Ein anderes Beispiel für Ko-Evolution ist die symbiotische Partnerschaft zwischen SWATCH und Siemens im Bereich der Telephonapparate.

In einer **symbiotischen Partnerschaft** müssen die Beiträge und Lasten der beteiligten Unternehmungen nicht symmetrisch verteilt sein. Auch wenn, genauso wie in der Natur, ein Partner Vorteile auf Kosten des anderen erzielt, ist der Gewinn für alle größer als wenn jeder für sich alleine wäre. Der italienische Brillenhersteller LUXOTTICA ist eine symbiotische Partnerschaft mit dem amerikanischen Schuhhersteller US Shoes eingegangen (Valdani 1996); alle Partner gewinnen durch die gemeinsame Ausrichtung ihrer Kernkompetenzen auf die Zufriedenstellung von Kunden, denen an ganz unterschiedlichen Points-of-Sale ein zusätzlicher, oft gar nicht erwarteter Nutzen angeboten wird (Hinterhuber /Handlbauer/Matzler 1997, S. 72). Die Ko-Evolution unterschiedlicher Partner aus unterschiedlichen Branchen kann einen ko-evolutionären Zyklus einleiten, wenn neue Partner, oft sogar Konkurrenten, sich dieser "Gewinn-Gewinn-Partnerschaft" anschließen. Beispiele hierfür sind die Forschungs- und Entwicklungskooperationen zwischen Automobilherstellern in präkompetitiven Bereichen.

Die Ko-Evolution kann sogar Konkurrenten zur Kooperation zwingen. Wie im Tierbereich, ist es häufig nicht im Interesse der Unternehmungen, den Gegner aus dem Markt zu verdrängen. Die Ko-Evolution erzeugt eine "stabile Instabilität" oder einen "dauerhaften Zustand von Ungleichgewicht"(K. Kelly 1994, S. 74). Dies allerdings nur so lange, als die Vorteile der Kooperation für alle Partner deren Opportunitätskosten übersteigen. Der folgende Satz Moltkes kann für die Gestaltung der Beziehungen in einer ko-evolutionären Partnerschaft nützlich sein: "Die Koalition ist vortrefflich, solange alle Interessen jedes Mitgliedes die selben sind. Bei allen Koalitionen gehen indes die Interessen der Verbündeten nur bis zu einem gewissen Punkt zusammen. Sobald es nämlich darauf ankommt, daß zur Erreichung des großen gemeinsamen Zwecks einer der Teilnehmer ein Opfer bringen soll, ist auf die Wirkung der Koalition meist nicht zu rechnen" (Hinterhuber 1990, S. 18).

Ko-Evolution ist vielseitiges und vielfältiges organisationales Lernen. SWATCH lernt von Mercedes-Benz und umgekehrt; beide Unternehmungen können das neue Wissen in ihren angestammten Bereichen wertsteigernd einsetzen. Die Partner in einer symbiotischen Ko-Evolution sind gleichzeitig Lehrende und Lernende, Gebende und Nehmende.

Die Zukunft eines ko-evolvierenden Systems ist nicht bestimmbar; viele Elemente der strategischen Führung dieses kreativen, neuen Systems werden erst im Lauf seiner Entwicklung festgelegt:

- Die Vision, das Leitbild und die Führungswerte entstehen graduell und spontan aus der "emergenten Ordnung" (Stahl 1996, S. 320)
- Die Strategie wird entsprechend den Aktionen der in den neuen Markt eindringenden Konkurrenten und der evolvierenden Erwartungen der Abnehmer fortgebildet;
- Die Führenden müssen mit den neuen Aufgaben wachsen oder, falls sie diesen nicht gewachsen sind, ausgewechselt werden.

Im Unterschied zum Schachspiel, zu politischen Wahlen, zum Sport oder Poker, ist die Ko-Evolution **kein** Nullsummenspiel. In einer symbiotischen Ko-Evolution gewinnen alle Partner, wenn auch nicht im gleichen Ausmaß. Koevolutionäre Beziehungen beruhen auf gegenseitiger Information und auf gegenseitigem Vertrauen. Information und Vertrauen verknüpfen die Partner in einem Netz gegenseitiger Wertsteigerung (Stahl 1996, S.320).

6. Zusammenfassung und Ausblick

> Ich war nie imstande, die Kunst des Aufgebens zu lernen
>
> Curt R. Nicolin

In der Wirtschaft wie im Leben ist alles ambivalent; nichts ist eindimensional. Die Ko-Evolution ist eine **indirekte** Strategie, und in der Strategie führt bekanntlich der Umweg oft am schnellsten zum Ziel. Bei der Ermittlung der Branchen und der Unternehmungen, die für eine Ko-Evolution in Frage kommen, geht es vor allem darum, die Grenzen und Widerstände zu überwinden, die die Tradition, die Kultur und die Gewohnheit der Führenden setzen. Unternehmungen, die sich an Vergangenes klammern, werden Opfer ihres Mangels an Einsicht. Das Leben kann nicht zurück, es ist unfähig, sich zu wiederholen. Jede Wegstrecke, die wir durchwandert haben, liegt für immer hinter uns. Die pro-aktive Einstellung der Führenden zur Ko-Evolution, ihre gemeinsame Sicht der Zukunft, die Überzeugung, daß für die Wertsteigerung der Unternehmung ein innovatives Konzept wichtiger ist als die Ausweitung der Marktanteile auf Kosten der Konkurrenten, das Gespür für Marktveränderungen, gegenseitiges Vertrauen, Offenheit, diese und andere **qualitative** Faktoren bestimmen den Erfolg einer symbiotischen Partnerschaft. Die Spezifität einer solchen Partnerschaft verlangt Ressourcen und Instrumente, die auf der Hervorbringung von neuem Wissen, auf Information und Kommunikation, auf Kreativität und Schnelligkeit sowie auf der Verbindung unterschiedlicher Kernkompetenzen beruhen. Im Krieg wie in der Wirtschaft gewinnt man durch Stellungnahme keine Schlacht, sondern nur durch Bewegung. Bewegung heißt Innovation, Entdecken neuer Möglichkeiten, Phantasie und Kreativität im Stellen von Fragen, an die andere nicht gedacht haben. "Was wir brauchen, sind bessere Fragen" (Hamel/Prahalad 1996, S. 237).

Die wichtigsten Ergebnisse sind:
(1) Der Hyperwettbewerb unserer Zeit spielt sich in **drei Arenen** ab.
(2) Leadership ist notwendig, um **aus dem Stellungskrieg auszubrechen.**
(3) **Leadership** ist in turbulenten Zeiten wichtiger als Management.
(4) **Das Gesamtbild sehen.** Strategisches Denken bewegt sich in der Regel innerhalb der Grenzen der Branche und des Marktsegments. Je mehr die Grenzen zwischen Branchen verschwinden, desto notwendiger ist eine kreative Ausweitung der Sicht in Richtung erfolgreicher Unternehmungen in anderen Märkten, mit denen durch Verknüpfung der jeweiligen Kernkompetenzen eine Ko-Evolution möglich ist. Es geht um den Entwurf eines evolutionären Szenarios, das für alle Beteiligten neue wertsteigernde Optionen erschließt.
(5) Die **Strategie** als Langzeitperspektive entsteht nicht aus der Summe der strategischen Absichten der Partner, sondern aus dem Ko-Evolutionsbild. Wenn das Ko-Evolutionsbild kein Wunschbild sein soll, dann muß es realistisch, wissenschaftlich-analytisch erarbeitet werden und allen Partner-Unternehmungen bekannt sein.
(6) Die Handlungsfreiheit der Partner-Unternehmungen im Rahmen der gemeinsamen Zielsetzung erfordert ein **Führen mit Direktiven**; Direktiven sind Richtlinien für das Handeln zur Erreichung der gemeinsamen Ziele (Hinterhuber 1997, S. 5ff.).
(7) **Ko-evolutionäres Lernen** ist ein Lernen, das auf das Verstehen der Beziehungen und Interaktionen zwischen unterschiedlichen Unternehmungen gerichtet ist und den Wert der gebündelten Kernkompetenzen erhöht. Die Ko-Evolution leitet neue Lernprozesse für alle Partner-Unternehmungen ein.
(8) **High Involvement.** Unternehmungen bringen in einer symbiotischen Ko-Evolution ihre Kernkompetenzen ein; sie passen sich den Besonderheiten der gemeinsamen Märkte an und versuchen darüberhinaus, die produktiven Kräfte in den unterschiedlichen sozio-kulturellen Kontexten sowohl für das gemeinsame Projekt als auch für ihre Kerngeschäfte zu nutzen.

Das neue Paradigma der Ko-Evolution ist noch eine Art "work-in-progress". Es deutet jedoch darauf hin, an **komplementäre** Formen der Unternehmungsentwicklung zu denken, die dramatische Leistungsverbesserungen sowohl für die eigene Unternehmung als auch für Partnerunternehmungen gewährleisten. Komplementäre Formen der Unternehmungsentwicklung beruhen auf Interaktionen, auf Vertrauen, auf Beziehungsnetzen und auf der operativen Verbindung von Kernkompetenzen unterschiedlicher Unternehmungen aus verschiedenen Branchen. Die Ko-Evolution ist ein Prozeß, in dem interdependente Unternehmungen in eine wechselseitige Evolution eingebunden sind. Die Bedeutung der Ko-Evolution geht über die der Konkurrenz und der Kooperation hinaus; die Ko-Evolution ist der Weg, der aus einem Stellungskrieg herausführt; er ist in dem Sinne ein Umweg, wie er den direkten Vergleich zwischen konkurrierenden Produkten und Dienstleistungen umgeht und durch die Vernetzung unterschiedlicher Kernkompetenzen oft ganz neue Möglichkeiten schafft.

Auch für die Ko-Evolution gilt der Ausspruch Nasreddins, des vielleicht größten Weisen der Weltgeschichte: "Versuche stets und in allem, das Nützliche für die anderen mit dem Angenehmen für dich selbst zu verbinden".

Literatur:

Bartlett, Ch.A., Goshal, S. (1995), Transnational Management, 2. Aufl., Chicago 1995

Brown, J.S. (1997), Innovation and the Social Mind, in: The Santa Fe Group and Knowledge Based Development (Eds.), Complexity and Technology, London 1997 (im Druck)

D'Aveni, R. (1994), Hypercompetition, New York 1994 (dt: Hyperwettbewerb - Strategien für die neue Dynamik der Märkte, Frankfurt, New York 1995)

Hamel, G., Prahalad, C.K. (1996), Competing in the New Economy: Managing out of Bounds, in: Strategic Management Journal, Vol. 17, (1996), S. 237-242

Hinterhuber, H.H. (1996), Strategische Unternehmungsführung, Band 1: Strategisches Denken, 6. Aufl., Berlin, New York 1996

Hinterhuber, H.H. (1997), Strategische Unternehmungsführung, Band 2: Strategisches Handeln, 6. Aufl., Berlin, New York 1997

Hinterhuber, H.H. (1990), Wettbewerbsstrategie, 2. Aufl., Berlin, New York 1990

Hinterhuber, H.H., Handlbauer, G., Matzler, K. (1997), Kundenzufriedenheit durch Kernkompetenzen, München 1997

Hinterhuber, H.H., Krauthammer, E. (1997), Leadership - mehr als Management, Wiesbaden 1997

Hinterhuber, H.H., Stahl, H.K. (1996), Die Unternehmung als Deutungsgemeinschaft, in: Technologie und Management, Vol. 45, (1996), No. 1, S. 8-13

Kelly, K. (1994), Out of Control, The New Biology of Machines, Social Systems, and the Economic World, Reading, Mass 1994

Mahbubani, K. (1995), The Pacific Way, in: Foreign Affairs", 1995, Nr. 1, S. 100-111

Mandl, H. (1994), Tagebuch meines letzten (42.) Dienstjahres bei der Waagner-Biro AG., Vervielfältigtes Manuskript, o.O. 1994

Rühli, E. (1996), Der Trend zum Hyperwettbewerb und seine Bewältigung im Rahmen des Neuen Strategischen Managements, in: Hinterhuber, H.H., Al-Ani, A. Handlbauer, G. (Hrsg.), Das Neue Strategische Management, Wiesbaden 1996, S. 115-126

Stacey, R.D. (1994), Strategic Management and Organisational Dynamics, 2. Aufl., London 1994

Stahl, H.-K. (1996), Zero-Migration, Wiesbaden 1996

Thurow, L.C. (1994), Das Ende des Kapitalismus, Frankfurt am Main 1994

Valdani, E. (1996), Dall'evoluzione alla coevoluzione. Dalla concorrenza all'ipercompetizione. Working Paper, Wirtschaftsuniversität Bocconi, Mailand 1996

Strategic Change Management
- Marktliche Wertschöpfung als Gegensatz zum Kostenabbau in operativen Prozessen

Jan S. Krulis-Randa
Rudolf Ergenzinger

Summary:

This article examines the concept of strategic change management. Global markets are the basis. They produce different social tranformations. The answer of a company is the strategic management of change, a total and long-term concept of change management directed towards the culture, strategy, and structure of a company. Better than a strategy of cost reduction is the strategy of increasing the market-oriented value of a company.

1. Verständnis der Grundbegriffe

Das Thema dieses Beitrages ist das strategische Management des Wandels. Die Betonung liegt dabei auf der Bezeichnung **strategisch.** Es scheint zunächst nützlich zu sein, die wesentlichsten Grundbegriffe zu erklären und ihre Bedeutung für die nachfolgende Auseinandersetzung zu bestimmen. Unter dem Begriff **strategisches Management** verstehen wir nach Rühli (1989, S. 50): „Strategisches Management bedeutet die erfolgsorientierte Globalsteuerung des Gesamtunternehmens unter dem primären Orientierungspunkt der Marktbeziehungen; Strategie-Schöpfung und Strategie-Durchsetzung sind dabei gleichermassen bedeutsam. Das strategische Management muss funktionsteilig die operative und taktische Führung ergänzen." Bei dieser Definition treten wesentliche **Kernelemente einer Unternehmungsstrategie** deutlich hervor (Rühli 1989, S. 16):

(a) **formal**
  - der umfassende Charakter,
  - die Langfristigkeit,
  - die hochaggregierte Ebene des Denkens und Handelns,

(b) **inhaltlich**
  - die fundamentale Erfolgsorientierung,
  - die Ausrichtung auf Tätigkeitsfelder mit Positionsstärke gegenüber der Konkurrenz,

- die Abgrenzung und Zuweisung zu den Problemfeldern, die operativ bzw. taktisch zu bezeichnen sind.

Rühli (1989, S. 19) betont ausdrücklich den Aspekt des strategischen Verständnisses: "Um den Begriff Unternehmungsstrategie nicht zu entwerten bzw. ihn stufengerecht zu erhalten, sollte daher vermieden werden, ihn mit Teil- und Detailproblemen zu beladen. Zu oft wird heute noch operativ-taktisches Kurzfutter unter dem Strategiebegriff verkauft". Im selben Sinne warnt auch Porter (1996, S. 61): "Operational effectiveness is not strategy ... The quest for productivity, quality, and speed has spawned a remarkable number of management tools and techniques: total quality management, benchmarking, time-based competition, outsourcing, partnering, reengineering, change management. Although the resulting **operational** improvements have often been dramatic, many companies have been frustrated by their inability to translate those gains into sustainable profitability. And bit by bit, almost imperceptibly, management tools have taken the place of strategy".

Die Begründung, warum wir unsere Auseinandersetzung mit dem Management des Wandels als strategisch bezeichnen, ist in der Art und Weise des gegenwärtigen gesellschaftlichen Wandels zu suchen. Dieser Wandel wird allgemein mit dem Begriff **Globalisierung** charakterisiert. Die Komplexität und die Tragweite des Globalisierungsphänomens verlangt eine umfassende, langfristige und fundamentale Anpassung der Unternehmung, also ein strategisches Management des unternehmerischen Wandels. Nur so gelingt es, den Umgang mit Unsicherheit, Komplexität, Dynamik usw. erfolgreich zu bewältigen. Zum Verständnis der Globalisierung wird folgende Definition beigezogen: "Globalisierung ist ein Prozess der Vernetzung von unterschiedlichen Kulturen und Regionen der Welt zu einem globalen System; es ist jedoch keine Integration zu einer kulturellen Einheit" (Krulis-Randa 1997, S. 126). Insofern ist die Globalisierung kein Schmelztiegel, aus dem eine globale, homogene Kultur entsteht.

Der **Prozess der Globalisierung** an sich ist nicht neu. Er begann bereits, als sesshafte Stämme nomadisiert wurden und entwickelte sich anschliessend weiter durch das Römische Imperium, den Kolonialismus, die Entdeckung Amerikas bis hin zur gegenwärtigen Erfassung des gesamten Planeten. Allerdings ist die gesellschaftliche Transformation des ausgehenden 20. Jahrhunderts durch eine aussergewöhnliche Beschleunigung der Globalisierung in Forschung und Technik gekennzeichnet, die zur bedeutenden Herausforderung der Unternehmung führt. Die Dynamik des Globalisierungsprozesses, seine Entwicklung, die Komplexität sowie die Tragweite dieses Phänomens verdeutlichen vier Aspekte (Kleps 1997, S. 93):

(1) **Moderne Völkerwanderung**

Das rasante Wachstum der Weltbevölkerung (6 Mrd. Menschen) bildet den Ausgangspunkt der Entstehung moderner Völkerwanderung von Regionen des Elends in die Oasen des Wohlstandes. Nach Angaben der Vereinten Nationen sind die Ströme dieser Kriegs- und Armutsflüchtlinge mittlerweile weltweit auf rund 200 Millionen angeschwollen.

(2) **Umweltbelastung des Planeten**
Raubbau, Waldsterben, Luft- und Gewässerverschmutzung, Ozonlöcher, Vernichtung der Regenwälder und Klimaveränderungen sind beherrschende Themen mondialer Diskussionen geworden.

(3) **Verschärfter Standort- und Global-Wettbewerb**
Die geopolitischen Veränderungen im Gefolge des Zusammenbruchs kommunistischer Herrschaftssysteme, die Durchsetzung marktwirtschaftlicher Ideen in einer immer grösseren Zahl von Ländern, die damit einhergehenden Liberalisierungsschübe in den aussermarktlichen Beziehungen und vor allem auch die Entwicklungen auf den Gebieten der Verkehrs- und Kommunikationstechnologien bilden die Grundlagen eines weiteren Globalisierungsprozesses. Dessen primäre Effizienz besteht in einer zunehmenden Intensivierung grenzüberschreitenden Wettbewerbs.

In vielen Industrien wird dies als **Hyperwettbewerb** bezeichnet. D'Aveni (1994, S. 218) versteht darunter folgendes: "Hypercompetitive behavior is the process of continuously generating new competitive advantage, thereby creating disequilibrium, destroying perfect competition, and disrupting the status quo of the marketplace".

(4) **Verschmelzung der Finanzmärkte**
Die Verschmelzung der internationalen Finanzmärkte ist auf der Basis der rasanten Entwicklungen der Informations- und Kommunikationstechnologien am weitesten fortgeschritten. Die sogenannten **Global Players** - wie beispielsweise Nick Leeson, der mit einer Spekulationspleite im Ausmass von über 1.5 Milliarden Dollars die Londoner Baring-Bank ruiniert hat oder George Soros, dem es gelungen ist, mit Spekulationen gegen das britische Pfund Sterling einen Gewinn von rund einer Milliarde Dollar zu erzielen und Grossbritannien aus dem Europäischen Währungssystem zu vertreiben - verdeutlichen diese einschneidende Dynamik und zeigen, wie labil ein solches System geworden ist.

Weitere Faktoren wie Deregulierung, Standardisierung, Mobilität und Dezentralisierung verstärken den Trend zur Globalisierung (vgl. z.B. Levitt 1983; Yip 1993). In diesem Zusammenhang stellt sich die berechtigte Frage, ob herkömmliche Methoden, Instrumente, Systeme, Problemlösungen noch die Möglichkeit bieten, obigen Herausforderungen erfolgreich begegnen zu können (Effizienz und Effektivität).

Das Verständnis dieser Grundbegriffe führt uns nun zu der Konklusion, dass der heutige gesellschaftliche Wandel eindeutig zu einem **strategischen Management des Wandels** führen muss. Eine Teilanpassung einzelner Funktionen oder operativer Prozesse, wie beispielsweise Total Quality Management (TQM), Benchmarking, Outsourcing oder Reengineering sind ungeeignet, den unternehmerischen Wandel erfolgreich durchzuführen. Der Grund besteht darin, dass sie nicht die Gesamtheit erfassen, sondern nur jeweils Ausschnitte aus einem Gesamten wie beispielsweise Prozess-Restrukturierung oder Ausgliederung einer Funktion. Das populäre Verständnis des Change Management ist die Steuerung und Regelung spezifischer Aspekte oder Funktionen wie Logistik oder die Ausgliederung von Funktionen. Das bestätigt auch das Verständnis des sogenannten integrierten Change Management von Thom (1997, S. 201 f.): "Das Konzept eines Management des Wandels umfasst **alle** geplanten, gesteuerten, organisierten und kontrollierten Veränderungen in den Strategien, Prozessen, Strukturen und in den Kulturen sozio-ökonomischer Systeme (z.B. privater und öffentlicher Unternehmungen)". Um diesem Gedankengut Nachhalt zu veschaffen, sei auf Rühli (1996, S. 11) verwiesen, der sich wie folgt äussert: "Ziel des strategischen Handelns von Unternehmungen ist es, Mehrwerte zu schaffen". Wir sind daher der Überzeugung, dass es nicht darum gehen kann, durch operative Massnahmen nur die Kosten zu senken.

2. Zunehmende Bedeutung des strategischen Change Management in der Gegenwart

Aus der Interpretation der Grundbegriffe ist deutlich hervorgegangen, dass die Globalisierung zwar nicht neu ist, aber die Dynamik und die Tragweite des Prozesses der weltweiten Vernetzung hat in den letzten Dekaden durch eine Kombination von vier Faktoren wesentlich zugenommen. Die **Erscheinungsformen des Globalisierungsprozesses** unserer Zeit sind wie eingangs erwähnt (ähnlich Kleps 1997, S. 93):
(1) Globale Mobilität,
(2) Globale ökologische Belastung,
(3) Globaler Hyperwettbewerb,
(4) Globaler Kapitalmarkt.
Ergänzend zu dieser Sichtweise und als Konsequenz der globalen Unternehmung sind die globale Wertschöpfung sowie die globalen Synergien zu erwähnen (vgl. Abb. 1).

Das Ergebnis dieser offensichtlich zunehmend dynamischen und komplexen Entwicklungen ist der Prozess der gegenwärtigen gesellschaftlichen Transformation. Unsere Zivilisation entwickelte immer wieder nach bestimmten Zeitabschnitten einen sprunghaften, starken Wandel. So beispielsweise die Zeit der Wende im 13. Jahrhundert (charakterisiert durch die Entstehung des Welthandels, der Universitäten, der europäischen Städte mit Zunftwirtschaft), nach

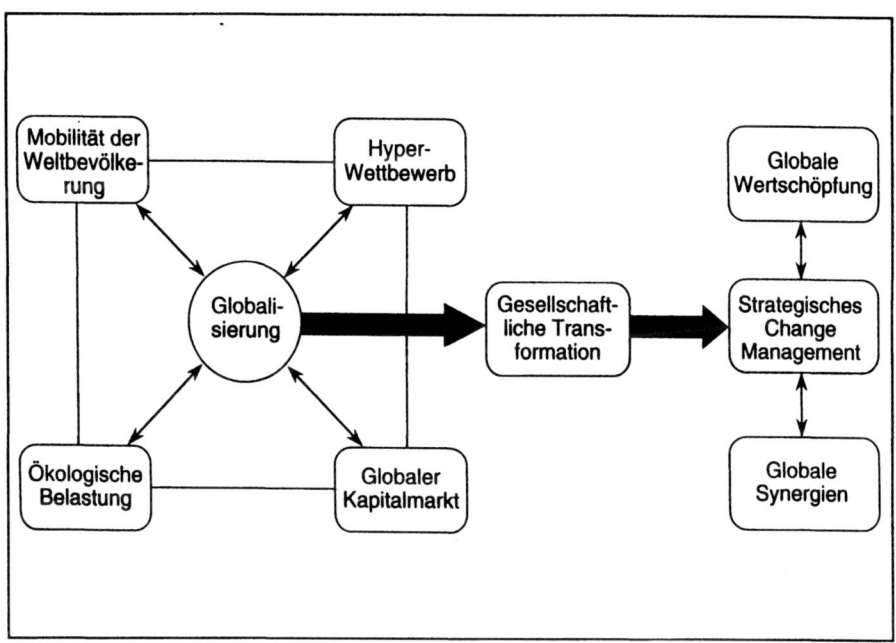

Abb. 1: Change Management als Konsequenz der Globalisierung

200 Jahren (ca. 1450 bis 1520) die Zeit der Renaissance (mit Buchdruck und der Entdeckung von Amerika), nach 250 Jahren (ca. 1776 bis 1860) die Industrielle Revolution (aber auch die Amerikanische Revolution, die Entstehung der modernen Demokratie und die Ideologien des Kapitalismus, Sozialismus und Kommunismus), und nun erleben wir heute die Transformation der Post-Moderne (oder wie es Peter Drucker (1993) nennt, den Post-Kapitalismus), die im 21. Jahrhundert eine neue Gesellschaft hervorbringen wird. Es wird allerdings diesmal keine Transformation der westlichen Zivilisation sein, sondern eine verwestlichte Transformation der globalen Gesellschaft.

Der gegenwärtige gesellschaftliche Wandel wird bereits in der Praxis von zahlreichen Unternehmungen erfahren. Es ist nicht überraschend, dass in der Wirtschaftspraxis wie auch in der Fachliteratur (Bleicher 1992 Doppler/Lauterburg 1994; Reiss 1995; Scholz 1995; Stamm 1995; Mary 1996; Pettigrew/Whipp 1996) eine intensive Auseinandersetzung mit dem Phänomen des **Change Management** festzustellen ist. In unserem Beitrag zu dieser Auseinandersetzung stellen wir die folgende These auf:

Der Prozess der Globalisierung führt zur gesellschaftlichen Transformation, und dieser Transformation kann eine Unternehmungsführung nur mit einem strategischem Management des Wandels begegnen, d.h. einem allumfassenden, ganzheitlichen und langfristigen Change Management der unternehmerischen Kultur, Strategie und Struktur.

Das Schema dieser Logik wird in Abb. 1 dargestellt. Gewiss wird je nach Standort, Branche oder Wirtschaftssektor der Unternehmung eine spezifisch unterschiedliche Strategie eingeführt. Strategien können sehr differenziert sein und müssen situativ entwickelt werden. Allen unterschiedlichen Arten von Strategien gemeinsam sind drei **wesentliche Aspekte des Strategiebegriffs:**
(a) Globalsteuerung des Gesamtunternehmens,
(b) Primäre Ausrichtung nach den Marktbeziehungen,
(c) Schaffung von Mehrwert.
Dadurch unterscheidet sich das strategische Management des Wandels von dem heute mehrheitlich diskutierten Change Management der unternehmerischen Prozesse in den Bereichen Kosten, Qualität, Service und Zeit (magisches Viereck) mit dem Ziel, nachhaltige Effizienzsteigerungen in den messbaren ökonomischen Grössen zu erzielen (z.B. Halbierung der Durchlaufzeit, Verdoppelung des Umsatzes pro Mitarbeiter, Reduktion der Mitarbeiter). Die primäre Ausrichtung der Re-Organisationsansätze ist die Steigerung des Return on Investment (ROI) durch Effizienzsteigerungen dank Kostenabbau. Mit anderen Worten: Das Ziel ist **Shareholder Value** anstatt **Customer Value**.

3. Unzulänglichkeit der Re-Organisation von operativen Prozessen für die Lösung der Anpassungsprobleme in der Zeit der dynamischen Globalisierung

Die Effizienzsteigerung der unternehmerischen Prozesse ist keine hinreichende Reaktion auf die substantielle Transformation unserer Gesellschaft. Im Gegenteil: Sie führt in eine Sackgasse, aus der es schwer sein wird, herauszukommen. Nachfolgend begründen wir diese Aussage. Zuerst sei jedoch eine treffende Bemerkung eines akademischen Kollegen erlaubt. Henry Mintzberg (1996, S. 65) von der McGill University in Montreal schrieb kürzlich: "There is no reengineering in the idea of reengineering. Just reification, just the same old notion that the new system will do the job. ... Why don't we just stop reengineering and delayering and restructuring and decentralizing and instead start thinking?" Was Mintzberg kritisiert ist die reine Umsetzung (reification) des alten Konzeptes in die Realität neuer Umsystemfelder, anstatt in der neuen Situation Neues zu erfinden und dazu braucht man zunächst neue Denkprozesse. In diesem Sinn bezeichnet auch Rühli (1996, S. 16) die hochaggregierte Ebene des Denkens und Handelns als ein wesentliches Kernelement einer Unternehmungsstrategie.

Die verschiedenen Ansätze der Re-Organisation von operativen Prozessen sind für die Lösung von Problemen, die aus dem externen Druck der neuen Systemumwelt entstanden sind, ungeeignet. Das Management des Wandels von unternehmerischen Prozessen und Strukturen führt zwar zur betrieblichen Effizienzsteigerung, nicht aber zu einer neuen strategischen Position der Unternehmung in der Dynamik der Globalisierung. Die Steigerung der Wirksamkeit von betrieblichen Strukturen und Prozessen ist keine Strategie, sondern eine rein operative Funktion des täglichen Management. Für die Entwicklung einer langfristigen Marktposition der Unternehmung weist sie zwei grundsätzliche Schwächen auf:

(1) **Rasche Imitierbarkeit**

Eine Steigerung der betrieblichen Wirksamkeit bedeutet eine bessere Abwicklung von **ähnlichen** Aktivitäten als es die Konkurrenz tut. Die Verbesserung der operativen Wirksamkeit beinhaltet betriebliche Prozesse, aber nicht nur. Nebst der Rationalisierung der Prozesse kann die Verbesserung durch neue Technologien oder Motivation der Mitarbeiter und professionelles Management erreicht werden. Eine kontinuierliche Verbesserung der operativen Wirksamkeit ist notwendig, um die Rentabilität zu erreichen. Deswegen sind in den letzten 10 Jahren so viele neue operative Programme entstanden wie TQM, time-based competition, benchmarking, empowerment oder learning organization. Die Popularität des Outsourcing und der virtual corporation entstand aus der Erfahrung, dass Aktivitäten, die nicht effizient durchgeführt werden, besser zu eliminieren sind. Die Schwäche dieser Ansätze besteht in der raschen Imitierbarkeit durch die Konkurrenz. Dadurch schwindet nach kurzer Zeit der Wettbewerbsvorsprung. Die höhere Wirksamkeit der betrieblichen Prozesse bewirkt zwar eine Senkung der Kosten der rationalisierten Aktivitäten und damit auch der Preise des Outputs sowie der Gewinnmargen. Es ist empirisch nachweisbar, dass die Industriezweige zwar eine reale Verbesserung der operativen Wirksamkeit erreicht haben, aber für die einzelnen Unternehmungen gab es keine Gewinnverbesserung (Luftfahrt, Druckereien usw.). Die Ergebnisse der Produktivitätssteigerungen haben die Kunden, die Lieferanten der Rationalisierungsinstrumente und die Unternehmensberater einkassiert.

Dabei ist zu sagen, dass die Rendite gewiss eine unabdingbare Voraussetzung für den Fortbestand einer Unternehmung sowie ein wichtiges Mittel zur Realisierung unternehmerischer Ziele ist, doch sind sie für viele visionäre Unternehmungen kein Ziel an sich (Collins/Porras 1995, S. 85). Und wenn sich diese Denkweise durchsetzt, kann eine ausschliessliche Fokussierung auf die betriebliche Effektivität ohne Einbezug der Strategie nicht zu langfristigen Wettbewerbsvorteilen führen.

(2) **Wachsende Homogenität der Konkurrenten**

Die zweite Schwäche des Change Management der operativen Wirksamkeit ist die zunehmende Angleichung der Aktivitäten aller Konkurrenten. Je mehr benchmarking praktiziert wird, um so mehr sehen sich alle ähnlich. Der Wettbewerb konzentriert sich damit nur auf die Wirksamkeit der betrieblichen Prozesse. Die Philosophie der Steigerung operativer Wirksamkeit führt schliesslich zu Fusionen von konkurrierenden Firmen in derselben Branche. Beim Fehlen der strategischen Vision und Phantasie gibt es scheinbar keine bessere Idee als den Konkurrenten aufzukaufen und die operativen Aktivitäten weiterhin zu rationalisieren. Die Kostensenkung stärkt zwar den **Shareholder Value,** aber nur kurzfristig. Der ansteigende Preisdruck verunmöglicht eine Investition in die langfristige Marktposition der Unternehmung. Deswegen führt die zunehmende Homogenität des Wettbewerbs die gesamte Industriebranche in die Degenerationsphase.

Die Steigerung der Wirksamkeit der operativen Prozesse durch Rationalisierung und Innovation der Technologie, kombiniert mit Marketing-Strategie, wäre eine **ideale Kombination,** weil beide für den unternehmerischen Erfolg wesentlich sind. Die Schwierigkeit liegt in der diametralen Philosophie beim Change Management der betrieblichen Operationen und beim Strategic Change Management der Marktpositionierung. Ziel der operativen Massnahmen ist, besser zu sein als die Konkurrenz und Ziel der Marktstrategie ist, anders zu sein als die Konkurrenz und etwas Besonderes anzubieten (nicht Besseres!), was schwer zu imitieren ist. Diese zwei sehr unterschiedlichen Denkweisen lassen sich schwer kombinieren. Der eine Ansatz möchte dieselben Aktivitäten wie die Konkurrenz besser machen, der andere Ansatz möchte andere Aktivitäten als die Konkurrenz sie macht.

Die Autoren der Ansätze Business Reengineering, Total Quality Management oder Organisationsentwicklung betonen zwar wiederholt, dass "bei allen Definitionen von Prozessen die Befriedigung der Wünsche (interner und externer) Kunden im Mittelpunkt steht" (Thom 1997, S. 204). Nur, es fehlt eine genauere Beschreibung, wie die Marketing-Strategie entwickelt und durchgesetzt wird. Unglaubwürdig scheint die Vorstellung, dass ein Reengineering-Zar (Fachpromotor), der bewusst undemokratisch die Umsetzung der neuen Lösungen durchsetzen soll, fähig sein kann, eine Marketing-Strategie fundamental zu überdenken. Auf die Frage, die am Anfang des Reengineering-Denkprozesses stehen sollte, nämlich "warum machen wir das überhaupt?", kann ein Fachpromotor keine strategisch-gerechte Antwort geben (vgl. Hammer/Champy 1994, S. 48). Ebenfalls ist es schwer vorstellbar, dass ein Change Catalyst (Machtpromotor), der in einer Organisationsentwicklung aus dem Client System, also ganz demokratisch aus den Mitgliedern des zu wandelnden Systems, eine neue Positionierungs-Strategie in der Zeit der Globalisierung aktivieren kann. Der Widerspruch zwischen den beiden Denkhaltungen, der operativen und der strategischen, ist riesig gross.

4. Wege zur Gewinnsteigerung

Es gibt zwei Wege zur Gewinnsteigerung: Entweder kann die Gewinnmarge (1) durch Rationalisierung der betrieblichen Aktivitäten und daraus resultiert Kostenreduktion oder (2) durch Wertschöpfung des marktlichen Angebotes und daraus resultiert Preiserhöhung verbessert werden. Beide Wege lassen sich schwer kombinieren, weil sie unterschiedliche und teilweise widersprüchliche Aktivitäten einsetzen. Das Denken und Handeln ist verschieden, und es braucht ein anderes Wissen und eine andere Mentalität. Der **erste Weg der Kostenreduktion** (sog. Denominator Management) ist inputorientiert und einfacher, weil er das Bestehende und Bekannte optimiert. Es ist auch verständlich, dass dieser Weg populärer ist. Es ist der Weg der Unternehmensberater und basiert auf technischem Know-how, auf dem Fachwissen der Effizienzsteigerungen von ökonomischen Kerngrössen wie Kosten, Qualität, Service und Zeit.

Der **zweite Weg der Wertschöpfung** (sog. Numerator Management) ist outputorientiert und bedeutend schwieriger, weil auf diesem Weg das Neue und Unbekannte kreiert wird. Er wird heute von wenigen, aber meistens erfolgreichen Unternehmungen beschritten. Dieser Weg der Wertschöpfung ist die Domäne der visionären Unternehmer mit tiefgehenden, fachlichen Branchenerfahrungen. Das bedingt auch neue Visionen und neue Kompetenzen, die sich wiederum in neuen Wertschöpfungsstufen niederschlagen. Im Zusammenhang mit visionären Unternehmen meinen Collins/Porras (1995, S. 10), dass alle visionären Produkte und Dienstleistungen, alle Ideen letztendlich veralten, sogar Märkte überleben sich und können verschwinden. "Visionäre Unternehmen hingegen florieren über längere Zeiträume, über mehrere Produktlebenszyklen und mehrere Generationen tatkräftiger Unternehmensführer".

Mentalitätsmässig bedeutet die **Inputorientierung** die Ausrichtung nach dem Shareholder Value. Der Kapitalgeber erwartet für seine Investition eine interessante (v.a. eine materielle) Kompensation. Die Schwäche dieses Konzeptes ist, dass man nicht genau feststellen kann, was für einen bestimmten Shareholder interessant ist. Allgemein wird vermutet, dass die Shareholders eher kurzfristigen Gewinn erwarten. Die **Outputorientierung** richtet sich nach dem Customer Value. Ziel der unternehmerischen Tätigkeiten ist die Wertschöpfung des Angebotes aus Sicht der Kunden zu gestalten, die man sich im bestimmten Marktsegment ausgewählt hat. Das Interesse liegt beim Ausbau einer längerfristigen Beziehung und Partnerschaft mit den Kunden, die der Unternehmung für das Angebot zahlen. Die Bemühungen um die Idealkombination beider Wege, die zur höchsten Leistung führen, werden in der Theorie und Praxis intensiv gesucht (vgl. dazu Tab.1).

Nach Porter (1985) gibt es zwei grundsätzliche Typen des Wettbewerbsvorteils: Kostenführerschaft oder Differenzierung. In jeder Branche kann nur eine Unternehmung die tiefsten Kosten haben, alle anderen Mitbewerber müssen ihr Angebot differenzieren. Besonders in den entwickelten Volkswirtschaften mit höheren Lohnkosten führt in der Regel die schwierigere Differenzierungsstrategie zum Erfolg. Die beste Praxis ist eine möglichst hohe Kundenwertschöpfung zu relativ tiefen Kosten (theoretisch gesehen würde sich der optimale Punkt in der Mitte der Kurve befinden), wobei die strategische Positionierung der Unternehmung richtungsweisend ist (Abb. 2).

Kostenreduktion der Geschäftstätig-keit (Denominator Management)	Ertragssteigerung durch Wertschöp-fung (Numerator Management)
• Reduzieren und Restrukturieren • Outsourcing wo möglich • Benchmarking • Reengineering • Automatisierung • Rationalisierung der Logistik	• Wertsteigerung des Angebotes zu höheren Preisen (Qualität) • Wertsteigerung durch Zusatznutzen (Service) • Öffnung neuer geographischer Märkte • Erschließung neuer Segmente oder Nischen • Customization • Kreieren neuer Nachfrage

Quelle: In Anlehnung an Kotler 1997.

Tabelle 1: Wege zur Gewinnerzielung

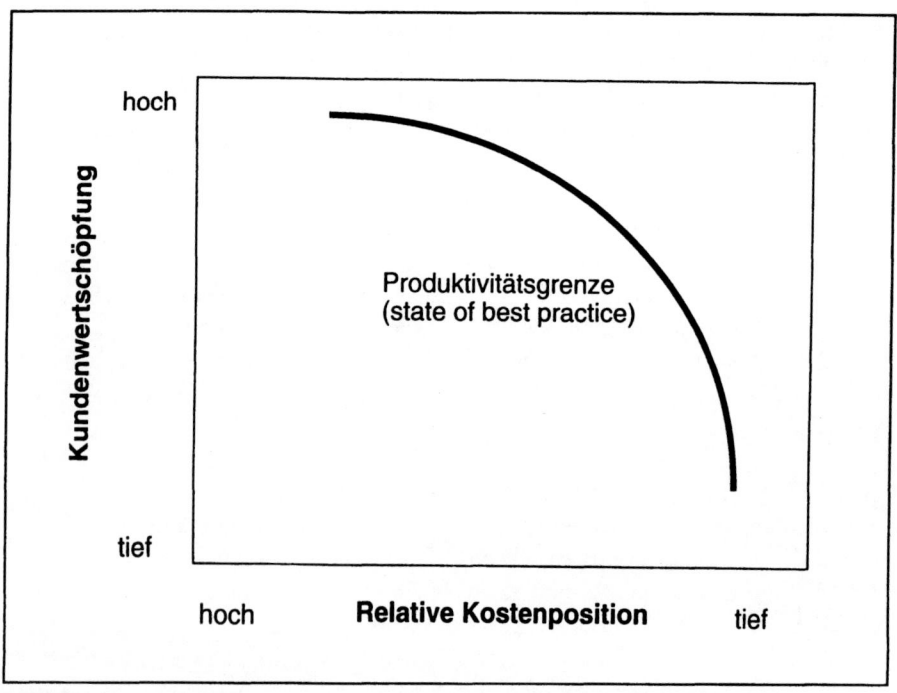

Quelle: Porter 1996, S. 62.

Abb. 2: Operationale Effektivität gegen strategische Positionierung

5. Management des Wandels durch die Strategie der marktlichen Wertschöpfung

Das strategische Change Management reagiert auf die Herausforderung der gesellschaftlichen Transformation, die durch die Globalisierung verursacht wurde, mit Re-Positionierung der Unternehmung in den sich wandelnden Umwelt-systemen. Der primäre Orientierungspunkt des strategischen Management sind die Marktbeziehungen. Demzufolge ist die **strategische Marktanalyse** die wesent-liche Ausgangsphase. Mit der zunehmenden Globalisierung und Deregulierung der Märkte wird eine genaue strategische Marktanalyse immer wichtiger, aber gleichzeitig auch schwieriger. Der Hauptgrund dafür ist im Wandel der fundamen-talen Logik der Wertschöpfung zu sehen. Die Wertvorstellungen, Werthaltungen und Wertschöpfungsprozesse sind nicht absolut, sondern wandelbar.

Der **Wert eines Produktes** oder einer Dienstleistung ist subjektiv. Es gibt keinen allgemein gültigen, objektiven Wert. Was für einen Menschen wertvoll erscheint ist für einen anderen wertlos. Auf dem Markt entsteht ein messbarer Tauschwert, ausgedrückt in monetären Einheiten in Form eines Marktpreises. Der Marktpreis ist ein Ergebnis der Intensität von Angebot und Nachfrage. Da das Verhältnis zwischen Angebot und Nachfrage variiert, ist auch der Tauschwert nicht beständig.

Bereits Adam Smith unterscheidet neben dem Tauschwert (**value in exchange**) den Wert im Gebrauch (**value in use**). Der Wert im Gebrauch ist der Nutzen, den ein Individuum durch Gebrauch eines Produktes und dessen Kombination mit anderen Produkten subjektiv erfahren kann. Der Wert, den ein Produkt oder eine Dienstleistung im Gebrauch bei einem Individuum generieren kann, bestimmt seine Bereitschaft, dieses Produkt oder diese Dienstleistung auf dem Markt zu erwerben. Somit bestimmt der Nutzwert (value in use) die Intensität der Nach-frage und beeinflusst, zusammen mit anderen Marktfaktoren (Wettbewerbssitua-tion, Erhältlichkeit, Substitutionsmöglichkeit), den Tauschwert. Nun ist mit der zunehmenden wirtschaftlichen Entwicklung neben dem Nutzwert (value in use) noch ein dritter, subjektiver Wert zu unterscheiden. Es ist wie in Abb. 3 dargestellt, der subjektiv empfundene, emotionale Wert der Zufriedenheit und des Glücks (**value of happiness**). Der emotionale Wert des empfundenen Glücks, beispielsweise beim Besitz eines impressionistischen Gemäldes, bestimmt ebenfalls den Wert des Angebotes auf dem Markt, beispielsweise bei einer Auktion.

Dieses dreidimensionale Wertverständnis, wie in Abb. 3 dargestellt, ist nicht nur von theoretischem Interesse. Die Ausgangsphase der gegenwärtigen strategischen Marktanalyse fängt mit der Analyse der wertgenerierenden Prozesse beim potentiellen Kunden an, weil diese den erzielbaren Tauschwert beeinflussen oder den Wettbewerbsvorteil erschaffen. Deswegen ist dieser Denkansatz sehr praxisorientiert und bietet eine brauchbare Anregung für die wirksame Marktanalyse in der gegenwärtigen Lage.

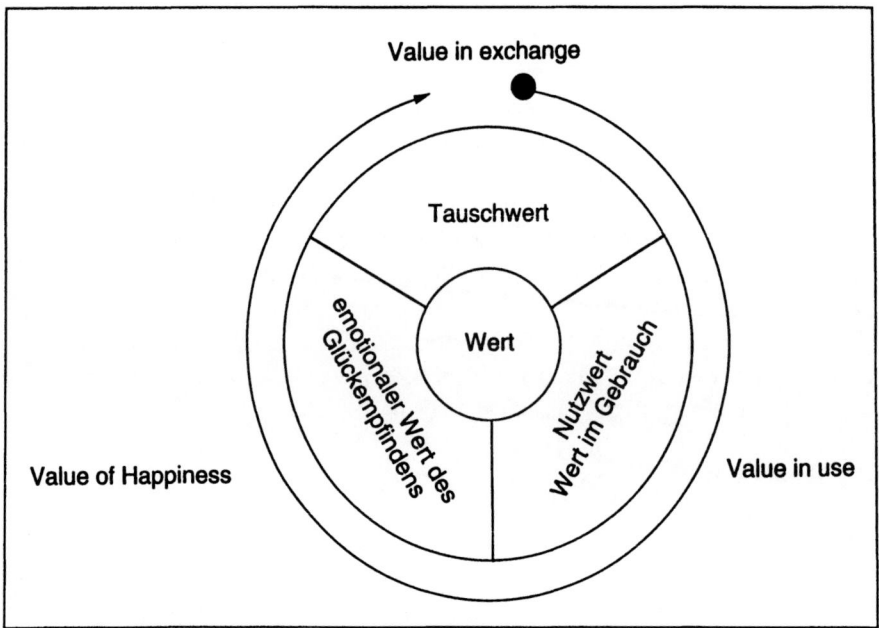

Abb. 3: Drei Sinngehalte des Wertbegriffs

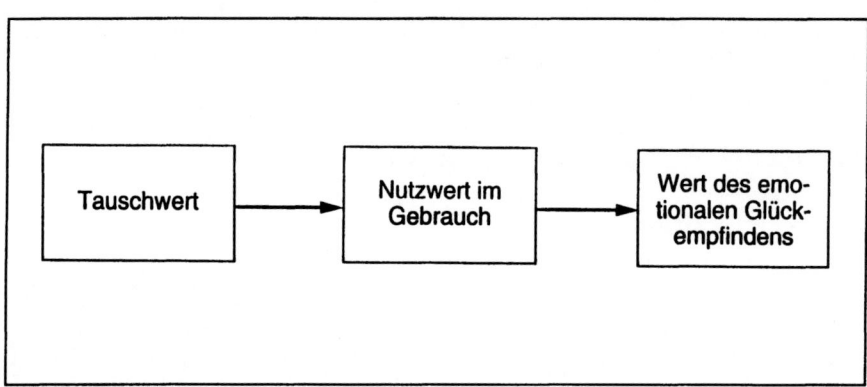

Abb. 4: Gesamtwert eines Angebots

Der Gesamtwert eines Angebotes weist aus Sicht der Kunden drei Komponenten auf (Abb. 4):

(a) Tauschwert:
Die Analyse konzentriert sich auf die Wertvorstellungen der potentiellen Kunden bezüglich des Marktpreises. Aus der Analyse wird die strategische Segmentierung der Kundengruppen nach ihrer Kaufkraft und Zahlungsbereitschaft abgeleitet. Liegt der Marktpreis eindeutig zu hoch, wäre es in der Regel falsch, die Konkurrenzpreise zu unterbieten (diese falsche Praxis

ruinierte bereits einige Industrien wie beispielsweise die Luftfahrt). Richtig ist, die weiteren Komponenten des Gesamtsystems zu analysieren

(b) Nutzwert im Gebrauch
Hier befasst sich die Analyse mit der Frage, für welchen Nutzen das Produkt oder die Dienstleistung gebraucht wird. Wird ein Fahrrad beispielsweise als ein Transportmittel auf dem Weg zur Arbeit gebraucht oder für die Freizeitgestaltung? Nach dieser Analyse werden Kunden in Marktsegmente gegliedert. Die Differenzierung des Marktes erlaubt die Entwicklung einer auf das spezifische Nutzenpotential fokussierten Marketing-Strategie, die dem Kunden einen höheren Wert im Gebrauch verschafft. Dadurch können die zu hohen Marktpreise (der Tauschwert) kompensiert werden.

(c) Wert des emotionalen Glückempfindens
Nebst dem Nutzen im Gebrauch eines Produktes bzw. einer Dienstleistung empfindet der Kunde beim Erwerb des Angebotes eine für ihn wertvolle subjektive Zufriedenheit. Auch dieses Wertempfinden muss analysiert werden. Dadurch wird die Segmentierung der potentiellen Kunden nach den typischen immateriellen Wertvorstellungen möglich. Schon die Freundlichkeit und das sympathische Lachen des Verkäufers bedeutet mehr Zufriedenheit beim Einkauf. Der Wert des Glückempfindens ist sehr unterschiedlich, je nach Segment des Marktes und sollte mit spezifischer Wertschöpfung befriedigt werden.

Die Mehrdimensionalität des Wertempfindens spielt in den Märkten der gegenwärtigen Entwicklungsphase der Wirtschaft und Gesellschaft eine zunehmend bedeutende Rolle. Deswegen ist auch die differenzierte strategische Marktanalyse für eine erfolgreiche Wettbewerbsstrategie auf praktisch allen Produkte-Märkten heute notwendig.

Die strategische Marktanalyse (die Betonung liegt auf der **strategischen** Marktanalyse im Vergleich zur Marktanalyse für die kurzfristigen, täglichen Operationen, die sich nach wie vor auf die Positionierungsmassstäbe wie Marktanteil, Rentabilität, Lebenszyklus, Wachstum usw. stützt), die auf der neuen Logik des Wertschöpfungssystems beruht, fokussiert sich auf zwei Schwerpunkte:
(a) Das **Wissen** bzw. die Kernkompetenz (die Fähigkeiten, Fertigkeiten und das Know-how) der Unternehmung.
(b) Die **Beziehungen** bzw. die Kunden und Marktpartner der Unternehmung, mit denen ein Netzwerk besteht oder aufgebaut werden kann.
Das Wissen allein, ohne die Beziehungen zu den Marktpartnern, genügt nicht. Offensichtlich sind die Kompetenzen der Unternehmung ohne die Bereitschaft der Kunden, für diese Kompetenzen zu bezahlen, wertlos. Die Kernkompetenz der Unternehmung ist das akkumulierte Wissen in der Technologie, in der spezialisierten Expertise, in den Prozessen der Herstellung und Logistik, aber auch auf

32

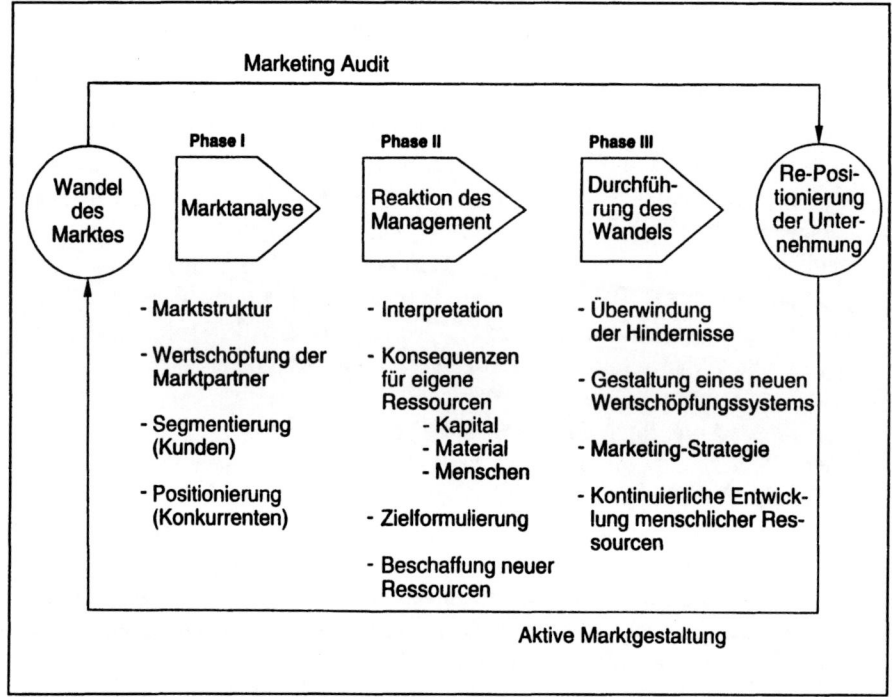

Abb. 5: Strategische Marktanalyse

der Basis von Kundenbeziehungen. Wie eine Studie des Internationalen Institutes für Lernende Organisation und Innovation zeigt, trägt die Ressource Wissen zu 60 bis 100 Prozent zur Wertschöpfung des Unternehmens bei (Wirtschaftswoche 41/1997, S. 127). Die Studie belegt auch, dass einer Unternehmung erhebliche Wettbewerbsvorteile entgehen, weil die Verantwortlichen das Wissen der Mitarbeiter nur ungenügend/unzureichend kennen bzw. einsetzen. Daher ist es unabdingbar, inskünftig vermehrt das latente Wissen mittels geeigneter Instrumente zu erfassen und zu nutzen.

Die Beziehungen der Unternehmung zu den Kunden ist in der Tat der Zugang zu den Wertschöpfungsprozessen der Kundschaft. Jeder Kunde, ob ein Endkonsument oder ein Industriebetrieb, braucht verschiedene Inputs für seine Wertschöpfungsprozesse. Die Inputs eines Lieferanten haben für den Kunden insofern einen Wert, als diese ihm eine eigene Wertschöpfung ermöglichen. In diesem Sinne erreicht die Unternehmung einen Gewinn nicht von den Kunden, sondern aus den Wertschöpfungsprozessen der Kunden.

Als Hauptaufgabe der strategischen Marktanalyse gilt es abzuklären, wie das Wissen (die Kompetenz) mit den Beziehungen (den Kunden und Marktpartnern) integriert werden soll und kann. Um die bestehenden Beziehungen erhalten zu können, muss die Unternehmung ihr Wissen kontinuierlich ausbauen. Die wachsende Kernkompetenz öffnet neue Beziehungen und ermöglicht neue Wertschöpfungsprozesse. Die neue Logik der Wertschöpfung und die strategische Marktanalyse, die auf ihr beruht, stellen die Integrations-möglichkeiten zwischen Kompetenzen und Kunden dar. Eine solche Analyse bedingt drei Schritte (vgl. Abb. 5).

Phase I: Die Marktanalyse im engeren Sinne

Die eigentliche Marktanalyse ist nur der erste Schritt in der ganzheitlichen strategischen Analyse, die zur Repositionierung der Unternehmung in einem wandelnden Markt führt. Eine strategische Marktanalyse muss auch die Möglichkeiten der Umsetzung in eine effektive Strategie miteinbeziehen. Deswegen folgen auch noch zwei weitere Schritte. Im ersten Schritt wird die Struktur des Marktes wahrgenommen. Die Marktstruktur wird durch eine möglichst vollständige Analyse der Werthaltungen und Wertschöpfungs-möglichkeiten der Marktpartner (Lieferanten, Vermittler, Kunden, Assoziierungs-kandidaten) erfasst. Erst danach kann die Marktseg-mentierung nach den Kriterien der Verhaltensweisen von Kunden durchgeführt werden und die Positionierung der eigenen Unternehmung gegenüber der Konkurrenz entworfen werden. Die Positionierung ist aus der Sicht der Kunden und nicht nach der Meinung der Unternehmensführung zu skizzieren.

Phase II: Die Reaktion des Management

Der zweite Schritt ist ebenso wichtig wie der erste. Er bezieht sich auf die erwähnten Schwerpunkte **Wissen und Beziehungen** der eigenen Unternehmung. In diesem Schritt wird die Interpretation der Marktdaten sichergestellt und die Konsequenzen für eigene Ressourcen (Kapital, Material, Menschen) analysiert. Danach soll erst die neue Zielformulierung erfolgen und die Möglichkeiten der Beschaffung von neuen, noch fehlenden Ressourcen müssen überprüft werden.

Phase III: Die Durchführung des Wandels

Der dritte Schritt ist die Durchführung des Wandels in der Unternehmung. Die Marktanalyse wird erst dann strategisch, wenn sie auch in eine Strategie umgesetzt werden kann, sonst bleibt es nur eine Konzeption. Dieser Schritt bedeutet zunächst die Überwindung der bestehenden Hindernisse, dann der Entwurf eines neuen Wertschöpfungssystems von mehreren Aktivitäten der Unternehmung und ihrer Partner (vgl. dazu Abb. 6, die beispielsweise ein Wertschöpfungssystem in Kombination verschiedener Aktivitäten darstellt), ferner die Formulierung der Marketing Strategie und schliesslich die kontinuierliche Entwicklung der lernfähigen menschlichen Ressourcen. Daraus ist bereits ersichtlich, dass die strategische Marktanalyse nicht ein einmaliger Akt ist, sondern ein kontinuierlicher Prozess. Dies wird in Abb. 5 durch die Rückkoppelung der re-positionierten Unternehmung mit ihrer aktiven

34

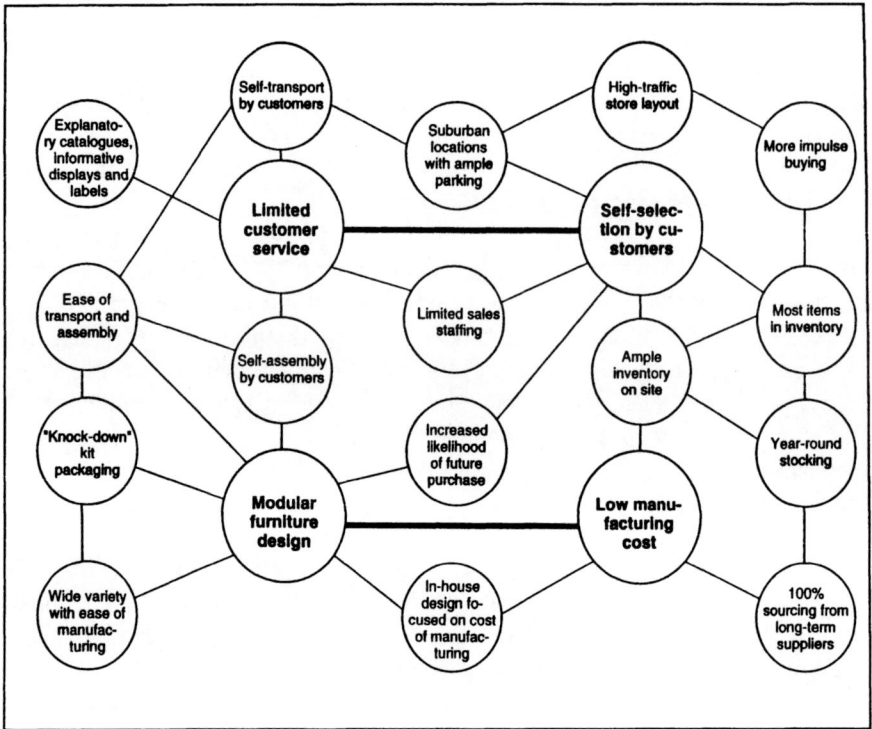

Quelle: Porter 1996, S. 71.

Abb. 6: Mapping Activity System

Marktgestaltung dargestellt. Der Kreislauf wird durch Marketing Audit gewährleistet, welcher wie ein Finanzaudit die kontinuierliche Überwachung des externen Wandels sicherstellt.

Die strategische Marktanalyse stellt das Management vor eine wesentliche Entscheidung: Entweder sein Angebotssystem im Sinne der Steigerung des Wertschöpfungssystems so zu erneuern, dass eine bessere Konstellation entsteht oder durch einen dynamischen Konkurrenten erworben, restrukturiert zu werden und eine neue Rolle in der Fusion spielen zu müssen.

Die zeitgemässe Marktanalyse befasst sich schwerpunktmässig nicht mehr mit der Positionierung von bestimmten Aktivitäten innerhalb einer Wertkette, um einen Mehrwert zu erzeugen, sondern mit dem Wertschöpfungssystem an sich. Es geht nicht um eine lineare Addition des Wertes in einer Kette, sondern um die Neugestaltung der Wertschöpfung innerhalb eines Netzwerkes mit einer Vielfalt von gleichzeitig werterzeugenden Beziehungen.

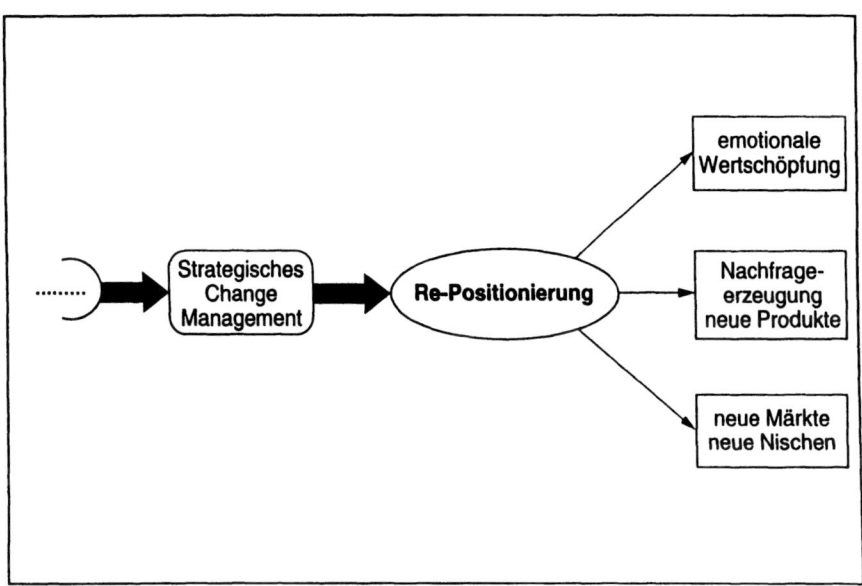

Abb. 7: Alternativen der Wertschöpfung infolge Repositionierung

Das Wertschöpfungssystem ist eine Kombination von Akteuren (Lieferanten, Marktpartner, Konkurrenten, Interessengruppen, Kunden, politische Entscheidungsträger), die gemeinsam einen Wert ko-produzieren. Die Erfindung neuer Prozesse der Wertschöpfung ergibt sich aus der Rekonstruierung der Rollen und Beziehungen, die zur Kreierung neuer Werte führen. Diese Vorstellung der Wertschöpfung in der Zeit der Diskontinuität und Transformation der Märkte verlangt eine ganzheitliche strategische Marktanalyse, die sich nicht nur auf das Produkt oder auf die Kunden oder auf die Konkurrenz bezieht, sondern auf alle Partner des globalen Marktes.

Die sehr differenzierten Möglichkeiten der strategischen Position im Markt sind situativ zu bestimmen. Es bieten sich folgende **Alternativen der Wertschöpfung** an (vgl. Abb. 7 in Verbindung mit Abb. 1):
(a) emotionale Wertschöpfung (bspw. Nike: Michael Jordan, Tiger Woods; Benetton: Darstellung der Realitäten) - z.B. die Verbindung mit einem Star und dem Produkt Schuh als Kultobjekt sowie Nike als cult-firm,
(b) Nachfrageerzeugung und Produktinnovation (bspw. Nestlé: Kaffee in Asien; Nike: Golf Tiger Woods; Internet: Bücher, CD),
(c) Marktinnovation und Nischenstrategie (Ikea: Asien/kids furniture).

6. Schlussfolgerungen

Wie der Beitrag verdeutlicht, besteht in vielen Unternehmungen im Rahmen der Restrukturierung bzw. Verbesserung der Produktivität oft das Problem, die betriebliche Effektivität anhand vorgegebener Konzepte zu fokussieren, die jedoch rein operational wirken, dabei die Entwicklung erfolgreicher Strategien vernachlässigen. In diesem Sinn hat Marketing versagt. Gerade in einer von Komplexität und Dynamik geprägten Umwelt ist eine spezifische und neuartige Denkweise gefragt. Kotler (1997) betrachtet die **gegenwärtige Marketing Malaise** unter drei Aspekten: (1) zu wenig an den Kundenwünschen fokussiert, (2) zu wenig an den Zielgruppen der Konsumenten ausgerichtet und (3) zu wenig innovativ und kreativ in bezug auf neue Nachfrager.

Es bedingt deshalb eine umfassendere Sicht. Das bedeutet auch, die Sichtweise nicht nur von aussen anch innen zu praktizieren, sondern auch von innen nach aussen. Unternehmungen müssen sich auf das Besondere konzentrieren und nicht nur gleiche Aktivitäten etwas besser machen als die Konkurrenz. Denn langfristig resultieren daraus keine Wettbewerbsvorteile, da Nachahmung keine Differenzierung bewirkt. Dauerhafte Wettbewerbsvorteile ergeben sich nicht aus der Imitation bzw. Nachahmung, sondern resultieren aus der marktlichen Wertschöpfung. Denn eine unreflektierte Aneignung überalterter Ideen, patentrezeptartiger Konstrukte (Modelle, Empowerment) und Konzepte (Prozesse, Methoden) sind in Folge einer hohen Veränderungsdynamik nicht mehr adäquat. Sie bilden höchstens Denkanstösse, jedoch angesichts einer wachsenden Komplexität und Dynamik werden sie ohne Einbezug der Strategie zu keiner erfolgreichen Transformation im Sinne einer marktlichen Wertschöpfung führen.

Strategisches Change Management wird zu einer wesentlichen Herausforderung für das Management. Und gerade deshalb kann eine einseitige Fokussierung gängiger Managementmethoden wie TQM, Outsourcing usw. nicht geeignet sein (sie führt zwar zu Produktivitäts- und Rentabilitätssteigerung, jedoch nicht zu einer zukunftsgerichteten strategisch-orientierten Sichtweise); es bedarf vielmehr einer spezifisch strategischen, wirtschaftlichen, organisatorischen und kulturellen Sichtweise (umfassende, gesamtheitliche Sicht). Eckpfeiler eines solchen Change Management ist somit nicht eine rein operationale Vorgehensweise, sondern muss durch Re-Positionierung der Unternehmung in einem sich wandelnden Umweltsystem erfolgen. Das aber bedingt eine strategische Marktanalyse, die schlussendlich in einer marktlichen Wertschöpfung mündet und so einen **Customer Value** generiert.

Eine Konzentration auf betriebliche Effektivität, wie sie in den letzten Jahren von vielen Unternehmungen praktiziert wurde, führt langfristig zu keinem Wettbewerbsvorteil und somit auch zu keinem Fortschritt. Denn anstelle eines Human Resource Value entstand ein Personalabbau, mit dem zwar eine Rentabilitätssteigerung erzielt werden konnte. Es wäre jedoch vermessen und zeugt von keiner strategischen Vision bzw. von einem eng begrenzten unternehmerischen Denken, der Effektivität und Rentabilität mehr Bedeutung beizumessen als der Strategie.

Gefragt ist daher ein neues Denken. Das bedeutet aber auch, den Status quo laufend in Frage zu stellen, auch bezüglich der Strategie, was nichts anderes heisst, als sich von bestehenden, bislang erfolgreichen Denkmustern zu verabschieden. Für das Management führt das zu einer intensiven Auseinandersetzung mit einem neuen strategischen Denken (Strategieentwicklung) im Zusammenhang mit Führungskompetenz. Nur so gelingt es, sich von einseitig betrieblichen Verbesserungen zu lösen und die Strategie wieder zur Kernaufgabe zu machen, nach der sich die operativen Prozesse zu richten haben. Dies ist nur dann erfolgreich, wenn wir uns von einer direkten Linearität verabschieden und uns eine neue Sichtweise (Nichtlinearität) von der Zukunft aneignen. Betriebliche Effektivität ohne strategische Ausrichtung wird keine Wettbewerbsvorteile schaffen.

Anhang

Anlässlich des 7. Zürcher GSBA-Management Kongresses zum Thema Change Management erfolgte innerhalb des Workshops VII eine schriftliche Umfrage. Dabei wurden 75 Fragebogen verteilt; ausgefüllt und ausgewertet wurden 45 (=60%). Folgende Ergebnisse brachte die Umfrage (für detailliertere Informationen wenden Sie sich bitte an die Autoren):

- Folgende Branchen waren vertreten: 45% aus Industrie, 31% aus Dienstleistungen (v.a. Banken), 13% aus EDV/Informatik, 7% aus Handel, 4% Verschiedenes.

- Die meisten Unternehmungen verfolgen als Zielsetzung den Shareholder Value, gefolgt vom Stakeholder Value sowie anderen Zielen (langfristige Marktführerschaft, sustainable enterprise usw.).

- Über 75% stimmten mit der Aussage überein, dass in der heutigen Transformation sowohl ein operatives wie strategisches Change Management angebracht ist. Gründe sind zur Hauptsache in der Reaktion auf die Globalisierung, stetig ändernde Marktbedürfnisse, Erkennen neuer Marktchancen zu finden.

- Eine weitere wichtige Frage beschäftigte sich mit dem Inhalt eines strategischen Change Management: Hier wurden v.a. Aspekte geäussert wie Reflexion und ständiges Zweifeln der Wettbewerbsposition, langfristige Ausrichtung (Vision, Mission), rasche Reaktion auf Kundenbedürfnisse.

38

- Über 90% sahen Change Management bezüglich Unternehmenserfolg als unverzichtbar an - die Probleme der Umsetzung liegen generell im Überzeugen der Mitarbeiter, in allgemeinen Widerständen/Blockaden, im Fehlen eines ganzheitlichen Konzeptes, im Management/ alte Strukturen, in der Kommunikation sowie häufig auch in kulturellen Gegebenheiten und fehlender Vision.

- Interessant waren die Aussagen, welchen Weg (Instrumente) die Unternehmungen zur Performancesteigerung wählen, wobei zu betonen ist, dass Instrumente wie Business Reengineering, Total Quality Management, Lean-Management usw. von fast 50% als Modetrends bezeichnet wurden.

Beim Aspekt Kostenreduktion wurden am meisten genannt: Outsourcing, Total Quality Management und Reengineering.

Beim Aspekt Wertschöpfungssteigerung befanden sich folgende Instrumente an vorderster Stelle: Erschliessung neuer Segmente, Öffnung neuer geographischer Märkte und Customization.

Literatur:

Bleicher, K. (1992), Change Management als unternehmerische Herausforderung, Wachstum als Leitmotiv der Unternehmensentwicklung, in: Thexis, Vol. 9, (1992), No. 2, S. 4-13

Collins, J., Porras, J. (1994), Visionary Companies - Visionen im Management, München 1995

D'Aveni, R.(1994), Hypercompetition, New York 1994

Doppler, K., Lauterburg, Ch. (Hrsg.) (1994), Change Management, Frankfurt, New York 1994

Drucker, P. (1993), Post-Capitalist Society, New York 1993

Hammer, M., Champy, J. (1994), Business reengineering, Frankfurt, New York 1994

Kleps, K. (1997), Droht Europa den Anschluss zu verlieren?, in Neue Zürcher Zeitung, Nr. 224, 27./28. September 1997, S. 93

Kotler, Ph. (1997), Über Marketing, ZfU Marketing-Veranstaltung vom 6./7. Oktober 1997, Zürich

Krulis-Randa, J. (1997), Human Resource Management als Wettbewerbsvorteil in globalen Märkten, in: Siegwart, H., Dubs, R., Mahari, J. (Hrsg.), Meilensteine im Management - Human Resource Management, Stuttgart, Zürich, Wien 1997, S. 124-135

Levitt, T. (1983), The globalization of markets, in: Harvard Business Review, Vol. 61(1983), No. 5/6, S. 92-102

Mary, M. (1996), Change-Management als Chance, Zürich 1996

Mintzberg, H. (1996), Musings on Management, in: Harvard Business Review, Vol. 74 (1996), No. 5, S. 61-67

o.V. (1997), Erhebliche Verluste, in: Wirtschaftswoche 1997, No. 41, S. 127

Pettigrew, A., Whipp, R.(1996), Managing Change for Competitive Success, Oxford, Cambridge 1996

Porter, M. (1996), What is strategy?, in: Harvard Business Review, Vol. 74 (1996), No. 6, S. 61-78

Porter, M. (1985), Competitive Advantage, New York 1985

Reiss, M. (1995), Implementierung, in: Corsten, H., Reiss, M. (Hrsg.), Handbuch Unternehmungsführung, Wiesbaden 1995, S. 292-301

Rühli, E. (1996), Strategische Führung bei Hyperwettbewerb, in: Staffelbach, B., Wehrli, H.P. (Hrsg.), Markt- und menschenorientierte Unternehmensführung, Bern 1996, S. 9-29

Rühli, E. (1989), Strategische Unternehmungsführung heute, in: Rühli, E. (Hrsg.), Strategisches Management in schweizerischen Industrie-Unternehmungen, Bern 1989, S. 11-53

Scholz, Chr. (Hrsg.) (1995), Internationales Change-Management - Internationale Praxiserfahrungen bei Veränderung von Unternehmen und Humanressourcen, Stuttgart 1995

Stamm, M. (1995), Controlling und Change Management, in: Controller Magazin, 1995, Heft 5, S. 280-284

Thom, N. (1997), Management des Wandels, in: Die Unternehmung, Vol. 51(1997), No. 3, S. 201-214

Yip, G.S. (1992), Total global strategy: Managing for worldwide competitive advantage, New York 1992

Change and the Learning Organization

Salvatore Belardo
Jackov Crnkovic

Zusammenfassung:

Die lernende Organisation ist ein neuer Ansatz zum Management des Wandels. Ausgangspunkt ist die heute extrem schnelle Vervielfachung des Wissens. Für ein Unternehmen ist es eine Herausforderung, schneller als die Konkurrenz zu lernen. Es wird herausgearbeitet, wie ein Unternehmen sich zu einer erfolgreichen lernenden Organisation entwickeln kann.

1. Introduction

When asked, "how do you know whether an organization has learned," a student of management commented, "if it has survived." At first this appears to be a rather naive or even evasive answer. It is, however, quite profound, and raises a number of questions concerning one of the more interesting new age management approaches to change, the Learning Organization. The Learning Organization has become as popular as other transforming ideas such as Reengineering, and Total Quality Management (TQM). However, unlike Reengineering or TQM, the benefits of which can be observed by monitoring process measures of performance, such as cost, timeliness, and quality, the benefits of the Learning Organization are intangible and therefore hard to measure.

In order to understand the organizational importance of learning and its by-product knowledge, consider for a moment a company's intangible assets, that is, the difference between net assets and market value. For Microsoft, the net assets and market value for the year 1995 were $4.5 billion and $49.1 billion, respectively. This can be interpreted to mean that the intangible assets, which consist of know-how, knowledge, and other results of learning (i.e. patents, copyrights, etc.), were approximately ten times the net assets. The same is true of many corporations. In recognition of these important intangible assets, firms have become increasingly interested in the Learning Organization. In an attempt to benefit from the knowledge of its employees, General Motors has announced the appointment of a senior level, chief learning officer to coordinate and disseminate the company's global knowledge. Other organizations including General Electric, Merck, Dow Chemicals, Skandia AFS, Hughes Communication, and Andersen

Consulting, have also recognized the importance of organizational learning in today's rapidly developing knowledge economy. The chief learning officer will be to the knowledge economy what the chief information officer is to the information economy.

In order to survive, organizations must change. Jack Welch, the CEO of General Electric Company put it succinctly when he concluded, " when the rate of change outside the firm is greater than the rate of change inside, the end is in sight." The connection between knowledge, learning, and beneficial change such as that envisioned by Welch, has been well established by science. Science posits that systems fail due to the phenomenon of entropy (i.e., the disorder that occurs in any closed system). General Systems Theory states that only by the importation of resources from outside, can the system be re-energized, and entropy arrested (Kast/Rosenzweig 1972). Similarly, organizations change when resources, in the form of new knowledge, are imported from outside, especially from other domains and disciplines. While any organization can change, change without the benefit of learning is risky, and inefficient. Changes that result from learning, however, foster the kinds of innovation that result in competitive advantage and ensure survival.

Ray Stata, CEO of Analog Devices Inc., provides a sense of the immediate importance of organizational learning in his prophetic statement: "the rate at which individuals and organizations learn may be the only sustainable source of competitive advantage" (Stata 1988). The need to learn faster than the competition poses a daunting challenge for many organizations today because of two interrelated forces. The first stems from the ever decreasing lifecycles of products and services, that is the time from initiation to maturity and decline, and the second from the rapidly increasing amount of information and knowledge available from literally thousands of sources. The first force is readily observable when one considers the computer and telecommunications industry, where new hardware and software are introduced at a dizzying speed. An example of the speed of change in the computer industry can be observed when one looks at components such as disk drives. The life-cycle for these critical components has been decreasing to the point where it is currently less than nine months (Gilson 1994). According to Peter Drucker (1991), the Industrial Revolution increased productivity 50 fold. In 25 years since the microprocessor was invented, computer power has increased 1,000 fold. This is equivalent to an Industrial Revolution per year. The second factor was confirmed in a study conducted by Professor Barbara Sizemore (1995). She estimates that the sum of humankind's knowledge doubled between the years 1750 and 1900, then doubled again between 1900 and 1950, then again between 1950 and 1960, and again between 1960 and 1965. Assuming this trend continues, by the year 2020, knowledge will double every 75 days. While some may question what constitutes knowledge (e.g., explicit, tacit, declarative, procedural), there is no question that knowledge is more readily available today, due to a large extent, because of new modes of dissemination such as the Internet. The Internet is doubling in size every year, and the World Wide Web every 90 days. Metcalfes law argues that each new connection adds value in proportion to the square of the number of users.

While faster learning is necessitated by the continuing decrease in product life-cycles, learning is confounded by the amount and variety of knowledge available. Building an organization that can manage these two forces and learn faster than the competition has, therefore, become a key survival factor for most organizations. None other than Peter Senge, considered by many to be one of the principal architects of the concept of the Learning Organization recently concluded that there is no such thing as a Learning Organization (Senge 1994). We concur, and believe that the problems that inhibit the development of Learning Organizations are not unlike those that confronted the early developers of Expert Systems. It wasn't until these pioneers of Expert Systems recognized that the problems they faced were too complex to rely on a single perspective or discipline that they began to achieve dramatic successes. We propose that the developers of Learning Organizations will need to learn how to synthesize knowledge from a number of disciplines including, computer science, cognitive psychology, and organizational behavior, just as the developers of Expert Systems did. Because Learning Organizations are far more complex than the current definitions suggest, a more comprehensive definition is needed in order to better understand how to develop them. To this end, we present a multi-disciplinary definition, which identifies disciplines from which a better understanding might be found.

In this manuscript, we present a research agenda that focuses attention on questions that need to be addressed in order to understand and overcome the impediments to the successful development of Learning Organizations. In the next section we develop our own definition of the Learning Organization by building on and extending the works of others such as Argyris/Schon (1974), Senge (1990), Kim (1993), Nevis/DiBella/Gould (1995) and Cohen/Sproull (1996). After that, we examine key elements of our definition, focusing on critical questions such as: how do people learn, how do we elicit knowledge, and what is required to ensure that knowledge is elicited, shared, and utilized. In the conclusion, we pose a number of research questions and identify disciplines from which possible answers might be found.

2. The Learning Organization

There are numerous definitions of the Learning Organization. Several of the more descriptive definitions are presented below. Senge (1990) for example defines the Learning Organization as follows:

> Learning Organizations are places where people continually expand their
> capacity to create the results they truly desire, where new and expansive
> patterns of thinking are nurtured, where collective aspirations are set free
> and where people are continually learning to learn together.

This definition emphasizes the importance of team learning as well as of what
Argyris/Schon (1974) and Schon (1996) describe as deutero learning or learning
how to learn.

In his book Visionary Leadership, Nanus (1992), maintains that:

> Organizational Learning is facilitated when there is openness and trust, that
> allow people to embrace change and experimentation without feeling
> personally threatened. It also helps if the culture supports widespread
> participation in decision making, an entrepreneurial ethic and a diversity of
> skills and viewpoints.

In the above definition the author recognizes the importance of culture and values
as they relate to learning. Here Nanus recognizes that for learning to occur,
organizations must establish a culture where risk-taking is encouraged and the
fear that inhibits learning and, hence, innovation, is eliminated.

More prescriptive definitions of the Learning Organization are found in two of
Senge's works, and in a more recent article by Nevis/DiBella/Gould (1995). In his
seminal article, "The Leaders New Work: Building Learning Organizations"
(1990), and in the book, **The Fifth Discipline: The Art and Practice of the
Learning Organization** (1990), Senge described what he believes are the
disciplines or skills required by the leaders of the Learning Organization. These
are:

(1) **Shared vision:** Senge points out that a shared vision ensures that everyone
has a picture in his/her mind of where the organization is going. Without
shared vision, there will not be an awareness of the need or the motivation to
learn and change.

(2) **Surfacing and testing mental models:** Mental models are defined as deeply
ingrained assumptions, generalizations, or even pictures or images that
influence how we understand the world and how we take action. Mental
models are active, they shape how we act. In order to ensure that the best
ideas get put into practice, it is essential that leaders ensure that defensive
routines that people employ to protect themselves from embarrassment do
not inhibit the articulation of new and innovative ideas. Surfacing and testing
mental models is an important means of facilitating communication and
ensuring learning.

(3) **Systems thinking:** Senge, concludes that successful leaders are, to a large
extent, systems thinkers. Systems thinking is too broad a definition to convey
here; but suffice it to say, it consists of numerous skills needed to help people
see the big picture. This is necessary, in order to help correctly identify the
problem that needs to be addressed rather than the obvious symptoms. One of
the important underlying features of systems thinking is the idea that "there is
no outside." In other words, people, the organization, and the cause of the

problem are part of a single system. Systems thinkers recognize that assessing blame is counter productive, and in fact does, little to help identify the real problem.

(4) **Team Learning:** In discussing the relationship between truth and learning, Immanuel Kant, the great German philosopher, noted "that apart from speculation, there are only two ways I can increase my fund of knowledge, by experience and by what others tell me" (Infield 1963). Leaders must be able to ensure that information and knowledge are shared so that team learning occurs and synergy, a primary benefit of team learning, results.

(5) **Personal Mastery:** This is essential to the Learning Organization because it recognizes the importance of continuous individual learning to the success of the organization. Maslow noted that there exists within individuals a hierarchy of needs ranging from survival needs at the lowest level to self actualization at the highest and that how a person behaves is dependent upon the degree to which his various needs have been satisfied. In order to encourage personal mastery, leaders must recognize that learning occurs differently in individuals, at different times, in different places, and for different reasons.

As noted above, Senge recently concluded that there is no such thing as a Learning Organization, nevertheless, he did note that five operating principles are beginning to emerge. These principles are:

(1) The Learning Organization embodies new capabilities including love, compassion, humility; learning, Senge notes, is a human activity.

(2) Learning Organizations are built by communities of servant leaders. Senge notes that our conventional notions of leadership are imbedded in heroic myths, which hold that those higher up in the organization must be more important and more knowledgeable than those lower in the organization. For organizations to become Learning Organizations, leaders must recognize that winning ideas will undoubtedly come from others in the organization, often below them in the hierarchy. Senge's observation tends to confirm what Nonaka/Takeuchi (1995), conclude about the important role of the middle manager in knowledge creating companies.

(3) Learning arises through performance and practice. Learning is too important to leave to chance. While certainly some of what we learn, we learn by insight, much of what we learn, we learn by trial and error, and by practice. The operative expression here is trial and error. No one plays the guitar like Andres Segovia did without years of practice.

(4) Process and content are inseparable. Systems thinking as noted earlier, suggests that there is no outside. Senge notes that it is impossible to think of new process oriented designs without addressing the way people think. He rightfully criticizes management educators as treating technical issues and behavioral issues separately. In an earlier work, Leavitt (1965) described the problems that result when one organizational variable is changed without due

consideration of the other variables. In recognition of this principle, management consulting firms have begun to integrate systems development and change management efforts in order to more effectively develop and implement computer applications. Furthermore, there exists a kind of recursive relationship between information technology (IT) and transforming ideas such as the Learning Organization. While IT enables Organizational Learning, it also facilitates learning by promoting the sharing of information and knowledge across functions and especially across disciplines.

(5) Learning is dangerous. Quite simply, it means that we often encounter knowledge that challenges what we know. To acknowledge such incongruities would logically require us to change, in other words to unlearn what we have accepted to be true. Given that our mental models are deeply ingrained assumptions and images that influence how we act, changing them requires a great deal of commitment and effort. Change is hard work; and because it threatens the status quo, resistance to change is inevitable.

Nevis/DiBella/Gould (1995) present an even more prescriptive approach to building Learning Organizations. They contend that all organizations engage in some form of collective learning and propose three learning related factors that determine success: well developed competencies, an attitude that supports continuous improvements in value-adding activities, and the ability to renew or revitalize itself by unlearning those things that inhibit innovation. Further, they present several assumptions, the most important of which is that the learning process has identifiable stages: knowledge acquisition, knowledge sharing, and knowledge utilization. Each prescriptive approach by itself does not present a complete enough understanding of what is required to build a Learning Organization. Senge's definition recognizes the important role that leadership plays in building Learning Organizations, not only in creating and communicating vision, but in directing resources and creating a culture conducive to continuous learning and knowledge sharing. Senge's definition, however, does not provide prescriptions for building such a culture. Answers to questions, such as why people learn and when they learn, are critical to understanding how to develop a culture that is conducive to continuous learning and knowledge sharing. None of the definitions discussed above really consider how people learn as being germane to building Learning Organizations.

Nevis/DiBella/Gould (1995) recognize that organizational learning requires that knowledge sources be identified and that knowledge must be elicited, represented, and stored so that it can be effectively shared and utilized by others. Yet their definition does not discuss how this can be accomplished efficiently and effectively. Experience has shown that whatever system design is employed to support activities such as these that it must be easy to employ. Anyone who has ever attempted to develop true knowledge based systems will confirm that the elicitation process is the bottleneck in development process; it is hard, laborious, and error prone. Finally, the definitions presented above recognize that in order for knowledge to be of value, it must be utilized in ways that enhance and extend one's capabilities. Yet the definitions do not offer ways of valuing knowledge and learning.

What is needed is a definition that incorporates the best of each of the descriptive and prescriptive definitions, yet one that accounts for the deficiencies presented above. To this end, we propose the following definition.

> People learn and organizations benefit when the results of learning are shared and utilized in meaningful ways. In order to benefit from shared learning and to ensure that important recipes are not lost, knowledge, the result of insights and learning in practice, must be identified, elicited, represented, stored, disseminated and used effectively. To do this organizations must create a culture whereby knowledge and learning are valued, where individuals will be encouraged to engage in continuous generative learning and willingly share their knowledge with the entire organization.

This definition suggests that those intent on building Learning Organizations can and must benefit from the research and findings from a multitude of disciplines. Stratton (1964), contends that, "today's complex problems require new unities that will bring together many different resources and bring about a new synthesis of knowledge, joining together the contributions of physical and biological scientists, economists, political scientists, engineers, and philosophers." He goes on to say that the task of welding together these components of learning offers the highest intellectual challenge of our time.

The above definition and the following sections are an attempt to do just that, to weld together the various components necessary to understand and develop Learning Organizations. The underlined words are considered key aspects of the definition. The following six sections examine the key words and associated issues that need to be addressed if we ever hope to build true Learning Organizations and not simply electronic mail (e-mail) systems that pass as such.

3. Building Learning Organizations: A Multidisciplinary Prescription

3.1. Learning: Getting What Is Outside, In

Our definition noted that people learn and that organizations benefit when the results are shared. Researchers from education and educational psychology have conducted considerable research concerning how people learn and have proposed several theories. Equally important is research concerning when people learn, why they learn, what they learn, and even where they learn. One theory suggests that humans learn by experience or by trial and error, sort of like learning how to ride a bicycle. Piaget (1980), the noted Swiss psychologist, suggested that learning by experience could be divided into two basic questions:

(1) how does what is outside a person get in? and

(2) how does what is inside a person get out? He suggested that the answer to the first question involves accommodation or the shaping of internal meaning making structures by experience. These internal meaning making structures are similar to the mental models described by Senge and others. The answer to the second question, he proposed, involved the process of "play" which can be described as the assimilation or imposition of internal meaning making structures on experience.

Another theory posits that learning can be explained by higher mental processes such as decision making, information processing, understanding in terms of perception, awareness and insight. Insight is the sudden perception of relationships among elements of a problem situation. Kohler (1927) described an example of insight learning as the learning that occurred when chimpanzees in a cage suddenly recognized that by stacking boxes they would be able to reach bananas that could not be reached otherwise. Koffka (1963) and Lewin (1938) describe other cognitive theories of learning, such as Gestalt and Life Space.

The education and psychology literature is replete with theories and the results of clinical trials that shed light on this important aspect of Learning Organizations. In building a Learning Organization, however, it is important to understand not only how people learn but also when they learn. Experiments suggest that learning occurs all the time. In one well-documented experiment, three groups of mice were presented with three similar puzzle mazes. In one maze a food reward was given to the mice once they reached the reward end. The group that was given the reward made it to the end significantly faster than the other two groups. When mice in the second group were given a reward after they successfully made it to the end of their puzzle maze, their speed the very next time was almost as fast as that of the first group; and it only took several trials to increase their speed to that of the first group. One conclusion that can be drawn is that learning occurs all the time, but will it not be exhibited until there is a reward or recognition.

What individuals learn can be viewed in terms of the accepted theories. For those who subscribe to a behavioral notion of learning, it can be assumed that what individuals learn will be a function of what brings them closer to their basic needs. The cognitive school of learning suggests that individuals will learn wholes or gestalts related to expectancies.

Where individuals learn is important as well. Students who participate in remedial programs similar to those designed to help improve perfomance on standardized tests such the Graduate Management Aptitude Test (GMAT), are advised to study in a room similar to the room where the actual test will be given. Evidence of the importance of context can be observed in everyday life. For example, if we see someone on the street we may not remember his or her name. However, when we see the individual in context in a bank, a school, or on the job, it is easier to remember his or her name. New approaches to learning recognize this fact and emphasize the need for context based learning experiences. While people learn, learning benefits the organization when it is shared. In order for knowledge to be shared it must be elicited from those who possess it.

3.2. Elicitation: Getting What Is Inside, Out

Researchers in cognitive psychology suggests that what a person knows about a particular subject can not be described according to one type of knowledge (e.g., classificatory knowledge, knowledge of concepts, etc.). They conclude that there does not exist an all-encompassing taxonomy of knowledge. However, for most narrowly defined problems in a given domain, knowledge can be classified according to the following four types: knowledge of facts and heuristics, classificatory knowledge, knowledge of concepts and relations, and knowledge about routine procedures. The cognitive psychologists have devised means of eliciting the various types of knowledge, recognizing that different techniques are needed for different types of knowledge (Gamack/Young 1984).

The first column of Table 1 shows the four different types of knowledge mentioned above and the third column some possible elicitation techniques for each type of knowledge. Examples of the knowledge employed by an experienced commercial loan officer are provided in column two.

Elicitation is a difficult and demanding aspect of building Learning Organizations; choosing the right technique, applying it properly and interpreting the results correctly are critical to getting the knowledge that "experts" possess. Even when the correct approach is employed there is no guarantee that the knowledge that

Type of Knowledge	Example of Knowledge	Possible Elicitation Techniques
– Concepts and Relations – Routine Procedures – Facts and Heuristics – Classificatory Knowledge	– Portfolio Modeling – Calculation of risk, credit worthiness – What to do if assumptions are violated – Choosing among candidate tests R.O.I, NPV, etc.	– Repertory Grid – Protocol Analysis – Memory Probe Techniques – Sorting Tasks

Table 1: Different Types of Knowledge and Possible Elicitation Techniques

has been elicited is the right knowledge. One of the authors had an experience a number of years ago when he attempted to elicit knowledge about signal processing from an expert in the field, using a memory probe technique. As a result, 238 rules were elicited from the expert. Later it was discovered that the 238 rules represented explicit knowledge, the type that could be found in training manuals, but not the tacit knowledge that could distinguish an expert from a novice. It wasn't until a special chauffeured memory probing technique (the chauffeur was a colleague of the expert) was employed that 18 significantly different rules emerged. These rules were based upon the heuristics that the expert had devised as a result of experience and were deemed to be significantly more valuable in solving signal processing problems than the other 238 rules. As was noted above, mental models are active; they are changed as a result of learning. As such, any system for eliciting knowledge must be capable of continuously updating the knowledge base. In order to store and process knowledge, it must first be represented.

3.3. Representation

As noted above, the efficiency and effectiveness of the knowledge elicitation process is highly dependent upon the elicitation techniques employed. Once the knowledge has been elicited, it must be represented so that it can be stored on a computer and effectively managed. The computer system, whether part of a decision support system, a knowledge based system, an expert system, or a Learning Organization, cannot process knowledge that cannot be represented. Computer scientists have done a considerable amount of work in this important area.

Knowledge representation can be described as the study of how reality can be represented and the kinds of reasoning that can be applied to such representations. Knowledge representation is just as important when building a Learning Organization as it is when building a computer based expert system, because it is through the process of representing knowledge that important organizational knowledge such as values, goals, and vision can be stored, disseminated and institutionalized.

A number of different representation schemes exist, including entities, facets, objects, frames, scripts, rules, and networks. The type of elicitation technique will influence the representation technique employed. For example, the result of protocol analysis does not translate easily into rules. The selection of the type of representation raises questions that include the tradeoffs between representational adequacy and effectiveness, fidelity, and the computational cost of translating and storing information. While it is difficult to compare representation techniques, a simple comparison of the efficiency of programming languages should illustrate the point about representation techniques, since the representation model employed will, in addition, determine the computer language used to store and process the knowledge.

One of the classic elicitation/representation problems can be found in the following:

Solve for each letter in the following relationship

Donald   Let D = 5; all letters must be between 0 and 9
+ Gerald
Robert

This problem is often presented to students in courses dealing with Artificial Intelligence in order to demonstrate the problems encountered when one tries to capture, represent and disseminate the knowledge that underlies the solution. When the above problem was solved using the programming language C, it took approximately 40 times longer to solve than when programmed using the A.I. language PROLOG.

The problem with most representation approaches is that they are rather artificial. People do not tend to represent what they know in terms of scripts or semantic nets. Objects, it has been argued, tend to be more orthogonal to human mental models of the world. Considerable work remains to be done, however, in developing representational schemes that are easy to understand and use, and yet capture, represent, and communicate the tacit knowledge necessary for in-depth learning.

3.4. Dissemination

Once the relevant knowledge has been identified, elicited, and represented, it must be disseminated. During the management information systems era, managers used to say "there is so much information that we are drowning in it." Today with data/information warehouses, and the plethora of information providers, the situation is far worse. Managing data that exists on various internal and external data bases continues to be a key success factor for organizations, especially those organizations intent on gaining advantages from information and from knowledge.

Many organizations like General Motors have attempted to disseminate knowledge through internal information communication systems, such as e-mail. Others have attempted to use Internet technologies or Groupware technologies, such as Lotus Notes.

Since its founding in 1982, Sun Microsystems has used Internet technologies internally to share information throughout its organization. All new employees learn to use e-mail, Stp, and a Usnet style news reader to keep up to date. Sun's slogan is "The Network is the Computer." Today Sun has more than 1000 internal web servers in operation, publishing approximately 250,000 Web and other electronic pages. Sun says "we now see (the Web) as a key part of our information infrastructure, as a way to save time and money by efficiently distributing information throughout the company" (Business Week, February 26, 1996). Sun estimates that various intranet applications have saved the company millions of dollars. They state that document distribution through the intranet that includes on line documentation, manuals, policies and procedures, work flow approvals, employee self-services, and information systems support has saved them $25 million per year.

Many other companies have also taken advantage of these technologies, including Hewlett Packard, US West, Morgan Stanley, Eli-Lily, Silicon Graphics, and Visa International. Applications range from the communication of bond positions and interest rates to traders throughout the world, to world-wide planning concerning how to schedule clinical trials and submissions for new drugs in 120 countries, (Sprout, Fortune, November 27, 1995).

In addition to Internet technology, firms have begun to employ a proprietary technology known as Lotus Notes. Lotus Notes is an architecture designed to support many types of groupware applications but primarily different place-different time applications. Lotus Notes is a text/document based database with hypertext links. It consists of a graphical user interface (GUI) for presentation and retrieval and is a network of independent distributed databases. An excellent example of the use of Lotus Notes is Andersen Consulting's Knowledge Xchange. The Knowledge Xchange consists of widely disseminated Notes applications used by managers, and partners; junior staff are just beginning to use it. The Knowledge Xchange is used for basic communication (HR, Training), Project Communications (Memos, Draft, Deliverables), Project Information (Staff Availability), Technical Information (Technology Discussions), Project Reports (Billing Standard Forms), and Staff Evaluations.

Knowledge Xchange began as an experiment to automate "Knowledge Capital." It was started because of the simultaneous need for e-mail standards, the desire to leverage project experience and networks, and to share competitive data across offices. As a result of the Knowledge Xchange, Andersen Consulting believes team interactions have been greatly improved. The Knowledge Xchange has provided simpler and faster access to corporate level information; new networks of experts have been established with critical technical and applications experience; and it has significantly reduced paper flow. However, the Knowledge Xchange has also created some problems. Experts complain that they are swamped with requests for information. In addition, the Xchange is often incongruent with older organizational paradigms. For example, senior staff have several roles which tend to conflict with groupware and collaborative models. A more critical analysis of the Knowledge Xchange raises questions concerning whether organizational learning is actually taking place. Does the Knowledge Xchange capture information? The answer is definitely yes. But is it capturing and disseminating knowledge? Is learning taking place? Is the knowledge that is being disseminated used to facilitate innovation and achieve other organizational goals and objectives? Here the answer gets a bit murky.

3.5. Utilization

Perhaps one of the reasons it has taken organizations so long to recognize human knowledge as the most important capital asset is because traditional accounting methodologies are inappropriate for valuing such intangibles. Various accounting procedures such as the market approach method, the cost approach, and the income method all have problems with intangible assets. For example, if the market approach is used, it is difficult to determine whether a certain price would have a close relation to the value of the same intangible in a different setting. We think we know the answer to this for physical assets, but we cannot be certain. With the income approach, questions concerning appropriate discount rates for knowledge, and the determination of an identifiable and limited useful life present real problems.

Yet companies recognize the need to measure and value knowledge. Measuring knowledge is a tremendous value in rapidly changing knowledge-based industries such as computer hardware and software, the financial and services industries, and especially for consulting firms. Skandia AFS, a Scandinavian based insurance firm, has started including an addendum on its annual report that describes important non-financial measures. As Leif Edvinsson, Director of Intellectual Capital at Scania, notes:
- The issue is not to measure financial capital only, but to have a balanced system of measurements that will end up creating financial capital.
- Several new age methods for valuing knowledge are beginning to appear in the literature.

DOW Chemical has devised a six stage process which it employs in its polyolefin plastics business. Other methods include Economic Information Analysis, the NCI method, and Sveiby's Method (1995). Sveiby's method, for example, involves three main indicators for examining a company's intangible assets: competence, that is who are the experts; internal structure measured by such things as investments in information technology; and external structure which deals with variables, such as customer satisfaction. These new methods attempt to capture important factors involving intangible risks and benefits. They do not, however, offer much more information than traditional methods in terms of valuation.

There are a number of pitfalls associated with including intangibles in financial statements, including inherent management bias to overstate the value of intangibles, and the fear of disclosing competitive secrets. Nevertheless, organizations must recognize the importance and value of these critical assets so that they can better manage them. As a representative from one of the Big Six consulting firms commented recently regarding Learning Organizations. " I would love to be able to sell Learning Organization systems to our customers, but how do we justify their investment?"

3.6. Culture

Nearly every definition of a Learning Organization alludes to the importance of a culture of openness and trust which, as Nanus notes, allows people to embrace change and experimentation without fear. As in any of the new age management approaches, trust is a key success factor, perhaps the most important factor of all. Like other transforming ideas, participation and cooperation are critical to implementation success. Philosophers have long understood that the key to cooperation is trust. However, trust is something that takes a considerable effort to develop, yet, can be destroyed by a single act.

Philosophers have proposed ethical systems as ways of creating trust. Whether in the form of religious laws such as the Ten Commandments, or social contracts such as the Bill of Rights, these systems are intended to minimize the inefficiencies in human relations that impede the communication, cooperation, and participation necessary for successful business activities. Magda Ratajski (1994) provides the rationale for trust when she states: "if everyone cheated, trust would not exist. Barring this, every party to every transaction would be suspicious of everyone else, and in such a system, business people would spend valuable time, energy, and resources on self-protection and retaliation. In such a system there would be little incentive to take risks or to innovate." Fukuyama (1995) believes that trust should be viewed as an important component of social capital since, as he argues, "widespread distrust imposes a tax on economic activity that high-trust societies do not incur." Robert Krikorian (1984) notes that every business decision and action has an ethical dimension and that they all depend on trust. He goes on to say that "we must compete in the arena of values, not efficiency, and productivity or performance; the public already assumes that." Creating a culture that ensures trust depends upon the values that the organization practices through its various dealings with key stakeholders. It is these values that characterize the ethical organization.

Not only will trust help organizations achieve the maximum benefits that new age management techniques promise, but for a number of organizations, especially those that have commoditized their products or services, trust can serve as a competitive weapon. Just as firms have employed cost, innovation, and quality as competitive thrusts, we believe that, in the future, trust will become an important strategic thrust.

4. Recommendations

The above sections provide a blueprint for building a Learning Organization, however, the building blocks needed to construct such an organization are yet to be quarried. The following section presents several questions that are representative of the type of questions that must be addressed if we hope to adequately understand and build Learning Organizations. It is our hope that the following questions will stimulate the thinking that is necessary to help formulate additional research questions.

4.1. Learning

The above discussion raises a number of research questions not the least of which is: is there an organizational analog to individual learning? Kim (1993) noted that Organizational Learning is more complex and dynamic than individual learning. The neurologist Damasio suggests that emotion plays an important role in learning, explaining not only when, but why, individuals learn (Lemonick 1995). He states, for example, that a person who invests in the stock market will become motivated to learn about the market when an investment goes badly. What, then, is the organizational equivalent of emotion? The answer to these questions, we believe, will require the combined research efforts of scholars from disciplines such as education, psychology, and, even, sociology, who have studied individual learning and the importance of social factors as they relate to group processes such as team learning and decision making.

4.2. Elicitation

Another major research question for builders of Learning Organizations, is how can efficient and effective elicitation techniques be developed and employed as part of a cooperative, work computer-based environment? Currently, elicitation techniques, such as the Repertory Grid, are available on the Internet. They are, however, difficult to use and interpret; determining the elements and constructs needed to employ a Repertory Grid, usually requires someone well versed in the technique and/or the domain of study. Other elicitation techniques such as Probing Memory or Protocol Analysis, require a great deal of interactivity and human interpretation. Solutions to this problem will require the combined research efforts of people from cognitive psychology, computer science, and information science. While the cognitive psychologists have devised a number of ways to help individuals make explicit what they know about a particular task or concept, the computer and information scientists have done research on developing more natural man-machine interface features.

4.3. Representation

Another major question for builders of Learning Organizations to contemplate, is how can the variety of tacit knowledge be efficiently represented, processed, and updated? As with data bases, knowledge bases will need to be updated as learning progresses and new mental models emerge. Answers to the above question, we believe, will result from the combined efforts of biologists, computer scientists, psychologists, and linguists, who have worked to develop neural network systems as a way of mimicking human learning. Neural networks can learn by trial and error, and can be very effective in helping to manage the conflicts that arise in, and as a result of, team learning.

4.4. Dissemination

Another question deals with modes of dissemination and in particular with concerns about whether the information and knowledge disseminated via these modes actually promotes in-depth or double-loop learning. Considerable research remains to be done, especially since there is a growing trend in both industry and education to employ these technologies for distance learning applications and also to create virtual universities. The answer to this question will come not only from academic disciplines such as education, but from industry as well. The development of private (for-profit) educational entities, such as the University of America and the Virtual University, will provide a rich vein of research material. Considerable information concerning the use of the Internet, Lotus Notes, and intranet technology will also be available from companies such as SUN, Andersen Consulting and several of the other firms identified above.

4.5. Valuing Knowledge

Perhaps one of the more difficult questions concerns how to value humans and their most precious capital, knowledge. The development of methods to better value these important assets will come from academia, industry, and government. As firms become more virtual or knowledge based organizations, the need to identify, manage, and ultimately tax these assets will spur the research needed to devise and implement new accounting standards. The current Generally Accepted Accounting Principles (GAAP), do not provide for such considerations.

4.6. Culture

Finally, we believe that the ultimate question for builders of Learning Organizations will be how to create a culture of trust that will ensure the necessary exchange of knowledge that is fundamental to all learning. Organizations must be seen as being trustworthy if organizational learning is to occur. As one manager commented to one of the authors recently, " why should I share my most precious resource with this company when they will probably say thank you as they escort me to the door after they have gotten what they want."

Bayles (1989) identified seven factors that he felt were necessary to ensure trust: honesty, candor, competence, diligence, loyalty, fairness, and discipline. Others, in describing values essential to interpersonal relationships, add factors such as caring and pursuit of excellence. Factors such as loyalty and candor are difficult to quantify and, therefore, present problems when we attempt to measure them.

Creating a culture that is conducive to continuous, purposeful learning will require that the organization determine and enshrine the values that are necessary to ensure trust. It means that these organizations must find ways to implement these values throughout the various levels in the organization so that they will influence every decision and every action. The answers to these questions, we believe, will require the combined research efforts of philosophers, psychologists, sociologists, and organizational behaviorists.

The above is not meant to provide a definitive set of questions. Rather, it is our hope that they, along with the discussion presented earlier, will serve as a guide to help generate a more complete set of research questions that will help those interested in developing a better understanding of this important new age transforming idea.

Bibliography:

Argyris, C., Schon, D.A. (1974), Theory in Practice, Increasing Professional Effectiveness, San Francisco 1974

Bayles, M.D. (1989), Professional Ethics: Second Edition, Belmont, CA. 1989

Business Week, Here Comes The Intranet, February 26, 1996, pp. 76-82

Cohen, M.D., Sproull, L.S. (1996) (Editors), Organizational Learning, Thousand Oakes, Ca. 1996

Fukuyama, F. (1995), Trust: The Social Virtues of the Creation of Prosperity, New York 1995

Gamack, J.G., Young, R.M. (1984), Psychological Techniques for Eliciting Expert Knowledge, in: Research and Development in Expert System, Edited by M.A. Bramer, Proceedings of the Fourth Technical Conference of the British Computer Society, 1984

Gilson, I. (1994), Telephone Interview Conducted in Los Angeles, May 3, 1994

Infield L. Trans. Immanuel Kant (1963), Lectures on Ethics, New York 1963

Kast, F.E., Rosenzweig, J.E. (1972), General Systems Theory: Applications for Organization and Management, in: Academy of Management Journal, December 1972, pp. 447-465

Kim, D.H. (1993), The Link Between Individual and Organizational Learning, Sloan Management Review, Fall 1993, pp. 37-50

Koffka, K. (1963), Principles of Gestalt Psychology, A Harbinger Book, New York 1963

Kohler, W. (1927), The Mentality of Apes, Translated by Ella Winter, New York 1927

58

Krikorian, R. (1994), Ethical Conduct: An Aid to Management, Executive Speeches, August-September, 1994, pp. 74-77

Leavitt, H. (1965), Applied Organizational Change in Industry: Structure, Technological, and Humanistic Approaches, in: J. G., March (Ed.), Handbook of Organizations, Chicago, Ill 1965

Lemonick, M.D. (1995), Glimpses of the Mind, Time Magazine, July 17, 1995, pp. 44-52

Lewin, K. (1938), The Conceptual Representation and the Measurement of Psychological Forces, Durham, N.C., Vol. I, No. 4, 1938

Nanus, B. (1992), Visionary Leadership: Creating a Compelling Sense of Direction in Your Organization, San Francisco 1992

Nevis, E.C., DiBella, A.J., Gould, J.M. (1995), Understand Organizations as Learning Systems, in: Sloan Management Review, Winter, 1995, pp. 73-84

Nonaka, I., Takeuchi, H. (1995), The Knowledge Creating Company: How Japanese Companies Create The Dynamics Of Innovation, New York 1995

Piaget, J. (1980), The Equilibrium of Cognitive Structure: The Central Problem of Intellectual Development, New York 1980

Porter, M.E. (1990), The Competitive Advantage of Nations, New York 1990

Ratajaski, M.(1994), Individual and Corporate Ethics, Executive Speeches, August-September, 1994, pp. 64-66

Schon, D.A. (1996), Conversations with Don Schon in Monterrey Mexico, August 30, 1996

Senge, P.M. (1994), Creating Quality Communities, Executive Excellence, June 1994, Vol. 11, Issue 6, pp. 11-13

Senge, P.M. (1990), The Leaders New York: Building Learning Organizations, in: Sloan Management Review, Fall 1990, pp. 7-23

Senge, P.M. (1990), The Fifth Discipline: The Art and Practice of the Learning Organization, New York 1990

Sizemore, B. (1995), Digital Equipment Corporation Internal Report, 1995

Sprout, A. (1995), The Internet Inside Your Company, in: Fortune, November 7, 1995, pp. 161-168

Stata, R. (1989), Organizational Learning: The Key to Management Innovation, in: Sloan Management Review, Vol. 30, Iss. 3, Spring 1989, pp. 63-74

Stratton J.A. (1975), in: Interdisciplinary Research in the University Setting, Edited by G.W. Leckie, The Center for Settlement Studies, University of Manitoba, November 1975

Svieby, E. (1995), Svieby Knowledge Management Home Page T+P://www2.eis.net.au/~Karl-eirk/Index.html, 1995

Implementing Partnering Relationships:
A Change Process Model

Douglas K. Macbeth
David Boddy
Beverley Wagner
Marilyn Charles

Zusammenfassung:

Ein geeignetes Beziehungsmanagement verlangt eine langfristige Kooperation von Unternehmen z. B. auf Angebots- und Nachfrageseite. Wesentliche Prinzipien der Partnerschaft sind u.a. gemeinsame Planungsprozesse, Austausch von Mitarbeitern, Offenlegung von Kosten, Informationsaustausch, gemeinsame Verbesserungsprogramme. Vorgestellt wird ein Modell zur Strukturierung von Veränderungsprozessen; die einzelnen Elemente werden im Detail beschrieben. Die besondere Bedeutung verschiedener Arten des Lernens wird herausgearbeitet.

1. Need for a Change in Business Relationships

It has become clear over the past number of years that traditional ways of competing were limited by our view of appropriate ways of behaving which are now being challenged by new paradigms. In particular that the adversarial process which results in a zero sum game might be counter productive when applied in areas away from the pure market place. In such markets the assumption is that there is an infinite supply of both customers and suppliers and that the only differentiating factor between the offerings of the suppliers is in the cost of their commodity produce. Further implied is the belief that after the deal has been struck then there need never be an occasion when the two parties will need to interact again. In such circumstances the only opportunity to gain an advantage is in the single transaction and so the trial of negotiating skills and will to succeed proceeds and even an agreeable outcome in the sense that the deal has been done leaves both parties wondering about what might have been if only... .

Of course many business situations are not single transactions. In fact they often take place within very long established trading arrangements. In such circumstances a short term maximising strategy can be seen as limiting the potential for both parties to build a successful future together. The zero sum game also forces each party to build defences against the other taking short term advantage of some form of relative superiority (apart from the one that customers always think is theirs ie the decision to purchase). The defences that are built tend to fall into catagories of information manipulation, inventories of material and time and layers of decision making authority to evaluate and protect against the risks of doing the business. In addition the limitation of current business to only the current purchase order creates pressures on suppliers to market themselves to other potential customers and on customers to search for alternative sources in case of need or to use anyway in a multi-sourcing strategy to bring pressure to bear on current suppliers to obtain price concessions.

All of these factors do nothing to increase the value added in terms of final customer satisfaction while doing a great deal to increase costs in the chain of supply between each customer and supplier playing these traditional games. Once recognised for what they are, these wasteful practices can be subject to serious questioning and hopefully removal as part of a wide ranging quality and customer responsiveness improvement process. In this way collaborating business entities can see their relative position in an interconnected chain of supply from raw materials through to final satisfied consumer with each customer and supplier link trying to remove as much waste as sensible, consistent with current operating conditions.

2. Principles of Partnering

Macbeth/Ferguson (1994) summarize the **characteristics of a partnering relationship** as being one in which the partners engage in activities such as shared design processes; open book costing; interchange of staff; developing shared visions of their business; creating long term commitments to each other; and engaging in joint improvement projects. Sako (1992) argued that the costs of doing business with another organization are not fixed and can be reduced through investing in building the relationship. An implication of this is that a move towards partnering has significant implications for the internal as well as the external operations of the firm. For example Kanter (1989) argues that supplier-customer partnerships require a more collaborative web of interfunctional relationships within each company in order to improve the flow of information between departments necessary to support closer working with the partner.

It is clear from the above discussion that Partnering is an approach to business which is not appropriate for all relationships. Rather its application is likely to be restricted to those important few whose support to the final satisfaction of the downstream customer is so important that all sensible effort needs to be devoted to ensuring that this particluar link does not fail causing the customer to fall into serious difficulty. When considering any complex product / service package it becomes obvious very quickly that it is not sensible to build a business on total supply capability or 'one stop shop'. While customers might wish to deal with a major supplier or systems integrator performing this service nevertheless no supplier could afford to invest in keeping at the leading edge of all such interdependent technologies. By design therefore the organisation has to source some of this technology from others more expert in that field and integrate their technology with their own and others to provide the customer satisfaction expected. This detail is often of no interest whatsoever to the final customers who want their needs satisfied but are not interested in how much is produced in the supplier's house and how much is bought in from elsewhere. Failure to supply according to expected criteria becomes a problem for the integrator and by implication, by contract or by relationship, all other upstream suppliers. This threat to the supply chain is also its opportunity since by removing the wastes discussed earlier the whole chain becomes more able to compete in the final market place with other chains of customers and suppliers for the consumers' money.

The decision about moving towards this more collaborative way of working has to be based on an understanding of the opportunities in prospect but also of the effort needed to make it happen to mutual benefit. This cannot be done for reason of copying other companies successful implementations if it is done only to follow some other's lead. Rather the issues underpinning the approach need to be evaluated to test the appropriateness of this solution. Undoubtedly the approach pays off financially. In a report covering the results of a project in Switzerland between ABB Power Generation Ltd and Schmiedewerk Stoos AG lead times were reduced from eight weeks to three and price reductions of 10-23% across a range of products were agreed with the customer at no long term disadvantage to the supplier (SCMG 1995a). Clearly this is also an approach which has paid off very well for a number of the Japanese Automotive companies but the approach has been successful in many other sectors as well. It is therefore worth taking time to consider the particular context of the company's market and seeing to what extent collaboration might be used to deliver similar benefits.

The **timescale** is important. Relatively quick results as reported can be achieved within a number of months but the real strategic leverage will come through collaborative working on core design areas in order to design out the wastes and manage the logistics flow more efficiently. This opportunity comes more intermittently and only when both parties are satisfied that each is both capable and trustworthy enough to share in market sensitive developments of this kind. The need for this kind of strategic alignment between the parties is clearly not something which happens overnight so the relationship development timescale has to recognise that the relationship has to be expected to extend for long enough into an unknown future such that these collaborations have time to bear fruit.

It is also recognised that while customers always have the right not to buy they are however as dependent on the supplier's performance as the supplier is on having a good customer. In this, **relative size and importance of spend** can be an important factor which will not always be in the customer's favour especially the closer we go to raw materials in the ground where economies of scale still apply. Circumstances between customers and suppliers therefore do not need to be equal but the treatment given one to the other has to be equitable. That is to say that the other party has legitimate interests and requirements which should be met wherever possible, within agreed boundaries.

Trust is evidently important in such environments since no one shares their future with those they do not trust. Trust takes time to build since all of us look for evidence that the trust will not be taken advantage of. What is important therefore is that the organization collectively recognises its responsibility to act in a way which allows trust to grow without putting it into jeopardy through an ill thought out opportunistic attempt to score quick points in the old zero sum game. Even more important is what Sako calls goodwill trust. This is behaviour that goes beyond what is the minimum expected response to support the partner's needs in the belief that this will be remembered later and that there will be a later situation which recognises the cost of the current additional effort. This is the way in which mutual obligations grow and how exceptional performance comes to be normal.

Partnering relationships are about complementary sets of skills developed in different market environments but with a common interest in the supply of a good or service. In order to make the operational improvements needed to remove waste from the chain, **information exchange**, to allow the other party to operate as efficiently as possible, is needed. Operationally this will relate to customer order processing data and / or forecasts and the speedy transmission of up to date order patterns is in everyone's interest. Conversely a customer trying to satisfy their own demanding customer by promising a delivery their supplier cannot support is not actually satisfying customer requirements, they are in fact sowing the seeds of failure by promising unachievable performance. Understanding the joint processes, the logistics flows and delays in the system can permit a more realistic promise to be made thereby allowing the customer to make its contingent plans to use the delivered goods or services.

Complementary partners however have major roles to play to support each other's future development. A customer should understand its market place and the likely demands coming from that quarter while a supplier deals with other customers as well as its own inbound supply chain they are therefore in a position to scan the supply side horizon for any new opportunities or threats which might be seen to impact on the business environment in which the chain is operating. Thus preferred suppliers act as the eyes and ears of their preferred customer who remains that way by sharing their vision of future developments downstream.

Continuous operational improvement is the incremental way of removing wastes from the chain and many little improvements add up to a clear performance gap from the chasing competitors. This must go on in every area of operation but needs to be supported on occasion by a more fundamental and possibly radical **redesign** of the complete system. In some cases running faster only keeps up with the pace of the fleetest runners in the race. What is needed is to find a way of changing the rules of the race in such a way that no matter how hard the competitors run they cannot catch up. This would be unethical behaviour on the athletics track but in business it is what strategy in action is all about. Radical redesign offers the chance to redefine what the business activity has to be and to radically improve customer value creation. Here again the ideal would be to retain such knowledge between the partners without sharing with competitors but often all that can be controlled is the speed at which the competitors obtain enough information in order to manufacture their own version to compete in the market place.

3. Structuring the Change Process

Pettigrew's (1987) model presents change as a historical process interacting with both an internal and an external environment. Content refers to the particular area of transformation under consideration, in this case partnering in the supply chain. That is undertaken with certain results in mind, which are in practice influenced by choices made in designing the content of the change, and in the process of change - shaped both by history and by interaction with the internal and external environment. In the new model we will build on the ideas of Content and Process but locate them in a Control and Learning system.

Buchanan/Boddy (1992) argued that significant change can be viewed from three perspectives, each with different implications for those trying to make it happen. The **project management** perspective predicts that successful implementation will depend on using established techniques of project management (Locke 1992; Owens 1993), such as setting clear goals and milestones. The **participative management** perspective emphasises the benefits of establishing a sense of ownership of the change amongst those whose support will be needed (Mumford/ Weir 1979; Kotter/Schlesinger 1979). Particular attention should be given to providing opportunities for the exchange of ideas, and the encouragement of alternative views (Pugh 1993) to build wide support. The **political perspective** stresses that change is likely to impinge on many different interests pulling in different directions, and possibly pursuing personal as well as organizational goals (Pfeffer 1992; Pettigrew 1987). This implies that implementation will depend not only on using project management and participative skills, but also on political skills.

4. Relationship Improvement Process

SCMG Ltd have a developed process (the Relationship Positioning Tool) to both measure the business relationship between organizations and also facilitate their improvement towards best in class levels (Macbeth 1996). They have also developed a strategic overview model of how to manage the change process (SCMG 1995). Some of the common prescriptions on how to introduce change suggest a structure in three parts.

Getting started and structuring the projekt a clarity of goals is often recommended, with Slevin/Pinto (1986), Kanter (1985) and Kotter/Schlesinger (1979) all predicting that clear goals lead to more successful projects. In the case of partnering we would also expect that the prospective partners would need to have agreed with them. Several writers draw attention to the management structure and resourcing of change projects: in the specific context of partnering Macbeth/Ferguson (1994) propose establishing a senior team with a specific mandate. Change should have a strong and well-respected backer or champion (Freeman 1982), while others argue that the perceived capability of the change agent or project manager will be important to success (Stanislao/Stanislao 1983; Hamilton 1988).

When planning the detail the agenda for the change is set (referred to in the model as the Content Agenda), and a sense of ownership created amongst those affected. A consistent theme in studies of both technical and organizational innovation is the systemic nature of change, with change in one element needing to be at least consistent with others (Leavitt 1988), and Boddy/Buchanan (1992) note the many facets of the change agenda which need to be anticipated by the project manager.

Partnering implies changes in roles and responsibilities within both organizations, leading Kanter to suggest that the main obstacle to partnering is the need for "managing the changes in each of the partners' own organizations" (Kanter 1989, p. 189). Structural changes may also extend to altering the pay and reward systems (Macbeth/Ferguson 1995), who also recommend that partnering initiatives be supported by changes in technology and information systems. There is a long tradition that change will be made easier if there is wide consultation and sharing of ideas (Pugh 1993; Mumford 1979; Stanislao/Stanislao 1980). Kotter and Schlesinger (op. cit.) recommend educating people about the change and Recardo (1991) also stresses intensive communication.

The implementing of the change refers to the series of practical actions needed to turn plans into operational reality, and of embedding change into the organization's normal ways of working. Again advice is offered by Kanter (1989), Stanislao/Stanislao (1983), Boddy/Buchanan (1992), and Slevin/Pinto (1986) on matters such as anticipating ripple effects, timing, and resources. The reality in many situations is that putting all of this is in place can be difficult when each party has to do something different to what has, until then, been normal practice. The problem has been that models such as Pettigrew's tend to focus only on one organization and are more static in their action than is the reality for organizations in a supply chain environment where the pace of change can be dramatic. The need is therefore to recognise and develop a model of change that captures the interconnectedness of the change process in the organizations and the nature of the organizational and business environment in which they operate and which allows managers to work through the emerging issues in a coherent and structured way.

Much of the underlying thinking in operational management is informed by considerations of total quality and it is from there that we take this concept. **Continuous improvement** recognises that business cannot afford to remain still, it must be constantly striving to improve in every aspect of its activity and as already highlighted this is also a key feature in successful supply chains. The Deming Cycle of Plan, Do, Check and Act has been modified in the model to represent the essentially sequential and cycling nature of continuous inprovement so we have created the cycle of Analysis, Decision, Act and Review.

In the **Analysis stage** the criticality of the change is recognised. In some cases this will be at the margins of the organization perhaps as some form of pilot study while at others it amounts to betting the company on a successful outcome. These variations will be reflected in the degrees of management commitment and interest. There will also be a difference if the concepts are being considered for the first time or if the change is part of a roll out programme building on prior experience and success. The largest part of the analysis comes from the evaluation of the gap between current practice and the currently understood vision of best practice that might be achievable. (The earlier application of the Relationship Positioning Tool will also have produced some indications of gaps in performance.) In the new model the exercise will involve the use of the Content Agenda about which more shortly. It is also necessary to consider the priorities for action since there may be opportunities to gain relatively easy successes on which more demanding projects can build. It may also be the case that the vision is not as demanding as it might be and so action to reposition the overall targets may also be called for.

Given the completed analysis, **Decisions** have to be made firstly on the intermediate objectives to be set since in any major change programme the journey from current performance to desired future capability will not be achievable in one step. With these in mind the decision revolves around what combinations of activities in the Process Agenda we will use to progress the decision. The Process Agenda essentially determines HOW the change is to be implemented. The actual implementation then needs to be planned according to normal project management processes. The ACT stage is simply that - do what you planned!

Review comes at the predetermined intervals and covers the normal control practice of measuring achievements against the contents agenda plans and against the actions taken from the process agenda. This is closing the performance gap but not yet considering the learning which has been achieved. We will return to that later.

In order to capture the dynamics and interaction between the facets of the organization which need to be considered we have chosen to represent them as part of a circular diagram. This represents the nature of the processes we have observed in a major research study now nearing completion (Macbeth et al. 1997) in which consideration of the implications of possible improvement actions cycles round the issues in an unpredictable and individualistic way. The contention is however that this process is necessary but normally inefficiently operated such that some detail is omitted or discussed and not captured so that subsequent implementation is problematic because of the item so ignored. Fig. 1 shows the **Content Agenda** in outline.

These same considerations operate with different degrees of importance and aggregation at other levels inside each organization such that a decision at regional or head office level will similarly impact the other segments and will cascade through the organization finally having an impact on the detailed interorganizational level where people are in daily or hourly contact.

As the relationships evolve issues which appear to be in one segment very quickly are seen to impact many others. For example the desire to remove time and paper wastes through communication by EDI looks to be a Technology issue but clearly implementing such a change should recognise the impact on the Business Processes between the organisations; will affect what People skills are required or no longer needed; might cause Structures to change in accounts payable or produc-

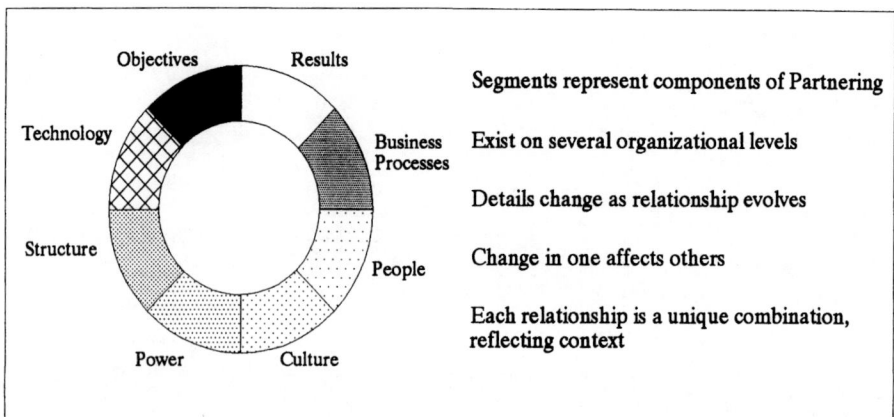

Fig. 1: Content Agenda Segments

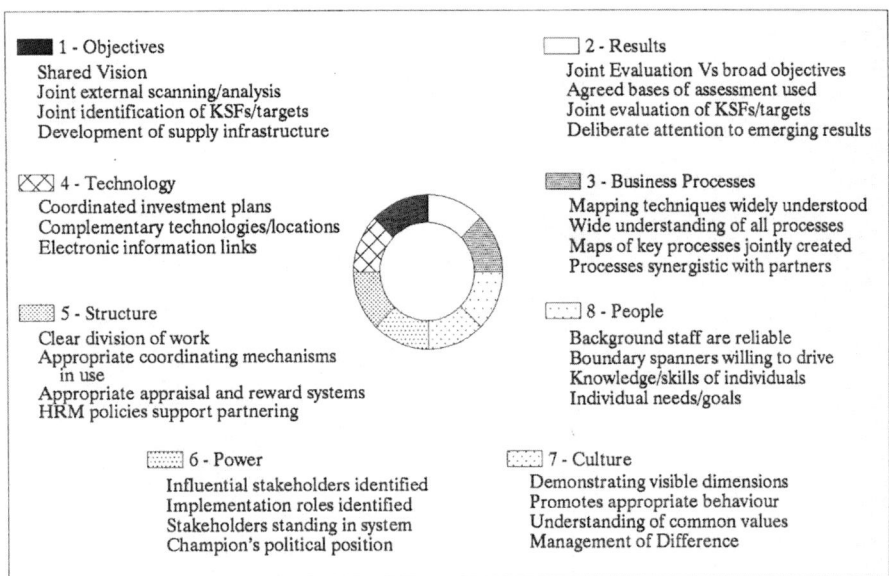

Fig. 2: Content Agenda - Segments and Activities

tion planning and logistics; might change the balance of Power or influence and might be constrained by a prevailing Culture of control rather than trust and empowerment; and if not consistent with the declared Objectives will undoubtedly fail to obtain the hoped for Results. This example serves to demonstrate how issues cross between segments often setting off other chains of consideration and it is therefore no wonder that what results is less than a complete statement of what was intended to be a considered and coherent strategy of change items.

Within each of these segments of course there is much more detail and we will be producing a hypertext document to allow for the expansion of these segments into four associated activities and up to five sub elements for each activity (see Fig. 2). The details of these are focused on the issues recognised during the research process to be important in the partnering context but we are strongly of the view that this conceptualisation of the process of agenda setting within a major organizational change is one that can be developed for other contexts as well.

The underlying principle of the **Process Agenda** is that there are essentially two choices to make in implementing a change. These are that an individual can take reponsibility to initiate the change on their own or that some form of institutional mechanism is employed. Of course these things are not mutually exclusive. Often a significant individual can make the breakthrough in determining what it is that should be done but even supreme leaders do not work alone and given the complexity of the changes we are discussing and the potential for covert sabotage by

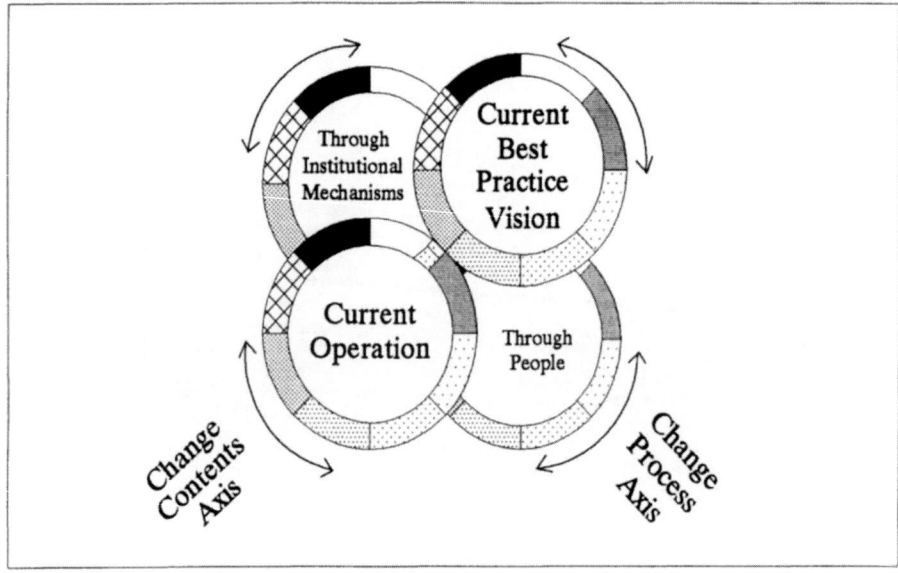

Fig. 3: Content and Process Axes

disaffected members of either organization it is clear that groups organised in new ways and working to a given set of rules have to make it happen. Thus the Process Agenda operates through People and / or Institutional Mechanisms.

The factors under the People heading include consideration of their: knowledge and skills in operating within the factors of the Content Agenda and within the Process Agenda; their ability to work and exert influence within the institutional mechanisms often without formal authority; and their inherent needs and goals for development and advancement. These can be grouped under a set of necessary skills as: project management and political influencing; communication; personal effectiveness and group working.

Factors under Institutional Mechanisms include: group membership; levels and responsibilities; rules, procedures and documentation; and appropriate coordinating mechanisms eg joint strategic review committees, joint process mapping teams, etc. We therefore recognise the two action agenda axes as shown in Fig. 3. The analysis process therefore highlights gaps between current practice and the current best practice vision probably in a mixture of the content agenda factors and once decisions are made to modify the chosen activities the process agenda information is used to plan the implementation through a mix of individual and institutional methods.

5. Capturing the Learning

It is now clear that a major issue in implementing partnering is how the parties learn. The model is a way of **organizing and storing accumulated knowledge** about the factors which help or hinder partnering. As a diagnostic tool, it can be used by the parties or an external observer to describe the unique combination of elements which make up the relationship. Those elements embody explicit or tacit knowledge. Explicit knowledge is that which has been codified into procedures and systems. Tacit knowledge is the unconscious or habitual ways of doing things - the skills and procedures developed amongst the players in that partnering relationship. It can be individual or shared.

There is nothing mysterious or secret about **tacit knowledge** and it is a familiar part of our everyday life. Indeed, it is that very familiarity which tends to lead us to overlook its importance when dealing with such a deep issue as what thinking and knowing is all about (Goranzon/Josefson 1988, p. 54). There are two ways in which tacit knowledge can be described. Firstly there are the things we could say if we wanted to, but choose not to. This type of knowledge could be articulated and when not shared may be interpreted as "knowledge equals power". Secondly, there is knowledge which by its very nature is incapable of precise articulation. We know things without being able to put what we know clearly into words and often it requires considerable effort to articulate a situation to the point where others understand (Goranzon/Josefson 1988, pp. 54-60). These limits of description and nuance are transferable only when the context of the exchange is familiar to the participants, i.e. "by relying on the pupil's intelligent co-operation for catching the meaning of the demon-stration" (Polanyi 1967, p. 5).

The importance of context cannot be over emphasised as it is through shared experience that knowledge and learning can be built. . ."Therefore, when I receive information by reading a letter and when I ponder the message of the letter, I am subsidiarily aware not only of the text, but also of all the past occasions by which I have come to understand the words of the text, and the whole range of this subsidiary awareness is presented focally in terms of the message" (Polanyi 1958, p. 92). Cohen/ Levinthal (1990, p. 131) have termed this "absorptive capacity".

Basic knowledge such as that held in routine procedures is explicit and formal and is the focus of training programmes to learn approved procedures for completing tasks (Dibello/Spender 1996, p. 748). Basic knowledge is formalised to the degree that it can be codified. However, Nelson/Winter (1982) would argue that much of the detailed knowledge of organizational routines is tacit.

As knowledge is translated from tacit to explicit, learning is encased in programmes and standard operating procedures which individuals execute routinely. As success accumulates, organizations grow complacent and generate inertia, which increases as new members are socialised and prescribed new roles (Starbuck 1996) . Thus **explicit knowledge** becomes dysfunctional when it has become static and out of date. Explicit knowledge is only of use if work processes, procedures and documentation are orderly and regularly maintained. Should current practices become inappropriate or ineffective, individuals will ignore the organizational procedures or implement them in their own way, relying on experience and tacit knowledge. It is important to capture this tacit knowledge by means of reformulating rules, procedural systems etc., thereby converting the tacit knowledge into new explicit knowledge. Krusterer (1978, p. 178) calls tacit knowledge, "supplementary knowledge" and explains that it is developed informally by workers as they acquire expertise from each other. This knowledge is usually unavailable to managers not involved in the system of activity. Thus, managers often make changes to a production system not knowing that they are disturbing the relationship between the production system and supplementary or tacit knowledge that keeps it functioning (Dibello/Spender 1996, p. 749).

Organizations are more likely to develop a **learning culture** with open channels when there is dialogue and no barriers to information flow. Organizational learning also involves acquiring information about threats and opportunities in the organization's external environment. Thus, organizational members have boundary scanning roles - "as monitor, the manager scans his environment for information, interrogates his liaison contacts and his subordinates, and receives unsolicited information, much of it as a result of the network of personal contacts he has developed" (Minzberg 1996).

Tacit knowledge may be defined as knowledge usually not verbalised and not explicitly taught. All organizations possess huge untapped bodies of experience that, if stored, retrieved and interpreted, could lead to considerable improvements in performance (Huber 1996, p. 827). This is echoed by Hastings (1996) who states that in practice very little of an individual's experience or expertise is drawn upon by organizations that only benefit from the visible top of the "know- how" iceberg. Only by maximising the return from an organization's know-how investment will there be a significant source of future competitive advantage (Hastings 1996, p. 127). Winter (1980) describes how knowledge possessed by an organization may be tacit knowledge in the sense that:- the tacit knowledge is possessed by individuals associated with the organization; related expressible knowledge may be possessed by other members outwith the organization. "we know someone who knows about. . .".

A multitude of relationships enables the organization to function in a coordinated way via rules which are not known as such by most of the participants eg top decision makers are often uninformed regarding details of what happens when their decisions are implemented. They create concepts and a vision that may suggest very little, but in reality people within the organization are capable of describing it to each other. Therefore, more and more, individuals need to know how to access relevant information outside the organization (Hastings 1996, p. 120). That is, they must not only know how to identify and access their own experience and expertise in many spheres of knowledge, but they must also be able to access other people's expertise within and outwith the organization.

In the field of **exploiting knowledge** the following implications are important:
- Efficiency and effectiveness of organizational performance requires that explicit and tacit knowledge are constantly renewed to create new tacit and new explicit knowledge, thereby developing and enlarging both individual and organizational learning.
- Outcomes of inadequate management with regards to explicit knowledge might include organizational rigidity and inability to change. Out of date systems and processes do not stand up in a dynamic, competitive environment.
- Inability to capture tacit knowledge will result in loss of learning, confusion and abuse of power, as individuals follow their own agendas.
- Firms need to systematically manage the creation and integration of knowledge to achieve superior performance.

While the strategic importance of knowledge is recognised, the challenge is how to identify, capture, retain and access knowledge. Organizational learning is arguably the only means of achieving sustainable competitive advantage. Understanding factors affecting the rate of learning within firms, its persistence and its transfer, is of great practical as well as theoretical importance.

Unique knowledge is a source of competitive advantage. For example Doz (1989) argued that "the role of the acquisition and development of unique non-tradable assets (i.e. knowledge) is the key factor that differentiates companies which successfully achieve a strategy versus those that do not succeed in achieving the same strategy", and similar points have been made by Itami (1987) and Tomer (1987). Kay (1993) has postulated that creating knowledge through a network of relational contracts is one of three sources of distinctive capabilitiy. The difficulty is that only when the knowledge from experience is captured, organised, disseminated and used will it help performance. Organizations learn from experience haphazardly (Huber 1996) and rarely capture it in ways that can be transformed into available knowledge (Dibello/Spender 1996; Lipshitz et al. 1996). They find it hard to generate potentially useful information from everyday activities (Karnoe 1996) which can be captured, stored and made available for future use (Weick 1996).

These knowledge isues are particularly significant in partnering. The usual difficulties are compounded and threaten the creation, spread and retention of knowledge (Hastings 1993; Spender 1996). They include: a lot to learn, as the process is complex; solutions are discovered during the task; solutions are human as well as technical; staff are physically distant with intermittent contact; staff change jobs

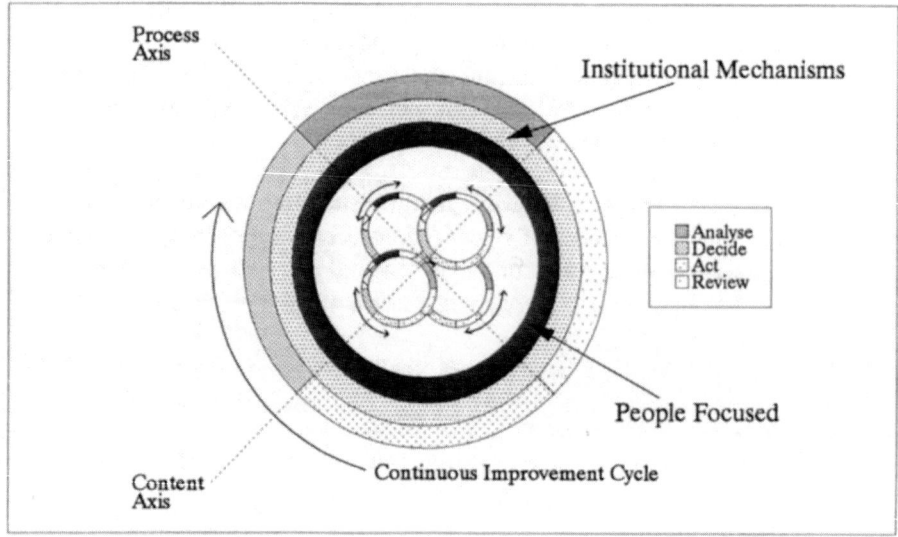

Fig. 4: The Complete Partnering Change Process

frequently. Yet the benefits may be greater. The knowledge created in the course of building a relationship is unique and non-transferable. If partnering is strategically important to the companies or the sector, those who learn how to do it, and the skills of how to do it, gain relatively.

Using the change model to both surface existing knowledge and capture new knowledge as it is created between the partners to create mutually beneficial performance in the market place becomes one of the key strategic issues of the coming years. Fig. 4 pulls all of this together to demonstrate the continuous improvement process operating at the two process levels and driven by the gap analysis embodied in the content and process agendas.

Bibliography:

Boddy, D., Buchanan (1992), Take the Lead, Prentice Hall International (UK) 1992

Christopher, M. (1992), Logistics and Supply Chain Management: Strategies for Reducing Costs and Improving Services, London 1992

Cohen, W. M., Levintha, D. A. (1990), Absorptive Capacity: A New Perspective on Learning and Innovation, in: Administration Science Quartlery, Vol. 35 (1990), pp. 128-152

Debresson, C., Amesse, F. (1991), Networks of Innovators: A Review and Introduction to the Issue, in: Research Policy, Vol. 20 (1991), pp. 363-379

Dibello, L., Spender, J. C. (1996), Constructive Learning: A New Approach to Deploying Technological Systems into the Workplace, in: Journal of Technology Management, Special Issue on Unlearning and Learning for Technological Innovation, Vol. 11(1996), pp. 747-758

Doz, Y. (1989), Knowledge as a Corporate Asset, Presentation to European forum for Management Development Research Conference, Barcelona, 1989

Freeman, C. (1982), The Economics of Industrial Innovation, London 1982

Gemser, G., Leeders, M.A.A.M., Wisnberg, N.M. (1996), The Dynamics of Inter-Firm Networks in the Course of the Industry Life cycle: The Role of Appropriability, in: Technology Analysis and Strategic Management, Vol. 18, No. 4, pp. 439-453

Goranzon, B., Josefson I. (eds.) (1988), Knowledge, Skills and Artificial Intelligence, London 1988

Hamilton, E. (1988), The Facilitation of Organizational Change: An Empirical Study of Factors Predicting Change Agent Effectiveness, in: Journal of Applied Behavioural Science, Vol. 24, No. 1, pp. 37-59

Hastings, C. (1993), The New Organization: Growing the Culture of Organizational Networking, London 1993

Huber, G. P. (1996), Organizational Learning: a Guide for Executives in Technology Critical Organizations in: Journal of Technology Management, Special Issue on Unlearning and Learning for Technological Innovation, Vol. 11, pp. 821-832

Itami, H et al. (1987), Mobilizing Invisible Assets, 1 ed. Cambridge 1987

Karnoe, P. (1996), The Social Process of Competence Building, in: Journal of Technology Management, Special Issue on Unlearning and Learning for Technological Innovation, Vol. 11, pp. 770-789

Kanter, R.M. (1985), Managing the Human Side of Change, in: Management Review, 1985, pp. 52-56

Kanter, R.M. (1989), Becoming PALs: Pooling, Allying and Linking across Companies, in: Academy of Management Executive, Vol III, No.3, pp. 183-193

Kay, J. (1993), Foundations of Corporate Success: How Business Strategies Add Value, Oxford 1993

Kotter, J.P., Schlesinger, L.A. (1979), Choosing Strategies for Change, in: Harvard Business Review, March/April 1979

Krusterer, K.C. (1978), Know-how on the Job: The Important Working Knowledge of the "Unskilled worker", Boulder (Co.) 1978

Leavitt, H.J. (1965), Applied Organizational Change in Industry: Structural, Technological and Humanistic Approaches, in: J.G. March (ed.), Handbook of Organizations, Chicago 1965

Lipshitz, R., Popper, M., Oz, S. (1996), Building Learning Organizations: the Design and Implementation of Organizational Learning Mechanisms, in: Journal of Applied Behavioural Science, Vol. 32 (1996), pp. 292-305

Locke, D. (1992), Project management, 5th Edition, Aldershot 1992

Macbeth, D.K., Ferguson, N. (1994), Partnership Sourcing: An Integrated Supply Chain Approach, London 1994

Macbeth, D. K, Boddy, D., Charles M., Wagner B. (1997), Implementing Partnering in the Supply Chain, Report on grant number GRK 21252. EPSRC, Swindon

Macbeth, D. K. (1996), Partnering in Internationally Competitive Supply Chains: Principles and Operational Management, in: Berndt, R. (Hrsg.) Global Management, Berlin (1996), pp. 245-261

Mintzberg, H. (1996), The Manager's Job: Folklore and Fact, in: Harvard Business Review, July/ August 1996

Mumford, E., Weir, M. (1979), Computer Systems in Work Design - The_ETHICS Method, Associated Business Press 1979

Nelson, R., Winter, S. (1982), An Evolutionary Theory of Economic Change, Belnap 1982

Owen, A.A. (1993), How to Implement Strategy, in: Mabey, C., Mayon-White, B. (eds.), Managing Change, Open University, Milton Keynes, pp. 143-150

Pettigrew, A.M. (1987), Context and Action in the Transformation of the Firm, in: Journal of Management Studies, Vol. 24, No. 6, pp. 649-670

Polyani, M. (1958), Personal Knowledge, London 1958

Polyani, M. (1967), The Tacit Dimension, London 1967

Pugh, D. (1993), Understanding and Managing Organization Change, in: Mabey, C., Mayon-White, B. (1993), Managing Change, Open University, Milton Keynes, pp. 108-112

Pfeffer, J. (1992), Managing with Power, Boston 1992

Recardo, R. (1991), The What, Why and How of Change Management, in: Manufacturing Systems, May 1991, pp. 52-58

Sako, M. (1992), Prices quality, and trust: inter-firm relations in Britain and Japan, Cambridge University Press, London 1992

SCMG (1995a), Report on Eureka Project EU1024, SCMG Ltd, Glasgow 1995

SCMG (1995b), Relationship Improvement Process, SCMG Ltd, Glasgow 1995

Slevin, D.P., Pinto, J.K. (1986), The Project Implementation Profile: A New Tool for Project Managers, in: Project Management Journal, September 1986, pp. 57-65

Spender, J.C. (1996), Organizational Knowledge, Learning and Memory: Three Concepts in search of a Theory, in: Journal of Organizational Change Management, Vol. 9, No. 1

Starbuck, W.H. (1996), Unlearning Ineffective or Obsolete Technologies, in: Journal of Technology Management, Special Issue on Unlearning and Learning for Technological Innovation, Vol. 11, pp. 725-737

Stanislao, J., Stanislao, B.C. (1983), Dealing with Resistance to Change, in: Business Horizons, July/August 1983, pp. 74-78

Tomer, J.F. (1987), Organizational Capital: the Path to Higher Productivity and Well-Being, Praeger Publishers 1987

Weick, K. (1996), The Role of Renewal in Organizational Learning, in: Journal of Technology Management, Special Issue on Unlearning and Learning for Technological Innovation, Vol. 11 (1996), pp. 738-746

Winter, S.G (1980), Knowledge and Competence as Strategic assets, in: Teece, D. J. (ed.), The Competitive Challenge: Strategies for Industrial Innovation and Renewal, New York 1980

Zweiter Teil

**Change Management
und
Management Education**

Change Management in der Management Andragogik

Albert Stähli

Summary:

The actual changes in the environment of a company lead to the need of a relevant concept of change management. Main conditions are that managers are willing to accept changes and are able to manage changes. To achieve this, institutions of management education have to fulfill specific challenges. In the field of executive development the concept of management andragogic is relevant. The developed MBA-programs help executives to manage change. Particulary important is the concept of the genetic growing case study. International cooperations of business schools, like the cooperation between the GSBA Zürich and State University of New York at Albany in the framework of their Dual MBA Degree, help executive managers to manage the consequences of globalisation.

1. Den Wandel annehmen!

Die klassische Weisheit des Heraklit - panta rhei, alles fließt - eröffnet sich erstaunlicherweise jeder Manager-Generation aufs Neue. An der Schwelle des 21. Jahrhunderts sehen sich viele europäische Unternehmen vor gewaltigen Umwälzungen in Politik und Gesellschaft, deren Auswirkungen in zunehmendem Maße sowohl den makroökonomischen Rahmen - Wachstumsschwäche, anhaltende Arbeitslosigkeit, steigende Budgetdefizite - als auch das traditionelle betriebswirtschaftliche Kalkül irritieren. Viele der gelernten und geübten Handlungsanleitungen als Reaktion auf ökonomische Problemstellungen erweisen sich als wirkungslos, vielfach schlimmer noch, sogar als kontraproduktiv. Die steigende Zahl der Insolvenzen, die boomende Manager-Weiterbildungsindustrie, der immer erratischere Aufstieg und Fall sogenannter „Management-Gurus" liefern unangreifbare Zeugnisse der herrschenden Unsicherheit in den Führungsgremien der Wirtschaft. Doch Unsicherheit führt leicht in die Handlungsverweigerung, in die tödliche Paralyse. „Viele Unternehmen (und Unternehmensführer) sind heute in Gefahr oder bereits im Begriff, unterzugehen. Nach zehn Jahren des Umstrukturierens und mitten in Umbau- und Revitalisierungsprozessen kämpft eine Firma nach der anderen darum, ihre Marktposition zu halten. Wie verändern Turbulenzen, Trendbrüche und Nachfragemacht das Wesen des Wettbewerbs? Genügen bewährte Erfolgspraktiken und gängige Prosperitätsrezepte, um den kommenden

Turbulenzen zu begegnen? ... Vier von fünf Wirtschaftsführern in Europa glauben es nicht" (The Phoenix Group 1996).

Als Reaktion auf die wachsende Komplexität der Wirtschaft und die neuerliche Erkenntnis, daß „alles fließt", stellen die weitaus meisten Führungskäfte Fragen nach der Richtung: Wohin geht der Trend? Wohin werden sich die europäischen Währungen nach Einführung des Euro entwickeln? Wohin orientieren sich die neuen, dynamischen Wettbewerber aus dem Fernen Osten? An welchen Bereichen sollte man die Ressourcen ausrichten, um in Zeiten der Unsicherheit ein höchstmögliches Maß an Treffgenauigkeit zu erreichen? Die Grundfrage dabei lautet immer: Wie schafft man die schnellere und wirtschaftlichere Bewältigung einer zunehmenden Vielfalt sich rasch ändernder Aufgaben? (Doppler/Lauterburg 1996, S. 47). Mit anderen Worten: Wie lautet die Lösung für eine Gleichung, deren fixe Größen schwinden und die nur mehr aus Variablen besteht?

Zweifelsohne besteht eine der größten Herausforderungen der Gegenwart darin, den Wandel anzunehmen und sich auf eine Welt einzulassen, die sich noch rascher und tiefgreifender verändern wird. Wer dies nicht wahrhaben will und sich nicht bewußt damit auseinandersetzt, wird künftig keine Überlebenschance mehr haben. Diese Erkenntnis gilt ausnahmslos für alle Unternehmen, Organisationen und Institutionen - und selbstverständlich auch für die Business Schools. „Dieses Gesetz gilt auch für das Lernen von Managern und Unternehmen, denn Wettbewerb ist wie Evolution ein Ausleseprozeß, in dem diejenigen, die sich besser und schneller anpassen, überleben. Wer hingegen die Anpassung nicht oder zu langsam bewältigt, wird eliminiert (Thommen 1995, S. 13). Denn die Zeiten, in denen es noch sichere Nischen für all diejenigen gab, die mit geschlossenen Augen dem Wandel zu trotzen vermeinten, sind endgültig vorüber.

2. Zur Rolle der Unternehmensführung im Change Management

Anders als noch vor wenigen Jahrzehnten von der Wissenschaft postuliert, ist es nicht allein Aufgabe des Managements, anstehende Veränderungsprozesse **zu gestalten**. In Zeiten permanenten Wandels ist es zunächst noch wichtiger, die Notwendigkeit von Veränderungen zu **erkennen und im ganzen Unternehmen die Bereitschaft dafür zu schaffen**. Insofern „...verstehen wir Managementlehre als Lehre von der Unternehmensführung, die sich durch ein systemtheoretisch orientiertes und interdisziplinäres Vorgehen darum bemüht, gestalterisch auf den Ablauf des Systems Unternehmung bei Einbezug der relevanten Kontextvariablen Einfluß zu nehmen" (Stähli 1996).

In den vergangenen zehn Jahren wurden zahlreiche Ansätze zum Veränderungsmanagement diskutiert und umgesetzt - mit durchaus unterschiedlichen und schlecht prognostizierbaren Erfolgen (vgl. Hochschule St. Gallen 1997). Zu den am häufigsten praktizierten Ansätzen gehören das **Total Quality Management**

(TQM) und das Business Process Reengineering. Das Business Process Reengineering untersucht die Unternehmensprozesse mit dem Ziel einer radikalen Verbesserung der Elemente Kosten, Qualität, Service sowie Zeit und mündet im Ergebnis zu einer entsprechenden Neugestaltung der Prozesse (vgl. Berndt 1997). TQM geht als ganzheitlicher Ansatz über die reinen Geschäftsprozesse hinaus und berücksichtigt auch „weiche" Prozesse und Faktoren, wie zum Beispiel Kundenorientierung, Führung, Kommunikation, Unternehmenskultur und das Commitment der Mitarbeiter (vgl. Berndt 1995).

Die meisten Gründe für das Scheitern von Change Management-Vorhaben liegen freilich im Bereich des menschlichen Verhaltens. Die **Widerstände gegen Veränderungen** kommen sowohl aus dem Management als auch aus der Mitarbeiterschaft, und zu den häufigsten Ursachen hierfür zählt die Angst (vor Veränderungen) bei den Betroffenen (vgl. Degen 1996):

(1) Die Betroffenen haben die Ziele, die Hintergründe oder die Motive einer Maßnahme nicht verstanden - möglicherweise, weil sie unzureichend kommuniziert wurden.

(2) Die Betroffenen haben verstanden, worum es geht, aber sie glauben nicht, was man ihnen sagt - möglicherweise fehlt ihnen das Vertrauen in die Glaubwürdigkeit der Manager.

(3) Die Betroffenen haben verstanden und sie glauben auch, was ihnen gesagt wurde, aber sie wollen oder können nicht mitziehen, weil sie sich von den vorgesehenen Maßnahmen für sich keine positiven Konsequenzen versprechen - auch hier liegen eventuell Vertrauensdefizite und/oder mangelnde Erfahrung mit Teamprozessen vor.

Bei Führungskräften kommt durch die Verlagerung von der Struktur- zur Prozeßverantwortung und durch die Verlagerung der Entscheidungskompetenz auf die Ausführungsebene (Empowerment der Mitarbeiter) ein weiterer Angstfaktor hinzu, nämlich die Angst vor Kontrollverlust. Untersuchungen zufolge wiegt diese in Veränderungsprozessen stärker als die Angst vor Positions- und Statusverlust (Doppler/Lauterburg 1996). Eine weitere Ursache für das Scheitern ist die mangelnde Selbstverpflichtung (Commitment) des obersten Managements. Die Betroffenen auf allen Ebenen hören zwar die Botschaft und verstehen sie möglicherweise auch, aber sie richten ihr eigenes Verhalten stark danach aus, wie sich ihre jeweiligen Führungskräfte verhalten, das heißt, ob diese Manager das, was sie sagen, auch ernst meinen und für sich umsetzen (Tushman/Anderson 1997).

Hieraus lassen sich im Hinblick auf den zu erwartenden **Erfolg von Veränderungsprozessen** nachstehende Schlußfolgerungen ziehen:

(1) Von entscheidender Bedeutung für den Erfolg eines Change Management-Vorhabens ist die glaubwürdige Kommunikation der anstehenden Veränderungen gegenüber den Mitarbeitern.

(2) Die Glaubwürdigkeit des Managements steht in einer direkten Beziehung zu seiner tatsächlichen Bereitschaft, die Veränderungen - gleichwohl, ob für den einzelnen positiv oder negativ besetzt - für sich mitzuvollziehen.

(3) Change Management bedarf damit der gelebten Überzeugung, das heißt der inneren Zustimmung des gesamten Managements. „In Zeiten existentieller Herausforderung wird nur der gewinnen, der wirklich zu führen bereit ist, dem es um Überzeugung geht und nicht um politische, wirtschaftliche oder mediale Macht - ihren Erhalt oder auch ihren Gewinn" (Herzog 1997, S. 353).

Wenn dieses heute die vorrangige Aufgabe der Unternehmensführer ist, dann stellt sich als nächstes die Frage, ob und inwieweit die Führungskräfte in Unternehmen, Organisationen und Institutionen im Rahmen ihrer beruflichen Ausbildung sowie des Managements und Executive Developments darauf vorbereitet werden. Konsequenterweise schließt sich gleich daran die Frage an, ob und inwieweit die für das Management Development verantwortlichen Institutionen zeitgemäße Inhalte, Lehr- und Lernmethoden sowie die wachsende Globalisierung der Wirtschaft ins Kalkül ziehende Lernorte anbieten. **Denn wenn von den Führungskräften heute zu Recht verlangt wird, zu veränderungsbereiten und veränderungsfähigen „Managern des Wandels" zu werden, so müssen sich die Management-Weiterbildungsinstitutionen die Frage gefallen lassen, wie sie diese neue Nachfrage seitens der Wirtschaft in ihrem Angebot umsetzen.**

3. Management-Andragogik im Executive Development

Ausgehend von der Erkenntnis, daß eine Unternehmung kein statisches, von seiner Umwelt isoliertes Gebilde ist, sondern eben in ständiger Wechselwirkung mit ihr steht, wurde von Ulrich (1970) der systemtheoretisch fundierte Ansatz einer Managementlehre entwickelt, der sich über die als zu statisch empfundene klassische Betriebswirtschaftslehre erhebt. Im Rahmen dieses Ansatzes kommt dem didaktischen Konzept der **Management-Andragogik** besondere Bedeutung zu.

Jede Art von Weiterbildung benötigt entsprechende Methoden. Ist die Weiterbildungsmaßnahme als Management oder Executive Development definiert, so liegt nahe, nach Methoden zu fragen, die dem Alter und der professionellen Erfahrung dieses Personenkreises gerecht wird (vgl. Abb. 1). Bei der Entwicklung von Executive Potential ist dabei jene Personengruppe angesprochen, die bereits über ausreichende Erfahrung im Management der operativen Ebene verfügt und sich in der Lebensdekade zwischen 30 und 40 Jahren befindet. Hall (1976, S. 54) beschreibt diese Lebensphase treffend als „advanced": „At this point the person is not so concerned with fitting into the organization (moving inside) as he is with moving and mastering it."

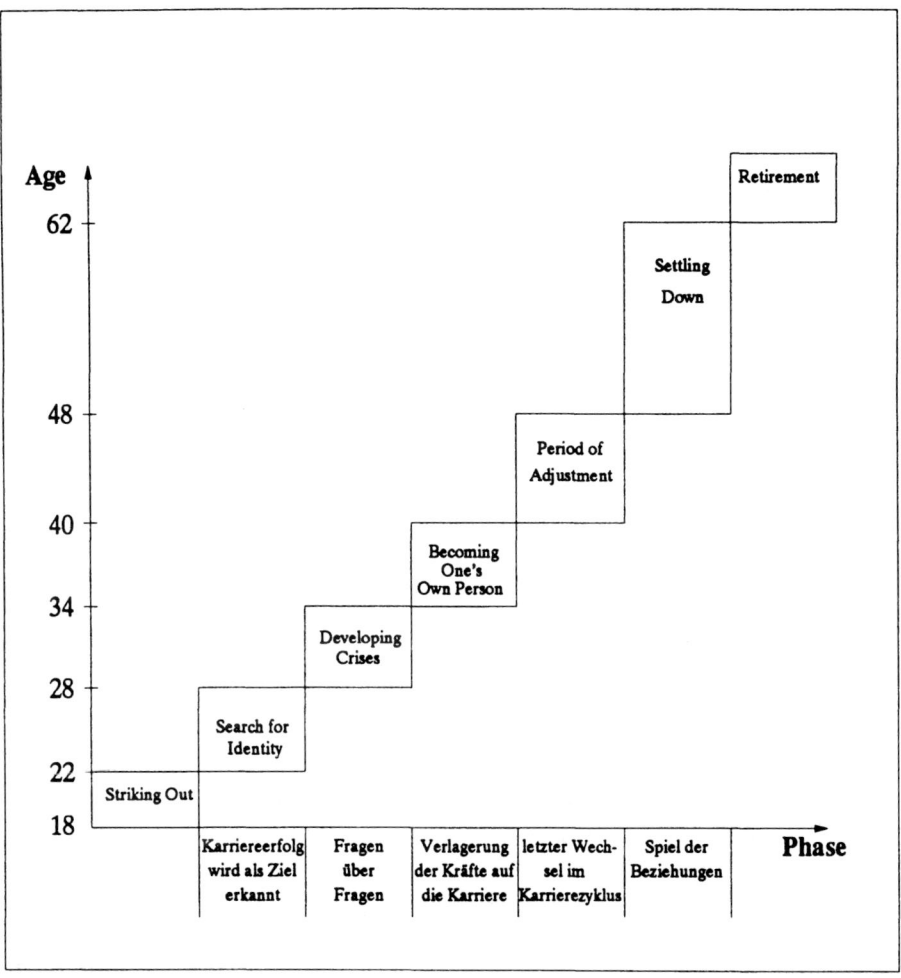

Quelle: Stähli 1988, S. 31.

Abb. 1: Lebenszyklen Erwachsener (Adult Life Cycles)

Dabei soll die Weiterbildung von Management bewußt auf einer speziellen, adäquat bezeichneten methodischen Grundlage stehen und nicht einfach als eine Form von berufsbezogener „Erwachsenenbildung" deklariert werden. Seine didaktische Ergänzung findet der systemtheoretische Ansatz im Management Development folglich im bildungstheoretischen Konzept der Andragogik. Denn im Gegensatz zur Pädagogik, die sich um die Erziehung junger, unmündiger Menschen zu mündigen Persönlichkeiten bemüht, steht im Mittelpunkt der Andragogik der bereits mündige, erwachsene Mensch. Die Management-Andragogik stellt eine zielgruppenbezogene Untergruppe der agogischen Wissenschaften dar (vgl. Abb. 2). Da es sich hier um Lernprozesse, speziell das Veränderungslernen, von

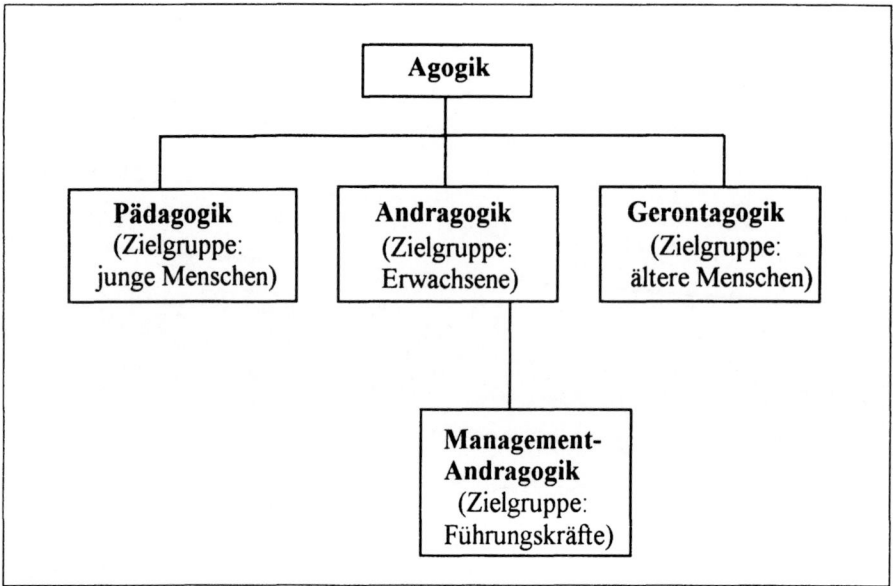

Abb. 2: Agogische Wissenschaften

Führungskräften handelt, läßt sich die Management-Andragogik wie folgt definieren: „**Management-Andragogik ist jener Bereich der Erwachsenenbildung, der sich mit der Weiterbildung von Führungskräften in offenen soziotechnischen Systemen befaßt. Sie setzt ihre Inhalte und Methoden in Beziehung zu den jeweiligen persönlichen und professionellen Bedürfnissen, Erfahrungswerten und Lebenszyklen der Studienteilnehmer. Dabei ist der laterale Lerntransfer obligatorischer Bestandteil ihres gesamten interdisziplinären Curriculums. Neben der Erarbeitung zeitgemäßer systemorientierter und global ausgerichteter Instrumente der Unternehmensführung wirkt die Management-Andragogik auf der Grundlage eines komplexen Menschenbildes und integriert die Berücksichtigung ethischer Prinzipien und Verantwortung gegenüber ökonomischer, politischer, sozialer und ökologischer Umwelt als Handelsorientierung**" (Stähli 1988, S. 22).

Das Ziel management-andragogischer Lernprozesse ist die Vermittlung von Fähigkeiten zeitgemäßer und erfolgreicher Unternehmensführung in zunehmend komplexen und sich fortwährend diskontinuierlich entwickelnden Märkten. „Die Organisation 'Unternehmen' muß sowohl in ihrer Gesamtheit als auch in ihrer Verflochtenheit mit der Umwelt analysiert, verstanden und gelenkt werden. Dazu bedarf es eines ausreichend differenzierenden Analyse- und Strukturierungsmodells, das die wichtigsten Unternehmensfunktionen beleuchtet. Dieses findet sich im betriebswirtschaftlich-systemtheoretischen Modell" (Stähli 1995).

Maßgeblich für Selbstverständnis und Problemlösungsvorgehen dieser Managementlehre sind ein optimales Instrumentarium zur Analyse der Unternehmung als offenes sozio-technisches System und der maximale Anwendungsbezug, die möglichst reibungslose Transfergelegenheit des gewonnenen Wissens in die betriebliche Realität. Der systemorientierte Ansatz eignet sich zur Beschreibung und Analyse verschiedener für die Unternehmensführung relevanter theoretischer Dimensionen (vgl. Stähli 1988. S. 12):

(1) zur Beschreibung (weil notwendig zu berücksichtigender Einflußfaktoren) der Welt und der Volkswirtschaft,

(2) zur Analyse der Unternehmenssituation, vielfach vernetzt mit verschiedensten Faktoren der sie umgebenden Umwelt (Kontextvariablen materieller und immaterieller Natur),

(3) zur Beschreibung und Analyse der internen Unternehmensstruktur und einem entsprechenden Anforderungsprofil an die Unternehmensleitung,

(4) zur Grundlegung lernpsychologischer Implikationen des Management resp. Executive Development,

(5) schließlich als Zusammenfassung all dieser zu berücksichtigenden Faktoren zur Grundlegung eines entsprechenden Fallstudienmodells und seiner praktischen Ausarbeitung und zur Bewertung des daraus resultierenden Lösungsvorschlages.

Die Organisation „Unternehmen" muß sowohl in ihrer Gesamtheit als auch in ihrer Verflochtenheit mit ihrer Umwelt verstanden, analysiert und gelenkt werden. Den systemtheoretischen Ansatz auf Unternehmungen zu übertragen, ist in der heutigen Zeit rasch aufeinanderfolgender Veränderungen nicht nur statthaft, sondern gleichsam zwingend geboten. Mehr noch: Die Fähigkeit des Überlebens von Unternehmungen ist unmittelbar mit den Fähigkeiten des Managements verknüpft, ein **Konzept für das Management des Wandels** entwickeln und durchsetzen zu können. Dieses sollte alle erkennbaren, geplanten, gesteuerten, organisierten und kontrollierten Veränderungen in den Strategien, Prozessen, Strukturen und in den Kulturen sozio-ökonomischer Systeme umfassen und die Grundfragestellung beantworten: „Wie können Unternehmungen den Herausforderungen eines sich häufig, unregelmässig und fast unvorhersehbar wandelnden Umsystems begegnen sowie durch ein pro- und reaktives Vorgehen ihr langfristiges Überleben und ihre fortlaufende Zielerreichung sichern?" (Thom 1997, S. 202).

Die zentrale Rolle in Veränderungsprozessen von Unternehmen kommt unbestreitbar dem Management der Unternehmen zu. Das Management wirkt an den Schaltstellen im organisatorischen Netzwerk, ist Initiator, „Lotse" und Organisator der Veränderung von Prozessen. Hierzu benötigen die Führungskräfte jedoch entsprechende Kenntnisse und Fähigkeiten (Skills), um das System Unternehmen erfolgreich in sich diskontinuierlich entwickelnden Märkten zu steuern. Diese Qualifikationen nach abgeschlossener beruflicher Grundausbildung zu vermitteln und weiterzubilden ist das Ziel des Managements- oder Executive Developments.

Derart neue und anspruchsvolle „Skills", wie sie aber gerade von „Managern des Wandels" erwartet werden, können über die klassischen Hochschul- und Universitätsausbildungen nicht vermittelt werden. Die Notwendigkeit einer die Tertiärausbildung ergänzenden Management-Weiterbildung liegt damit auf der Hand. Wie freilich noch zu zeigen ist, korrespondieren häufig auch die dort angewandten Lehrmethoden nicht mehr mit den aktuellen Herausforderungen der Wirtschaft. Die traditionellen Lehrmethoden, die heute im Bereich Management Development eingesetzt werden, wurden in den 60er, 70er und 80er Jahren dieses Jahrhunderts entwickelt. Sie zielten im Kontext der damals weitgehend stabilen ökonomischen Systeme mehrheitlich auf die Herausbildung und Förderung funktionaler und analytischer Fähigkeiten sowie auf die Verbreiterung des Erfahrungswissens des Einzelnen.

Gegen Ende der 80er Jahre begann sich das **business environment** weltweit dramatisch zu verändern. Japan, China und die früheren Schwellenländer Südostasiens entwickelten sich zu ernstzunehmenden Mitbewerbern auf den Weltmärkten und bedrohten die angestammten Terrarien der Industrienationen. Die früheren Länder des Ostblocks entdeckten die Vorzüge des freien Marktes. Und mit atemberaubender Geschwindigkeit zogen neue Informations- und Kommunikationstechnologien in die Unternehmen ein und verlangten von den Führungskräften vermehrtes technologisches Wissen und darauf ausgerichtete komunikative Fähigkeiten. Diese großen weltökonomischen Verschiebungen ließen die stabil geglaubten gesellschaftlichen und sozialen Strukturen nicht unberührt. Gelernte Werte wie Kontinuität, Arbeitsplatzsicherheit, Eindimensionalität der Berufsausbildung und -tätigkeit oder das Primat hierarchischer Strukturen waren auf einmal nicht länger sakrosankt (vgl. Küng 1980), sondern wurden insbesondere bei Führungskräften durch neue Anforderungen wie Flexibilität, Kommunikationsfähigkeit, Führung und Zusammenarbeit im Team ersetzt. Und diese Verlagerung hält weiter an (vgl. Angehrn/Doz/Atherton 1995). „The new skills, necessary to manage in the turbulent nineties, are evolving, by increasing the breadth and depth of executives´ skill base to be able to:
- operate internationally across continents and have a good understanding of cultural differences;
- select essential data, interpret signals, determine clear objectives and act rapidly, often on the basis of excessive though incomplete information;
- be flexible and adopt continuous learning as a philosophy of life;
- get things done with others.

Parallel zu diesem neuen Anforderungsprofil an die Individuen wird das Idealbild der lernenden Organisation konzeptionell weiterentwickelt. Organisationen aber lernen nach Senge (1996) nur, wenn einzelne Menschen etwas lernen. Ohne individuelles Lernen gibt es keine lernende Organisation, und um dieses Ziel zu erreichen, muß das permanente Lernen sowohl in den Individuen als Wert verankert werden als auch durch die Organisation selbst unterstützt werden. Pointiert ausgedrückt: Management Development ist eine Grundvoraussetzung, um das Unternehmen als Ganzes in eine lernende Organisation zu verwandeln.

Erfolgreich eingesetztes Management Development muß dabei neben den Zielen und Bedürfnissen der Unternehmensführung auch die individuellen Motive der jeweiligen, in den Prozeß des Management Development involvierten, Persönlichkeiten berücksichtigen. Im Rahmen eines Forschungsprojektes ermittelte Regula Schräder-Naef als wesentliche ökonomische Einflußfaktoren, die die Entscheidung Erwachsener für die Aufnahme einer Weiterbildungsmaßnahme begünstigen (Schraeder-Naef 1996): „Druck von aussen, die Wirtschaftslage, eine unbefriedigende berufliche Situation, mangelnde Entwicklungsmöglichkeiten, Bedrohung oder Verlust des Arbeitsplatzes ...". Allerdings ist mit Sattelberger (1997) davor zu warnen, das Angebot des Management Development allein am Angstverhalten oder an der primären Karriereorientierung der Führungskräfte auszurichten; insbesondere im Hinblick auf die Erfolgschancen von Veränderungsprozessen sind Reife, Eigenverantwortlichkeit und die Fähigkeit zur Selbstverpflichtung von Führungskräften vorauszusetzen.

Während die Unternehmen für die mittlere Managementebene intern durchgeführte Weiterbildungsmaßnahmen bevorzugen, um die oben skizzierten Aufgabenstellungen zu erfüllen, so gilt für die Weiterbildung des Topmanagements, dass dieses vor allem in externen Institutionen des Management Developments aus- und weitergebildet werden soll (vgl. Stähli 1993, S. 56 f.). Während die unternehmensinternen Weiterbildungsveranstaltungen die Ausrichtung der Curricula (Lerninhalte und Strukturen) an den Unternehmensbedürfnissen weitgehend sicherstellen, da sich die Seminare vorrangig an der Unternehmenspolitik orientieren, bergen sie doch die Gefahr des „Blinden Fleckes": Es kommt nicht zu einem Erfahrungsaustausch mit Führungskräften anderer Organisationen und Wirtschaftszweige. Deshalb senden selbst große Unternehmen mit eigenen Weiterbildungs- und Trainingsabteilungen ihre Manager mit dem größten Potential zunehmend in externe Institutionen der Management-Weiterbildung (vgl. Stähli 1994).

Diese erfüllen, wenn sie denn international angelegt sind, eine weitere Forderung im Katalog der Eigenschaften und Fähigkeiten an veränderungsreaktive Führungskräfte: Das heutige globale Umfeld verlangt multikulturell bewanderte, mehrsprachige und international versierte Manager. „Business schools, as responsible educators of `future generations of managers` must continue to train students to critical thinkers. Additionally, they must ensure that students understand the complexities of operating in a global marketplace" (vgl. Stumpf et al. 1997; vgl. auch Abb. 3).

Durchführen organisatorischer Veränderungen

☐

Schaffen eines intakten sozialen Arbeitsumfeldes

☐

Abbau hierarchischer Schranken

☐

Leistung erzeugen durch Synergie

☐

Flexibilisierung der Arbeitsformen und Arbeitszeiten

☐

Organisieren von Lernen und Entwicklung

☐

Frauen erobern Schlüsselpositionen

☐

Management von Konflikt- und Krisensituationen

☐

Entlassung von Mitarbeiterinnen und Mitarbeitern

☐

Aushalten innerer Zielkonflikte und Widersprüche

☐

Steuerung und Kontrolle durch Kommunikation

☐

Zukunftsplanung aufgrund komplexer Szenarien

☐

Integration durch Visionen und Leitbilder

Quelle: Doppler/Lauterburg 1996, S. 31.

Abb. 3: Herausforderungen, die in Zukunft den Berufsalltag
im Management prägen

4. Der Master of Business Administration (MBA)

Die im Zuge erfolgversprechenden Change Managements notwendigen „Managerial skills" werden in Europa traditionellerweise nicht über die Ausbildung der tertiären Phase (Universität) vermittelt, da diese Institutionen vom Selbstverständnis her im Prozess der Wissensvermittlung stark die klassischen akademisch-theoretischen Positionen favorisieren (s. Stähli 1996, S. 25). Während in den Vereinigten Staaten die beste Management-Ausbildung und - Weiterbildung über private Business Schools als MBA (Master of Business Administration) angeboten wird, stellen marktwirtschaftlich operierende Bildungseinrichtungen auf Hochschulniveau im deutschsprachigen Raum immer noch die

Junior-MBA-Programme		Executive MBA-Programme	
Merkmale	- Vollstudium auf dem Campus - akademisch - keine oder geringe Berufserfahrung - intensiv und interaktiv - hohe Studiengebühren, hohe Nebenkosten - kaum Entsendung durch Firmen - attraktiv für Hochschulabsolventen - Auswahl nach GMAT (Graduate Management Admission Test) und TOEFL (Test of English as a Foreign Language)	**Merkmale**	- berufsbegleitend - berufserfahrene Fach- und Führungskräfte - Alter zwischen 30 und 40 Jahren - oft Entsendung durch Firmen - Auswahl nach beruflicher Erfahrung und Managementpotential - hoher Praxisbezug - Projektarbeit mit Bezug auf das Unternehmen - keine Berufsunterbrechung, geringe Ausfallzeiten - hohe Studiengebühren, geringe Nebenkosten
Formen		**Formen**	
(a) Zweijährige Vollzeitprogramme	- ursprüngliche Form der Ausbildung - typisch für die USA - Durchschnittsalter 26 bis 28 Jahre	(a) Part-time-Executive-Programme	- 18 bis 36 Monate - regelmäßig einzelne Lehrveranstaltungen an Abenden oder Wochenenden - lokales Teilnehmerumfeld - geringe Internationalität
(b) Einjährige Vollzeitprogramme	- Weiterentwicklung des US-Modells - typisch für Europa - sehr intensiv Durchschnittsalter 28 bis 30 Jahre	(b) Modulare Programme	- 18 bis 36 Monate - verteilt auf mehrere ein- bis vierwöchige Präsenzmodule - Wechsel von On-the-job- und Off-the-job-Perioden - hohe Verträglichkeit mit dem Beruf - internationale Zusammenarbeit - intensiv und interaktiv
(c) Part-time-Programme	- 18 bis 36 Monate - höheres Durchschnittsalter der Teilnehmer - gewisse Berufserfahrung - Finanzierung durch Beruf - relativ verschult - weniger intensiv und interaktiv als ein Vollzeitprogramm - geringe Internationalität - kostengünstiger - lokale Schule	(c) Distance-Learning-Programme	- Fernstudium - Unterstützung durch einzelne Workshops - 36 bis 48 Monate - sehr flexibel - wenig interaktiv - geringe Internationalität - keine Abwesenheitszeiten

Quelle: Thommen 1995, S. 23.

Abb. 4: Überblick über MBA-Typen

Ausnahme dar. Die langsame, aber stetige Zunahme solcher Bildungsinstitutionen in Deutschland und der Schweiz ist nachfrageinduziert und bestätigt die These, daß weder die Reaktionsfähigkeit auf sich schnell ändernde Weiterbildungs-Bedürfnisse des Marktes noch die Engpaßverhältnisse der traditionellen Hochschulen in bezug auf weiter steigende Studentenzahlen und daher vielfach angespannte Finanzlagen geeignet sind, Management-Weiterbildung erfolgreich durchführen zu können - jedenfalls nicht, solange sie keine relevanten Teile der Managementausbildung in ihre Curricula integrieren, um beispielsweise auch Medizinern oder Pädagogen ein Grundverständnis vom Management einer Klinik oder einer Bildungseinrichtung zu vermitteln (vgl. Kozminski 1994).

Aufgrund ihrer praxisnahen Konzeption haben die MBA-Ausbildungsprogramme daher zunehmend an Attraktivität gewonnen. Allein im Ursprungsland des MBA stieg die Zahl der Business Schools von 1965 bis heute von 400 auf rund 800 Schulen mit jährlich mehr als 80000 Absolventen. Der MBA als ein akademischer Nachdiplomstudiengang an einer Business School, der ein bereits absolviertes Erststudium ergänzt, unterstützt die mit dem Management Development zu erreichenden Ziele in mehrerer Hinsicht besser als ein Zweit- oder Aufbaustudium an einer klassischen Hochschule:

- Der Studiengang ist praxisorientiert und stellt daher eine sinnvolle Ergänzung des theoretischen Wissens der Hochschulabsolventen dar.
- Die Unternehmen - letztlich die „Kunden" der MBA-Absolventen - präferieren in ihrer weit überwiegenden Mehrzahl die private Business School als geeignetsten Lernort.
- Management Development über die MBA-Ausbildung ist aufgrund der Heterogenität des Lehrkörpers - neben Theoretikern unterrichten auch Führungskräfte mit eigener Management-Praxis - in der Regel sowohl zeitlich als auch inhaltlich deutlich näher am aktuellen Geschehen auf den Märkten angesiedelt. Während die klassische Hochschulausbildung das Grundverständnis für wirtschaftliche Zusammenhänge lehrt und die Absolventen erst im Laufe ihrer Berufstätigkeit mit Entscheidungssituationen aus dem praktischen Alltag konfrontiert werden, sind Theorie und Praxis in der MBA-Ausbildung eng miteinander verzahnt.
- Die Lehr- und Lernmethoden der Business Schools erlauben insbesondere dann einen hohen Grad an Transfermöglichkeiten des Gelernten in den Führungsalltag, wenn die Weiterbildungs- und Praxisphasen in einem regelmäßigen Rhythmus wechseln.

Hinsichtlich der von Führungskräften geforderten Internationalität leisten europäische Business Schools einen höheren Beitrag als amerikanische Programme: „Der Vielfalt von Kultur, Mentalität, Sprache und individuellem Erfahrungshintergrund wird ein deutlich höherer Stellenwert beigemessen" (Schneider 1996, S. 6). Wie dringend notwendig diese interkulturelle und internationale Ausrichtung ist, macht auch diese Aussage deutlich: „For some time now graduate schools of business have felt the pressure to internationalize their teaching and learning environments to meet the needs of their students, their communities, and a more globally active marketplace. Technological developments, particulary in the areas of communications and information systems, have facilitated the flow of goods, services, and capital across national and cultural boundaries. New responsibilities have been placed in schools of business to deliver services which are relevant in a rapidly changing global environment. Internationalization of business education is not a matter of choice for most institutions; it is a necessity driven by the need to remain competitive and to be effective in satisfying the needs of key stakeholders (Stumpf et al. 1996).

Zweifelsohne ist die normative Ausbildung ein wesentlicher Bestandteil der betriebswirtschaftlichen Hochschulausbildung, doch vor dem Hintergrund des permanenten Wandels wird die Frage immer drängender, ob sie die genügende Praxisnähe bietet. Zu Recht weist Dubs (1996, S. 311) darauf hin, daß „Praxisnähe ... nicht mit `Ausbildung zur Berufsfertigkeit` verwechselt werden darf, sondern die Studierenden müssen fähig werden, grundlegende und aktuelle Problemstellungen in der Unternehmung und ihren Umwelten zu erkennen und zu verstehen, um in kompetenter Weise unter Berücksichtigung reflektierter normativer Annahmen nach innovativen Lösungen zu suchen, diese in Diskussionen auf ihre Plausibilität hin zu untersuchen sowie mit dem aktuellen Erkenntnisstand zu vergleichen."

Sowohl in den Vereinigten Staaten - dem Herkunftsland der MBA-Ausbildung - als auch in Europa werden diese Weiterbildungsgänge zumeist von privaten Institutionen angeboten. Dies entspricht auch mehrheitlich dem Wunsch der Wirt-

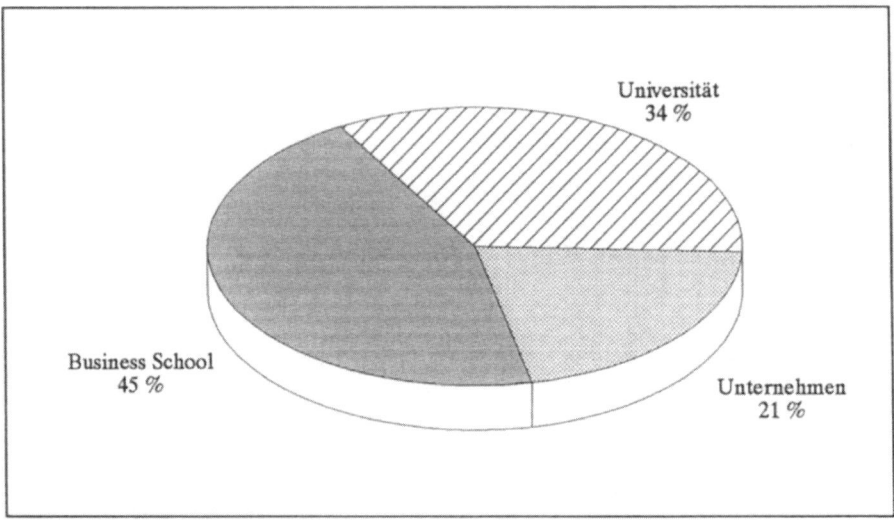

Abb. 5: Die präferierten Lernorte der Management-Weiterbildung (MBA-Studiengang)

schaft, die den privaten Einrichtungen offensichtlich nicht nur ein höheres Maß an Effizienz und Effektivität zuschreibt, sondern auch die von privaten Institutionen getroffenen Qualitätssicherungsmaßnahmen hoch bewertet (vgl. Abb. 5).

Darüber hinaus zeichnen sich insbesondere die privaten Business Schools in der Regel durch ein feststehendes und organisiertes Kontaktnetz zur Wirtschaft aus, wodurch der regelmäßige Austausch von Wissenschaft und Praxis gefördert wird. „Um stärker auf die aktuellen Bedürfnisse der Unternehmen eingehen zu können, unterhalten die Business Schools in Forschung wie in Lehre enge Kontakte zur Wirtschaft. Mit der zunehmenden Kundenorientierung verbunden ist eine größere Flexibilität und Vielfalt des Programmangebots, die eine Trendwende von standardisierten Konzepten mit geringer Arbeitsplatz-Relevanz hin zu berufsbegleitenden, modularen und firmenspezifischen Programmen bewirkt hat. Leistungsorientierte Mitarbeiter können so von den Unternehmen gefördert werden, die direkte Rückkopplung des Studieneffektes mit der aktuellen Berufstätigkeit verspricht Vorteile für beide Seiten, und nicht zuletzt können Probleme mit der Wiedereingliederung in den Beruf vermieden werden" (Bundesanstalt für Arbeit 1996, S. 206).

Insbesondere im Hinblick auf die von den Business Schools postulierte Fortentwicklung der Managerfähigkeit, die akzelerierenden Veränderungen in Wirtschaft und Gesellschaft mit unternehmerischen Konzepten zu bewältigen, sind „für das Lernen von Unternehmensführung ... der direkte Kontakt und die ständige, fest institutionalisierte Interaktion von Wirtschaft, Politik und Wissenschaft notwendig. Dabei muß, damit der Träger (Lernort) von Management- und Executive Development nicht erstarrt, sondern sich an den Bedürfnissen und der Nachfrage des Marktes orientiert und diese effizient und effektiv umsetzen kann, ein solcher Lernort - im weiteren als **Business School** bezeichnet - selbst nach marktwirtschaftlichen Prinzipien wirken, bei gleichzeitiger Gewährleistung bester Reputation" (Stähli 1993, S. 10).

Letztlich wird die Notwendigkeit für eine interkulturelle Management-Weiterbildung immer wieder von den Absolventen der Business School selbst betont. So sprach Jack F. Smith jr. (1997), Chief Executive Officer von General Motors und Absolvent eines MBA-Programmes, in einem im Internet (World Wide Web) publizierten Interview auf die Frage nach den künftigen Ansprüchen an die MBA-Programme der Business Schools gewiß nicht nur amerikanischen Führungskräften aus der Seele: „I think there needs to be a cross-fertilization of ideas between business schools and the corporate world to address the rapid pace of change occurring in the competitive arena. I strongly believe the business schools must emphasize team skills and techniques for managing in a global environment. A global perspective and a knowledge of other cultures and their competitive approaches is essential as American corporations move into global markets."

5. Gestaltung des Wandels in der Business School

Auf der Basis der klassischen MBA-Ausbildung nach amerikanischem Vorbild hat sich in Europa eine neue Weiterbildungskultur entwickelt. Nicht die Wissens-vermittlung steht im Vordergrund, sondern die Schulung der Entscheidungsfin-dung in anspruchsvollen strategischen Führungssituationen. Die praxisorientierten Management-Weiterbildungsprogramme nehmen aktuelle Trends des Wirtschafts-lebens auf und orientieren sich an den Bedürfnissen der Unternehmen. In der Schweiz hat sich die MBA-Kultur nach anfänglicher Skepsis etabliert. 1997 gibt es bereits 15 Bildungsinstitutionen, die ein MBA-Programm in der Schweiz anbie-ten.

Die fortdauernde Verkürzung der Produktionszyklen und die immer noch zuneh-mende Komplexität der Wirtschaftsabläufe zwingen die Führungskräfte, sich ei-nem permanenten Lernprozess zu unterziehen. Entscheidend für die kontinuierli-che Aufbereitung des Wissensstandes ist die zunehmende Globalisierung der Han-

Schule	Punkte
1. Rotterdam School of Management	20482
2. Manchester Business School	20237
3. Insead	20122
4. GSBA Zürich	19860
5. London Business School	19613,50
6. IESE	19374
7. Instituto de Empresa	19097
8. ISA	19080
9. Nijenrode	17983,50
10. IMD (Lausanne)	17623
11. SDA Bocconi	17262
12. Cranfield School of Management	16279,50
13. ESADE	16051
14. EAP Paris	15579
15. Stockholm School of Economics (SSE)	15460,50
16. The Helsinki School of Economics and Bus. Adm.	14221
17. Warwick Business School	13935
18. K.U. Leuven	13525
19. Ashridge Management College	12865,50
20. Henley - The Management College	11755,75

Quelle: Top Business 1992, S. 35.

Abb. 6: Rangfolge europäischer Business Schools

dels- und Wirtschaftsbeziehungen und der durchdringende Einsatz moderner Informations- und Kommunikationstechnologien. Wichtig ist daneben die Förderung und Schulung des interkulturellen Managements. Gemeint ist die Fähigkeit, mit größtmöglicher Flexibilität und Mobilität fremde Kulturen verstehen und akzeptieren zu können und mit internationalen Partnern - zunehmend auch mit ihren Kollegen in international besetzten Projektteams - kompetent und erfolgreich zu verhandeln und zusammenzuwirken. Führungskräfte müssen lernen, globale Geschäftsstrategien zu entwickeln, durchzusetzen und deren Umsetzung aktiv zu begleiten.

Ein Charakteristikum der MBA Ausbildungs-Methodik ist daher die Lösung von Fallstudien (case studies) in Gruppen, womit das analytische Denken und die Fähigkeit, im Team Entscheidungsgrundlagen zu erarbeiten, stark gefördert werden. Eingeführt wurde diese Lernmethode von der Business School der Harvard University. Sie galt während vieler Jahrzehnte als „Königsweg der Management-Weiterbildung". Die meisten Business Schools haben die klassische Case Study-Methode übernommen und wenden sie auch heute noch an. Vor allem in den USA gibt es MBA-Programme, in deren Verlauf bis zu 800 Fallstudien innerhalb von zwei Jahren durchgenommen werden. Bei den klassischen Fallstudien handelt es sich in der Regel um vergangenheitsbezogene Fälle (frühere Situationen in einem Unternehmen). Sie lassen daher jeglichen Aktualitätsbezug vermissen. Europäische Business Schools wenden alternativ vermehrt Fallstudien mit einer komplexen aktuellen Problemstellung an und verlangen ganzheitliche Lösungsvorschläge (Stähli 1992).

Eine weitere Besonderheit der MBA-Ausbildung liegt beim Executive MBA darin, daß der gesamte Weiterbildungsprozeß nicht nur Wissen vermittelt, sondern auch die Übertragung des Lernstoffes in die Praxis institutionalisiert. Erst der geplante und erfolgreiche Transfer des in Lernprozessen vom Management und Executive Development Gelernten in die Führungspraxis ist das ausschlaggebende Kriterium für die Effektivität und Effizienz der Qualifizierungsmaßnahmen für Führungskräfte. In dieser Forderung manifestiert sich auch der Anspruch an eine wirklich praxisnahe, lebendige Management-Weiterbildung.

6. GSBA: Veränderungen für die Zukunft durch den lateralen Lerntransfer

Den konsequenten Lerntransfer (vgl. Abb. 7) pflegt die Graduate School of Business Administration Zürich, GSBA, mit der **genetisch wachsenden Fallstudie**, bei der das Unternehmen des Studienteilnehmers oder ein ihm vertrautes Unternehmen das „Objekt" der Fallstudie ist. Die während des Studiums gewonnenen Erkenntnisse werden Schritt für Schritt in die Praxis umgesetzt. Die Studienteilnehmer profitieren von der Authentizität des Lehrstoffes (Living Case Study) und müssen Entscheidungen fällen, die sich in der Praxis verantworten lassen. Dieses

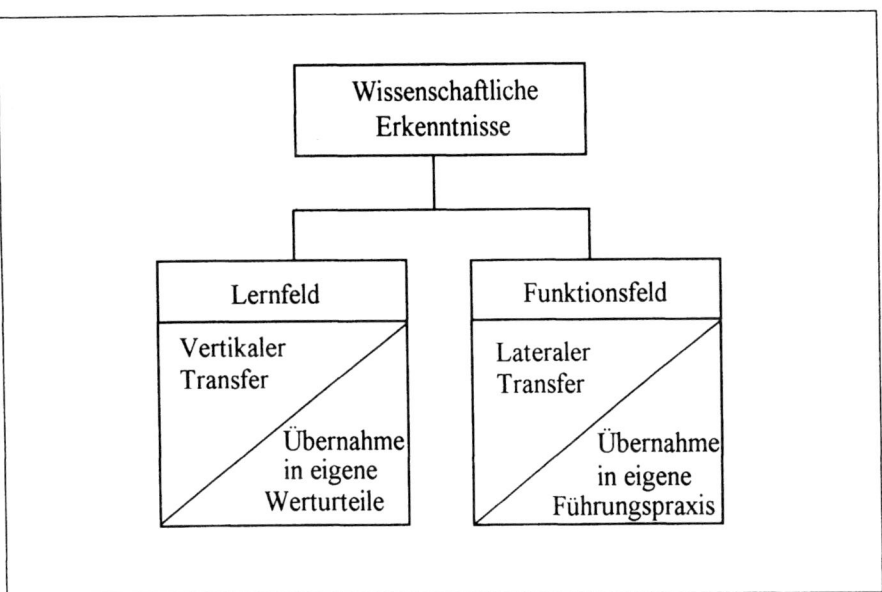

Abb. 7: Transfer-Dimensionen

Lehrelement schließt die didaktische Lücke zwischen kognitivem Wissenserwerb und sofortiger Umsetzung des Gelernten in die Praxis - Feuchthofen beschreibt dies als „fast dialektische Figur:" Das Planspiel bezieht emotionale und rationale Komponenten konstitutiv in den Lernprozeß ein, ohne aber einen der beiden Pole auf den jeweils anderen hin zu verkürzen (Feuchthofen 1997). Zusätzlich profitieren die Unternehmen direkt vom Know-how der MBA-Absolventen und Dozenten. Am Ende des Studiums erstellen die Studienteilnehmer eine These, die als „Masterplan" im Sinne des lateralen Lerntransfers auf das Unternehmen übertragen wird. Der Masterplan ist die aus der Arbeit in den Studienblöcken resultierende Unternehmensstrategie für das real existierende Unternehmen eigener Wahl. Es ist somit die Zusammenstellung einzelner Transferkonzepte zu verschiedenen betrieblichen Funktionsbereichen, ihre Zusammenfassung und Zielformulierung in Form eines Strategiehandbuches (vgl. Abb. 8).

Die Verpflichtung bestqualifizierter Dozenten stellt die Business Schools oftmals vor große Rekrutierungsprobleme. Vielfach werden relativ junge Lehrkräfte aus den USA herangezogen oder besonders talentierte MBA-Absolventen gefragt. Eine andere exemplarische Lösung dieses Problems hat die GSBA Zürich gefunden. Da ihr Executive MBA-Programm berufsbegleitend im Modulsystem (7 Blöcke à je 2 Wochen) absolviert wird, werden die Dozenten nicht vollzeitlich in Anspruch genommen. Dies erlaubt es, eine erstklassige Fakultät zu führen, deren Dozenten hauptberuflich für renommierte Hochschulen in den USA (Columbia, Cornell, Berkeley, SUNY und andere), Deutschland und der Schweiz tätig sind und an der GSBA Zürich ein zusätzliches Lehrpensum erfüllen.

94

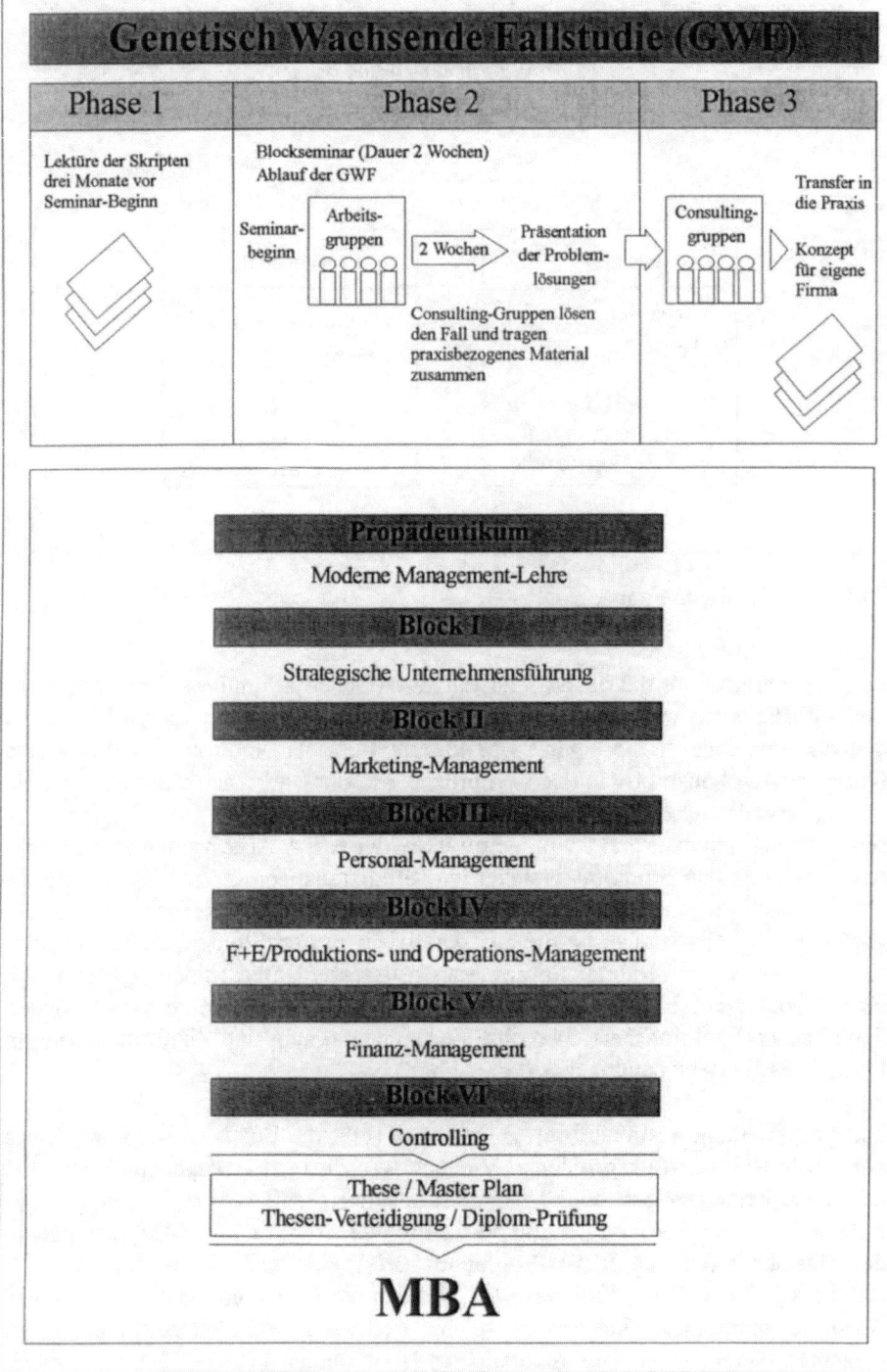

Abb. 8: Die Genetisch Wachsende Fallstudie (GWF)

Die Globalisierung der Wirtschaftsbeziehungen hat zur Folge, daß gute Business Schools besonderen Wert auf die Internationalität ihrer Programme und Lehrstrukturen legen. An der GSBA Zürich wird jeder Seminarblock von einem europäischen und einem amerikanischen Professor gemeinsam geleitet. Jedes Fachgebiet wird somit aus der Warte unterschiedlicher Managementkulturen betrachtet. Die Zulassung von Studienteilnehmern verschiedener Nationalitäten zum MBA-Studium ermöglicht einen intensiven interkulturellen Erfahrungsaustausch.

Die Internationalisierung der Wirtschaftsprozesse drängt zahlreiche Unternehmen, ihre Aktivitäten ebenfalls international auszurichten. So wird beispielsweise jeden Tag von neuen strategischen Allianzen mit ausländischen Organisationen berichtet, so bewegen sich immer mehr europäische Unternehmen in die Vereinigten Staaten und nach Asien.

Die Management-Ausbildung und ihre Träger können in diesem Prozeß nicht in der Rolle unbeteiligter Zuschauer am Rande des Geschehens verharren. Es genügt aber nicht - will die Business School ihrem Anspruch auf Praxisverankerung gerecht werden - etwa nur die Studienprogramme über ein Redesign des Curriculums mit global-wirtschaftlichen Lehrinhalten aufzufrischen - es kann sich das Gebot der Stunde stellen, auch die Aktivitäten der Business School selbst international auszurichten, in globale Netzwerke einzutreten und es dadurch den Studienteilnehmern zu ermöglichen, auch in praxi an diesem Globalisierungsprozess partizipieren zu können.

Im Sog der Globalisierung ist der Trend zur internationalen Kooperation zwischen Business Schools und Universitäten feststellbar. Seit 1996 bietet die GSBA Zürich in Kooperation mit State University of New York at Albany (SUNY) das Dual MBA-Programm an. Die SUNY ist die weltweit größte Universität mit 350000 Studenten, 27000 Fakultätsmitgliedern, 11 Research Universities und 27 Colleges. Die Studienteilnehmer absolvieren einen Teil ihres Studiums (zwei Blöcke) an der amerikanischen Partneruniversität und sind als reguläre Studenten an der SUNY eingeschrieben und können die gesamten Einrichtungen der Universität für ihre Arbeit nutzen. Sie gewinnen auf diese Weise neue Erfahrungen in einer ihnen weniger bekannten Management-Kultur. Zudem profitieren sie nicht nur von der Infrastruktur und dem Netzwerk des weltweit größten Universitäts-Systems, sondern von der solcherart verdoppelten Erfahrung im Management Development zweier Kontinente. Prof. Dr. Don Bourque, Dean, State University of New York at Albany, anläßlich der Unterzeichnung des Letter of Agreement über den Dual Degree: „The cooperation between our two institutions means that we can draw on a much larger pool of highly qualified faculty than business schools with only one faculty. The result is a higher quality teaching experience for program participants" - und damit ein deutlich höherer Lerngewinn bei den Teilnehmern. Die Studienteilnehmer legen einen Teil ihrer Prüfungen an der amerikanischen Universität ab und erhalten dadurch zusätzlich zum MBA-Diplom der GSBA Zürich auch das MBA-Diplom der SUNY, das von der amerikanischen Akkreditierungsbehörde AACSB voll anerkannt ist (Dual Degree; vgl. Abb. 9).

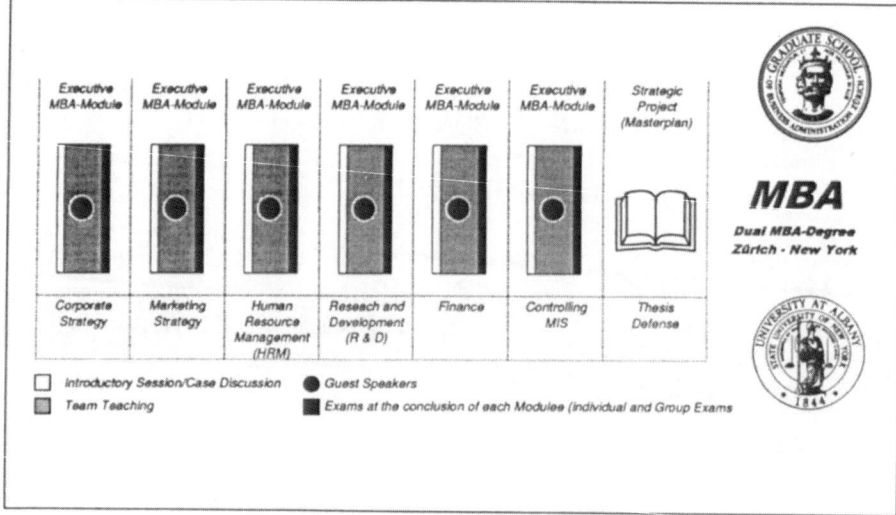

Abb. 9: Genetically Growing Case Study (within the context of
the Zuerich Executive MBA-Program)

Akkreditierungseinrichtungen für die Programme von Business Schools sind in
den USA, aber auch in Europa nicht unbekannt. Es gibt mittlerweile etliche Ver-
einigungen, die sich in Europa um Qualitätskriterien im Management bemühen.
Diese firmieren als Vereine der Anbieter, sind national organisiert und in ihrer
Wirkung in der Regel auf den nationalen Raum beschränkt. Solange die Akkreditierung der europäischen MBA-Programme nicht einheitlich geregelt ist, gilt die
AACSB-Akkreditierung weltweit immer noch als zuverlässigster Indikator für
eine qualitativ hochstehende MBA-Ausbildung (von den 2500 Schulen, die in der
Marktregion von AACSB ausbilden, sind gerade 315 akkreditiert.) Dies ist vor
allem für MBA-Absolventen von Bedeutung, die in einem amerikanischen oder
global agierenden Unternehmen tätig sind oder werden wollen.

Vor einigen Jahren auf den europäischen Markt getreten ist die Schweizer Stif-
tung Foundation for International Business Administration Accreditation
(FIBAA), die als aus der Wirtschaft geborene, anbieterneutrale Einrichtung vor
allem die verläßliche Qualitätsbewertung der in Europa angebotenen MBA-
Programme vornimmt. Träger der FIBAA sind die Bundesvereinigung der Deutschen Arbeitgeberverbände, der Deutsche Industrie- und Handelstag, der Schweizerische Handels- und Industrie-Verein - VORORT -, der Zentralverband
Schweizerischer Arbeitgeberorganisationen und die Vereinigung Österreichischer
Industrieller. Die fünf Spitzenorganisationen der Wirtschaft aus Österreich,
Schweiz und Deutschland gewährleisten, daß die FIBAA international ausgerichtet ist und in der Wirtschaft verankert bleibt, zumal der Stifungsrat über die Träger hinaus mit Unternehmensvertretern besetzt ist. „Eine zentrale Aufgabe der

FIBAA besteht darin, den Dialog zwischen Unternehmen und Business Schools aufrechtzuerhalten, um angesichts tiefgreifender Transformationsprozesse in der Wirtschaft flexible und rasche Lösungen in der Management-Qualifizierung sicherstellen zu können" (Brackmann 1994, S. 300 ff.). Bisher wurden drei Business Schools in Österreich akkreditiert. Weitere Business Schools in der Schweiz und Deutschland werden demnächst ihre Akkreditierung erhalten.

7. Schlußfolgerung: Den Wandel herbeiführen!

Es ist unübersehbar, daß Wirtschaft und Unternehmen mit dem akzelerierenden Tempo des Wandels werden umgehen lernen müssen. Zur Bewältigung dieser Herausforderung benötigen sie immer mehr veränderungsbereite, veränderungsfähige und veränderungsfreudige Führungskräfte - Manager, die den Sinn ihrer Aufgabe darin begreifen, mit unternehmerischem Blick den ihnen zur Verfügung stehenden Aktionsradius zu umreißen, wo immer möglich auszuweiten und proaktiv auf die Märkte zuzugehen. Umfassende Change-Programme werden in aller Regel immer nur von wenigen Menschen gestartet. Viele Versuche schlugen fehl. Wo die Transformationsbestrebungen dann erfolgreich ausgingen, hatten sich mit der Zeit aber immer mehr „Veränderer" zusammengetan. Wo jedoch schon im Frühstadium keine minimale kritische Menge zusammen kam, wurde anschließend auch nicht viel erreicht. Die Konsequenz aus dieser empirisch belegbaren (vgl. Kotter 1995) Feststellung ruft die neue und gleichzeitig so alte Forderung nach **Entrepreneuren** im Schumpeterschen Sinne auf den Plan - nach Menschen, deren Begeisterungsfähigkeit für das Neue erst die Bewältigung des Wandels möglich macht.

Diese Menschen zeichnen sich nicht durch das Festhalten am Bewährten, sondern gerade durch ihre Freude an der und über die Veränderung aus. Mehr noch, sie sind durch ihre Ausbildung und stetige Weiterentwicklung so geprägt, daß sie die Veränderungen der Märkte am liebsten selbst herbeiführen wollen. Es sind Menschen, die den Sinn wirklichen Managements nicht in der bloßen Reaktion auf sich wandelnde Märkte, Nachfragepräferenzen, Technologien, Arbeitsmarktstrukturen und gesellschaftliche Rahmenbedingungen betrachten, vielmehr setzen sie ihr Können und Wollen vorrangig dazu ein, erkennbare Veränderungen zu spüren, durch unternehmerisches Tun zu antizipieren und damit dem Wettbewerb stets eine Nasenlänge voraus zu sein.

Wenn die heutigen Einrichtungen des Management Development solche Manager hervorbringen und prägen wollen, müssen sie sich dem gleichen Anspruch stellen und über die fortlaufende Beobachtung der Bedürfnisse ihrer Märkte die aktive Gestaltung der Management-Weiterbildung stellen. Dieses Ziel, so hochgesteckt es auch immer sein mag, ist das einzig lohnenswerte und belohnenswerte in der Zukunft. Die GSBA Zürich leistet dazu ihren aktiven Beitrag.

98

Literatur:

Angehrn, A., Doz, Y., Atherton, J. (1995), Business Navigator - The Next Generation of Management Development Tools, in: EFMD Review, 1995, Nr. 1

Berndt, R. (Hrsg.) (1995), Total Quality Management als Erfolgsstrategie, Berlin u.a. 1995

Berndt, R. (Hrsg.) (1997), Business Reengineering, Berlin u.a. 1997

Brackmann, H. J. (1994), FIBAA: Gütesiegel und Impulse für den Markt, in: GdWZ, 1994, Nr. 5, S. 300 ff.

BfA (Hrsg.) (1996), Blätter zur Berufskunde, MBA-Master of Business Administration in Europa, Nürnberg 1996

Carl, P. (1992), Die Top 20 der europäischen MBA-Schulen, Landsberg/Lech 1992

Degen, R. (1996), Verhaltensänderung als kritischer Erfolgsfaktor im Veränderungsmanagement, Hamburg 1996

Doppler, K., Lauterburg, C. (1996), Change Management, Frankfurt, New York 1996

Dubs, R. (1996), Betriebswirtschaftliche Ausbildung in der Herausforderung, in: Die Unternehmung, 1996, Nr. 5, S. 311 ff.

Feuchthofen, J. E. u.a. (1977), Lernen in Gegensätzen, in: GdWZ, April 1977

Hall, D. T. (1976), Careers in Organizations, Glenview Ill. 1976

Herzog, R. (1997), Aufbruch ins 21. Jahrhundert, „Berliner Rede" vom 26.4.1997 , in: Bulletin des Presse- und Informationsamtes der Bundesregierung, 1997, Nr. 33

HS St. Gallen/ILOT (1997), Management of Change, Erfolgsfaktoren und Barrieren organisatorischer Veränderungsprozesse, München 1997

Kotter, J. P. (1995), Acht Kardinalfehler bei der Transformation, in: Harvard Business Manager, 1995, Nr. 3, S. 21 ff.

Kozminski, A. (1994), Looking ahead: Skills and Competencies in the new Europe, in: EFMD Forum 1994, Nr. 3

Küng, E. (1980), Wege und Irrwege in die Zukunft, Stuttgart 1980

Sattelberger, T. (1997), Freiheit mit Risiko: Vom Ende klassischer Karriere-Muster, in: GdWZ, 1997, Nr. 5

Schräder-Naef, R. (1996), Forschungsprojekt Bildungsbiographien Erwachsener, in: Nationales Forschungsprogramm 33, Bulletin 4, 1996

Senge, P. M. (1996), Die fünfte Disziplin, Stuttgart 1996

Schneider, M. (1996), MBA - Master of Business Administration in Europa, in: BfA (Hrsg.), Blätter zur Berufskunde, 2-IX A 27, Nürnberg 1996

Smith Jr., J. F. (1997), Interview im Internet, http://www.general-motors.com, 1997

Stähli, A. (1988), Management-Andragogik I, Zürich 1988

Stähli, A. (1992a), Harvard Anti Case, Management Andragogik, Bd. 1, London 1992

Stähli, A. (1992b), Europäische Lösung: Genetisch wachsende Fallstudie, Management Andragogik, Bd. 2, London 1992

Stähli, A. (1993), Management-Weiterbildung, Ziele, Inhalte, Methoden, Lernorte, Neuwied 1993

Stähli, A. (1994), Neue Wege in der Management-Andragogik, in: Berndt, R. (Hrsg.), Management-Qualität contra Rezession und Krise, Berlin u.a. 1994, S. 31 ff.

Stähli, A. (1995), Total Quality Management und Management Andragogik, in: Berndt, R. (Hrsg.), Total Quality Management als Erfolgsstrategie, Berlin u.a. 1995, S. 27 ff.

Stähli, A. (1996), Globalisierung in der Management-Andragogik, in: Berndt, R. (Hrsg.), Global Management, Berlin u.a. 1996, S. 19 ff.

Stumpf, S. u.a. (1996), Internationalizing Business Education, The Value Added Learning Model, in: Berndt, R. (Hrsg.), Global Management, Berlin u.a. 1996, S. 45 ff.

Stumpf, S. u.a. (1997), Internationalizing Business Education through the Management of Process: An Interdisziplinary Approach, in: Berndt, R. (Hrsg.), Business Reengineering, Berlin u.a. 1997, S. 247 ff.

The Phoenix Group (Anderson Consulting) (1996), Die Navigation des Unternehmens in stürmischen Zeiten, Zürich 1996

Thom, N. (1997), Management des Wandels, in: Die Unternehmung, Schweizerische Zeitschrift für betriebswirtschaftliche Forschung und Praxis, 1997, Nr. 3, S. 202

Thommen, J.P. (1995), Management-Kompetenz durch Weiterbildung, St. Gallen, Zürich 1995

Tushman, M.L., Anderson, P.C. (Hrsg.) (1997), Managing Strategic Innovation and Change, Oxford 1997

Ulrich, H. (1970), Die Unternehmung als produktives soziales System, Bern 1970

Changes Ahead for Russian Management Education - Reflections from the American Experience

Daniel J. McCarthy
Sheila M. Puffer

Zusammenfassung:

Die Management-Weiterbildung in Rußland ist schnell und intensiv vorangetrieben worden, um die Wirtschaftsreform von Rußland zu unterstützen. Diverse Programme sind von russischen und von westlichen Management-Trainer angeboten worden. In diesem Artikel werden die Weiterbildungsprogramme i.e. beurteilt. Außerdem werden zukünftige Entwicklungstrends aufgezeigt.

1. Introduction

Management education in Russia has been evolving at a rapid pace to facilitate economic reform toward a more market-oriented economy. A wide variety of programs and pedagogical techniques for Russian managers have been offered over the past several years by Russian and Western management specialists. The first part of this article assesses the effectiveness of some of these management education efforts and discusses the experiences of a number of institutions in designing programs and experimenting with pedagogical techniques. This is followed by a description of changes in Russian management education in the late 1990s. Next, key issues that emerged in American management education during the 1980s and 1990s are presented and related to emerging trends in Russia's management education programs. A number of strengths traditionally associated with Russian managers are then discussed as resources that can be drawn upon as management education evolves in Russia.

2. Early Efforts in Russian Market-Oriented Management Education

Management education has flourished in Russia since the country began its transition to a more market-oriented economy in the early 1990s. Many different approaches have been used by Russian and Western educators, academics, consultants and business managers with varying degrees of success (Holden 1994, 1995; Puffer 1992,1994a; Thach 1996; Vikhanski 1995; Warner/Denezhkina/Campbell

1993). The variability of such management education efforts can be seen from the experiences of numerous institutions in program design and choice of pedagogical techniques. The main features of program design relevant to Russian management development are program length, general and specialized programs, location, and faculty. Each of these is discussed below.

2.1. Program Length

Short-term or nondegree programs have ranged from informational seminars lasting a few hours to intensive programs lasting several months, and requiring a leave of absence from work. In more recent years, full-time and part-time degree programs have been developed at various Russian universities and institutes such as Moscow State University, the Russian Economic Academy (formerly the Plekhanov Institute of the National Economy), and the International Management Institute of St. Petersburg (IMISP). Such programs are completed within one to several years.

In the early days of economic reform, Russian management consultants and educators quickly flooded the market with short programs, often of questionable quality (Veselov 1992). Western consultants and educators soon followed, but many concentrated on programs of longer duration. Among the pioneers in intensive programs were Duke University (Puffer 1992), California State University at Hayward (Wiley/Kamath/MacNab 1992), Northeastern University (McCarthy 1991), the University of Manchester Institute of Science and Technology in the United Kingdom (Holden 1995), and Bocconi University of Milan, Italy. Some programs were offered in Russia, while others took place abroad. In addition to their degree programs, several leading business schools in Russia have also begun to develop high quality, shorter programs, including Moscow State University and the International Management Institute of St. Petersburg.

Some obvious factors related to program duration are the time managers have available for training, as well as program cost. Objectives are also important. Short programs can be effective when the objectives are to develop awareness of the topic or to make business contacts. The objectives of intensive programs are usually to foster learning, attitude and behavioral change, and practical application of concepts in the work place. Sometimes, however, programs can be too long, and participants experience information overload or boredom, and become distanced from their jobs. The longer degree programs are generally aimed at younger people who have more flexible schedules, with the objective of preparing them for business careers.

2.2. General and Specialized Programs

Some general management programs offered in collaboration with Western institutions, such as Duke University, were targeted at participants from a range of industrial sectors. This approach provided opportunities for developing breadth of knowledge and networks of colleagues, and seemed to work best for senior executives. Specialized programs were offered for key industries, such as a banking program at Middlesex Community College in Massachusetts (Puffer 1992), or for individual firms, such as the California State University program for the St. Petersburg Ship Building Works. The success of specialized or custom programs depended heavily on the willingness of faculty and administrators to understand the specific conditions of the firm or industry, and to provide tools and techniques for practical solutions. Five major types of business programs were also offered by Russian organizations namely, state university programs, those of municipal and other local schools or universities, academy or institute degree programs, executive education programs, and private school programs (Mockler/Chao/Dologite 1996).

2.3. Content

Two main issues regarding content are the relative importance of theory and practice, as well as the content mix of Western and Russian management. Practical application and "how-to" skills were the most useful and the best received. Theory also had to be included to some extent, since practical guidelines cannot cover all contingencies. A mix of Western and Russian content is desirable, but not always feasible. Western content is useful if participants have a point of reference, such as knowledge of the industry. Russian content was also considered to be useful for illustrating local conditions. However, in the early programs, the small amount of material available, as well as few success stories, were serious drawbacks.

2.4. Faculty

Management development programs were typically conducted with Western faculty exclusively, with Russian faculty exclusively, or at times with binational teaching teams. Several training programs were offered for Russian faculty. For instance, a consortium of American business schools led by Harvard Business School offered some in the U.S. (Hemp 1992). Others were conducted in Russia by such organizations as the Russian Management Faculty Association organized by Moscow State University. Program success depended on providing opportunities for Russian faculty to practice interactive teaching methods to supplement their traditional lecture styles, as well as offering ongoing support. The need for better preparation on the part of Western faculty was also frequently cited by Russian business schools which wanted these visitors to adapt their materials more to Russian conditions (Kozlova/Puffer 1994).

2.5. Location

Some programs were held entirely in the West, others entirely in Russia, and some were held in both locations. Having at least some portion of a program in the West was seen as being extremely valuable, as long as participants were serious about learning and avoided the temptations of shopping and sightseeing. Even a brief experience in a Western industrialized country could often make more of an impact than reading dozens of books. Site visits to companies, with a follow-up analysis in the classroom, were particularly effective but difficult to orchestrate. Multinational corporations such as Otis Elevator, McDonald's and Polaroid often sent their Russian employees abroad to corporate training programs, with successful results. Attitude change was a major outcome, with Russians often absorbing values like professionalism and optimism. Lastly, distance learning became an economical alternative. For instance, the Russian Foreign Economic School broadcast business modules on radio throughout the former Soviet Union, and local facilitators reinforced learning.

3. Pedagogical Techniques in Russian Management Programs

The major pedagogical techniques used in Russian management programs have been lectures, cases, games or simulations, and role plays. Human obstacles to using interactive pedagogical techniques effectively have included the shortage of trained Russian faculty members as well as their mindsets from the Communist period (Panevin/Rinefort/Payne 1992). An additional drawback was managers' experience with an impractical management education system that failed to improve industrial output under Communism. Environmental obstacles have included the chaotic political, legal, and economic conditions that have made it difficult to write business cases on Russian companies, or give useful advice on managerial decision making. Limited funding for development of course materials has also been a drawback.

The most effective techniques to encourage learning are interactive ones that foster attitude and behavior change. These pedagogies encourage involvement, accountability, initiative and risk taking, and emphasizing problem solving and taking action. Such characteristics were sorely undeveloped, and even discouraged, during the Communist period (Puffer 1994b). The major techniques employed in Russian management education are discussed below.

3.1. Lectures

Lecturing has been the traditional teaching method in Russia, although other techniques had been present to a slight extent during the Communist period (McNulty 1992; Puffer 1981). The lecture method has been effective for transmitting information, but it fails to promote analysis or skill practice because participants are not actively involved. Since Russian faculty and students traditionally have preferred the lecture method, it has been important to demonstrate to them the superior benefits of more interactive methodologies so as to reduce their initial resistance.

3.2. Cases

Western business cases have been used effectively by Western and Russian instructors who have been able to explain situations in the context of a market economy, and also create links to the Russian business environment. Another effective method has been team teaching by Western faculty and business executives who discuss their own experiences and give customized advice to Russian business managers. At first, only a few Russian cases were available. Although they worked well, they quickly became outdated because of the rapidly changing environment. However, Russian and Western faculty members continued to write numerous cases during the 1990s, and a substantial repertoire was developed. Many can be found in the Harvard Business School Catalog of Teaching Materials, the University of Western Ontario, Canada case catalog, the European Case Clearing House catalog, and the Russian Association of Management Development's journal, Management.

3.3. Games and Simulations

A number of interactive techniques had been used in Russia even during the Communist era (Wolfe 1993). For example, "open games" were elaborate simulations involving dozens of participants engaged in organizational and community change. Open games were conducted by skilled facilitators in isolated settings, and could last from several days to several weeks. Participants represented groups with different views of a very complex issue. The object of the game was usually to bring about deep personal, organizational, and social transformation on the part of participants. They were expected to question their values, and to experience self-determination, responsibility, and openness (Zhezhko 1992). Some critics have contended that such games are no longer necessary since Russians are now free to experiment directly in real-life situations. As such, they face many serious economic and managerial problems deserving immediate attention (Zhezhko 1992).

Russian experts have continued to create and utilize other organization development techniques (Walck 1993). And Western simulations have also been used effectively (Wolfe 1991). For example, senior executives from the Russian aviation industry competed in a computerized marketing strategy game, Brandmaps, during their training program at California State University (Wiley/Kamath/MacNab 1992). The simulation gave managers the opportunity to see the results of their decisions in the context of a market economy. Such hands-on learning experiences sought to accelerate their acquisition of knowledge about this unfamiliar economic system.

3.4. Role Plays

Some Russian managers also had experience with role plays during the Communist period. In particular, role playing about human resource issues such as leadership style, superior-subordinate relationships, decision making, and delegation were used in some executive programs. Innovative techniques included "paratheater," a sophisticated role play in which a manager would play the roles of a scriptwriter, director, and manager. "Dueling" was an exercise in which participants took turns being the boss and exercising power (Tarasov 1992). Such role plays could likely be effective to teach Western managerial practices under some circumstances. To be effective, care must be taken that trust is established with the participants, their status differences are understood, potential benefits are accepted, and Russian and Western facilitators are able to work together.

3.5. Summary of Techniques

A combination of pedagogical techniques can be a useful approach to developing Russian managers' ability to function in a more market-oriented economy. Effective features of training programs have included techniques which reduce resistance to interactive learning methods, the adaptation of Western concepts to a Russian context, an emphasis on practical application of knowledge and skills, and follow-up consultation with managers as they attempt to apply new techniques in their own work settings.

4. Russian Management Education Toward the End of the Century

By the mid-1990s, the initial phase of exploration and familiarization with the basics of a market system had come to a close. Russian business schools began to face the challenge of defining and structuring themselves to best serve the needs of Russian enterprises in the emerging market economy, while also ensuring their own survival. Educational institutions were no longer the stable, state-funded monopolies they once were. Now, like the businesses they serve, they must worry about financing their operations, satisfying their customers, and surpassing their competitors.

Much of the success of Russian business schools in this challenging environment will depend on how effectively they promote their mission, design their programs, develop curricula, attract talented faculty and students, and forge relationships with enterprises. Most importantly, in order to have a significant role in shaping Russia's transition to a market-oriented economy, Russian business schools must create a sustainable market for their products by persuasively showing that they can add value to managers' skills and abilities.

Three major observations were offered in 1996 by a leading Russian business educator, the director of the Moscow State University School of Business Administration. He noted that business schools would have to develop new teaching methods and technologies as well as materials to meet the changing needs of businesses. He predicted that the number of business schools would stabilize, noting that by 1996 the only survivors were those that had succeeded in establishing their own market niche. A third observation was a prediction that the number of masters-level programs would increase as the market need developed for graduates with advanced skills (Vikhanski 1996). A notable example was the launching at Moscow State's business school of a Graduate Program in Professional Accounting in the fall of 1996. The program was modeled after the long successful program at Northeastern University in Boston, and was also eveloped in collaboration with the Big Six American accounting firms in Moscow. The program attracted an entering class of 22 students (Kantrowitz 1997).

Russian management institutions have been developing programs that they expect will be effective in a market-oriented economy. The transition of these institutions has had to progress in concert with the changes in Russia's business environment. As much as in any other country, Russian management education institutions will have to serve the needs of the developing business sector. The success of their efforts, and indeed, their survival, will depend upon it. Much of their development over the past decade has been drawn, in part, from American models and experiences. All must remember, however, that Russian enterprise managers share a limited base of management knowledge and organizational culture with American educators (Vlachoutsicos/Lawrence 1996). Although Russian institutions must develop management education programs in their own unique fashion, they will likely continue to draw from developments in the American environment and elsewhere, which they see as being useful in achieving their own objectives.

5. Recent Changes in American Management Education

Many issues facing business schools in Russia are reminiscent of those that American business schools have confronted in recent years. American management education has been undergoing a major transition as a result of significant changes in the business, government, and social environments (McCarthy/Puffer/ Weihrich 1996). While certainly not as dramatic as Russia's abrupt shift from a command economy to a market economy, changes during the late 1980s and the 1990s threatened the viability of many business schools. They caused many management educators to radically redesign the content of their programs, as well as the pedagogies they employed. Even though changes had been made at several critical junctures over the past century, the major emphasis had been upon growth in both the size and number of business schools. In contrast, the more recent period of slower growth mandated that they focus on quality, accept downsizing, and increase their productivity.

To illustrate how American educators have been adapting in their own environment, some of the most recent issues and actions taken by various business schools are discussed here. The variety of measures already implemented by some schools, or being considered by others, underscores the fact that there are few easy answers. It has become clear that there is no one best way to run a business school. Nevertheless, Russian business educators, when facing decisions similar to those of their American counterparts, might wish to consider a number of actions, practices, and programs which might prove useful in their own environment.

5.1. Pressures for Change in American Management Education in the Late 1980s

By the late 1980s, competition for students at American universities intensified as a result of the sharp decline in the traditional college-age population, which dropped by nearly 25 percent from 1986 to 1994. The percentage of college students under age 24 decreased from 66 to 60 percent of all students enrolled, with a corresponding increase in older, part-time students from 1979 to 1994. The popularity of business education waned as undergraduate students majoring in business slipped from a high of 25 percent in the mid-1980s to 15 percent by the mid-1990s. The business community heavily criticized the lack of relevance and usefulness of business schools' programs. Their failure to meet the needs of business for improved quality and productivity in their operations compounded the problem. Many companies developed in-house training programs and sent fewer employees to business schools' management programs. At the same time, governments at the federal and state level, because of their own fiscal problems, substantially reduced funding to most higher educational institutions.

5.2. What Size to Be and What Standards to Employ?

Business schools could not afford to ignore these threats that challenged the way they had functioned for decades. Some universities tried to maintain enrollments and keep their size by lowering admission standards. Others took the painful step of cutting programs and personnel, while attempting to maintain their standards. The elite schools required no immediate action, but the least prestigious schools had little choice but to slash budgets and lower standards at the same time. Some institutions learned from bitter experience that it would take time to rebuild a reputation once it had been compromised for revenues.

5.3. What Markets to Serve?

The boom in American higher education extending from post-World War II through the 1980s had created a profusion of business programs at all academic levels to meet the huge demand. Some business schools restricted their focus to specific markets, such as exclusively serving undergraduate or graduate populations. However, a far greater number offered a full range of full-time and part-time degree programs at the undergraduate, graduate (MBA) and even doctoral levels, as well as non-degree career development programs for senior executives and middle managers.

Despite demographic projections and educational analysts' warnings, many business schools were unprepared for the sudden drop in demand and the resulting reduction in revenues, since higher education had been in a growth mode up to that time. Business schools reacted initially by trying to fill existing programs using more personalized and more appealing recruiting methods. Other measures included encouraging more applicants from abroad, targeting older, part-time students, and developing customized programs for corporations.

Such measures soon proved inadequate, however, and serious reviews of programs and curricula had to be undertaken as a long-term solution. Business schools began to downsize, re-engineer, and refocus their programs, just as many corporations had done in response to sharply increased competitive pressures. During the same period, the American Assembly of Collegiate Schools of Business (AACSB) expanded its criteria for accrediting business schools. These new policies gave schools an opportunity to differentiate themselves from competitors, design new programs, and develop new market niches.

Actions taken or considered by various business schools included eliminating entire programs, such as doctoral programs or executive education, and reducing the number of courses required for degrees. Many schools revised their curricula to make them more relevant to business conditions that had changed dramatically since the 1980s. For decades, curricula had been organized around functions such as marketing and accounting, and emphasized management techniques suitable for large, bureaucratic organizations primarily in the manufacturing sector. This sector had declined markedly to 12 percent of the economy by 1997, while the service and nonprofit sectors grew rapidly, and smaller, entrepreneurial firms gained in importance. As a result, new programs were developed in these areas. These included offerings in health care, entrepreneurship, and nonprofit management, as well as taxation and accounting specializations. In short, American business schools learned that they had to work more closely with businesses, and develop specialized market niches to respond to specific customer needs.

5.4. What Knowledge and Skills to Emphasize?

The 1990s corporate environment also required new knowledge and skills for a changing workforce. Many business schools surveyed corporations to learn which techniques were considered most valuable in making their organizations competitive and effective. Some surveys found that personal qualities of honesty and reliability were very important, as well as interpersonal skills in communication and team work. Emphasis was also placed on the ability to work with people of different ages, genders, and ethnic and racial backgrounds. Companies also wanted graduates to have more practical knowledge. Thus, critical thinking, problem solving skills, and a broad multidisciplinary approach to business issues gained in importance.

These new requirements were in sharp contrast to the way management had been taught for decades, when the general body of knowledge was divided into special courses each with its own subject matter. Examples included accounting, finance, marketing, and operations management, while others emphasized integration and processes such as strategic management and organizational behavior. The AACSB responded to the new demands from business by emphasizing ethics, an international perspective, legal issues, technology, and demographic diversity in its accreditation standards. Another consequence of the changes was that faculty no longer had the luxury of teaching esoteric theories and techniques without demonstrating their relevance for the business world. Understandably, finding the proper balance in their own curriculum between basic knowledge and pragmatic skills remained an unresolved issue in many business schools in the later 1990s.

5.5. What Teaching Methodologies to Use?

Developing students' knowledge and skills in the areas needed by business required new teaching methodologies. Case studies, class discussions, experiential exercises, team projects, and computer simulations, as well as lectures, had been used for many years. However, they needed to be refocused in light of the changing needs of business. In the past, these techniques had been isolated within specific functions. Simulations were used primarily in strategy and policy courses, and experiential exercises were featured in organizational behavior. Cases were used in many courses. One new trend involved the integration of functional subjects into multidisciplinary courses taught by faculty teams. Also, newer cases and simulations began to reflect a broader perspective, interpersonal skills became emphasized in technical subjects, and student teams became involved in projects with companies to help them solve actual problems.

5.6. Resistance to Management Education Reform in the U.S.

Many American business schools responded to the strong external pressures to change their programs, curricula, and teaching methodologies. For most, the cost was high in terms of money, time, and resistance by some faculty members and administrators. Other schools are still evaluating their programs, while some that tried to make changes were unsuccessful because of limited resources, inadequate leadership, or resistance to change.

While some faculty and administrators readily welcomed new approaches to management education, others understandably had many reasons to be less enthusiastic. Most reservations and resistance come from people with vested interests who felt threatened by the changes. Such feelings arose when people were given inadequate information about the reason for and nature of the changes, or were denied sufficient opportunity to participate. Some worried about losing status and prestige, and took offense that their prior contributions and talents seemed unappreciated. Another reaction was a lack of confidence in their ability to successfully develop new materials and teaching techniques, and some lacked the interest to do so. Further, the changes were at odds with some people's value systems. For instance, many faculty members argued that offering more applied programs and developing closer relationships with business, business schools was a "sell out" to corporate interests. They saw business schools losing their academic purity and independence. Even the business schools that successfully redesigned their programs recognized that resistance to change is a natural reaction. As such, it was to be expected, understood, and dealt with. This is precisely what many corporations had to do to be competitive. Like them, business schools had to manage change in their own organizations.

6. Building on Russia's Managerial Potential to Develop Business Education

American business schools' recent experience in re-engineering management education may help raise issues, anticipate problems, and suggest potential solutions for Russian business educators to consider as they design their own programs during a period of dramatic change. Like their American counterparts, Russian educators will need to make choices about academic standards and the growth objectives of their institutions. They will also have to target specific market segments such as undergraduate, graduate, and nondegree management programs. They will be required to determine the appropriate mix of theoretical knowledge and practical skills, as well as which teaching methodologies to employ. An inevitable challenge will be the necessity to manage resistance to change from faculty, administrators, students, and even company managers.

Russian business educators will have to continually develop a sound and relevant body of knowledge to establish business education as a respected academic discipline capable of thriving over the longer term. Concurrently, they will need to continually find ways of being responsive to their customers' immediate needs for practical solutions to their pressing business problems. The situation facing Russians is, of course, unique, and they themselves have the most insight into how to develop business schools that best meet their needs. Undoubtedly, each school will make choices that are suitable for itself and its customers, and different types of schools and programs will emerge. While recognizing a shortage of market-trained educators, Russia has a store of managerial talent that can be drawn upon to develop market-oriented business education. Some managerial strengths are highlighted below.

6.1. Ability to Cope With Adversity

In the former centralized economy, Russian enterprise managers faced highly challenging and unfavorable conditions. Many such managers demonstrated a strong ability to cope with adversity. For instance, many skillfully used their entrepreneurial abilities to meet demanding production plans set by central ministries, and often kept their plants operating in spite of inadequate resources. This pragmatic managerial style, combined with knowledge that business schools can provide about market-oriented management practices, should enable Russian managers to cope effectively with the challenges of their country's new economic conditions.

6.2. Proven Abilities and Pride in Achievement

Russian managers generally have faith in their own individual abilities to make decisions and solve problems (Puffer/McCarthy/Naumov 1997), and take pride in their achievements. These values can serve as a stimulus for positive developments in business education. Just as many Russians have made outstanding contributions to science, technology, the humanities, and sports, many also have the ability to work toward developing excellent business schools. Russian management educators should stress the important contributions that business professionals can make to help develop strong business schools.

6.3. Tradition of Strong Leadership

Russians can draw upon their traditional management style of providing strong leadership when promoting market-oriented business education. Competent leaders are respected, their authority is rarely questioned, and they typically receive support for their policies by those designated to implement them. Such leaders, who set a personal example by learning new management techniques and putting them into practice, can take the initiative in creating positive attitudes about management education. Russian managers have experience and skills in improving employees' personal lives by helping them with family, career, and other personal needs. This foundation can serve as a basis for building employee trust, and can facilitate employees' acceptance of new methods such as participative management and team building.

6.4. Eastern and Western Ways of Managing

One Russian educator has provided a tentative roadmap to guide their efforts by proposing that they draw from their own Eastern and Western heritage in developing programs and working with Russian businesses (Naumov 1996). Russians have the opportunity to make unique contributions to market-oriented business education that can enhance the theory and practice of management internationally. They can draw upon their rich cultural origins and create a unique blend of Eastern and Western ways. For instance, with their reliance on networking adopted from the West, and their strength in building close personal relationships brought from the East, Russians have the potential for developing new ways of managing interpersonal work relationships as well as relationships among organizations.

Russian business schools, too, can use these abilities to establish close relationships with enterprises. Such involvement might include training enterprise managers, providing consulting services, writing cases about their problems and successes, inviting managers to be guest speakers in programs, and forming alumni associations. Additionally, business schools and managers can create mutual commitments and obligations that forge long-lasting relationships and loyalties based on trust. In this way, market-oriented management education and practice can become tightly linked through personal as well as institutional relationships.

7. The Road Ahead for Russian Management Education

The opportunity to develop new types of management education and the requisite infrastructure is an exciting, yet daunting task. Programs must be developed, faculty trained, students attracted, textbooks and cases written, and methodologies developed. American business schools at the end of the century are still involved in their own process of change. Russian business educators will likely watch with interest the successes and failures of their American counterparts. They will adapt some useful practices from the Americans as well as from educators in other countries.

Yet, Russian management educators must find ways to best respond to the rapid changes in their own environment and the resulting threats to their institutions. In the turbulent environment of the later 1990s, they must change and adapt, and each school must try to find the best solution for its own specific circumstances. Undoubtedly, most successful measures will be based on their own styles and methods, drawing on their own history and traditions but adapted to the needs of the new market economy. They will utilize the managerial strengths which were developed in prior periods, but will modify them to fit Russia's current environment. Although they will borrow from others, they must develop their own distinctive form of management education.

Bibliography:

Hemp, P. (1992), Readying for market economy, in: The Boston Globe, 9 July 1992, pp. 29-30

Holden, N.J. (1995), Management Training in Russia: Issues in Course Design, Development and Evaluation. A Report with Special Reference to the Russian Construction Industry, Manchester, UK, Brooke Publications

Holden, N.J., Cooper, C. (1994), Russian managers as learners, in: Management Learning, Vol. 25 (1994), No. 4, 503-522

Kantrowitz, J. (1997), Cloning success in Moscow: Graduate accounting program establishes mirror project in Russia, in: The Northeastern Voice, Northeastern University, Boston, April 10, 1997, pp. 3, 5

Kozlova, T.V., Puffer, S.M. (1994), Private and public business schools in Russia: A survey of problems and prospects, in: European Management Journal, December, Vol. 12 (1994), No. 4, pp. 462-468

McCarthy, D.J. (1991), Developing a programme for Soviet managers, in: Journal of Management Development, Vol.10 (1991), No.5, pp. 26-31

McCarthy, D.J., Puffer, S.M., Weihrich, H. (1996), Contributions to management education by North American and European management programs, in: R. Berndt (ed.), Global Management, Berlin, Springer-Verlag, 1996, pp. 3-18

McNulty, N.G. (1992), Management education in Eastern Europe: 'Fore and after, in: The Academy of Management Executive, Vol. 6 (1992), No. 4, pp. 78-87

Mockler, R., Chao, Chian-Nan, Dologite, D. (1996), A comparative study of business education programs in China and Russia, in: Journal of Teaching in International Business, Vol. 8 (1996), No. 2, pp. 19-39

Naumov, A.I. (1996), Deputy director, School of Business Administration, Moscow State University, personal communication with the authors

Panevin, Y.L., Rinefort, F.C., Payne, S.L. (1992), East-West cooperation on Russian management development: Russian views and a U.S. response, in: Journal of Business Affairs, Vol. 18 (1992), No. 2, pp. 5-9

Puffer, S.M. (1981), Inside a Soviet management institute, in: California Management Review, Vol. 24 (1981), No. 1, pp. 90-96

Puffer, S.M. (ed.) (1992), The Russian management revolution: Preparing managers for the market economy, Armonk, New York, M.E. Sharpe, 1992

Puffer, S.M. (1994a), Education for management in a new economy, in: A. Jones (ed.), Education and Society in the New Russia, Armonk, New York, M.E. Sharpe, 1994, pp. 171-196

Puffer, S.M. (1994b), Understanding the bear: A portrait of Russian business leaders, in: The Academy of Management Executive, Vol. 8 (1994), No. 1, pp. 41-54

Puffer, S.M., McCarthy, D.J., Naumov, A.I. (1997), Russian Managerial Values, unpublished manuscript

Tarasov, V.K. (1992), Personnel-technology: The selection and training of managers, in: S.M. Puffer (ed.), The Russian Management Revolution, 1992, pp. 121-148

Thach, L. (1996), Training in Russia, Training & Development, Vol. 50 (1996), No. 7, p. 34.

Veselov, S. (1992), Biznes-obrazovanie v Rossii: Spros 50 raz bol'she predlozheniia (Business education in Russia: Demand is 50 times greater than supply), in: Biznes MN (Moskovskie Novosti), Vol. 40 (1992), No. 28, October, p. 15

Vikhanski, O.S. (1995), Viewpoint: Message from Moscow, in: Journal of Teaching in International Business, Vol. 7 (1995), No. 2, pp. 99-112

Vikhanski, O.S. (1996), Kuda idet biznes-obrazovanie v Rossii (Where business education is headed in Russia), in: Menedzhment (Management), Vol. 1 (1996, No. 3, pp. 10-27

Vlachoutsicos, C.A., Lawrence, P.R. (1996), How managerial learning can assist economic transformation in Russia, in: Organization Studies, Vol. 17 (1996), No. 2, pp. 311-325

Walck, C.L. (1993), Organization development in the USSR: An overview and a case example, in: Journal of Managerial Psychology, Vol. 8 (1993), No. 2

Warner, M., Denezhkina, E. Campbell, A. (1993), How Russian managers learn, Cambridge, UK: Cambridge University of Cambridge Judge Institute of Management Studies

Wiley, D.L., Kamath, S.J., MacNab, B. (1992), "Sedpro:" Three Soviet executive development programs at California State University at Hayward, in: S.M. Puffer (ed.), The Russian Management Revolution, 1992, pp. 201-220

Wolfe, J. (1991), On the transfer of market-oriented business games to Eastern bloc cultures, in: Social Science Computer Review, Vol. 9 (1991), No. 2, pp. 202-214

Wolfe, J. (1993), A history of business teaching games in English-speaking and Post-socialist countries: The origination and diffusion of a management education and development technology, in: Simulation and Gaming, Vol. 24 (1993), No. 4, pp. 446-463

Zhezhko, I.V. (1992), Open games as a method of personal transformation and motivation, in: S.M. Puffer (ed.), The Russian Management Revolution, 1992, pp. 158-177

Acknowledgment:

A portion of this article was adapted from the Introduction by S.M. Puffer (1996) in G.R. Teicher and A.D. Weinberger (eds.), White Paper to Reform Business Education in Russia, New York, Liberty Publishing House

Dritter Teil

Change Management und Corporate Strategy

Wandel von Unternehmensleitbild und Unternehmenszielen:
Eine Analyse anhand der Geschäftsberichte der größten Aktiengesellschaften aus vier europäischen Ländern

Reinhart Schmidt

Summary:

Corporate guidelines and corporate objectives are important elements of strategic management. The companies' orientations towards specific groups of stakeholders and changes of these orientations can be studied by the analysis of published annual reports. The empirical investigation concerning the largest listed companies from France, Germany, Switzerland and the UK for the financial years 1986 and 1996 results in a changing role of the stakeholders, especially of the shareholders.

1. Problemstellung

Ein Management des Wandels, das sich nicht in einem „muddling through" erschöpfen will, muß auf einem verläßlichen Orientierungsrahmen beruhen. In diesem Zusammenhang kommt Unternehmensleitbildern und Unternehmenszielen besondere Bedeutung zu. „Unternehmensgrundsätze", „Unternehmensleitbilder", „Grundordnungen", „Leitsätze für Führung und Zusammenarbeit", „Unternehmensphilosophien" , „Missions" haben - wie Gabele/Kretschmer (1983) feststellen - seit Mitte der siebziger Jahre große Bedeutung gewonnen. Diese Entwicklung ist wohl mit dem in diesem Zeitraum einsetzenden langfristigen Planungsbewußtsein zu begründen, das wiederum durch die Lehre von der strategischen Unternehmensplanung und -führung beeinflußt worden ist. So wurden in Deutschland auch erst Mitte der siebziger Jahre die ersten Lehrgänge über strategische Unternehmensplanung angeboten. Unternehmensleitbilder - die übrigens auch als „Absichten" bezeichnet werden (Kreikebaum 1981, S. 33) - beinhalten Ausssagen über die gewünschte Unternehmensentwicklung auf konzeptioneller Ebene, sie bestimmen „einen unternehmensbezogenen Organisations- und Handlungsrahmen, der zur gesteuerten Transformation der Organisationskultur beitragen und vor allem als Ausgangspunkt einer strategischen Planung dienen kann" (Gabele/Kretschmer 1983, S. 726). Neuerdings wird auch die Eigenschaft als Führungsinstrument betont (Matje 1996; Steinmann/Kustermann 1997). Da die Unternehmensleitbilder vom Top-Management formuliert werden, geben sie auch

Auskunft über die Werthaltungen der Unternehmensführung, so daß ein Wandel im Leitbild im Zusammenhang mit einem Wandel der Werthaltungen von Top-Managern untersucht werden kann (Albach 1994).

Adressaten der Unternehmensgrundsätze und damit auch der Unternehmensleitbilder sind verschiedenste Bezugsgruppen, nämlich die „Stakeholder" als diejenigen, die Ansprüche an das Unternehmen stellen. Empirische Untersuchungen (u.a. Gabele/Kretschmer 1983) haben ergeben, daß tatsächlich eine Fülle von Bezugsgruppen bei der Aufstellung des Leitbildes berücksichtigt wird: Mitarbeiter, Kunden, Anteilseigner, Gesellschaft und Öffentlichkeit, Lieferanten, Konkurrenz, Betriebsrat, Gläubiger und Verbände. Albach (1994) hat Führungsgrundsätze deutscher Großunternehmen daraufhin empirisch untersucht, inwieweit sich das Selbstverständnis vom Wesen des Unternehmens von 1975 bis 1991 geändert hat. Er konnte feststellen, daß 1975 noch das Verständnis vom Unternehmen als sozialer Einrichtung im Vordergrund stand, während 1991 das Unternehmen primär als Hersteller von Produkten, mit denen der Markt versorgt wird, gesehen wurde. Dies zeitigte auch in Konsequenzen für die Willensbildung des Top-Managements: Die Bedeutung von Bezugsgruppen, welche - indirekt - Einfluß auf die Entscheidungen haben, hat sich geändert und führt zu einem „bemerkenswerten Wertewandel". Während 1975 noch die Mitarbeiter im Vordergrund standen, waren es 1991 die Kunden, die den größten Einfluß auf Entscheidungen des Unternehmens hatten. Bezüglich der Rolle der Anteilseigner stellte Albach noch in einem Vortrag 1993 für 1991 fest: „Während in den Vereinigten Staaten das Top-Management den Shareholder-Value zu maximieren scheint, bewerten deutsche Manager dieses Ziel bisher nicht sehr hoch" (1994, S. 9). Ob diese Einschätzung 1996 noch gilt, wird die empirische Analyse zeigen.

Aufgrund der empfundenen Verantwortung gegenüber externen Bezugsgruppen, aber auch aufgrund des Drucks dieser Bezugsgruppen, sind vor allem die großen Unternehmen immer mehr dazu übergegangen, ihr **unternehmenspolitisches Leitbild oder Teile davon auch zu publizieren**. Dabei kann man auch noch - wie Hinterhuber (1990, S. 209) dies tut - eine Unterscheidung nach dem Umfang der Publikation des Leitbildes vornehmen, indem von „Leitsätzen" für den Teil des Leitbildes gesprochen wird, der nach außen mitgeteilt wird. Diese Unterscheidung ist jedoch nur aus interner Sicht sinnvoll, ein Externer wird den Vollständigkeitsgrad einer Artikulation des Leitbildes schwer beurteilen können.

Als das wichtigste Kommunikationsmedium für die extern wirksame Artikulation von Unternehmensleitbildern bzw. von Teilen dieser Leitbilder hat sich inzwischen der jährliche Geschäftsbericht erwiesen, der immer mehr nicht nur vergangenheits-, sondern auch zukunftsorientiert gestaltet wird. Im internationalen Vergleich ist erkennbar, daß der sog. Druckbericht (vgl. dazu Schmidt 1992) teilweise in (mindestens) zwei getrennte Druckstücke zerlegt wird, in einen Teil „Views" und einen anderen, klassischen Teil „Financial Statements". Damit suchen die Unternehmen offenbar mehr Freiheit für Darstellungen gegenüber anderen Zielgruppen als den Anteilseignern, und sie erreichen dadurch eher ein einheitliches Auftreten gegenüber der Öffentlichkeit. Diese Tendenz wird durch den Einsatz elektronischer Medien verstärkt werden.

Die Unternehmen gehen - so kann man empirisch feststellen - auch dazu über, ausgewählte **Unternehmensziele** zu publizieren. Unternehmensziele stellen konkrete Vorstellungen über zukünftig durch die Unternehmenspolitik zu erreichende Zustände dar. Die Unternehmensziele werden unter Berücksichtigung von Unternehmensanalysen und -prognosen sowie von Umweltanalysen und -prognosen aus dem Unternehmensleitbild abgeleitet. Empirische Untersuchungen von Fritz (1988) belegen die Rationalität strategischer Zielplanungen. Pantalone/Welch (1986) haben dabei den Nutzen einer **Publikation** von Unternehmenszielen aufgezeigt.

Die öffentlich zugänglichen Geschäftsberichte stellen also (inzwischen) eine Datenbasis dar, um einen Wandel des Unternehmensleitbildes und der Unternehmensziele empirisch zu untersuchen. Besonders interessant und grundsätzlich erfolgsversprechend erscheint dabei eine Vorgehensweise, wie sie hier eingeschlagen wurde. Es wird erstens ein Langfristvergleich angestellt (Geschäftsjahr 1996 gegenüber dem Geschäftsjahr 1986). Zweitens werden Aktiengesellschaften aus mehreren Ländern untersucht, hier aus den durchaus unterschiedlichen Ländern Deutschland, Frankreich, Großbritannien und der Schweiz (vgl. auch ähnliche Analysen für zwei Länder bei Brabet/Klemm 1994, bei Wahlquist 1996, und für Unternehmenskulturen bei Hoffmann 1987). Durch die hier gewählte Kombination von Zeitvergleich und internationalem Querschnittsvergleich können Tendenzen besser erkannt und begründet werden. Im folgenden werden auf Basis bisheriger Erkenntnisse zunächst Hypothesen entwickelt, es wird das gewählte Untersuchungsdesign beschrieben und diskutiert. Sodann werden für die jeweils zehn größten börsennotierten Aktiengesellschaften aus den Ländern D, GB, F und CH Analysen der Geschäftsberichte 1986 und 1996 vorgenommen, die Ergebnisse werden abschließend vergleichend kommentiert.

2. Hypothesen und Design

Hypothesen über einen Wandel in bezug auf Unternehmensleitbild und Unternehmensziele können aus dem Aufkommen neuer oder veränderter Ansprüche von Stakeholdern generiert werden. Es ist vor allem der Shareholder Value-Ansatz, der seit Beginn der achtziger Jahre wesentlich von Rappaport (1986) als Konzeption zur Umsetzung von Aktionärsinteressen im Unternehmen propagiert worden ist. Zwar ist der Ansatz nicht neu, er steht durchaus im Einklang mit bestimmten herkömmlichen Methoden der Aktienbewertung (vgl. dazu Schmidt 1993). Aber die wachsende Bedeutung und Konkurrenz einer internationalen Kapitalbeschaffung zwingt die Unternehmen, diesen Ansatz in das Unternehmensbild aufzunehmen. Spremann (1994, S. 307) prognostiziert, daß die Zukunft für Europa liquidere Märkte bringen wird, und er folgert: „Deshalb ist Shareholder Value als Managementprinzip in Europa unausweichlich."

Der Shareholder Value-Ansatz wird aber auch relativiert und in einer integrierenden Sichtweise behandelt (Brune 1996; Hill 1996, Meier-Scherling 1996). In der Literatur wird besonders das Dreieck von Kunden, Mitarbeitern und Aktionären stark diskutiert (vgl. dazu etwa Baetge 1997). Wagner (1997) stellt zusätzlich das Gemeinwohl einer marktorientierten Unternehmensführung gegenüber. Es muß daher überprüft werden, **welche Gewichte den verschiedenen Stakeholdern gegeben werden.**

Eine **Hypothese über den Wandel im Umfang der Artikulationen** zum Unternehmensleitbild und zu den Zielen folgt aus einer eigenen aktuellen Umfrage bei mehr als 100 Finanzchefs der größten deutschen Industrie-, Handels- und Verkehrsunternehmen im Rahmen eines internationalen Forschungsprojekts zur Kurz- und Langfristorientierung von Unternehmen (Schmidt 1998): 68,3% der Antwortenden stimmten - auf einer 5-er Skala gemessen - im höchsten Maße darin überein, daß die Anteilseigner heute mehr Informationen als vor zehn Jahren verlangen. Daraus resultiert die Hypothese, daß die Unternehmen sich dieser Erwartungshaltung bzw. diesem Druck angepaßt haben und entsprechend mehr - auch zum Leitbild und zu Zielen - veröffentlichen.

Albach (1994) konstatiert weiter einen Wandel der Werte deutscher Top-Manager in Richtung globaler Orientierung und auch die zunehmende Bedeutung ethischen Verhaltens sowie eine neue Einstellung gegenüber den Mitarbeitern. Es gilt zu prüfen, wie sich dieser Wandel im Zeitvergleich bis 1996 und im internationalen Vergleich darstellt. Die Analyse wird hier auf börsennotierte Unternehmen beschränkt, obwohl auch die Unterscheidung von notierten und nichtnotierten Unternehmen eine interessante Fragestellung beinhaltet (vgl. dazu Bosch 1990).

Als ein Verfahren zur Überprüfung der Hypothesen könnte die (ggf. computergestützte) Inhaltsanalyse in Form der aus der empirischen Sozialforschung bekannten Content Analysis in Frage kommen (vgl. dazu Schmidt 1981; Massenberg 1986; Wagner 1990). Eine Auszählung der dabei ermittelten Worthäufigkeiten setzt aber eine Großzahligkeit voraus, die an dieser Stelle nicht gewährleistet werden kann. Außerdem kann eine sachverständige individuelle Gesamtanalyse besser die Besonderheiten eines Einzelfalles berücksichtigen, was bei einer kleineren Stichprobe Vorteile bringt.

Am Lehrstuhl für Finanzwirtschaft und Bankbetriebslehre der Martin-Luther-Universität Halle-Wittenberg existiert aufgrund der Kooperation mit dem manager magazin ein Archiv von Geschäftsberichten aller börsennotierten deutschen Aktiengesellschaften und der 500 größten börsennotierten europäischen Aktiengesellschaften für die Geschäftsjahre ab 1986. Die mehr als 10.000 Geschäftsberichte stellen ein ideales Material für empirische Forschung dar. Dem Repertoire der Geschäftsberichte in Halle wurden für vier Länder (Deutschland, Großbritannien, Frankreich und Schweiz) die Berichte der jeweils nach dem Umsatz des Jahres 1996 größten Gesellschaften aus Industrie, Handel und Verkehr entnommen. Die vier Länder wurden ausgewählt, weil es sich einerseits um die drei größten europäischen Länder handelt, weil unterschiedliche Auffassungen im angelsächsischen Bereich gegenüber den Auffassungen in Zentraleuropa zu vermuten sind. Die Schweiz wurde einerseits aufgrund ihrer wirtschaftlichen und kulturellen Nähe zu Deutschland, aber andererseits aufgrund ihrer starken Eigenständigkeit herangezogen. Die jeweils größten Unternehmen der Länder wurden ausgewählt, weil es sich dabei in der Regel um große Publikumsaktiengesellschaften handelt und weil die größten Unternehmen wohl am stärksten mit der Problematik von Unternehmensleitbildern und deren Wandel befaßt sind. Auf die Einbeziehung von Banken und Versicherungen wurde hier verzichtet, um mehr Homogenität des Materials zu erreichen.

Im Rahmen des Zeitvergleichs könnte man natürlich mehr als zwei Geschäftsberichte aus dem Zeitraum von zehn Jahren heranziehen. Es ist aber zu erwarten, daß durch das lange Intervall von zehn Jahren ein möglicher genereller Wandel besser als durch eine Verlaufsanalyse identifizierbar wird. Selbstverständlich könnten auch Aktiengesellschaften anderer Länder und anderer Größenklassen untersucht werden. Auch muß die Analyse in bezug auf Banken und Versicherungen einer späteren Untersuchung vorbehalten bleiben; dabei wären die Erkenntnisse von Chiozzi (1997) zu verwerten.

Die Analyse der veröffentlichten Geschäftsberichte mit dem Ziel einer Gewinnung von Erkenntnisssen über einen Wandel bei Unternehmensleitbild und auch Unternehmenszielen ist ggf. nur mit Einschränkungen möglich. So kann ein Unternehmen zwar ein schriftliches Leitbild und entsprechende Unternehmensziele haben, jedoch werden die Sachverhalte bewußt nicht oder in unvollständiger Weise publiziert. Insbesondere kann die Vollständigkeit des publizierten Leitbildes extern nicht erkannt werden. Andererseits lassen Artikulationen, die erkennbar nur einen Ausschnitt darstellen sollen, Schlüsse auf die von dem Top-Management als wichtig empfundenen Sachverhalte zu.

Bei fehlender direkter Ansprache des Leitbildes kann aus bestimmten Formulierungen im Geschäftsbericht, die sich **indirekt** auf Leitbild und Ziele beziehen, auf das vorhandene Leitbild bzw. die Ziele rückgeschlossen werden. Dies gilt auch, wenn sich die Einstellung zur Publizität wegen gestiegener Ansprüche an die Investor Relations (vgl. dazu Günther/Otterbein 1996) in den letzten Jahren geändert hat, so daß die damaligen, kurzen Ausführungen mit den heutigen, umfangreicheren Artikulationen verglichen werden können. Auch kann sich zeigen, daß bestimmte Unternehmen in Geschäftsberichten praktisch **keine Aussage treffen**, die sich auf Unternehmensleitbild und Unternehmensziele bezieht. Im Vordergrund der Interpretation von Ergebnissen stehen daher die Unternehmen, in deren

Berichten sich für beide Jahre des Zehnjahreszeitraums Ausführungen zu Unternehmensleitbild und Unternehmenszielen finden.

3. Befunde und deren Interpretation

Die Befunde aus zehn Geschäftsberichten je Land der Jahre 1986 und 1996 - also aus 80 Geschäftsberichten - werden in Abb. 1 bis Abb. 4 dokumentiert, so daß damit zugleich eine umfangreiche und vergleichbare Datenbasis über Unternehmensleitbilder und Unternehmensziele öffentlich zur Verfügung steht. Die Interpretation der Befunde wird grundsätzlich ohne Nennung des jeweiligen Unternehmens vorgenommen, vielmehr wird als Abkürzung ein Länderkürzel und eine fortlaufende Unternehmensnummer je Land verwendet. Die Unternehmensnummern wurden dabei je Land gemäß der Umsatzrangfolge des Geschäftsjahres 1996 vergeben.

3.1. Deutsche Aktiengesellschaften

Die Befunde zu den größten zehn deutschen Aktiengesellschaften sind in Abb. 1 dokumentiert. Die Verlautbarungen der Vorstände für das Jahr 1986 zeigen kaum etwas von einem etwa vorhandenen Leitbild. In D5 findet sich nicht ein Satz, der im Sinne eines Leitbildes interpretiert werden kann, dieses Dokument kann als Musterfall einer traditionellen Berichterstattung im Geschäftsbericht klassifiziert werden. Die Ausführungen anderer Unternehmen sind allgemein auf Zielsetzungen ausgerichtet, wobei im Vordergrund die langfristige Unternehmenssicherung und die Wettbewerbsfähigkeit stehen (D1, D2, D6, D8). Daneben werden hochwertige Technik für die Kunden sowie Wachstum betont (D3). In D4 wird ein Höchststimmrecht befürwortet, um die „Unabhängigkeit des Unternehmens sicherzustellen". In D9 wird die Gewinnerzielung als Mittel zur Erlangung finanzieller Stärke des Unternehmens beschrieben. Nur in D7 wird - neben den Mitarbeitern - auf die Aktionäre verwiesen, und es wird - vorsichtig! - der Erhalt des Wertes des eingesetzten Kapitals propagiert, verbunden mit einer angemessenen Kapitalrendite.

Die Berichte über das Jahr 1996 zeigen gegenüber 1986 einen dramatischen Wandel. Die Existenz von Leitbildern wird deutlich, wobei das Bezugsgruppendreieck von Aktionären, Kunden und Mitarbeitern im Vordergrund steht (D1, D3, D5, D6). Immerhin in sieben von zehn Fällen wird in unterschiedlicher Form auf „Wertorientierung" (D1, D3, D4, D5, D10), „Wertsteigerung" (D9) und auf konsequente Ertragsausrichtung (D8) abgestellt, wobei in D8 sogar eine Zielrendite, allerdings als Gesamtkapitalrendte, angegeben wird. In D10 werden gleich mehrere konkrete Renditemaße genannt, nach denen das Unternehmen verfährt (vgl. auch den Überblick über alternative Performance-Maße bei Baden, 1994). Eine deutlich schwächere Aktionärsorientierung zeigt sich bei D2; bei diesem Unternehmen, an dem das Bundesland Niedersachsen maßgeblich beteiligt ist, „werden

D1: Daimler-Benz AG
„Die Strategie von Daimler-Benz ist auf eine langfristige Absicherung und damit auf Zukunftssicherung ausgerichtet. ... Dem Gewicht des Unternehmens in Staat und Gesellschaft sowie seinen Einflußmöglichkeiten entspricht eine Verantwortung, die wir voll anerkennen." (GB 1986, S. 19 u. 21)

„Eine angemessene Verzinsung für unsere Aktionäre, attraktive Produkte und Dienstleistungen für unsere Kunden sowie anspruchsvolle und sichere Arbeitsplätze für unsere Mitarbeiterinnen und Mitarbeiter: Das sind die Ziele, die wir im Rahmen einer wertorientierten Unternehmensführung verfolgen." (GB 1996, Innenseite)

D2: Volkswagen AG
„Der Volkswagen-Konzern hat im 100. Jubiläumsjahr des Automobils seine Anstrengungen zur Sicherung der Wettbewerbsfähigkeit auf den internationalen Märkten fortgeführt." (GB 1986, S. 8)

„Die Erschließung zusätzlicher Potentiale und Maßnahmen zur Verbesserung wollen wir nutzen, um Ihnen, den Eigentümern unseres Unternehmens, weiterhin attraktive Wertsteigerungen zu verschaffen. .... Die strategische Orientierung des Konzerns hin zur Globalisierung, Prozeßorientierung und Produktinnovation wirkt sich zunehmend positiv auf die Erreichung unserer wirtschaftlichen Ziele aus .... An einer positiven Weiterentwicklung werden unsere Aktionäre in angemessener Weise beteiligt." (GB 1996, S. 5 u. 22)

D3: Siemens AG
„Hauptziel des Unternehmens ist es, auf unseren Arbeitsgebieten technisch führend zu sein und unseren Kunden mit überlegener Technik besondere Vorteile zu bieten. .... Das Unternehmen will auch künftig schneller wachsen als der Markt." (GB '86, S. 1)

„Wir wollen die Wettbewerbsstärke des Unternehmens ausbauen und einen höheren Ertrag erwirtschaften. .... Wir wollen den Wert des Unternehmens weiter steigern und haben deshalb die Steuerung und Kontrolle der operativen Einheiten sowie die Anreizsysteme der Geschäftsverantwortlichen um Renditeziele ergänzt. Ein höherer Unternehmenswert kommt allen Beteiligten zugute: Ihnen, unseren Anteilseignern, ebenso wie unseren Mitarbeitern, ohne deren Motivation und Leistung kein Fortschritt möglich ist. Nicht zuletzt unseren Kunden, die uns die Lösung ihrer Probleme anvertrauen und denen wir mit unseren Leistungen zum Erfolg verhelfen. ... 'Siemens - das innovative Unternehmen', mit diesem Anspruch wollen wir in die Zukunft blicken, zum Nutzen unserer Kunden, unserer Mitarbeiterinnen und Mitarbeiter und auch zu Ihrem Vorteil." (GB '96, S. 2 u. 3)

D4: VEBA AG
„Ferner schlagen wir der Hauptversammlung die Einführung eines Höchststimmrechts vor, um - wie andere große deutsche Aktiengesellschaften - die Unabhängigkeit des Unternehmens sicherzustellen." (GB 1986, S. 9)

„Wir sind davon überzeugt, daß VEBA als Konglomerat auch in Zukunft erfolgreich sein wird. Voraussetzung ist, daß wir weiterhin eine wertorientierte Unternehmenspolitik verfolgen und die vielfältigen Konzernpotentiale systematisch und konsequent in Wertsteigerungen umsetzen. ... Wir betrachten die Führungskräfte des VEBA-Konzerns als Garant und Motor für die Umsetzung unserer wertsteigernden Unternehmenspolitik. ... Die weitere Internationalisierung ist eine unserer größten Herausforderungen, um nachhaltige Wertsteigerungen zu erzielen." (GB 1996, S. 8, 9 u. 16)

D5: Rheinisch-Westfälisches Elektrizitätswerk AG bzw. RWE AG
Im GB 1986 keine Ausführungen über Ziele oder Strategien.

„Unsere Zielsetzung ist eine langfristige Steigerung des Unternehmenswerts. Dabei werden wir zugleich unserer gesellschafts- und wirtschaftspolitischen Verantwortung gerecht. Nur ein leistungsfähiges und ertragsstarkes Unternehmen wird auf Dauer seinen Mitarbeitern sichere und attraktive Arbeitsplätze bieten und den Kundenwünschen im wettbewerblichen Umfeld gerecht werden können." (GB 1995/96, Deckblatt)

D6: Bayerische Motoren Werke AG
„BMW hat im Berichtsjahr die Zeichen gesetzt, um in den kommenden Jahren die Möglichkeiten der Märkte verstärkt zu nutzen und damit die Position des Unternehmens auf den Weltmärkten zu sichern und auszubauen ." (GB 1986, S. 26)

„Das Jahr 1996 setzt, trotz größten Aufwands für die Zukunft unseres Unternehmens, die lange Reihe besonders erfolgreicher Jahre für BMW fort. Damit bestätigt sich die Unternehmenspolitik von BMW: Unsere Investitionen in Produkte, Produktion und Mitarbeiter sind Investitionen in die Zukunft des Unternehmens - zum Wohl unserer Aktionäre, unserer Kunden und unserer Belegschaft." (GB 1996, S. 5)

D7: Hoechst AG
„Aktionär und Mitarbeiter tragen gemeinsam zum Bestand und Erfolg des Unternehmens bei. Für die Mitarbeiter haben wir die Arbeitsplätze und ein leistungsgerechtes Einkommen zu sichern. Für die Aktionäre müssen wir den Wert des eingesetzten Kapitals erhalten und für eine angemessene Kapitalrendite sorgen." (GB 1986, S. 6)

„Unser gemeinsames Ziel ist eine langfristige, nachhaltige *Wertsteigerung* des Unternehmens, die den Kapitalgebern, den Mitarbeitern, ganz generell dem Gemeinwesen zugute kommt. ... Wir konzentrieren uns auf ertragsstarke *Kerngeschäfte*, bei denen wir weltweit zur Spitze zählen wollen." (GB 1996, S. 4)

D8: BASF AG
„Die BASF legt auch künftig besonderen Wert auf die Sicherung ihrer Versorgung mit Rohstoffen und Grundprodukten, die Verstärkung ihrer Arbeitsgebiete spezieller und hochveredelter Chemieprodukte und auf die Erschließung neuer Gebiete und Märkte. ... Bei alledem baut sie auf den Erfindungsreichtum und die Leistungsbereitschaft ihrer Mitarbeiter und ebenso auf das Vertrauen ihrer Aktionäre." (GB 1986, S.1)

„Wir richten unser Unternehmen konsequent auf Ertrag und Rendite aus. ... Wir erwirtschafteten wieder erfreuliche Renditen. ... konnten wir die Gesamtkapitalrendite vor Zinsen und Ertragsteuern auf 11,4 Prozent steigern. Es ist unser Ziel, im Durchschnitt eines Konjukturzyklus mindestens 10 Prozent zu erreichen." (GB 1996, S. 3 u. 9)

D9: Bayer AG
„Wir konnten auch das vierte erfreuliche Geschäftsjahr in Folge dazu nutzen, finanziell noch stärker zu werden." (GB 1986, S. 4)

„Bayer ist forschungsorientiert und setzt bei seinen Kernaktivitäten auf die Technologieführerschaft. Dabei ist es unser Ziel, den Unternehmenswert nachhaltig zu steigern und im Interesse der Aktionäre, der Mitarbeiterinnen und Mitarbeiter und der gesamten Gesellschaft in allen Ländern, in denen wir vertreten sind, eine hohe Wertschöpfung zu erzielen." (GB 1996, Innenseite)

D10: VIAG AG
Im GB 1986 keine besonderen Ausführungen.

„Die langfristige Steigerung des Unternehmenswertes ist das primäre Ziel der VIAG. Zur Optimierung des Portfolios werden die Bestandteile laufend unter den Aspekten Rentabilität, Zukunftschancen und Marktpositionen überprüft. ... Finanzwirtschaftliche Kerngrößen sind dafür insbesondere die konzerneinheitlich definierten Kennziffern ROCE, ROS und ROI. Neben diesen Größen gibt es für die konkrete Steuerung der einzelnen Geschäftsfelder detaillierte Beurteilungskriterien, die als Werttreiber für die jeweiligen Aktivitäten identifiziert wurden." (GB 1996, S. 2 u. 9)

Abb. 1: Verlautbarungen aus deutschen Aktiengesellschaften

unsere Aktionäre in angemessener Weise beteiligt". Internationalisierung und Globalisierung werden in D2 und D4 angesprochen, das Kerngeschäft wird in D7 betont, und in D4 werden auch die Führungskräfte in ihrer Bedeutung für eine wertsteigernde Unternehmenspolitik herausgestellt.

Man kann für die größten deutschen Aktiengesellschaften also feststellen, daß sich die Einstellung durchaus stark gewandelt hat. Auch Baden (1996) findet, daß sich nunmehr auch deutsche Top-Manager verstärkt der Steigerung des Shareholder Value verpflichtet fühlen. Auf die Notwendigkeit einer solchen Orientierung wird auch in der deutschen Literatur hingewiesen (vgl. Günther 1994), Praxisberichte über die Anwendungsmöglichkeiten liegen vor (vgl. etwa Siegert 1995).

Andererseits bleibt die besondere Problematik des **Shareholder Value für deutsche Unternehmen bestehen** (vgl. auch Dufey/Hommel 1997). Eine wesentliche Einschränkung der strengen Verfolgung des Konzepts stellt offenbar die Mitbestimmung der Arbeitnehmer in Deutschland dar. So hieß es jüngst in der FAZ (o.V. 1997): „In Montanunternehmen ist die Abhängigkeit des Vorstandes von Gewerkschaften und Betriebsräten größer; die Gemeinsamkeit läßt sich nutzen zur Interessen- und Machtkonzentration als Gegenpol zur Kontrolle der Anteilseigner.In nicht paritätisch mitbestimmten Unternehmen muß der Vorstand dagegen größere Rücksicht auf die Interessen der Kapitaleigner legen; hier läßt sich auch innerhalb des deutschen Modells eher ein Konzept des Shareholder Value durchsetzen." So sind auch dezidierte Gegenbewegungen - nicht nur in der deutschen Öffentlichkeit, sondern auch in der deutschen Betriebswirtschaftslehre (Schmid 1996) - erkennbar. In Deutschland wird daher weiter stark über Shareholder Value gestritten werden.

3.2. Britische Aktiengesellschaften

Die Befunde zu den größten zehn britischen Aktiengesellschaften sind in Abb. 2 dokumentiert. Schon im Geschäftsjahr 1986 stellen die großen britischen Aktiengesellschaften die Aktionärsorientierung heraus, so wird in GB2, GB5 und GB9 das Dividenden- bzw. Gewinnwachstum angesprochen, in GB1 noch kombiniert mit dem „value to our shareholders". Andererseits werden auch schon die Bezugsgruppen der Aktionäre, Kunden und des Personals zusammen beachtet (GB4, GB7, GB9), in GB6 ergänzt um die Gemeinschaft. GB3 betont das Wachstum, verbunden mit Marketingzielsetzungen, GB2 und GB10 weisen schon für 1986 auf die Bedeutung des Kerngeschäfts hin. Ein gerade privatisiertes Unternehmen stellt die Marktversorgung in den Vordergrund (GB8).

Für das Geschäftsjahr 1996 bildet bei GB1 die Globalisierung den Schwerpunkt, GB2 und GB6 wollen „world leader" werden, wobei GB6 dabei auch auf die Orientierung an Aktionärszielen und Kundenzufriedenheit abstellt. Die Erweiterung

GB1: The British Petroleum Company p.l.c.
„Our aim continues to be that of enhancing the value to our shareholders of their stake in the company - both trough capital growth and trough a policy of improving our dividends whenever this is possible." (GB 1986, S. 2)

„To maintain competitive success we are developing our 'global reach' - the ability to grasp the best opportunities whenever and wherever they arise. ... BP's operations and actions influence the lives of people worldwide. As an international business we are striving to ensure that we make a positive impact: setting clear targets against which our performance on health, safety and the environment can be udged; working together with communities for mutual benefit; empowering our people to take responsibility for their own actions, allowing them the freedom to make a difference; achieving excellent financial performance for our shareholders." (GB 1996, S. 8 u. 15)

GB2: B.A.T. Industries p.l.c.
„It is most encouraging that the successful implementation of our declared strategies and the strong record of sustained dividend growth have won wider recognition in the stock market. ... In all these ways we are constantly reshaping the Group and concentrating its development on the four principal activities." (GB 1986, S. 2 u. 3)

„Our primary objective remains to provide shareholders, over the long term, with above average total returns. Our vision for developing the financial services and tobacco businesses as world leaders is absolutely clear." (GB 1996, S. 4)

GB3: Tesco PLC
„Tesco is committed to expansion and believes the best way to secure a healthy and growing share of the market is to be innovative and efficient both in the creation of high quality products and in the way they are produced, distributes and sold." (GB 1986/87)

„Tesco is committed to creating shareholder value through an innovative customer focused strategy implemented by our people. This strategy is based on the following principles: ... value for money ... customer service ... customer loyalty ... products ... stores" (GB 1996/97, Innenseite)

GB4: J Sainsbury plc
„ ... Sainsbury's will continue to excel, to the advantage of customers, shareholders and indeed the staff themselves." (GB 1986/87, 6)

„Group Objectives: To discharge the responsibility as leaders in our trade ... To provide unrivalled value to our customers ... The achieve the highest stands in efficiency of operation, convenience and customer service ... To offer our staff outstanding opportunities in terms of personal career development and in renumeration ... To generate sufficient profit to finance continual improvement and growth of the business whilst providing our shareholders with an excellent return on their investment." (GB 1996/97, Innenseite)

GB5: Hanson Trust PLC
„But far more important than our size is our commitment to growth. Over the past 21 years our earnings per share have grown at an average annual rate of 21 %. And every single year our dividends have grown, at an average of 24 %." (GB 1986, S. 8)

„The year has been dominated by the implementation of our plan to tontinue the demerger of Hanson's five Divisions into separately quoted companies ... We are convinced that the merits of this radical reorgnisation will be proved when the performance of these companies on their own is measured." (GB 1996, S. 2 u. 3)

GB6: Imperial Chemical Industries PLC
„ICI's principal objective is to improve the effectivenes of wealth reation within the Group, and hence its financial performance, to the benefit of shareholders, employees, customers and the communities in which the Goup operates." (GB 1986, Innenseite)

„We intend to be the world leader in the chemical industry in creating value for customers and shareholders." (GB 1996, S. 4)

GB7: BTR plc

„The growth in profit margins, a principal aim, was also very encouraging, resulting as it has from improvements in every facet of the conduct of our business. ... Each business strives to fulfil its own distrinct purpose, utilising certain common principles all directed towards meeting the requirements of the marketplace - the customer. In so doing it also affords satisfaction to suppliers, to employees and to shareholders." (GB 1986, S. 3)

„Improving returns to shareholders requires profitable growth, and the key to this is targeted investment in high growth activities, as well as increasing involvement in the rapidly growing areas of the world." (GB 1996, S. 6)

GB8: BG plc

„So British Gas is a big business, however you measure it. ... Our fundamental objective is to provide a safe and reliable gas supply, at a competitive price." (GB 1986/87, S. 1)

„Change ..., without precedent elsewhere, was bound to require major change within British Gas. New systems and business practices hat to be designed and implemented troughout our organisation and the culture and values, which served the Company well in the past, had to adapt to the new competitive environment. By far the most significant change was the completion of the demerger." (Annual Review 1996, Deckblatt)

GB9: Grand Metropolitan PLC

„We take a long term view in oder to sustain the quality of earnings and our record shows the wsdom of this policy. We will continue to add value to our operations through investment in established activities, strategic acquisitions and disposals, and by developing new areas of business ..." (GB 1986, S. 4)

„The group aims to strengthen this position through the consistent application of a number of key strategic initiatives. These comprise: growing brand equity; delivering quality financial performance primarily through organic growth; growing shareholder returns by managing for economic profit; developing and retaining talented people and collective senior management leadership." (Annual Review 1996, Innenseite)

GB10: SmithKline Beecham plc

„Beecham seeks to enhance shareholder value by superior performance, and is committed to supplying customers with quality products, providing employees with a challenging environment which encourages excellence, and to fulfilling its responsibilities to the communities in which it operates. To achieve these goals management commits the necessary financial and human resources to its core businesses and encourages innovative research and imaginative marketing throughout the company." (GB 1988, Innenseite)

„We plan to sustain and enhance the performance of your Company. We will have plenty of challenges but are better prepared than ever to meet them. We have a motivated worl force that knows that success generates success and that change is a way of life in a time of global healthcare reform. Our incentive systems are based on a pay for performance principle and we have implemented a programme that further aligns our executives' interests with the interests of our shareholders, including a requirement to own SB shares. We will continue to pursue increases in value creation that outperform our peers in the healthcare industry." (GB 1996, S. 6)

Abb. 2: Verlautbarungen aus britischen Aktiengesellschaften

zum Bezugsgruppendreieck von Aktionären, Kunden und Mitarbeitern findet sich bei GB3, GB4, GB9; dabei erwähnen GB1 und GB6 zusätzlich die Gemeinschaft. GB2 hält die reine Aktionärsorientierung bei, GB7 gibt ihr im Gegensatz zu 1986 größeres Gewicht. GB9 betont besonders den Aspekt eines organischen Wachstums, das früher privatisierte Unternehmen GB8 sieht „change" - die Anpassung an neue Systeme und Praktiken - als wesentliche Herausforderungen an.

Insgesamt zeigt sich bei den britischen Unternehmen eine schon 1986 zu beobachtende starke Orientierung an den Aktionärsinteressen. In der letzten Zeit scheint - wenn man den Verlautbarungen glauben kann - interessanterweise der Kreis der Bezugsgruppen stärker in Richtung von Kunden und Mitarbeitern erweitert zu werden. Auch spielt die Globalisierung eine große Rolle.

3.3. Französische Aktiengesellschaften

Die Befunde zu den größten zehn französischen Aktiengesellschaften sind in Abb. 3 dokumentiert. Im Geschäftsjahr 1986 stehen in Frankreich die Unternehmensleistung und Kompetenz im Vordergrund (F1, F3, F4, F8). Die Kunden werden von F1, F5 und F6 herausgestellt. F7 will Weltmarktführer bei gleichzeitiger Kunden- und Aktionärsorientierung sein, F9 gestaltet die Unternehmensstrategie zum Nutzen der Aktionäre und Mitarbeiter, und ausgerechnet ein stark staatsorientiertes Unternehmen F2 propagiert Wachstum und Schaffung von Wert für die Aktionäre. Ein großer Baukonzern (F10) sieht sich nur als Herausforderer.

Für das Geschäftsjahr 1996 kann ähnlich wie in Deutschland ein Vordringen der Aktionärsorientierung festgestellt werden. F2, F4, F7 und F9 nehmen diese alleinige Orientierung vor, F8 verkündet ein Kurzfristziel in englischer Sprache: **„boosting our share price in 1997"**. F1 und F6 betonen das auch in Deutschland und Großbritannien gefundene Bezugsgruppendreieck, in F6 ergänzt um die Belange der Umwelt. F10 will das Vertrauen von Kunden und Aktionären positiv beantworten. F5 betont Kundenorientierung und Internationalisierung, F3 bleibt bei dem Ziel der Branchenführung. In F9 wird auf ein Bonussystem zur Unterstützung der Aktionärsorientierung verwiesen.

Insgesamt kann für Frankreich ähnlich wie für Deutschland ein starkes Ansteigen der Aktionärsorientierung festgestellt werden.

3.4. Schweizerische Aktiengesellschaften

Die Befunde zu den größten zehn schweizerischen Aktiengesellschaften sind in Abb. 4 dokumentiert. Für das Geschäftsjahr 1986 werden in CH1 und CH8 **Ausführungen in Richtung von Zielen und Leitbildern vermieden.** Im Vordergrund der anderen Unternehmen steht die Unternehmensflexibilität (CH5, CH7, CH10). Daneben geht es um Wachstum (CH9), Marktpräsenz und Innovation (CH4) sowie um Produktqualität (CH6). CH2 stellt Produktivität und Rentabilität heraus, CH3 adressiert das Problem eines optimalen Gleichgewichts zwischen Zentralität und Dezentralität in einem international tätigen Konzern.

Zehn Jahre später ist auch für die Schweiz ein deutlicher Wandel zu festzustellen. In fünf von zehn Fällen werden nunmehr die Aktionäre bzw. Wertorientierungen erwähnt (CH2, CH3, CH6, CH8, CH9). In CH8 werden dabei ROCE-Ziele explizit angesprochen, CH7 will dort wachsen, „wo Wertzuwachs und Ertrag am

F1: Société Nationale Elf Aquitaine S.A.
„Tourné vers l'avenir, Elf Aquitaine consacre d'importants moyens au maintien de son haut degré de compétence. Il poursuit, à cet effet, un vaste effort de recherche, scientifique et technique, d'innovation et de perfectionnement des hommes." (GB 1986, S. 3)

„For Elf Aquitaine, the running of the company is, above all, an *état d'esprit*, bases on three simple guiding principles shared by everyone: ... Decisions taken in the long-term interests of shareholders ... Strategy of creating lasting value ... High-quality controls, both internally and externally ... Elf believes that the creation and preservation of value correspond to the best interests of ... its shareholders, who contribute their capital and their constructive demands, ... its customers, who will benefit from constand improving quality and reduced costs and, ... its personnell, who commit their skills and devotion to the development of their Company." (GB 1996, Innenseite)

F2: TOTAL Compagnie Française des Pétroles S.A.
„Our strategy for the coming years calls for continued growth and improved profitability to create value for shareholders." (GB 1996, S. 3)

„Une stratégie de ferme mise en œuvre de ces atouts avec le soutien constant de ses actionnaires lui permet d'envisager son avenir avec une confiante détermination." (GB 1986, S. 16)

F3: Peugeot S.A.
„L'objectif de PSA est de devenir vers 1992 le premier constructeur européen tant par le volume de ses ventes que par l'importance de son bénéfice." (HV-Ansprache 1987, S. 3)

„PSA Peugeot Citroën rassemble deux constructeurs automobiles généralistes, Automobiles Peugeot et Automobiles Citroën. Ces deux sociétés bénéficient ainsi d'une synergie industrielle, technologique et financière qui leur permet de former, ensemble ..." (GB 1996, S. 1)

F4: Compagnie Générale des Eaux S.A.
„L'action de la Compagnie dans les métiers de l'eau reste au centre de son histoire, comme de son avenir. ...Efficacité ... Productivité ... (GB 1986, S. 9)

„Our activities are entirely oriented towards the next century. They are our greatest strength and main source of pride. These activities enable us to pursue our objective of creating value for all our shareholders, and to eam a little more of their loyalty and confidence every day." (GB 1996, S. 3)

F5: Carrefour S.A.
„Par ses contacts avec les clients, par l'engagement de son personnel, ses liens avec ses fournisseurs et ses relations avec son environnement, Carrefour est quotidiennement à la recherche du mieux, de la satisfaction, de l'innovation, en un mot, de la QUALITÉ." (GB 1986, S. 15)

„Just as Carrefour forms part of these nations, so it is a sign of our times, when concern with the quality of products we sell, with customer satisfaction and market trends are allimportant. New supply chains, logistics tools, the implementation of more efficient sales concepts and the development of partnerships are all tokens of controlled growth. The investments we are making mean we can forcast continuing growth in our results, based on both the enhancement of our business activities and the development of new countries." (GB 1996, S. 2)

F6: Lyonnaise des Eaux S.A.
„Sa mission est de satisfaire sur le long terme les besoins de base des municipalités et de l'industrie. Il a pour ambition de contribuer à la qualité de la vie dans la cité, en proposant son expérience et son savoir-faire dans ces domaines d'activitiés." (GB 1986, S.5)

„Through its long-term partnerships with local governments, the group is pursuing a strategy rooted in the highest professional standards, providing a high quality service to customer, shareholder satisfaction, and caring for people and the environment." (GB 1996, S. 1)

132

F7: Compagnie de Saint-Gobain S.A.
„Il est, par ailleurs, essentiel d'accélérer notre développement international et d'être les leaders mondiaux de nos métiers. ... Déjà, la récente émission de certificats d'investissements est nue renforcer nos fonds propres. Mais la politique de développement que nous devons poursuivre exigera, pour l'avenir, des moyens importants. Le Groupe Saint-Gobain dispose d'hommes et de femmes de qualité et de vastes réserves d'énergie. C'est tout cela qu'il faut conjuguer pour mener un développement énergique et figurer parmi le leaders mondiaux de demain." (GB 1986, S. 4 u. 5)

„The Group's principal objective over the coming year will be to focus on profitable growth while seeking to increase shareholder value. All of the Group's Divisions will contribute to this effort, while a continual emphasis on Research and Development, Innovation, and Marketing will serve to accelerate internal expansion. New acquisitions will also play an important role ..." (GB 1996, S. 1)

F8: Rhône-Poulenc S.A.
„... konnten wir unser Eigenkapital im März 1987 durch die Emission von Vorzugsaktien um weitere 2,5 Mrd. FF. erhöhen. ... Die positive Entwicklung dieser Aktien ermöglicht der Gruppe ehrgeizige Zukunftsprognosen. Die Aufgabe unrentabler Unternehmen und unsere Pläne zur Steigerung der Produktivität sind ein Garant für zukünftige Rentabilität. ... Unsere Investitionspolitik, unser Engagement auf dem Gebiet der Forschung und Entwicklung sowie der Erwerb zahlreicher Unternehmen schaffen eine solide Grundlage für die Leistungsfähigkeit von morgen. ... Ein zusätzlicher Pluspunkt für die Gruppe wäre eine Privatisierung, da sie die oft so entscheidende finanzielle Flexibilität fördert." (GB 1986, S. 3)

„We are convinced that our decision to remain a diversified pharmaceutical group with interests in life sciences and high added-value specialty chemicals represents the best means of creating value for our customers and shareholders. ... We realize that, in order to stick to this decision in the long term, we will have to ensure that our market capitalization reflects the sum of the values of the individual businesses and their respective potential. This is why, notwithstanding the sharp rise recorded in 1996, we will continue to give priority to boosting our share price in 1997." (GB 1996, S.5)

F9: BSN S.A. bzw. Danone S.A.
„Ces diverses opérations donneront à BSN les moyens nécessaires pour conduire sa stratégie, au bénéfice de ses actionnaires et de son personnel. BSN grandit, BSN évolue, BSN s'internationalise." (GB 1986, S. 1)

„Increasing shareholder value is of prime importance to Danone Group, which is reviewing its current business mix and permanently monitors and analyses acquisition opportunities. Return on capital employed is now a key measure of performance and is used to determine bonuses for senior management at corporate and divisional level." (GB 1996, S. 5)

F10: Bouygues S.A.
„Bouygues tire sa cohésion des principes sur lesquels se fonde sa dynamique: la force de son management ... et la volonté de progrès qui anime chacun de ses 50.000 collaborateurs. Leur philosophie: être toujours des challengers." (GB 1986, S. 2)

„In all its areas of business, Bouygues has a distinctive approach based on modern working methods and a proven capacity for innovation. ... With the modern conception we have of our businesses and the means we employ to ensure they succeed and grow, we are responding ever more closely to the confidence that our customers and shareholders have placed in us." (GB 1996/97, S. 3)

Abb. 3: Verlautbarungen aus französischen Aktiengesellschaften

CH1: Nestlé S.A.
Im GB 1986 keine besonderen Ausführungen.

„The strategy followed over the past years has given a new business and half of its profits came from coffee. Since then, we have extended our presence into other regions of the world where we now hold strong and promising positions. For our products, too, we have developed a more balanced distribution of risks and better prospects for growth. In addition, I would like to highlight the increase in research and development spending, the strengthening of the Group's image and that of its brands, the major efforts made in management development as well as in controlling and mastering our costs." (GB 1996, S. 2)

CH2: ABB Asea Brown Boveri AG (früher: BBC)
„ ... eine Reihe von Maßnahmen, mit denen wir den Konzern aus der unzureichenden Ertragslage herauszuführen gedenken: Durchsetzung einer schlagkräftigen Organisationsstruktur im Konzern ... Verbeserung der Rentabilität, vor allem durch Elimination von Verlustquellen ... Reduktion der starken Abhängigkeit von der Stromerzeugung ... Förderung von Wachstumsgebieten. Diese Stoßrichtungen bleiben unverändert gültig. wir haben sie im Berichtsjahr durch das Ziel einer maßgeblichen Produktivitätssteigerung im ganzen Konzern ergänzt." (GB 1986, S. 7)

„Oberster Maßstab des Erfolgs sind die Zufriedenheit unserer Kunden und die langfristige Wertsteigerung für unsere Aktionäre. Seit der Konzerngründung sind unsere Aktien auf das 5,5fache ihres ursprünglichen Werts gestiegen. Der jährliche Kursgewinn von 23 Prozent liegt deutlich über dem Züricher Börsenindex." (GB 1996, S. 5)

CH3: Novartis AG (früher: Ciba-Geigy und Sandoz)
„Diese starke Dezentralisierung ermöglicht es, daß die Ciba-Geigy als Schweizer Konzern mehr als 95 Prozent ihrer Umsätze im Ausland tätigt. Eine der subtilsten und zugleich wichtigsten Aufgaben der Leitung eines derart strukturierten Konzerns ohne Heimmarkt ist die dauernde Herstellung eines optimalen Gleichgewichts zwischen der Festlegung allgemein gültiger Prinzipien und Richtlinien für den ganzen Konzern und der Delegierung möglichst vieler Entscheide an die Front des täglichen Geschäftes in aller Welt." (GB 1986, S. 16)

„Mit anhaltend starken Leistungen auf der Basis kontinuierlicher Innovation wollen wir in allen unseren Tätigkeitsbereichen eine Führungsposition einnehmen und halten. Unser langfristiger Erfolg beruht auf der Erfüllung der Erwartungen einer breiten Öffentlichkeit - unserer Kunden, unserer Mitarbeiter, unserer Aktionäre und der Gemeinschaft, in der wir leben und arbeiten." (GB 1996, S.5)

CH4: Roche Holding AG
„Wir betrachten es als eine Daueraufgabe der Unternehmensführung, den Belangen der Sicherheit größte Aufmerksamkeit zu schenken ... Unsere neue Konzernstruktur bildet die beste Voraussetzung, um unsere Präsenz am Markt in den nächsten Jahren bedeutend zu stärken und in unserer Forschung die Entwicklung bemerkenswert vieler innovativer Produkte abzuschließen." (GB 1986, S. 9)

„ ... , daß es unsere Kunden sind, die über unseren unternehmerischen Erfolg entscheiden. Darauf richten wir uns konsequent aus. Es gilt, die wirklichen Bedürfnisse des Marktes zu erkennen und ihnen mit innovativen Produkten und Dienstleistungen zu entsprechen. Dabei erweist es sich zunehmend als richtig, daß wir uns schon sehr frühzeitig auf unsere Kernaktivitäten konzentriert haben. So gehören wir heute in den meisten Gebieten, in denen wir tätig sind, zu den führenden Anbietern. ... Entscheidend ist, daß wir uns die Fähigkeit erhalten, uns vorausschauend und ohne Zögern auf die sich ändernden Marktbedürfnisse auszurichten." (GB 1996, S. 4)

CH5: „Holderbank" Financière Glarus AG
„Ebenso wichtig ist die Fähigkeit, sich stets mit neuen Situationen und Entwicklungstendenzen zu wandeln: Mithin flexibel zu bleiben. ... 'Holderbank' hat diese Flexibilität immer wieder unter Beweis gestellt." (GB 1986, S. 5)

„Wandel als Chance nutzen ... Im wirtschaftlich eher gesättigten Westeuropa hat sich die Nachfrage nach Baustoffen in letzter Zeit derart stark zurückgebildet, daß wir rasch Korrekturen vornehmen wollen. Wir verstehen dies vor allem als Chance, um neuen Perspektiven Platz zu machen. ... Allen Mitarbeiterinnen und Mitarbeitern sei wiederum bestens gedankt für ihren außerordentlichen Einsatz und ihre aktive Mitwirkung sowie für das große Engagement, unsere Produkte qualitäts- und umweltgerecht herzustellen und unsere Kunden optimal zu bedienen." (GB 1996, S. 10 u. 11)

CH6: Swissair AG
„Nach wie vor sind unsere Anstrengungen darauf ausgerichtet, ein einwandfreies Qualitätsprodukt zu erbringen." (GB 1986, S. 5)

„Die eingeleiteten Strategien und Maßnahmen bilden die Basis für eine Verstärkung der Leistungskraft der SAirGroup. Damit sollen deutlich verbesserte Jahresresultate erzielt werden, welche eine angemessene Verzinsung des Eigenkapitals sowie eine Erfolgsbeteiligung unseres Personals ermöglichen." (GB 1996, S. 6)

CH7: Alusuisse-Lonza Holding AG
„Auf die Frage «Wohin steuert ALUSUISSE?» sind wir heute in der Lage, eine klare Antwort zu geben. Abgestützt auf die verbleibenden Hauptbereiche Aluminium und Chemie wollen wir längerfristig ein führender Hersteller spezieller Materialien im Verpackungssektor, von Verbund- und keramischen Werkstoffen sowie von chemischen Spezialitäten sein. Wir wollen anwendungsorientierte Lösungspakete anbieten und Standarderzeugnisse nur noch verkaufen, wo Veredlungsaktivitäten auf eine Grundlastproduktion angewiesen sind. Unsere Organisationsstruktur richten wir auf größtmögliche Beweglichkeit zum Erkennen neuer Marktchancen und zur Zusammenarbeit mit unseren Kunden aus." (GB 1986, S. 5)

„1996 ist es uns in mehrfacher Hinsicht gelungen, wichtige unternehmerische Grenzen zu überschreiten. ... Wir werden unser Produktesortiment weiter in Richtung höherwertiger Produkte ausbauen. Mit einem nochmals gesteigerten Investitionsprogramm von rund CHF 800 Millionen wollen wir schwerpunktmäßig dort wachsen, wo Wertzuwachs und Ertrag am höchsten sind." (GB 1996, S. 2 u. 3)

CH8: Elektrowatt AG
Im GB 1986 keine besondere Ausführungen.

„Wirtschaftlicher Mehrwert durch übernormale Rentabilität: Neue Zielsetzungen ... Die Geschäftsleitung der Elektrowatt hat die übergeordnete Zielsetzung, eine übernormale Rentabilität zu erwirtschaften. Sie will einen Ertrag auf dem investierten Kapital (Return on Capital Employed, ROCE) erreichen, der über dem gewichteten Kapitalkostensatz liegt (Weighted Average Cost of Capital, WACC = normale Rentabilität). Nur so kann wirtschaftlicher Mehrwert für die Aktionäre geschaffen werden. Die ursprüngliche Zielsetzung einer Eigenkapitalrendite (Return on Equity, ROE) von 15 % hat Elektrowatt deshalb vor zwei Jahren mit spezifischen ROCE-Zielen für ihre Sparten und Geschäftsfelder ergänzt. Jede Sparte und jedes Geschäftsfeld hat nicht nur unterschiedliche Eigenkapitalkosten, sondern auch unterschiedliche Fremdkapitalkosten. ... Ein neues Managementkonzept ... Zur Zeit wird gruppenweit ein neues Managementsystem für das obere Kader eingeführt, das auf dem Leistungsprinzip basiert." (GB 1996, S. 10 u. 11)

CH9: Sulzer AG
„Für die nähere Zukunft ist einer weiteren Verbesserung der Ertragskraft besonderes Gewicht beizumessen, um damit die Voraussetzungen für das Wachstum des Unternehmens zu schaffen. Neben der Festigung des Aufbaus in den neuen Aktivitätsgebieten steht dabei bonders die Weiterentwicklung der bisherigen Produkte in den vom Markt schwergewichtig verlangten Segmenten im Vordergrund." (GB 1986, S.7)

höchsten sind". Eine bedeutende Rolle kommt in CH2, CH3, CH4 und CH5 den Kunden zu. Der „zugeknöpfte" Konzern CH1 läßt die Bedeutung der weltweiten Orientierung durchblicken, der neu formierte Konzern CH3 betont das Bezugsgruppendreieck einschließlich der Öffentlichkeit. CH10 hat ein sogen. SPRINT-Programm zur Bewältigung der Anpassung initiiert.

„Die umfassende und kritische Beurteilung der Lage des Sulzer-Konzerns wurde aus den drei Blickwinkeln Marktentwicklung, unsere eigenen Stärken und Schwächen sowie Unternehmenswertsteigerung vorgenommen. ... Ohne Zweifel haben die Fokussierungsanstrengungen der vergangenen Jahre entscheidend zur Wertsteigerung beigetragen. Diese liegt denn auch über dem relevanten in- und ausländischen Durchschnitt. Die Strategie mit Rückbesinnung auf unsere Stärken hat dazu geführt, daß wir in den heute von Sulzer bearbeiteten Märkten mehrheitlich zu den führenden Anbietern gehören." (GB 1996, S. 4)

CH10: Schindler Holding AG
„In dieses Umfeld gehört auch ... die Eigenkapitalerhöhung zur Stärkung der unternehmerischen Flexibilität." (GB 1986, S. 4)

„Mit dem Wegfall der geographischen Grenzen erscheint der alte Grundsatz «das richtige Produkt zur richtigen Zeit und zum richtigen Preis» in grellerem Licht und wird zum schonungslosen Prüfstein im heutigen Verdrängungswettbewerb. Gefordert sind daher eine markante Steigerung der unternehmerischen Effektivität sowie eine raschere Innovation von Produktangeboten und Leistungserstellung. Der schnelle Rhythmus der Veränderungen macht die Anpassungen im Unternehmen heute zu einem Marathon. Das überlagerte «SPRINT»-Programm ist aber notwendig, um in diesem Langstreckenrennen rasch und durchschlagend Produktivitätsfortschritte zu erzielen. ... Neben fortlaufenden Anpassungen an die Marktgegebenheiten galten im Berichtsjahr die Hauptanstrengungen im Kerngeschäft der Initialisierung von «SPRINT» - «Schindler's Program for Radical and Innovative New Thinking» in ..." (GB 1996, S. 5)

Abb. 4: Verlautbarungen der schweizer Aktiengesellschaften

Auch für die Schweiz läßt sich ein deutlicher Wandel in Richtung von Aktionärs-, aber durchaus auch Kundenorientierung feststellen. Besonders fällt auf, daß die großen schweizerischen Aktiengesellschaften inzwischen auch den Geschäftsbericht als wichtiges Instrument der Investor Relations erkannt haben.

4. Abschließender Vergleich und Ausblick

In der hier vorgenommenen empirischen Analyse von 80 Geschäftsberichten der zehn größten börsennotierten Aktiengesellschaften aus vier Ländern wurde versucht, einen möglichen Wandel von Leitbild und Unternehmenszielen aus externer Sicht zu identifizieren. Der Wandel des Leitbildes und wohl auch der Unternehmensziele ist in den letzten zehn Jahren im Gegensatz zu mancher Prognose durchaus als dramatisch zu bezeichnen. Insbesondere ist bei den größten börsennotierten Aktiengesellschaften in Deutschland, Frankreich und der Schweiz eine deutlich stärkere Aktionärsorientierung auszumachen. In Großbritannien kann die Existenz solcher Orientierungen am Shareholder Value dagegen schon für das Jahr 1986 festgestellt werden. Reine Aktionärsorientierungen sind jedoch auch 1996 vergleichsweise selten anzutreffen, die Kunden und die Mitarbeiter stellen - wie man den Verlautbarungen entnehmen kann - weitere wichtige Bezugsgruppen dar.

In der Literatur wird allerdings davor gewarnt, daß dem Unternehmensleitbild im Unternehmen selbst nicht gefolgt wird und nur verbindlich klingende Slogans formuliert und publiziert werden (so etwa Giblin/Amuso 1997). Auch ist empirisch nachgewiesen worden, daß sich das Unternehmensimage einer Aktiengesellschaft stark an der vergangenen Performance orientiert und sich entsprechend mit Performance-Änderungen durchaus schnell verändern kann (Schmidt 1991). Daher ist es für die Unternehmen besonders wichtig, das nach außen kommunizierte Leitbild - wenn es denn die Aktionäre stark herausstellt - auch erfolgsmäßig dauerhaft umzusetzen. Nur so können negative Reaktionen der Aktionäre an der Börse vermieden werden.

Wie stark sich Unternehmen vom allgemeinen Wandel herausgefordert fühlen, zeigt abschließend die Formulierung der Schindler Holding AG in ihrem Geschäftsbericht 1996 (CH10 in Abb. 4): „Der schnelle Rhythmus der Veränderungen macht die Anpassungen im Unternehmen heute zu einem Marathon".

Literatur:

Albach, H. (1994), Wertewandel deutscher Manager, in: Albach, H. (Hrsg.), Werte und Unternehmensziele im Wandel der Zeit, Wiesbaden 1994, S. 1-25

Baden, K. (1994), Alternative Ansätze zur Performance-Messung von Unternehmen, in: Höfner, K., Pohl, A. (Hrsg.), Wertsteigerungs-Management, Frankfurt, New York 1994, S. 116-149

Baden, K. (1996), Zum Wohl der Aktionäre, in: Manager Magazin, 1996, Nr. 4, S. 146-157

Baetge, J. (1997), Gesellschafterorientierung als Voraussetzung fuer Kunden- und Marktorientierung, in: Marktorientierte Unternehmensführung, Wiesbaden 1997, S. 103 - 117

Bosch, J. K. (1990), Empirical investigations into the goals of listed and unlisted firms with special reference to social responsibility, in: Tydskrift vor studies in ekonomie en ekonometrie, 1990, S.51-70

Brabet, J., Klemm, M. (1994), Sharing the vision: company mission statements in Britain and France, in: Long Range Planning, 1994, Nr. 1, S. 84-94

Brune, J. W. (1996), Der Shareholder-Value-Ansatz als ganzheitliches Instrument strategischer Planung und Kontrolle: eine Untersuchung unter Beachtung besonderer Rahmenbedingungen in der Bundesrepublik Deutschland, Diss. Köln 1996

Chiozzi, R.E. (1996), The forest by way of the trees, in: Bank Marketing, 1996, Nr. 12, S. 57-60

Dufey, G., Hommel, U. (1997), Der Shareholder-Value-Ansatz : US-amerikanischer Kulturimport oder Diktat des globalen Marktes? Einige Überlegungen zur "Corporate Governance" in Deutschland, in: Interkulturelles Management, Wiesbaden 1997, S. 183-211

Fritz, W. (1988), Unternehmensziele und strategische Unternehmensführung: neuere Resultate der empirischen Zielforschung und ihre Bedeutung für das strategische Management und die Managementlehre, in: Die Betriebswirtschaft, 1988, S. 567 - 586

Gabele, E., Kretschmer, H. (1983), Unternehmensgrundsätze als Instrument der Unternehmensführung, in: Schmalenbachs Zeitschrift für betriebswirtschaftliche Forschung, 1983, S. 716-726

Giblin, E.J., Amuso, L.E. (1997), Putting meaning into corporate values, in: Business Forum, 1997, Nr. 1, S. 14-18

Günther, T. (1994), Zur Notwendigkeit des Wertsteigerungs-Managements, in: Höfner, K., Pohl, A. (Hrsg.), Wertsteigerungs-Management, Frankfurt, New York 1994, S. 13-58

Günther, T., Otterbein, S. (1996), Die Gestaltung der Investor Relations am Beispiel führender deutscher Aktiengesellschaften, in: Zeitschrift für Betriebswirtschaft, 1996, S. 389-417

Hill, W. (1996), Der Shareholder Value und die Stakeholder, in: Die Unternehmung, 1996, S. 411-420

Hinterhuber, H.H. (1990), Wettbewerbsstrategie, Frankfurt, New York 1990

Hoffmann, F. (1987), Unternehmenskultur in Amerika und Deutschland, in: Harvard Manager, 1987, Nr. 4, S.91-97

Kreikebaum, H. (1981), Strategische Unternehmensplanung, Stuttgart et al. 1981

Massenberg, J. (1986), Strategie und Entwicklung deutscher Großunternehmen, Frankfurt. M., Bern, New York 1986

Matje, A. (1996), Unternehmensleitbilder als Führungsinstrument, Wiesbaden 1996

Meier-Scherling, P. (1996), Shareholder Value Analyse vs. Stakeholder Management: unternehmenspolitische Grundkonzeptionen als Ansätze zur Erweiterung der Theorie der Unternehmung, Diss. Fribourg 1996

o.V. (1997), Im Krupp-Thyssen-Konflikt wird über die Mitbestimmung gestritten, in: Frankfurter Allgemeine Zeitung, 13.12.1997, S. 23

Pantalone, C.C., Welch, J.B. (1986), The usefulness of public information about corporate goals, in: Quarterly Journal of Business and Economics, 1986, Nr. 4, S. 29-40

Rappaport, A. (1986), Creating Shareholder Value, New York 1986

Schmid, S. (1996), Nicht Shareholder-Orientierung, sondern Stakeholder-Orientierung! Plädoyer für eine Relativierung der einseitigen Ausrichtung am Shareholder Value, in: Diskussionsbeiträge der Wirtschaftswissenschaftlichen Fakultät Ingolstadt / Katholische Universität Eichstätt, Nr. 76, 1996

Schmidt, R. (1981), Diagnose von Unternehmensentwicklungen auf Basis computergestützter Inhaltsanalyse, in: Bratschitsch, R., Schnellinger, W. (Hrsg.), Unternehmenskrisen - Ursachen, Frühwarnung, Bewältigung, Stuttgart 1981, S. 353-379

Schmidt, R. (1991), Unternehmensimage, Unternehmensperformance und Börsenkurs, in: Demuth, A. (Hrsg.), Imageprofile '91, Düsseldorf, Wien, New York 1991, S. 29-35

Schmidt, R. (1992), Artikel „Druckbericht, Inhaltsanalyse", in: Handwörterbuch der Revision, 2. Aufl., Stuttgart 1992, Sp. 368-376

Schmidt, R. (1993), Das Shareholder Value-Konzept, in: Fritsch, U., Liener,G., Schmidt, R. (Hrsg.), Die deutsche Aktie, Stuttgart 1993, S. 277-296

Schmidt, R. (1998), Financial Markets, Corporate Governance and Short-term Pressures in Germany, in: Demirag, I. (Hrsg.), Corporate Governance, Accountability and Pressures to Perform: An International Study, Greenwich/CT (erscheint demnächst)

Siegert, T. (1995), Shareholder-Value als Lenkungsinstrument, in: Schmalenbachs Zeitschrift für betriebswirtschaftliche Forschung, 1995, S. 580-607

138

Spremann, K. (1994), Wertsteigerung als Managementprinzip in Europa?, in: Höfner, K., Pohl, A. (Hrsg.), Wertsteigerungs-Management, Frankfurt, New York 1994, S. 303-319

Stehr, C., Belzer, V. (Hrsg.) (1995), Sinn in Organisationen? oder: Warum haben moderne Organisationen Leitbilder?, München 1995

Steinmann, H., Löhr, A., Kustermann, B. (1996), Unternehmensleitbilder - Instrumente einer effizienten und sozialverträglichen Unternehmensführung, in: Forum Wirtschaftsethik, 1996, Nr. 1, S. 1-5

Wagner, H. (1997), Marktorientierte Unternehmensführung versus Orientierung an Mitarbeiterinteressen, Shareholder-Value und Gemeinwohlverpflichtung, in: Marktorientierte Unternehmensführung, Wiesbaden 1997, S. 87 - 102

Wahlquist, C. N. (1996), Inhalts- und Prozessanalyse von Unternehmensvisionen multinationaler Gesellschaften: komparative Untersuchung am Beispiel schwedischer und schweizerischer Unternehmen der Pharmaindustrie unter besonderer Berücksichtigung des Anspruchsgruppen-Ansatzes, Diss. St. Gallen 1996

Werner, U. (1990), Die Analyse des Lageberichts als Instrument empirischer Zielforschung, in: Schmalenbachs Zeitschrift für betriebswirtschaftliche Forschung, 1990, S. 1014-1035

The Key Role of Purchasing within Virtualizing Organizations

Jean Claude Som

Zusammenfassung:

Die Globalisierung der Wirtschaft und die Entwicklung von Telekommunikation und Informationstechnologie sind die Grundfaktoren, die am Ursprung der virtuellen Organisation (VO) liegen. Wir interessieren uns für zwei Fragen mit denen sich Firmen heutzutage befassen : (1) dem massiven Preisdruck die in den meisten Bereichen der Wirtschaft herrscht (Computer, Kleidung, Lebensmittel, Spielwaren, Dienstleistungen, usw.) und (2) der Rückkehr zu den Kernkompetenzen mit der resultierenden Zunahme der Abhängigkeit von Zulieferern.

Dieser Beitrag befasst sich mit der Beschaffung von externen Diensteistungen in Form von Temporär-Personal (TP) in Europa. In diesem Kontext wird aufgezeigt, wie die TP-Beschaffungsfunktion an : (1) direkten und indirekten Kostensenkungsprogrammen, (2) Beschaffung von Wettbewerbsvorteilen, und (3) Ankurbelung des Lerneffektes in der Organisation beitragen kann. Dabei werden TP-Beschaffungsziele und Strategien (z.B. strategische TP-Lieferanten Partnerschaften) diskutiert und mittels Modellierung und Simulierung geprüft. Abschliessend und auf Basis der neuen Management-Techniken werden Hinweise für die Einführung der Strategie vorgestellt.

1. Introduction

The globalization of the worldwide economy and the development of information technology (IT), in the last few years, are the underlying circumstances that are at the origin of the Virtual Organization (VO). In that context, the present paper looks at the aspect of procuring and managing external services, in the form of skilled temporary workers in Europe. Why is this of interest to the changing organization ? When elaborating their operations (ex. Value Chain Management, Cost Management, Process Management) and their structures to compete in the global world, companies have at least two major reasons for considering the particular domain of acquiring temporary human resources:

- Most sectors of commerce (computer, telecommunications, clothing, services, food, toys, etc.) experience a formidable pressure on prices. Cost efficiency is an everyday focus for a business to stay profitable and to survive. Establishing cost reduction strategies for acquiring temporary workers, is a natural objective of the Purchasing function,

- After a trend of diversification and growth-through-acquisition in the eighties, enterprises today tend to go back to their core competencies through divestitures. The new companies are increasingly dependent on their partners. Cooperating with suppliers becomes of strategic importance. The Purchasing department has to play a key role in integrating suppliers, for instance of temporary workers, into the issues of the company's business.

In what precedes, we imply that it is primarily the Purchasing's responsibility to take the lead in these issues; later on, we will argue why. What is quite undisputed is that the role of the Purchasing department has evolved dramatically over the last 40 years : From executing operational activities (buying the right material, at the right time, in the right quantity and at the right price); to this day, they have a Supply Management responsibility (Gasser 1995, p.2-6). Remarkably, there is very little management literature dealing with purchasing contract personnel. Typically, "Purchasing Management" books do not consider personnel acquisition at all. Authors mainly focus on tangible goods. For instance, Scheuing quotes : "Purchasing is not responsible for the acquisition of human resources" (Scheuing 1989). Referring to the Human Resources Organization (HRO) management literature, we notice that under "Human Resources (HR)-acquisition", authors concentrate on HR-planning and personnel selection of the fixed work force. The particularities of acquiring and managing temporary personnel (and temporary personnel suppliers), are not handled. We conclude that there is a gap in the management literature, concerning the acquisition and the use of contract personnel.

In practice, some companies, such as Ford, Microsoft, DEC, ICL, etc., have created (or are in the process of creating) dedicated organizations to manage the acquisition of contract personnel. Their experiences represent an inspirational source of ideas and empirical data. The present paper uses the opportunity to look at this particular domain, by taking on a European global supplier of IT in Europe, and an American automobile manufacturer as a basis for the discussion.

2. The Virtual Organization - Definition

Many authors make a distinction between the terms "Virtual Organization" (VO), "Virtual Corporation", "Virtual Company", etc. In our context, they all mean the same and we use them indifferently. To illustrate a Virtual Organization, consider the following structures :

- Individuals widely separated geographically, pool their skills to run a common business. These individuals, working away from a traditional office, build a Virtual Organization,

– A company relies to a great extent on third parties to conduct its business. It is part of a large network of companies, that are linked together via strategic partnerships, joint ventures, etc. : it represents a Virtual Organization.

Frequently, it is a combination of the above structures that build up a VO. To exist, a VO has to rely on supporting technologies such as telecommunications, networking and work group applications. The principal advantages of Virtual Organizations are : efficiency, productivity, speed, and higher levels of expertise (finding the right resource is not limited geographically anymore). Further, there is little corporate overhead and before all, it is an extremely flexible organizational model able to reorganize itself instantly to suit customer needs. Finally, it is a lifestyle for confirmed remote workers. But there are also many disadvantages, such as the sharing of knowledge which becomes difficult to manage, or the workers' "sense of belonging". These aspects will be developed later in this paper. The underlying reasons why corporations become or are Virtual Organizations are discussed in the section 3.2.

3. The Organization and its Environment

The breadth and depth of examination of each element depends on its relation with the particular aspect being considered : procuring and managing contract personnel.

3.1. Economic and Cultural Environments in Europe

The general economic situation in Europe has been moody for years now. In most countries, the unemployment rate exceeds 10%. Although there are signs in specific sectors of commerce for a recovery (ex. high-tech), it is unlikely that "easy years" like the sixties again will return. The only way for Europe to regain a competitive position in the world, and to give a boost to its economy, is the accomplishment of the EC's free trade vision. As a result of deregulation (for instance the free circulation of people, goods, services), work capacity will increasingly move from low wage to high wage countries. However, due to the many different cultures and languages in Europe, this movement will be limited to specific jobs. For example, a software programmer may well provide his services across countries, whereas jobs that are close to the customers, (economy of proximity) can hardly be exported (ex. lawyers).

3.2. The Employment Paradigm Shift and the Virtual Organization

Signs about a revolution at work are coming from the USA : There is a move in people's mind from being an "employee" (protected, secured, managed) to becoming an "independent" (exposed, at risk, empowered). This paragraph discusses this trend from a European perspective, and demonstrates how companies affect (and are affected by) that trend.

Many authors predict an employment paradigm shift. For example, Handy alleges that less than half of the work force in the industrial world will be in proper full-time jobs, in organizations, by the beginning of the twenty-first century (Handy 1991). An organization that is moving in this direction **(the organization is virtualizing)**, implies that Management deals with the following questions :

- What parts of the company should be made variable, or outsourced (security, administration, mailroom services, cleaning, sales, IT operations, finance, manufacturing, training, purchasing, etc. are just a few examples), and why ?
- What is the cost of flexibility ? Replacing a regular with a variable work force may well reduce, for example, human resource's administrative workload (less employees to care for). But sourcing variable personnel through agencies increases also the direct costs (agency's margin). On the positive side though, going outside gives access to a wide choice of skilled resources that can hardly be developed internally. Where is the trade off ? In the end, the questions are : "Does a variable work force cost more or less than regular employees ?", and "does an external expert help provide a competitive advantage ?"
- What about issues such as unions' resistance, people's "sense of belonging", company philosophy and ethics, security, people's commitment, etc. ? These will undoubtedly be impacted by an increase of the proportion of variable versus regular personnel.

Fig. 1 shows graphically the transformational process of building a "**Core Company**". Core company means the basic organization necessary to execute core competencies. Although core competencies will not be discussed, understanding how the employment paradigm shift is likely to impact Purchasing is of interest.

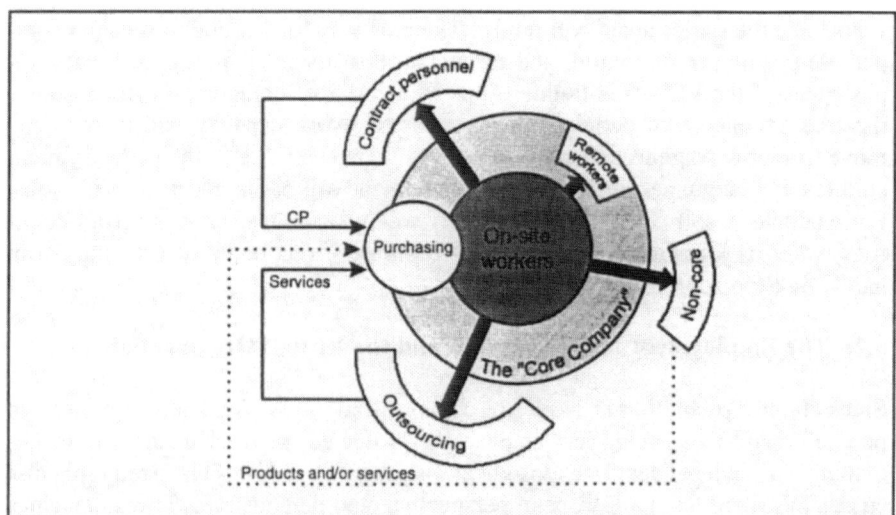

Fig. 1: Building the „Core Company": Implications on Purchasing

On-site and remote workers build the "Core Company". Remote workers are on the company's payroll but not in the office (ex. sales people working from home). Their "sense of belonging" can be characterized as medium. The principal advantage of having remote workers is the possibility to reduce office space, i.e. property assets. On-site and remote workers build a Virtual Organization (VO).

Non-core activities can be discontinued or sold. When activities are sold, the objects of the deal are usually people and assets (tangible and/or intangible). Selling a business activity results in reduced revenue. Whether the margin decreases or not depends on how profitable the activity was, and whether products or services now need to be bought or not from the outside. For example Digital sold its disk technology activity (research, engineering and production) to Quantum and now obtains the finished products from the latter.

Outsourcing is the displacement of activities to outside companies. These activities represent support work that is necessary to the business. The work is provided by suppliers as a service. Outsourcing results in a decrease in head count and in assets. Revenue is not directly impacted and the company's margin may go up or down (depending on how much the work cost the company when it was performed by a regular work force versus the price the company pays for outsourcing the service). There is little a "sense of belonging" between a supplier and his customer.

Contract personnel is the solution to the problem of a company's cyclical labor needs. In order to quickly adapt to changes in market demand, companies adjust the fixed work force to lower levels and engage contract personnel when a labor

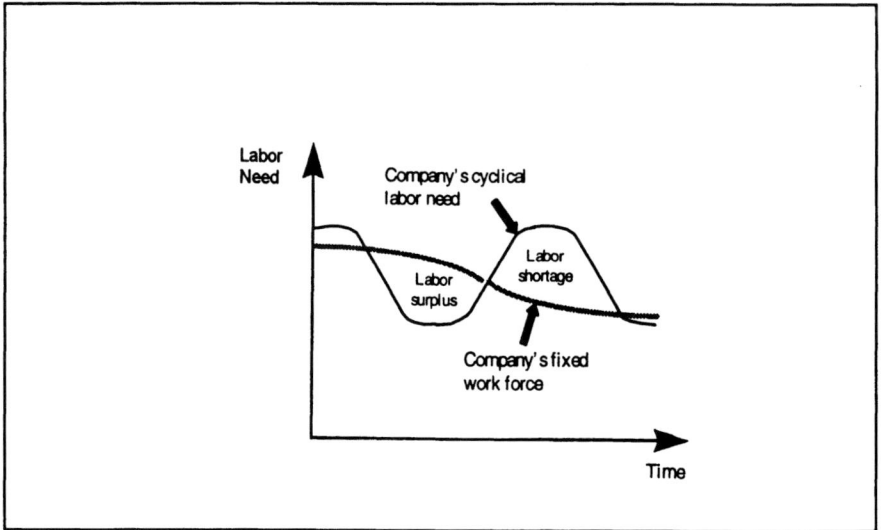

Fig. 2: A Company's Cyclical Labor Need

shortage occurs (see Fig. 2). Margins are theoretically reduced by using contract personnel instead of a regular work force (because of agency's margin). But what proportion of the work force should be variable ? More than 50% believes Handy (Handy 1991). For Europe this seems to be excessive. Why ? To explain, let us develop and comment two basic scenarios. In the first scenario, companies take the initiative and start to lay off people and to re-engage temporary workers instead. This will be interpreted by the employees as a method to lower salaries. As a result, unions and political parties will immediately resist change. In the second scenario, people change their mind set with regards to work : they are more entrepreneurial and more independent. In this scenario, the move towards a flexible work force comes from the employees. Thinking about what is most likely to happen in Europe, we believe that resistance will predominate, for two reasons : First, the entrepreneurship spirit exists to a much lesser extent in Europe than in the USA, and second, most European countries (the United Kingdom, Germany, France, etc.) have strong unions.

Even though no radical change in the European work force will happen in the short term, we expect a slow but steady increase of the demand for contract personnel in the coming years. Recognizing this trend is important from an acquisition perspective. For procuring CP it has to be professionally managed to minimize the associated direct and indirect expenses, and to satisfy requesters' needs.

3.3. Political/Legal Environment

There is a substantial amount of legislation regulating the employment of people in all European countries. Beside constantly dealing with unions, companies also have to be knowledgeable about an increasing number of laws, and have to face a growing number of public-interest groups (ex. media publics). The European Community's (EC) motto is "deregulation", for instance, free circulation of people. Deregulation here is not a synonym for "reduced worker protection". Rather a harmonization of the laws regulating employment will occur with the European Union. But this is still a long way off. In our system of procuring and managing contract personnel, the intervention of political groups, especially in a context such as the one discussed in the previous section, can be expected.

3.4. Technological Environment

The revolution of telecommunications and IT and their combination enables remote workers to connect to the company's systems and work with applications and data as if they were at the office. The advent of Virtual Organizations (VO), relies entirely on such new technologies and can not exist without these.

4. Definition and Categories of Temporary Workers

High-Skilled temporary workers or contract personnel (CP), can be characterized as being employed by agencies, and hired by companies for short periods of time. They are mainly used to absorb workload peaks or provide skills unavailable in the company. For management and reporting purposes, larger companies typically organize their Purchasing function around different commodities such as "travel", "telecommunications", "distribution/transportation", etc., and generally also a commodity group called "contract personnel" (CP). According to the type of work/skills or services provided, the commodity group "contract personnel" is subdivided into categories. An IT supplier (who uses CP for both its internal needs and for resale within customer projects), would typically distinguish three main categories : (1) contract labor, (2) contractors and (3) consultants. The characteristics of each category are described in Table 1. According to the proportion of spending among the three categories, a Purchaser can set priorities and develop adequate strategies for each section.

Commodity Category	Job Particularities	Payment	Preferred Suppliers	Skill Types
Contract Labor	Used on a short term. Limited time basis. Work supervised and managed by the company. Administrative or operative work. Internal use.	Typically on an hourly basis.	Global and country specific agencies.	Switchboard/reception operator; General clerk; Secretary; Word processing operator; etc.
Contractors (technical consultants)	Used on a short term. Limited time basis. Work supervised and managed by the company. IT or project support/ management work. Internal use or rsale.	Time and material basis or fixed price basis.	Specific agencies and/or software houses.	System analyst; Computer operator; Service delivery engineer; Technical designer; IT consultant; Translation services; etc.
Consultants	Used for independent advise, knowledge and professional expertise. Use their own tools, processes, practices. Set their own working hours. Can work on a company site, customer site, or in their own premises. Internal use or resale.	Generally fixed price basis.	Self employed; Partnership; Corporate entities.	Marketing consultant; Lawyer; Financial consultant; HRO consultant; Recruitment consultant; Outplacement consultant; etc.

Table 1: Job Characteristics of Contract Personnel (CP) Categories

146

4.1. The Contract Personnel Industry

The CP industry has low entry barriers. It is easy for new suppliers to quickly establish themselves. CP providers can be self-employed individuals, partnerships (loosely coupled Associates/Consultants), agencies (ex. Manpower), software groups (ex. Interskill Services SA) or consulting firms (ex. Andersen Consulting, Coopers & Lybrand). Due to the persistent weakness of the European economy, many suppliers (particularly individuals and agencies), have had to give up in the last couple of years. The competition among those left is quite strong, reinforcing in some domains (i.e. agencies) the bargaining power of companies with a sizable need for temporary manpower services.

4.2. Pricing for Contract Personnel Services in the Global Context

Agencies generally have a fixed margin policy. In Switzerland the margin situates between 20% and 30%. If more is bought from a supplier, a sort of "volume pricing" applies : the hourly rate of a contractor's agency drops by roughly 5% if a contract lasts between 3-6 months, and 12% if it lasts more than 6 months. The costs for a "technical consultant" range from $80 to $130 per hour. If contracted directly, professionals would cost 20% to 30 % less (the agency's margin), but the indirect costs are higher due to the time spent in negotiating and maintaining individual contracts.

Many suppliers operate internationally. Concluding preferred partnerships with international suppliers, represents for multi-national companies a good potential for lowering costs (supply base consolidation, "export work" from high wage to low wage countries). In that context, an overview of the salaries and working hours in different countries is of top interest : the relative gross income per hour of engineers in Europe is provided in Fig. 3 (we assume that "Engineers" - from an income point of view - is closest to our "technical consultants" category). Thus, the calculated range for relative hourly gross income for technical consultants in Europe ranges from 6% to 121% (reference : Switzerland = 100%). It is obvious that money can be saved by "exporting" certain working skills, from low income countries to high income countries. Likely importing countries are Germany, Austria and Switzerland; exporting countries could be the United Kingdom, Israel, or Eastern countries such as Hungary (provided that skilled resources are available). Of course, the savings would be somewhat offset by other costs (travel, lodging, car, etc.), if the contractee had to be temporarily moved. However, certain jobs can be performed at distance (ex. programming), making this approach worth consideration.

City:	Relative gross income per year	Weekly working hours	Vacation per year paid working days	Number of work hours per year	Relative number of work hours	Relative gross income per hour
Luxemburg	127%	40	27	1864	104%	121%
Frankfurt	113%	39	31	1786	100%	113%
Vienna	102%	38	30	1748	98%	104%
Copenhagen	99%	37	25	1739	97%	101%
Zurich	100%	40	22	1904	100%	100%
Paris	96%	39	25	1833	103%	94%
Dusseldorf	89%	38	30	1748	98%	91%
Brussels	74%	37	22	1761	99%	75%
Oslo	72%	38	21	1816	102%	70%
Dublin	69%	38	27	1771	99%	69%
London	69%	39	20	1872	105%	66%
Helsinki	63%	38	25	1786	100%	63%
Milan	64%	39	25	1833	103%	62%
Stockholm	59%	39	26	1825	102%	57%
Madrid	56%	40	30	1840	103%	55%
Tel Aviv	55%	43	24	2030	114%	49%
Athens	33%	40	22	1904	107%	30%
Budapest	12%	41	25	1927	108%	11%
Prague	6%	43	23	2038	114%	6%

Number of weeks per year: 52

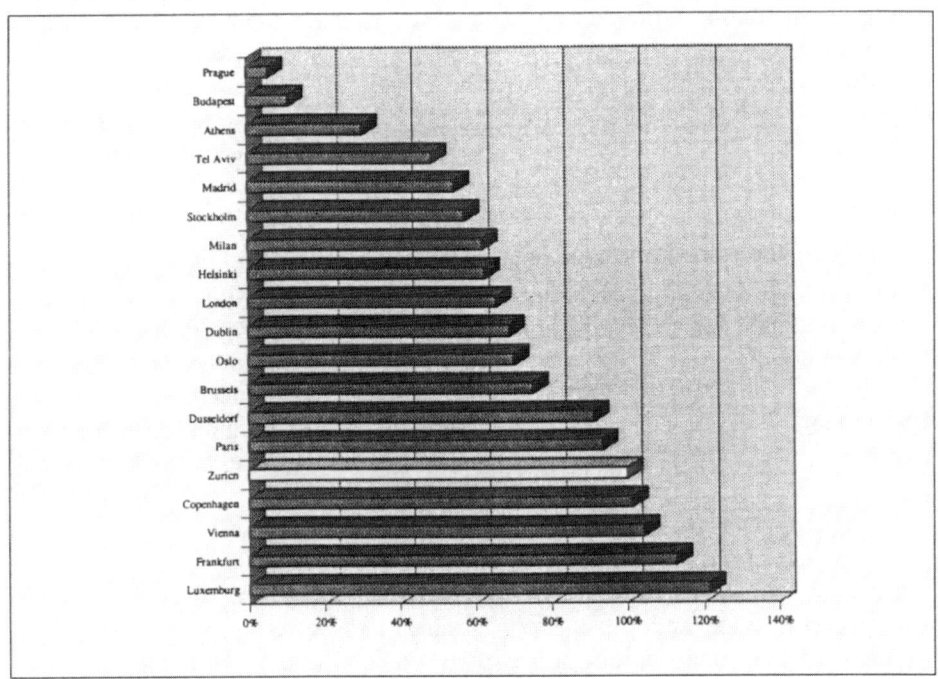

Source: UBS, Prices an Earnings Around the Globe, 1994 Edition (adapted).

Fig. 3: Relative Gross Income per Hour of Engineers in Europe

5. The Virtualizing Organization and Contract Personnel Acquisition

5.1. Virtual Organization - Challenges for Purchasing

Nowadays, many companies have been organized around Business Lines, (also called Business Units) with Profit and Loss (P&L) responsibility. Business Lines have advantages (i.e. manageability, accountability), but also drawbacks. For instance, Business Lines tend to develop their own processes at a country level. CP acquisition (CPA) is one example. As a result, uncoordinated and immature procurement strategies emerge with following typical consequences :

- The supply base is too wide. Economy of scale cannot be fully achieved,
- Requesters (typically Managers) spend too much time searching and acquiring candidates,
- Contracting with suppliers is inconsistent, costly and very slow. Cooperation is frequently started without a valid contract, because the negotiation process often takes up several weeks. This represents a high business risk for the company,
- Ordering and administrative processes are complex and slow. Acquiring and placing CP can take up several weeks, negatively impacting the productivity of a team,
- Dealing with a wide supply base is also at the expense of the Accounts Payable function : the number of invoices is proportional to the size of the supply base,
- Supplier management is limited. For instance, there is no continuous improvement program in place, nor are there rewards for supplier excellence practiced,
- IT is not adapted to new business models. Reporting is limited, and does not fulfill the businesses' and the CP acquisition's information needs.

Due to the growing number of CP hired, the task of procuring and managing external human resources is gaining great importance. Developing and operating efficient and effective acquisition strategies is one factor to remaining profitable and competitive.

When a CP supply base is vast and unstable, it is unpractical to objectively evaluate its performance and capabilities. Dealing with fewer, preferred suppliers, would make performance tracking easier. It would also allow to reduce the indirect costs (less parties to deal with) as well as the direct costs (supply base consolidation, "export work" from high wage to low wage countries).

5.2. Needs of the Requester for Contract Personnel

Every division, function, department, etc., in a company may use CP for carrying out work (internal use). Many companies, especially IT suppliers, are also consumers of CP for resale. For them, the proportion of CP used for resale (customer projects) versus own consumption is largely a factor of three to four. The needs of a requester for CP are summarized :

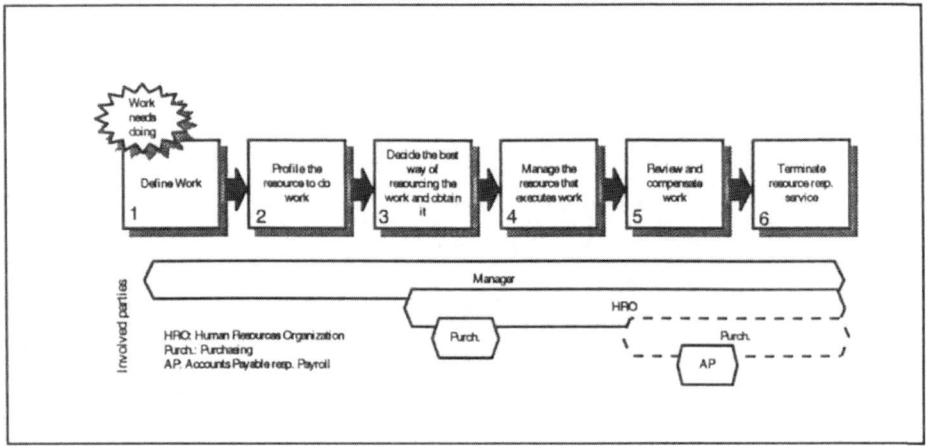

Fig. 4: Approach to Resourcing Work

Accessible high quality skills with expertise in a particular field, at competitive rates,
- Ease of recruitment (quick and easy processes),
- Flexibility to obtain the most appropriate partner,
- Meeting company's customer and project deadlines (controlled risk),
- Cultural and language compatibility,
- Obtaining decision support and critical information to run their businesses (i.e. statistics about CP profiles, costs, etc.).

5.3. Processes to Resourcing Work

The general approach to resourcing work is represented in Fig. 4, assuming that the work can be accomplished :
- by an internal human resource (fixed work force/"permanent" or "regular" personnel),
- by an external human resource (variable or temporary work force/"contract" personnel),
- through an external service (outsourced).

Resourcing work is a major task in the Manager's job : a good reason for him being involved in each step. But being involved does not mean that he has to do everything himself. In fact, Managers often waste too much time, for example in searching/pre-screening external temporary skills. Looking at HRO, we note that its degree of participation is strongly dependent on whether a permanent resource is needed ("hiring", therefore high participation), or a non-permanent resource is sufficient, ("acquisition", therefore low, or no involvement at all). Purchasing becomes involved only when a non-permanent resource is sought. However this often happens too late : once the candidate has already been selected. The Purchaser then just does the administrative work (which is frustrating). As a result,

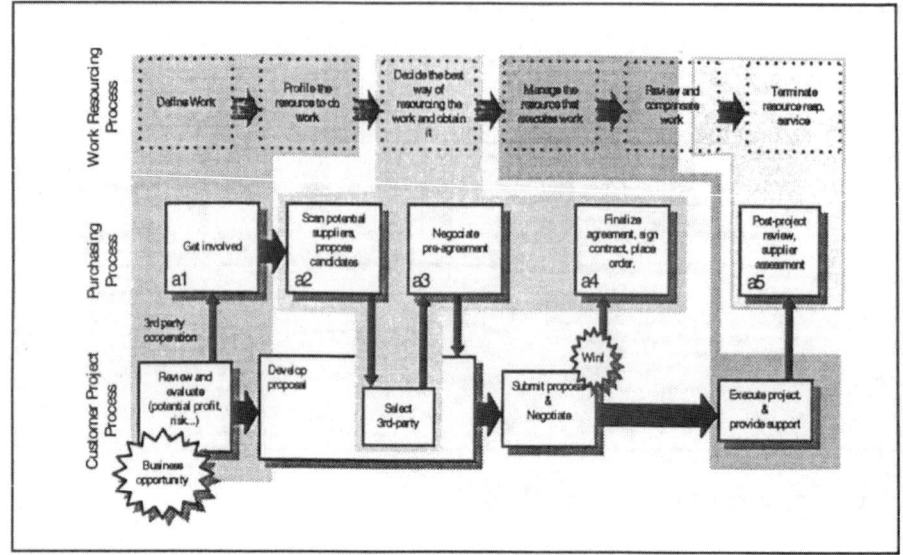

Fig. 5: Customer Project and CP Procurement Processes

purchasing strategies cannot be pursued (i.e. effective use of preferred suppliers to reduce costs, etc.), and even more important, the business risk for the company increases when formal agreements and contracts are not signed, as frequently happens. In a later step, Purchasing should perform a supplier evaluation. In reality, this is not done systematically, and so another opportunity to accumulate and disseminate knowledge disappears. Finally, Accounts Payable pays the invoice for a temporary work force, (or an external service), or payroll pays the salary to a regular employee.

An important distinction must be made between resourcing work to satisfy internal needs and resourcing work for reselling. In the latter case, the CP procurement process is tightly imbedded in the customer project process as represented in Fig. 5. The purchasing process is "driven" by the customer project process. Frequently, Purchasing gets involved only at stage "a4". Such situations tend to occur when (1) time and competitive pressure are such that slow and complicated processes (i.e. purchasing process) have to be "forgotten for a while, at least until the project is won", (2) the potential customer dictates the third-party to work with, or (3) some decision maker decided to bring "friends" in. It is obvious that once the third-party to work with on the project has been selected, there is almost no margin left for the Purchaser to negotiate the best conditions for the company. If later the partner is unable to fulfill what is expected from him and no formal contract had been previously signed, the company is penalized. As the number and $-volume of projects increase, it is important that a risk management program be put in place.

6. Purchasing : Role and Organization

6.1. Set of Objectives : Benefits and Limitations

The set of objectives proposed in Table 2 can be taken as an example applicable to any European CP Purchasing function of a multinational company, whose variable work force represents an important part of the total work force, and that has a significant bargaining power, (ex. : an IT solutions supplier). We assume that it is fully in line with corporate objectives (such as "increase shareholder value", "define core competencies", "build a flexible organization", "make the overall cost structure more competitive"), and that it is supported by all the concerned entities (Business Lines, HRO, and Finance). The set of objectives aims at creating a new CP acquisition system, able to satisfy higher standards in cost efficiency, quality and speed.

The following discussion explains (1) how the objectives address the weaknesses and the threats discussed earlier, (2) on which strengths and opportunities they rely on and (3) what the assumptions and limitations are.

Objectives	Measurements
Create and promote X preferrred European suppliers, and nominate and pro mote Y preferred national suppliers, in 6 months.	X international agreement(s) signed and Y national suppliers nominated and promoted until dd-mmm-yy.
Have 50% of all next year's spending with preferred suppliers (international and national).	End-of-year report: 50% or more of total CP spending with the preferred suppliers.
Develop a specific CP Supplier management program and start using it with all prefferred suppliers.	Supplier management programs formally engaged with all preferred suppliers by the end of the year.
Provide a complete procurement service able to satisfy every CP need in the company (internal and external use).	The procedure is set up, implemented and operational in one or two pilot country(ies) (UK, France, Germany, Holland or Switzerland) by end of the year.
Work out a concept destined to share and utilize the knowledge about the CP market, suppliers, clients, customers and competitors.	A detailed plan is presented (including objective 6) to Senior Management and the implementation approved and funded, within 3 months.
Define and develop the underlyng IT necessary to effectively support objectives 4, 5 and 6	Specifications for the application are available within 3 months, and a first operational version within 6 months.
Have 100% of all active suppliers under contract within one year.	No supplier works for the company without a contract signed by the end of the year.

Table 2: Contract Personnel Acquisition: Set of Objectives

Objective 1: Preferred International and National Suppliers

In a study about the strategic impact of long-term purchasing partnerships (Graham 1994), it was reported that the development of such partnerships is a significant contemporary trend. The main reason for this trend is that firms recognize the advantages of coalitions, particularly in implementing specific purchasing strategies (ex. continuous improvement programs or TQM-ISO 9000), and in achieving desired outcomes (ex. improved quality of processes, decreased buying organization's and supplier's total costs). The above, plus : (1) the strong bargaining power of customers in the CP industry in general, (2) the own company's strong bargaining power in particular, and its global presence, (3) the existence of established international suppliers (ex. Manpower), represent a propitious combination of elements to enter various partnering relationships. The benefits expected from supplier partnering are manifold :

- Through optimization of the leverage opportunities (getting volume prices by sourcing more CP work from less suppliers) :
  - Reduced expenses,
  - Improved competitive position in customer projects (resale of CP), for instance more price-competitive offers, higher margins, or a combination of both.
- International supplier networks can help export work opportunities (i.e. skills needed for a project), from high wage to low wage countries :
  - Same benefits as above (expenses, competitive position),
  - Additional business opportunities for the supplier.
- Reduced need to recruit new suppliers (assuming that the preferred partners are able to satisfy the majority of the requester's needs) :
  - Reduction of the number of costly and lengthy new contract negotiation processes,
  - Stabilizing the supply base.
- Decreased number of payments, (assuming that suppliers are paid monthly for all resources provided, instead of invoicing and paying them on a per-contractee basis) :
  - Process simplification (for buyer and supplier),
  - Reduced number of cases, therefore reduced indirect costs (for buyer and supplier).
- Through the possibility of hiring the same contractees repeatedly, decreased necessity for preparation and training, (because they start to know the company and the working environment) :
  - More cost and time efficient,
  - Increasing work quality.

According to a study that examined the partnership sourcing practices of 11 companies residing in the UK, nine major benefits of partnering relationships with suppliers were reported (Akacum 1995). Three of them may be relevant to our own environment : (1) improved resolution of problems, (2) improved service, and (3) faster delivery. But Akacum also observed some limitations of the partnering concept : (1) suppliers feel that customers want to use the partnership to cut price, (2) the time spent in establishing the relationship is often seen as "a lot of time for nothing", (3) the agreed terms and conditions tend to limit the possibility to exploit more attractive market opportunities.

It is critical that the designated preferred suppliers are the right ones, those that are able to satisfy the majority of the requester's needs. Overall, the benefits of a supplier partnering outweigh the disadvantages. Supporting this assertion are the conclusions of the study mentioned earlier : "the degree of success for purchasing strategy implementation and desired outcome achievements increases with long-term strategic purchasing partnerships, and accelerates markedly after three years" (Graham 1994).

Objective 2 : Fifty Percent of Spending with the Preferred Suppliers
The benefits for entering strategic business partnerships are discussed in detail above. The leverage effect results from directing more business to fewer (preferred) suppliers. Objective 2 is a means to consciously focus Purchasers on this aspect. But how much is right, and realistic ? This question is developed in section 6.3. The critical success factor is that the suppliers are to be able to provide the needed skills, in the requested amount, and at the right moment.

Objective 3 : Contract Personnel Supplier Management Program
Purchasing of many large companies provide generic supplier management programs, but they generally do not suit the particular needs of procuring and managing CP. Therefore, the development of an adapted supplier management program, specific to the CP context, is proposed. The focus of such a program should be on aspects such as : (1) Total Quality Management (TQM) of the supplier and the contractee, (2) performance (ex. response time), etc.

Objective 4 : Complete Procurement Service
Such a service is meant to satisfy all CP demands within the company. A pilot implementation should be run in one country, and if the results are conclusive, gradually be deployed in other countries. The benefits expected from this service are :
– Through a professional and complete procurement service (search, supplier acquisition, pre-selection, etc.) :
  – Increased productivity of the requester,
  – More motivated Purchasers (because they will be more involved in projects earlier, and less in carrying out the administrative burden).
– Because of the execution of the procedures by professionals :
  – Reduction of the number of costly after-the-fact cases.

Given the organization and procedures with which CP acquisition work is usually carried out, the acquired knowledge is disseminated geographically and linguistically, functionally (Business Lines, Central Acquisition, HRO), and personally.

Objective 5 : Shared Knowledge Concept

There is barely an effective mechanism in place to retain that knowledge, share it and utilize it broadly. To build an organization that can adapt to change, that is able to avoid the repetition of past mistakes, that can retain critical knowledge that would otherwise go lost, it is proposed to develop a concept for enhancing organizational capability. This aspect is elaborated in section 7.

Objective 6 : Information Technology

Most of the objectives defined above have to rely on IT. It was reported earlier that purchasing applications are usually not adapted to the particularities of CP procurement and management. Technology is not the most important piece in a change process (people are), but without it, no one would envisage commencing.

Objective 7 : All Suppliers under Contract

Making sure that all the suppliers working with the company have a valid contract aiming at decreasing the business risk. A side effect, may also be a "natural selection", (i.e. not all suppliers may be able or willing to fulfill the company's terms and conditions), which will lead to an increased use of a smaller number of (preferred) suppliers.

6.2. Strategic Alternatives and Selection

The strategy definition consists in identifying all the routes presented to a company, and choosing the one that will best bring it to its goals.

Strategic Alternative 1 : Decentralization

Let each Business Line resolve the problems in its own way, at a country level.

PRO's :	CON's :
• No direct investments occurring outside of profit and loss (P&L) domains (Business Lines and countries are typically P&L carriers).	• Different, uncoordinated and immature procurement strategies are developed by Business Lines at country levels, • Impossible to achieve economies of scale, Difficult to implement effective global strategic partnerships with suppliers (the same supplier may be approached by different Business Lines, or country Purchasers).

Strategic Alternative 2 : Coordinate
Have Business Lines participate in strategic and operational planning with central Purchasing, (defining and implementing common strategies for improvement, etc.).

PRO's :	CON's :
• No imposed "dictatorial" approach.	• Unclear responsibilities (overlapping domains between a central CP Purchaser and a Business Line), • Still difficult to achieve economies of scale. Requires a lot of coordination in planning (objectives, measurements, strategies).

Strategic Alternative 3 : Outsource Procurement
Outsource all the CP procurement activities.

The Question of Core Activity. In the objectives defined earlier, the aspect of building long-term supplier relationships has been developed. Envisioning the possibility of creating a sustainable competitive advantage, by tightening the relationships with CP suppliers, implies that the role of Purchasing is strategic (Akacum 1995). The expected results from the partnership are for the supplier : obtain more business, benefit from mutual learning (market knowledge, customer need information, business processes, etc.), and, for the company : obtain the best people (contractees), faster, and to the best conditions. The resulting knowledge embodied in the individuals (CP Purchasers), should be translated into an accessible company asset (that subject is elaborated later in this paper). Another aspect that has been discussed earlier is the Political/Legal environment. Tracking the performance of individuals, retaining and utilizing the obtained information is strictly regulated by most European countries. For that and all the above, outsourcing CP Purchasing is not the way to go.

Strategic Alternative 4 : Regroup and Focus
Divide CP procurement and management resources into two highly focused entities : (1) A single-point-of-contact CP Service Administration Group, (2) A highly-skilled CP Purchaser Group. Each entity reports to one unique Management Authority.

PRO's :	CON's :
• Best chances for a successful implementation of long-term supplier relationships, • The planned changes aim at improving problems that are common to the whole company from a centralized approach, • Two distinct entities, relieving Purchasers from the administrative burden, and requesters (Managers) from lengthy and costly search tasks, • Single source for defining and implementing the best CP acquisition related strategies, • Easier to fix purchasing goals and measure the achievements globally, • Individuals can better be motivated (career path, sense of belonging, challenge, responsibilities, etc.).	• Implies change, i.e. organizational trauma, • May not be in line with organizational strategy, i.e. "Business Lines are responsible for developing processes to support their objectives", • Senior management exposure in case of failure (those who will go for the change).

Strategy Selection

Based on the PRO's exposed previously, the strategic alternative 4 is selected because it promises the highest degree of improvement. The concerns showed in the CON's will be addressed in section 7. But first, we look in gaining the confidence in the objectives, which is the subject of the next section.

6.3. Testing the Objectives

Cost reduction is a major concern of every private company. Reducing costs by exploiting the leverage-effect-potential is a typical practice used in Purchasing. It consists in reducing the supplier base, and buying more from the remaining suppliers with a volume discount. To increase the leverage effect in subsequent years, objective 1 and objective 2 (see section 6.1), have been defined as : "increase the number of preferred suppliers" and "increase the spending with preferred suppliers to 50%", respectively. It means that the preferred suppliers would be rewarded with additional business in exchange of a volume discount. Fixing objective 2 at 50% is somewhat arbitrary; it raises questions that are addressed hereafter.

Questions about the Objectives:

– How much work has to be moved from non-preferred to preferred suppliers to reach objective 2 ?
– Is objective 2 realistic or not ?
– What are the savings and is it worth the effort ?

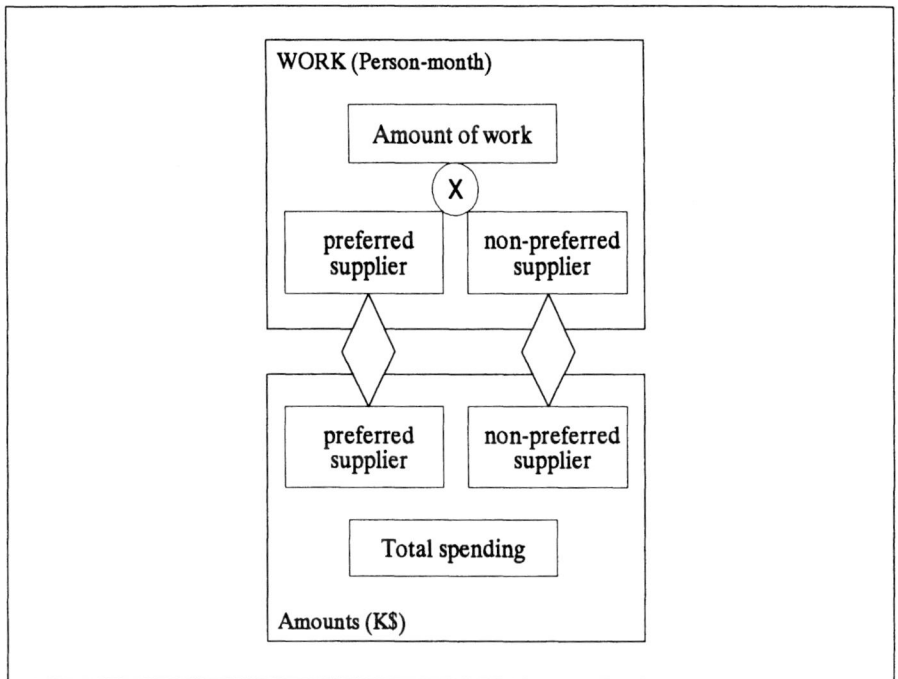

Fig. 6: Leverage-Effect System

To provide answers to these questions in multiple contexts, (i.e. different CP categories, different countries, pace of implementation, varying need for CP, etc.), we model and simulate the portion of the acquisition system that mimics the leverage effect. We use a dynamic modeling tool, allowing time and space compression. The tool we have used is called ithink® and comes from High Performance Systems Inc.

Fig. 6 is a representation of the leverage-effect system. There are two main parts : "WORK (measured in Person-month)" and "Amounts (K$)". The vertical unit translation from the upper to the lower part takes place when WORK is multiplied by a monthly rate for the WORK procured, (i.e. Person-month x K$ per Person-month). There are also two main columns : preferred supplier and non-preferred supplier. The circle with an "X" in its middle and surrounded by the rectangles "Amount of work", "preferred supplier" and "non-preferred supplier" splits the amount of work between the two columns.

Leverage-Effect Model, Simulations and Results:
The system diagram (Fig. 6) is mapped and modeled with ithink® : this step consists in laying out the infrastructure with stocks and flows. The resulting Leverage-Effect Model is shown in Fig. 7. Then the parameters are programmed. We hypothesize a set of data representing :

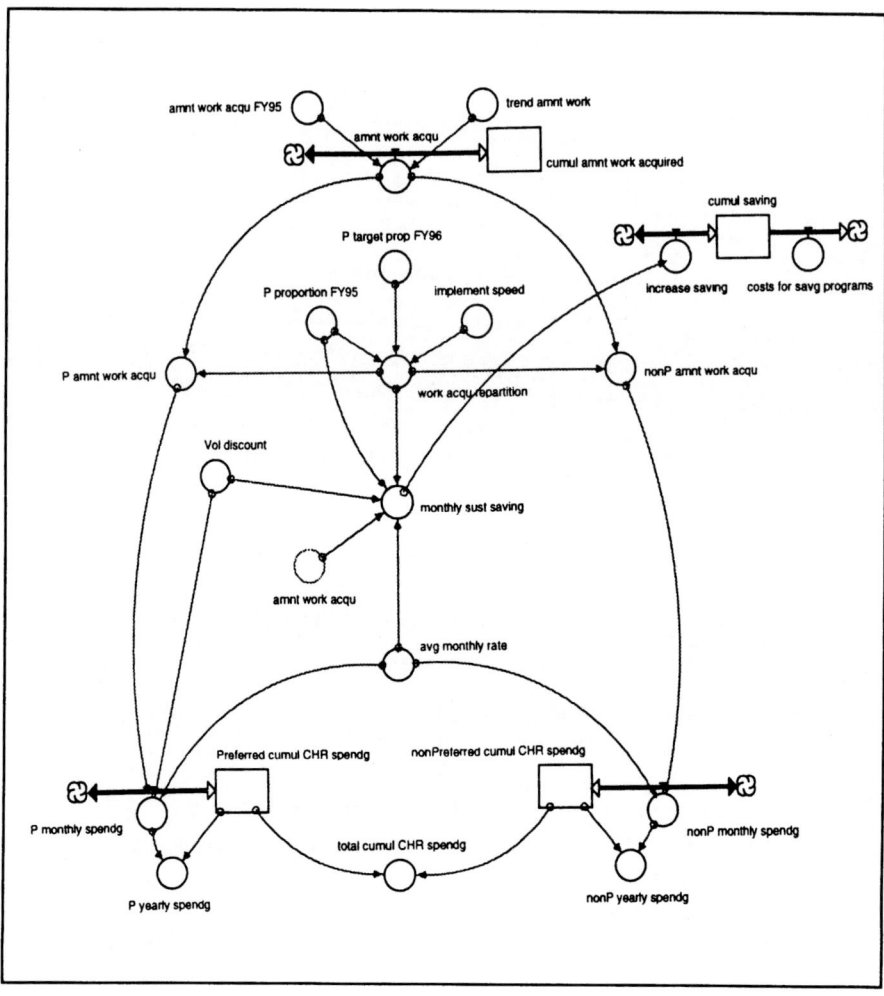

Fig. 7: Leverage-Effect Model

- The system's initial state (based on historical data) :
  - last year's total spending for CP in Europe : $200 million,
  - last year's spending with preferred suppliers : $57 million (28.5% of total spending),
  - last year's volume discount obtained from the preferred suppliers : 10%,
  - last year's average monthly rate for each Person-month procured : 12.8K$ (80$ hourly rate x 8 hours x 20 days),
  - last year's amount of work procured : 16'120 Person-months. This is calculated as the amount of work from preferred suppliers which was 4'948 Person-months ($57mio divided by : 12.8K$ minus 10%) plus the amount of work from non-preferred suppliers which was 11'172 Person-months ($200mio minus $57mio, divided by 12.8K$),

- last year's proportion of work from preferred suppliers : 0.31 (4'948 divided by 16'120 Person-months). A proportion of work of 0.31 means that 3 out of 10 CP Person-months have been procured from preferred suppliers.
- The system's state change (based on 12-month projected data) :
  - preferred suppliers' volume discount : 10% (same as the year before),
  - next year's average monthly CP rate : 12.8K$ (same as the year before),
  - amount of work procured : 16'120 Person-months (same as the year before),
  - proportion of work sourced through preferred versus non-preferred suppliers : variable that will be set to different values during the simulation process, until objective 2 is reached,
  - "system inertia" : When the field (Purchasers) is told that it has to spend 50% of the total spending for CP, with preferred suppliers, it is going to take some time to implement one change. To account for this in our model, we apply a fifth-order exponential smooth to any increase of the last year's initial value "proportion work preferred versus non-preferred" (the exponential's "averaging time" used in our model is 5 months).
- The system's results (data that will provide answers to our questions) :
  - total cumulated CP spending,
  - cumulated spending with preferred suppliers (objective 2),
  - cumulated saving.

Fig. 8 shows the system state change we want to simulate.

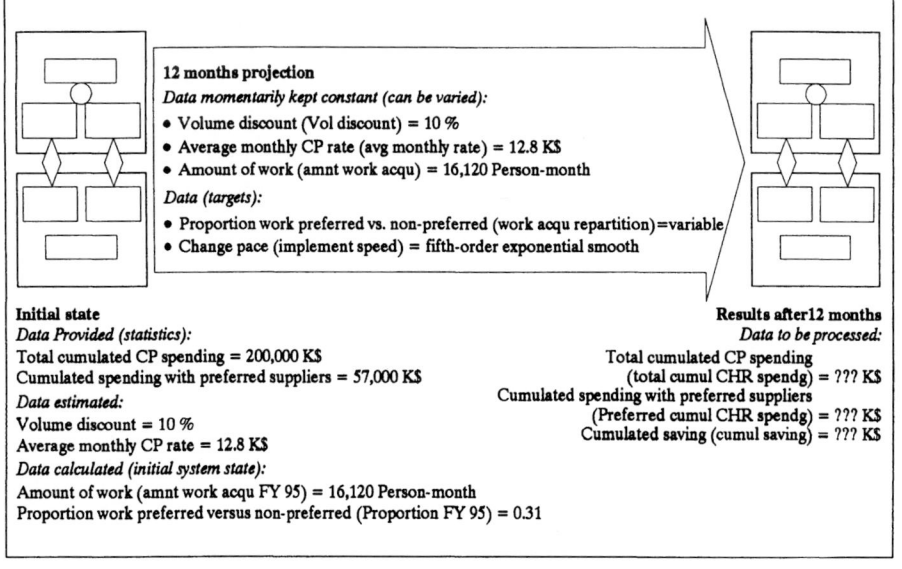

Fig. 8: Leverage-Effect System: State Change

The first, run over a 12 months period which was made with a target "proportion of work from preferred suppliers" of 0.5, curve 1 in Fig. 9 shows how it smoothly changes from 0.31 to 0.5. Curve 2 represents the cumulated $ amount spent with preferred suppliers. We see that it reaches only about $80 million in month 12, which is about 40% of the total spending (curve 3); 10% short of objective 2 (see section 6.1). After several more trials, we find that objective 2 can be attained with a target "proportion of work from preferred suppliers" of 0.68 (see Fig. 10).

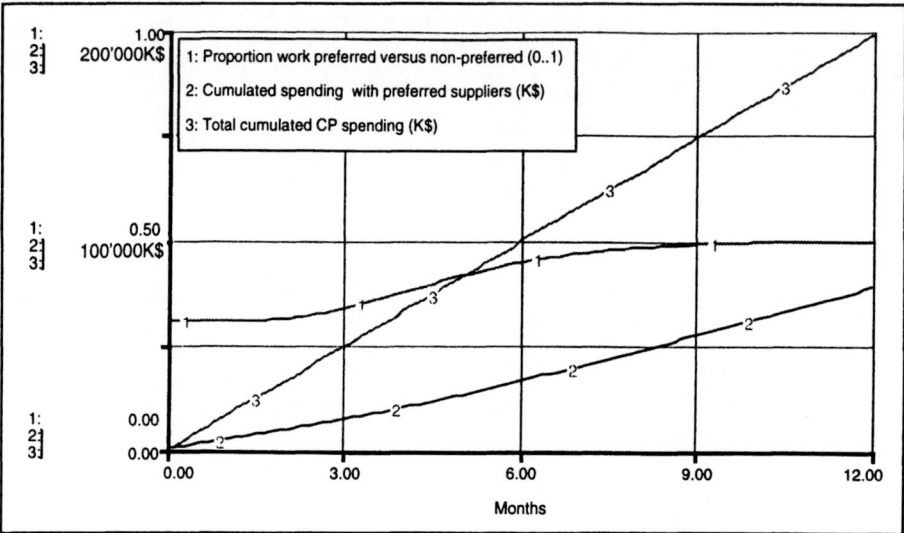

Fig. 9: Leverage-Effect System Simulation 1

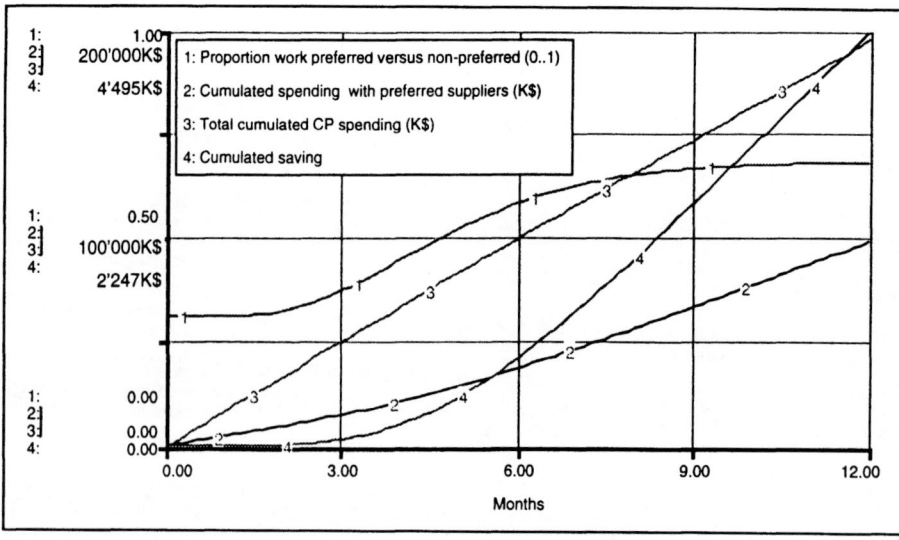

Fig. 10: Leverage-Effect System Simulation 2

Given all the assumptions previously made, this means that to reach objective 2, a target of 7 out of 10 CP Person-months from preferred supplier(s) should be pursued. The curve number 4 in Fig. 10 shows the saving during the whole period which cumulates at $4.495 million at the end of month 12.

Changing some or all the projected data, (volume discount, average monthly CP rate, total amount of work, change pace), will allow to verify the pertinence of objective 2 under different circumstances, and help to comprehend the system's behavior. Yet is our model rather simple. There are several aspects that have not been considered. But modeling is a rolling process : new elements can continuously be added. Useful extensions are :
- Types of CP : Contract Labor, Contractors, Consultants. This level of detail would enable to assign more realistic values to the "average monthly rate" and the "volume discount" for each type of CP,
- The country dimension : develop one "Leverage-Effect Model" per country and interconnect them. This step would permit to set a detailed leverage-effect objective at the country level and take wage variations into account,
- Net saving, i.e. show the net saving (saving minus costs of saving-program) directly in the model by adding a "cost-saving-program-system" into the model,
- Other saving systems (such as "export work from high to low wage countries),
- CP-organization (people and processes) and embed it into the model.

Conclusions about Systems Modeling:
Systems modeling is about creating microworlds. It is a powerful method to better understand our environment, and the interrelationships of the elements that constitute the system. The dynamics of the system are studied by playing with the microworld (simulating the model). The learning resulting from microworlds can be great and it is increasingly used to extend a company's knowledge. Senge regards microworlds as the technology of the learning organization (Senge 1994, p. 313).

6.4. Organizational Structure

The organizational structure of the Purchasing function is the key in implementing the recommended strategy (see section 6.2). Building the two entities "CP Service Administration Group" and "CP Purchaser Group", is represented in Fig. 11. CP acquisition (CPA) individuals are spread among the countries and grouped in the two dedicated entities. CPA entities in the countries report to the central Purchasing function, but are remote-managed by local Finance/Purchasing functions. The dotted line relating HRO to "CP Administration Service" indicates that synergies could be pursued in CPA administration activities, (HRO and CPA have similar tasks when it comes, for example, to assessing a person's performance).

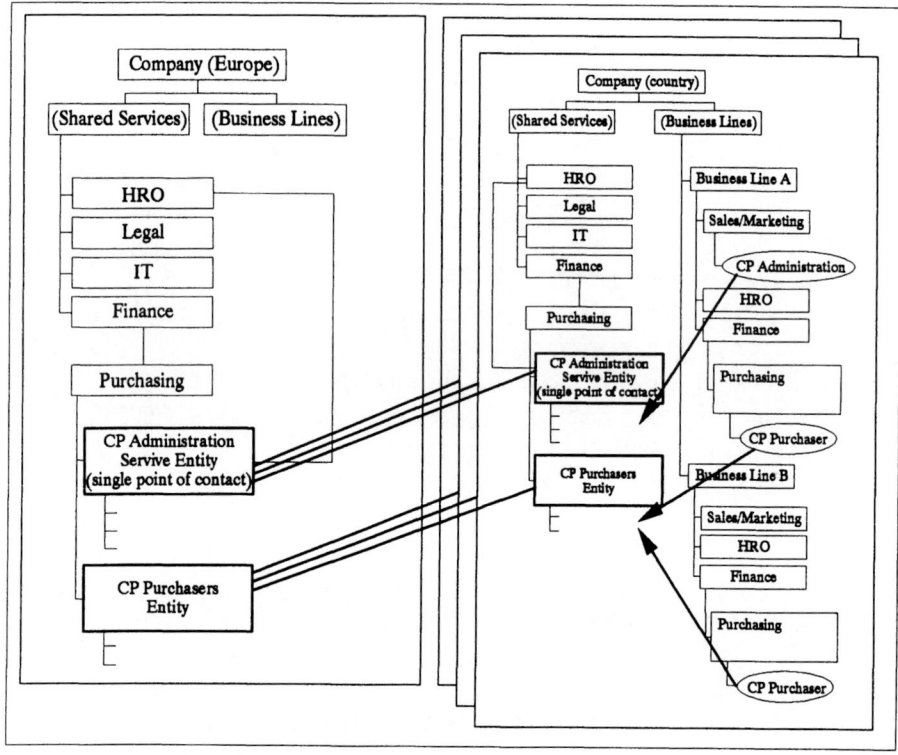

Fig. 11: Purchasing Organization Chart

The CP Purchaser is sole responsible for supplier selection (negotiation, contracting, risk management), supplier development (supplier management, quality insurance/TQM) and assessment of the "CP Administration" entity. He is also co-responsible, together with CP Administration, for requester satisfaction. The "highly focused CP Purchaser" we advocate means that he will have to spend most of his time with his suppliers, requesters (company internal), and possibly, company's external customers. The CP Purchaser is also responsible for learning from comparison. He builds up relationships with Purchasers from other organizations, exchanges information and shares knowledge (Benchmarking). Performance measurements for the CP Purchaser ought to be defined in two domains: quantitative goals (objective 2 defined earlier), and qualitative goals (supplier satisfaction, requester satisfaction).

CP Administration Service Entity: This is the single point of contact for all CP requests. It relies on IT (Decision Support Systems - DSS) for finding the best sourcing solution, i.e. the best supplier, the best candidate. CP Administration provides Management with the reports they need (Management Information System - MIS). It also has the role of the "guard" for the CP knowledge repository (see section 6.5.). The Service entity is responsible for the availability of up-to-date supplier and contractees information. Performance measurement is based on the service they provide, for instance, response time, placement timing, requester and customer satisfaction, etc.

6.5. IT and Purchasing

Brandmier demonstrates that the chances for success are maximized (1000% Return on Investment - ROI) when a high degree of change in Management is combined with a high degree of change in Technology (Belardo 1995). If the degree of change in technology is high, and the degree in management is low, then the ROI is 10%; and if it is the other way around, (high degree of change in management and low in technology) the ROI is 100%. To support the strategy recommended earlier (see section 6.2), a state-of-the-art IT solution has to be developed. There are two main areas in CPA where IT has to be applied :

(1) **Reporting**: provides CP related information, i.e. "how much has been spent for consultants with supplier X in the last quarter ?". This kind of information is statistical. It is provided by applications generally called MIS (Management Information System),

(2) **Operational Decision Making**: supports CP related decisions. It mainly helps find the best contractees and the best suppliers to execute a specific work. The application analyses various inputs (i.e. suppliers' and CP's capabilities, costs, etc.) and produces a list of candidates from which to choose. This kind of application is usually called DSS (Decision Support System).

The information pyramid hierarchy is represented in Fig. 12 (Belardo 1995). The levels to concentrate on for CPA activities are the first three from the bottom, as described.

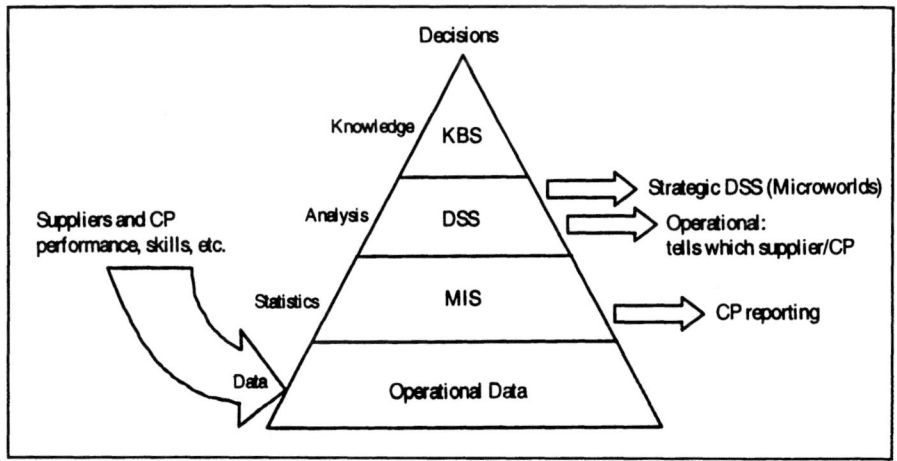

Source: Adapted from Belardo 1995.

Fig. 12: The Information Pyramid

Operational data includes information about suppliers and CP. It should be the responsibility of the CP Administrator and the CP Purchaser to collect information about the contractees and the suppliers, respectively. In general, the data collected for each case should be reasonably significant but short, such as to keep operations effective and efficient. The CP Administrator, together with the requester, assesses, for example the contractees' skills, performance, billing rate, etc. and enters the information into the database. On his side, the CP Purchaser tracks the suppliers' capabilities (qualitative, technical, commercial) and reports the information to be entered into the database.

The DSS solution proposed here is situated at an operational level. Its functionality can be extended by adding conceptual business models (i.e. the Leverage-Effect Model developed in the section 6.3.), enabling Managers to test strategies and objectives (run sensitivity or "what-if" analyses). The use of such Strategic DSS (Belardo et al. 1994) accelerates learning for example by creating a common systems understanding among team members or enabling players to simulate the future effects of their decisions.

With the support of IT, the following benefits can be expected :
- Process improvements such as : (1) faster ordering process (DSS provides immediate supplier/candidate screening), (2) easier and more flexible CP reporting (MIS generated reports include all the relevant, up-to-date statistics needed by the management),
- Direct cost reduction through the automatic sourcing preference given to preferred suppliers (with whom volume prices have been negotiated),
- Indirect cost reduction because the requesters do not spend their time searching for possible candidates: they go directly to the much more efficient centralized professional sourcing service,
- Steady sharable knowledge increase due to the ability to effectively track, store and retrieve supplier and CP performance data,
- Reliable supplier data due to CPA applications providing a focused work frame to CP staff,
- Motivated Purchasers because their administrative burden has been replaced by more interesting tasks, such as supplier management.

7. Inducing Change Successfully

7.1. What Changes ?

Implementing the strategy means inducing change in a system, and being ready to deal with the system's response. The organizational structure and the IT advocated previously, will certainly generate organizational trauma if not handled properly. Before defining a change strategy to avoid this trauma, one may first identify the parties impacted by the change.

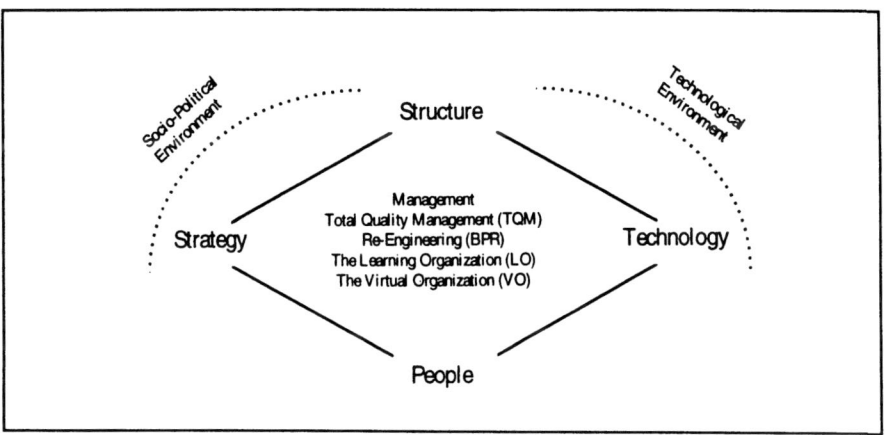

Source: Adapted from Belardo 1995.

Fig. 13: Managing Change - The Scott Morton Model

7.2. Who is Impacted by Change ?

Targets can be grouped into 3 categories: (1) Individuals (ex. Business Line Managers, CP Purchasers, etc.), (2) Groups (ex. MIS Department, Finance, Legal, HRO, etc.), and (3) Organizations (ex. Business Lines, CP Suppliers, Unions, etc.). Different approaches to change : the "psychological approach", "social psychological" and "sociological approach" are to be associated with the targets Individual, Group and Organization, respectively, as suggested by Sashkin and Morris (1984) (Belardo 1995).

7.3. The Strategy for Change

General strategies for change can be can be grouped in three categories: (1) Empirical-Rational, (2) Normative-Re-Educative and (3) Power Coercive. **Power Coercive** strategies are based on the assumption that power is legitimate : authority can be used to influence people. **Empirical-Rational** strategies are built upon the assumption that people are guided by reason: they will adopt change if they are made knowledgeable. **Normative-Re-Educative** strategies assume that the underlying norms that motivate people to take actions are of socio-cultural type (Making people more knowledgeable is not enough for change to be adopted: the attitudes, values, skills, etc. have to be addressed first).

7.4. Managing the Change

The Scott-Morton Model depicts the way for managing change (see Fig. 13). "Structure" covers the organization and the processes (control, measurement, co-ordination); "Technology" is about CPA information systems; and "People" deals with tasks, assessments; "Strategy". New Age Management Techniques are briefly reviewed in the context of what we intend to achieve. Relevant characteristics are pointed out and related to where they may be of use.

Benchmarking is a business management technique aimed at achieving competitive advantage by learning from comparison. Benchmarks can be carried out on two levels: strategic benchmarking and process benchmarking. Process benchmarking focuses on aspects such as delivery performance, customer service, order fulfillment, etc. Strategic benchmarking compares values at the business level such as profit potential, shareholder value or innovation potential. On a process level, it would be interesting to know for example: (1) How many staffing specialists do Ford's PeopleNET use, and how much spending do these specialists manage?, (2) How wide is the supply base and how many dedicated Purchasers work on it?, (3) How do the processes perform (speed, quality, costs)?, etc.

Total Quality Management (TQM). TQM was born in the production process environment and has moved to virtually all types of processes since (ex. customer service, software development). TQM's underlying idea is that all employees can contribute to raise quality. The conclusion is that employees have to be placed in a favorable environment enabling them to produce quality, i.e. they are "empowered". For assessing quality, an international quality accreditation standard, ISO 9000 has been created. Purchasing is also concerned with TQM because quality begins upstream, where the acquired products and services are produced. The CP supplier management program proposed earlier (see objective 3) includes TQM aspects.

Business Process Reengineering (BPR). Reengineering calls for asking fundamental questions about the business: "what is the company here for?", "if we were starting from scratch, what would we look like ?" Reengineering is a dramatic approach to change business processes (Hammer 1990). To be successful, it uses an imposed top-down procedure. BPR and TQM are incompatible, i.e. they cannot take place at the same time, rather they are used sequentially. In our situation, we did not opt for a complete redesign of everything in Purchasing.

Learning Organization (LO). The LO is discussed in section 7.6.

Virtual Organization (VO). In section 2 we briefly exposed the advantages and drawbacks of the VO. Even though purchasing staff are spread among many countries, they are still "white-collar" employees in the sense that they remain on-site workers. Their "sense of belonging" goes first to the Business Line they work for, then to their country, and finally to the "virtual Purchasing organization". Regrouping those people in the entities as we suggest it with strategy 4 (see section 6.2) would strengthen their sense of belonging in favor of the virtual Purchasing organization.

7.5. Who is Responsible for Change?

Obtaining the active support of Senior Management is a critical success factor for beginning to implement change. According to Kotter, step 1 of a BPR effort consists in "Establishing a Sense of Urgency" by sharing concerns, (actual and potential crises, but also major opportunities), with concerned managers and "form a powerful guiding coalition", a group with enough power to lead the change effort (Kotter 1995). Senior positions in the organization to be brought together are : the European CP Purchasing Manager and Business Line Managers of the pilot country(ies). The European Purchasing Manager should be the project's sponsor who obtains Senior Management's "green light" to go ahead with the necessary funding. But not to forget are the employees themselves who know what needs to be done to improve operations; they should be made responsible for communicating with the hierarchy. This becomes obvious when one knows "The Iceberg of Ignorance", whereby problems known by first-line employees, reach supervisors, general supervisors and top Managers at a penetration rate of 74%, 9% and 4%, respectively (Whiteley 1991).

7.6. Purchasing: a Learning Organization ?

The Learning Organization (LO) is about the conscious acceleration of learning. It must be "conscious" because learning requires reflection, as expressed by Handy: "The Wheel of Learning is a circle that rotates from Question -> Theory -> Test -> Reflection, and back to Question" (Handy 1991). According to Handy and many other authors, the acceleration of organizational learning is becoming THE competitive differentiator of the decade.

Learning activities take place simultaneously within three overlapping spheres : (1) the Individual Sphere (by reading, experimenting), the Team Sphere (by sharing experiences with colleagues, suppliers, customers), and (3) the System Sphere (by developing systemic processes to acquire, retain, use, and communicate organizational learning).

What is essential to a LO can best be summarized with Senge's five disciplines : "Personal Mastery", "Mental Models", "Shared Vision", "Team Learning" and "Systems Thinking" (Senge 1994, p.5). All the disciplines are to be developed consecutively as a whole. Their interrelationship can be seen as the following : Systems Thinking integrates the whole, but, it requires Team Learning; Team Learning requires individuals committed to Personal Mastery; learning takes place at the personal, team, and organizational levels when Mental Models are unearthed, changed, and shared; and finally, the learning is accelerated when personal, team, and organizational Visions are Shared.

Who is responsible for learning? Everyone. Extending on "Who is Responsible for Change?", we suggest the following:

- Every individual has to take responsibility for his own life (be proactive),
- The Organization. European Purchasing is responsible for providing the structures (tools, resources, etc.) to CPA,
- The leaders. Leaders are responsible for (1) building organizations where people can continually expand their capabilities, (2) creating a climate of openness where divergent views are encouraged, (3) coaching, i.e. helping people to gain more insightful views of current reality (instead of teaching them the "correct" view of reality), (4) listening and asking questions: build trust because the human dimension prevails over the technical side of a problem.

How we can best encourage learning in the CPA context is contained in following tips:
- "The only thing that is constant, is Change". Therefore concentrate on change, get used to it,
- Encourage experimentation. Individuals and companies learn from mistakes. Senge says "A mistake is an event, the full benefit of which has not yet been turned to your advantage" (Senge 1994). But, for mistakes (and successes) to be a learning vector, companies have to develop mechanisms to store and retrieve related information,
- Another dimension is the "learning lab" that enables experimental learning. As it is generally recognized that learning by playing is a good way to learn, "microworlds" are developed for Managers to play with the reality. The main advantage of computer based microworlds (such as ithink®) is the possibility to compress time and space. The demonstration of its power is provided in section 6.3.,
- Learn from the external environment. Customers, suppliers, other companies are among the most important entities for focusing learning. Suppliers and CP requesters understand each others needs and the best ways to satisfy them in a win-win perspective,
- Intentionally acquire, share, and utilize organizational memory to enable learning from past experience. Lessons about successes and failures have to be recorded for later reviewing. Because CP suppliers will always exist, it makes sense to build a system that enables learning from experience as described in section 6.5.

7.7. The Change Process

The **Implementation** steps are described in the steps below:
- Establish a sense of urgency and decide whether something needs to be done or not,
- Name a leader - "a senior executive who authorizes and motivates the overall reengineering effort" (Hammer 1994, p.102),
- Name a project Manager,

- Build a cross functional team (i.e. Business Lines, central Purchasing, HRO, IT) with the task to design the new entities (CP Service Administration Group and CP Purchasers Group) and define the specifications of the CP applications. Some aspects of this process are: (1) Build a shared vision, (2) Encourage people to adopt different mental models that better reflect competitive and workplace realities, (3) Establish a budget,
- Obtain approval and funding from senior management,
- Develop CP acquisition applications,
- Implement changes in pilot countries and monitor for one year,
- Analyze results and deploy the model in other countries.

Finally, there are two other programs that are not directly linked to the change process, but are worth being pursued: (1) set up a benchmarks partner and compare the processes, and (2) introduce the use of a systems modeling and simulation tool.

7.8. Barriers to Overcome

Finally some **potential problems** are discussed:
- Overcome the 7 learning disabilities (Senge 1994, p.17):
  - "I am my position" and "The enemy is out there": people with little sense of responsibility for the results produced when all positions interact. For example, Business Lines' disinterest in a global approach to optimize the leverage effect,
  - "The illusion of taking charge": being proactive is often seen as an antidote of being reactive. True proactiveness comes from seeing how we contribute to our own problems. For example, see the reasons why Business Lines and countries tend to build their own CP acquisition procedures,
  - "The fixation on events": if people's thinking is dominated by short term events, they cannot learn how to create,
  - "The parable of the boiled frog": pay attention to the subtle as well as the dramatic. For example, that a rapid increase in knowledge will be the key competitive differentiator in the next decades,
  - "The delusion of learning from experience": people learn best from experience, but they never directly experience the consequences of many of their important decisions. The use of a systems modeling and simulation tools (microworlds) can help compress time and space,
  - "The myth of the management team": all too often, teams in business tend to spend their time fighting for turf ... and pretending that everyone is behind the team's collective strategy, maintaining the appearance of a collective team.
- Overcome fragmentation: CPA is a systemic major challenge. It should not be fragmented into pieces and resolved at this level,
- Beware cross-functional barriers: CPA knowledge has to be gathered, stored and utilized on a broad base, across functions, Business Lines, and countries, Change results in organizational trauma and loss of trust.

A **set of solutions** is provided as an idea compendium to help dealing with the above shortfalls (Belardo 1995):
- Lewin and Schein change model (Unfreeze-Change-Refreeze),
- Covey's 7 habits: be proactive, begin with the end in mind, prioritize, think win/win, seek first to understand then to be understood, synergize, reflect on what you are doing,
- Bennet's 10 virtues: self discipline, compassion, responsibility, friendship, work, courage, perseverance, honesty, loyalty, faith,
- Bary's 10 core values: caring, honesty, accountability, promise keeping, pursuit of excellence, loyalty, fairness, integrity, respect for others, responsible citizenship,
- Belardo's ethical organization: is based on trust building. The ethical organization value principles are:
  - inclusiveness (distribute responsibility, seek ways to create synergy),
  - consistency (choose a task worthy your efforts, believe in yourself, set standards high),
  - truthtelling (admit mistakes quickly and publicly, humility is the best guarantor of truth, do not give the impression of stealth or impropriety),
  - discipline (know your limits, establish goals and make them explicit, make your goals and your performance public).

8. Conclusion

The report started off with the "core company" and the "pressure on prices", as two of the major companies' concerns today's globalizing economy. To stay profitable and to survive, companies are evolving. In this context, we have looked at the particular aspect of acquiring and managing Contract Personnel (CP) in Europe, and we have demonstrated that the Purchasing function had a key role to play in these processes. A CP acquisition concept, aiming at reducing direct and indirect costs, at developing strategic supplier partnerships, and at accelerating the learning process, is proposed and tested. The scope of the present paper could be extended further with the Benchmarking. It would be interesting, for example, to learn more about other companies' CP acquisition processes and Purchasing organizations, (ex. how many staffing specialists do they employ, and how much spending do these specialists manage?, how are the processes performed with regard to speed, quality, costs?, etc...). In essence, we have seen that to work professionally and to contribute effectively to the company's challenges, the procurement and management of CP has to be performed by dedicated service entities supported by specific IT applications.

Bibliography:

Akacum, A., Dale, B.G. (1995), Supplier Partnering : Case Study Experiences, in : International Journal of Purchasing and Materials Management, January 1995, pp.38-44

Belardo, S. (1995), The Key to Succeeding in a Global Economy : Human Knowledge as Capital, in: presentation handout to Workshop I of the V. Zürcher Management Kongress organized by GSBA-Zurich, Zurich, 15. September 1995

Belardo, S., Duchessi P., Coleman, J.R. (1994), A Strategic Decision Support System at Orell Fussli, Jounal of Management Information Systems. Spring 1994, Vol. 10, No 4, pp.135-157

Ford (1993), PeopleNET, Video by Ford, USA 1993

Gasser, A. J. (1995), Purchasing as Profit Maker, Aarau 1995

Graham, T., Daugherty, P.J., Dudley, W.N. (1994), The Long Term Strategic Impact of Purchasing Partnerships, in: International Journal of Purchasing and Materials Management, October 1994, pp.13-18

Hammer, M. (1990), Reengineering Work : Don't Automate, Obliterate, in: Harvard Business Review, July-August 1990, pp.104-112

Hammer, M., Champy, J. (1994), Reengineering the Corporation : a manifesto for business revolution, New York 1994

Handy, Ch. (1991), The Age of Unreason, Harward University Press, Cambridge 1991

Kotter, J.P. (1995), Leading Change : Why Transformation Efforts Fail, in: Harvard Business Review, March-April 1995, pp.59-67

Sashkin, M., Morris, W. C. (1984), Organizational behavior : Concepts and experiences, Englewood Cliffs 1984

Scheuing, E.E. (1989), Purchasing Management, Englewood Cliffs 1989

Senge, P.M. (1994), The Fifth Discipline : the Art and Practice of the Learning Organization, New York 1994

Union Bank of Switzerland - UBS (1994), Prices and Earnings Around the Globe, Zurich 1994

Whiteley, R.C. (1991), The Customer-Driven Company : A Road Map for Competitive Advantage, Addison-Wesley 1991

Implementation of a Tactical Strategy in China by a German Company

Godwin Wong
Peter Oswald

Zusammenfassung:

China bietet für viele Anbieter ein enormes Marktpotential. Auch wenn in China der Wettbewerb immer noch vor allem über den Preis ausgetragen wird, so werden doch Güter mit passenden Kundennutzen durch ein entsprechendes Premium honoriert. Unterschiede in der Kultur und im 'chinesischen' Kundennutzen, sowie das spezifische Umfeld, erfordern eine adaptive Strategie. Eine Change Management Denke, um Dinge 'besser' und 'anders' zu tun als der Wettbewerb, ist zwingend notwendig. Nur so können vorhandene Chancen voll genutzt werden.

1. Introduction

The vast population of China and the country's economic growth over the past decade has created a huge market with enormous potential. The growth of Gross Domestic Product (GDP) in the China averaged more than 10% in the last six years (Fig. 1) and will be around 11% in 1997. This rapid growth has translated into China's foreign reserves of US$ 123 billion (July 1997, without Hong Kong), second only to Japan worldwide (USA: US$ 55 billion). The inflation was below 10% in 1996 and continues to decline in 1997.

Cultural differences make it difficult for western firms to get a foothold in this market. If one is to simply classify the Chinese culture and the German culture into two rough categories, the Chinese culture can be considered as „reactive", which are those cultures that prioritize courtesy and respect, listening quietly and calmly to their interlocutors and reacting carefully to the other side's proposal. The German are more „linear-actives", those who plan, schedule, organize, pursue action chains, do one thing at a time (Lewis 1996, p. 5). But characterizing a national culture does not mean that every person in the nation has all characteristics assigned to that culture (Hofstede 1992, p. 225). It is only but a simply generalization. Every business, regardless of its size, product or service, faces in China a marketplace of ever-increasing competition and complexity. Most organizations have to make significant changes on a continuing basis in a way they do

174

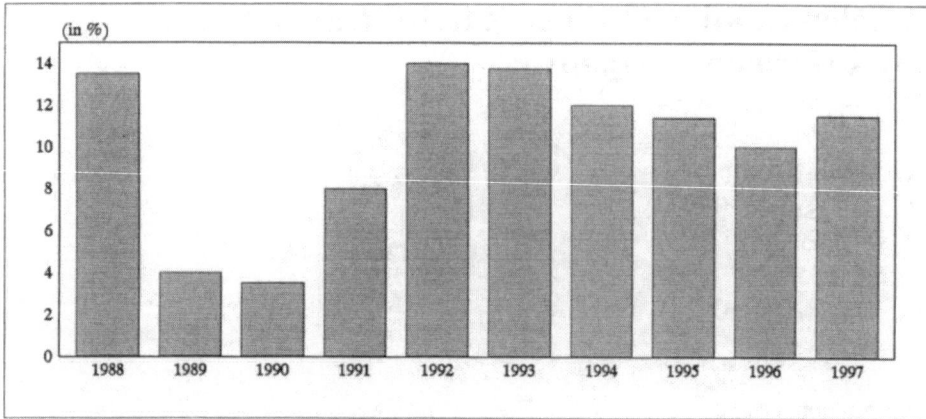

Source: n. a. 1996; n. a. 1997.

Fig. 1: China´s Percentage of GDP Growth

business in order to successfully compete in this difficult environment. Interwoven into the discussion in this paper is the experience of Brückner, the world-leading German manufacturer of biaxial film stretching systems.

Successful companies like Brückner have learned over the past few years that they have to make major changes in their organization, focus, use of people, and design and delivery of products and services. Companies which are serious about their performance must commit to making change a key element in the culture of their company, and they have to understand that the change drivers are in the market and cannot be ignored.

2. Business Environment in China

As China is a centrally governed country, most of the macro environment forces are determined by the government.

2.1. China's Way of Reforming

The political peace in China depends mainly on how successful a reform or change will be managed. William Overholt explained the basics of China's success by comparing its strategy with that of the Soviet Union. The differences between Chinese and Soviet performance derive from profoundly different economic and political strategies. Much of the West long believed a myth that China was an impoverished version of the Soviet Union which must inexorably follow the latter's failures - because, after all, both were communist countries. On the contrary, China has been following a model of development more similar to South Korea than to its formerly communist comrades. (Overholt 1993, p. 5-6).

2.2. Political and Social Stability

Jiang Zemin, who has succeeded Deng Xiaoping, got his legitimacy from his appointment by Deng Xiaoping. Jiang Zemin (Party Leader and State President) has emerged as the dominant person, and is a 'first among equals' for several years within a narrow circle of two or three top leaders, like Li Peng (Premier) and Zhu Rongji (Senior Vice Premier). All news indicates that state president and party chief Jiang Zemin is consolidating his position and one can expect a collective leadership with a stable policy.

Further inflation and the deepening reforms have led to an increase in inequalities. According to official statistics, the average urban income was 3 times higher than the average rural income in 1994, while the ratio was only 1.8 in 1978, and 2.9 in 1993. A survey done in 1994 showed that the average yearly income of a farm peasant was 678 Yuan against 2,221 for a person who worked in town (Beja 1995, p. 117). Despite these inequalities - as far as the rural income is growing too and nutrition is secured for this group - no serious instability has occurred.

2.3. Economic Environment

A consensus is emerging among economists that China's leaders have finally adopted a more unified, realistic strategy for setting the nation on the road to sustainable economic growth. China enjoyed a GDP increase of 9.7% in 1996. Over the period 1978-1994, real gross national product (GNP) growth in China has averaged some 9% per annum, about triple the rate recorded by the advanced economies grouped in the Organization for Economic Cooperation and Development (OECD). Among the world's leading exporting economies, China rose from thirty-second in 1979 to eleventh place in 1995 (3% of total world export). The Chinese have become quite money-minded (Soledad 1997, p. 32).

2.4. Exchange Control

China pursues a policy of centralized control and unified management of foreign exchange by the state. The Bank of China is the specialized foreign exchange bank. Other financial institutions may engage in foreign exchange transactions only with the approval of the State Administration of Exchange Control (SAEC). The Chinese currency, Renmimbi, is not a freely convertible currency, although China is planning to introduce free convertibility gradually in preparation for its membership application to the WTO (People's Republic of China 1995). Since 1996, the Renmimbi is convertible for 'current accounts'.

2.5. The Chinese Consumer Market

If one focuses only on the urban population in China, this market comprises approximately 100 million households, which use cigarettes, personal-care products such as soap, toothpaste and shampoo - wrapped in packaging material - every day (Cromie 1995, p.33). Household incomes in China are highly disposable. Purchasing power of household income in urban China is relatively higher than other developing markets, because many basic household expenses such as housing, transportation, medical care and education are covered by the state or work unit.

2.6. Business Mentality and Values

It is usually the case that for each contract, several quotations from different suppliers will be solicited in the beginning. The standard procedure is to select the two or three lowest offers and launch parallel negotiations with these suppliers. Companies with superior technology but high prices will be told that they will also have to compete on price. The Chinese believe foreigners should pay handsomely for the privilege of being in China and doing business there. They see no contradiction in charging everything the market will bear. Their rationale is that foreigners are there for their own selfish motives, to make profit, and can leave if they do not want to pay the price (De Mente 1994, p. 177). Chinese managers have been shown to be relatively risk-aversive. With their limited financial resources and their less experience as buyer, the Chinese place more emphasis on purchase value, than customers from other countries (Tse 1996, p. 357 ff.). Chinese see collective welfare and social concern as more important than personal enjoyment and feeling. They value social and moral goals more than personal goals and competence (Bond 1991, p. 38).

3. A Case in Action: Brückner

3.1. Brückner Maschinenbau GmbH

The German firm Brückner is the world-leading manufacturer of biaxial film stretching systems for use in factories. Brückner's core competencies are in designing these complex machines, finding the suppliers of the hardware, then putting everything together. To be close to the customer Brückner established subsidiaries in the USA, France, Great Britain and Hong Kong (Brückner Far East). For more than 30 years, Brückner has been active in the Chinese market. Fig. 2 shows the total sales from the whole German Plastic and Rubber Machinery Industry to China between 1983 and 1995. Brückner's average market share of the overall industry supply was around 15%.

Brückner's turnover in the eighties and early nineties was on average around 150 mill Deutsche Mark. This figure has doubled in the recent years, with the Chinese market being a major contributor towards this growth. Brückner's annual turnover has in the last six years been between 150 and 320 million DM worldwide and between 15 and 120 million DM in China. Sales in China have averaged about 35-40% of worldwide sales over the last years (Fig. 3).

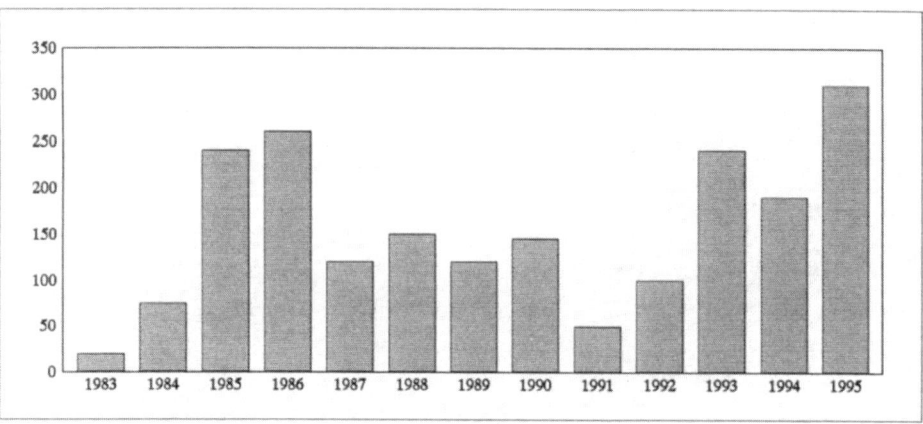

Source: n. a. 1996b.

Fig. 2: German Export of Rubber and Plastic Machinery to China

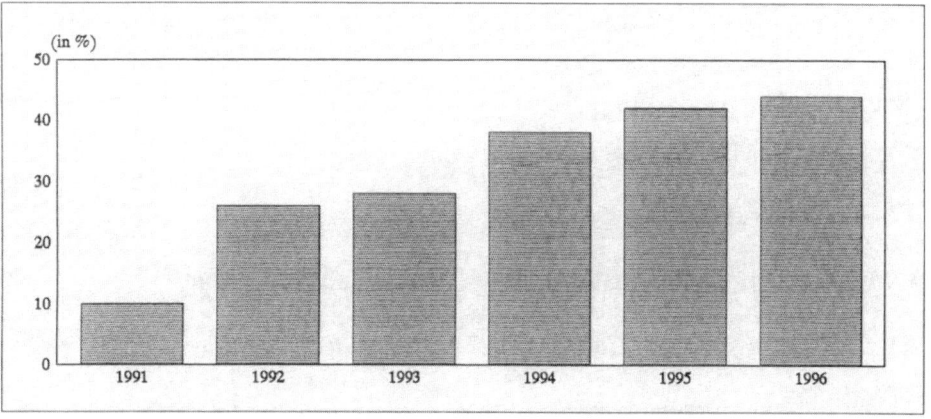

Fig. 3: Brückner's Portion of China Sales to Total Sales

3.2. Change Management to Match the Chinese Market

With change management thinking, Brückner produced breakthrough results in the Chinese market. Brückner focused on the 'Chinese' customer delivered value and aligned its strategy with the Chinese value system. The total customer value is the bundle of benefits customers expect from a given product (Fig. 4). As different cultures judge the single benefits differently, the products and services have to be adjusted to the Chinese market. Based on Brückner's experience, the Chinese customers associate with product value the attributes 'quality & reliability' and they appreciate very much the service value. The investment costs has to meet their tight limited budget. The expendable costs are secondary.

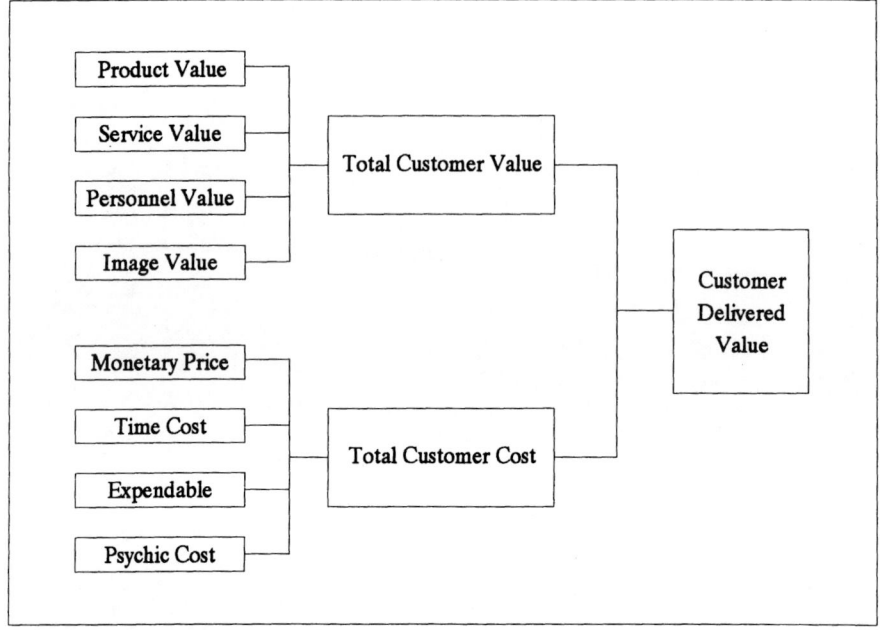

Source: Kotler 1994, p. 38.

Fig. 4: Factors Determining Customer Value

4. Management Change: How to Reduce Costs and Add Value

4.1. Corporate Strategy: Cost Saving Through Local Manufacturing

To **reduce manufacturing costs** and to enable the customer to save a portion of import tax, Brückner manufactures certain parts in China. To achieve the required quality standard, to keep schedules and to save know-how, one has to be deeply involved. The involvement in the manufacturing process can be a quasi-backward integration for some companies. A selective backward integration may lower the costs and put pressure on competitors who cannot afford such integration (Porter 1980, p. 210). To avoid costly investments in manufacturing facilities, the easiest way for Brückner was to cooperate with qualified manufacturers within China.

4.2. Business Strategy: Differentiation through Superior Product Support Service

To **add value,** corporate strategy should enable a company to perform one or more of the value-creation functions at a lower cost, or perform one or more of the value-creation functions in a way that allows for differentiation and a premium price (Hill 1995, p. 257 ff.). Brückner's business strategy does not only focus on

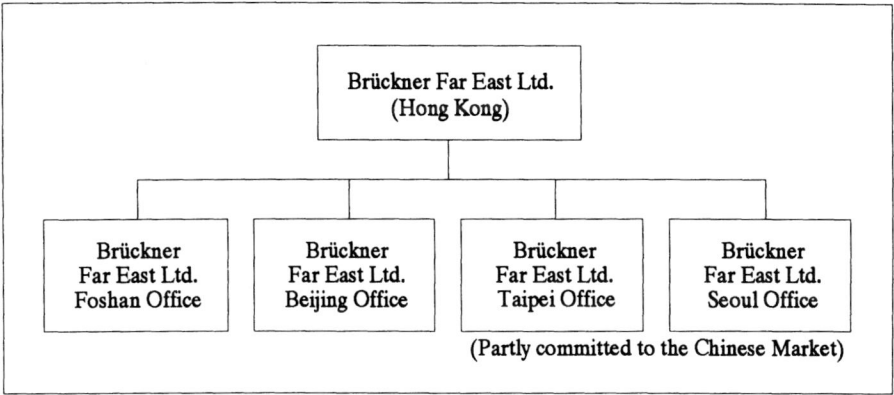

Fig. 5: Brückner's Organization to Serve the Chinese Customer

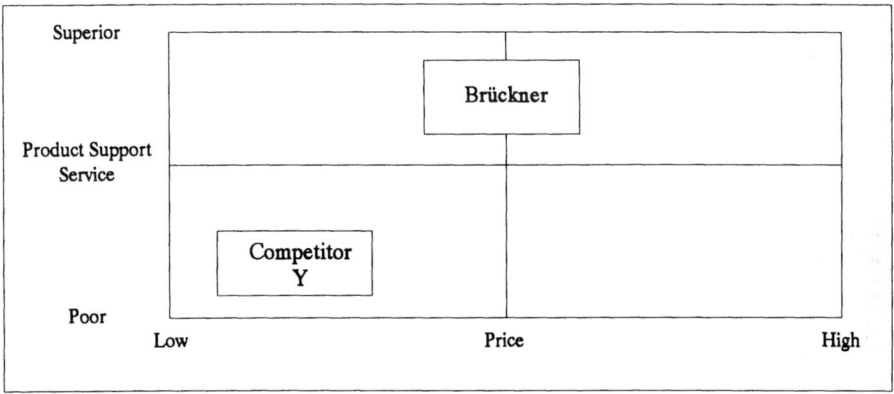

Fig. 6: Positioning of Brückner on the Chinese Market

the cost in order to minimize the total customer cost, but also differentiate, to **maximize the total customer value.** The most important way - where Brückner gained competitive advantages - was and is the Product Support Service.

Brueckner Far East is running five offices in Far East (Fig. 5), three of those are exclusively taking care of the Chinese customers. The other two offices are partly committed to China. In order to close the cultural gap, to be really close to the customer and to find a common understanding, most of the Brueckner Far East staff is Chinese. The positioning - as shown in Fig. 6 - in the medium price segment still allows Brückner to reap a premium through differentiation on service quality.

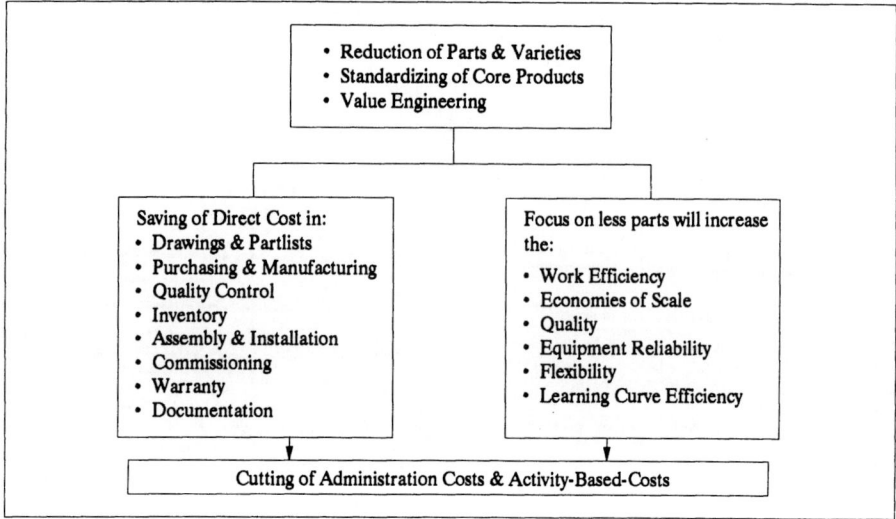

Source: Oswald 1997.

Fig. 7: Cost Cutting Through Reduction of Parts & Varieties

4.3. Functional Strategy: Value Engineering and Standardized Core Products

Some German firms at times seem to be more technology driven than customer driven. This results in over engineered products, which the Chinese customers do not see and appreciate all the advantages and they are not willing to pay a higher price for it. Brückner continuously investigates how **to cut costs** in order to bring more profitable equipment to the Chinese market not only with the right level of quality and functionality, but also with appropriate prices for the Chinese customer. Companies have to design the cost out of their products when they set initial levels of quality and functionality in order to gain and hold the market leadership (Cooper/Chew 1996, p. 88). This can be achieved by reducing the number of parts and through value engineering in order to gain economies in parts and manufacturing. The latter is focusing on reducing the varieties. By reducing the number of parts, not only the material cost of the 'eliminated' parts has to be considered (Fig. 7), but also other direct and indirect costs - like activity based costs (quality control costs, etc.) - caused by those within the process chain.

A further cost benefit was achieved by standardizing core products or large parts of it, while customizing peripheral or parts of the product. Reducing the amount of equipment allows Brückner to focus on the smaller number of products, which will improve the quality of the products themselves. The design of the core product (Fig. 8) has to focus on the biggest common need of the customers and the peripheral parts can be optionally added and implemented modularly in the production line.

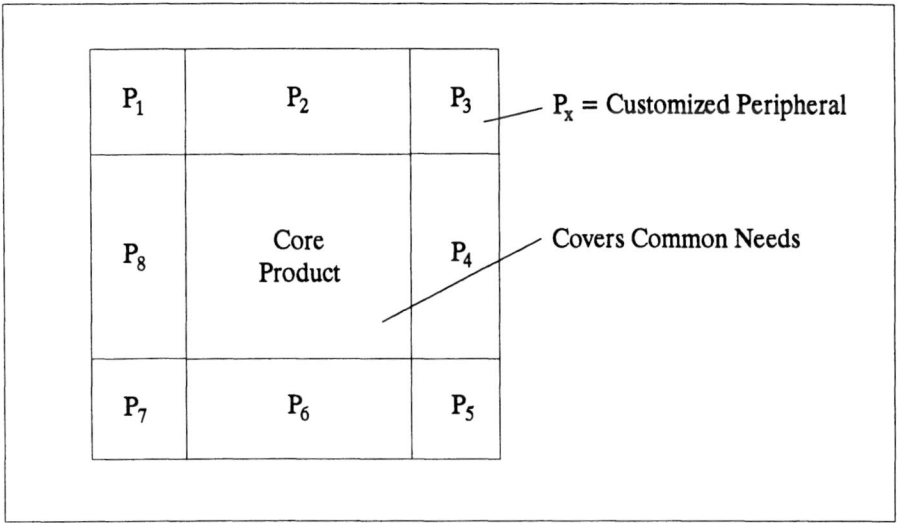

Source: Oswald 1997.

Fig. 8: Cost Saving Through Standardized Core Products

4.4. Results

Brückner's strategy in China focuses on a superior product support service, value engineering, standardized core products, its core competencies, local manufacturing, understanding of Chinese business culture, and making changes within Brückner to accommodate the needs and requirements of the Chinese. The strategy mix, will not only bring down the customer's monetary price and the expendable cost, but also increase the product and service value (Fig. 9). Brückner is not only performing similar activities, but also performing similar activities 'different' from its competitors. 'Better' means competing on cost and price, and 'different' means competing on customer service. Simon analyzed in his book 'Hidden Champions': While the hidden champions adjust performance to customer's requirements, their main selling point is superior value not price. Service also plays an important role in the value they deliver (Simon 1996, p.113).

The evidence that Brückner is right with its approach is indicated by its position as market leader in China with a market share above 60%. The other 40% are shared by four to five competitors. Based on this success, Brückner Far East grew from a small liaison office to an organization with different branches as seen in Fig. 5 earlier.

182

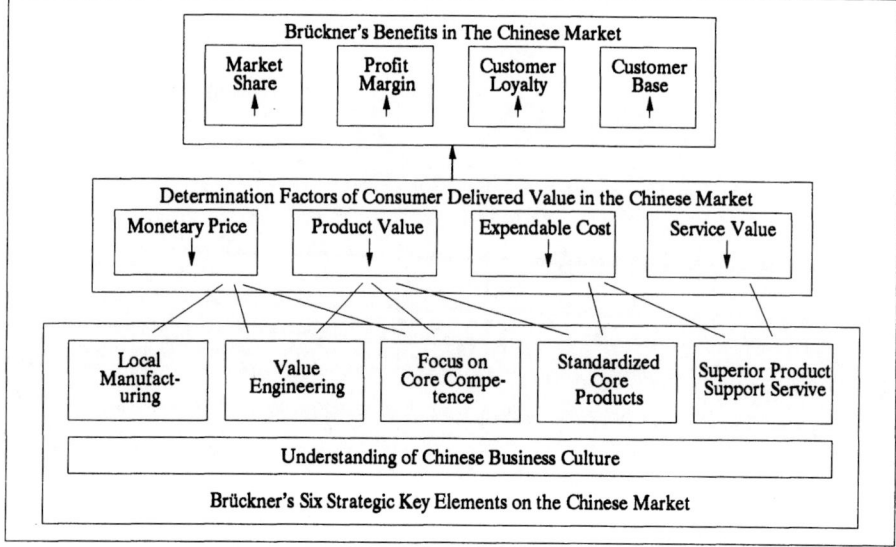

Source: Oswald 1997.

Fig. 9: Brückner's Six Strategic Key Elements on The Chinese Market

5. Recommendations

5.1. Product Design and Manufacturing

The aforementioned strategy will force companies to move from a product driven to a customer driven company. The more the business becomes customer driven, the more important it is that the business achieves a local match with its market. It means understanding how the products and services appeal to the customers and there environment. Core products, which focus on fundamental needs common to all countries - such as reliability and economy - can be marketed globally with minimal modifications. Furthermore, companies should also benefit from a global strategy, in order to reap competitive advantage on the global market place. Global strategy should be the flexible combination of many elements (Yip 1992, p. 2).

Every functional or value-adding activity, from R&D to manufacturing to customer service, is an opportunity for globalization. The extreme global strategy as shown in Fig. 10 would mean that companies spread all their value-adding-activities in countries where the costs are minimal but within the same result. Of course such a big step cannot be done overnight and the extreme global strategy does not fit in every business. But the strategy can be tailored to individual needs and will deliver a higher competitive advantage than without this approach.

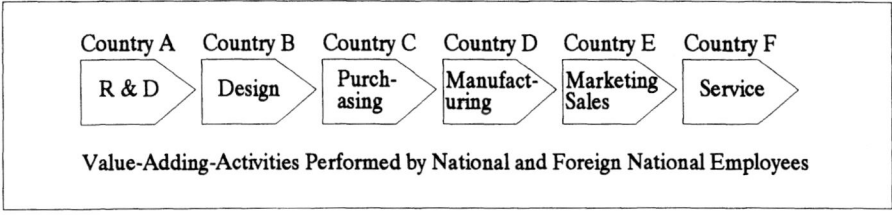

Source: Oswald 1997.

Fig. 10: Extreme Global Strategy

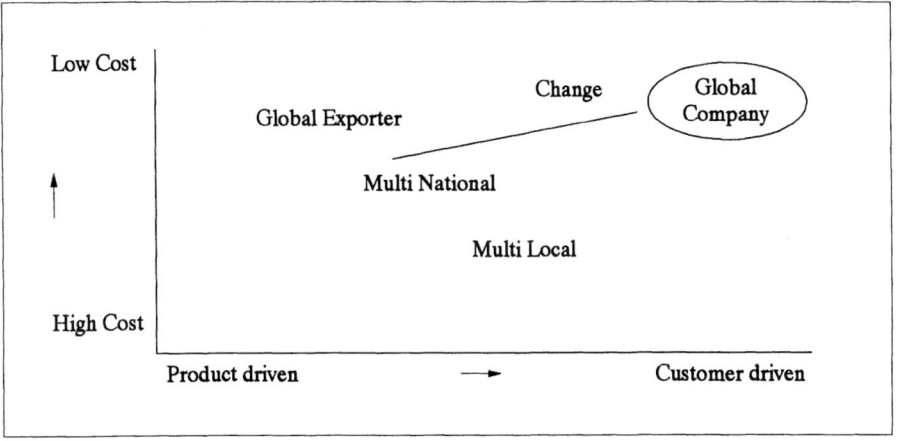

Source: Daniels 1994, p. 24.

Fig. 11: Change to a Global Company

The major difficulties of organizing a company for global operations lies in the psychology of managers who are used to thinking by a country-based line of authority rather than by line of opportunity. Lots of creative ideas for generating value are overlooked because such managers are captive to nation/state-conditioned habits of mind (Ohmae 1995, p. 112). However there is a risk associated with the creation of a global mindset at the top only, or among a selected group of people only (Dowling/Schuler/Welch 1994, p. 215). The globalization strategy enable companies to move from a product driven and rather high cost company to a customer driven and low cost company (Fig. 11).

5.2. Different Ways to Invest in China

Companies which want to enhance their presence in China have different possibilities:
- Service Center,
- Representative Office,

- Wholly Foreign Owned Enterprise (WFOE),
- Equity Joint Venture,
- Cooperative Joint Venture.

Service centers may provide after-sales service, maintenance, and spare parts for machinery and equipment sold to end-users in China. But service centers themselves are not permitted to market the main products that they service. Service centers have an independent legal person status in China and therefore must have a separate name, articles of association, registered capital and at least eight full-time staff. Revenues from service centers may be shared between Chinese and foreign parties in accordance with contract stipulations.

Representative offices are the easiest and the most popular method of maintaining a fixed presence in China, but strict limits apply to their scope of operations. Basically, representative offices may not engage in 'direct business operations'. They may, however, engage in promotional and support activities on behalf of their head offices.

Wholly foreign-owned enterprises (WFOE) involve equity from only one or more foreign parties. Unlike joint ventures, WFOEs have no Chinese partners or shareholders. The scope of operations of wholly foreign-owned enterprises is more restricted than for equity or cooperative joint ventures e.g. WFOEs are generally prohibited from engaging in service industries and focus on manufacturing plants for high-quality products. Wholly foreign owned enterprises are Chinese legal persons with limited liabilities.

Equity joint ventures (EJV) are separate entities with a Chinese legal person status and limited liability. Equity joint venture law requires that equity joint venture contracts be governed by Chinese law. EJVs have the right to hire and fire Chinese employees, to own and use property, and to independently engage in management and production activities within their permitted scope of operations. Risks, profits and liability are shared strictly in accordance with the individual capital contributions of the parties. Foreign parties are required to contribute at least 25% of a joint venture's total registered capital.

Cooperative joint ventures (CJV) have to be export oriented or technologically advanced. Generally two types of CJVs are possible: a 'pure' CJV and a 'hybrid' CJV. A pure cooperative joint venture does not have a separate legal identity. It is, in effect, a partnership with each party jointly and severally liable for its operations. Taxes, profits, management and other operational matters are handled as specified in detail in the joint venture contract. A hybrid CJV shares some characteristics of an equity joint venture. It is a separate Chinese legal person and has limited liability. Profits may be distributed as agreed by the parties, and other operational matters are handled as specified in the joint venture contract.

The **right organization** to realize local manufacturing and to establish a superior service organization, firms should consider two different forms of business organization. To establish a service organization one could open a Service Center or a Representative Office in South China. Since the representative office can be established very easily and without any PRC-partner, this organization form is recommended. The right organization form for local manufacturing should allow firms to use its company name, which will also mean the parts can be declared 'Made by ....' and to avoid any fixed assets investments. Only the CJV, only the hybrid cooperative joint venture allows one to use its company name (e.g. .... China Ltd.) as this form has a separate Chinese legal identity. The most important and most critical issue in establishing a joint venture is to find the right partner.

5.3. Major Issues Upon Entry into China

The choice of the right partner is most critical to the success of a joint venture. Potential partners will undoubtedly be judged on a range of criteria, but in the Chinese context, there are two which must not be neglected: a genuine commitment to working with the foreign partner in an honest business relationship, and strong relationship with the different levels of government which are necessary to facilitate the joint venture company to be able to work. Most foreign-investment projects do not require national approvals, even then it is worthwhile for the foreign partner to open and maintain channels to the central government (Batey 1994, p. 111). The key to a successful joint venture is a relationship of trust with the partner. Chinese tend to do business with friends, and the best way to do business is to become friends. To avoid the 'same bed, different dreams' phenomenon, foreign investors have to be direct and frank about their objectives in entering into a joint venture.

To develop a balanced set of allegiances, the expatriate managers must first develop a clear set of objectives that are acceptable to both partners and periodically updated. Next, the expatriate must be given considerable autonomy and discretion in implementing these objectives. A high level of discretion gives the expatriate the flexibility to resolve conflicting objectives in ways that benefit the joint venture and, consequently, both contracting parties (Hamrick 1995, p.165). Expatriate managers must balance Western management methods and concepts with Chinese styles. In regard to the cultural differences and the newly created cooperation, it is clear that as much as possible has to be considered and fixed in the joint venture contract, but the most important success factor is TRUST. There is usually an inverse relationship between rules and trust: The more people depend on rules to regulate their interactions, the less they trust each other and vice versa. To build up trust, both parties have to understand their partners' culture (Fukuyama 1995, p. 8).

The German Business Association (GBA) made a survey in 1996 to find out some major experience made by foreign parties in founding and running a joint venture

Company	1	2	3	4	5
City in CHINA	Shunde	Shanghai	Zhaoqing	Xiamen	Liuzhou
JV-Form	CJV	CJV	CJV	EJV	EJV
Major Incentive to Found a JV	distribution network of PRC-partner	growing market, avoid import barriers	growing market, avoid import barriers	growing market, avoid import barriers	growing market, avoid import barriers
Shares	60 %	100 %	100 %	55%	51 %
Searching for CHINA-Partner	company own selection	company own selection	company own selection	provincial government	company own selection
JV-Contract Negotiation	company own lawyer	external lawyer	external lawyer	company's management	external lawyer
Production Focus	to keep the quality standard	to keep the quality standard	to keep the quality standard	customized & quality	to keep the quality standard
Recommendation	to hold the majority	to hold the majority	a high majority	a high majority	training of local staff

Source: GBA 1996.

Fig. 12: Experiences of German JV-Partners

in China. The essential features and feed backs are listed in Fig. 12. Note that the German partners all have major shareholder status.

5.4. Strategic Audit to Control Change Management

The evaluation of the validity of the new strategy must not be based simply on the performance of its competitors on the Chinese market, but rather on comparison between returns derived from the actual strategy and those from the proposed strategy. A major problem in evaluating strategic performance is that all information they receive passes through the filter of management perspective (Gordon 1995, p. 105). Since a maximization of the profit margin will result in a declining market share and vice versa, both data have to be considered together and an optimum of both values has to be aspired to have. The results and the strategy have to be reviewed in strategic audit as mapped out in Fig. 13. The frequency of such meetings should be once every three years. It has to be considered that these meetings should not be so frequent that strategic review is confused with an operating review or that the minor changes in key indicators are incorrectly interpreted as significant trends. Simultaneously the organization has to provide an ongoing support of 'doing things better and differently' once the changes are implemented.

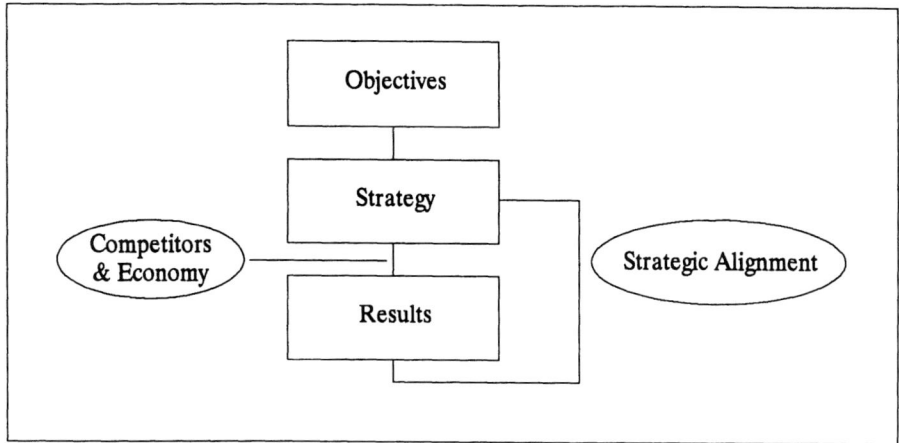

Source: Oswald 1997.

Fig. 13: Strategic Audit

Bibliography:

Barnard, G. (1995), Cross-Cultural Communication: A Practical Guide, London 1995

Barrington, S. (1997), Canada Speaks to Chinese Markets: Vancouver Takes on Flavor of Hong Kong, in: Advertising Age, Vol. 68, No. 2, Jan.13, 1997, p. I12

Batey, P. (1995), Doing Business in China, Selecting a Joint Venture Partner, New York u.a. 1995

Beja, J. P (1995), The Year of the Dog: In the Shadow of the Ailing Patriarch, in: China Review 1995, The Chinese University Press 1995

Bond, M.H. (1991), Beyond the Chinese Face: Insights from Psychology, Oxford University Press 1991

Bristol, M. (1996), Making Connections Between Cultures, in: Social Education, Vol. 60, No. 7, Nov-Dec 1996

Bucknall, K.B. (1994), Culture Guide to Doing Business in China, 1994

Carroll, S. J. (1997), Ethical Dimensions of International Management, 1997

China & North Asia Monitor (1996), Vol. 3, No. 3 , March 1996

Cooper, R.C., Chew, W.B (1996), Control Tomorrow's Costs through Today's Designs, in: Harvard Business Review, January- February 1996

Cromie, R. (1995), Chinese Consumer Market, Doing Business in China, New York u.a. 1995

Daniels, L., Daniels, C. (1994), Global Vision, New York u.a. 1994

De Mente, B. L. (1994), Chinese Etiquette & Ethics in Business, 1994

Deresky, H. (1997), International Management; Managing Across Borders and Cultures, 2nd ed., 1997

Dowling, P.J., Schuler, R.S., Welch, D.E. (1994), International Dimension of Human Resource Management, Belmont 1994

Dresser, N. (1996), Multicultural Manners New Rules of Etiquette for a Changing Society, New York 1996

Earley, P. C. (1997), The Transplanted Executive: Why You Need to Understand How Workers in: Other Countries See the World Differently, New York 1997

English, L. M. (1995), Business Across Cultures Effective Communication Strategies, White Plains 1995

Far Eastern Economic Review (1997), Economic Indicators, Selected Asian Countries, September 1997

Fukuyama, F. (1995), Trust: The Social Virtues and the Creation of Prosperity, London 1995

GBA (1996), Joint Venture Foundation in PRC, German Business Association of Hong Kong 1996

Gordan, D. (1995), A New Tool for Boards: The Strategic Audit, in: Harvard Business Review, July - August 1995

Gross, A., Dyson, P. (1997), China: Managing the Culture Gap, in: HR Focus, Vol. 74, No. 2, Feb. 1997

Gulbro, R., Herbig, P. (1995), Negotiating Successfully in Cross-cultural Situations, in: Industrial Marketing Management, Vol. 25, Issue 3, 1995

Hamrick, C.A. (1995), Doing Business in China, Managing a Manufacturing Enterprise, New York u.a. 1995

Hill, C., W. L., Jones Gareth, R. (1995), Strategic Management Theory, 1995

Ho, Yin-ping (1995), Foreign Trade and China's Growing International Presence, in: China Review 1995, The Chinese University Press 1995

Hofstede, G. (1992), Transnational Management, Motivation, Leadership, and Organization: Do American Theories Apply Abroad?, Irwin 1992

Kotler, P. (1994), Marketing Management, Englewood Cliffs 1994

Lewis, R. D. (1996), When Cultures Collide: Managing Successfully across Cultures, London 1996

n. a. (1996a), China Growth Bit Realistic, in: South China Morning Post, 1996, March 05

n. a. (1996b), German Exort to China, in: China Plastic and Public Journal, 1996, February

Nowak, L., Dong, D. (1997), Intercultural Difference Between Chinese and Americans in: Business, in: Business Communication Quarterly, Vol. 60, No. 1, Mar. 1997, p.115-123,

Ohmae, K. (1995), The End of the Nation State: The Rise of Regional Economies, London 1995

Oswald, P. (1997), Strategic Alignment of a German Plastic Machine Producer with the Chinese Market, Graduate School of Business Administration (GSBA) Zürich 1997

Overholt, W. H. (1993), China: The Next Economic Superpower, London 1993

People's Republic of China (1995), International Tax and Business Guide, Deloitte Touche Tohmatsu International 1995

Porter, M.E. (1980), Competitive Strategy, London 1980

Puffer, S. M. (1996), Management Across Cultures; Insights from Fiction and Practice, Cambridge 1996

Redding, S. G. (1995), International Cultural Differences, Aldershot 1995

Schneider, S. (1997), Managing Across Cultures, London, New York 1997

Schuster, C. P. (1996), Global Business: Planning for Sales and Negotiations, Fort Worth 1996

Simon, H. (1996), Hidden Champions; Lessons from 500 of the World's Best Unknown Companies, in: Harvard Business School Press, 1996

Slate, E. (1993), Success Depends on an Understanding of Cultural Differences, in: HR Focus, Oct., Vol. 70 Issue 10, 1993

Soledad, G. (1997), Asiamoney, June 1997, p. 32.

South China Morning Post (1996), Li Sets Tone for Stable Growth, March 14, 1996

South China Morning Post (1996), WTO Quest Sees Li Promise More Tariff Cuts, March 02, 1996

Tse, D.T. (1996), Understanding Chinese People as Consumers: Past Findings and Future Propositions, in: The Handbook of Chinese Psychology, edited by Bond, M.H., Oxford University Press 1996

Yip, G.S. (1992), Total Global Strategy, Englewood Cliffs 1992

Managing Change in the US Defense Industry
- The Case of Lockheed Martin's Acquisition of Loral

Jonathan B. Welch

Zusammenfassung:

Mit dem Ende des Kalten Krieges war der Verteidigungsetat der USA ständig gesunken. Die Rüstungsindustrie sah sich gezwungen, eine geeignete Anpassungsstrategie zu finden. Manche Firmen blieben wie zuvor im Rüstungsgeschäft, manche zogen sich zurück. Lockheed Corporation andererseits zog eine Wachstumsstrategie auf der Basis von Mergers und Acquisition heran und entwickelte sich zum führenden globalen Unternehmen in der Rüstungsindustrie.

1. Introduction

Driven by concerns over the federal budget deficit and with the Cold War coming to end, the total US defense budget steadily declined between 1985 and 1995. The decline in the portion of the budget that impacts defense contractors decreased from $128 billion to $78 billion. Defense Secretary William Perry made the comment, "We expect companies to go out of business and we will stand by and let that happen." Confronted by the new defense landscape, defense firms had to decide on appropriate strategies. Some tried to maintain the status quo while others decided to liquidate. Lockheed Corporation, on the other hand, decided to grow through acquisition, consolidate, provide turnkey packages and become the leading global company in the industry.

2. The Loral Opportunity

Only a few months after its creation from one of the largest mergers in history between Lockheed and Martin Marietta Corporation, Lockheed Martin (LMT) was faced with an opportunity in 1996 to acquire the defense electronics firm, Loral Corporation, for approximately $9 billion. There appeared to be an excellent strategic fit, in part, because of Loral's focus on what was so important to the future in the defense industry, electronics and international growth. Loral appeared willing to be acquired by the right company at the right price. As the defense industry was becoming a constellation of mega-companies, it may have realized the need to merge to stay at the forefront.

LMT, convinced of a sound strategic fit with Loral, turned its attention to valuing and financing the proposed acquisition. It was under some time pressure to act quickly because other firms were interested in acquiring Loral. Furthermore, government regulators, concerned with the decreasing number of defense firms, might decide to stop the merger wave in the defense industry before the deal could be completed.

3. Valuation

Was $9 billion too high a price to pay? It would be the highest price per dollar of sales revenue (136%) ever paid for a defense firm up to that time. By contrast, in the early 1990s most acquisitions were made at 40%-60% of sales revenue.

One estimate of the "free cash flows" of the business units of Loral that LMT wanted to buy was $600 million per year. This was clearly insufficient to support a $9 billion price tag. Consequently, additional cash flows would have to be realized from integration cost savings, synergies and portfolio shaping.

Integration cost savings were estimated in the $300 million per year range. The areas where these economies might be achieved were extensive: headquarters; centralized services; procurement; data systems; payroll; accounts payable; capital expenditures; R&D; field offices; site consolidation and best practices. Synergies might come in the form of winning contracts that might not have been awarded to LMT without Loral's participation. These additional "wins" could be in the order of $100 million per year.

Portfolio shaping meant divestiture of some non-core businesses as well as excess real estate after the acquisition. For example, the former COO of Loral who had joined LMT with the acquisition, bought a group of former Loral businesses from LMT for $480 million. Another potentially valuable piece of Loral Corporation was Loral Space, the portion of the business involved with satellite systems and telecommunications. Although LMT was required to spin-off Loral Space because of anti-trust concerns, it was able to retain a 20% ownership interest. The upside potential of this piece of the acquisition was appealing for two reasons. First was the growth potential of telecommunications. Secondly, Loral Space would be run by the former Chairman and CEO of Loral, Bernard Schwartz. Schwartz was highly regarded by Wall Street for his ability to create value for shareholders.

When the value of integration cost savings, synergies and portfolio shaping were added to the initial $600 million of "free cash flows", and considering the growth potential of defense electronics internationally, one estimate made by the author of the present value on a discounted cash flow basis of Loral to LMT was $15 billion. All told then, $9 billion appeared to be a fair price for LMT and its shareholders. No wonder LMT's investment bankers, Bear Stearns & Company, provided a favorable fairness opinion.

4. Financing

Arranging the financing was critically important because the transaction did not have a financing contingency - a way out should financing not be available. This was the case because, after appropriate analysis, LMT was highly confident the financial markets would support and fund the deal.

The first cut at the financing decision was choosing the best proportions of debt and equity capital to finance the acquisition. Because LMT was concerned that issuing equity might dilute its EPS, it decided to finance the deal with 100% debt capital. Although using so much debt capital would nearly double its debt ratio from approximately 35% to nearly 70% and place its credit ratings in jeopardy, the finance staff was confident that enough cash flow would be generated after the acquisition to service and pay down the debt quickly and bring the debt ratio back in line with historical levels and industry norms.

The plan was to utilize short term debt initially and then replace it with longer term financing. A backstop bank facility for $10 billion was considered essential both to provide a formally available source to bridge fund the transaction and to provide traditional working capital requirements. J.P. Morgan was given the assignment to line up the banks. From the time the proposed merger was announced on January 7, 1996 to the time of the bank meeting on January 29, 1996, where it was agreed by a syndicate lead by Morgan Guarantee Trust Company, Bank of America and Citibank to provide the required financing, only three weeks had elapsed. This was one of the first signals that financial markets were favorably impressed with the acquisition.

Although bank financing was available, LMT preferred to use commercial paper to bridge fund the transaction because it was cheaper by 5-10 basis points. The subsequent, longer term financing strategy utilized by LMT might best be described as "filling in the yield curve". Financing of the magnitude to acquire Loral was so big relative to the size of financial markets and investor depth that it could even impact yields in the Treasury market. Consequently, LMT spread their financing over a spectrum of maturities where they had gaps.

The first of two issuances of longer term debt for $3.5 billion was planned for May, 1996 and managed by Goldman Sachs. It was an historic issue, being the largest non finance company investment grade debt issue ever. The first issuance was comprised of six tranches with notes due in 1999, 2001 and 2006; and debentures due in 2016, 2026, and 2036. The second issuance was scheduled for $1.5 billion in June, 1996 and was to be led by First Boston. Three tranches included notes due in 1998, 2004 and 2008. Overall the maturity structure was weighted towards rapid repayment.

LMT was effective dealing with the credit rating agencies: Moody's, Standard & Poor's, Duff & Phelps and Fitch Investor Services. The credit agency reviews included detailed discussions not only of the financial impact of the transaction, but about strategic, operating and marketing benefits as well. Each agency took a different perspective on how to weight the quantitative factors vs. the qualitative ones. LMT felt fortunate when Moody's assigned an A3 longer term rating, down from A2. Standard & Poor's announced a rating of BBB+, down from A+. Duff & Phelps and Fitch also assigned an A- rating to the longer term debt. All the agencies assigned the Company's commercial paper '2' level ratings, down from the previous '1' level ratings.

As an example of the impact of lower ratings on financing availability, consider the commercial paper market. Companies with a rating of '1' can finance in a $600 billion market. With a rating of '2' the market shrinks by approximately 90% to $60 billion. This happens because money market mutual funds are limited by internal investment and external regulatory guidelines in the amount they can invest in lower rated paper. Had LMT's ratings been lowered more than they were by the credit rating agencies, it could have made financing difficult especially if overall credit markets conditions simultaneously tightened, or it could have made the cost of financing unattractive.

Another concern for LMT was that while they waited for US and European regulatory reviews of the Loral acquisition to conclude, and before the financing plan could be implemented, the low interest rates that prevailed in January, 1996 would rise. With a multi-billion dollar financing program planned, the exposure was significant. Consequently, they considered an interest rate hedge to protect against rising interest rates. LMT was contemplating putting on one of the largest interest rate hedges in history and engaged the investment banking firm, Goldman Sachs, to provide analytical and advisory services. The objective was to identify and neutralize risk, not speculate.

After careful consideration and review by LMT's Board of Directors, the primary vehicle utilized was a forward swap. Although the technical details are daunting, it worked as follows. An interest rate swap was sold by LMT. As interest rates rose during the first several months of 1996, the value of the swap vehicle declined as do other financial instruments such as Treasury securities when interest rates rise. Several months later, LMT unwound the swap by buying it back at a lower price than they had sold it, thus creating a gain. Overall, LMT had a gain of approximately $150 million on the hedge. Although transaction costs were involved, the gain largely offset the cost of the higher interest rates they had to pay on that portion of the financing program that was hedged.

5. Summary and Concluding Observations

Lockheed Martin's record of managing change in the declining US defense industry is impressive. LMT aggressively pursued its goal to grow through acquisition, consolidate, provide turnkey packages and become the leading global company in the industry. The acquisition of Loral was an integral part of the mosaic.

Effective financial management provided the funding to implement LMT's bold strategic plan. It utilized financial leverage in the Loral acquisition to minimize its cost of capital and maximize shareholder value. The role of investor relations convincing the banks and credit rating agencies about the merits of the acquisition and selling the deal to Wall Street investors was instrumental to its success.

LMT's longer term financial results reflect its "Mission Success" motto described in its Annual Report as "LMT's commitment to provide superior performance and total customer satisfaction in every goal we set and every task we undertake". For example, from March 1995 when the Lockheed-Martin Marietta merger was completed to the present (August 1997), a period including the Loral acquisition, LMT's stock price has doubled. When dividend reinvestment is included, this represents a compound annual rate of growth of approximately 35%. Investors have been enamoured with LMT's ability to manage change.

Recently, Lockheed Martin announced the acquisition of Northrop Grumman for $11.6 billion. With this acquisition, LMT will become a company with $36 billion annual sales and 230,000 employees. The new Company appears to be well positioned for global growth in an industry which increasingly demands economies of scale and cost efficiency. Three major US aerospace-defense companies remain after the recent consolidation: Lockheed Martin; Raytheon; and Boeing/Mcdonnell Douglas. Consequently, any future consolidation may involve companies based in countries outside the US.

Acknowledgment:

This article is based, in part, on a case study prepared by the author entitled, „Lockheed Martin & Loral". The case study benefited form insight provided by Walter E. Skowronski, Vice President & Treasurer, Lockheed Martin Corporation. Errors or omissions in the article are solely the responsibility of the author.

Vierter Teil

Change Management im Marketing

Markenmanagement im Zeitalter von Konzentrationsprozessen und Machtverschiebungen auf mehrstufigen Märkten

Ralph Berndt

Summary:

This article considers typical trends of consumer behavior and retailing and deals with producers of product brands. Concentration processes in the fields of retail and production and the resulting shifts of power at multistage markets are developed. The principles of successful management of product brands are presented with respect to different marketing instruments. The cooperative systems of brand management like category management or efficient consumer response are analysed.

1. Mehrstufige Märkte im Wandel

Betrachtet man die **Distributionssysteme von Konsumgüterherstellern,** so ist der **indirekte Vertrieb** auf mehrstufigen Märkten der Normalfall; der **Direktvertrieb** auf einstufigen Märkten (Beispiele sind Avon Cosmetic oder Eismann-Tiefkühl-Service) ist eher eine Ausnahme in dieser Branche. **Mehrstufige Märkte** werden in der Abb. 1 charakterisiert; sie zeichnen sich tyischerweise aus durch
- eine Vielzahl an Konsumenten (privaten Haushalten),
- eine begrenzte Anzahl an Handelsunternehmen (-ketten), welche Produkte in verschiedenen Kategorien (Warengruppen) anbieten und unter denen ein Konkurrenzkampf besteht,
- eine begrenzte Anzahl an Produzenten, welche Markenartikel aus verschiedenen (Produkt-) Kategorien anbieten und zwischen denen ebenfalls ein Wettbewerb besteht.

Im Vergleich zum Direktvertrieb auf einstufigen Märkten sind beim indirekten Vertrieb auf mehrstufigen Märkten einige Besonderheiten gegeben:
- i.d.R. besteht für einen Produzenten nur die Möglichkeit einer **unverbindlichen Preisempfehlung,** welcher seitens des Handels nicht gefolgt werden muß;
- das Handlungsfeld der **Marketing-Kommunikation** eines Produzenten ist viel breiter;
- es können sowohl eine **Push-Strategie** (konzentrierte Marketing-Maßnahmen gegenüber dem Handel, der den Artikel ordern und seinen Konsumenten anbie-

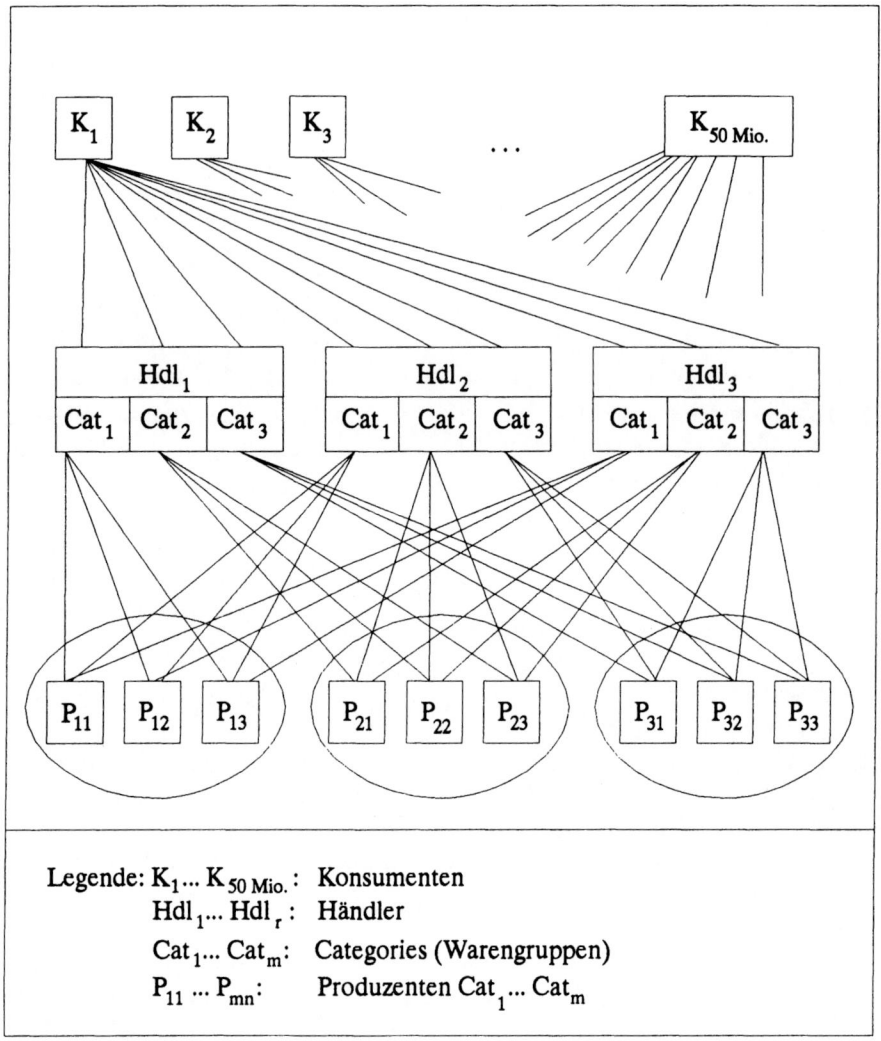

Legende: $K_1 ... K_{50 \text{ Mio.}}$: Konsumenten
Hdl$_1$... Hdl$_r$: Händler
Cat$_1$... Cat$_m$: Categories (Warengruppen)
P_{11} ... P_{mn}: Produzenten Cat$_1$ ... Cat$_m$

Abb. 1: Mehrstufige Märkte

ten soll) oder eine **Pull-Strategie** (konzentrierte Marketing-Maßnahmen gegenüber den Konsumenten, die einen Artikel nachfragen und den Handel dazu bewegen sollen, den Artikel zu ordern) verfolgt werden, wobei **Mischstrategien** denkbar sind.

Grundsätzliches Ziel der Marketing-Maßnahmen sollte es u. a. sein, einen möglichst hohen **Markenwert (Brand Equity)** zu erreichen. Durch die Kennzeichnung eines Produktes (einer Dienstleistung) mit einer Marke versucht der Markeninhaber, sein Angebot gegenüber der Konkurrenz abzuheben. Bei dem Wert einer Marke handelt es sich dabei um einen Nettowert in dem Sinne, daß die auf die Marke (als Markenzeichen) zurückzuführenden ökonomischen Wirkungen (Umsätze, Marktanteile, Gewinne, Kapitalwerte) relevant sind (zu den Ansätzen der Markenbewertung zählen diverse praxisorientierte Verfahren (z. B. das Nielsen-Modell und das Interbrand-Modell) sowie mehrere theoretische Verfahren; i.e. vgl. z. B. Sander 1994; Berndt 1995a, S. 34ff.). Daneben lassen sich **spezifische Marketingziele** eines Markenartikelproduzenten

- gegenüber den Konkurrenten (ökonomische Ziele wie z. B. Gewinn-, Erlös- oder Marktanteilssteigerung sowie psychologische Ziele wie z. B. Imageverbesserung),
- gegenüber dem Handel (wie z. B. Steigerung der Macht auf mehrstufigen Märkten) und
- gegenüber den (einzelnen) Konsumenten (wie z. B. Steigerung der Markentreue)

identifizieren.

Von besonderer Bedeutung sind die **typischen Trends**
- beim Konsumentenverhalten,
- beim Handel und
- bei den Produzenten (Markenartiklern).

Beim **Konsumentenverhalten** sind derzeit national und z.T. auch international folgende Trends zu beachten:
- **stagnierende Kaufkraft** bei sogar sinkenden Realeinkommen,
- **Zukunftssorgen** in manchen Bevölkerungs- (Ziel-)gruppen (z. B. Rentner, Jugendliche, Auszubildende),
- vergleichsweise **geringe Markentreue** - insbesondere dann, wenn funktionale Unterschiede bei konkurrierenden Produkten fehlen,
- **hybrides Konsumverhalten** (preisorientierten Einkauf bei einem Discounter und gleichzeitiger qualitätsorientierter Einkauf bei einer Top-Boutique),
- **Wertewandel** in der Gesellschaft (z. B.stärkere Freizeit-, Gesundheits- und Umweltorientierung),
- **Low Involvement** der Konsumenten gegenüber der Werbung (kein besonderes Interesse an Produktinformationen, die über Werbemaßnahmen vermittelt werden sollen),
- **Informationsüberlastung** der Konsumenten (eine Anzeige im „Stern" wird im Durchschnitt nur 1,9 Sekunden gelesen; 95 % der in Anzeigen enthaltenen Informationen werden nicht wahrgenommen).

Folgende **Handelstrends** können festgestellt werden:
- **Umsatzbegrenzungen** aufgrund der stagnierenden Konsumentennachfrage,
- **Konzentration** im Handel (in den letzten 15 Jahren deutliches Marktanteilswachstum des konzentrativen und kooperativen Handels in Deutschland zu Lasten des nicht-organisierten Handels); im internationalen Rahmen Handelskonzentration durch Firmenaufkäufe und Handelskooperationen (vgl. Abb. 2 und 3),

202

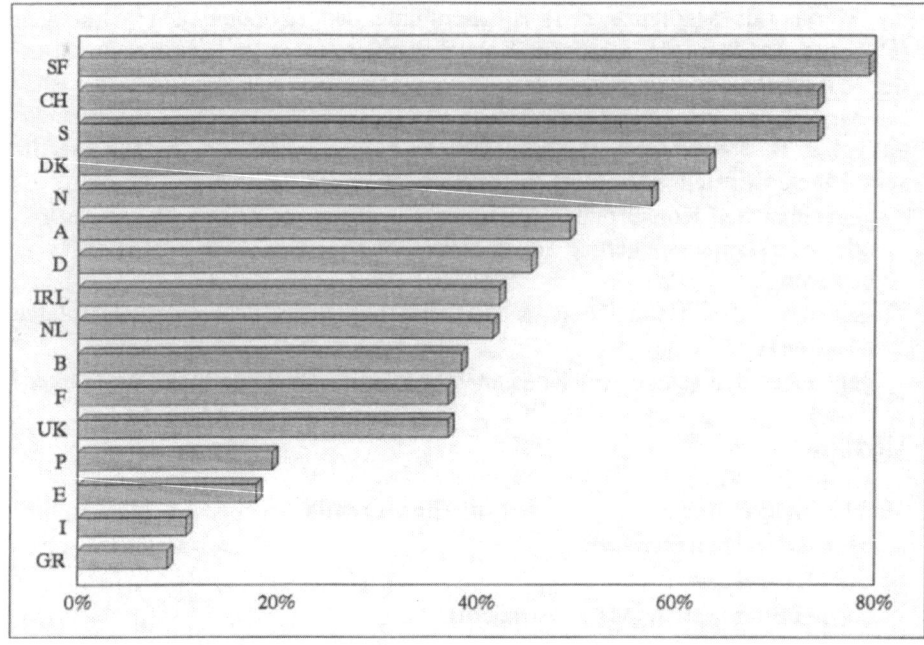

Quelle: Holliger 1994, S. 243.

Abb. 2: Anteil der drei größten Handelsorganisationen pro Land

- weitere **Heterogenität der Betriebsstätten** des Handels (mit einer besonderen Bedeutung großflächiger Betriebstypen, welche schon im Jahre 1993 Umsatzanteile von 82% bei den Lebensmitteln, 75% im Bereich Drogerie/Parfüm, 70% bei den Haushaltsgeräten, 69% bei der Unterhaltungselektronik sowie 54% bei Papier und Schreibwaren erreichten),
- Einsatz **neuer Informationstechniken** (z. B. Scanner-Technik), welche es erlauben, sehr schnell eine Vielzahl an Absatzinformationen bezüglich jeder relevanten Marketing-Fragestellung auszuwerten (zur typischen, regelmäßigen Nutzung von Scanner-Daten s. i. e. Hallier 1996, S. 47ff.; vgl. auch Taylor 1997); die Verbreitung von **Scanner-Kassen** in Europa läßt die Abb. 4 erkennen,
- zunehmende Bedeutung der **Eigenmarken** des Handels (die sog. Handelsmarken, die im Lebensmittelhandel in Großbritannien schon einen Umsatzanteil von 30%, in Belgien, Frankreich und Deutschland von knapp 25% erreichen; ein detaillierter Überblick für die USA findet sich bei Jain/Tucker (1996, S. 90)); die Eigenmarken des Handels werden häufig durch Markenartikelproduzenten (zusätzlich) hergestellt,
- Tendenz möglichst **niedriger Abgabepreise** gegenüber dem Konsumenten (während zwischen 1985 und 1994 die kommunalen Gebühren um mehr als

	Umsatz Schätzung Mrd SFr.	Deutsch- land	Öster- reich	Schweiz	Nieder- lande	Frank- reich	Gross- britannien	Italien
A. M. S.	105	ALLKAUF	-	MIGROS	AHOLD	CASINO	ARGVIL	RINA- SCENTE
C. E. M.	N. V.	EDEKA					BOOKER	CONAD/ CRAI
E. M. D.	69	MARKANT	ZEV	-	MARKANT	SOCAIP	-	ABO SELEX
EURO- GROUP	39	REWE		COOP	VENDEX	PARDOC	-	-
BIGS	N.V.	SPAR/ GEDELFI	SPAR	SPAR	UNGRO	-	SPAR	DESPAR
DEURO- BUYING	62	METRO	HUMA METRO	-	MAKRO	CAPRE- FOUR/ EURO- MARCHE (METRO)	ASDA (MAKRO)	METRO (Einzel- handel)
INTER- COOP	75	-	KON- SUM	-	EURO- COOP	-	CWS	COOP
Umsatz- anteil im LH inkl. ALDI, HOFER		84 %	59 %	47 %	54 %	44 %	34 %	37 %

Die 7 wichtigsten europäischen Einkaufsgenossenschaften:

A.M.S. (CH) INTERCOOP (DK)	=	Associated Marketing Service
E.M.D. (CH) DEURO-BUYING (CH)	=	European Marketing Distribution
BIGS (GB) EUROGROUP (B)	=	Buyung International Gedelfi/SPAR
C.E.M (8) DIFRA (F)	=	Cooperation Eropéene de Marketing

Quelle: Holliger 1994, S. 244.

Abb. 3: Einkaufskonzentration der 7 europäischen Einkaufsgenossenschaften

40% und die Lebenshaltungskosten um mehr als 20% stiegen, erhöhten sich die Einzelhandelspreise um etwa 15%),
- Tendenz möglichst **niedriger Einstandspreise** gegenüber den Produzenten,
- Optimierung der eigenen **Kostenlage** (z. B. durch Servicebegrenzungen).

Auf der **Produzentenseite** sind folgende Trends erkennbar:
- stetiger **Konzentrationsprozeß,** der die Wettbewerbssituation erschwert,
- **Markenartikel ähneln** sich immer mehr, da funktionale Unterschiede kaum noch bestehen,
- die **Werbung** erscheint als austauschbar, da häufig dieselben Motive verwandt werden,

204

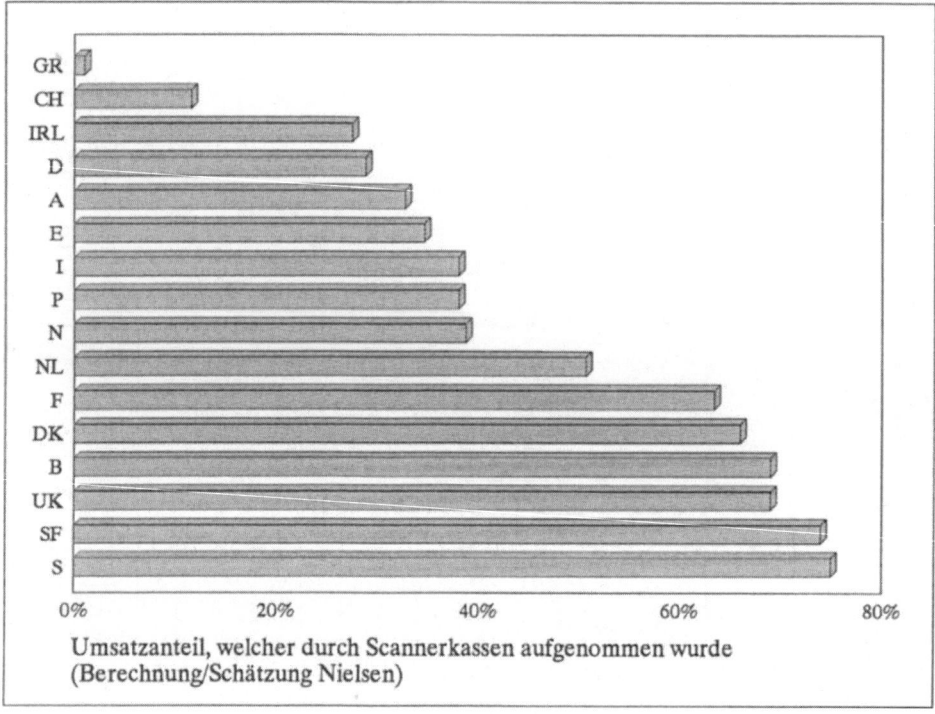

Umsatzanteil, welcher durch Scannerkassen aufgenommen wurde
(Berechnung/Schätzung Nielsen)

Quelle: Holliger 1994, S. 247.

Abb. 4: Scanning-Penetration in Europa (Basis 1993)

- steigende **Marktmacht des Handels** (schon aufgrund höherer Umsatzanteile; vgl. Abb. 5),
- die Einwirkung auf die **Preispolitik des Handels** wird als schwierig eingeschätzt (der Handel profiliert sich häufig über den Preis),
- die Absatzmöglichkeiten werden durch die **Eigenmarken-Politik** des Handels begrenzt.

Zusammenfassend ist festzustellen, daß die heutigen Rahmenbedingungen des Marketing für Markenartikel vergleichsweise schwierig sind. **Konzentrationsprozesse** auf der Produzenten- und auf der Handelsseite führen sowohl horizontal als auch vertikal zu einer höheren Wettbewerbsintensität. Daneben hat sich der Anteil der konfliktträchtigen Beziehungen zwischen Produzenten und Handel deutlich erhöht, z. B. im Jahre 1994 von 7,6% auf 18,7% mehr als verdoppelt (vgl. Zentes 1996, S. 26f.); die Hauptkonflikt-Potentiale sind in der Preis- und Konditionenpolitik, in der Sortimentspolitik und im Bereich Entsorgung/Recycling gegeben.

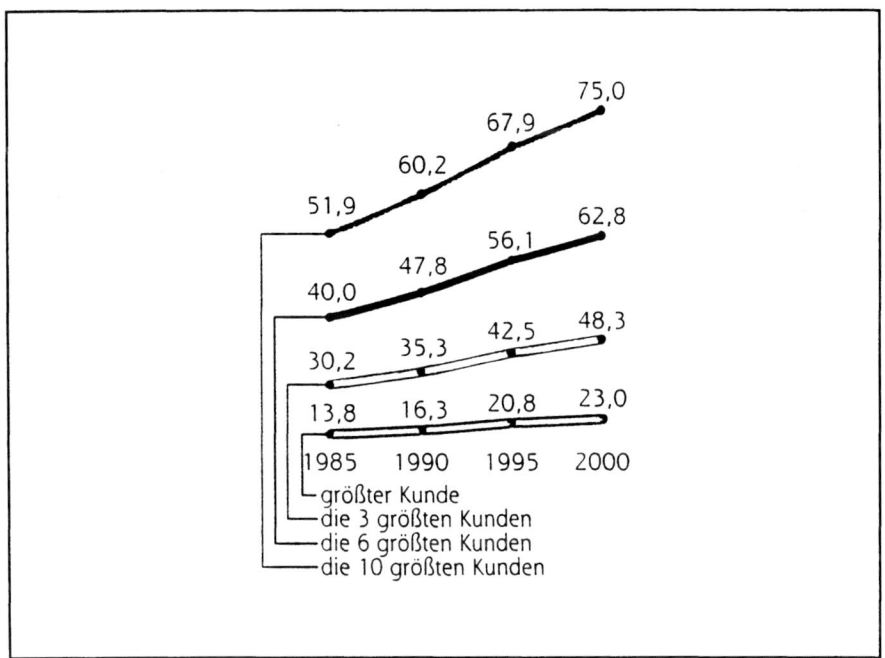

Quelle: o. V. 1997a.

Abb. 5: Entwicklung des Umsatzanteils der ... größten Handels-Kunden
(kumulierter Umsatzanteil in %)

Ob und in welchem Maße **Machtverschiebungen** zwischen einer Handelsorgani-
sation und einem Markenartikelproduzenten entstehen, hängt von der Führung
und der resultierenden Stärke einer Marke ab. Bei einer starken Marke, die durch
hohe Aufmerksamkeits- und Erinnerungswerte, ein positives Image und eine hohe Markentreue gekennzeichnet ist und als Erstmarke im Handel gelistet wird, ist
offensichtlich eine große Marktmacht beim Produzenten gegeben. Bei schwächeren Marken hingegen, die durch Handelsmarken ausgetauscht werden können,
liegt hingegen eine deutlich größere Marktmacht beim Handel. In welcher Weise
eine Führung von Marken erfolgen sollte wird im folgenden i.e. untersucht.

2. Erfolgreiche Führung von Markenartikeln

2.1. Die Marketinginstrumente im Überblick

Damit unter den aktuellen Rahmenbedingungen mehrstufiger Märkte die Markenpolitik eines Produzenten erfolgreich ist, muß
- eine **innovative Markenpolitik** durchgeführt werden,
- eine **Marketing-Kommunikation** realisiert werden, welche den heutigen Bedingungen des Konsumentenverhaltens entspricht,

- eine **Preis- und Konditionenpolitik** gefunden werden, bei der die Interessen aller Marktpartner (Produzenten, Handel, Konsumenten) gleichzeitig in angemessener Weise beachtet werden,
- eine zielgruppenspezifische Auswahl der **Distributionskanäle** erfolgen,
- schließlich eine geeignete Abstimmung aller Marketing-Maßnahmen im Rahmen des **Marketing-Mixes** gefunden werden, so daß im Ergebnis ein hoher Markenwert erreicht wird.

2.2. Markenpolitik

Im Rahmen der **Markenpolitik** sollten echte Produktinnovationen, unverwechselbare Topmarken, kreiert werden, welche die Nummer 1 im Markt werden können, also als Erstmarken vom Handel gelistet werden. Voraussetzung hierfür ist, daß erkennbare Produktvorteile gegeben sind, die zu einer wahrnehmbaren Nutzensteigerung beim Konsumenten führen. Erworbene Schutzrechte (z. B. eingetragene Warenzeichen) müssen verteidigt werden; die Markenpiraterie ist zu bekämpfen. Im Umfeld von Topmarken können **Produktlinien** aufgebaut werden. Auch die Bedeutung von **Produktvariationen** darf nicht unterschätzt werden; regelmäßig muß analysiert werden, ob durch Relaunches Markttrends begegnet werden können.

Walker/Keefe (1998) unterscheiden mehrere **Marken- (Branding-)strategien,**
- das Anbieten einer dominanten Firmenmarke (dominant corporate brand),
- eine duale Markenstrategie i. S. einer gleichzeitigen Verwendung einer Firmen- und einer Produktmarke (dual branding strategy),
- die Führung individueller Produktmarken (individual product brands)
sowie im internationalen Kontext
- eine standardisierte oder lokale Produkt- und Markenstrategie und
- die Verwendung einer internationalen Firmenmarke.
Eine generelle Überlegenheit einer dieser Markenstrategien ist nicht zu verzeichnen; die **situative Vorteilhaftigkeit** der einzelnen Strategien wird von Walker/Keefe herausgearbeitet (vgl. den entsprechenden Beitrag in diesem Sammelband).

2.3. Marketing-Kommunikation

Für kurzlebige Konsumgüter muß durch die **Marketing-Kommunikation** eine Markentreue aufgebaut werden. Bei langlebigen Konsumgütern, bei denen nur ein vergleichsweise geringer Anteil der Konsumenten in einer High-Involvement-Situation, der weit größere Anteil low-involviert ist, sollte **eine zweigleisige Kommunikations-Strategie** erwogen werden. Die High-Involvierten können z. B. durch Special-Interest-Medien erreicht werden; für die Werbemittelgestaltung gilt in diesem Fall, daß der Text (detaillierte Produktinformationen) im Vergleich zur Bildkommunikation eine große Bedeutung hat.

Für die Low-Involvierten ist - wie generell im Falle von kurzlebigen Konsumgütern - folgende **Werbemittelgestaltung** (vgl. Berndt 1995a, S. 403ff.) heranzuziehen:

- **Dominanz der Bildkommunikation** (wenig, aber etwas Text zur Steigerung der Glaubwürdigkeit einer Anzeige),
- **Vorrang der erlebnisorientierten Kommunikation** (da eine Differenzierung von Produkten nach sachlichen/funktionalen Eigenschaften in vielen Branchen nicht mehr gegeben ist, muß für ein Produkt - durch den Einsatz emotionaler Werbung - ein Erlebnisprofil geschaffen werden),
- **Aufbau von Schlüsselbildern** (z. B. Schemabilder wie „das rassige Pferd", „die schlafende Schöne"), die einen positiven emotionalen Gehalt und einen engen Bezug zum Produkt haben sollten,
- **Einsatz visueller Präsenzsignale** durch die Visualisierung eines Markennamen oder durch die Verwendung konkreter Symbole (wie Esso-Tiger oder Lacost-Krokodil),
- **Anstreben einer integrierten Marketing-Kommunikation** (Abstimmung aller Kommunikations-Maßnahmen in inhaltlicher, formaler und zeitlicher Hinsicht; vgl. i.e. Berndt 1995b).

Bei mehrstufigen Märkten ist die Kommunikationspolitik eines Markenartiklers mit den Kommunikations-Maßnahmen des Handels abzustimmen (vgl. Abb. 6). Grundsätzlich hat ein Produzent dabei drei Möglichkeiten,

- die Marketing-Kommunikation gegenüber Konsumenten (in Abb. 6: Marketing-Kommunikation 1),
- die Marketing-Kommunikation gegenüber dem Handel (Marketing-Kommunikation 2) und

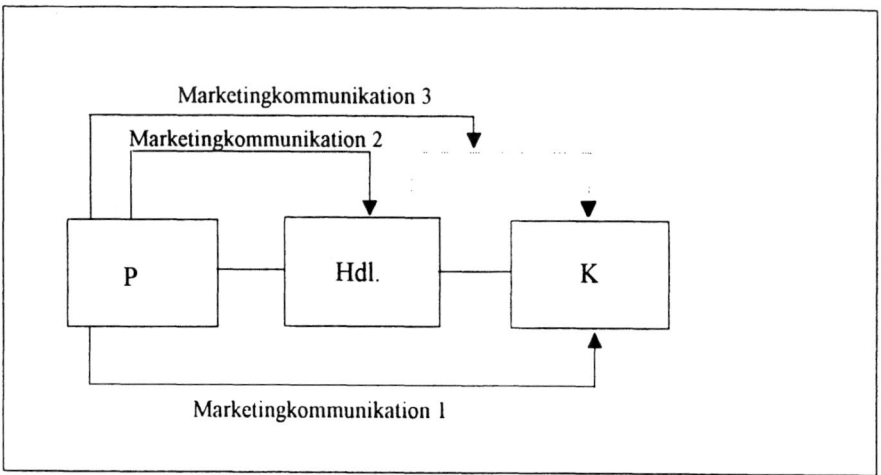

Abb. 6: Grundsätzliche Möglichkeiten der Marketing-Kommunikation eines Produzenten auf mehrstufigen Märkten

– die Beteiligung an Kommunikationsmaßnahmen des Handels (Marketing-Kommunikation 3).

Bei den Low-Involvierten soll durch die Marketing-Kommunikation bewirkt werden, daß das eigene Produkt zum Evoked-Set der Konsumenten gehört; durch geeignete Marketing-Maßnahmen gegenüber dem Handel (z. B. angemessene Sales Promotions) muß dann erreicht werden, daß der Konsument das eigene Produkt als Problemlösung wählt.

Handelsorientierte **Sales-Promotions-Maßnahmen** können auch als Verteidigungsmittel gegen die Einführung von Handelsmarken eingesetzt werden. Durch Rabattsysteme, In-Store-Promotions oder Anzeigen auf der Rückseite von Kassenbons können Handelsunternehmen dazu bewegt werden, den angebotenen Markenartikeln eine besondere Beachtung zu schenken (vgl. Jain/Tucker 1997, S. 98f.).

2.4. Preispolitik

Die **Preisbildung** auf mehrstufigen Märkten läßt die Abb. 7 erkennen; wesentliche Einflußfaktoren der Abfolge „Kosten pro Stück" - „Abgabepreis an Handel"-"Einstandspreis des Handels" - „Verkaufspreis des Handels" sind aufgeführt. Offensichtlich ist ein **Zielkonflikt** zwischen Produzent und Handel: Ein Produzent ist tendenziell an einem hohen Abgabepreis an den Handel, der Handel dagegen an einen niedrigen Einstandspreis interessiert. Damit sind **partnerschaftliche**

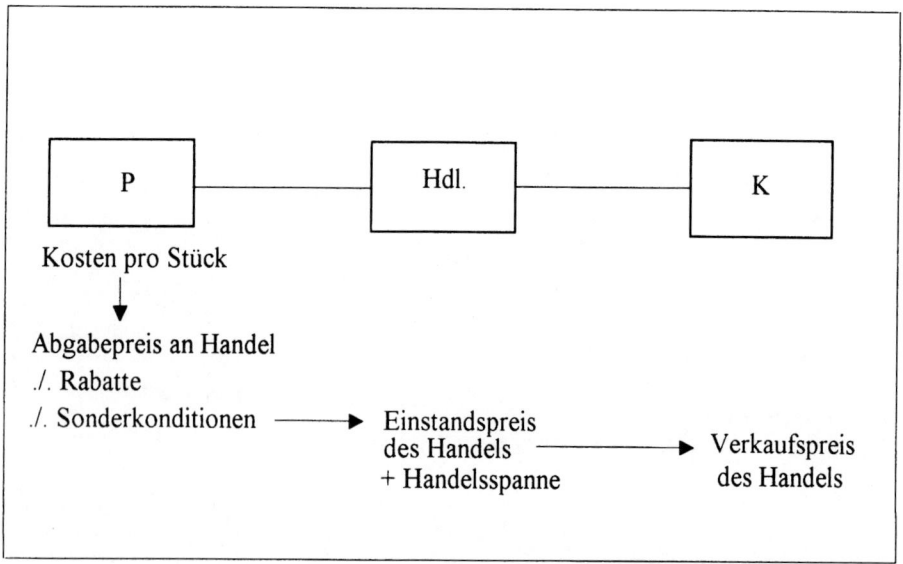

Abb. 7: Preisbildung auf mehrstufigen Märtken

Verhandlungen zwischen Produzenten und Handel unumgänglich. Darüber hinaus kann ein Produzent Wettbewerbsvorteile erringen durch
- Reduktion der Produktionskosten,
- Optimierung von Sonderaktionen zum Vorteil von Handel und Produzenten,
- Preisbündelung bei Produktpaketen zur Stützung schwächerer Marken durch stärkere Marken und
- Kundenbindungsmaßnahmen (z. B. Miles & More).

Bei der **Preissetzung für einen Markenartikel** auf mehrstufigen Märkten sollten gemäß Jain/Tucker (1997, S. 98) folgende Aspekte beachtet werden:
- Grundsätzlich sollte für einen Markenartikel eine Prämie (ein Preisaufschlag) gegenüber der jeweiligen Produktklasse verlangt werden.
- Der Preisaufschlag darf nicht so hoch sein, daß der Handel dazu verleitet wird, konkurrierende Eigenmarken zu einem deutlich niedrigeren Preis anzubieten.
- Im Falle, daß Eigenmarken des Handels schon existieren, sollten in jedem Marktsegment die Preislücken zwischen jedem Markenartikel und jeder Handelsmarke (im Hinblick auf das Handels- und das Konsumentenverhalten) beobachtet werden.
- Auch die Preiselastizitäten (im Sinne von Änderungen der Absatzmenge bei Preisänderungen) sollten für alle angebotenen Produkte gemessen werden.
- Auf der Basis dieser Daten sollte dann die Prämie (der Preisaufschlag) für einen Markenartikel festgelegt werden.

2.5. Distributionspolitik

Die grundsätzlichen Möglichkeiten der **Distributionspolitik** eines Markenartikelproduzenten auf mehrstufigen Märkten liegen in
- der Auswahl der Absatzwege und
- der Verkaufspolitik (dem Einsatz von Außendienstmitarbeitern).

Die **Absatzwege-Wahl** hat zielgruppenspezifisch zu erfolgen. Ein angemessener Distributionsgrad ist anzustreben, um durch die Verfügbarkeit eigener Markenartikel das Phänomen der Markentreue (bei kurzlebigen Konsumgütern) bzw. die Zugehörigkeit zum Evoked-Set (bei langlebigen Konsumgütern) ausnutzen zu können. Im Rahmen der **Verkaufspolitik** sind alle Entscheidungstatbestände (Ziele, Zielgruppen, Verkaufsbudget, Umfang des Außendienstes, Verkaufsbezirke, Verkäufer-Akquisition, -Selektion und -Schulung, Außendienst-Steuerung, Planung von Außendienstbesuchen, Planung von Verkaufsgesprächen) angemessen festzulegen (siehe hierzu i.e. Berndt 1995, S. 485 ff.).

Welche Bedeutung diese Marketing-Instrumente in verschiedenen Problemsituationen aus der Sicht der Praxis haben, ist Otzen-Wehmeier in einer **empirischen Studie** nachgegangen, wobei u. a. zum einen die frühen 90'er Jahre, zum anderen die Zeit „nach dem Jahr 2000" berücksichtigt worden sind. Für die Zeitspanne „**frühe 90'er Jahre**" ist eine Expertenbefragung durchgeführt worden. Für sieben

Relevantes Problemfeld	Anpassungsreaktion / Lösungsansatz / Strategie der Markenartikler
1. Steigende Konfliktintensität durch selektives und zurückhaltendes Beschaffungsverhalten des Handels sowie ruinöser Preiskampf im Handelswettbewerb	• Konzentration auf Premiummarken und / oder Erweiterung des Sortiments durch preiswertere Marken • Eigehen konstruktiver Partnerschaften mit ausgewählten Handelskunden
2. Verschärfung des Problems der Nachfragemacht	• Machtgewinn durch Marktanteilsgewinn, entweder über intensivierte Werbung, Promotions oder Akquisitionen von Wettbewerbern • Unterstützung alternativer Absatzmittelformen, Direktvertrieb • konsequentes Markenartikelmarketing: Machtgewinn durch Consumer Pull, Innovationen, Differenzierung
3. Verschärfung des Problems Konditionen- druck und Gewinneinbussen	• Kostenstrategien: • Kosten bei eigener Beschaffung, Produktion, F&E, Logistik etc. reduzieren • durch Schnittstellenmanagement Kosten in der Zusammenarbeit mit dem Handel senken • Überkapazität in der Branche beseitigen: • herstellereigenes Angebot und Kapazitäten reduzieren • mittelständische Handelsmarken-Produzenten akquirieren, die für Überkapazität sorgen
4. Arbitragegeschäfte bei international standardisierten Sortimenten	• Harmonisierung der Netto-Netto-Preise • Definition von Preisbandbreiten • Supranationale Preiskoordination durch die Unternehmenszentrale

5. Verschärfung des Problems Handels- markenkonkurrenz	• Solo-Markenstrategie:
	• Preise senken und gleichzeitig verstärkter Einsatz von Werbung und Promotions
	• Konzentration auf Top-Marken
	• Innovation und Differenzierung bei bestehenden Marken
	• Dual-Brandingstrategie:
	  Handelsmarken herstellen, ... um Goodwill im Handel zu erzielen
	  um mittelständische Konkurrenz zu verdrängen
	  um die eigenen Kapazitäten auszulasten
	  um sich Eintritt in einen Absatzkanal zu verschaffen

6. Der europäische Konzentrationsprozess im Lebensmittelhandel erfordert eine suprana- tionale Ausrichtung des Vertriebs	• Abschottungsstrategie: Blockierung der Geschäftsbeziehung zu Euro-Accounts • Annäherungsstrategie • Aufbau von Geschäftsbeziehungen über Euro-Pilotprojekte • Aufbau eines Euro-Key-Account-Managements
7. Probleme des Herstellers mit den unter- schiedlichen Handelssystemtypen	• Signalisieren von Gesprächsbereitschaft gegenüber attraktiven und durchsetzungsfähigen Euro-Accounts

Quelle: Otzen-Wehmeyer 1995, S. 208.

Abb. 8: Problemfelder und zugehörige Anpassungsreaktionen/Strategien von Markenartikel-Produzenten in den frühen 90er Jahren

relevante Problemfelder (siehe erste Spalte der Abb. 8) sind die in derselben Abb. aufgeführten Anpassungsreaktionen/Strategien für Markenartikel-Produzenten identifiziert worden.

Für die Zukunft (**„nach dem Jahr 2000"**) erwarten die befragten Experten su- pranationale Beziehungen zwischen multinationalen Markenartikelproduzenten und Euro-Accounts des Handels. Für den Handel werden international standardisierte Sortimente erwartet; ein Großteil der Beschaffungsentscheidungen wird von europäischen Einkaufszentralen getroffen werden. Als erstes werden die Euro-Filialisten ihre „Euro"-Sortimente supranational listen und ein entsprechend hohes Einkaufsmachtpotential haben (siehe i.e. Otzen-Wehmeyer 1996, S. 201). Die Produzenten haben eine schwierige Wettbewerbssituation zu erwarten, die u.a. durch eine kostengünstigere Produktion (Standardisierung der Produktion) zu begegnen ist. Die Distributionsorganisation muß auf die erwarteten Euro-Accounts der Handelsorganisationen ausgerichtet werden. Entsprechend muß das Key-Account-Management der Markenartikler international orientiert werden; Euro-Key-Account-Manager der Produzenten werden den Euro-Key-Accounts des Handels gegenübergestellt (vgl. auch Diller 1992).

Zusammenfassend ist festzustellen, daß nur im (selbstverständlich angestrebten) Ausnahmefall ein innovativer Markenartikel entwickelt und angeboten wird, der als Nr. 1 vom Handel gelistet und für den eine Marketing-Führerschaft im Rahmen des vertikalen Marketing besteht. Im Normalfall ist es situativ abhängig, in welchem Maße sich ein Markenartikel im Handel durchsetzt. Erforderlich sind (dann) kooperative Marketing-Konzepte, im Rahmen derer eine (teamorientierte) Zusammenarbeit zwischen Industrie und Handel angestrebt wird; mögliche Kämpfe zwischen Markenartiklern und Handelsmarken sollten aber verhindert werden.

3. Kooperative Systeme des Markenmanagement

Zu den kooperativen Systemen des Markenmangement zählen zunächst die (theoretischen) Ansätze der **Preisbildung auf mehrstufigen Märkten** (vgl. Ott 1992, S. 255ff.); für gewisse Kombinationen von Marktformen (z. B. bilaterales Monopol auf dem Produzenten-Händler-Markt und Monopol auf dem Händler-Konsumenten-Markt oder Polypol sowohl auf dem Produzenten-Händler-Markt als auch auf dem Händler-Konsumenten-Markt) werden optimale Abgabepreise an den Handel als auch optimale Endverbraucherpreise bestimmt, wobei davon ausgegangen wird, daß alle relevanten Informationen mit Sicherheit vorliegen. Die theoretischen Ansätze sind dahingehend zu kritisieren, daß die unterstellten Marktformen-Kombinationen wenig realitätsnah sind und eine Beschränkung allein auf die Preispolitik erfolgt. Daneben sind in letzter Zeit verschiedene **kooperative Systeme in der Praxis** wie
- Category-Management oder
- Efficient Consumer Response
entwickelt worden, welche - in differenzierter Weise - die Verteilung der Informations- und Distributionsmacht zwischen Handel und Industrie beeinflussen (vgl. Abb. 9).

212

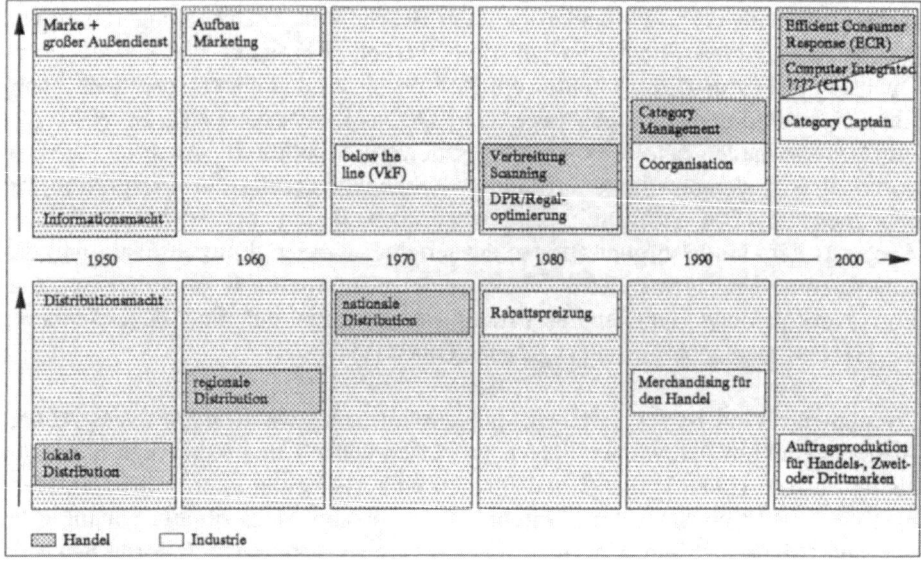

Quelle: Hallier 1995, S. 105.

Abb. 9: Die Verteilung von Informations- und Distributionsmacht zwischen Handel und Industrie im Zeitablauf

3.1. Category-Management

Category-Management (vgl. z. B. Milde 1994; Holliger 1994; Behrens 1994; Zenor 1994) beinhaltet das konsequente Management einer Warengruppe durch ein Handelsunternehmen, wobei kompetente Produzenten sowohl als Lieferant als auch als Berater einbezogen werden. Während ehemals separate Vorstellungen dominierten (für den Key-Account-Manager eines Produzenten die optimale Plazierung seiner Markenartikel, für den Zentraleinkäufer eines Handelsunternehmens der möglichst große Deckungsbeitrag einer (jeden) Warengruppe), wird im Rahmen des Category-Management eine gemeinsame Zielsetzung, die Optimierung einer Warengruppe des Handels, in der ein Markenartikel eines Produzenten enthalten ist, verfolgt. Offensichtlich ist, daß ein Category-Management nur dann funktionieren kann, wenn eine **vertrauensvolle Zusammenarbeit** und ein intensiver Informationsaustausch zwischen Handel und Produzenten erfolgt. Insbesondere müssen Informationen in erheblichem Maße getauscht werden. Durch Einsatz der **Scanner-Technik** fallen im Handelsbetrieb sehr detaillierte Informationen an, die in den verschiedensten Weisen ausgewertet werden können. Hierbei kann ein Markenartikelhersteller sein spezifisches **Marketing-know-how** - im besten Falle als Category-Captain - einbringen.

```
                Absatzplanung
   Category Gewinn          Regaloptimierung

   Einkauf      CATEGORY MANAGER      Promotions

   Bestandsführung                    Preispolitik
                Sortimentsplanung
```

Quelle: Nach Milde 1994, S. 345.

Abb. 10: Verantwortungsbereich des Category Manager

Der **Prozeß des Category-Management** (vgl. z. B. Milde 1994, S. 344ff.; Holliger 1994, S. 246f.; Pretzel 1996, S. 23ff.) umfaßt 5 Teilphasen, welche immer wieder durchlaufen werden sollten:
- die **Analyse der Categories** (Warengruppen) beim einzelnen Handelsunternehmen, deren Stärken und Schwächen; Ermittlung der relevanten Trends,
- die **Analyse des Kundenpotentials** (detaillierte Bestimmung des Kundenverhaltens beim Handelspartner und bei konkurrierenden Handelsunternehmen in Abhängigkeit von der jeweiligen Marketingpolitik),
- **Planung** der angemessenen **Merchandising-Strategie** (sowohl aus Handels- als auch aus Produzentensicht; den Verantwortungsbereich eines (handelsseitigen) Category-Managers läßt die Abb. 10 erkennen).
- **Implementierung** der ausgewählten Merchandising-Strategie (auf der Basis vorab durchgeführter Tests),
- **Ergebniskontrolle** (in Form von Soll-Ist-Vergleichen sowohl aus Handels- als auch aus Produzentensicht und Einleitung von Änderungsmaßnahmen).

Auf allen Stufen des Planungs-, Realisierungs- und Kontrollprozesses des Category-Management sind angemessene Verfahren der **Informationsgewinnung und -verarbeitung** einzusetzen;
- auf der ersten Stufe sollte ein (repräsentatives) Handelspanel befragt werden,
- auf der zweiten Stufe kann auf ein geeignetes Konsumentenpanel zurückgegriffen werden.
- Simulationsverfahren sind auf der dritten Stufe hilfreich,
- geeignete Testkonstruktionen und varianzanalytische Auswertungsverfahren kennzeichnen die vierte Stufe,
- Soll-Ist-Vergleiche und darauf basierende Abweichungsanalysen können auf der fünften Stufe eingesetzt werden.

Category-Management ist mit klassischen **Organisations-Konzepten** (vgl. Abb. 11) nicht mehr vereinbar. Während bisher funktionale Organisationsstrukturen im Handel dominierten, gliedern sich die Organisationsformen im Rahmen des Category Management nach strategischen Geschäftseinheiten (Categories, vgl. Abb. 12).

214

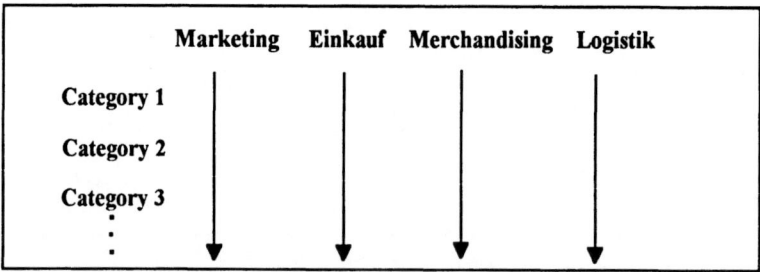

Quelle: Pretzel 1996, S. 23.

Abb. 11: Traditionelle funktionale Organisationsform des Handels

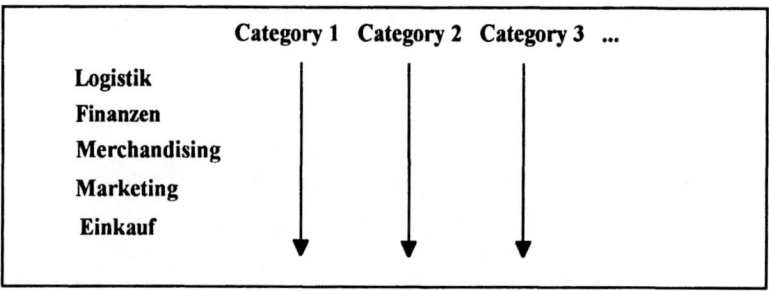

Quelle: Pretzel 1996, S. 23.

Abb. 12: Category-Management-Organisation im Handel
(Funktionen eines Category Managers)

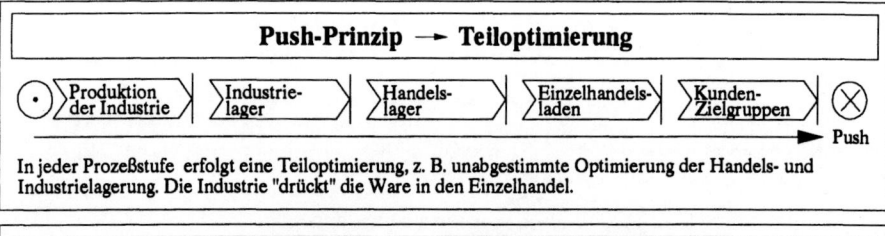

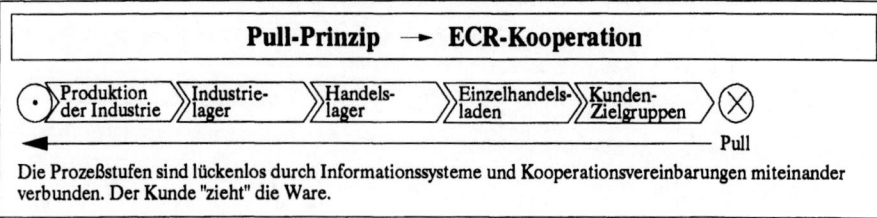

Quelle: Dantzer 1996, S. 56.

Abb. 13: Ersetzung des Push-Systems in der Distributionslogistik zwischen
Industrie und Handel durch ein Pull-System

Empirische Erkenntnisse zum Category Management in der Bundesrepublik Deutschland liefert eine Studie von Hahne (1997). Eine Befragung von 60 Konsumgüterherstellern ergab, daß

- in 70% der Fälle Category Management bekannt ist und im eigenen Unternehmen angewandt wird,
- mehr als 80% der Befragten Category Management als Implementierung eines Warengruppendenkens und etwa zwei Drittel der Befragten Category Management als Konzept einer intensiven Zusammenarbeit zwischen Produzenten und Handel wahrnehmen,

wobei folgende **Aufgaben** im Rahmen des Category Management als besonders wichtig angesehen wurden:

- Konzeption handelsgerichteter Verkaufsförderungs- und Merchandising-Maßnahmen,
- Produktprogrammplanung im Hinblick auf die Sortimentsanforderungen des Handels,
- direkte Zusammenarbeit mit dem Handelspartner,
- Kombination von Produktmanagement und handelsgerichtetem Marketing.

3.2. Efficient Consumer Response

Das Konzept des Efficient Consumer Response (vgl. z. B. Dantzer 1996; Tietz 1995; Zentes 1996) beinhaltet eine **intensive Zusammenarbeit** auf allen Stufen einer Warenflußkette zwischen Produzent und Konsument auf der Grundlage einer genauen Kenntnis des Konsumentenverhaltens; es ist durch **integrierte Steuerungs- und Rationalisierungskonzepte** sowohl der Waren- als auch der Informationsprozesse gekennzeichnet (grundsätzlich läßt sich das Efficient Consumer Response-Modell mit den Just-in-Time-Konzepten zwischen Zulieferern und Herstellern in der Automobilbranche vergleichen).

Im Rahmen des Efficient Consumer Response-Ansatzes wird die traditionelle Push-Strategie auf mehrstufigen Märkten durch eine Pull-Strategie ersetzt. (vgl. Abb. 13). Zwei gleichzeitig verfolgte **Zielsetzungen** kennzeichnen das Konzept,

- extern die Maximierung der Kundenzufriedenheit,
- intern die Minimierung der Kosten auf allen Stufen der Warenflußkette.

Der Efficient Consumer Response-Ansatz umfaßt zum einen das **Category Management**, zum anderen das **Supply Chain Management**; die erstgenannte Zielsetzung ist im Rahmen des Category Management, die zweitgenannte Zielsetzung im Rahmen des Supply Chain Management relevant (zum Wertketten-Management vgl. Fantapié Altobelli 1995, S. 135ff.).

Im Rahmen des Efficient Consumer Response-Modells können **vier Basisstrategien** unterschieden werden (vgl. Abb. 14), die sich auf die Lagerhaltung, das Bestellwesen, die Sales Promotions und die Produktinnovationen beziehen. Gegenstand des **Efficient Store Assortments** sind die Bestands- und Regaloptimierung

216

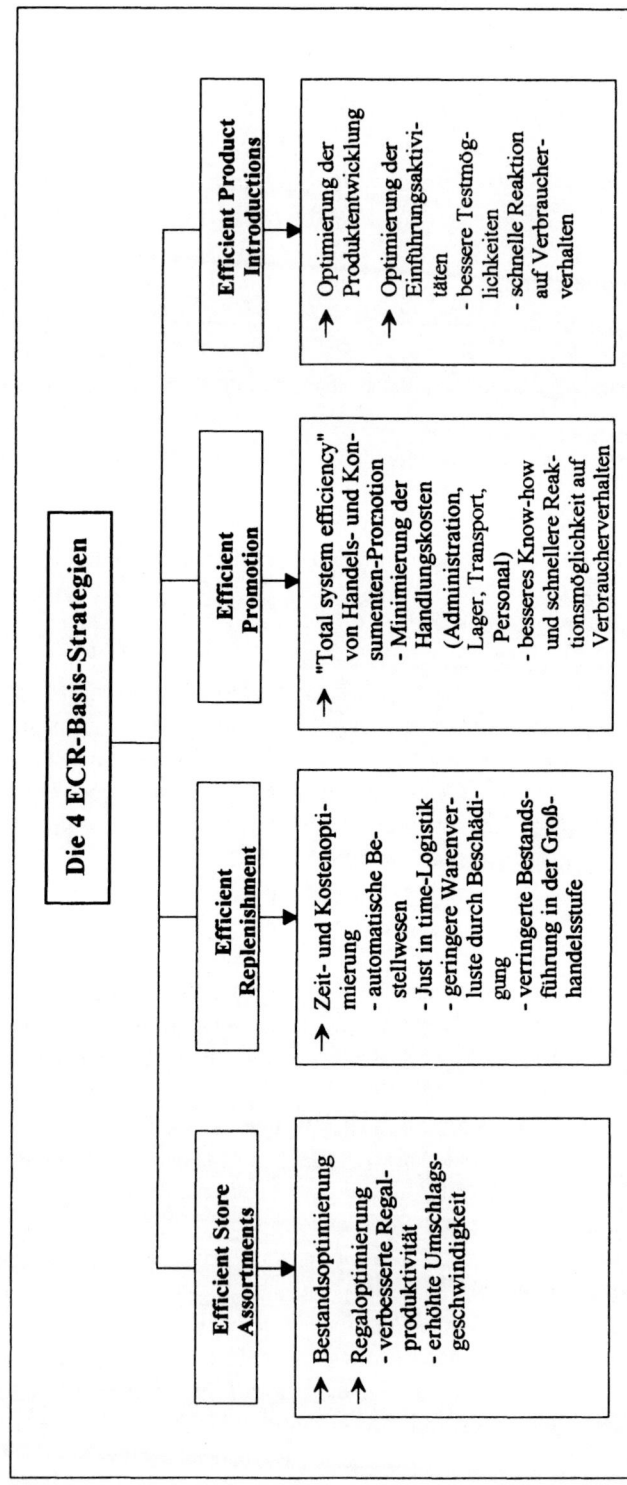

Quelle: Pretzel 1996, S. 22.

Abb. 14: Basisstrategien des Efficient Consumer Response

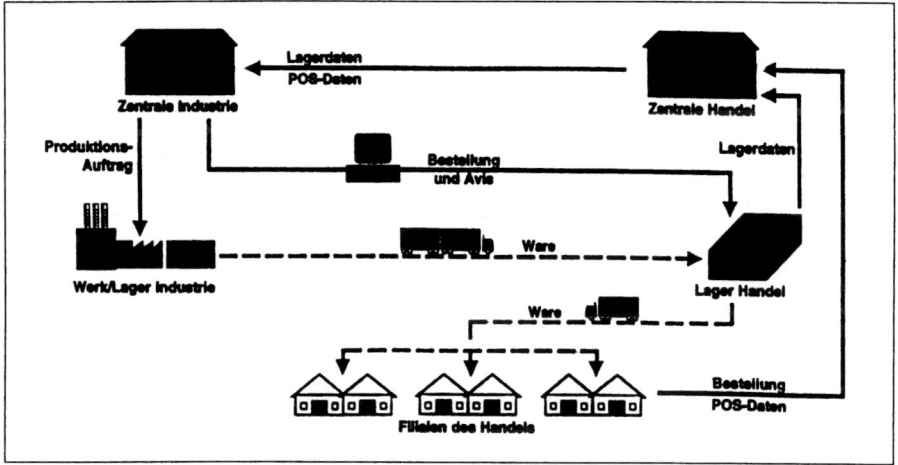

Quelle: Dantzer 1996, S. 56.

Abb. 15: Continuous Replenishment zwischen Industrie und Handel

im Handel; dabei werden Ziele wie höhere Regalproduktivität und höhere Um-schlagsgeschwindigkeit verfolgt (vgl. hierzu i. e. Ring 1992; Günther/Mattmüller 1993). Hauptaufgaben des **Efficient Replenishment** sind die Zeit- und die Ko-stenoptimierung, welche durch eine angemessene Logistikstrategie (vgl. Abb. 15) erreicht werden sollen (ein interessantes Beispiel hierzu findet sich in o.V. 1997b). Im Rahmen der **Efficient Promotions** sollen in zielgerechter Weise angemessene handels- und konsumentengerichtete Sales Promotions-Maßnahmen entwickelt werden. Gegenstand der vierten Basisstrategie, der **Efficient Product Intro-ductions**, ist die Optimierung der Produktentwicklung und der Produkteinfüh-rung sowohl aus Produzenten- als auch aus Handelssicht.

In einer aktuellen empirischen Studie haben Homburg/Grandinger/Krohmer (1996) den aktuellen und den geplanten **Entwicklungsstand des Efficient Con-sumer Response**, die bestehenden und die geplanten Kooperationen zwischen Produzenten und Handel in der Bundesrepublik Deutschland hinterfragt. Befragt wurden 52 Markenartikelproduzenten aus der Verbrauchsgüterindustrie, die zu den Lieferanten des deutschen Lebensmitteleinzelhandels gehören. Dabei zeigten sich für die einzelnen Strategie-Bereiche des Efficient Consumer Response fol-gende **Tendenzen**:

– Im Strategiebereich **Efficient Replenishment** wird insbesondere die Planung der Lagerbestände auf der Grundlage von Point-of-Sales-Daten erheblich zu-nehmen.

– Entsprechendes gilt für den Aufgabenbereich „**Efficient Store Assortments**"; auch hier wächst die Bedeutung der Point-of-Sales-Daten.

– Für den Bereich **Efficient Promotion** werden ebenfalls nachhaltige Änderun-gen erwartet; die Vorauskäufe des Handels sollen reduziert werden; Niedrig-preis-strategien auf Dauer werden erwartet; Rabatte und Sonderkonditionen sollen eingeschränkt werden.

- Was den Stragegiebereich **Efficient Product Introductions** angeht, werden insbesondere zwei Entwicklungen erwartet: Der Handel soll stärker in die Produktentwicklung einbezogen werden; außerdem werden mehr Produkttests in Handelsgeschäften vorausgesagt.

3.3. Zusammenfassende Beurteilung der kooperativen Systeme des Markenmanagements

Kooperative Systeme des Markenmanagement wie Category Management oder Efficient Consumer Response beinhalten eine enge Zusammenarbeit zwischen Industrie und Handel, im Rahmen derer permanent sehr detaillierte Informationen vom Handel an die Produzenten fließen. Dies setzt voraus, daß eine **echte Vertrauensbasis** gegeben ist, die Zusammenarbeit **dauerhaft** und **vertraglich geregelt** ist. In die vertraglichen Regelungen müssen alle Aspekte der Zusammenarbeit aufgenommen werden, um eventuelle Konfliktpotentiale möglichst klein zu halten. Zu den wesentlichen Voraussetzungen einer effizienten Managementpolitik gehören weiterhin eine konsequent und dauerhaft angelegte Informationsbeschaffung, die sich sowohl Handels- als auch Konsumentenpanels bedient, sowie eine Umorientierung im Hinblick auf bestehende Organisationskonzepte innerhalb des Handels. Aufgrund der Konzentration auf einzelne Warengruppen ist der Übergang zu einer organisatorischen Gliederung, die sich an strategische Geschäftseinheiten ausrichtet, erforderlich.

4. Zukunftsperspektiven

Welche Rollenverteilung zwischen Handel und Produzenten in der Zukunft bestehen wird, hängt entscheidend davon ab, wie sich die **(interaktive) Informationstechnologie** entwickeln wird. Virnich (1996) prophezeit für das zukünftige Einkaufsverhalten der Konsumenten revolutionäre Änderungen; er erwartet aufgrund der Multimedia-Fortschritte ein **virtuelles Retailing** der Art Online-Shopping, Scanning, Teleshopping, Heimlieferdienste (vgl. hierzu auch Reinhardt u.a. 1997; Gattiker/Kelley/Janz 1996, S. 422ff.). Dies wird begleitet durch **innovative Marketing-Konzepte** wie multimediales Kochbuch, interaktive Rezepte, interaktive Werbespots (vgl. i.e. Fantapié Altobelli/Hoffmann 1996). Eine geringere Bedeutung erhält dann die Verpackungspolitik.

Der Handel muß analysieren, ob diese Trends der Informationstechnologie seine derzeit erstarkte Marktmacht schmälern wird. Neben dem verstärkt auftretenden **Convenience Shopping** (Einkaufen in Tankstellenshops, Kiosken/Trinkhallen, Bäckereien oder Getränkemärkten mit Zusatzsortimenten; vgl. o.V. 1996, S. 8ff.) können sich die heutigen mehrstufigen Märkte zu **einstufigen Märkten** entwickeln; die zu erwartenden weitergehenden Konzentrationsprozesse auf Produzentenseite können dann Machtverschiebungen wieder zur Produzentenseite verstärken.

Literatur:

Behrens, C. (1994), Category Management: Handel und Hersteller in Kompetenz-Partnerschaft, in: absatzwirtschaft, 1994, Nr. 10, S. 108-114

Berndt, R. (1995a), Marketing 2, Marketing-Politik, 3. Aufl., Berlin u.a. 1995

Berndt, R. (1995b), Integrierte Kommunikation und Total Quality Management, in: Berndt, R. u.a. (Hrsg.), Total Quality Management als Erfolgsstrategie, Band 2 der Schriftenreihe der GSBA Zürich, Berlin u.a. 1995, S. 221-242

Berndt, R. (1996), Marketing 1, Käuferverhalten, Marktforschung und Marketingprognosen, 3. Aufl., Berlin u.a. 1996

Berndt, R., Sander, M. (1994), Der Wert von Marken, Begriffliche Grundlagen und Ansätze zur Markenwertbestimmung, in: Bruhn, M. (Hrsg.), Handbuch Markenartikel, Band 2, Stuttgart 1994, S. 353-1371

Bruhn, M. (Hrsg.) (1994), Handbuch Markenartikel, Band 1-3, Stuttgart 1994

Dantzer, U. (1996), Efficient Consumer Response, Von der Teiloptimierung zum echten Erfolg, in: Logistik heute, 1996, Nr. 10, S. 56-58

Diller, H. (1992), Euro-Key-Account-Management, in: Marketing ZFP, 1992, S. 239-246

Fantapié Altobelli, C.(1995), Wertkette, Schnittstellen-Management und Total Quality Management, in: Berndt, R. (Hrsg.), Total Quality Management als Erfolgsstrategie, Band 2 der Schriftenreihe der GSBA Zürich, Berlin u.a. 1995, S. 135ff.

Fantapié Altobelli, C.(1998), Marketing im interaktiven Zeitalter, in: Berndt, R. u.a. (Hrsg.), Unternehmen im Wandel - Change Management, Band 5 der Schriftenreihe der GSBA Zürich, Berlin u.a. 1998

Fantapié Altobelli, C., Hoffmann, S. (1996), Die optimale Online-Werbung für jede Branche, München, Hamburg 1996

Förster, H. (1996), EDI - Eine Voraussetzung zur Gewinnsteigerung durch ECR; in: CPC Deutschland (Hrsg.), Efficient Consumer Response, Mainz 1996, S. 57-68

Gattiker, U.E. (1998), Benchmarking, Innovation and Reengineering: Should We Pull the Plug on the Internet of Make it Serve Better?, in: Berndt, R. u.a. (Hrsg.), Unternehmen im Wandel - Change Management, Band 5 der Schriftenreihe der GSBA Zürich, Berlin u.a. 1998

Gattiker, U.E., Kelley, H., Janz, L. (1996), Today's Information Highway and Tomorrow's Organization: Managing Privacy, Marketing and Strategic Issues Successfully, in: Berndt, R. (Hrsg.), Global Management, Band 3 der Schriftenreihe der GSBA Zürich, Berlin u.a. 1996, S. 417ff.

Hahne, H. (1997), Category Management, Interface zum Handel, in: absatzwirtschaft, 1997, Nr. 3, S. 72-76

Hallier, B. (1996), ECR - Keine Revolution sondern Evolution, in: CPC Deutschlang (Hrsg.), Efficient Consumer Response, Mainz 1996, S. 47-55

Holliger, P. (1994), Category Management, Mehr als nur eine vorübergehende Modeerscheinung?, in: Marktforschung, Thexis-Fachbuch für Marketing, St. Gallen 1994, S.. 242-249

Homburg, C., Grandinger, A., Krohmer, H. (1996), Efficient Consumer Response, Erfolg durch Kooperationen mit dem Handel, in: absatzwirtschaft, 1996, Nr. 10, S. 86-92

Interbrand (1990), Brands, London 1990

220

Irrgang, W. (1991), Präferenzstragtegie zur Motivation des Handels - Marktforschung für vertikales Marketing, in: Marktforschung & Management, 1991, Nr. 2, S. 67ff.

Jackel, B. (1997), Merkmale markentreuer Konsumenten, in: Gesellschaft zur Erforschung des Markenwesens (Hrsg.), Markendialog, Wiesbaden 1997, S. 41-63

Jain, S.C., Tucker, L.R. (1997), A New Era of Brand Warfare: Preventing Private Label Inroads, in: Berndt, R. u.a. (Hrsg.), Business Reengineering, Band 4 der Schriftenreihe der GSBA Zürich, Berlin u.a. 1997, S. 89-102

Kaas, K.P., Gegenmantel, R. (1995), Ökonomische Determinanten der Macht auf dem Lebensmittelmarkt, in: Zeitschrift für Betriebswirtschaft, 1995, Nr. 8, S. 885-904

Kapferer, J.N. (1995), Strategic Brand Management, New Approaches to Creating and Evaluating Brand Equity, London 1995

Klein, H. Lachhammer, J. (1996), Efficient Consumer Response, Die Aufgaben des Beziehungs-Managements, in: absatzwirtschaft, 1996, Nr. 2, S. 62-66

Milde, H. (1994), Category Management - die stille Revolution, in: Markenartikel, 1997, Nr. 7, S. 343-346

Mulhern, F.J. (1997), Retail marketing: From distribution to integration, in: International Journal of Research in Marketing, 1997, Nr. 2, S. 103-124

Murphy, J.M. (1990), Brand Strategy, Cambridge 1990

Ott, A.E. (1991), Grundzüge der Preistheorie, 3. Aufl., Göttingen 1991

Otzen-Wehmeyer, E. (1996), Internationales vertikales Marketing, Wiesbaden 1996

o.V. (1996), Convenience Shopping, Executive Summary in: CPC Deutschlang (Hrsg.), Convenience Shopping, Mainz 1996, S. 7ff.

o.V. (1997a), Wachsender Druck auf „mittelstarke" Marken, in: Markenartikel, 1997, Nr. 1, S. 13ff.

o.V. (1997b), Efficient Replenishment, Täglich flexibel auf Ereignisse reagieren, in: absatzwirtschaft, 1997, Nr. 5, S. 48-50

Pretzel, J. (1996), Gestaltung der Hersteller-Handel-Beziehung durch Category Management, in: Markenartikel, 1996, Nr. 1, S. 21ff.

Reinhardt, A. u.a. (1997), Zooming Down the I-Way, Alternative carriers and nimble startups have united PC's, E-mail, fax, and video, in: Business Week ,1997, April 7, S. 54-59

Ring, N.G. (1992), Die Funktionen des Sortimentsgroßhandels unter besonderer Berücksichtigung eines Regaloptimierungssystems, in: Zeitschrift für betriebswirtschaftliche Forschung, 1992, Nr. 6, S. 566-585

Sander, M. (1994), Die Bestimmung und Steuerung des Wertes von Marken, Heidelberg 1994

Sander, M. (1995), Steigerung des Markenwertes durch Total Quality Management, in: Berndt, R. u.a. (Hrsg.), Total Quality Management als Erfolgsstrategie, Band 2 der Schriftenreihe der GSBA Zürich, Berlin u.a. 1995, S. 199-220

Sander, M. (1997), Markenführung zur Erhaltung von Markenloyalität, in: Gesellschaft zur Erforschung des Markenwesens (Hrsg.), Markendialog, Wiesbaden 1977, S. 77-82

Schulz, R., Brandmeyer, K. (1989), Die Marken-Bilanz, Ein Instrument zur Bestimmung und Steuerung von Markenwerten, in: absatzwirtschaft, 1989, Nr. 7, S. 364-371

Taylor, P. (1997), Electronic revolution in the retailing world, in: Financial Times, 3.9.1997, S. III

Tietz, B. (1995), Efficient Consumer Response, in: Wirtschaftswissenschaftliches Studium, 1995, Nr. 10, S. 529-530

Tochtermann, T. (1997), Category-Management ein Flop?, in: absatzwirtschaft, 1997, Nr. 9, S. 134-136

Trommsdorff, V. (1997), Markenmanagement und Kommunikation, Vortrag auf der 25. Jahrestagung der Deutschen Werbewissenschaftlichen Gesellschaft, Bonn 1997

Virnich, H.G. (1996), Das Einkaufen von morgen - „Darf's ein bißchen Mehrwert sein?, Vortrag beim Unilever-Forum Marketing, Hamburg 1996

Walker, O.C. jr., Keefe, L.M. (1998), Corporate Identity and International Branding Strategies, in: Berndt, R. u.a. (Hrsg.), Unternehmen im Wandel - Change Management, Band 5 der Schriftenreihe der GSBA Zürich, Berlin u.a. 1998

Zenor, M.J. (1994), The Profit-Benefits of Category Management, in: Journal of Marketing Research, Vol. 31 (May 1994), S. 202-213

Zentes, J. (1996), ECR - eine neue Zauberformel, in: CPC Deutschland (Hrsg.), Efficient Consumer Response, Mainz 1996, S. 24-46

Markenführung unter geänderten Kommunikationsbedingungen

Matthias Sander

Summary:

Brand communication is one of the most relevant tasks of branding. Without brand communication it is not possible to create strong brands. Meanwhile the circumstances of brand communication have varied. New media and a fragmenting process in the media scene in Germany mean new challenges for brand managers. In this article, the new situation is described and possibilities for handling the new situation are explained.

1. Ausgangssituation

Die Rahmenbedingungen für die Kommunikationspolitik der werbetreibenden Wirtschaft haben sich in Deutschland in den letzten Jahren entscheidend verändert. In besonderer Weise stellen die Veränderungen in der Medienlandschaft eine neue Herausforderung für werbetreibende Unternehmen dar, da bisherige Werbestrategien unter den neuen kommunikativen Bedingungen an Wirkung verlieren. Die Veränderungen in der Medienlandschaft sind dadurch gekennzeichnet, daß sich einerseits klassische Werbemedien zunehmend in einem Segmentierungsprozeß befinden, andererseits sind in den letzten Jahren neue Medien hinzugekommen, die das grundsätzlich nutzbare Medienspektrum erweitert haben. Zudem steigen die Werbeinvestitionen weiter mit der Folge, daß die Informationsüberlastung seitens der Umworbenen insgesamt zunimmt. Es ist daher die Frage nach der Wirksamkeit von Werbung bzw. ihrer Änderung unter diesen Bedingungen zu stellen; gleichzeitig ist nach Lösungen zu suchen, um die Wirkung kommunikationspolitischer Maßnahmen zu verbessern. Diese Entwicklungen sind insbesondere für markenführende Unternehmen von Bedeutung, da kommunikationspolitische Aktivitäten für Markenartikel wesensinhärent sind und für die Unternehmen damit einen entscheidenden Erfolgsfaktor darstellen.

2. Kommunikationspolitische Ziele der Markenführung

Ausgangspunkt jeglicher Planung des Einsatzes von Kommunikationsinstrumenten sind die verfolgten **Ziele**. Kommunikationspolitische Ziele lassen sich im er-

224

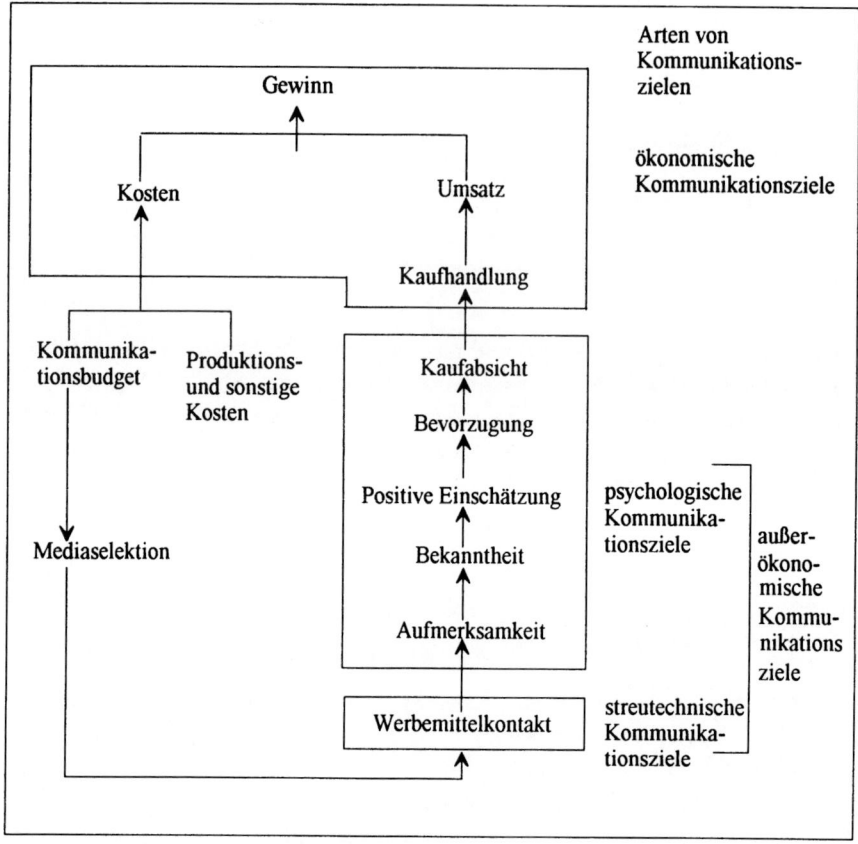

Abb. 1: Auf Basis eines individuellen Wirkungsprozesses abgeleitete Kommunikationsziele

sten Schritt in generelle und spezielle Ziele einteilen. **Generelle** kommunikationspolitische Ziele sind (vgl. Schweiger/Schrattenecker, 1992, S. 49)
– die Erhaltung und Sicherung des erreichten Absatzes (Erhaltungs-/Erinnerungskommunikation),
– die Abwehr gewisser Bedrohungen des Marktanteils durch die Konkurrenten (Stabilisierungskommunikation)
– Steigerung des Absatzvolumens bzw. Erhöhung des Marktanteils (Expansionskommunikation) sowie
– die Durchsetzung neuer Erzeugnisse und/oder Erschließung neuer Märkte (Einführungskommunikation).

Aus diesen generellen Kommunikationszielen können **spezielle** Ziele abgeleitet werden, welche in streutechnische, psychologische und ökonomische Kommunikationsziele eingeteilt werden können (vgl. Sander 1993, S. 270 ff.). Abb. 1 verdeutlicht die einzelnen auf Basis eines individuellen Modells der Werbewirkung abgeleiteten kommunikationspolitischen Ziele. Infolge des nur mittelbaren Wirkungszusammenhanges zwischen kommunikativen Maßnahmen und ökonomischen Zielen wird dabei häufig auf psychologische und auf streutechnische Ziele ausgewichen (vgl. Berndt 1995, S. 333 f.; Gleich 1997, S. 331); psychologische und streutechnische Ziele weisen einen stärkeren Zusammenhang zwischen kommunikativer Maßnahme und eingetretener Zielwirkung auf.

"Klassische" außerökonomische Werbeziele wie Imageverbesserung oder Bekanntheitsgradsteigerung einer Marke sind inzwischen ergänzt worden um weitere außerökonomische Ziele. Eine besondere Rolle spielt dabei die sog. Aktualisierung der Marke (vgl. Hattemer 1991, S. 486 ff.). Unter Aktualisierung einer Marke kann der Versuch der Heraushebung der Marke aus der Informationsflut verstanden werden, um sie ins Gespräch und damit möglichst ins evoked set der Zielgruppenmitglieder zu bringen. Die Marke selbst ist dabei insofern von Bedeutung, als sie gerade in einer Situation der Informationsüberlastung als Ankerpunkt dienen kann und damit eine Orientierungshilfe für den Verbraucher darstellt (vgl. Simon 1997, S. 230).

In mittelfristiger Hinsicht ist zu beachten, daß die verfolgten Kommunikationsziele und die damit verbundene Kommunikationsstrategien keinen häufigen Änderungen unterzogen werden, da hierdurch die Kontinuität der Markenführung durchbrochen wird und das Vertrauen der Konsumenten in die Marke erschüttert werden kann; Kontinuität ist dabei relativ zu verstehen in dem Sinne, daß über einen längeren Zeitraum die Ziele und das kommunikative Konzept durchaus variieren können, allerdings immer unter Ausrichtung an einer **zentralen Leitidee** mit einer inhaltlich-formalen Klammer im Rahmen der konkreten Umsetzung des Konzepts. Die Orientierungsfunktion der Marke wird untergraben, sofern die einzelnen Werbekampagnen nicht aufeinander abgestimmt sind. Eine Marke kann auf diese Weise ihre Identität verlieren und wird konturlos. Fraktale Marken entsprechen also nicht einer effizienten Markenführung (vgl. Lachmann 1996, S. 22 f.; Simon 1997, S. 234; Sander 1997, S. 80 f.).

Hinzuweisen ist in diesem Zusammenhang auf die Tatsache, daß in der Praxis formulierte Kommunikations- bzw. Werbeziele häufig nicht den Anforderungen genügen, die an sie zu stellen sind; insbesondere sind sie nicht in der Lage, den Planungsprozeß für kommunikationspolitische Aktivitäten zu steuern (vgl. Steffenhagen/Siemer 1996). Untaugliche Kommunikationsziele sind z. B. allgemeine Absichtserklärungen ("Durchsetzung der Markenartikel-Idee"), unspezifizierte Globalziele ("Image-Bildung") sowie unklare Bedeutungen verwendeter Ausdrücke ("Aufrechterhaltung des guten Standing am Markt"). Werden derartige Ziele zugrunde gelegt, so ergibt sich u.a. das Problem, daß das Ausmaß der Zielerreichung im Rahmen der Zielkontrolle aufgrund einer mangelnden Operationalisierung dieser Ziele gar nicht ermittelt werden kann.

3. Die derzeitigen Kommunikationsbedingungen in Deutschland

3.1. Werbeinvestitionen in Deutschland

Die Werbeinvesitionen in Deutschland betrugen im Jahre 1996 insgesamt 55,1 Mrd. DM; dies entspricht einem Anteil am Bruttoinlandsprodukt von 1,56% (vgl. ZAW 1997, S. 9 ff.). 37,5 Mrd. DM hiervon stellen Einnahmen der Werbeträger dar. Für 1997 wird ein Anstieg der Werbeinvestitionen auf 56,4 Mrd. DM (+2,4%) bzw. 38,5 Mrd. DM (+2,7%) prognostiziert. Aus derzeitiger Sicht kann diese Prognose als vorsichtig bewertet werden: Die Werbeinvestitionen in den klassischen Medien (Print, Fernsehen, Hörfunk, Plakat) stiegen in Deutschland in der ersten Jahreshälfte 1997 gegenüber dem Vorjahreszeitraum um 3,5% auf 13,36 Mrd. DM (vgl. o. V. 1997a, S. 6). Ein besonders starkes Wachstum verzeichnete dabei die Werbung im privaten Fernsehen mit einer Zunahme um 10,5%. Leichte Steigerungsraten konnten auch Publikums- und Fachzeitschriften verzeichnen, Zeitungen hingen büßten knapp 1% Werbeeinnahmen ein, Plakate sogar fast 13%. Abb. 2 zeigt die Entwicklung dieser Medien gegenüber dem Vorjahreszeitraum im einzelnen auf.

	Jan.-Juni 1997 Millionen Mark	Jan.-Juni 1996 Millionen Mark	Veränderung in Prozent
Print	6424,7	6383,8	0,6
Zeitungen	2834,5	2861,0	-0,9
Publikumszeitschriften	3163,7	3107,2	1,8
Fachzeitschriften	426,5	415,6	2,6
Elektronik	6593,0	6129,0	7,6
Fernsehen	5781,1	5318,5	8,7
öffentlich-rechtlich	434,4	479,0	-9,3
privat	5346,7	4839,5	10,5
Hörfunk	812,0	810,8	0,2
öffentlich-rechtlich	302,5	301,1	0,5
privat	509,6	509,7	0,0
Plakat	341,3	391,6	-12,9
Endsumme	**13359,1**	**12904,8**	**3,5**

Quelle: o.V. 1997a, S. 6.

Abb. 2: Bruttowerbeumsätze klassischer Medien

Rang	Branchen	Jan.-Juni 1997 in TDM	Jan.-Juni 1996 in TDM	Veränderung in Prozent
1	Auto-Markt	1.478.202	1.405.547	4,7
2	Massenmedien	1.185.174	1.048.855	11,5
3	Handelsorganisationen	810.551	756.323	7,1
4	Pharmazie Publikums-werbung	586.173	569.643	2,8
5	Schokolade und Süßwaren	547.965	503.243	7,0
6	Banken und Sparkassen	405.928	422.177	-3,9
7	Bier	396.711	407.678	-2,8
8	Telekommunikation	345.113	31.374	1000,0
9	Spezialversender	321.106	323.814	-1,0
10	Milchprodukte	276.732	248.655	11,2

Quelle: o.V. 1997b, S. 18.

Abb. 3: Werbeintensität einzelner Branchen

Die Werbeintensität einzelner Branchen zeigt Abb. 3 auf. Neu hinzugekommen zu den 10 werbeintensivsten Branchen in Deutschland ist der wachstumsträchtige Bereich der Telekommunikation. Wie anhand von Abb. 3 deutlich wird, bestehen branchenübergreifend stark unterschiedliche Werbeintensitäten; immerhin wird in der Automobilindustrie mehr als fünfmal soviel wie in der Milchbranche in Werbung investiert. Auffällig ist zudem die Tatsache, daß sich unter den zehn werbeintensivsten Branchen immerhin drei Wirtschaftsbereiche befinden, die im Halbjahresvergleich ihre Werbeausgaben reduzierten. Im Ganzjahresvergleich 1995/1996 konnte ein Rückgang der Werbeausgaben unter den ersten zehn Plätzen nicht festgestellt werden (vgl. ZAW 1997, S. 13). Ob der Rückgang der Werbeausgaben bei den Bereichen "Banken und Sparkassen", "Bier" und "Spezialversender" am Ende des Jahres 1997 im Ganzjahresvergleich zu 1996 in ein positives Wachstum umgewandelt werden kann, bleibt abzuwarten.

Insgesamt zeichnet sich der deutsche Werbemarkt derzeit durch ein vergleichsweise verhaltenes Wachstum aus. Es ist davon auszugehen, daß ein stärkeres Wachstum der Werbeinvestitionen einsetzt, sobald die Konjunktur, die derzeit stark vom Export geprägt ist, auf die Inlandsnachfrage übergreift. Diese Situation darf jedoch nicht darüber hinwegtäuschen, daß die Entwicklung bei den einzelnen Werbeträgern sehr unterschiedlich ist; während beispielsweise bei den Tageszeitungen von einer Stagnation gesprochen werden kann, boomen nach wie vor die Werbeinvestitionen in das private Fernsehen.

3.2. Veränderungen der Medienlandschaft in Deutschland

Die Medienlandschaft in Deutschland ist gekennzeichnet durch einen Segmentierungsprozeß bei gleichzeitiger Erweiterung des zur Verfügung stehenden Medienspektrums. Der **Segmentierungsprozeß** äußert sich darin, daß sich bei vielen bestehenden Medien das Angebot vergrößert. Abb. 4 zeigt die Veränderung der Anzahl der Werbeträger von 1991 bis 1996 in Deutschland auf. Lediglich geringen Rückgängen bei Tages- und Wochenzeitungen stehen z. T. enorme Zuwächse bei allen anderen Werbeträgern gegenüber. Besonders eindrucksvoll läßt sich diese Entwicklung anhand der Anzahl der verfügbaren Fernsehprogramme nachvoll-

Mediengruppe	Anzahl		Veränderung
	1991	**1996**	**Prozent**
Tageszeitungen	418	408	-2,4
Wochenzeitungen	29	28	-3,4
Anzeigenblätter	1.088	1.279	+17,6
Publikumszeitschriften	589	745	+26,5
Fachzeitschriften	917	978	+6,7
Kundenzeitschriften	43	58	+34,9
Branchen-Fernsprechbücher			
Gelbe Seiten	79	94	+19,0
Massendrucksachen/Infopost	-	-	-
Bundesweite TV-Programme (deutschsprachig)	7	22	+214,3
Regionale TV-Programme	54	71	+31,5
Bundesweite, regionale und lokale Hörfunkprogramme	187	233	+24,6
Plakatanschlagstellen	282.000	391.292	+38,8
Filmtheater	3.741	4.025	+7,6

Quelle: ZAW 1997, S. 20.

Abb. 4: Entwicklung der Werbeträger von 1991 - 1996

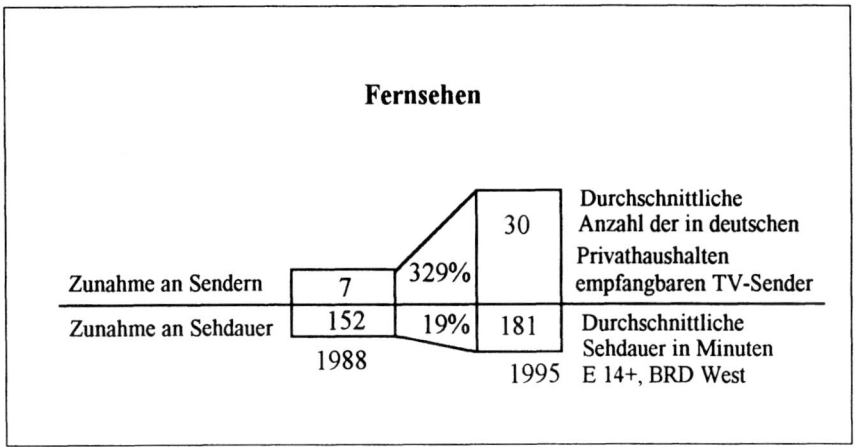

Quelle: Hüther 1996, S. 347.

Abb. 5: Entwicklung der Anzahl von Fernsehsendern und Sehdauer

ziehen. Wie Abb. 5 zeigt, vergrößerte sich das Angebot an Fernsehkanälen im Zeitraum von 1988 bis 1995 - gemessen an der Zahl der in deutschen Privathaushalten durchschnittlich empfangbaren Sender - um mehr als 300% von 7 auf 30 Programme; gleichzeitig stieg die durchschnittliche Sehdauer in demselben Zeitraum lediglich um 19% von 152 Minuten auf 181 Minuten bei der Erwachsenenbevölkerung. Dies bedeutet, daß im Durchschnitt die Sehdauer pro Fernsehkanal von 21,7 Minuten auf nur noch 6 Minuten geschrumpft ist. Ergänzend ist darauf hinzuweisen, daß die tatsächliche Nutzung der einzelnen Fernsehkanäle seitens der Umworbenen sehr stark um diese Durchschnittswerte streut; Abb. 6 zeigt die Marktanteile der bedeutendsten Fernsehkanäle in Deutschland für den Zeitraum August 1997 auf. Offensichtlich findet also ein verstärkter Wettbewerb um die Aufmerksamkeit der Mediennutzer bzw. Fernsehzuschauer statt. Neben den Vollprogrammanbietern bemühen sich dabei zunehmend Spartenprogrammanbieter um die Gunst der Zuschauer (vgl. Hüther 1996, S. 347 f.).

Die **Erweiterung des Medienspektrums** äußert sich hingegen in einer zunehmenden Anzahl zur Verfügung stehender Werbeträgerarten, wobei insbesondere die Entwicklung der Neuen Medien wie z. B. dem Internet sowie dem digitalen Fernsehen und dem digitalen Hörfunk als interaktive Medien eine Rolle spielt. Diese Medien - insbesondere das Internet - implizieren grundsätzlich andere Nutzungsweisen seitens der Umworbenen im Vergleich mit den herkömmlichen Medien mit der Folge, daß auch der kommunikative Auftritt durch die werbetreibende Wirtschaft in diesen Neuen Medien anders gestaltet werden muß (vgl. z. B. Fantapié Altobelli/Hoffmann 1996).

230

Unternehmen	Zuschauer ab 3 Jahren		Zuschauer 14-19 Jahre	
	August 1997	±zu Juli 1997	August 1997	±zu Juli 1997
ARD	16,0	1,0	11,8	1,0
RTL	14,7	-0,1	17,1	0,2
Dritte Programme	11,5	-2,1	8,5	-1,8
ZDF	13,2	0,5	8,5	0,3
Sat.1	12,7	0,7	13,3	0,9
Pro Sieben	9,2	-0,1	14,1	-0,3
RTL 2	3,6	-0,2	4,8	-0,2
Kabel 1	3,5	-0,0	3,9	-0,2
Vox	3,2	0,0	4,3	0,1
Super-RTL	2,3	-0,1	2,0	-0,1

Quelle: o.V. 1997c, S. 54.

Abb. 6: Marktanteile ausgewählter Fernsehprogrammanbieter im August 1997

Insgesamt ist in Deutschland damit eine **Fraktionierung der Medienlandschaft** zu konstatieren; sowohl Breite (Anzahl unterschiedlicher Werbeträgerarten bzw. Medien) als auch Tiefe (Anzahl der Werbeträger pro Medium) der Medienlandschaft haben zugenommen. Die Mediaselektion als wesentliche Stufe des Kommunikations- bzw. Werbeplanungsprozesses hat daher für die werbetreibenden Unternehmen erheblich an Komplexität gewonnen. Hinzu kommt, daß die Werbewirkungsforschung gerade bei den Neuen Medien noch erhebliche Lücken aufweist. Andererseits ist auch von einer Veränderung der Werbewirkung bei den bestehenden, klassischen Medien auszugehen, da - wie am Beispiel des Fernsehens dargelegt - bei nur unterproportional gestiegener Mediennutzung der Informations- und damit auch der Werbeoverload insgesamt zugenommen hat. Für die Markenartikelindustrie bedeutet dies, daß eine effiziente Markenführung nur dann stattfinden kann, wenn im Rahmen des Einsatzes der kommunikationspolitischen Instrumente die skizzierten neuen Rahmenbedingungen konsequent in der Mediaplanung beachtet werden.

4. Reaktionsmöglichkeiten der Werbewirtschaft auf die neuen Kommunikationsbedingungen

Reaktionsmöglichkeiten der werbetreibenden Unternehmen liegen einerseits in der Art der Kommunikation mit den Zielgruppen, andererseits in der Gestaltung der werblichen Informationen. Konkrete Ansatzpunkte bieten damit

Mediengesteuerte Instrumente	Product Publicity
Zwischenformen	Symposien Messen Events
Unternehmensgesteuerte Instrumente	Außendienst Direktwerbung Mediawerbung Händlerwerbung Unternehmenswerbung - Markenerweiterung
Sonderformen	Lobbying Schulungen Markttests Subskriptionspreise Comarketing und Lizenzvergabe

Quelle: Möhrle 1995, S. 70.

Abb. 7: Überblick über die Prämarketing-Instrumente

– innovative Kommunikationsinstrumente sowie
– neue Formen der Werbemittelgestaltung.

Beide Handlungsalternativen zielen darauf ab, sowohl die Kontakt**qualität** als auch die Kontakt**quantität** bzw. **Kontaktwahrscheinlichkeit** seitens der Umworbenen mit dem Werbemittel zu erhöhen.

4.1. Innovative Kommunikationsinstrumente

In den letzten Jahren haben sich neuartige Kommunikationsinstrumente herausgebildet, welche u.a. als Antwort auf die skizzierten kommunikativen Rahmenbedingungen zu verstehen sind. Zu diesen Kommunikationsinstrumenten zählen das Prämarketing sowie das Eventmarketing. Unter **Prämarketing** im weiteren Sinne sind sämtliche Marketing-Maßnahmen zu subsumieren, welche vor der eigentlichen Produkteinführung im Markt stattfinden; in erster Linie sind dies Informations- und Vertriebsaktivitäten (vgl. Simon 1989, S. 82). Prämarketing im engeren Sinne umfaßt lediglich die Vorankündigung eines Produktes durch Einsatz kommunikationspolitischer Instrumente, also ebenfalls bevor das Produkt selbst auf dem Markt ist bzw. käuflich erworben werden kann (vgl. auch Möhrle 1995, S. 9 ff.). Übergeordnetes Ziel des Prämarketing ist die Bedarfsschaffung bereits vor der Markteinführung des Produkts. Abb. 7 gibt einen Überblick über die zur Verfügung stehenden Prämarketing-Instrumente, aus denen ein Prämarketing-Mix erstellt werden kann.

Vorteile der Vorankündigung liegen u.a. in der kommunikativen Überbrückung verlängerter Entwicklungszeiten eines Produktes sowie in der Vorprägung des Produktes in den Köpfen der Konsumenten; durch die Vorprägung bzw. Einbringung des Produkts in das evoked set der Konsumenten wird die Möglichkeit der Verhinderung eines Ausweichens auf Konkurrenzprodukte infolge der frühzeitigen Bindung an das angekündigte Produkt geschaffen. Problematisch ist allerdings der schnellere Alterungsprozeß vorangekündigter Produkte, da sie bereits als vertraut gelten, wenn sie auf den Markt kommen; dieses Problem ist insbesondere für Produkte relevant, für welche das Design von besonderer Bedeutung ist (z. B. Autos). Auch sollte die Prämarketing-Phase nicht zu lange dauern, da die Geduld der Umworbenen im Hinblick auf die Erhältlichkeit des Produkts begrenzt ist; ein "ewiges Hinhalten" der Nachfrager ist also nicht möglich bzw. kann sich im Hinblick auf die Wirkung der Prämarketing-Maßnahmen sogar als schädlich erweisen.

Eine empirische Untersuchung, die im Jahre 1996 am Lehrstuhl für Absatzwirtschaft an der Universität Tübingen in der Kraftfahrzeugbranche durchgeführt wurde, führte u. a. zu folgenden Ergebnissen: Als **Ziele** des Prämarketing werden insbesondere eine Interaktion mit Stakeholdern, die Schaffung von Unternehmens- und Produktliniengoodwill, die Überbrückung von "Innovationsleerzeiten" sowie die Absicherung des Neuprodukterfolges bei gleichzeitiger Erhöhung des Marktpotentials verfolgt. **Zielgruppen** von Prämarketing-Maßnahmen sind in erster Linie die Verbraucher bzw. Verwender der umworbenen Produkte, der Handel sowie die Lieferanten. Gesellschaftliche Zielgruppen sowie der Kapitalmarkt sind ebenfalls von Bedeutung, wenn auch mit schwächerer Ausprägung. Die **Budgetierung** von Prämarketing-Maßnahmen erfolgt dabei überwiegend anhand des Verfahrens "Gemäß Ziel und zu lösender werblicher Aufgabe" (vgl. hierzu z. B. Berndt 1995, S. 344 f.); hierbei handelt es sich um eine Vorgehensweise, welche auch aus theoretischer Sicht - im Gegensatz zu anderen Budgetierungsverfahren, die in der Praxis ebenfalls angewandt werden - sinnvoll ist. Als **Prämarketing-Instrumente** werden nahezu alle in Abb. 7 genannten Instrumente eingesetzt, wobei die Sonderformen nur eine untergeordnete Rolle spielen. Bemerkenswert ist das Ergebnis, daß ein großer Teil der befragten Unternehmen (ca. 35%) keine **Kontrolle** der erzielten Prämarketing-Wirkungen durchführt; dies dürfte insbesondere auf die Schwierigkeit der Messung der Prämarketing-Wirkungen zurückzuführen sein. Als mögliche **Probleme** des Prämarketing wurden in erster Linie Goodwillverluste bei Nichteinhaltung des Markteinführungstermins oder der angekündigten Produktqualität, die Interventionsgefahr bzw. rechtzeitige Reaktionsmöglichkeit seitens der Konkurrenz sowie die Kannibalisierung im eigenen Produktionsprogramm gesehen.

Als weiteres innovatives Kommunikationsinstrument ist dem **Event-Marketing** eine zunehmende Bedeutung zu bescheinigen; die Gründung von Event-Agenturen hat Konjunktur (vgl. o.V. 1996, S. 8). Allgemein umfaßt Event-

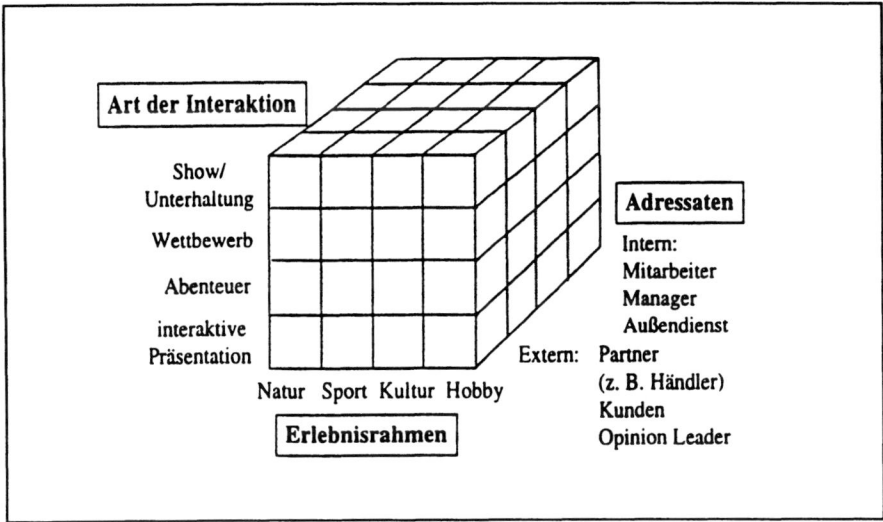

Quelle: Zanger/Sistenich 1996, S. 235.

Abb. 8: Dimensionen des Event-Marketing

Marketing "alle Bestandteile moderner Kommunikation, die dazu beitragen, eine Erlebnisstrategie zu entwickeln und zu vermitteln" (Zanger/Sistenich 1996, S. 234). Als Events sind dabei Ereignisse in Form erlebnisorientierter firmen- oder produktbezogener Veranstaltungen zu verstehen, die zu einer starken Aktivierung der potentiellen Konsumenten durch emotionale und physische Reize führen. Die Dimensionen des Event-Marketing zeigt Abb. 8.

Allgemein darf beim Event-Marketing von einer hohen Qualität der erzielten Kontakte infolge der hohen Attraktivität des Umfeldes ausgegangen werden. Es erscheint realistisch, dem Event-Marketing ein hohes Potential im Hinblick auf eine dialogische Kommunikation von Markenbotschaften zu unterstellen (vgl. Zanger/Sistenich 1996, S. 240). Hierauf aufbauend kann eine emotionale Bindung der Konsumenten an die Markenwelt erfolgen. In welchem Maße jedoch überhaupt Kontaktquantitäten geschaffen werden können, hängt vom konkreten Event ab; generell ist jedoch davon auszugehen, daß bei gegebenem Budget das Ausmaß der erzielten Kontakte vergleichsweise klein ist, d. h. Event-Marketing eignet sich besonders für kleinere, eng umrissene Zielgruppen.

Im Hinblick auf die erzielten Wirkungen erscheint insbesondere die **Kombination** von Prämarketing- und Event-Marketing-Maßnahmen bzw. die Einbindung von Events in Prämarketing-Maßnahmen sinnvoll (vgl. auch Abb. 7); auf diese Weise lassen sich werbliche Synergieeffekte in Form besonders hoher Kontaktqualitäten und -quantitäten erzielen. In der Automobilindustrie konnte dieses Konzept bereits erfolgreich umgesetzt werden.

Generell gilt, daß eine **Integration** kommunikativer Maßnahmen in zeitlicher, inhaltlicher und formaler Hinsicht anzustreben ist, um kommunikative Wirkungen bei gleichbleibendem finanziellen Input verstärken zu können (vgl. Berndt 1995, S. 436 ff.). Im Hinblick auf innovative Kommunikationsinstrumente bedeutet dies, daß zumindest überprüft werden sollte, ob auch die **Neuen Medien**, insbesondere das Internet, in das Spektrum der zu belegenden Werbeträger mit aufgenommen werden sollte. Die unterschiedliche Erreichbarkeit von Zielgruppen über die einzelnen Medien sowie die z. T. stark divergierenden Nutzungsgewohnheiten für die einzelnen Medien machen in diesem Zusammenhang eine medienspezifische Anpassung der werblichen Inhalte allerdings zur absoluten Notwendigkeit.

Um eine Aussage im Hinblick auf die **ökonomische Vorteilhaftigkeit** der aufgezeigten innovativen Kommunikationsinstrumente treffen zu können, müssen die erzielbaren Wirkungen jeweils in Relation zum Ausmaß des notwendigen Einsatzes finanzieller Mittel gestellt werden. Eine in der Praxis häufig verwendete Kennziffer ist der Tausenderkontakt-Preis, welcher die Kosten für 1000 geschaffene Kontakte angibt (vgl. z. B. Berndt 1995, S. 385 ff.). Diese Kennziffer ist allerdings um die Qualität der geschaffenen Kontakte zu bereinigen, da andernfalls keine sinnvolle Aussage beim Vergleich alternativer Kommunikationsinstrumente möglich ist. Probleme entstehen in diesem Zusammenhang in der konkreten Operationalisierung der Qualitätsunterschiede, z. B. in Form eines Gewichtungsfaktors. Angedeutet wurden darüber hinaus bereits Probleme bei Wirkungsmessungen, welche z. B. an psychologischen Zielen (wie Image, Aufmersamkeit, Bekanntheit) ansetzen. Generell weist die Wirkungsforschung gerade bei den innovativen Kommunikationsinstrumenten wie Prämarketing und Event-Marketing noch erhebliche Lücken auf.

4.2. Neue Formen der Werbemittelgestaltung

Im folgenden wird in erster Linie auf den Bereich der Fernsehwerbung eingegangen, da dieses Medium - wie dargestellt - in der Vergangenheit die stürmischste Entwicklung vollzogen hat und nach wie vor die höchsten Zuwachsraten aufweist. Gleichzeitig liegt hier ein Schwerpunkt neuer Werbemittelgestaltungsansätze. Näher eingegangen wird im folgenden auf

– das Programmsponsoring,

– Sonderwerbeformen sowie

– die Tandem- bzw. Reminderwerbung.

Als innovative Gestaltungsform im Bereich der TV-Werbung hat sich das **Programmsponsoring** inzwischen etabliert. Das Sponsoring bestimmter Sendungen, welche hohe Reichweiten aufweisen (z. B. Sportereignisse, Wettervorhersage) oder eine hohe Affinität der Seherschaft mit der angestrebten Zielgruppe besitzen (z. B. eine bestimmte Serie oder ein bestimmtes Fachmagazin für Special-Interest-Zielgruppen), ist insbesondere deshalb interessant, weil die Werbemittelkontaktwahrscheinlichkeit sehr hoch ist. Durch die Nennung des Sponsors zum Beginn und zum Schluß der jeweiligen Sendung darf im Vergleich mit herkömmlichen Plazierungen innerhalb eines Werbeblocks von einer deutlich höheren Wahrscheinlichkeit der Werbemittel- bzw. Werbebotschaftswahrnehmung ausgegangen werden. Dies gilt insbesondere für die Werbung vor Beginn der Sendung, da bei rechtzeitigem Einschalten ein Werbemittelkontakt zwangsläufig zustande kommt; am Ende der Sendung wird jedoch häufig bereits umgeschaltet (z. B. während des Abspanns), so daß hier von einer tendenziell geringeren Werbemittelkontaktwahrscheinlichkeit ausgegangen werden muß. Darüber hinaus sind positive Effekte im Hinblick auf die Einstellung der Umworbenen zum Programmsponsoring denkbar, da u. U. der Eindruck vermittelt werden kann, daß der Sponsor durch die finanzielle Unterstützung zum Entstehen der jeweiligen Sendung beigetragen hat; in diesem Fall bestehen auch positive Einflüsse auf die Kontaktqualität.

Von ähnlichen Effekten ist bei **Sonderwerbeformen** wie die Werbeuhr im öffentlich-rechtlichen Programm (z. B. in der ARD vor den Hauptnachrichten um 20 Uhr) auszugehen. Zumindest im Hinblick auf die Kontaktquantität lassen sich dieselben Aussagen wie beim Programmsponsoring ableiten; rechtzeitiges Einschalten führt zu zwangsläufigen Werbekontakten, welche nicht umgangen werden können, seitens der Umworbenen aufgrund der Furcht, Teile der nachfolgenden Sendung verpassen zu können, aber auch nicht umgangen werden wollen bzw. hingenommen werden. Zu ähnlichen Effekten führt die Strategie, Teile einer Sendung durch eine kurze Werbepause abzuspalten (z. B. die Wettervorhersage von den Nachrichten). Wesentliche Einflußgröße auf die Werbeblockreichweite ist hier die Werbeblocklänge: Einerseits steigt das Ausmaß an möglicher Werbeinformation mit der Werbeblocklänge naturgemäß, andererseits sinkt die Wahrscheinlichkeit mit zunehmender Werbeblocklänge, daß der nachfolgende - die Sendung in der Regel abschließende - Teil noch gesehen wird, weil ab einem bestimmten Punkt die Attraktivität des Schlußteils nicht mehr ausreicht, die Umworbenen auf dem gewählten Fernsehkanal zu halten. In diesem Moment sinkt die Werbeblockreichweite wieder. Prinzipiell handelt es sich hier um das Problem der Bestimmung der optimalen Werbeblocklänge wie bei herkömmlichen Werbeblöcken auch, allerdings stehen in diesem konkreten Fall Sendungen im Mittelpunkt, welche früher nicht unterbrochen wurden (z. B. Nachrichten). Gegenüber herkömmlichen Werbeblöcken sind diese Werbeblöcke zudem deutlich kürzer.

Eine weitere neuartige Gestaltungsmöglichkeit stellt die **Tandem- bzw. Reminder-Werbung** dar. Hierunter versteht man die verkürzte Wiederholung eines Hörfunk- oder Fernsehspots im gleichen Werbeblock. Empirische Untersuchungen haben sich bereits mit der Wirkung derartiger Spots auseinandergesetzt. So konnte Fahr (1995) zeigen, daß Spot- und Detailerkennung für Tandem-Spots sowohl bei freier als auch bei gestützter Abfrage deutlich besser waren als bei Single-Spots. Die Detailerinnerung bezog sich dabei in erster Linie auf diejenigen Inhalte, die in beiden Teilen des Tandems identisch waren. Ein wesentliches Ergebnis der Untersuchung ist in der nicht negativeren Einschätzung von Reminder-

bzw. Tandem-Spots gegenüber Single-Spots zu erkennen. Die Spotwiederholung in demselben Werbeblock führt also offensichtlich nicht zu Reaktanzerscheinungen bei den Umworbenen. Ähnliche Ergebnisse erhielten Mattenklott et al. (1995) in ihrer Untersuchung der Wirkung von Tandem-Spots. Sie konnten nachweisen, daß Tandem-Spots besser und schneller erinnert wurden, d. h. sie wurden bei ungestützer Abfrage häufiger an erster Stelle genannt als Single-Spots. Umstritten ist hingegen die Wirkung der Tandem-Spots auf die umschlossenen Werbespots. Während bei Fahr (1995) ein - nicht signifikanter - positiver Effekt auf den umschlossenen Spot festgestellt werden konnte, wird an anderer Stelle von einer Verdrängung der Erinnerung der zwischen den Tandem-Spots beworbenen Produkte ausgegangen (vgl. z. B. Tödtmann 1995, S. 100).

Offensichtlich sind Reminder-Spots in der Lage, innerhalb kurzer Zeit zentrale Werbeinhalte an die Zielgruppe zu transportieren; die Erinnerungsleistungen der Umworbenen wird signifikant erhöht. Gleichzeitig wird diese Werbemittelgestaltung vom Publikum akzeptiert, d. h. sie wird nicht als störend oder aufdringlich empfunden. In diesem Zusammenhang ist darauf hinzuweisen, daß bei Tandem- bzw. Reminderspots der zweite Spot merklich kürzer als der erste Spot sein sollte; wird er nicht lediglich als gekürzte Fassung des ersten Spots gestaltet, sondern inhaltlich variiert - z. B. als kurze Weiterführung des ersten Spots mit denselben inhaltlichen Anknüpfungspunkten - so kann die Attraktivität dieser Spots durchaus noch gesteigert werden. Hierdurch sind offensichtlich weitere positive Effekte im Hinblick auf die Werbewirksamkeit dieses Gestaltungsansatzes gegeben.

5. Schlußbetrachtung

Die Veränderungen in der Medienlandschaft haben dazu geführt, daß herkömmliche Werbekonzepte nicht mehr die erwünschte Wirkung erbringen. Das Werbeverhalten der werbetreibenden Wirtschaft und insbesondere der Markenartikelindustrie hat sich an den neuen Gegebenheiten auszurichten, damit die Kommunikationspolitik dieser Unternehmen nach wie vor in der Lage ist, Produkte bzw. Marken auf kommunikativem Wege wirkungsvoll zu unterstützen. Dabei ist zu beachten, daß eine intensive - und wirkungsvolle - Kommunikationspolitik ein zentraler Erfolgfaktor für die Schaffung und Aufrechterhaltung starker Marken ist.

Die dargelegten neuen Kommunikationsbedingungen sollten jedoch nicht als Bedrohung, sondern eher als Chance aufgefaßt werden, Marken effizient führen zu können. Durch die Neuen Medien sowie den dargestellten Segmentierungsprozeß in der Medienlandschaft ist die Möglichkeit geschaffen worden, Streuverluste bei der werblichen Ansprache zu minimieren; gleichwohl ist hierdurch ein höherer Aufwand im Hinblick auf die Mediaselektion gegeben, welche komplexer und unübersichtlicher geworden ist. Soll die kommunikative Unterstützung von Marken nicht an Wirkung verlieren, so ist es unausweichlich, sich intensiv mit den neuen kommunikativen Bedingungen und ihren Implikationen für den Einsatz des kommunikationspolitischen Instrumentariums auseinanderzusetzen. Bei geschickter Auslotung der durch die neuen Kommunikationsinstrumente und werblichen Gestaltungsansätze gegebenen Potentiale ist gegenüber früheren Situationen durchaus die Möglichkeit der Wirkungserhöhung kommunikativer Maßnahmen - bei gleichem Budget - gegeben.

Literatur:

Berndt, R. (1995), Marketing 2 - Marketing-Politik, 3. Aufl., Berlin, Heidelberg, New York 1995

Fahr, A. (1995), Erfolgreicher per Tandem (I)? - Ergebnisse einer empirischen Untersuchung von Reminder-Werbung, in: Media Spectrum, 1995, Nr. 10, S. 20 - 24

Fantapié Altobelli, C., Hoffmann, S. (1996), Die optimale Online-Werbung für jede Branche, München, Hamburg 1996

Gleich, U. (1997), Aktuelle Ansätze und Probleme der Werbeforschung, in: Mediaperspektiven, 1997, Nr. 6, S. 330 - 338

Hattemer, K. (1991), Medien tragen Marken zum Erfolg, in: Markenartikel, 1991, Nr. 11, S. 486 - 489

Hüther, R. (1996), Strategien des digitalen Fernsehens am Beispiel des Deutschen Sportfernsehens (DSF), in: Zeitschrift Führung und Organisation, 1996, Nr. 6, S. 347 - 349

Lachmann, U. (1996), Fraktale Markenführung? Fraktale Werbung?, in: Marketing Journal, 1996, Nr. 1, S. 22 - 23

Mattenklott, A. et al. (1995), Erfolgreicher per Tandem (II)? - Werbung als Single- und als Tandem-Spot: Erinnerung und Akzeptanz, in: Media Spectrum, 1995, Nr. 10, S. 26 - 31

Möhrle, M. (1995), Prämarketing- Zur Markteinführung neuer Produkte, Wiesbaden 1995

o. V. (1997a), Privat-TV sahnt weiter ab, in: Horizont, 1997, Nr. 30, S. 6

o. V. (1997b), Werbepower der Top five, in: Horizont, 1997, Nr. 30, S. 18

o. V. (1997c), ARD gewöhnt sich an Höhenluft, in: werben & verkaufen, 1997, Nr. 37, S. 54

o.V. (1996), Inflation der Events, in: werben & verkaufen, 1996, Nr. 6, S. 8

Sander, M. (1993), Der Planungsprozeß der Werbung, in: Berndt, R., Hermanns, A. (Hrsg.), Handbuch Marketing-Kommunikation, Wiesbaden 1993, S. 261 - 284

Sander, M. (1997), Markenführung zur Erhaltung von Markenloyalität, in: Gesellschaft zur Erforschung des Markenwesens (Hrsg.), Markendialog, Wiesbaden 1997, S. 77 - 82

Schmalen, H. (1992), Kommunikationspolitik, 2. Aufl., Stuttgart, Berlin, Köln 1992

Schweiger, G., Schrattenecker, G. (1992), Werbung, 3. Aufl., Stuttgart 1992

Simon , H.-J. (1997), Was läuft falsch in der Markenführung?, in: Marketing-Journal, 1997, Nr. 4, S. 228 - 234

Simon, H. (1989), Die Zeit als strategischer Erfolgsfaktor, in: Zeitschrift für Betriebswirtschaft, 1989, Nr. 1, S. 70 - 93

Steffenhagen, H., Siemer, S. (1996), Untaugliche Werbezielformulierungen der Praxis, in: Marketing ZFP, 1996, Nr. 1, S. 45 - 54

Tödtmann, C. (1995), Ans Messer, in: Wirtschaftswoche, 1995, Nr. 26, S. 97 - 100

Zanger, C., Sistenich, F. (1996), Event-Marketing - Bestandsaufnahme, Standortbestimmung und ausgewählte theoretische Ansätze zur Erklärung eines innovativen Kommunikationsinstruments, in: Marketing ZFP, 1996, Nr. 4, S. 233 - 242

ZAW (Hrsg.) (1997), Werbung in Deutschland 1997, Bonn 1997

Corporate Identity and International Branding Strategies

Orville C. Walker, Jr.
Linda M. Keefe

Zusammenfassung:

Der Bezug zwischen der Corporate Identity und verschiedenen möglichen Markenstrategien (dominierende Firmenmarke, Firmen- und Produktmarke, dominierende Produktmarke, keine ausgeprägte Marke) wird i.e. untersucht. Ausgangspunkt der Untersuchung ist eine Analyse des Markenwertes und seiner Determinanten aus Konsumentensicht. Es werden Bedingungen entwickelt, unter denen die verschiedenen Markenstrategien von Vorteil sind.

1. Corporate Identity and International Branding Strategies

Corporate identity can either distinguish a company or make it invisible. A strong identity reflecting unique competencies, character, and values can make a firm stand out from its competitors and give it a sustainable edge in the marketplace. On the other hand, firms with a bland or unfocused identity - who either try to be all things to all people or send conflicting signals - fade into the background. Corporate identity flows from the communications, impressions, and personality projected by an organization. It is shaped by the firm's mission and values, its internal culture and personnel, its functional competencies, the quality and design of its products and services, its marketing communications, the image generated by various corporate activities, and many other factors. A strong and positive identity can aid a firm's ability to attract and hold the loyalty of customers, improve the morale and productivity of employees, appeal to investors, and maintain good relations with the larger society. As one authority argues, "The company with the stronger, more consistent, more attractive, better implemented and manifested reputation will emerge on top" (Olins 1993).

As more companies around the world have learned the importance of projecting strong and consistent identities, they have begun to develop formal programs to manage the way those identities are projected to both internal and external audiences. Firms as diverse as Caterpillar, Disney, and London Transport are implementing formal Corporate Voice programs. "Corporate Voice" is the total net effect of all the ways a company communicates to all of its various audiences. Thus, Corporate Voice programs attempt to establish criteria and guidelines to help ensure that all the messages and sensory images a firm communicates are consistent and reflect the company's unique values, personality, and competencies. Such guidelines are typically aimed at helping employees make consistent decisions concerning corporate messages and images delivered across the full range of audiences and communications channels - including the design and use of the corporate logo, internal employee communications, the annual report and other communications with investors, dealer brochures and point-of-sale materials, packaging, advertising and sales promotion messages, and even the design, positioning, and brand identities of individual products (Keefe 1995).

1.1. The Relation Between Corporate Identity and Product Marketing Strategies

One major rationale for instituting a strong Corporate Voice program is that it provides a tool for more closely integrating the individual marketing strategies and programs for a firm's various product or service offerings with the corporation's overall identity and competitive strategy. This, in turn, can help improve the effectiveness and efficiency of those individual marketing efforts. By focusing on a common core of corporate values and attributes, every impression generated by each product's design, packaging, advertising, promotional materials, and the like can help reinforce and strengthen the impact of all the other impressions the firm communicates to its various target customers, dealers, and other audiences. Thus, a strong corporate identity and consistent corporate voice can help a firm achieve a bigger „bang" for its limited marketing bucks. For example, by consistently focusing on core values and competencies concerned with providing high quality family entertainment, Disney has created an identity which helps stimulate consumer demand and generates marketing synergies across a wide range of product offerings - from movies to TV programs to licensed merchandise to theme parks.

While the promise of enhanced efficiency and marketing synergies to be gained from a strong corporate identity and a consistent corporate voice hold obvious attractions, many managers - especially those responsible for marketing individual products - question whether a strong corporate voice is **always** a good thing. Given that most medium to large-sized corporations compete in multiple and diverse product categories, might some of those firms' many products and services benefit from a more independent identity - one that is divorced from or even inconsistent with, the identity of the larger organization? And given that many firms sell their product's and services across many different global markets at different stages of development, might they be more successful in at least some of those markets by tailoring each product's identity to fit the local circumstances?

1.2. Corporate Identity and Branding Strategies

At the most basic level, such questions about the proper balance between a strong and consistent corporate identity on the one hand versus unique and independent identities for individual product or service offering on the other lie at the heart of a firm's branding strategy. Should the corporation's own identity and logo be adopted as the brand name for all or most of the firm's products in markets around the world, as is the case in some high-tech (e.g., IBM, Siemens) and service (e.g., Sofitel hotels, British Airways, McDonald's) industries? Should individual products be given unique brand names and identities - perhaps even multiple brand names across different markets - while the identity of the source company is demphasized or even hidden? Or should products carry both a corporate and an individual name and identity, as in the case of various software products from Microsoft (e.g., Microsoft Windows, Microsoft Word, Microsoft Office, etc.). In view of the large number of firms pursuing each of these three different branding strategies around the world, all three are obviously viable. The important question is what variables or conditions are likely to make one of these branding strategies more efficient and effective - and thus mor profitable over time - than the other two?

2. Purpose

This paper develops a framework to help guide managers' decisions concerning which of the alternative branding strategies outlined above are best suited to their firm's circumstances. The framework builds upon the concepts of customer-based brand equity, the various kinds of brand associations or knowledge that build equity for a particular brand, and the relative importance customers attach to different kinds of brand associations. We begin by briefly reviewing the existing literature describing the various components of a customer's knowledge about a particular brand's attributes and potential benefits and how that knowledge, in turn, affects the brand's equity from the customer's perspective. We then discuss how the different components of brand knowledge may flow from characteristics of the product itself, or from characteristics and the corporate identity of the sponsoring firm. Next, we examine some circumstances affecting the relative importance to customers of product-specific versus company-based attributes, benefits, and associations, and we offer some propositions concerning how various product, market, and company characteristics are likely to influence the relevance of these two types of brand knowledge. These propositions suggest conditions under which each of the three branding strategies are most appropriate. Finally, we speculate about how some specific differences across international markets might impact the effectiveness of each branding strategy.

3. Brand Equity and Brand Knowledge

3.1. What is Brand Equity?

The term „brand equity" has two basic meanings. One is essentially financial: It refers to the value the financial markets place on a brand over and above its physical assets. This definition treats brand equity as the „goodwill" that appears on a balance sheet to explain the difference in the purchase price of a brand and its asset value. Although of great interest for mergers and acquisitions, however, the brand goodwill concept is of limited value at the product management level. The second meaning of brand equity, and the one we focus on here, is the value a given customer attaches to a product or service carrying a specific brand relative to the value he or she would attach to an unbranded product or service. Cus-tomer-based brand equity, in other words, is the differential effect of **brand knowledge** on a custumer's response to the marketing of the brand (Aaker 1991; Keller, 1993). A brand is said to have positive equity when customers react more favorably to an element of the brand's marketing mix (e.g., price, an advertise-ment, a sales presentation, etc.) than they would to the same marketing mix ele-ment for an unbranded version of the same product or service. Given that a brand's equity in the marketplace is based on customers' (or potential customers') knowledge and beliefs about the brand, a crucial question is: What constitutes brand knowledge? What are the components or dimensions of that knowledge?

3.2. The Components of Brand Knowledge

A **brand** is "a name, term, sign, symbol, or design, or combination of them which is intended to identify the goods and services of one seller or group of sellers and to differentiate them from competitiors" (Kotler 1994, p. 444). **Brand knowl-edge**, then, consists of all the bits of information - both positive and negative - that a customer **associates** with a particular brand within his or her memory. As diagrammed in Figure 1, these bits of information - or "brand associatons!" - can be grouped into several categories: (1) awareness of the brand, (2) product-related and non-product-related attributes associated with the brand, (3) benefits associated with the brand, and (4) secondary associations (adapted from Keller 1993). As Figure 1 also indicates, a customer's image of - and knowledge about - a given brand is also affected by the favorability, strength, and uniqueness of the brand associations in each of the above four categories. However, to make the following discussion more manageable and clearly focused, we will not examine these aspects of brand knowledge in detail in this paper. Interested readers can find more information about the effects of the favorability, strength, and unique-ness of brand associations on a customer's brand knowledge and the equity of that brand in Keller (1993).

Brand awareness. A first, necessary condition for the accumulation of brand knowledge in a customer's memory is that the customer is aware that the brand exists. The customer must be able to recognize the brand's name and/or visual symbols and to recall the brand's existence, and other information associated with the brand, when considering a purchase within the product or service category to which the brand belongs. Without such awareness, it is unlikely that a brand would make it into the customer's "consideration set" or "approved supplier list" - the handful of brands that receive serious consideration for purchase.

Product-related attributes. Another key component of a customer's image of, and knowledge about, a brand is his or her perceptions concerning the brand's attributes. Attributes are descriptive features that characterize a product or service; what a customer thinks the product or service is or has and what is involved with its purchase and use. **Product-related attributes** are features directly related to the product or service's ability to perform the function(s) sought by the customer. While specific product-related attributes vary across product and service categories, they typically include features related to the product's physical composition (e.g., size, weight, component materials, etc.), service features (e.g., delivery time, availability of spare parts, etc.), and performance characteristics (e.g., energy efficiency, speed, durability, etc.). While many product-related attributes are tangible, some may be intangible, such as style or the empathy of service personnel.

Non-product-related attributes. Non-product-related attributes are external aspects of the product or service that do not directly affect its functional performance but may nevertheless influence its purchase or consumption (Keller 1993, p. 4). For example, the price of the product or service is considered a non-product-related attribute because it obviously affects the purchase process but typically does not relate directly to the product's performance or service function. Price is a particularly important attribute association because customers often have strong beliefs about the price and value of particular brands, an sometimes rely on price as a signal of the brand's quality (Rao/Monroe 1989). They may also categorize brands according to their relative price (i.e., "expensive" brands versus „cheap" brands) (Blattberg/Wisniewski 1989). Similarly, packaging often plays an important role in the purchase and consumption process, particularly for consumer goods, but in most cases does not directly impact the product's functional performance.

User imagery reflects a customer's perceptions about the type of person or organization - defined by characteristics such as sex, age, income, social status, company size, etc. - that typically purchases a given brand. Similarly, usage imagery reflects a customer's perceptions about where and in what types of situations a brand is typically used. Taken together, these two sets of image attributes can help determine a brand's personality. Plummer (1985) reports that customers often characterize brands by personality descriptors, such as "youthful", "colorful", or "conservative." These associations seem to reflect customers' images of a brand's users and usage situations, as well as emotions or feelings evoked by the brand.

Benefits. Not all of the various attributes associated with a product or service are equally relevant or important to all potential buyers. This is because different buyers may have different applications for - or different needs to be satisfied by - the same product or service. Thus, benefits reflect the personal value customers attach to the various attributes associated with a brand - that is, what customers think the product or service can do for them.

As indicated in Figure 1, benefits can be divided into three categories according to the kinds of customer needs or motivations they address (Park/Jaworski/ MacInnis 1986): (1) functional benefits, (2) experiential benefits, and (3) symbolic benefits. **Functional benefits** reflect the more intrinsic and utilitarian advantages thought to be gained from using the product or service, and they usually correspond to product-related performance or service attributes. These benefits are often linked to a customer's desire to solve or avoid a specific problem. Thus, a Mercedes automobile's ability to safely and reliably transport a person from one place to another provides functional benefits. Likewise, dependable just-in-time delivery by a supplier that reduces the buyer's parts inventory and working capital provides a functional benefit to that buyer.

Experiential benefits reflect what the customer thinks it feels like to use the product or service. These benefits also usually correspond to product-related attributes. They satisfy experiential needs such as the desire for sensory pleasure, variety, or stimulation. A Mercedes' ability to negotiate winding roads at high speeds may provide experiential benefits; at least to some drivers.

Symbolic benefits derive from more external advantages of using the product or service. They usually correspond to non-product-related attributes and relate to underlying needs for social approval, self expression, or esteem. Thus, the exclusivity and prestige of owning a Mercedes may provide symbolic benefits to some customers.

Secondary associations. Finally, some of the knowledge and beliefs a potential customer has about a given product or service may not be derived directly from personal experience or from information gleaned from promotional materials or word-of-mouth. Instead, some brand knowledge may be **inferred** from perceived linkages between the brand and other entities, such as the company that makes it, its country of origin, or members of its distribution channel. In some instances, particularly when consumer products or services are involved, secondary associations may also derive from a celebrity spokesperson or endorser of the product or service, or from events sponsored by the brand. Such perceived linkages - or sec-

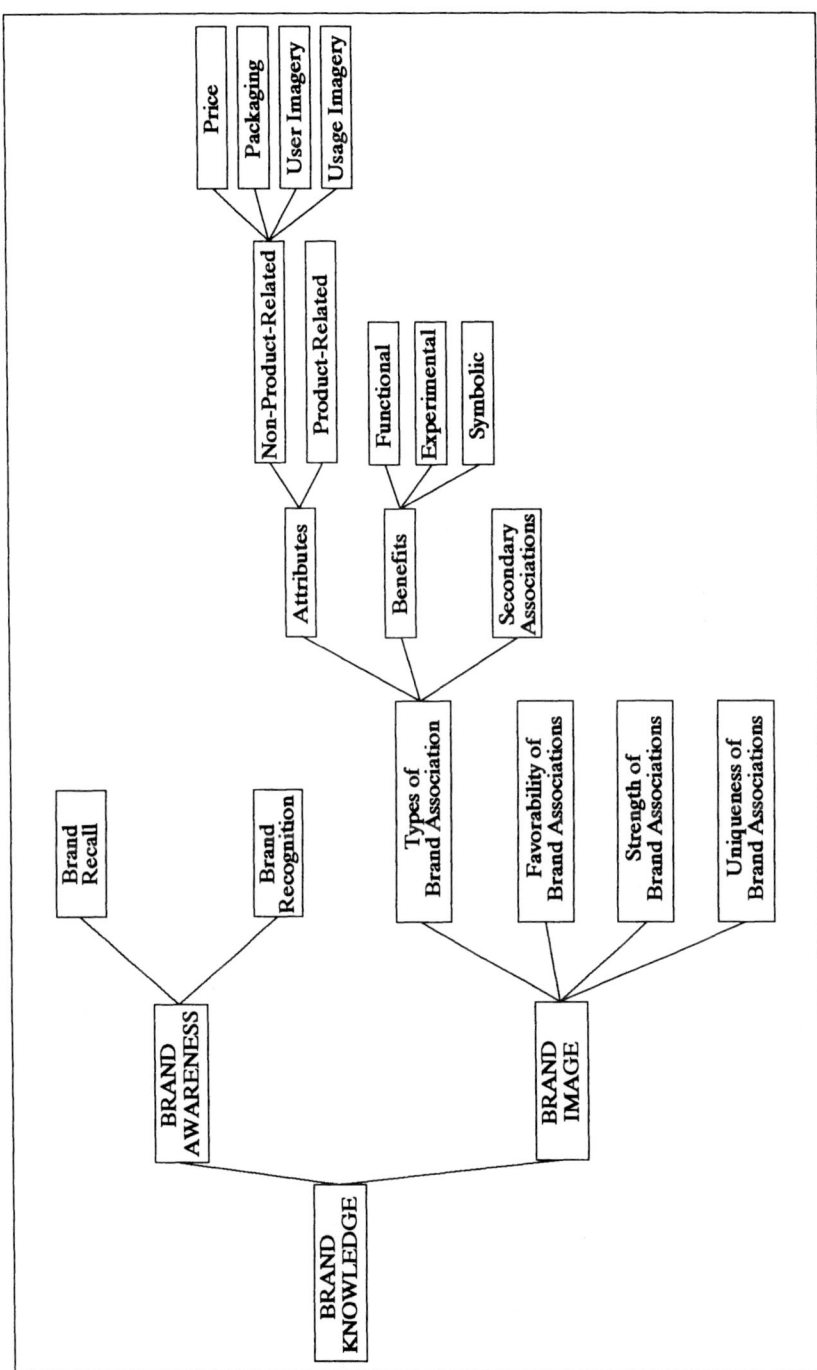

Fig. 1: Dimensions of Brand Knowledge

ondary associations - may lead customers to transfer attributes or benefits associated with the other entity to the brand itself. Thus, the perceived quality and reliability of Mercedes cars may be influenced, in part, by both the company's and Germany's reputations for technological sophistication, engineering expertise, and attention to detail. Similarly, products sold through Tiffany's, while from different manufacturers and carrying different brands, may all benefit from that retailer's prestigious and exclusive image.

4. The Focus of Brand Associations

The existing literature on customer-based brand equity is generally not concerned with the **focus** of the various associations and beliefs a customer holds concerning a given brand - that is, whether those associations focus directly on characteristics of the product or service itself, elements of its marketing program (e.g., its price, packaging, etc.), augmentations or supplementary services provided by the manufacturer (e.g., just-in-time delivery), or relationships with other entities (e.g., the source company, country of origin, channel members, etc.). All that matters, as suggested by Figure 1, is the favorability, strength, and uniqueness of those brand associations which, together with brand awareness, determine the customer's differential response to marketing efforts for the brand (Keller 1993, p. 10).

For purposes of developing a brand strategy for a product or service, however, the focus - as well as the relative importance - of customers' brand associations are critically important. If most of the important associations in the customer's memory focus on attributes or benefits flowing directly from the product or service itself, or from aspects of its specific marketing program, then development of a unique brand name and symbols for that product or service may be the most appropriate strategy to adopt. On the other hand, when many associations important to the customer flow from attributes of or benefits provided by the company that makes or supplies the product or service, a corporate brand - or at least a dual brand that prominently identifies the manufacturer - may make more sense. With this point in mind, then, the first column of Figure 2 lists a number of associations related to a customer's awareness of a product, perceptions of its product-related and non-product-related attributes, its various potential benefits, and other secondary associations which flow directly from aspects of the product or service itself or its specific marketing program. The second column of the Figure lists a similar set of associations which flow from the firm that makes or supplies the product or service, or from company-wide marketing, distribution, or service activities or competencies that impact that firm's indiviudal offerings. These two lists are merely suggestive and are by no means exhaustive. But when combined with the likely importance of these various kinds of product knowledge to a potential customer when making a purchase decision, they provide some insights into the appropriateness of incorporating a strong corporate identity as part of the branding strategy for that product or service offering.

Product Associations	Focus on Product/Service or its Marketing Program	Focus on Manufacturer/ Supplier
Awareness	- Product Advertising/Promotion - Dedicated Salesforce	- Corporate Advertising/Promotion - Corporate/Divisional Salesforce - Other Elements of the "Corporate Voice"
Product-Related Attributes	- Component Materials - Size- Weight - Quality - Speed - Flavor/Taste - Energy Efficiency - Ease of Use - Style/Fashion - Durability - Compatibility - Serviceability	- Delivery Time - Sales Engineering/Systems Design - Installation - User Training - User Assistance/Trouble Shooting - Spare Parts Availability - Service Time - Service Reliability
Non-Product-Related Attributes	- Price - Packaging - Availability - Warranty - Imagery of Product Users - Imagery of Usage Situations	- Competence of Sales & Support Personnel - Empathy/Helpfulness of Sale & Support Personnel - Credit Policies - Imagery of Corporate Customers
Functional Benefits	- Relative Performance - Performance Reliability - Speed - Efficiency- Convenience - Nutrition - Versatility - Safety - Low Cost/Superior Value	- Creative Problems Solutions - System Solutions - Superior Logistics/Inventory Management - Superior Maintenance/Reduced Downtime - Reduced Waiting Time - Design/Manufacturing Flexibility
Experiential Benefits	- Sensory Performance - Variety/Line Breadth/Customization - Cognitive Stimulation - Risk	- Training/Skill Development Programs - Facilities/Ambiance - Warmth/Friendliness of Sales & Support Personnel
Symbolic Benefits	- Prestige/Status of Product Ownership - Exclusivity of Product Ownership - Customization; Opportunities for Self-Expression	- Prestige/Status of Corporate Image - Exclusivity/Status of Corporate Customer or Clients
Secondary Associations	- Status/Reputation of Dealers or Distributors	- Customer Orientation of Company - Quality/Performance of Other Company Products or Services - Company's Reputation for Technology Leadership - Company's Reputation for Innovativeness - Company's Reputation for Quality - Company's Reputation for Reliability - Company's Reputation for Design - Company's Reputation for Service/ Responsiveness

Fig. 2: The Focus of Product Knowledge

5. The Importance of Product-Specific versus Company-Based Associations - Some Branding Implications

The strategic implications of the relative importance of product-specific versus company-focused brand associations for alternative branding policies are summarized in matrix form in Figure 3. The Figure specifies some of the conditions under which each set of brand associations is likely to be relatively important and

248

		Importance of Company-Related Associations	
		High	**Low**

Importance of Product-Specific Associations	**Low**	**CORPORATE BRAND DOMINANT**
		Conditions:
		• Corporate competencies or programs add significant value for target customers
		  - Service business
		  - Industrial goods
		  - High technology product/systems
		• Product quality difficult to judge before use
		• Company offer a single line, or closely related product lines
		• Strong, positive Corp. identity reputation
		• Limited marketing resources expenditures
		
		Examples:
		• Sony electronics
		• Siemens industrial & telecommunications prods.
		• McKinsey consulting services
		• Mercedes automobiles
		IBM computers
			MINIMAL EMPHASIS ON BRAND
			Conditions:
			• Little differentiation across alternatives
			• Low price is critical decision variable for most customers
			
			Examples:
			• Private lables/store brands
			• Generic pharmaceuticals
			• Agricultural commodities

	High	**DUAL BRAND**
		Conditions:
		• Common core of company competencies/ programs important to most customers, but specific features/benefits targeted at different segments
		• Company offers diverse, but compatible product lines
		• Strong, positive Corp. identity/reputation
		• Limited marketing resources/expenditures
		
		Examples:
		• Compaq computers
		• Microsoft software
		• British Ariways Club World, Club Europe, etc.
		• Fidelity Mutual Funds
			PRODUCT BRAND DOMINANT
			Conditions:
			• Multiple offerings in same product category targeted at diverse market segments
			  - Different quality levels
			  - Different service levels
			  - Different price points
			• Firm offers diverse array of inconsistent or incompatible products
			• Customers seek experiential or symbolic benefits
			• Substantial marketing resources/expenditures
			
			Examples:
			• Marlboro cigarettes
			• Sassoon hair care products
			• Cadillac automobiles
			• Scotch tape

Fig. 3: Brand Strategy Matrix Importance of Company-Related Associations

each alternative branding policiy is therefore likely to be appropriate. The rationale for each of the conditions listed in the matrix is examined in more detail in the following sections.

5.1. Dominant Corporate Brand

When the perceived importance of attributes or benefits flowing from the company that makes the product or service is high relative to the attributes and benefits associated with the product itself, a branding strategy in which the corporate name or identity plays a dominant role is likely to be most appropriate. The important question, of course, is under what circumstances the perceived importance of associations focused on the source company is likely to be relatively high. An examination of Figure 2 suggests that a large proportion of the company-based attributes and benefits that might be associated with a particular offering involve activities or competencies directly related to providing service to customers. For example, attributes such as service time and reliability and the competence and helpfulness of company personnel, benefits like creative problem solutions and skill development, and secondary associations such as the firm's customer orientation and its reputation for service quality and responsiveness all relate to the firm's ability to deliver timely, high-quality customer service. In many service industries, such company-based associations are virtually the only criteria potential customers have for evaluating the likely quality of a firm's service offering before making a purchase. This is because many services are by nature intangible and are often tailored to the specific needs of individual customers; particularly in industries characterized by high levels of direct contact between the firm and its customers (e.g., professional services such as business consulting, law, medicine, and education) (Chase 1978). Thus, their content and quality is hard for customers to judge **a priori** except by inference based on knowledge of the sponsoring firm's competencies and reputation. Consequently, a strong corporate identity - and branding strategy featuring a strong corporate identification - can have a great influence on customers' purchase decisions for such service. Thus, all else equal:

Proposition 1: A dominant corporate brand is more likely to be used by firms in service rather than manufacturing industries, particularly when high levels of customer contact are involved.

Of course, services can also substantially augment the value customers receive from physical products. Supplementary services such as sales engineering, quick and reliable delivery, installation, user training, and repair can provide important functional benefits to users. Once again, the likely quality and timeliness of such services depends largely on the sponsoring firm's competencies, experience, and reputation based on past performance. While such services sometimes play an important role in the marketing of consumer durables, such as automobiles and personal computers, they tend to be even more critical for industrial markets where purchase cycles are shorter, purchase volumes are larger, and products often are more complex. Indeed, the development of alliances between suppliers and their customers in such markets is becoming increasingly common as a means to facilitate the delivery of such supplementary services. Thus:

Proposition 2: A dominant corporate brand is more likely to be used by firms in industrial goods rather than consumer markets, particularly when the product is relatively complex and supplementary services add significant value for customers.

Supplementary services like sales engineering, system design, user training, and creative troubleshooting are likely to add even more value when the product is not only complex but also technically innovative and therefore unfamiliar to the buyer. For such complex innovations, superior service is not only necessary to enable the customer to gain full value from the product, but also to help lower the perceived risk involved in being an early adopter of unfamiliar technology. In other words, a strong identification of the product with the sponsoring firm's technical and engineering competencies and past successes in introducing new technologies - as is the primary theme of Siemens' advertising in the U.S. market - can help reassure potential customers and speed the adoption process. Thus:

Proposition 3: A dominant corporate brand is more likely to be used by firms who are technical innovators in their industries than by firms who are technical followers.

Another reason why a dominant corporate identity is often appropriate for technically innovative products is because potential customers may have difficulty judging the likely quality and performance levels of such unfamiliar offerings. As mentioned earlier, the intangible and customized nature of professional services make their quality and value hard for customers to judge a priori. Similarly, some products - particularly those which are technically innovative and complex - are hard for customers to evaluate without actually buying and using the product. In such cases, some sellers may try to reassure potential buyers by allowing them to try out the product without making a major financial commitment; as when customers are encouraged to test drive a new car. A more efficient way to signal potential customers that the product is of high quality is simply for a sponsoring firm with a strong reputation as a technical innovator and producer of quality products to put that reputation on the line by associating itself directly with the product (Rao/Ruekert 1994).

Of course, there is some risk to the sponsoring firm in pursuing such a strategy. If customers are disappointed by the product's performance, the firm's reputation could be damaged. But that is exactly why a strong association between a new product and reputable manufacturer is so reassuring to potential customers. They know the firm would be reluctant to risk its reputation by putting its corporate brand on products that fall below its historical standards. Thus:

> **Proposition 4:** A dominant corporate brand is more likely to be used by firms producing "experience" goods that are hard to evaluate before purchase.

Moderating variables. All of the above propositions are moderated by the existing competencies, past experience, and reputation of the sponsoring firm. In other words, while the preceding propostions all suggest situations where a dominant corporate identity may be an appropriate branding strategy, such a strategy makes most sense when the firm already has a strong, positive identity among target customers. For example, Sony's history as an innovator in the consumer electronics industry facilitates the adoption of new innovations introduced under the corporate brand, such as the Sony Discman. And McDonalds' reputation for consistent quality control helps customers world-wide know what to expect when they eat at any McDonalds' restaurant. Thus:

> **Proposition 5:** A dominant corporate brand is more likely to be used by firms with a well-established, positive corporate identity among its target customers.

Unfortunately, a firm's corporate identity may be based on competencies or secondary associations that are not equally relevant or important to all potential customers across different product or service categories, or even to all customer segments within a single category. Even corporate attributes that are considered positive and relevant in one market context or by one market segment may be viewed as irrelevant - or even as a disadvantage - in another context or segment. For instance, Toyota's reputation as a cost-efficient manufacturer of reliable cars has contributed to its success in the low and medium-priced segments of the automobile market. But the firm feared its low-cost, mass-market identity would be a negative association in the luxury car segment where customers likely consider selectivity, prestige, and innovative engineering more important brand attributes. Consequently, Toyota committed substantial resources to create a distinct brand image for its Lexus automobiles; even going so far as to establish a separate dealer organization to sell and service its cars. For other examples of firms with strong corporate identities who have developed separate brands for markets where the company's identity was irrelevant or inconsistent with customer preferences and desired benefits, see "Brands Disown Their Parents," Fortune, September 5, 1994, p. 15. This suggests, then, that the appropriateness of a dominant corporate brand is moderated by the scope of the corporation's competitive strategy; by the breadth and diversity of the firm's product lines and the heterogeneity of the various market segments it targets. Thus:

> **Proposition 6a:** A dominant corporate brand is more likely to be used by firms with a single product line, or a limited number of complementary lines, than by firms competing in a large number of diverse product or service categories.
>
> **Proposition 6b:** A dominant corporate brand is more likely to be used by firms targeting a single market segment, or a limited number of segments seeking similar attributes and benefits, than by firms targeting a broad range of customer segments with different needs and preferences.

Finally, the attractiveness of a dominant corporate brand may also be moderated by the marketing resources avaiblable within the firm, and its managers' willingness to commit those resources across its various product lines and target markets. As mentioned earlier, a dominant corporate brand - as one part of a strong Corporate Voice program - can help a firm gain greater efficiency in its marketing programs. By focusing on a common core of company attributes and values, every impression generated by each product's design, packaging, advertising, and other promotional materials can reinforce and strengthen the impact of all the other impressions communicated to potential customers. While finding ways to increase the efficiency of marketing expenditures is of growing interest to many firms in today's competitive environment (Sheth/Sisodia 1995), it is of particular concern to companies who have limited marketing resources relative to the number of products they wish to promote and/or target markets they hope to communicate with. Thus:

> **Proposition 7:** A dominant corporate brand is more likely to be used by firms with limited marketing resources relative to their number of product offerings and/or target markets than by firms with more substantial resources relative to their requirements.

5.2. Dual Branding

As indicated in Figure 3, when potential customers attach high levels of importance to **both** product specific and company-related attributes, benefits, and associations, a dual branding strategy which prominently features both the corporate identity and an individual product brand is likely to be appropriate. Once again, the important question is under what conditions the perceived importance of both product-related and company-based associations is likely to be high. Many of the conditions where we expect potential customers to attach substantial importance to company-based attributes and associations have already been described in the preceding section. Thus, one might expect dual branding to occur under some of the same circumstances as the use of a dominant corporate brand;

especially when (a) the firm is in a service business or is selling complex products where timely, high-quality services from the supplier can add substantial value for customers, (b) it is selling products or services that are technically complex and/or dificult for customers to objectively evaluate before purchase, and (c) the sponsoring firm has developed a strong, positive identity based on core competencies or past performance outcomes that are relevant across its various product categories and customer segments.

Obviously, though, dual branding also requires some additional conditions which favor an **emphasis on individual product names as well as on the corporate brand**-conditions which magnify the perceived importance of individual attributes or benefits associated with different products within the firm's set offerings. One situation where this is often the case is when a firm presents multiple offerings within a product category, each targeted at a unique segment of customers. While there may be a common core of company-related attributes (e.g., a reputation for technical leadership or good customer service) that are relevant to customers in all of the targeted segments, each segment may also seek somewhat different product-specific attributes or benefits. Separate product names can help signal such product-specific differences and aid customers in associating different attributes with the appropriate offerings from a given supplier. For instance, while Microsoft clearly identifies itself as the corporate sponsor of all its software products, different offerings also carry individual product names - such as Windows 95 or Word - to help potential customers identify the specific applications each was designed for and their unique features. Thus:

> **Proposition 8:** A dual branding strategy is more likely to be used by firms with relatively broad product lines incorporating offerings with unique attributes or benefits targeted at separate market segments, but where there is a common core of company-specific attributes that are important across segments.

A different, though closely related, situation involves firms offering products or services in multiple categories or industries. Once again, a common core of company-related attributes may be relevant across many or all of the firms various businesses, but customers in the different categories may also attach great importance to attributes or benefits that are unique to that category. For instance, the 3M Company manufactures more than 65,000 different products in a variety of consumer and industrial goods businesses. Given that the firm's strong reputation for innovativeness, technical competence, and reliable service is relevant to customers across many of its businesses, the corporate logo is featured prominently on most of the firm's products. But individual product or product-line names are also used to identify offerings targeted at specific markets (e.g., dentists or automotive manufacturers) or specific applications (e.g., Post-it Notes or Scotch-Brite

Never-Rust scouring pads). It is also interesting to note that strong emphasis on the 3M logo as part of the firm's dual branding strategy emerged - at least in part - out of a desire to increase the efficiency of the company's promotional efforts (as suggested by Proposition 7); an important consideration for a firm with 65,000 different product offerings around the world. Thus:

Proposition 9: A dual branding strategy is more likely to be used by firms which compete in many diverse, but relatively compatible, businesses or product categories.

Finally, a dual branding strategy may sometimes evolve when a firm accumulates a number of established brands from other companies through mergers or acquisitions. In such circumstance, dual branding enables the acquiring firm to signal that its competencies and reputation are now behind the product while simultaneously preserving any equity accruing to the original product name. Thus:

Proposition 10: A dual branding strategy is more likely to be used by firms which offer a substantial proportion of products obtained from other companies through merger or acquisition.

5.3. Dominant Product Brand

The conditions favoring the use of separate brands for individual products - where the sponsoring firm's identity is de-emphasized or even hidden - involve situations whre associations with the attributes or reputation of the sponsoring firm are relatively unimportant to most potential customers compared to product-specific associations. In general terms, such situations are the opposite of those described in the preceding propositions. Specifically, we expect firms to emphasize individual product brands when: (a) they are selling consumer nondurable goods rather than more technically complex durables, industrial products, or professional services where ancillary services provided by the sponsoring firm are likely to be important purchase criteria; (b) they are selling familiar "search" products which are relatively easy for customers to evaluate prior to purchase rather than more complex "experience" goods where the firm's competence and repuation may serve as important signals of product quality; and (c) they are selling non-technical products or offerings based on familiar technologies rather than technically innovative products or services.

In addition, the kinds of benefits being sought by customers may also play a role. Specifically, experiential benefits such as sensory pleasure or stimulation, or symbolic benefits such as social approval or self-expression, tend to flow directly from attributes of the product itself or its marketing program (e.g., performance characteristics, style, opportunities for customization, price, etc.), or from associations with other product users or use situations (e.g., endorsements by sports stars or other public figures, etc.). Individual product brands are more likely to capture and reflect such product-specific associations. Thus:

Proposition 11: Individual product brands are more likely to be used in product categories where experiential and/or symbolic benefits are relatively important to most potential customers.

Earlier, Propositions 8 and 9 argued that dual branding strategies are likely to be pursued by firms with broad product lines offering unique benefits to separate market segments, and by firms competing in many diverse businesses or product categories. However, dual branding strategies are appropriate in such situations **only if** there is also a common core of company-specific attributes or benefits that appeal to customers in most of the targeted segments and if customers perceive the firm's various businesses and product offerings to be reasonably compatible with one another. When these conditions are not met, it often makes more sense for firms to use separate brand names for each product in the line, or for each business or product category, while de-emphasizing the corporation's identity. For example, Toyota created a separate brand for its Lexsus automobiles to disassociate the line from the low-priced image of the parent company, and meat packing firms typically use separate brands for consumer products versus pet foods since many customers may be reluctant to buy packaged meats carrying the same brand or corporate identity as the food they buy for their dogs and cats. Thus:

Proposition 12a: Individual product brands are more likely to be used by firms with relatively broad product lines incorporating offerings with unique attributes or benefits targeted at separate market segments when there is no common core of company-specific attributes that are important across segments.

Proposition 12b: Individual product brands are more likely to be used by firms which compete in many diverse businesses or product categories which customers perceive to be inconsistent or incompatible with one another.

Finally, many of the variables that we have argued moderate the use of a dominant corporate brand also work in reverse to influence the appropriateness of a strategy emphasizing individual brand names. Thus, individual product brands are more viable when the parent firm has sufficient financial and human resources to support, promote, and manage multiple brands effectively. Similarly, individual product brands may be more appropriate for firms which lack a strong, positive corporate identity, or whose identity may generate some unfavorable associations in at least some of the product-markets in which it competes - as was Toyota's concern in the luxury car market.

5.4. Minimal Brand Emphasis

Historically, unbranded products have been confined primarily to commodities which are difficult to differentiate in the marketplace on the basis of unique product attributes or benefits, such as agricultural products or component parts supplied to original equipment manufacturers. Increasingly, however, firms have found ways to differentiate even the most basic commodities. In some cases they have accomplished this via an infusion of continous technical improvements or rigorous quality control, and have begun emphasizing corporate brand names as signals of superior technology or product quality. For example, Intel aggressively promotes its corporate identity to help build demand among end-users for each new generation of chips it supplies to various computer manufacturers, and food processors such as Dole market high quality fresh vegetables under their corporate brands.

More commonly, firms are adding value to mundane commodity products by developing innovative supplementary services, such as the formation of logistics alliances with major customers. While such services help differentiate the offerings of one supplier from another, the perceived value of such services in the eyes of potential customers depends on the suppplier's competencies, capabilities, and reputation. Thus, as more firms in mature, commodity businesses seek new ways to differentiate their offerings from the competition, it seems likely they will also increase their emphasis on corporate brands to help customers identify and develop loyalty to those offerings. Indeed, the trend toward the development of strong corporate brands for previously unbranded commodities and components is already well underway and we expect it to continue.

6. International Implications for Branding Strategy

A number of academic articles in recent years have addressed questions of branding strategy across international markets (e.g., Onkvisit/Shaw 1989, Jain 1989, Roth 1995). In general, the existing literature explores conditions affecting the appropriateness of **standardized versus localized products and brands** across national boundaries. It suggests, for instance, that the use of standardized global brands is more likely when a firm is targeting countries (a) that are similar in their socioeconomic characteristics and in their physical, political, and legal environments; (b) that are culturally compatible and have similar patterns of customer behavior and lifestyles, (c) in which the firm's competitve position is relatively similar and where it faces the same competitve adversaries, and (d) that do not impose legal restrictions or financial penalties on foreign brands (Jain 1989).

It is important to note that the existing literature does not directly explore the appropriateness of strong corporate brands across international markets. However, there are close parallels between the decision to use a standard international brand versus localized brands and the decision to adopt a corporate brand versus individual product brands. In most cases firms that promote a standard brand across national boundaries also pursue a corporate branding strategy; their corporate identity serves as their global brand. On the other hand, the adoption of local brands for different countries virtually dictates the use of different brand names for individual product or service offerings. Therefore, many of the conditions identified in the marketing literature as favoring the use of a standard brand across countries should also favor the use of a strong corporate branding strategy.

However, the framework outlined in Figures 2 and 3 which distinguishes the sources of brand equity on the basis of the relative importance customers attach to product-specific versus company-related attributes, benefits, and associations can contribute some additional insights concerning when a strong corporate brand might be appropriate in global markets. For example, it seems likely that company-related associations - such as the perceived competencies of the firm, the value-enhancing services it provides customers, and its reputation for technical innovation and product quality - all speak to universal customer needs and desires that are likely to be quite constant across countries. Consequently, products and service offerings for which such company-related associations are relatively important to customers - such as professional services (Propositon 1), complex industrial products and consumer durables (Proposition 2), technically innovative products (Proposition 3), and "experience" goods and services which are difficult for customers to evaluate prior to purchase (Proposition 4) all seem likely candidates for the use of a dominant corporate branding strategy across global markets.

However, the above propositions assume that the sponsoring firm will be able to **deliver the same levels** of competence, customer service, and quality in international markets as they do in their home market. If this is not the case, the use of a strong corporate brand might be ineffective, and it might even damage the image and reputation of the company around the world. Therefore, the appropriateness of a global corporate brand is moderated by the kind of market entry strategy the firm employs. Corporate brands are likely to be most appropriate in global markets where the sponsoring firm has a high degree of control over its product quality and relations with customers. Such control is most likely in markets which the firm has entered via direct investment or joint ventures in which it has a controlling interest. Corporate branding is less appropriate for firms which rely on import agents or licensing agreements-where the sponsoring firm has less direct control over quality and service performance - to enter international markets. Thus:

> **Proposition 13:** An international corporate brand is more likely to be used by firms that enter foreign markets via direct investment or joint venture than those that rely on import agents or licensing agreements.

On the other hand, offerings for which product-specific attributes are relatively more important to customers in making purchase decisions are more likely candidates for individual and localized product brands or for dual branding strategies. This is especially true for products where the product-specific attributes and benefits sought may vary substantially across countries with different cultural and socioeconomic characteristics, such as consumer nondurables that offer primarily experiential or symbolic benefits (Proposition 11), or that are consumed in different usage situations in different countries (Jain 1989; Roth 1995).

Finally, many of the same factors that influence the adoption of individual product brands in a firm's home market are also likely to dictate individual and localized brands in international markets as well. Such is most probably the case for firms (a) competing in diverse and incompatible businesses within a host country; (b) offering diverse product lines targeted at distinct segments within a host country who attach little importance to any common company-related attributes or associations, or (c) firms which have a weak or inappropriate identity within the host country.

7. Conclusion

We have shown that an analytical framework that separates the various associations that underlie customers' knowledge about a brand - and therefore the brand's equity in the marketplace - into product-specific versus company-related associations can produce a wealth of propositions concerning the circumstances where different branding strategies are likely to be most appropriate. It is important to keep in mind, though, that the propositions presented here are by no means exhaustive. There are no doubt many additional factors affecting the adoption and effectiveness of different branding strategies. More critically, our propositions are speculative. While we have provides examples which seem to support each proposition, we would remind readers of the scientific dictum that, „For example is not proof." Therefore, we offer our conceptual framework and its propositions in the hope that it will stimulate further research and analysis. In the meantime, we hope that practicing managers will a least find the framework provocative, and perhaps even find it useful as an aid to making branding decisions in their organizations.

Bibliography:

Aaker, D. A. (1991), Managing Brand Equity, New York 1991

Boddewyn, J.J., Soehl, R., Picard, J. (1986), Standardization in International Marketing: Is Ted Levitt in Fact Right? in: Business Horizons, Vol. 29 (1986), pp. 69-75

Blattberg, R. C., Wisniewski, K. J. (1989), Price-Induced Patterns of Competition, in: Marketing Science, Vol. 8 (1989), pp. 291-309

Chase, R. B. (1978), Where Does the Customer Fit Into a Service Operation?, in: Havard Business Review, November-December 1978, pp. 139-74

Jain, S. C. (1989), Standardization of International Marketing Strategy: Some Research Hypotheses, in: Journal of Marketing, Vol. 53 (1989), pp. 70-79

Keefe, L. M. (1995), Corporate Voice in Relation to Product Brands, in: Design Management Journal, Vol. 6 (1995), pp. 45-49

Keller, K. L. (1993), Conceptualizing, Measuring, and Managing Customer-Based Brand Equity, in: Journal of Marketing, Vol. 57 (1993), pp. 1-22

Kotler, P. (1994), Marketing Management: Analysis, Planning, Implementation, and Control, Englewood Cliffs 1994

Onkvisit, S., Shaw, J. J. (1989), The International Dimension of Branding: Strategic Considerations and Decisions, in: International Marketing Review, 1989, pp. 22-34

Plummer, J. T. (1985), How Personality Makes a Difference, in: Journal of Advertising Research, Vol. 24 (1985), pp. 27-31

Rao, A. R., Monroe, K. B. (1989), The Effects of Price, Brand Name, and Store Name on Buyers' Perceptions of Product Quality: An Integrative Review, in: Journal of Marketing Research, Vol. 26 (1989), pp. 351-57

Rao, A. R., Ruekert, R. W. (1994), Brand Alliances as Signals of Product Quality, in: Sloan Management Review, Vol. 36 (1994), pp. 87-97

Roth, M. S. (1995), The Effects of Culture and Socioeconomics on the Performance of Global Brand Image Strategies, in: Journal of Marketing Research, Vol. 32 (1995), pp. 163-175

Sheth, J., Sisodia, R. S. (1995), Feeling the Heat, in: Marketing Management, Vol. 4 (1995), pp. 8-23

Marketing im interaktiven Zeitalter

Claudia Fantapié Altobelli
Stefan Hoffmann

Summary:

„New Media", „Interactive Media" and „Multimedia" are key-words drawing more and more attention during the last years. Developments in the field of information and communication technology, for example digitalisation and data compression procedures, lead to the progress of new communication platforms and therefore supplement the „classic" media-mix, consisting of print and television, by innovative media like internet and CD ROM. In spite of their little reach compared to classic media, it is agreed that new challenges occur, especially to the creative agencies, to develop innovative contents and designs for new media.

1. Einführung

„Neue Medien", „interaktive Medien" und „Multimedia" sind Schlagworte, die in den letzten Jahren immer stärkeres Interesse auf sich ziehen. Fortschritte in der Informations- und Kommunikationstechnologie, etwa Digitalisierung und Datenkompressionsverfahren, haben zur Entwicklung neuer Kommunikationsplattformen und damit zu einer Ergänzung des „klassischen" Medienmix aus Print und TV um innovative Medien wie Internet und CD ROMs beigetragen. Trotz der im Vergleich zu den klassischen Medien bislang eher geringen Reichweite besteht Einigkeit darüber, daß die neuen interaktiven Medien große Potentiale für die werbende Wirtschaft bergen; gleichzeitig entstehen aber auch neue Herausforderungen, insbesondere für die Kreativbranche, welche für die Neuen Medien innovative Inhalte und Präsentationsformen entwickeln muß.

2. Einsatzmöglichkeiten interaktiver Medien im Marketing

2.1. Die Neuen Medien im Überblick

Die rasanten Fortschritte in der Informations- und Kommunikationstechnologie haben zu einer Fülle neuer Medien geführt, welche unter dem Begriff „Multimedia" subsumiert werden können. Zur begrifflichen Abgrenzung von Multimedia

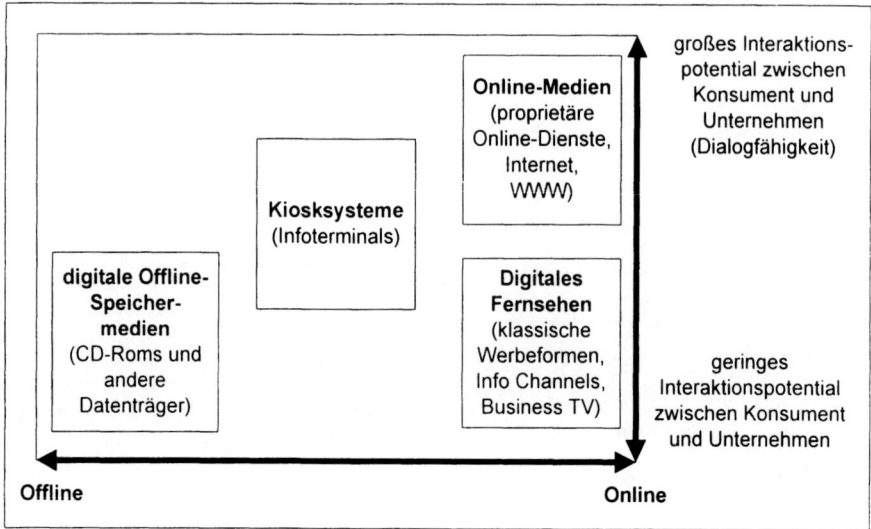

Quelle: In Anlehnung an Fink/Meyer 1996, S. 56; Booz, Allen & Hamilton
1995, S. 28.

Abb. 1: Systematik von Multimedia

lassen sich dabei folgende Kriterien heranziehen (vgl. Silberer 1995, S. 4 f.; Hünerberg/Heise 1995, S. 1 ff.; Schierl 1996, S. 40 f.):

- Durch **multimodale** Informationstechnologien werden mehrere Sinne der menschlichen Wahrnehmung angesprochen. In diesem Sinne sind sämtliche audiovisuellen Technologien - etwa das Fernsehen - in der Lage, multimodal zu kommunizieren.
- **Interaktivität** ist das eigentliche Kennzeichen von Multimedia. Interaktive Technologien erlauben es dem Nutzer, Inhalte gezielt zu selektieren und damit aktiv in den Kommunikationsprozeß einzugreifen; speziell bei Online-Medien (vgl. Abschn. 2.5.) ist sogar eine echte **Dialogfähigkeit** gegeben, d.h. die Möglichkeit einer Two-Way-Kommunikation.
- Darüber hinaus liegen bei multimedialen Anwendungen die Informationen in **digitaler** Form vor oder werden digital bearbeitet. Dies erlaubt die Speicherung und Übertragung einer erheblich größeren Datenmenge als bei analogen Technologien.

Eine Systematik der neuen Medien kann dabei nach mehreren Kriterien erfolgen (vgl. Abb. 1). Zum einen kann zwischen Offline- und Online-Medien unterschieden werden. Während **Offline-Medien** Datenträger umfassen, auf denen vorproduzierte Informationen gespeichert und von einem PC-Arbeitsplatz aus lokal abgerufen werden können (z.B. CD ROMs), stellen **Online-Medien**, wie das Internet, netzgebundene Verteil- und Abrufdienste dar, die eine Informationsübertragung in Echtzeit wie auch den Dialog zwischen Sender und Empfänger ermöglichen. Zum anderen kann nach dem Ausmaß der Interaktion zwischen Medien, die nur interaktive Abrufmöglichkeiten gestatten, und solchen, die eine „echte" Dialogfähigkeit bieten, unterschieden werden. Zu den wichtigsten Neuen Medien zählen im einzelnen:

- das digitale Fernsehen,
- Kiosksysteme,
- CD ROMs und
- Online-Medien.

2.2. Digitales Fernsehen

Anders als bei der herkömmlichen TV-Technologie muß das Programm beim digitalen Fernsehen in Form von digitalen Daten vorliegen; über Satellit, Kabelnetz oder terrestrische Sender wird das digalisierte Programm zu den TV-Haushalten übertragen. Durch die Digitalisierung können wesentlich mehr Programme ausgestrahlt werden als bei analoger Übertragung; darüber hinaus profitieren die Fernsehzuschauer von einer höheren Bildqualität (vgl. Schrape 1996, S. 7 f.). Interaktiv wird das digitale Fernsehen dann, wenn zwischen Zuschauer und Sender ein Rückkanal geschaltet wird: Über **Video-on-Demand** kann der Nutzer z.B. individuell von einem Video-Server Angebote abrufen und sich das eigene Programm selbst zusammenstellen. Die größere Programmvielfalt erlaubt es darüber hinaus, bspw. bei sportlichen Ereignissen wie Autorennen, die Sendung aus mehreren Perspektiven gleichzeitig zu übertragen, indem für jede Perspektive ein separater Kanal eingerichtet wird; der Zuschauer kann dann - quasi als eigener Regisseur - seine favorisierte Perspektive auswählen.

Damit die Zuschauer das digitale Fernsehangebot nutzen können, benötigen sie eine spezielle Hardwarekomponente, die sog. Set-Top-Box, welche die empfangenen digitalen Signale analysiert und für herkömmliche Fernsehgeräte nutzbar macht. Mittelfristig ist dabei mit der Entwicklung neuer Fernsehgeräte zu rechnen, in denen diese Komponente bereits integriert ist (vgl. Booz Allen & Hamilton 1995, S. 37; Schrape 1996, S. 9).

Digitale Programmangebote können grundsätzlich gebührenfrei oder gebührenpflichtig angeboten werden, wobei gebührenfreie Programme voraussichtlich eher die Ausnahme darstellen werden. Hinsichtlich der Abrechnungsmodalitäten ist dabei zwischen „**Pay-per-Channel**" und „**Pay-per-View**" zu unterscheiden: Während beim Pay-per-Channel-Konzept die Zuschauer bestimmte verschlüsselte Kanäle abonnieren, entrichten sie beim Pay-per-View-Konzept lediglich für einzelne Sendungen ein Entgelt (vgl. Schrape 1995, S. 27); von der sog. Smart Card, die wie eine Telefonkarte funktioniert, werden die Nutzungsgebühren abgebucht.

Im Rahmen des **Marketing** kann das digitale Fernsehen zunächst als Plattform für die herkömmlichen TV-Werbeformen wie Werbespots, Sponsoring und Product

Placement genutzt werden (vgl. Glabus/Peters 1997, S. 77 f.). Des weiteren können spezielle Werbekanäle („Informercial Channels") für weiterführende, detailliertere Werbeinformationen oder Teleshopping-Kanäle für den Verkauf von Produkten eingerichtet werden. So ist etwa ein „Automobilkanal" denkbar, über den in Verbindung mit redaktionellen Beiträgen informative Promotion-Filme über einzelne Fahrzeuge ausgestrahlt werden. Befindet sich der Zuschauer im Kaufentscheidungsprozeß, so kann er über diesen Kanal für ihn relevante Informationen selektiv abrufen (vgl. Heinemann 1997, S. 123 ff.; Kroff 1995, S. 264). Einen Schritt weiter geht das **Business-TV**, bei dem Unternehmen die Peripherie des digitalen Fernsehens nutzen und eigene Fernsehprogramme für Mitarbeiter und Kunden anbieten. Richtet sich das Programm an die Mitarbeiter, so kann es zur internen Kommunikation und Schulung eingesetzt werden; sind Kunden die Zielgruppe, so kann z. B. der Gebrauch von Produkten vorgeführt werden (vgl. Schäfer 1997, S. 49 f.).

Die für digitale Fernsehangebote entstehenden **Kosten** sind sehr unterschiedlich (vg. Schrape 1995, S. 106 ff.). Spartenprogramme, z.B. für die Bereiche Gesundheit, Wirtschaft, Wissenschaft, verursachen jährliche Kosten in Höhe von 100 - 150 Mio. DM; bei einem Abo-Preis in Höhe von z.B. 20 DM/Monat wären damit rd. 416.000 - 625.000 Abonnenten erforderlich, sofern die Finanzierung ausschließlich über Gebühren erfolgt. Im Rahmen einer Finanzierung durch Werbung liegt die erforderliche durchschnittliche Zuschauerzahl - bei einem TKP von 30 DM und 15 % Werbezeit pro Tag - hingegen bei nur rd. 40.000 Zuschauern. Die Kosten eines Teleshopping-Programms sind wesentlich geringer und reichen von 25 Mio. DM bis zu 80 Mio. DM (mit TV-Mantelprogramm) pro Jahr; für das Betreiben eines Video-on-Demand-Dienstes wird von Kosten in Höhe von 200 $ pro angeschlossenem Haushalt ausgegangen.

2.3. CD-ROMs

Größte Bedeutung unter den mobilen Offline-Speichermedien hat die CD-ROM erlangt. Auf ihr können Texte, Ton, Stand- und Bewegtbilder in digitalisierter Form gespeichert werden. Neben der hohen erzielbaren Bild- und Tonqualität ist insb. die hohe Speicherkapazität hervorzuheben: Während eine herkömmliche Diskette 1,4 MB Speicherplatz umfaßt, kann eine CD-ROM mit einer Kapazität von bis zu 650 MB wesentlich umfangreichere und multimediale Informationen bereitstellen; in naher Zukunft ist mit einer weiteren Steigerung der CD-ROM-Speicherkapazität zu rechnen (vgl. Hünerberg/Heise 1995, S. 8 f.). Hinsichtlich der **Inhalte** besteht das größte Interesse der Nutzer vor allem für Auskunftssysteme, Lernprogramme, Lexika und Datenbanken, wohingegen CD-ROMs mit Produktinformationen, Werbung und verkaufsfördernden Inhalten vergleichsweise weniger nachgefragt werden (vgl. Spiegel Verlag 1996, S. 58).

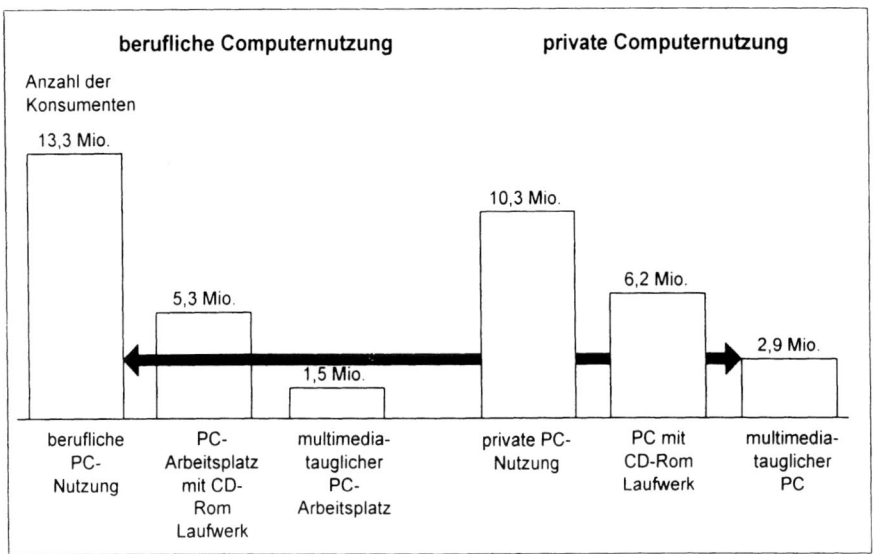

Quelle: Spiegel Verlag 1996, S. 31-59.

Abb. 2: Verbreitung von Multimedia-PCs in Betrieben und privaten Haushalten

Voraussetzung für die multimodale Nutzung der CD-ROM ist nicht nur das Vorhandensein eines CD-ROM-Laufwerks, sondern auch die Multimediatauglichkeit des verwendeten PCs; dies erfordert das Vorhandensein einer Soundkarte sowie von Lautsprechern. Wie aus Abb. 2 ersichtlich wird, sind heute in privaten Haushalten weniger als die Hälfte der mit CD ROM ausgestatteten PCs multimediatauglich; dabei ist die Multimediatauglichkeit der Endgeräte die Voraussetzung dafür, daß CD-ROMs seitens der Unternehmen für Marketingzwecke eingesetzt werden können.

Das Spektrum der **Marketing-Möglichkeiten** mit dem Offline-Medium CD-ROM ist sehr weitreichend. Einen ersten Einsatzbereich stellt die **Produkt- und Leistungspräsentation** dar. Parallel zur Markteinführung von neuen Modellreihen bieten Automobilhersteller neben den klassischen Prospekten bereits CD-ROMs als Informationsmaterial an. Auf diesen Promotion-CD-ROMs erhält der Nutzer u.a. interaktiv abrufbare Informationen über Preise von einzelnen Modellvarianten und kann menügesteuert sein Wunschauto mit Sonderausstattungen zusammenstellen (vgl. Jäschke/Albrecht 1996, S. 180). Neben Gebrauchsgütern mit extensiver Kaufentscheidung ist die CD-ROM auch für die Produktpräsentation von standardisierten Investitionsgütern geeignet (vgl. Heimbach 1997, S. 39); aber auch viele Dienstleister nutzen bereits die CD-ROM als Marketinginstrument. Die Lufthansa und die Deutsche Bahn präsentieren beispielsweise ihre aktuellen Flug- bzw. Fahrpläne auf CD-ROM.

Vor allem für den Versandhandel ist die CD-ROM zur **Sortimentspräsentation** sehr geeignet. Die großen deutschen Versandhandelsunternehmen offerieren bereits seit einigen Jahren ihre Kataloge auf CD-ROMs. Die Auflage der halbjährlich simultan mit den Print-Katalogen erscheinenden CD-ROMs liegt bei dem Versandhaus Quelle bei immerhin 300.000 Stück und beim OTTO-Versand bei 170.000 (vgl. Heimbach 1997, S. 40 ff.).

Geringe Bedeutung hat die CD-ROM hingegen im Bereich der **Werbung**. Obwohl sich reichweitenstarke CD-ROM-Publikationen wie Telefonbücher, Fahrpläne usw. gut als Insertionsmedien eignen, wird diese zusätzliche Einnahmequelle bisher nur von sehr wenigen Anbietern ausgeschöpft.

Entscheidend für die Erreichung der anvisierten Zielgruppen per CD-ROM ist nicht nur deren Inhalt, sondern auch die Vermarktung (vgl. Bruhn 1997, S. 12). Diese kann durch folgende Maßnahmen unterstützt werden:

- Print- und TV-Anzeigen müssen auf die CD-ROM verweisen, die bei Interesse per Fax, Telefon oder E-mail bestellt werden kann.
- In zielgruppenaffinen Zeitungen und Zeitschriften können CD-ROMs ähnlich wie Produktproben beigelegt werden. Aber auch über Kooperationen mit großen Computerhandelsketten kann die CD-ROM beim Neukauf eines Computers vertrieben werden.
- Darüber hinaus eignet sich der Direktvertrieb, bei dem auf bestehende Adressdaten zurückgegriffen wird, zur zielgruppengenauen Penetration.

Die Produktionskosten von qualitativ hochwertigen CD-ROMs sind im Vergleich zu den Reproduktionskosten relativ hoch: Für die Gestaltung und Programmierung sind Ausgaben bis zu einer Million Mark keine Seltenheit. Die Kosten für die Vervielfältigung betragen hingegen nur etwa 2 Mark pro Stück; insgesamt werden daher oftmals sogar die Herstellungskosten für einen vergleichbaren Printkatalog unterschritten (vgl. GfK/Horizont/MGM 1997, S. 27; Jäschke/Albrecht 1996, S. 180).

2.4. Kiosksysteme

Bei Kiosksystemen handelt es sich um frei zugängliche Computerterminals, die vom kommunizierenden Unternehmen am Point-of-Sale oder Point-of-Interest aufgestellt werden und für den Anwender multimedial aufbereitete Informationen bereithalten. In technischer Hinsicht handelt es sich um herkömmliche PCs, welche entweder auf CD-ROM gespeicherte Informationen bereitstellen, oder aber um hybride Systeme mit einem Online-Offline-Mix, d.h. neben dem Zugriff auf offline gespeicherte Daten wird der Zugang zu einem Online-System (z.B. Internet) ermöglicht. Im Vergleich zu herkömmlichen PCs zeichnen sich Kiosksysteme durch eine leichtere Bedienbarkeit aus, u.a. durch die sog. Touch-Screen-Technik (vgl. Rieke 1996, S. 116).

Grundsätzlich können zwei Typen von Kiosksystemen unterschieden werden (vgl. Bruhn 1997b, S. 13). **Point-of-Interest-Systeme** (Point-of-Information bzw. Point-of-Fun) besitzen primär informativen oder unterhaltenden Charakter und sind dem Pre-Sales-Bereich zuzuordnen. Mit Informationen über Produkte in Kaufhäusern oder auf Messen sollen die Nutzer zum Kauf angeregt werden (vgl. Silberer 1995, S. 16 f). Der eigentliche Kaufakt erfolgt nicht am Terminal, sondern in herkömmlicher Form über einen Verkäufer. **Point-of-Sale-Systeme** beinhalten hingegen neben den informativen Elementen auch Transaktionsfunktionen, welche die mit einem Kauf verbundene Austauschbeziehungen ermöglichen. So können z.B. Bestellungen, Reservierungen und Buchungen direkt am Terminal vorgenommen werden; einige Systeme ermöglichen darüber hinaus auch die Bezahlung mittels Eingabe entsprechender Daten wie Kreditkartennummer o.ä. Solche Systeme müssen eine hybride Struktur besitzen: Zeitlich invariante Daten (z.B. Produktpräsentationen) werden lokal gespeichert, wohingegen variante Daten (z.B. Preislisten, Rückkopplungen bei Buchungen und Bestellungen) online über die Netzanbindung übertragen werden (vgl. Hensmann/Meffert/Wagner 1996, S. 11). Trotz der vielfältigen Einsatzbereiche beginnt die Verbreitung von Kiosksystemen im Vergleich zu den übrigen Neuen Medien allerdings bereits zu stagnieren (vgl. GfK/Horizont/MGM 1997, S. 15).

2.5. Online-Medien

Online-Medien sind netzgebundene Abrufdienste, welche zum einen durch einen kommerziellen Betreiber zentral organisierte Dienste umfassen (proprietäre Online-Dienste), zum anderen offene Systeme mit dezentraler Struktur wie das World Wide Web (WWW) des Internet. Innerhalb der Neuen Medien nehmen Online-Medien, insb. das Internet, eine herausragende Stellung ein.

Ursprünglich für militärische Zwecke konzipiert und später von akademischen Institutionen „entdeckt", hat das **Internet** seinen Siegeszug mittlerweile auch im kommerziellen Bereich angetreten. Mit knapp 20 Millionen angeschlossenen Rechnern weltweit (Stand: Juli 1997) - davon über 700.000 in Deutschland - ist Internet der mit Abstand größte zusammenhängende Online-Verbund der Welt (vgl. Internet Domain Survey 1997, o.S.). Die Zahl der Nutzer ist eine Vielfaches davon: Allein in Deutschland wird von 3,75 Mio. aktiven Online-Nutzern ausgegangen (vgl. Spiegel Verlag 1996, S. 60). Abb. 3 zeigt die weltweite Entwicklung der Host-Rechner von 1981 - 1997. Erheblich beschleunigt wurde die Diffusion des Internets durch die Einführung des World Wide Web (WWW) im Jahre 1992, welcher mit seiner intuitiven Benutzeroberfläche und der Integration multimedialer Elemente die Benutzerfreundlichkeit des Internets erheblich verbesserte und das Medium zu einer attraktiven Marketingplattform machte (vgl. Fantapié Altobelli 1997, S. 5).

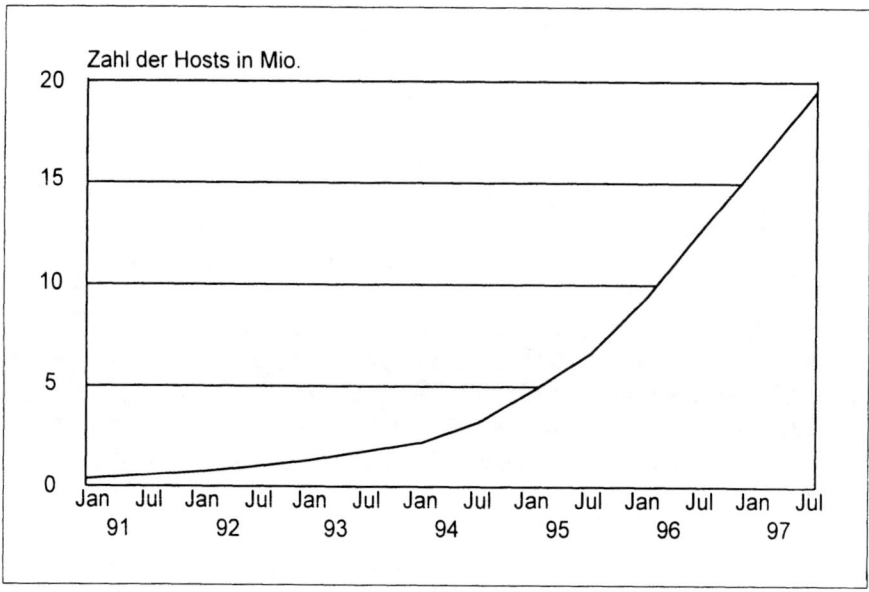

Quelle: Internet Domain Survey (1997), http://www.nw.com

Abb. 3: Weltweite Entwicklung der Host-Rechner im Internet 1991-1997

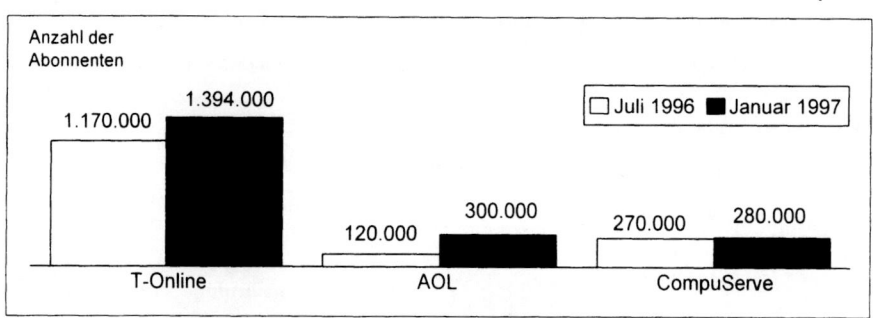

Quelle: MGM Mediareport 1997, S. 5.

Abb. 4: Abonnenten der proprietären Online-Dienste im Vergleich

Zu den kommerziellen, proprietären Online-Diensten zählen T-Online, CompuServe, AOL (America Online) sowie MSN (Microsoft Network). Abb. 4 zeigt die bisherige Entwicklung der proprietären Online-Dienste in Deutschland. Zu beachten ist hierbei, daß alle in Deutschland verfügbaren proprietären Dienste einen Zugang zum WWW ermöglichen, so daß die kommerziellen Dienste zunehmend eine reine Providerfunktion für den Internetzugang übernehmen. Während die Internet-Nutzung bis auf die anfallenden Telefongebühren kostenlos ist, sind für die Nutzung kommerzieller Online-Dienste an die Betreiber zusätzliche

	monatliche Gebühr	zeitbezogene Gebühr	inhalts- bezogene Gebühr	Internetnutzung	Zugangsknoten
T-Online	DM 8	DM 0,06/min DM 0,02/min	z.B. DM 0,30/ min (Fahr- planauskunft)	DM 3/h	zum Ortstarif
CompuServe	US$ 9,95 (5 Stunden frei)	US$ 2,95/h	je nach Information	-	12 Knoten
AOL	DM 9,90 (2 Stunden frei)	DM 6/h	-	-	60 Knoten
MSN	DM 12 (2 Stunden frei)	DM 6/h	-	-	36 Knoten

Quelle: Neue Mediengesellschaft Ulm 1996.

Abb. 5: Gebührenstruktur für proprietäre Online-Dienste in Deutschland

Gebühren zu entrichten; Abb. 5 zeigt die Tarifstruktur in kommerziellen Online-Diensten im Überblick.

Der deutsche Online-Dienst **T-Online** (früher BTX bzw. Datex-J) hat sich nach erheblichen Widerständen mit mittlerweile über 1,3 Mio. Teilnehmern (Stand: Januar 1997) etablieren können. T-Online hält zu unterschiedlichen Themenbereichen wie Finanzen, Nachrichten, Unterhaltung Informationen bereit; am stärksten genutzt wird jedoch das Homebanking, das lange Zeit die „Killer-Applikation" und den Hauptgrund für die Anschaffung von T-Online darstellte (vgl. Fugmann/Hoffmann/Pfleiderer 1996, S. 14). Auch in Zukunft wird sich T-Online als Breitband-Online-Dienst „für jedermann" positionieren. Im Gegensatz zu T-Online entstand der Online-Dienst **CompuServe** in den USA aus rein privater Initiative. CompuServe ist ein gebührenpflichtiges, geschlossenes Teilnetz im Internet (vgl. Cole 1996, o.S.). Der Betreiber übernimmt die Planung, Installation und Kontrolle für die Mitglieder, was eine deutlich bessere Übersichtlichkeit des Systems zur Folge hat (vgl. Fantapié Altobelli 1996, S. 5). Die Nutzerzahlen von CompuServe sind allerdings stagnierend; in Deutschland wurde CompuServe erst kürzlich von AOL überholt. In Zukunft will sich CompuServe verstärkt im Segment der Geschäftskunden positionieren.

Der derzeit wachstumsstärkste Dienst ist **AOL**, welcher aus einem Joint Venture von Bertelsmann mit America Online im November 1995 entstand. Die Angebote von AOL besitzen starken Entertainment-Bezug. In Zukunft sollen auch lokale

Informationen (z. B. Stadtmagazine, Fahrpläne von öffentlichen Nahverkehrsmitteln u.a.) in das Angebot aufgenommen werden; außerdem will AOL vor allem jüngere Zielgruppen ansprechen. Auch hier ist die Verzahnung mit dem Internet sehr eng. Darüber hinaus hat AOL mittlerweile CompuServe übernommen.

Mit der Einführung von Windows 95 ging auch **MSN** an den Start. Wie bei CompuServe stellt das Angebot von MSN ein Teilnetz des Internet dar; auch WWW-Nutzer können ohne Gebühren auf Teile von MSN zugreifen. Die Angebotepalette von MSN ist allerdings noch relativ schmal, so daß der Dienst derzeit keine ernsthafte Konkurrenz für T-Online, AOL und CompuServe darstellt. Ebenso wie AOL will MSN seine Angebote in Richtung Unterhaltung ausbauen (vgl. Hoffmann 1997, S. 14).

Die **Marketing-Möglichkeiten** in Online-Medien sind vielfältiger Natur. Die gebräuchlichste Form des Online-Marketing ist das Einrichten einer **Information-Site** als eigenständiger Auftritt eines Unternehmens mit einer Eingangsseite (Homepage) und hierarchisch angeordneten tieferliegenden Seiten. In der Regel enthält eine Information-Site neben Produkt- und Unternehmensinformationen auch ergänzende Komponenten wie Online-Beratung oder Online-After-Sales-Service, unterhaltende Komponenten wie Gewinnspiele sowie Komponenten mit Zusatznutzencharakter wie Börseninformationen (vgl. Fantapié Altobelli/Hoffmann 1996a, S. 24 ff.).

Inhaltlich sind auch bei den privat betriebenen Diensten keine Einschränkungen vorgegeben, außer bei Verstößen gegen Gesetze und Verordnungen. Unterschiedlich sind die **Kosten**, um bei den einzelnen Diensten eine Informations-Site einzurichten. Während in CompuServe keine Gebühren anfallen, sind bei T-Online für die Eingangsseite 350 DM/Monat bei deutschlandweitem bzw. 50 DM/Monat bei regionalem Angebot zu entrichten, darüber hinaus 8 bzw. 2 Pf. Pro Monat für jede weiter Seite (vgl. Deutsche Telekom 1996, o.S.). Der Zugang zum Internet erfolgt i.d.R. über kommerzielle Provider, so daß die dort anfallenden Kosten erheblich variieren können; je nach Umfang und Qualität des Auftritts fallen monatliche Kosten an, die sich i.d.R. zwischen 200 und 8000 DM bewegen (vgl. Fantapié Altobelli/Hoffmann 1996b, S. 7).

Online-Banner beinhalten die Plazierung von Markenzeichen oder Firmenlogos auf häufig besuchten Seiten anderer Anbieter, welche als Werbeträger fungieren (z. B. Spiegel online), aber auch auf Suchmaschinen wie Web.de, Lycos oder Yahoo. In diesem Sinne sind Banner die „eigentliche" Online-Werbung. In T-Online sind Banner auf internen Telekom-Seiten nicht möglich, wohl aber auf Seiten anderer Anbieter. Das Entgelt ist Verhandlungssache und richtet sich i.d.R. nach der Größe des Banners wie auch nach der Zahl der Abrufe der Datei. Auch in CompuServe ist das Schalten von Bannern grundsätzlich möglich; am weitesten verbreitet ist diese Marketing-Form jedoch im Internet. Abb. 6 zeigt die für die Banner-Plazierung in ausgewählten Seiten des WWW anfallenden Kosten.

Medien	Pixel-Größe	Preis in DM	Plazierungsdauer
Tageszeitungen			
www.bild.de	400x70	30.000,-	4 Wochen
www.welt.de	340x50	2.000,-	1 Woche
www.zeit.de	330x50	1.250,-	1 Woche
www.abendblatt.de	160x35	1.000,-	1 Woche
www.mopo.de	328x53	520,-	1 Woche
www.taz.de	120x100	5.400,-	4 Wochen
Publikumszeitschriften			
	137x60	3.500,-	4 Wochen
www.allegra.de	600x50	10.000,-	4 Wochen
www.amica.de	120x180	3.000,-	4 Wochen
www.autobild.de	600x50	10.000,-	4 Wochen
www.cinema.de	600x50	10.000,-	4 Wochen
www.fitforfun.de	432x50	30.000,-	4 Wochen
www.focus.de	400x80	5.400,-	4 Wochen
www.geo.de	100x75	500,-	4 Wochen
www.gong.de	400x80	3.200,-	1 Woche
www.spiegel.de	60x340	3.000,-	4 Wochen
www.sportbild.de	40x60	5.000,-	4 Wochen
www.stern.de	110x52	1.200,-	4 Wochen
www.tvtoday.de	600x50	10.000,-	4 Wochen
www.tvspielfilm.de			
Online-Medien			
	468x60	120,-	1000 Kontakte
www.web.de	180x60	0,35	1 Kontakt
www.netguide.de			
Fernsehen/Funk			
	400x30	2,-	Adclick
www.pro-sieben.de	60x300	8.000,-	4 Wochen
www.rtl.de	45x60	6.000,-	4 Wochen
www.rtl2.de	250x60	3.700,-	4 Wochen
www.vox.sw			

Quelle: Media Daten & Fakten 1997a, S. 80-135.

Abb. 6: Preise und Plazierungsdauer für Online-Banners bei führenden deutschen Online-Plattformen

Online Shopping beinhaltet den Verkauf von Produkten über einen virtuellen Marktplatz (z.B. eine „Shopping Mall", vgl. ausführlich Fantapié Altobelli/Fittkau 1997). Bei CompuServe muß dem Betreiber zunächst ein Konzept vorgelegt werden, das von CompuServe überprüft wird; außerdem verlangt CompuServe einen Mindestumsatz von 3000 $/Monat. Bei T-Online ist das Einrichten einer Shopping Mall uneingeschränkt möglich; die Telekom fungiert als Inkasso-Unternehmen und stellt dem Kunden den Kaufpreis des Artikels unter Einbehaltung von 2 % Provision über die Telefonrechnung in Rechnung. Die Integration der angebotenen Produkte in eine Shopping Mall ist auch im Internet uneingeschränkt möglich; die Kosten können von 50 bis 2500 DM betragen. Im Gegensatz zu den proprietären Online-Diensten ist jedoch bei der Übertragung von z.B. Kreditkarteninformationen die Gefahr des Mißbrauchs nicht ausgeschlossen.

3. Die Neuen und die klassischen Medien im Vergleich

Für viele Unternehmen stellt sich die Frage, welche Vorteile neue Medien im Vergleich zu den klassischen Medien bieten und - innerhalb der Gruppe der neuen Medien - welcher Kommunikationstechnologie der Vorzug zu geben ist. Im folgenden werden die neuen Medien miteinander sowie mit den klassischen Medien Print und TV anhand der Kriterien
- Multimedialität,
- Reichweite,
- Kontaktqualität,
- Aktualität,
- Verfügbarkeit,
- Globalität und
- Kontrollierbarkeit
verglichen.

3.1. Multimedialität

Alle neuen Medien beinhalten eine multimodale Technologie, welche bei den klassischen Medien nur beim Fernsehen gewährleistet ist; aufgrund der hohen Ladezeiten von Bildinformationen sind multimodale Anwendungen in Online-Medien jedoch noch mit Problemen behaftet. Im Vergleich zu den klassischen Medien bieten neue Medien auch den Vorteil der Interaktivität, d.h. der selektiven Abrufbarkeit von Informationen; Online-Medien und hybride Kiosk-Systeme ermöglichen darüber hinaus eine „echte" Two-Way-Kommunikation i.S. einer Dialogfähigkeit.

3.2. Reichweite

Ein Defizit der neuen Medien liegt in der noch geringen Reichweite. Erst wenige Millionen Deutsche sind Online-Nutzer; die reichweitenstärkste deutsche Online-Publikumszeitschrift Focus online z.B. erreicht gemessen an den Visits nur rd. 1 Mio. Kontakte pro Monat (vgl. PZ-online 1997). Auch die Auflagen von CD ROMs bewegen sich derzeit in der Größenordnung von einigen Hunderttausend, so daß diese Medien lediglich eine Ergänzungsfunktion zu den klassischen Medien übernehmen können. Die Zielgruppenpotentiale für Sparten-Programme im digitalen Fernsehen werden hingegen mit 5 - 6 Mio. Zuschauern beziffert (vgl. Schrape 1995, S. 107), so daß das digitale Fernsehen durchaus attraktive Zielgruppenpotentiale birgt. Die Ausbreitung von Kiosksystemen stagniert hingegen bereits.

3.3. Kontaktqualität

Die insgesamt geringe Reichweite der neuen Medien muß relativiert werden durch die erheblich bessere Kontaktqualität (vgl. Hoffmann 1997, S. 19). Der Nutzer wird nicht passiv der Werbebotschaft ausgesetzt, wie dies bei TV-Spots oder

Printanzeigen der Fall ist, sondern wählt aktiv und bewußt die Informationen, die er benötigt; bei aktiven Angeboten führt die Selbstbestimmtheit zu Verweildauern von mehreren Minuten. Interaktive Medien sind daher hervorragend geeignet, um hochinvolvierte Zielgruppen mit einem konkreten Produktinteresse zu erreichen (vgl. Fantapié Altobelli 1997, S. 11).

3.4. Aktualität

Online-Medien und hybride Kiosksysteme bieten den Vorteil der permanenten Aktualisierbarkeit der angebotenen Informationen; dies gilt - mit Einschränkungen - auch für kommerzielle Sendungen im Rahmen des digitalen Fernsehens. CD-ROMs und Offline-Kiosksysteme erfordern hingegen eine vollständige Neuauflage, wie dies auch bei herkömmlichen Printkatalogen der Fall ist.

3.5. Verfügbarkeit

Marketing-Informationen in Online-Medien und in Kiosk-Systemen sind sofort verfügbar, wohingegen eine CD-ROM i.d.R. erst geordert werden muß. Die Nutzung von Online-Medien und CD-ROMs ist allerdings am Vorhandensein eines multimedia-tauglichen PCs gebunden, wohingegen die Nutzung digitaler Fernsehprogramme lediglich eine Aufrüstung des vorhandenen TV-Geräts erfordert.

3.6. Globalität

Online-Marketing ist nicht nur zeitlich, sondern auch räumlich unbegrenzt. In den Web-Server eines Unternehmens können sich Nutzer weltweit einloggen. Die übrigen neuen Medien sind hingegen eher für den nationalen oder gar lokalen Einsatz geeignet. Auch bei den klassischen Medien besitzen die meisten Sender bzw. Printtitel einen regionalen oder nationalen Charakter; eine Ausnahme bilden supranationale Satellitenprogramme wie MTV und internationale Printtitel wie Time.

3.7. Kontrollierbarkeit

Die Reichweite sowie die Wirkung von TV- und Printkampagnen können nur über verschiedene Erhebungen (GfK-Fernsehpanel, Media Analyse usw.) und Werbetests (Recall-, Recognitiontest usw.) abgeschätzt werden (vgl. Behrens 1996, S. 145 ff.). Der direkte Erfolg in Form von Absatzsteigerungen läßt sich nicht exakt bestimmen, da auch andere Faktoren den Markt beeinflussen. Über Zugriffsdaten läßt sich die Nutzung von Online-Auftritten genauer bestimmen als es bei klassischen Medien über Panels und Erhebungen der Fall ist. Eine vielfach erwünschte exakte Kontrolle des User ist allerdings auch bei Online-Medien nicht möglich. Die Reichweite von CD-ROMs kann nur über den Abverkauf bzw. Vertrieb von CD-ROMs gemessen werden.

4. Fazit

Auf lange Sicht ist zu erwarten, daß sich Online-Anwendungen aufgrund der beschriebenen Vorteile sowie der fortschreitenden Verbesserung der technologischen Infrastruktur als Multimedia-Applikation im Marketing durchsetzen werden. Mittelfristig stellen Kombinationslösungen aus Offline und Online einen adäquaten Ansatz dar. Konstante Rahmeninformationen können, hochwertig aufbereitet, offline präsentiert werden. Aktuelle Informationen (z.B. Preise, Buchungssituation) und erweiterte Funktionen (z.B. Bestellverfahren) werden online ergänzt (vgl. Fink/Meyer/Wamser 1995, S. 470). Die klassischen Massenmedien werden jedoch nie ihre Bedeutung zur Bekanntmachung von Produkten und zur Einstellungsbildung verlieren.

Literatur:

Behrens, G. (1996), Werbung, München 1996

Booz, Allen & Hamilton (Hrsg.) (1995), Zukunft Multimedia: Grundlagen, Märkte und Perspektiven in Deutschland, Frankfurt/Main 1995

Bruhn, M. (1997), Multimedia-Kommunikation, München 1997

Cole, T. (Hrsg.) (1996), Internet Praxis: Der Wegweiser für das größte Datennetz der Welt (Loseblattsammlung), München 1996

Fantapié Altobelli, C., Fittkau, S. (1997), Formen und Erfolgsfaktoren der Online-Distribution, in: Trommsdorff, V. (Hrsg.), Handelsforschung 1997/1998: Positionierung des Handels, Jahrbuch der Forschungsstelle für Handel Berlin (FFH) e.V., Wiesbaden 1997, S. 397-415

Fantapié Altobelli, Hoffmann, S. (1996a), Werbung im Internet: Wie Unternehmen ihren Online-Werbeauftritt planen und optimieren, München 1996

Fantapié Altobelli, C., Hoffmann, S. (1996b), Online-Marketing, in: Weidner, L.E. (Hrsg.), Handbuch Kommunikationspraxis, 14. Nachlieferung 6/1996, Teil F/II/4, S. 1-13

Fink, D.H., Meyer, N. (1996), Multimedia: Wie Visionen zu Geld werden, in: Absatzwirtschaft, 1996, Nr. 3, S. 56-62

Fink, D.H., Meyer, N., Wamser, C. (1996), Multimedia-Einsatz im Marketing, in: Marketing Journal, 1995, Nr. 6, S. 468-470

Fugmann, J., Hoffmann, S., Pfleiderer, R. (1996), Infratest Burke: Die ForeRunner der Multimedia Generation: Online-Survey von Infratest Burke, München 1996

GfK, Horizont, MGM (Hrsg.) (1997), Multimedia-Barometer, München 1997

Glabus, W., Peters, R. H. (1997), Nichts ist unmöglich: Spitzensport im Abo-TV krempelt das Mediengeschäft um, in: Wirtschaftswoche, 1997, Nr. 43, S. 77-78

Heimbach, P. (1997), Marktkommunikation mit digitalen Offline-Medien, in: Silberer, G. (Hrsg.), Interaktive Werbung, Stuttgart 1997, S. 23-70

Heinemann, C.(1997), Werbliche Kommunikation im interaktiven Fernsehen, in: Silberer, G. (Hrsg.), Interaktive Werbung, Stuttgart 1997, S. 197-225

Hensmann, J., Meffert, H., Wagner, P.O. (1996), Marketing mit multimedialen Kommunikationstechnologien - Einsatzfelder und Entwicklungsperspektiven, Arbeitspapier Nr. 101, Wissenschaftliche Gesellschaft für Marketing und Unternehmensführung, Münster 1996

Hoffmann, S. (1997), Optimales Online-Marketing. Analyse der Marketingmöglichkeiten im Medium Online und methodische Ansatzpunkte zur anwendergerechten Gestaltung, Diss. Hamburg 1997

Hünerberg, R., Heise, G. (1995), Multi-Media und Marketing: Grundlagen und Anwendungen, Wiesbaden 1995

Internet Domain Survey (1997): http://www.nw.com, Stand Juli 1997

Jäschke, M., Albrecht M. (1996), New Media - Von der Euphorie zur Investitionsentscheidung, in: Markenartikel, 1996, Nr. 5, S. 178-184

Kroff, G. (1995), Multimedia Online - Die Welt am Draht?, in: Markenartikel, 1995, Nr. 6, S. 260-264

MGM Mediareport (1997), Daten - Fakten - Trends: Telekommunikation: Online-Dienste und Internet, München 1997

Neue Mediengesellschaft Ulm (Hrsg.) (1996), Online: CompuServe, Internet, T-Online, AOL, Europe Online, MSN, München 1996

PZ-online (1997): http://www.pz-online.de, Stand: Oktober 1997

Rieke, H.J. (1996), Neun Thesen zu Strategie und Aufbau interaktiver PoS-Kiosksysteme, in: Absatzwirtschaft, 1996, Nr. 5, S. 116-117

Schäfer, M. (1997), Gestaltungsaspekte für Business TV Anwendungen, in: Bullinger, H.J., Broßmann, M. (Hrsg.), Business Television: Beginn einer neuen Informationskultur in den Unternehmen, Stuttgart 1997, S. 35-61

Schierl, T. (1996), Multimedia ante portas, in: Marketing Journal, 1996, Nr. 1, S. 40-44

Schrape, K. (1995), Digitales Fernsehen: Marktchancen und ordnungspolitischer Regelungsbedarf, München 1995

Schrape, K. (1996), Marktperspektiven für Online-Medien in der Schweiz, Vortrag anläßlich des New Media Day der MGM MediaGruppe München in Zürich, Basel 1996

Silberer, G. (1995), Marketing mit Multimedia im Überblick, in: Silberer, G. (Hrsg.), Marketing mit Multimedia, Grundlagen, Anwendungen und Management einer neuen Technologie im Marketing, Stuttgart 1995, S. 3-32

Spiegel Verlag (1996), Online-Offline: Hauptergebnisse, Codeplan, Hamburg 1996

Spiegel Verlag (1997), Online-Offline: Nutzer-Typologien, Hamburg 1997

Einkauf im Wandel - von der Versorgungserfüllung zum Strategischen Beschaffungsmarketing

Udo Koppelmann

Summary:

The main elements of the strategic procurement concepts required for today´s business are discussed. Particulary important are the situations analysis, the demand analysis, the procurement market analysis, the analysis of suppliers, the negotiations with suppliers, the procurement market research and control. The author discusses how to design the elements of strategic procurement.

1. Probleme des Einkaufs heute

Lean-Management, Business-Reengineering, wertschöpfungsorientiertes Prozeßkettendenken haben auch dazu beigetragen, die bisherige Beschaffungs- oder Einkaufspraxis kritisch zu überprüfen. Aussagen wie „Wenn wir doch nur dürften, wie wir wollen" oder „Man fragt uns ja nicht" oder „Der Einkauf ist der Mülleimer des Unternehmens" zeigen bereits, wo Schwachpunkte liegen. Andererseits gibt es natürlich Unternehmen, die den immensen Wertschöpfungsbeitrag der Beschaffung erkannt haben und daraus Konsequenzen zogen. Dies deutet bereits die folgende, einfache Rechnung an:

Annahmen (Bruttobetrachtung):
60 % Einkaufs/Absatzvolumen
4 % Bruttoumsatzrendite $60 \times \boxed{5 = 75} \times 4$
5 % Einkaufskostenreduktion/ja
100 Mio. Umsatzerlöse

Unter der Annahme der genannten Bedingungen haben also eine 5 %ige Kostensenkung der Beschaffung und eine 75%ige Umsatzsteigerung den selben Gewinneinfluß. Die wesentlichen „Rationalisierungsreserven" liegen heute in Beschaffung und Entwicklung. Deshalb müssen diese Bereiche hinsichtlich ihrer Ergebnisbeiträge professionalisiert werden. Das gibt es manches zu tun.

(1) Der Einkauf wird vielfach auf die **Ausführungsfunktion** reduziert. Die Entwicklung (z. B. Konstruktion, F + E, Design) legt fest, was zu kaufen ist, die

Produktion sagt, wann man was in welcher Menge benötigt. In vielen Fällen kann nicht einmal über den Preis verhandelt werden, wenn der Lieferant bereits durch die Konstruktion feststeht. Man könnte den Einkauf fast abschaffen. Bestellschreiben können auch andere! Worin liegt die Motivation, Beschaffungsmarktkenntnisse zu erarbeiten, wenn sie keiner nutzt? Diese Aussagen lassen sich prolongieren.

(2) Eine **Strategielücke** kennzeichnet vielerorts den Beschaffungsbereich. Eine repräsentative Erhebung im Jahr 1955 durch uns ergab, daß 76 % der Unternehmen im Beschaffungsbereich keine Mehrjahresplanung kennen. Viele Unternehmen sind stolz und präsentieren damit ihre Modernität durch den Verweis auf die Verwendung des SAP R/3-Programms. Hierbei handelt es sich aber lediglich um ein operatives Abwicklungsprogramm. Etwa die Hälfte der Unternehmen kennen keine Beschaffungsmarktforschung. Damit bleibt unerklärlich, auf welcher Basis langfristige Planung erfolgen soll. Während andere Abteilungen (Produktion, F + E, Marketing, Finanzen) selbstverständlich langfristig planen, herrschen diesbezüglich in der Beschaffung eher archaische Zustände.

Der Fortschritt einer Disziplin zeigt sich auch in ihrer **Methodenreichhaltigkeit**. Die folgende Abb. 1 zeigt, daß davon im Beschaffungsbereich wohl

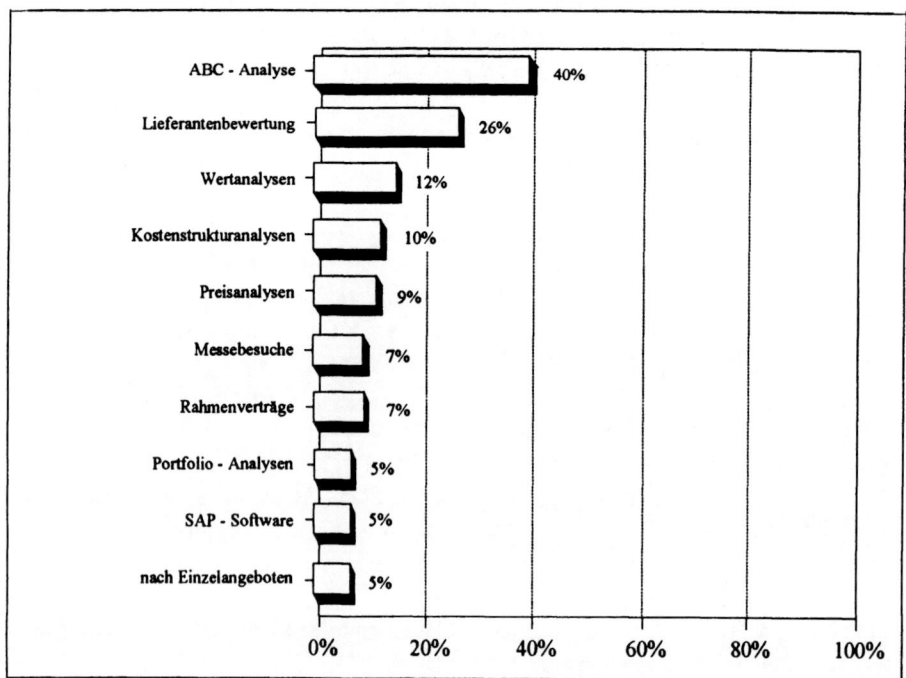

Abb. 1: Methoden im Zusammenhang mit Beschaffung

kaum die Rede sein kann. Offensichtlich kommt hier auch ein erstaunliches Methodenverständnis zum Ausdruck.

(3) Das Beschaffer-Lieferantenverhältnis ist vielfach noch durch **Gegnerschaft** gekennzeichnet. Durch den Aufbau potemkinscher Dörfer, durch willkürlichen Informationsaustausch, durch Mißtrauen werden die Verhandlungsgespräche mit dem Lieferanten nicht gerade gefördert. In der Absicht, einen guten Abschluß zu Lasten des Lieferanten zu erzielen, werden Verhandlungen geführt, die davon ausgehen, daß der Verlustpreis vom unmittelbaren Beschaffungskonkurrenten schon ausgeglichen werde. Von einer Motivation zu einer fairen **Partnerschaft** ist selten etwas zu spüren. Das Preisboxen gleicht einem Fingerhakeln, bei dem man unterstellt, selbst in der stärkeren Position zu sein. Ist man in der schwächeren Position, versucht man sie zu verschleiern, sonst hat man eben Pech gehabt. Unersichtlich bleibt, was das mit modernem Management zu tun haben soll.

(4) Alle reden von Prozeßorientierung, aber jeder will die Prozeßführerschaft in der Hoffnung, dann die eigenen Ideen am besten umsetzen zu können. So zementiert man altes Funktionsdenken. Einigkeit besteht eigentlich darin, daß durch **funktionsübergreifendes Teamdenken** Zeit und Kosten gespart sowie die Lösungsqualität gesteigert werden kann. Das gesamte Beschaffungsteam verantwortet die Qualität der Versorgungsentscheidungen, alle müssen überzeugt werden, Majoritätsentscheidungen zu Lasten eines Funktionsbereichs sollten tunlichst unterlassen werden. Das ist noch unüblich.

(5) Auch ein **Kompetenzgap** kann nicht übersehen werden. Dies kann eine faktische Kompetenzlücke sein, wenn nicht gerade die fähigsten Mitarbeiter in die Beschaffung delegiert wurden. Das kann aber auch eine Imagelücke sein. Eben weil man die Mitarbeiter als „Bestellschreiber und -verwalter" mißbraucht, haben sie gar nicht die Chance, ihre Fähigkeiten zu zeigen.

2. Visionen für eine strategische Beschaffung

Nur wenn man Vorstellungen darüber entwickelt, welche Zustände man für erstrebenswert hält, kann man Maßnahmen des Wandels ergreifen.

(1) An die Stelle der unternehmensinternen wie -externen Funktionsegozentrik muß das **Win-Win-Denken** treten. Es muß dafür gesorgt werden, daß jeder gewinnt. Das gilt sowohl intern für die beteiligten Funktionsbereiche als auch extern zum Lieferanten. Im Team muß bei der Bedarfsfeststellung gemeinsam um die für das Gesamtunternehmen beste Lösung gerungen werden. Sie ergibt sich nicht aus der Addition der Teiloptima. Wenn die insgesamt beste Lösung nicht offenkundig ist, müssen Lösungsalternativen bezüglich ihrer Lösungsbeiträge simuliert werden. Führt auch das zu keinem eindeutigen Ergebnis, sind Verhandlungslösungen unvermeidlich.

Das gleiche gilt für die Lösungsgenerierung mit dem Lieferanten. Wenn nur einer die Gewinner- und der andere die Verliererposition einnimmt, fällt die Begründung schwer, warum der Verlierer am Geschäft interessiert sein soll. Der verlierende Lieferant wird wohl kaum investieren, sich wenig Mühe um Qualität, Zeit- und Mengenzuverlässigkeit usw. machen. Nur gemeinsam kann man in einem komplizierten Anreiz-Forderungskalkül zu deutlichen Effizienzsteigerungen gelangen.

(2) Mit der **Kundenorientierung** ist es im Unternehmen noch nicht weit her. Zentraler Bezugspunkt der Funktionsorientierung aller muß die Orientierung am Engpaß der Unternehmensplanung bleiben. Und das ist in Wettbewerbswirtschaften der Kunde, der Absatzmarkt. Daraus folgt die **Dienstleistungsorientierung** aller Funktionsbereiche. Es interessiert nicht, was der einzelne Funktionsbereich für die beste Lösung hält, sondern was alle gemeinsam aus Kundensicht für den besten Lösungsbeitrag halten. Jeder ist Dienstleister. Die Beschaffung hat damit interne Kunden (Produktion usw.), die ihrerseits für externe Absatzkunden arbeiten. Und sie hat externe Lieferanten als Reverse-Kunden, die gepflegt werden müssen, damit sie zielgerecht arbeiten.

Um die Kundenorientierung besonders zu betonen, ist eine Aufspaltung des Beschaffungsmanagers in drei Schwerpunkte denkbar:
- den Bedarsmanager,
- den Lieferantenmanager,
- den Informationsmanager.

Aufgabe des **Bedarfsmanagers** ist es, unternehmensinterne Entscheidungskonflikte um die zieloptimale Feststellung der Bedarfsanforderungen zu lösen. In seinem Team kommt dem Absatzmarketing (z. B. Produktmanagement) insofern große Bedeutung zu, als der Produktmanager den Kundenbedarf definiert, aus dem dann die Gestaltungsvorschläge, die Produktionsanforderungen usw. abgeleitet werden. Das Ringen um die gesamtoptimale Lösung setzt das Ermitteln, Diskutieren, Verändern, Prüfen vor Ort voraus.

Demgegenüber arbeitet der **Lieferantenmanager** meist außerhalb des Unternehmens. Das frühzeitige Entdecken auftauchender Probleme, das Entwickeln von Problemlösungshilfen, auch die Pflege und der Aufbau von Lieferanten gehört zu seinen Aufgaben. Je mehr Systemlieferanten das Geschehen bestimmen, je kleiner die Lieferantenzahl also wird, um so mehr kann man den im Absatz bekannten Key-Account-Managementgedanken auf den Beschaffungsbereich übertragen. Zu seinen Aufgaben kann es auch gehören, sich um die gesamte Lieferantenpyramide zu kümmern.

Und Aufgabe des **Informationsmanagers** ist es schließlich, neben der internen Informationsgewinnung (Kontrollinformationen, Benchmarking) besonderes Gewicht auf die Beschaffungsmarktforschung zu legen, damit Entscheidungen auf guter Informationsgrundlage und nicht erst nach langem Suchen getroffen werden können.

281

(3) Die Orientierung am **Wertschöpfungsprozeß** muß auch konsequent für die gesamte Versorgung mit den Inputfaktoren gelten. Dieser Prozeß muß die Grundlage für die an der Planung beteiligten Funktionsbereiche darstellen. Es muß deutlich festgelegt werden, wer welche Lösungsbeiträge bis wann (Milestones) vorzustellen hat. Leistungsverweigerungen können neben Personalkonsequenzen auch zu Kostenkonsequenzen in Form von Kostenbelastungen führen. So können beispielsweise nachträglich Anspruchsänderungen aus dem Absatz mit den daraus resultierenden Kosten dem Produktmanagement angelastet werden, wenn eine ungenügende Anspruchsbeschreibung den Ausgangspunkt der Planung bildete.

3. Theoretische Positionen

Das Beste für praktisches Handeln ist eine gute Theorie. Zumindest zwei Theorien können als Fundament herangezogen werden.
(1) Auf Simon/March/Cyert geht die sogenannte **Koalitionstheorie** zurück, die in Abb. 2 dargestellt wird. Eine Koalition überlebt nur so lange, wie die Partner den Eindruck haben, nicht übervorteilt zu werden. Für die Input-Koalition bedeutet das, daß Verkäufer **und** Einkäufer Nutzen aus dem Austauschpro-

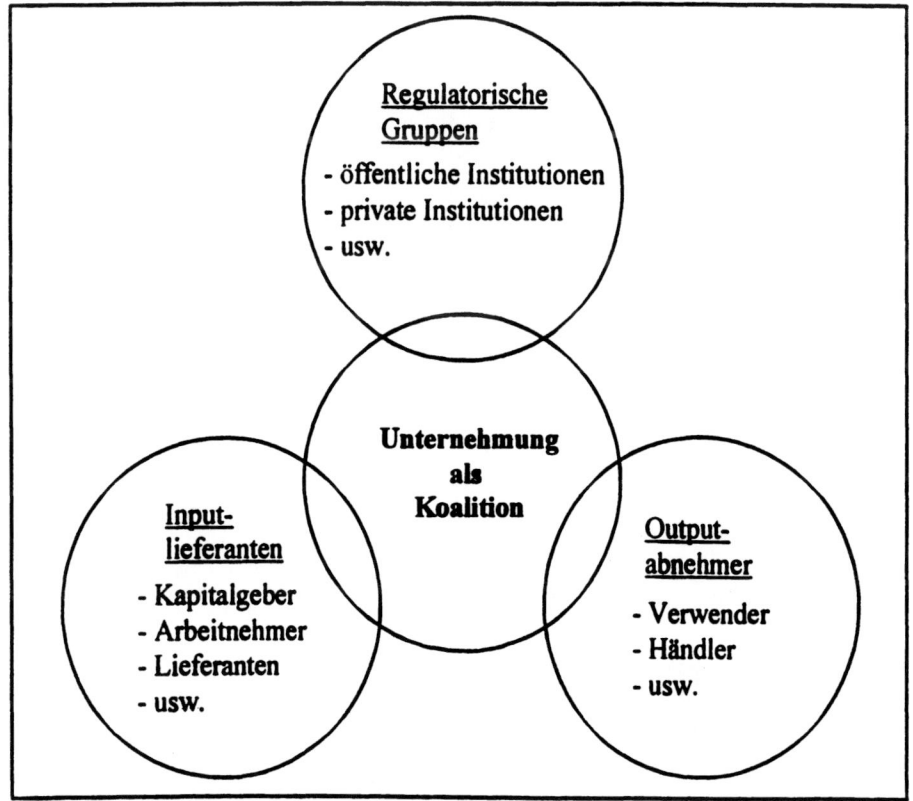

Abb. 2: Koalitionstheorie

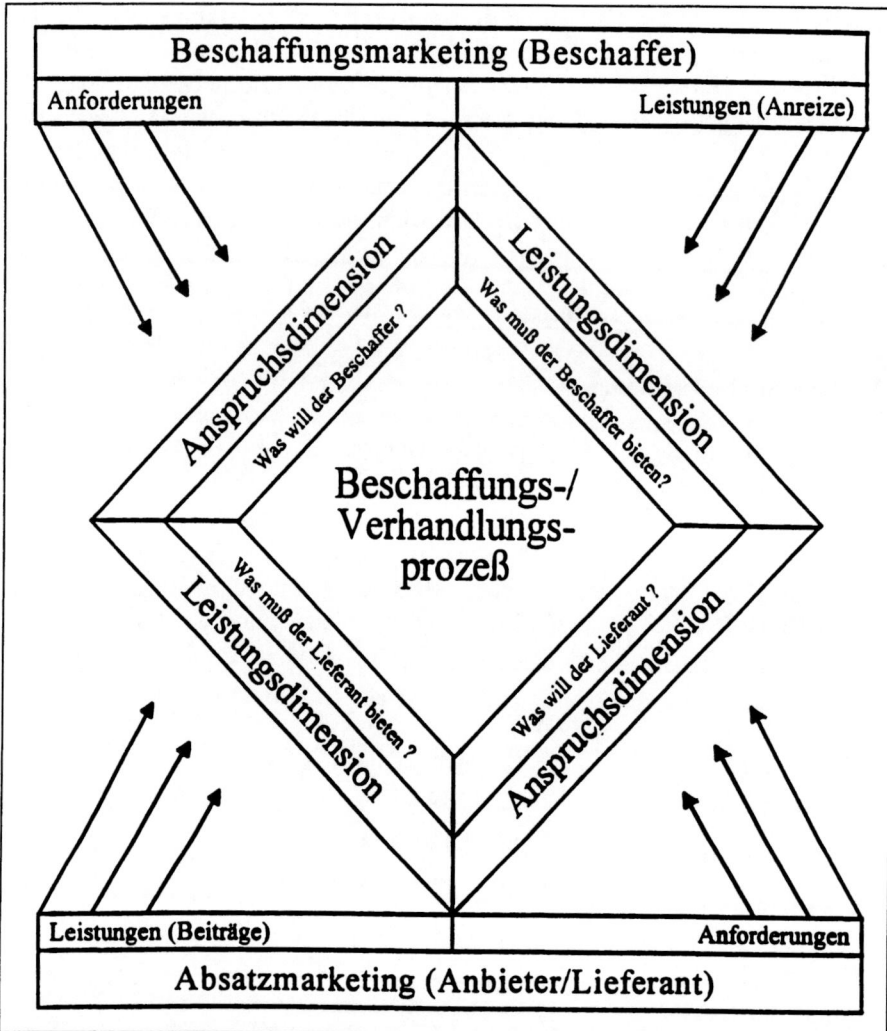

Abb. 3: Anreiz-Beitrags-Theorie

zeß ziehen müssen. Bleibt bei diesem Geschäft für den Lieferanten nichts übrig, sinkt seine Bereitschaft zur Investition, reduziert er seine Qualitätsanstrengungen, nutzt er die nächstbeste Gelegenheit, die Nutzenwaage zu seinen Gunsten umzukehren, aus dem Geschäft auszusteigen usw.

(2) Eng mit der Koalitionstheorie verknüpft ist die **Anreiz-Beitrags-Theorie** (vgl. Abb. 3). Als Beschaffer muß man seine eigenen Anforderungen (Bedarfe) kennen. Man wird sie mit den Leistungen des Lieferanten konfrontieren. In Verhandlungen wird man dann prüfen, welche Anforderungen der Lieferant stellt, die man dann mit eigenen Anreizen zu befriedigen sucht. Die erste

Konfrontation ist der Normalfall des Beschaffungsverhaltens. Bei den Anforderungen wird der Preis als wichtigste Größe mitgenannt. Im Sinne einer faiiren Partnerschaft wesentlich erfolgreicher ist es allerdings, wenn man genauer prüft, was man als Beschaffer dem Lieferanten anbieten kann, was bei ihm mehr bewirkt (→ Bereitschaft zur Preissenkung) als es den Beschaffer kostet. Das setzt voraus, daß man sich um die Analyse der Lieferantenanforderungen systematisch kümmert, daß man dann prüft, welche der Anforderungen man erfüllen kann (→ Beschafferleistungen) und was die Erfüllung kostet. Bei den meisten Unternehmen hapert es bereits an der eigenen Leistungsanalyse und noch viel seltener ist das Wissen um die damit verbundenen Kosten ausgeprägt. Wenn man sich jedoch darum bemüht, den Wertschöpfungsprozeß zu verbessern, wird man auch das prüfen müssen.

4. Handlungskonsequenzen

Um die Konsequenzen für das strategische Beschaffungshandeln aus den bisherigen Überlegungen ableiten zu können, benötigen wir eine Prozeßstruktur, die
- das Beschaffungsdenken und -handeln widerspiegelt,
- den Mitwirkungsprozeß anderer Prozeßbeteiligter transparent macht.
In den bisherigen Überlegungen hat sich die in Abb. 4 dargestellte Struktur als zweckmäßig erwiesen. Sie wurde bereits mehrfach in Unternehmen als Grundlage eines Wandlungsprozesses empirisch überprüft. Folgt man diesem Prozeß in seinem neuartigen Verständnis auch in der inhaltlichen Ausprägung, dann wird der Wandel von erfüllungsorientiertem Einkauf zum strategischen Beschaffungsmarketing offenkundig. Dies sei zum besseren Verständnis überblicksweise erläutert.

(1) In der **Situationsanalyse** wird der Ausgangspunkt der Planung erfaßt und geprüft. Am Anfang steht die **Konstellationsprüfung**. Was kann das Beschaffungshandeln jetzt und morgen stören? Mit welchen Störquellen muß man rechnen? Kann man sie mit geeigneten Maßnahmen verhindern? Ist ihre Verhinderung besonders wichtig?

Bei der **Potentialprüfung** geht es um die Ermittlung der eigenen Fähigkeiten, Stärken und Schwächen. Wer über keine Beschaffungsmarktforschung verfügt und auch nicht die Mittel zu ihrer Etablierung besitzt, wird kaum sinnvoll über global sourcing nachdenken können. Neben der Ermittlung des Potential-Ist geht es also auch darum, sich Gedanken darüber zu machen, was zielbezogene/projektbezogene Potentialänderungspläne bewirken und kosten.

Die Beschaffungszielprüfung leitet sich zum einen aus den Unternehmenszielen ab. Zum anderen müssen Beschaffungsziele je Projekt priorisiert und konkretisiert werden. Als Zielalternativen können genannt werden:
- Beschaffungskosten senken,
- Beschaffungsqualität steigern,

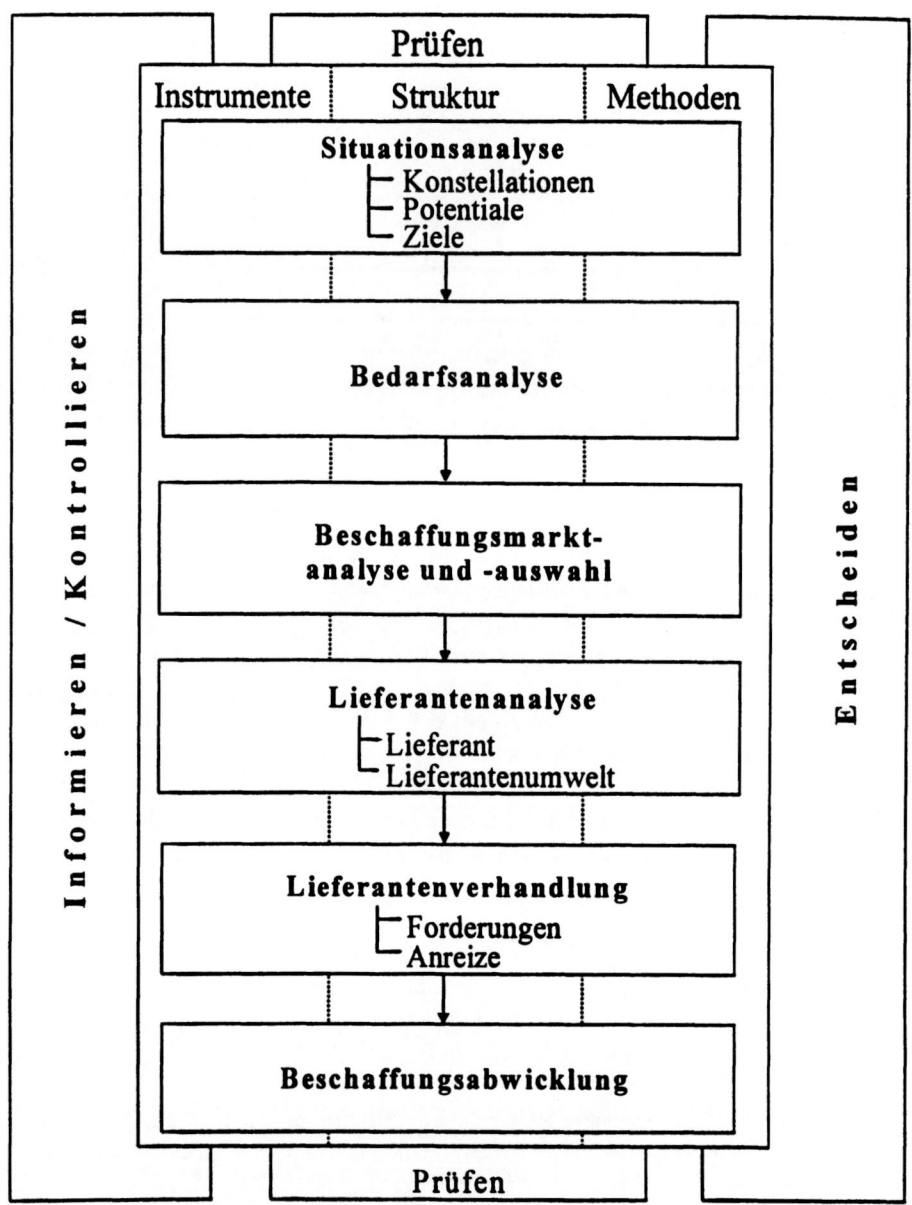

Abb. 4: Beschaffungsmarketingprozeß

- Beschaffungsflexibilität steigern,
- Beschaffungsrisiko senken.

Durch Festlegung des Hauptziels und der Nebenziele lassen sich Zielkonflikte vermeiden. Diese Ziele müssen auch mit anderen Funktionsbereichen abgestimmt werden, um kontraproduktive Zielsysteme zu vermeiden. Aus diesen noch sehr generellen Zielen müssen konkrete Instrumentalziele abgeleitet

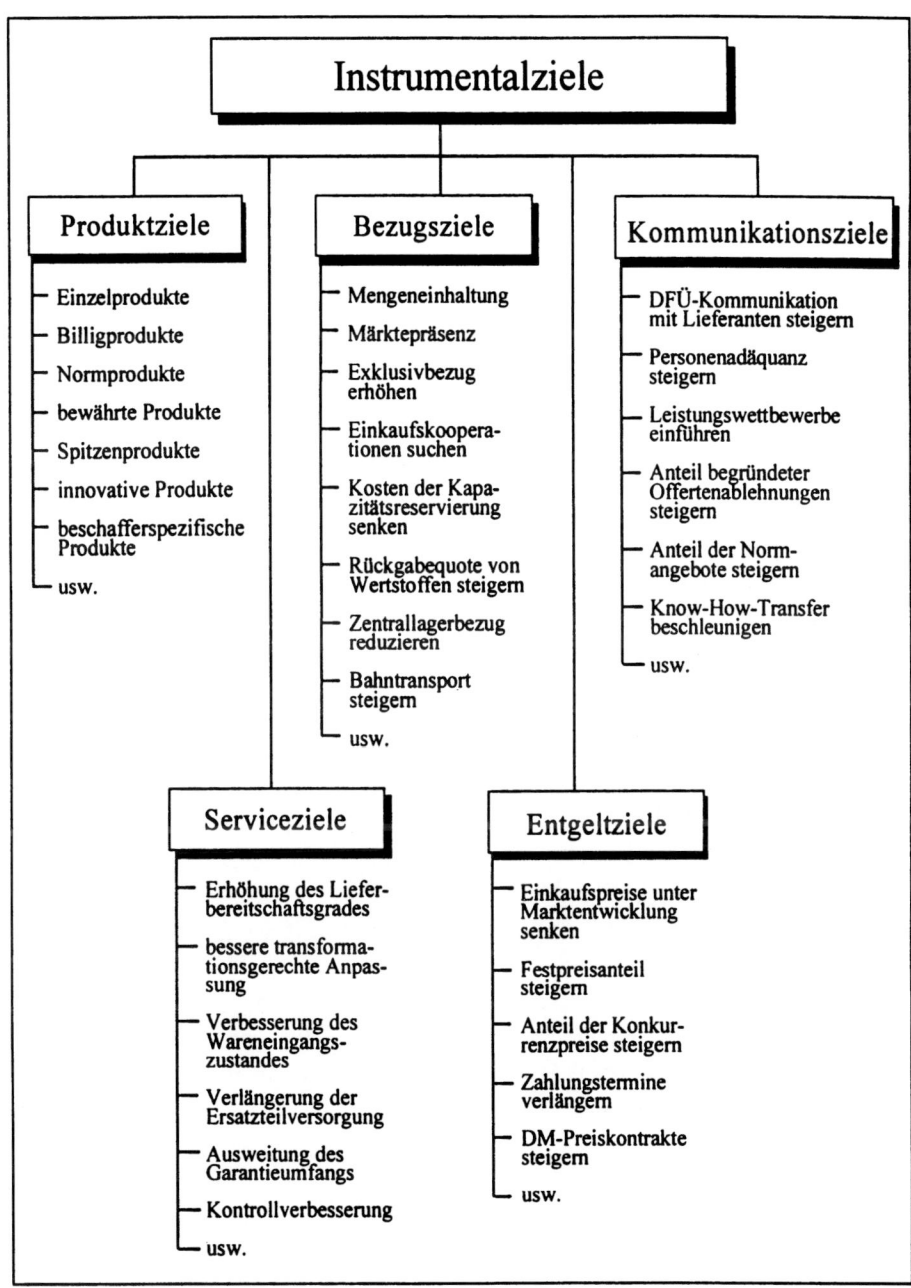

Abb. 5: Instrumentalziele

werden, um genauere Handlungsvorgaben für die Mitarbeiter zu generieren. Beispiele enthält die Abb. 5.

Bei der Umsetzung der Instrumentalziele helfen Strategien als Wege zum Ziel. Auch sie kann man so, wie gerade geschehen, ordnen. Als Produktstrategien erkennen wir Simultaneouns Engineering, Standardisierung, Null-Fehler-Qualität, Modularisierung. Beispiele für Bezugsstrategien sind Single/Multiple Sourcing, Local/Global Sourcing, Vorratshaltung/Just-in-Time-Versorgung usw.

(2) Der zentrale Handlungspunkt der Beschaffung liegt in der **Bedarfsanalyse**. Fehler, die hier gemacht werden, können nur zufällig durch noch so intelligente spätere Handlungen beseitigt werden. Zum einen geht es darum, gemeinsam mit anderen Funktionsträgern den Bedarf zu erheben. Dazu dient der in Abb. 6 dargestellte Bedarfsanforderungspool, der unternehmensspezifisch erweitert oder konzentriert wird.

Dann muß jeweils aus der marktbezogenen Kundenperspektive gefragt werden, ob die zusammengestellten Bedarfe
- überhaupt nötig sind,
- warum auf sie nicht verzichtet werden kann,
- ob die geplante Intensität unbedingt nötig ist,
- ob der Kunde das auch alles honoriert.
Bereits an dieser Stelle kann der Beschaffungsmanager (Bedarfsmanager) sein Wissen um die Realisierungsmöglichkeiten auf den Märkten mit in die Diskussion einbringen. Dazu gehören auch Hinweise auf Möglichkeiten und Grenzen. Zur aktiven Marktbearbeitung (→ Innovation) gehört dann allerdings die stärkere Betonung der Möglichkeiten und weniger die eher verhindernde Betonung der Grenzen.

(3) Wenn man gemeinsam festgelegt hat, was man unbedingt benötigt, dann muß das Arbeitsfeld aufgespannt werden, innerhalb dessen man nach Realisierungsmöglichkeiten sucht - die **Marktanalyse** steht an. Die bisherigen Arbeitsergebnisse (Konstellationen, Ziele und Bedarfe) lenken die Suche. Wir müssen also Marktauswahlkriterien entwickeln, die uns die Analyse erleichtern. Man kann mit dem in Abb. 7 dargestellten Merkmalskatalog arbeiten.

Um zu zeigen, wie man damit arbeiten kann, sei das Portfolio von Abb. 8 erläutert. In das Spannungsfeld Lieferer-/Beschafferkonkurrenz wurde ein Marktwürfel integriert, der, bezogen auf die erwähnten Beschaffungsobjektziele, Soll-Suchpositionen andeutet. Deutliche Abweichungen gesuchter oder gefundener Märkte müssen zum Nachdenken und zum Begründen führen.

(4) Erst nach der Eingrenzung des Suchfeldes ist auch die **Lieferantenanalyse** sinnvoll. Zumindest drei grundsätzliche Aspekte müssen geprüft werden:
- In der Lieferantenzahlentscheidung schlägt sich nieder, ob man der Single-, Multiple- oder System-Sourcing-Strategie folgen will.

Objektanforderungen

Mengenanforderungen

große Menge
kleine Menge
hohe Mengenflexibilität
hohe Mengenkonstanz

Leistungsanforderungen

Gestaltungsmittelakzeptanz
Gestaltungsleistungsakzeptanz
Gestaltungsmittelveränderbarkeit
Leistungsveränderbarkeit
Langlebigkeit
Leistungskonstanz
Einsatzvariabilität
Leistungssichtbarkeit
hoher Technologiestand
Werkzeugherstellungs- und instand-
haltungsfähigkeit
Werkzeug- und Materialbeistellungs-
akzeptanz

Modalitätsanforderungen

Zeitanforderungen

kurze Entwicklunsgzeit
kurze Produktionszeit
kurze Lieferzeit
Bereitstellungszeitpunkteinhaltung
Lieferzeitpunkteinhaltung
flexible Termingestaltung

Ortsanforderungen

Lagerzugänglichkeit
Transportmittelanbindung
Lieferortakzeptanz

Informationsanforderungen

Informationskompetenz
Informationsbereitschaft
Problemlösungsbereitschaft
Geheimhaltung
Marktinformationen
Anwendungsberatung
Marketingzusammenarbeit

Lieferungsanforderungen

Lieferzuverlässigkeit
Verpackungs- und Transportschutz
verarbeitungsgerechte Anlieferung
Vorrangbelieferung
Exklusivbelieferung
Lieferantensicherheit

Entgeltanforderungen

Preis x
Bereitschaft zur Kostenanalyse
Preissicherheit
lange Zahlungsziele
Leasingmöglichkeiten
leistungsbezogene Rabatt-
staffelung
Mindermengenzuschlagsverzicht

Serviceanforderungen

Kundendienstbereitschaft
Recyclingbereitschaft
erweiterte Objektgarantie
Nachkaufsicherheit
Servicekapazität

Abb. 6: Bedarfsanforderungen

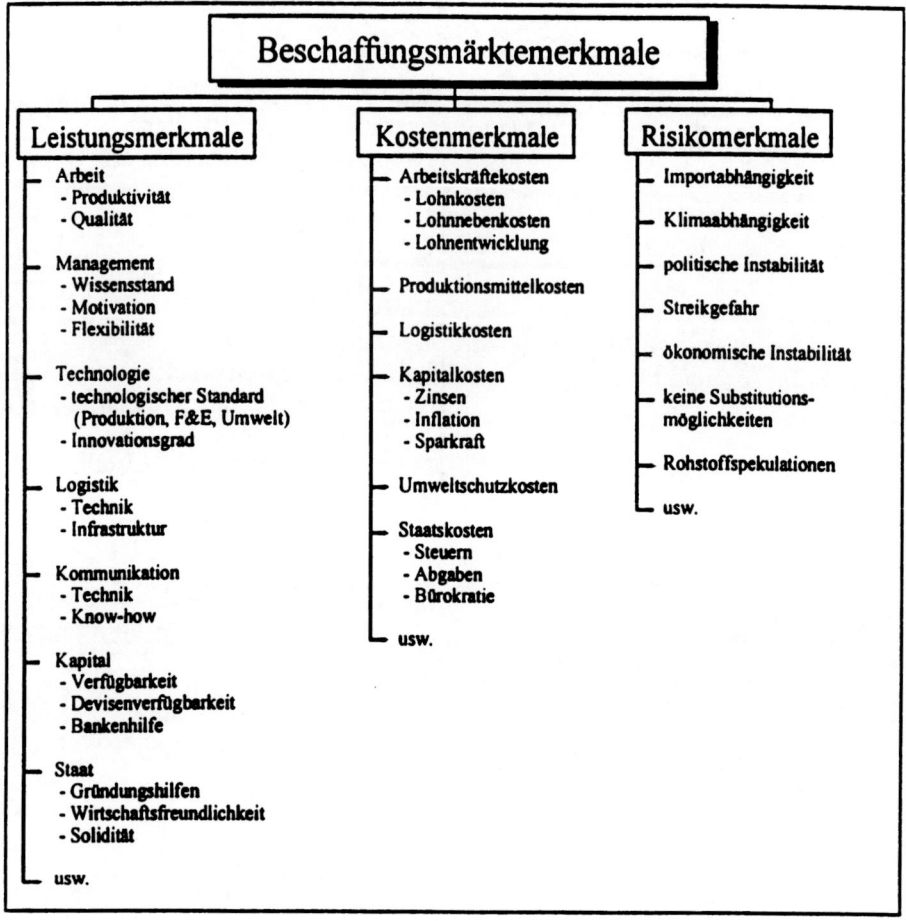

Abb. 7: Wichtige Beschaffungsmärktemerkmale

- Mit der Lieferantenbindungsentscheidung wird festgelegt, ob man Stamm-
lieferanten, Wechsellieferanten oder auch Aufbaulieferanten präferiert.
- Mit der Lieferantenqualitätsentscheidung wird geprüft, wer welche Bedarfs
anforderungen erfüllen kann und will.

Auf die letzte Fragestellung konzentrieren sich die folgenden Überlegungen.
Das Lieferantenauswahlverfahren gleicht einem Trichtermodell (vgl. Abb. 9).
Die Identifikation möglicher Lieferanten kann dadurch erfolgen, daß man
nach solchen Ausschau hält, die das gewünschte Bedarfsobjekt bereits genau
so (→ Katalogware) herstellen oder in der gewünschten Branche tätig sind,
also Ähnliches herstellen oder über Fertigungsprozesse verfügen, welche die
Belieferung mit dem Gewünschten vermuten lassen. An diese Unternehmen
kann man sich mit einem systematischen Selbstauskunftsfragebogen wenden.
Einige wichtige Fragenkreise enthält die Abb. 10.

289

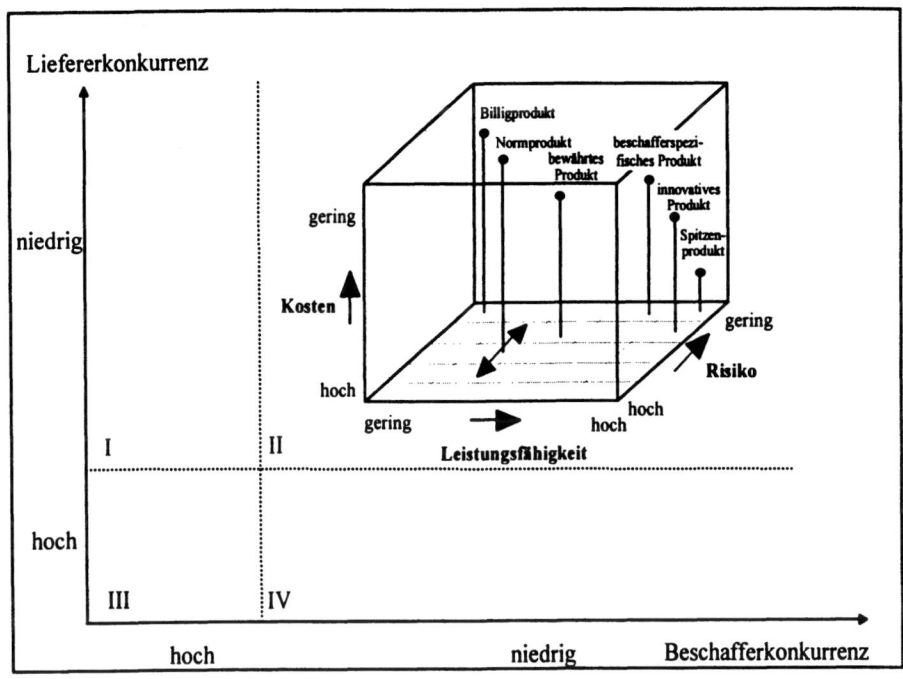

Abb. 8: Zur Konkurrenzabhängigkeit der Märkteposition

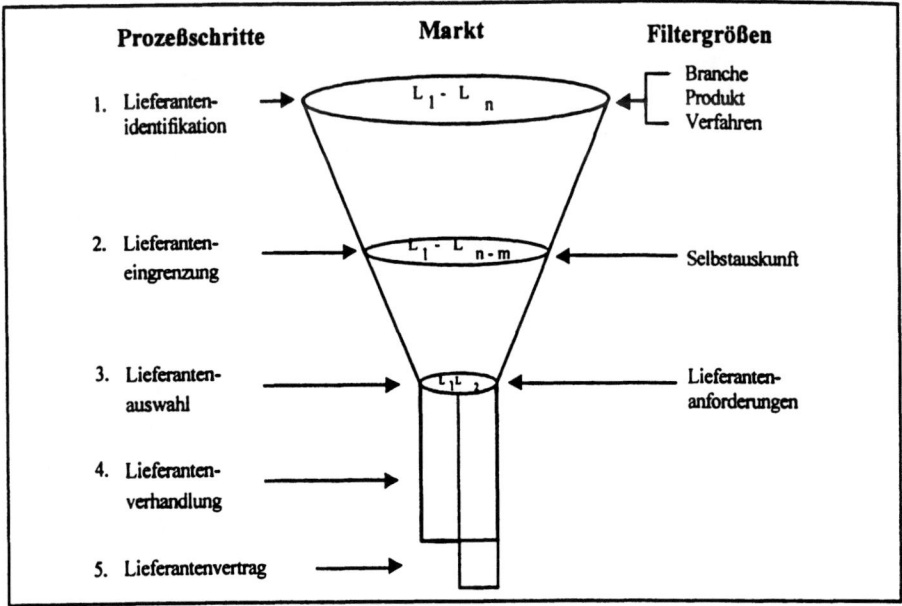

Abb. 9: Ein Trichtermodell der Lieferantenauswahl

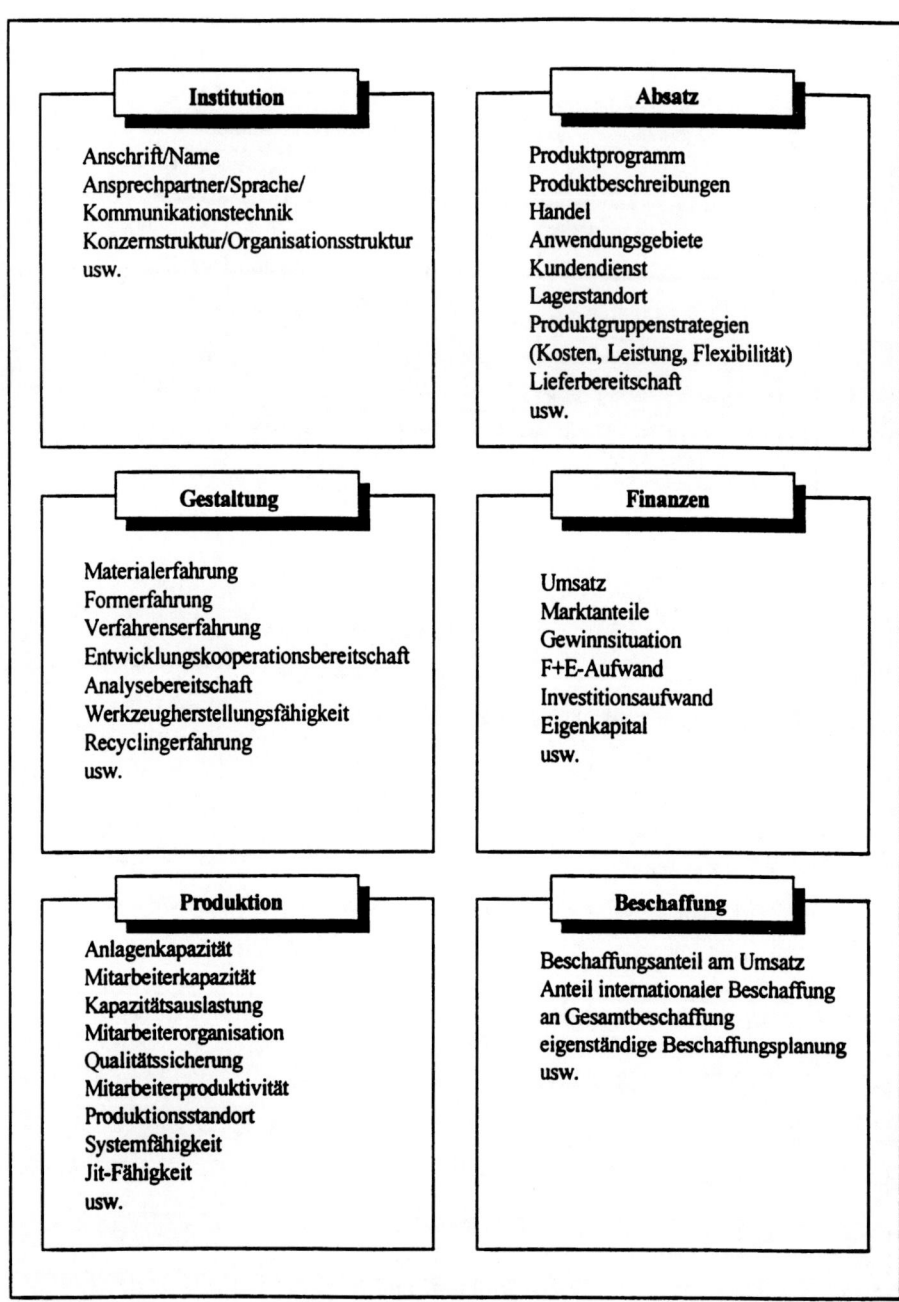

Abb. 10: Struktur eines Selbstauskunftsfragebogens

Die Sorgfalt und die Inhalte der Antwort zeigen dann in bezug zum Beschaffungsobjektziel, wer in den näheren Auswahlkreis einbezogen werden sollte. Diese Lieferanten werden mit der Bedarfsanforderung konfrontiert, es handelt sich jetzt um die Lieferanforderungen. Zuerst wird man die Lieferanten aussondern, die sowohl heute als auch höchstwahrscheinlich morgen nicht in der Lage sind, die Bedarfsanforderungen so zu erfüllen, wie man sich das vorstellt. Das investierende Wachsen des Lieferanten ist mit Chancen und Risiken verbunden, die genau abgewogen werden müssen - ohne Dynamik bliebe alles beim alten. Zusätzlich zu den Lieferantenanforderungen müssen die Marktanforderungen geprüft werden, um zu vermeiden, daß sich der richtige Lieferant im falschen Markt befindet.

(5) Nur mit sehr wenigen (z. B. drei) potentiellen Lieferanten lohnt sich die langwierige **Lieferantenverhandlung**. Man kann sich den Gesamtprozeß so vorstellen, wie er in Abb. 11 dargestellt ist. Aus dem Target Price ergibt sich das Target Costing als Oberpreis. Mit Hilfe der Einkaufskostenanalyse kann man den Unterpreis unter optimalen Bedingungen errechnen. Damit hat man das Preisband umschrieben, innerhalb dessen man sich bei den folgenden Verhandlungen bewegt. In den Verhandlungen geht es darum, durch die Kombination der beschaffungspolitischen Instrumente (Beschaffungsmix) den Lieferanten zu einem Angebot zu bewegen, das den eigenen Anforderungen möglichst entspricht. Wenn Absatzmix und Beschaffungsmix identisch sind, erfolgt der Vertragsabschluß. Der Weg dorthin ist meist mit harten Verhandlungen gepflastert. Der Pflastergrund baut dabei auf der Anreiz-Beitrags-Theorie auf. Allgemein bedeutet das, im gegenseitigen Gespräch einen Weg zu finden, der insofern zielführend ist, als er beiden Seiten Vorteile verschafft.

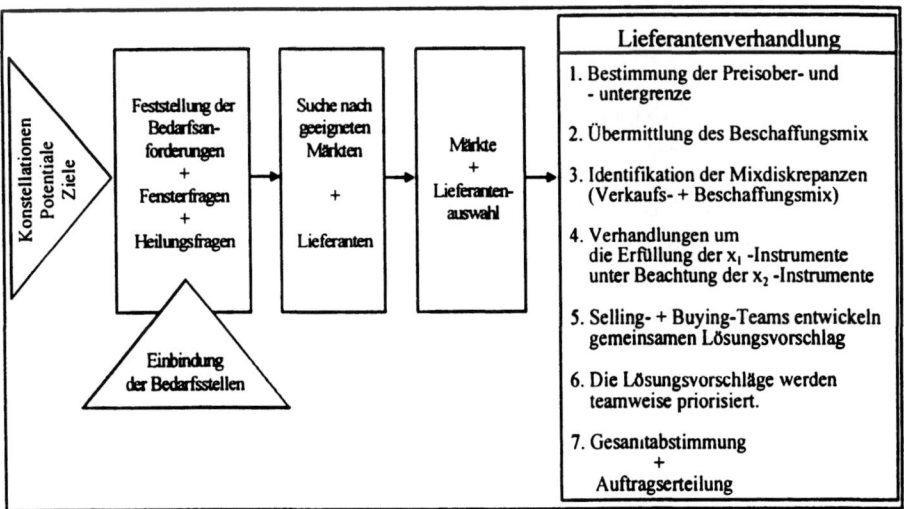

Abb. 11: Der Beschaffungsverhandlungsprozeß

Und konkret heißt das, durch zähes Austarieren der anreiz- und beitragsorientierten Beschaffungsinstrumente einen Weg zu finden, dessen beschaffungspolitische Instrumente weniger kosten als sie bewirken. Um eine Vorstellung davon zu erhalten, wie komplex dieses forderungs- und anreizpolitische Kalkül aussieht, sei lediglich ein Überblick über die produktpolitischen Instrumente gegeben (vgl. Abb. 12).

In Verhandlungen des eigenen Buying-Teams mit dem Selling-Team des Lieferanten muß nun nach der für beide Seiten bestmöglichen Lösung gesucht werden. Wenn Mercedes anläßlich der Eröffnung der neuen Motorenfabrikation in Stuttgart darüber berichtet, daß durch Zusammenarbeit von Konstruktion und Produktion trotz aufwendigerer Gestaltung eine 30 %ige Kostensenkung gelungen sei, um wieviel mehr muß dann bei gemeinsamer Arbeit über eine noch längere Prozeßstrecke möglich sein! Nach Vertragsabschluß erfolgt die Beschaffungsabwicklung. Es kann sinnvoll sein, diesen Tätigkeitsbereich in die Logistik zu verlagern.

(6) Damit die geschilderten Tätigkeiten dem ökonomischen Prinzip gehorchend vollzogen werden können, sind **Informationen** vonnöten. Dabei muß in externe Informationen (→ Beschaffungsmarktforschung) und interne Informationen (Kontrollinformationen, Controlling, Benchmarking) unterschieden werden.

Bei der **Beschaffungsmarktforschung** geht es zunächst darum festzulegen, für welches Beschaffungsobjekt vorrangig Marktforschung betrieben werden soll. Generell wird man sich auf wichtige (kosten-, leistungsbedeutsame) Objekte beschränken. Nach dieser Auswahl ist es nötig zu fixieren, welche Informationen benötigt werden. Dazu kann die Übersicht von Abb. 13 dienen.

Die Leistungsinformationen (→ Bedarfsanforderung) und die Marktinformationen (→ Marktanforderungen) wurden bereits erwähnt, so daß wir uns auf die Anforderungs- und Konkurrenzinformationen konzentrieren können. Die Anforderungsinformationen sind deshalb so wichtig, weil sie einen wesentlichen Baustein für anreiz-beitrags-orientierten Verhandlungsprozesse bilden. Sie decken Möglichkeiten auf, mit welchen Handlungsinhalten (Anrei-zen) man Lieferanten für sich gewinnen kann (vgl. Abb. 14).

Die Informationen über Beschafferkonkurrenten benötigen wir deshalb, um insbesondere bei begrenzten Angebotskapazitäten Störmanöver der Konkurrenz prognostizieren zu können. Informationen über die Liefererkonkurrenz soll ufschluß über deren Potential und deren Aktivitäten geben. Im nächsten Schritt muß geprüft werden, wie man die gewünschten Informationen unter Beachtung des ökonomischen Prinzips erhalten kann. Aus welchen Quellen und mit welchen Methoden kann man die benötigten Informationen erhalten?

Produktpolitik		

| Instrumental-variable | Variablenausprägung | |
	Forderungen	Anreize
Produkt-entwicklungs-politik	Eigenentwicklung Lieferantenentwicklung Partnerentwicklung Drittentwicklung Neuentwicklung Weiterentwicklung	
Produkt-gestaltungs-politik	Gestaltungsvorschriften Leistungsvorschriften geringe Gestaltungstoleranzen Beschaffermarkierung Lieferantenmarkierung Produkteinpassung Produktanpassung	
Produkt-herstellungs-politik	geringe Realisationstoleranzen Materialbeistellung Werkzeugbeistellung	
Produkt-modifikations-politik	Produktvereinheitlichung Produktdifferenzierung Produktveränderung Produktleistungskonstanz Produktleistungs-veränderbarkeit	
Produkt-programm-politik	Produktselektionspolitik Produktmixpolitik	
Produkt-verwendungs-politik	Produktgestaltungszusagen Produktverwendungszusagen	

━━ weniger wahrscheinlich ━━━ wahrscheinlich ━━━━━ sehr wahrscheinlich

Abb. 12: Produktpolitische Instrumentalvariablen und Variablenausprägungen

Beschaffer	Lieferant
Anforderungen →	Leistungsinformationen
Leistungen →	Anforderungsinformationen
Beschafferkonkurrenz-informationen	Liefererkonkurrenz-informationen
allgemeine Märkteinformationen	

Abb. 13: Informationsblöcke der Beschaffungsmarktforschung

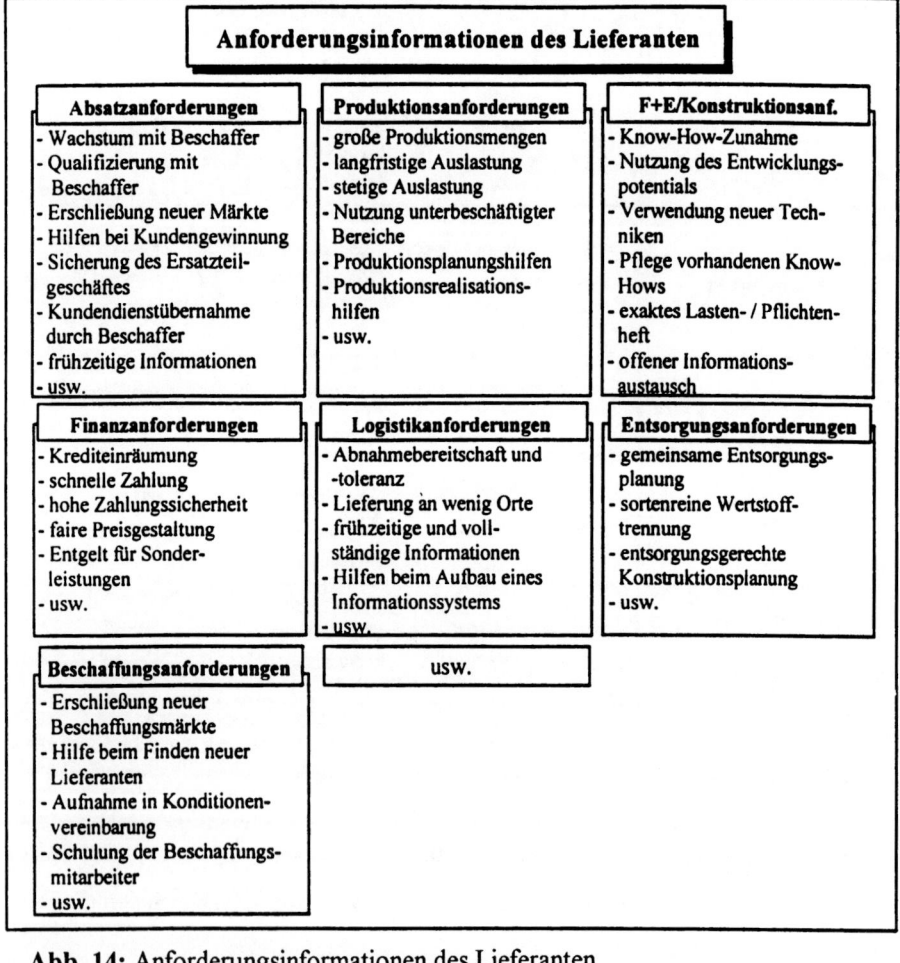

Abb. 14: Anforderungsinformationen des Lieferanten

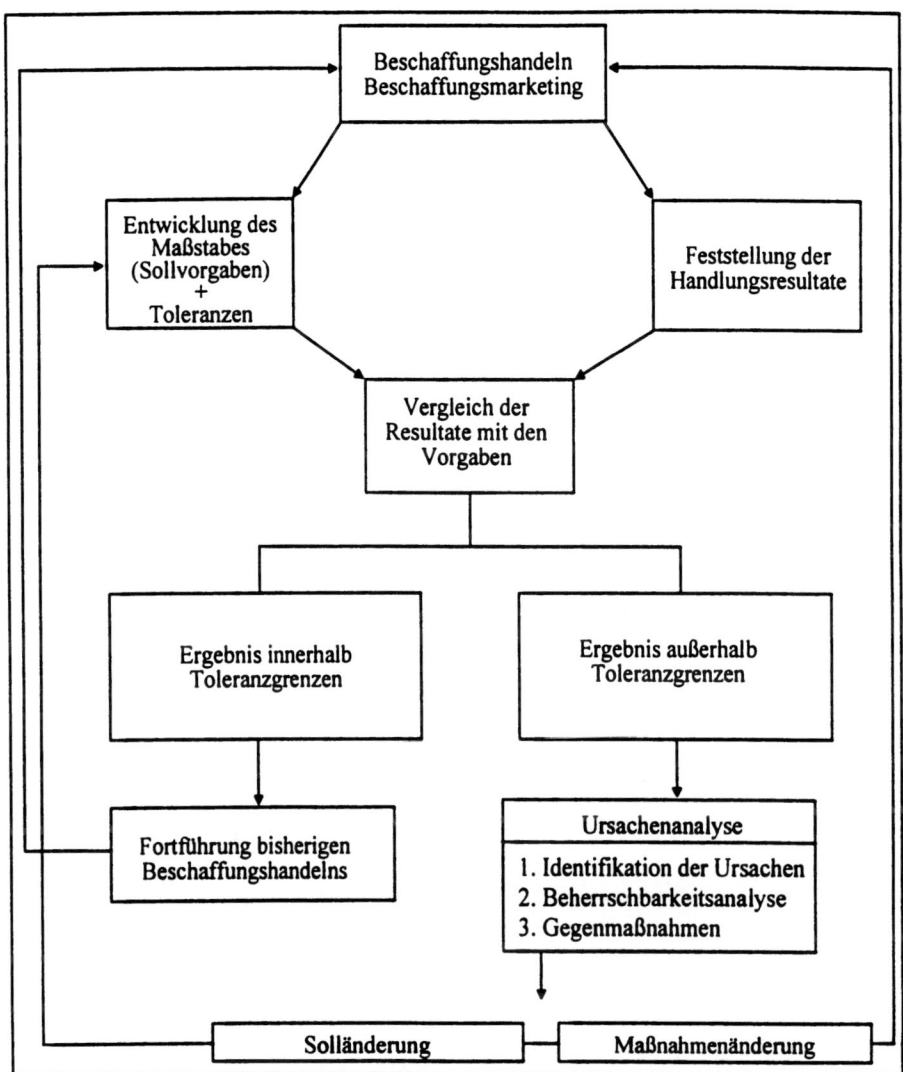

Abb. 15: Stufen des Kontrollprozesses

Marktforschung zeichnet sich dabei durch systematische Erhebung und Aus-
wertung aus. Und schließlich muß überlegt werden, wie man die gewonnenen
Informationen darstellt. Weil keiner Zeit hat, sind Informationsgräber zu vermeiden und Informationen so übersichtlich und einsichtig bei Konstanz der
Darstellungsform zu präsentieren, daß die Gehalte schnell und zielführend in
die Entscheidungen einbezogen werden.

Beschaffungskontrolle kann als Soll-Ist-Vergleich verstanden werden (vgl.
Abb. 15). Bewegen sich die Ist-Abweichungen außerhalb des fixierten Tole-
ranzbereichs, muß geprüft werden, woran die Abweichung gelegen hat. Es

kann sein, daß sich die Umweltzustände außerhalb des eigenen Einflußbereichs verändert haben (z. B. Nachfrageexplosion → Lieferengpässe). Vor allem dann aber, wenn das selbstverantwortete Ist vom geplanten Soll abweicht, muß geprüft werden, wodurch man das hätte vermeiden können (Lernen für Maßnahmenkorrekturen), oder ob das Soll zu anspruchsvoll gesetzt wurde (Sollkorrektur). Um diese Abweichungen schnell zu identifizieren, sind Kontrollkennzahlen hilfreich. Im Rahmen des **Controlling** ermöglichen sie schnell zu steuernde Eingriffe. Gemessen an best-practice-Partnern können **Benchmarkinggrößen** zeigen, wo man im Problemlösungsvergleich mit anderen Unternehmen steht. Wir haben vielfältige Kennzahlen zusammengestellt aus den Bereichen Bedarfsbezogenheit, Funktions- und Instrumentalbezogenheit.

5. Entscheidungsbezug

Der Lösung von Unternehmensproblemen kann man sich wissenschaftlich unterschiedlich zu wenden. Man kann etwas beschreiben. Im Rahmen dieses **Beschreibungszusammenhanges** der Theorie wird versucht, durch Realitätsabstraktion ein Modell zu kreieren, das möglichst viel der Realität jenseits der 1 : 1-Abbildung erfaßt. Der geschilderte Beschaffungsprozeß entspricht diesem Gedanken. Dies macht den deskriptiven Teil einer induktiv gewonnenen Theorie aus.

Theorie hat meist auch eine erklärende Komponente (→ **Erklärungszusammenhang**). Bei der abstrahierenden Realitätsabbildung geht es auch darum, Gesetzmäßigkeiten, Zusammenhänge, Erklärungen des Warum zu erarbeiten. Wieso scheitern so häufig eindeutig preisorientierte Beschaffungsverhandlungen? Wie kann es gelingen, ein größeres Kostensenkungspotential anzuschieben als durch die alleinige Konzentration auf die Preisdruckpolitik? Die Anreiz-Beitrags-Theorie liefert einen derartigen Erklärungsansatz, wenn man sich gleichzeitig um die Alternativenausweitung bemüht. Eine neue Theorie forciert also nur dann den Wandel, wenn man gleichzeitig auch den Handlungsraum erweitert.

Und schließlich kann Theorie auch die Frage nach dem **Zweck** (→ **Verwendungszusammenhang**) beantworten. In der Betriebswirtschaftslehre interessiert uns aus der Unternehmensperspektive die Frage, wie das ökonomische Prinzip realisiert werden kann. Das bedeutet im Beschaffungsbereich vorrangig, wie ein gesetztes Ziel möglichst mit geringem Input erreicht werden kann. Dies kann man auf verschiedenen Wegen versuchen. In der noch dominierenden praktisch normativen Entscheidungstheorie werden durch starke Realitätsreduktionen mit Hilfe formaler Lösungsalgorithmen optimale Entscheidungen generiert. Dies ist bei der hohen Problemkomplexität, wie sie meist bei Beschaffungsentscheidungen vorliegt, nicht oder nur unter schwierigsten Bedingungen möglich. Deshalb haben wir uns durch die Analyse faktischer Entscheidungen in der Realität um die Entwicklung von Entscheidungsoperatoren bemüht, die man als Entscheidungs-

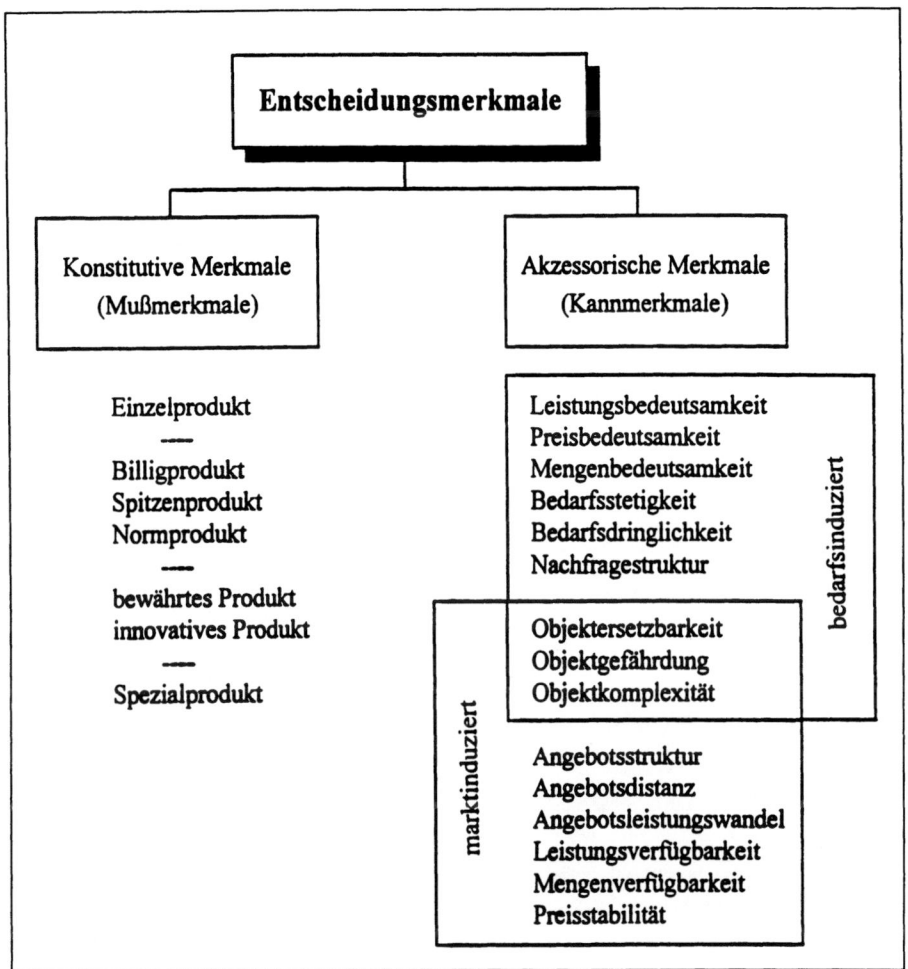

Abb. 16: Entscheidungsmerkmale

Wennbedingungen auffassen kann. Sie reflektieren die spezifische, jeweils anders akzentuierbare Entscheidungssituation des Praktikers, die ihn zu der Aussage führt, in dieser spezifischen Situation sich so und nicht anders entscheiden zu müssen. Diese Wenn-Bedingungen nennen wir Entscheidungsmerkmale. Aus einer Vielzahl möglicher haben sich die in Abb. 16 wiedergegeben. Die konstitutiven Entscheidungsmerkmale entsprechen den bereits genannten Produktzielen. In der jeweiligen Entscheidungssituation wird nur eines dieser Produktmerkmale eine Rolle spielen. Hinzutreten können mehrere akzessorische Merkmale.

In allen Stufen des Entscheidungsprozesses kann nun geprüft werden, welche der entwickelten Alternativen im konkreten produktbezogenen Entscheidungsfall handlungsrelevant sind und welche nicht. Als Beispiel mag die Entscheidungsma-

Bedarfsanforderungen	(Objektmerkmale) Bedingungen	Einzelprodukt	Billigprodukt	Normprodukt	bewährtes Produkt	Spitzenprodukt	innovatives Produkt	beschaferspezifisches Produkt	Mengenbedeutsamkeit	usw.
Mengenanforderungen	große Menge		x_1	x_1	x_2				x_1	
	kleine Menge	x_1				x_2	x_2	x_2		
	hohe Mengenflexibilität			x_2					x_2	
	hohe Mengenkonstanz				x_1	x_1	x_1	x_1	x_1	
Leistungsanforderungen	Gestaltungsmittelakzeptanz	x_1			x_1	x_1	x_1	x_1		
	Gestaltungsleistungsakzeptanz	x_1			x_1	x_1	x_1	x_1		
	Gestaltungsmittelveränderbarkeit						x_2			
	Leistungsveränderbarkeit					x_1	x_1	x_1	x_2	
	Langlebigkeit	x_2			x_1	x_2	x_2			
	Leistungskonstanz			x_1	x_1				x_1	
	Einsatzvariabilität	x_2		x_1						
	Leistungssichtbarkeit					x_1	x_1			
	hoher Technologiestand	x_1				x_1	x_1	x_1		
	Werkzeugherstellungsfähigkeit	x_2					x_2	x_2		
	Werkzeug- u. Materialbeistellungsakzeptanz					x_2			x_3	
Zeitanforderungen	kurze Entwicklungszeit					x_2	x_1	x_1		
	kurze Produktionszeit		x_1			x_2			x_1	
	kurze Lieferzeit		x_1	x_1		x_2			x_1	
	Bereitstellungszeitpunkteinhaltung			x_1	x_1				x_1	
	Lieferzeitpunkteinhaltung	x_2	x_1	x_1	x_1				x_1	
	flexible Termingestaltung			x_2	x_2					
Ortsanforderungen	Lagerzugänglichkeit			x_3	x_2				x_2	
	Transportmittelanbindung			x_2	x_2				x_2	
	Lieferortakzeptanz	x_2		x_2	x_2				x_2	
Lieferungsanforderungen	Lieferzuverlässigkeit	x_1		x_2	x_1	x_1	x_1	x_1	x_1	
	Verpackungs- und Transportschutz	x_2				x_2	x_2	x_2		
	verarbeitungsgerechte Anlieferung	x_1	x_1	x_2					x_1	
	Vorrangbelieferung					x_2	x_2	x_1		
	Exklusivbelieferung					x_2	x_2	x_1		
	Lieferantensicherheit	x_1				x_1	x_1	x_1	x_1	
Entgeltanforderungen	Bereitschaft zur Kostenanalyse	x_1				x_1	x_2	x_2	x_1	
	Preissicherheit	x_2				x_2			x_2	
	lange Zahlungsziele	x_2						x_3		
	Leasingmöglichkeiten	x_2								
	leistungsbezogene Rabattstaffelung					x_2			x_2	
	Mindestmengenzuschlagsverzicht				x_2	x_2				
Serviceanforderungen	Kundendienstbereitschaft	x_1				x_1	x_1	x_1		
	Recyclingbereitschaft	x_2	x_1	x_2	x_2	x_2	x_2	x_2	x_1	
	erweiterte Objektgarantie	x_1			x_2					
	Nachkaufsicherheit				x_1					
	Servicekapazität	x_3				x_3	x_3	x_3		
Informationsanforderungen	Informationskompetenz	x_2				x_1	x_1	x_1		
	Informationsbereitschaft	x_2				x_1	x_1	x_1		
	Problemlösungsbereitschaft	x_1				x_1	x_1	x_1		
	Geheimhaltung					x_2	x_2	x_1		
	Marktinformation					x_2	x_2	x_2		
	Anwendungsberatung	x_2				x_2	x_2	x_2		
	Marketingzusammenarbeit					x_2	x_2			

Abb. 17: Von Bedingungen abhängige hierarchisierte Bedarfsanforderungen

trix für die Bedarfsanforderungen dienen (vgl. Abb. 17). In Abhängigkeit vom jeweiligen Merkmal (Bedingung) müssen die X_1-Anforderungen im Regelfall genannt werden. X_2 erscheint wünschenswert, auf X_3 kann man zur Not verzichten. Hinzufügungen und Streichungen bedürfen der Begründung. Somit hat man ein für jedermann nachvollziehbares Entscheidungsprotokoll, das die Zusammenarbeit erleichtert und für Entscheidungskontinuität sorgt. Mit dieser strategisch orientierten und entscheidungsbezogenen Betrachtungsweise gelingt der Übergang vom eher abwicklungsorientierten Einkauf zum Beschaffungsmarketing.

Change Management
und
Operations-Management

Die Praxis der Steuerung cross-funktionaler Teams zur Steigerung der Effektivität und Effizienz von Geschäftsprozessen

Claus W. Gerberich

Summary:

The old functional and hierarchic structures of organizations can no longer meet the demands of the international competition today. Management structures have to follow the actual process orientation. An important vision is the integrated concept of managing customer oriented business processes. Cross-functional teams need to be created.

1. Neues Denken und Handeln in dynamischen, erfolgreichen Unternehmen

In allen Branchen wird immer stärker erkannt, daß die alten funktionalen und hierarchisch geprägten Strukturen nicht mehr den Anforderungen des modernen, internationalen Wettbewerbs gerecht werden. Die Ausrichtung des Unternehmens, der Mitarbeiter und der Führungs- und Entscheidungsstrukturen auf die Prozeßorientierung wird immer wichtiger. Dazu gibt es heute in der Wissenschaft, der Beratung und der Unternehmenspraxis eine Fülle von Ansätzen, Schlagworten und Methoden. Viele sind nur ein Mantel für althergebrachten Kostenabbau und zeigen nicht viel von einer grundlegenden Neugestaltung der Unternehmen. Die besten Beratungskonzepte oder integrierte Informations Systeme wie SAP\R3 haben nur dann einen Sinn und einen Nutzen, wenn die Mitarbeiter in neuen Kategorien denken und handeln. Die althergebrachte Abteilungsstruktur und das Abteilungsdenken müssen überwunden werden. Ein neues cross-funktionales Denken und Handeln der Mitarbeiter muß durch eine Veränderung der Entscheidungs- und Kompetenzstrukturen begleitet werden. Die Vision ist das integrierte Führen und Steuern von kundenorientierten Geschäftsprozessen. Geschäftsprozeßorganisation setzt daher voraus, daß im Unternehmen immer mehr cross-funktionale Teams gebildet werden, diese untereinander vernetzt werden und daß mit diesen Teams alle wesentlichen Geschäftsprozesse geplant, realisiert und gesteuert werden.

2. Praxiserkenntnisse aus der angewandten Prozeßforschung

Folgende Erkenntnisse haben wir aus zahlreichen Forschungsprojekten zur angewandten Prozeßforschung als Rahmenbedingungen für die Praxis der Prozeßorganisation gezogen:
- Teamarbeit wird immer erfolgsentscheidender und setzt sich immer mehr in der Praxis durch.
- Teamarbeit ist der Schlüssel zur Kundenzufriedenheit.
- Cross - funktionale Aufgaben- und hierarchieübergreifende Teams unterliegen speziellen Gesetzmäßigkeiten und bedürfen einer speziellen Steuerung, um erfolgreich zu sein.
- Cross-funktionale Teams sind wesentliche Bausteine einer lernenden Organisation.
- Lernende Organisationen haben die besseren Zukunfts- und Wettbewerbschancen.
- Cross-funktionale Teams müssen über das gesamte Unternehmen entwickelt und vernetzt werden.
- Cross-funktionale Teams schaffen eine höhere Flexibilität im Unternehmen.
- Cross-funktionale Teams beschleunigen dramatisch die Geschäftsprozesse.

Aber auch diese Praxiserkenntnis haben wir gefunden: Nach dem Wandel sind die Unternehmen nicht wieder zu erkennen. Es hat sich eine neue Unternehmenskultur entwickelt.

3. Merkmale von Best of Class Unternehmen

Erfolgreiche Weltklasse-Unternehmen - Best of Class - arbeiten aktiv gestaltend durch ganzheitliches Denken und Handeln im gesamten Unternehmen. Die traditionellen Grenzen des Unternehmens werden dabei immer wieder bewußt überschritten: gemeinsame Produktentwicklungsteams mit Lieferanten, Innovationsworkshops mit Kunden, Benchmarking mit Unternehmen aus anderen Branchen zur Prozeßverbesserung, Management von Netzwerken in virtuellen Unternehmen, Pflege und Führung von strategischen Allianzen. Diese Unternehmen erreichen immer wieder Quantensprünge in der Verbesserung und hören nicht auf, besser zu werden. Best of Class Unternehmen nutzen intensiv das Leistungspotential ihrer Mitarbeiter, um innovativ und flexibel am Markt zu reagieren. Sie erreichen einen Spitzenplatz im Mitarbeitermotivations- und Zufriedenheitsportfolio, mit hohen Werten der Motivation und Qualifikation.

Produkt- und Prozeßinnovationen sind dabei gleichwertig. Kein neues Produkt ohne die dafür adäquaten Prozesse. Die Teams denken sowohl in neuen Produkten als auch in der Neugestaltung der dazu relevanten Prozesse. Produkt und Prozeß sind zu einer Einheit geworden. Kundenbedürfnisse wechseln schnell. Best of Class Unternehmen erfüllen nicht nur bestens die aktuellen Kundenanforderungen, sondern sind immer schon einen Schritt voraus. Sie denken schon heute in den morgen wichtigen Kundenwünschen und haben entsprechende Leistungsangebote vorrätig oder im Aufbau.

Produktlebenszyklen verkürzen sich dramatisch. Innovationszeiten würden tendenziell länger aufgrund der steigenden Komplexität der Produkte, die Märkte verlangen aber immer schneller das Nachschieben von neuen Produkten. Dies kann jedoch nicht erreicht werden durch den Einsatz von höheren finanziellen Ressourcen, sondern erfordert neue Arbeitsformen in cross-funktionalen Teams. Kunden erwarten den absoluten Mehrwert, Kundenbindung, Kundenloyalität und Kundenenthusiasmus sind Erfolgsvoraussetzungen geworden. Schaffen von Kundennutzen ist nur durch ein neues Denken im cross-funktionalen Team möglich. In den alten Strukturen werden immer wieder die eigenen Ziele oder die Interessen der Abteilung in den Vordergrund gestellt.

Diese Best of Class-Merkmale erreichen die Unternehmen nur durch engagierte Mitarbeiter, die sich in ihrer Leistung voll entfalten können. Rahmenbedingungen und Impulse müssen Führung und Organisation schaffen. Business Reengineering, kontinuierliche Unternehmensverbesserung, Kundenorientierung und schlanke Unternehmensführung haben immer mehr das Element neuer Arbeitsstrukturen und Arbeitsorganisation im Rahmen zeitgemäßer Führung entstehen lassen. Das cross-funktionale, das Aufgaben- und hierarchieübergreifende, sich selbst steuernde Team, das von der Produktentwicklung, der Produktgestaltung bis über den Fertigungs- und Auslieferungsprozeß hin die Unternehmensflexibilität gewährleistet, wird zum Schlüssel, um die Spitze zu erklimmen.

4. Die Rolle cross-funktionaler Teams

Cross-funktionale Teams bedürfen einer besonderen Steuerung und Begleitung. Coaching und permanente Unterstützung sind für die Aufrechterhaltung von Motivation und Leistungsbereitschaft erforderlich. Führungsaufgaben definieren sich neu; Führen heißt immer mehr Coachen als Anweisen. Führen heißt, die Prozeßteams begleiten und motivieren. Betriebsräte und Mitarbeitervertreter sind von Anfang an in das Projekt einzubinden. Mögliche Ängste und Befürchtungen werden immer wieder auftreten, diese gilt es abzubauen und durch Offenheit in den Zielen der Veränderung zu entkräften. Eine positives Vertrauensklima ist aufzubauen. Dies erfordert auch neue Formen der Information und Kommunikation. Best of Class Unternehmen nutzen cross-funktionale Teams mit Erfolg zur Sicherung ihrer Spitzenstellung.

5. Die Wege der Veränderung

Management des Wandels ist heute überlebenswichtig. Nur die Unternehmen, die es beherrschen, sich permanent zu verändern, werden Überlebenschancen haben.

- **Ziele des Wandels**
  Dabei ist es wichtig, jeweils die richtigen Ziele des Wandels zu finden und zu definieren, z.b. Welches sind meine Kernkompetenzen und meine Kernfähigkeiten? Orientierung am Markt und am Best of Class Unternehmen hilft, die richtigen Ziele zu wählen.
- **Weg des Wandels**
  Ebenso ist es aber wichtig, den „richtigen" Weg des Wandels, der spezifisch auf mein Unternehmen zugeschnitten ist, zu finden und zu wählen. Grundsätzlich werden heute zwei unterschiedliche Wege in der Beratung und Unternehmenspraxis erprobt und realisiert:
  (1) Der Weg des radikalen Wandels in Form des Business Reengineering.
  (2) Der Weg des sanften, evolutionären Wandels im Rahmen der Organisationsentwicklung des KVP und des KAIZEN.

Beide Wege haben ihre Erfolge, beide Wege haben ihre Mißerfolge. Dies zeigt, daß es nicht einen einzigen richtigen Weg gibt, sondern daß eine Ausrichtung auf die Art der notwendigen Veränderung, auf die Strukturen und die Kultur des Unternehmens erfolgen muß.

6. Entscheidungskriterien für den richtigen Weg der Veränderung

Für den einzuschlagenden Weg der Veränderung in der Praxis sind folgende Kriterien zur Prüfung notwendig:

(1) Kriterien der Umwelt

- Ökonomische Aspekte wie die Globalisierung von Geschäften, veränderte Konjunkturverläufe, neue Rolle der Käufer in den Märkten.
- Technologische Aspekte wie die Entwicklung und der Reifegrad von Technologien oder Investitionen in Forschung und Entwicklung.
- Rechtlich-politische Aspekte wie die Produzentenhaftung oder Zoll- und Handelsabkommen bzw. die Einflüsse des Steuerrechts.
- Sozio-kulturelle Komponenten für die Wahl des Weges der Veränderung wie die Qualifikation der Bevölkerung, die Mobilität und Lernbereitschaft oder vorhandene Sozialvereinbarungen zwischen den verschiedenen Interessengruppen in der Gesellschaft.
- Ökologische Komponenten wie der Wandel durch ein verändertes Umweltbewußtsein oder neue Umweltmanagement-Anforderungen an die Unternehmen.

(2) Kriterien des Unternehmens

Neben den Kriterien der Umwelt spielen die unternehmerischen Kriterien eine entscheidende Rolle für die Wahl des Weges der Veränderung. Dabei sind die strategischen Geschäftsfelder, die Aufbau- und Ablauforganisation, die traditionelle Unternehmenskultur, die vorhandene Technik zu berücksichtigen, aber auch die Eigentumsverhältnisse. Auf der psychologischen Seite sind die Rolle und die Erwartungen der Mitglieder des Managements und der Mitarbeiter von besonderer Bedeutung. Dazu zählen insbesondere das Wahrnehmungsvermögen, die persönlichen Ziele und die Bereitschaft zur Kooperation. Entscheidend ist aber auch die gegebene Unternehmenssituation. In einer komfortablen Situation wird es sehr schwer sein, eine radikale Veränderung zu realisieren, während in der Liquiditäts- oder der Erfolgskrise sehr viel eher die Bereitschaft gegeben ist, einen radikalen Wandel vorzunehmen.

Gerade in der strategischen Krise ist ein völliger Wandel notwendig. Hier gilt es, neue Produkte zu finden, neue Technologien zu entwickeln, neue Märkte zu erschließen und neues Verhalten in den Kundenbeziehungen zu erproben. Dies geht nur über einen mehrjährigen Wandel, der alle Komponenten der Produkt/Marktbeziehungen und alle Ebenen einbeziehen muß.

7. Der Weg des radikalen Wandels von Organisation und Geschäftsprozessen

Das Konzept des Business Reengineering von Hammer/Champy basiert auf einem radikalen Wandel, einer revolutionären Veränderung des Unternehmens und seiner Strukturen. Der gesamte Prozeß zwischen dem Erkennen der Kundenbedürfnisse und dem Erreichen der Kundenzufriedenheit ist völlig neu zu gestalten. Ziel ist es dabei, jeweils durch die radikale Neugestaltung Quantensprünge in den Erfolgsfaktoren Zeit, Qualität, Kosten und Flexibilität zu realisieren. Die eingefahrenen, bewährten Abläufe werden dabei jedoch nicht als Basis genommen. Die Erfahrungen, die die Mitarbeiter in vielen Jahren gesammelt haben, werden sogar als Hindernis für das radikale Umdenken gesehen.

Im Business Reengineering ist daher das Denken in Richtung „Wie können wir es besser machen?" fehl am Platze. Hier geht man immer von der Frage aus, „Wie sollten wir den Prozeß gestalten, wenn wir völlig neu aufsetzen und dabei eine deutlich höhere Kundenzufriedenheit erreichen wollen?" Hier steht daher nicht das Arbeiten mit cross-funktionalen Teams im Vordergrund, sondern primär die Überlegung zu neuen Informationstechniken, die es erlauben, Prozesse völlig neu zu gestalten.

Eine Fehlerferndiagnose bei Computern und Netzwerken erlaubt damit eine gänzlich andere Gestaltung von Serviceprozessen als die klassischen Prozeßschritte der Auftragsannahme, der Kundenklassifzierung, der Auftragsqualifizierung und Einsatzplanung der Techniker und der Logistik der Ersatzteile. Auch in der Umsetzung der Gedanken und Gestaltungswege spielt das cross-funktionale Team nicht die entscheidende Rolle. Hier gilt primär die Anordnung des Top - Managements, das aufgrund seiner Machtposition die neuen Wege anordnet. Die Umsetzung und das Arbeiten im neuen Prozeß erfolgt dann über neue Teams, die den Gedanken der Cross-Funktionalität bewahren, Sie werden aber neu geschaffen und bilden sich nicht aus den alten Strukturen heraus. Parallel mit den neuen Techniken und Abläufen erhalten die Mitarbeiter auch das Empowerment, um für den neuen Prozeß auch die Verantwortung zu zeichnen.

Diese Vorgehensweise kann hervorragend als Denkansatz für einen Organisationswandel genommen werden; sie hat jedoch erhebliche Probleme in der Praxis erfolgreich realisiert zu werden. Die Rolle und Aufgaben der Mitarbeiter im Prozeß des Change Managements sind nicht durchgängig gegeben, und es fehlen oft die notwendigen Informationen zur zielgerichteten Realisierung des Veränderungsprozesses. Im radikalen Business Reengineering dominieren viel stärker die neuen Konzepte der Prozeßveränderung, der Branchen-Referenzprozesse und der Informationstechnologien als die kontinuierliche Entwicklung der Veränderung durch die Mitarbeiter.

8. Der Weg der schrittweisen Organisationsveränderung und Unternehmensentwicklung

Die Grundgedanken der Organisationsentwicklung gibt es schon lange. In der Vergangenheit war es jedoch mehr das Denken in Schüben der Veränderung. Bei einer historischen Betrachtung von Unternehmen und ihrer Organisation ausgewählter Branchen haben wir festgestellt, daß sich in den Jahrzehnten nach dem zweiten Weltkrieg die Strukturen in den Unternehmen immer wieder deutlich in größeren Zeitabständen verändert haben. Dies war jedoch noch nicht getragen von den Mitarbeitern und ihren Einstellungen, sondern von Strategien und Grundsatzüberlegungen des Managements. Genau in diese Denkweise paßt die Formulierung „Structure follows Strategy".

Heute geht man jedoch mehr davon aus, das Ziel zu verfolgen, das Menschenbild zu wandeln und die Einstellungen, Werte und Verhaltensweisen der Mitarbeiter zu verändern, um daraus permanent Impulse für Veränderungen zu schaffen. Veränderungen müssen von den Mitarbeitern getragen werden. Berater oder die Führung haben allein die Rolle der Change Agents. Sie sollen helfen, die Veränderungsprozesse zu begleiten, dürfen diese aber nicht dominieren.

Dabei stehen **zwei grundlegende Prinzipien** immer wieder im Vordergrund:
- Hilfe zur Selbsthilfe,
- Betroffene zu Beteiligten machen.

Das Prinzip Hilfe zur Selbsthilfe wird vom Leitprinzip getragen, daß der Change Agent Impulse für Veränderungen gibt, daß diese aber dann von den Mitarbeitern selbst aufgenommen und umgesetzt werden. Das Prinzip **Betroffene zu Beteiligten** machen geht davon aus, daß die vom Wandel betroffenen Personen am Wandlungsprozess aktiv mitarbeiten, um den Prozeß zu verstärken und zu beschleunigen.

9. Voraussetzungen schaffen für die permanente Organisationsentwicklung

Für die Erfüllung dieser beiden Prinzipien müssen jedoch im Unternehmen erst die Voraussetzungen geschaffen werden.

(1) **Das Beseitigen überlanger Hierarchien und Entscheidungswege**
Die Hierarchien verändern die Bereitschaft, Verantwortung zu übernehmen und selbst Anstöße für Veränderungen zu schaffen. Hierarchien erzeugen Schnittstellen, die erheblich effizienzmindernd für Prozesse sein können.

(2) **Die Machtbeziehungen sind neu zu regeln**
Die Formen der Zusammenarbeit müssen stärker auf das Team ausgerichtet werden. Es ist zu verdeutlichen, daß nur im Team gemeinsam Probleme erkannt, die richtigen Ursachen gefunden und gelöst werden können. Es ist eine Kultur gegenseitigen Vertrauens aufzubauen. Dieses gegenseitige Vertrauen ist im Team zu entwickeln und zwischen den einzelnen Teams zu fördern. Offenheit und Transparenz sind dazu wichtig.

Diese Voraussetzungen sind über **zwei Stellhebel** zu bewirken:

(1) **Die strukturellen Maßnahmen**
Bei den strukturellen Regeln sind die Grundelemente einer Prozeßorganisation zu entwickeln und einzuführen. Der Organisationsplan ist entsprechend anzupassen, die Prozesse sind zu ermitteln und die Prozeßverantwortung ist festzulegen. Kernprozesse und Unterstützungsprozesse sind zu definieren und ihre Verflechtung ist zu regeln. Nahtstellenvereinbarungen helfen, alt eingefahrene Schnittstellen und ihre Probleme zu beseitigen. Die Rollen der einzelnen Prozeßmitglieder sind dann im Rahmen der Prozesse neu zu definieren. Durch die Ermittlung der Geschäftsprozesse wird der Rahmen für die Erreichung der Organisationsentwicklungsziele geschaffen.

(2) **Die personellen Maßnahmen**
Hier ist bei den Mitarbeitern anzusetzen. Diese sind durch entsprechende Förder- und Qualifizierungsmaßnahmen auf die neuen Aufgaben im Rahmen der Prozesse und die neuen Kompetenzen vorzubereiten und zu trainieren. Durch diese Qualifizierungsmaßnahmen sind die Fähigkeit zum Erkennen notwendiger Veränderungen und zum Bewältigen der Veränderungen zu fördern und zu unterstützen. Ohne Coaching wird sich kein Erfolg einstellen. Die Mitarbeiter fallen schnell in die aus der alten Hierarchie gewohnten Verhaltensweisen zurück.

10. Entscheidungskriterien für die Wahl des Veränderungsansatzes

Der radikale Ansatz des Business Reengineering und des Organisationswandels durch eine kontinuierliche Entwicklung unterscheiden sich deutlich in der Methodik und im Vorgehen. Menschenbild und Machtverständnis differieren erheblich. Keines der Vorgehen ist immer richtig und geeignet, die spezifische Problemsituation im Unternehmen zu lösen.

In der **strategischen Krise** müssen neue Ideen entwickelt und neue Kräfte generiert werden. Der Ansatz des Balanced Scorecard zeigt den richtigen vernetzten Weg auf. Hier ist die Wandlungsbereitschaft zu fördern und alle sind auf das neue Ziel auszurichten. Dazu eignet sich die kontinuierliche Veränderung im Rahmen der Organisationsentwicklung ideal. Voraussetzung für den Erfolg des Wandels im strategischen Krisenbereich ist das Schaffen von ganzheitlichen denkenden abteilungsübergreifenden Teams.

In der **Erfolgskrise** ist es sinnvoll, den ersten Anstoß für die Neuausrichtung durch ein Business Reengineering für die zentralen Kernprozesse des Unternehmens zu schaffen und dann über Teams die Veränderung im Rahmen eines kontinuierlichen Prozesses zu verbessern.

In der **Liquiditätskrise** ist keiner der beiden Ansätze allein möglich und sinnvoll. Hier muß primär darauf geachtet werden, daß das Unternehmen über die Phase des Liquiditätsengpasses in kurzer Zeit hinwegkommt. Hier sind Liquiditätsprogramme über das gesamte Unternehmen und über alle Bereiche notwendig. Ebenso ist es hier wichtig, schnell Kostensenkungen zu realisieren und die Kostenstruktur zu verbessern. Aber auch in der Liquiditätskrise spielt die langfristige Vision eine bedeutende Rolle. Sonst ist in der Liquiditätskrise die Motivation für ein überdurchschnittliches Engagement schnell verpufft.

11. Die Rolle des Prozeßpromoters

Veränderungen bedürfen Anstöße. Veränderungen bedürfen Personen, die hinter diesen Veränderungen stehen. Der **Prozeßpromoter** ist die Person, die ein crossfunktionales Prozeßteam zusammenbringt und zusammenschweißt. Er hat die Beteiligten immer wieder zu inspirieren und Impulse zu setzen. Ebenso hat er die wichtige Aufgabe, bei aufkommenden Konflikten eine Lösung zu suchen und zu helfen, daß das Team die Lösung erzielt. Er kann nicht anweisen, sondern er hat zu motivieren und Prozesse zu moderieren. Daher ist es für den Erfolg wichtig, möglichst früh schon den zukünftigen Prozeßpromoter auszuwählen. Seine Fähigkeiten liegen insbesondere im Bereich der sozialen Kompetenzen und des ganzheitlichen Denkens und Handelns. Er benötigt Kommunikationsfähigkeit, Teamfähigkeit und Koordinationsgeschick.

Für den Erfolg des Veränderungsmanagements ist jedoch hilfreich, wenn der Prozeßpromoter von einem **Machtpromotor,** der die Macht im Unternehmen hat, um Veränderungen anzustoßen und von verschiedenen **Fachpromotoren,** die die fachliche Kompetenz der Veränderung beherrschen, permanent unterstützt wird. Der Machtpromotor ist im Business Reengineering von besonderer Bedeutung. Er soll Impulse setzen, Sanktionsmacht haben und im Grenzfall auch Widerstand brechen. Der Fachpromotor ist oft deckungsgleich mit dem Prozeßpromoter. Es ist zu empfehlen, denjenigen Fachpromotor als Prozeßpromotor zu wählen, der wesentlichen Einfluß auf die Gestaltung der Prozesse und auf die Wertschöpfung im Prozeß hat.diese drei Promotoren haben unterschiedliche Rollen, aber haben sich ideal im Veränderungsmanagement zu ergänzen.

12. Die neue Rolle der Ressource Mitarbeiter

Bei der Ausrichtung des Unternehmens auf cross-funktionale Teams zur Steuerung der Geschäftsprozesse gewinnt die Ressource Humankapital dramatisch an Bedeutung. Mitarbeiter-, Kunden- und Investorenloyalität sind sehr eng miteinander verbunden. Bricht die Loyalität ab, beginnt die Erosion des Profits. Unternehmen müssen sich daher zu Wert- und Emotionsgemeinschaften entwickeln, die ihre Fähigkeitspotentiale und Kernkompetenzen schätzen und pflegen. Sie bauen damit langfristig loyale Partnerschaften auf. Basis der Zusammenarbeit in cross-funktionalen Teams werden leistungsorientierte Kontrakte zwischen den Teammitgliedern und den anderen Teams in der Wertschöpfungskette. Dies führt auch zu völlig neuen Bildern der Karriere. Lernen und Leistung sind engstens miteinander verknüpft. Die bisherige lineare Karriere wird ersetzt durch ein Portfolio an Projekten, horizontalen Bewegungen in Prozessen und immer wieder durch den Start von neuen Aufgaben im Rahmen der persönlichen Kernkompetenzen. Die Geradlinigkeit der Karriere wird stärker in der Zukunft durch Zickzackbewegungen im Prozeß- und Projektfeld des Unternehmens geprägt. Dadurch werden völlig neue Vertragsbeziehungen im Human Resource Bereich geschaffen. Thomas Sattelberger, Leiter Führungskräfte der Lufthansa, bringt dies auf folgende Formel: **„Wir geben Dir Sinn und Wertschätzung, solange Du Spitzenleistungen erbringst und Dein Geistkapital gibst".**

13. Wichtige Erfolgsfaktoren zur Steigerung der Effektivität von Geschäftsprozessen

Erfolgreiches Prozeßredesign hat verschiedene Aspekte simultan zu beachten:
(1)   Auswahl weniger Kernprozesse zur Neugestaltung und Optimierung
(2)   Personalabbau darf nicht im Mittelpunkt des Projektes stehen. Dies führt zu Innovationsblockaden und zu Sperren gegenüber Veränderungen.
(3)   Die Notwendigkeit der Veränderung muß klar sein und deutlich herausgestellt werden.

(4) Der Leidensdruck muß offen signalisiert werden.

(5) Angst und Problembewältigungsfähigkeit der Mitarbeiter muß gegeben sein.

(6). Die Geschäftsführung muß hinter dem Projekt und dem Umsetzungswillen stehen.

(7) Klare Führung durch das Top-Management und die Struktur cross-funktionaler Teams in der Projektarbeit müssen sich ergänzen.

(8) Die Veränderungen müssen vorgelebt werden.

(9) Das faktische Verhalten des Managements ist entscheidend, nicht die Reden und Konzepte.

(10) Alle Beteiligten müssen im Verhalten permanent trainiert und gecoacht werden.

Nur bei einem gleichzeitigen Beachten aller Erfolgsfaktoren und einer permanenten Überprüfung gibt es eine Chance auf einen Erfolg des Veränderungsmanagements.

14. Gründe für ein Scheitern des Neugestaltens von Geschäftsprozessen

Leider scheitern zahlreiche Effizienzsteigerungsprozesse. Die Ursachen sind vielfältig, haben aber immer folgende Muster:

(1) Nach großen Ankündigungen wird schnell wieder bei den ersten Problemen ein Rückzieher gemacht.

(2) In schwierigen Phasen fehlt das wechselseitige Vertrauen.

(3) Die Projektverantwortung und die Linienverantwortung sind schlecht abgegrenzt.

(4) Die falschen Leistungsmaßstäbe werden etabliert. Das Ausrichten am Best of Class scheitert.

(5) Die Projektmitarbeiter wurden falsch ausgewählt oder schaffen die Doppelbelastung mit ihren regulären Aufgaben nicht.

(6) Die Betroffenen werden zu spät eingebunden.

(7) Das Projektmanagement mit Zeiten, Meilensteinen und Verantwortungszuordnung zeigt Schwächen.

Diese Hürden müssen allen bewußt sein und können mit gezielten Maßnahmen überwunden werden. Permanentes Benchmarking zeigt Ziele, Hürden und Wege des Überwindens auf.

15. Kundenorientierung durch cross-funktionale Teams

Cross-funktionale Teams ermöglichen eine völlig andere Form der Bearbeitung von Kundenwünschen und Kundenproblemen. Sie ermöglichen die Rundumbearbeitung von Kundenproblemen. Dadurch werden Schnittstellen in der Leistungserstellung vermieden, die Qualität der Leistung erhöht, die Kosten reduziert, die Prozeßzeiten dramatisch beschleunigt und deutliche Wettbewerbsvorteile möglich. Gerade für die auf den Kunden ausgerichteten Kernprozesse ist dies von be-

sonderer Bedeutung. Diese schaffen für den Kunden einen wahrnehmbaren Nutzen. Der organisatorische Ansatz der Rundumbearbeitung eines Prozesses funktioniert aber nur dann in der Praxis, wenn parallel dazu bei den Prozessen verschiedene Varianten untersucht und separat betrachtet werden. Die Segmentierung der Prozesse kann dabei nach folgenden Kriterien erfolgen:
(1) Segmentierung nach der Problemhaftigkeit bzw.
(2) Segmentierung nach den Kundengruppen.

16. Cross-funktionale Teams vermeiden Schnittstellen

Ein permanent bohrendes Problem in den Unternehmen ist die **immerwährende Problemsituation mit Schnittstellen.** Cross-funktionale Teams schaffen jedoch ein völlig anderes Denken und Handeln. Sie denken vom Output zum Input, den zur Verfügung stehenden Ressourcen und Kapazitäten. Dadurch werden Schnittstellen vermieden. Schnittstellen entwickeln sich langsam und leise, aber später jedoch lähmen sie das gesamte Unternehmen. Die bestehende Organisation und vorhandene Organisationshandbücher und Abteilungsegoismen fördern sie sogar permanent. Nur dadurch kann das Schlagwort Kundenorientierung zum Leben gebracht werden. Das cross-funktionale Team hat den permanenten Zwang der Rückkopplung zum Kunden. Woran jedoch erkennt man im Unternehmen Schnittstellen und ihre Gefährlichkeit? Schnittstellen äußern sich im Verhalten und in Äußerungen von Mitarbeitern. Zwei Typen von Schnittstellen können dabei auftreten:
- **Horizontale Schnittstellen**
  Hier erhalten Sie in einem Prozeß immer wieder die Antwort: **Dafür bin ich nicht zuständig.** Dies ist ein deutliches Zeichen, daß der Mitarbeiter primär nach innen orientiert ist, funktional ausgerichtet ist und nicht zum Kunden hin denkt und handelt.
- **Vertikale Schnittstellen**
  Hier erhalten Sie die Antwort des im Prozeß Tätigen: **Das darf ich nicht entscheiden.** Dies ist ein Signal, daß im Prozeß die Kompetenzen und Zuständigkeiten nicht scharf definiert sind. Auch hier dominiert die interne Machtsicht vor der Kundensicht. Entscheidungskompetenzen dürfen nicht aufgrund interner Stellung und Macht geregelt werden, sondern allein aus der Gesamtsicht des Kunden. Wenn es Führungskräfte gibt, die nicht auf die Entscheidungskompetenzen verzichten wollen, dann haben diese auch die Prozeßkompetenz zu übernehmen und alle ihre Entscheidungen dem Kunden gegenüber zu verantworten.

17. Permanente Beurteilung der Leistung von cross-funktionalen Teams

Der Nutzen cross-funktionaler Teams im Rahmen der Unternehmensentwicklung und dem Management von Veränderungen setzt ein effizientes Steuerungssystem voraus. Diese Messung der Leistung von Teams hat zwei Bausteine:

(1) Die Messung der Leistung
Dies bezieht sich auf Output-Kennzahlen und auf Kennzahlen im Prozeßablauf und Prozeßverhalten. Dazu ist die Messung der Erreichung der Erfolgsfaktoren der Qualität, der Zeit und der Kosten geeignet.

(2) Die Messung der Performance der Teammitglieder und jedes einzelnen
Neben den harten Faktoren sind die weichen Faktoren im Messen bei crossfunktionalen Teams von großer Bedeutung. Das **360 Grad Assessment** hilft alle Perspektiven der Beurteilung zu beachten. Dies sind die Teammitglieder, die Mitarbeiter, die Vorgesetzten und die vor- oder nachgeschalteten Teams.

18. Erfolgreiches Wissensmanagement durch cross-funktionale Teams

Wissen wird zum entscheidenden Erfolgsfaktor im Wettbewerbskampf. Cross - funktionale Teams in der Prozeßorganisation sollen die Voraussetzung schaffen, daß Wissen überall erfaßt, systematisch gefördert und weiterentwickelt wird. Ein hervorragendes Wissensmanagement schafft folgende Vorsprünge gegenüber der Konkurrenz:
- Verbesserte Produktqualität,
- stärkere Innovationskraft,
- größere Kundennähe,
- höhere Produktivität,
- mehr Kreativität,
- kürzere Durchlaufzeiten,
- stärkeres Wachstum.

Cross - funktionale Teams schaffen die Bündelung von Kräften und Kompetenzen. Um cross-funktionale Teams im Wissensmanagement erfolgreich zu machen, sind die immer wieder auftretenden Barrieren zu beseitigen. Nach einer Untersuchung des Fraunhofer Instituts für Arbeitswirtschaft und Organisation sind dies folgende Barrieren:
- Zeitmangel,
- fehlendes Bewußtsein,
- Unkenntnis über Wissensbedarf,
- Wissen als Machtfaktor,
- fehlende Anreizsysteme,
- fehlende Transparenz,

- zu starke Spezialisierung der Mitarbeiter,
- mangelnder Wissensaustausch,
- hemmende Unternehmenskultur.

Das Management und die Prozeßverantwortlichen haben die Hemmnisse zu beseitigen. Den Teammitgliedern muß garantiert werden, daß sie sich durch die Preisgabe ihres Wissens im Team nicht überflüssig machen. Ebenso müssen die Entscheider aktiv miteinbezogen werden, damit diese nicht die Befürchtung haben überflüssig zu werden. Die Berührungsängste müssen abgebaut werden.

19. Klimaänderung im Unternehmen

In zahlreichen Projekten zur Einführung von cross - funktionalen Teams im Rahmen der Entwicklung einer Prozeßorganisation konnten wir immer wieder folgende Wirkungen feststellen. Es haben sich nicht nur die harten Zahlen der Efizienz und der Effektivität dramatisch verbessert, sondern es wird dadurch ein völlig neues Unternehmensklima geschaffen. Wesentliche Wirkungen waren:

- Verbesserte Unternehmenskultur,
- organisierte Austauschmöglichkeiten,
- transparenz zu den Wissensbedürfnissen,
- transparenz der Aufgabenfelder,
- speziell geschaffene Freiräume,
- gegenseitiger Wissensaustausch,
- verbesserte IT - Infrastruktur,
- Leistungsprämien für Teams,
- verbesserte Karrierechancen,
- nichtmonetäre Anreizsysteme,
- individuelle Prämien.

Das richtige Motivieren und Führen durch cross-funktionale Teams schafft zufriedene Mitarbeiter, zufriedene Kunden, zufriedene Partner und zufriedene Aktionäre.

Change Management
und
Finance Management

Shareholder-Value-Konzepte für das Management von Unternehmen im dynamischem Umfeld

Manfred Steiner
Hermann-Josef Tebroke

Summary:

Classic performance measures have to be seen critically with respect to the management of companies working in the environment of a dynamic changing world. They are based only on information from the external accountancy and exclude future uncertain incomes. The shareholder-value-concept involves an assessment and controlling approach which enables the correct decisions to be made in order to increase the value of a company on a long-term basis.

1. Strukturwandel – Ursachen und Konsequenzen für das Management

Moderne Wirtschaftsunternehmen agieren in einem nicht-statischen sozialen und ökonomischen Umfeld. In zurückliegenden Perioden bewährte Strategien und Instrumente sind keine Garanten für zukünftigen Unternehmenserfolg. Ihr Wert für das Unternehmen läßt sich nicht einmalig feststellen und dann in der Erfolgsrechnung fortschreiben, sondern ist systematisch zu überprüfen – grundsätzlich regelmäßig vor dem Hintergrund der Ergebnisse aktueller Umfeldanalysen und Zukunftsprognosen und zudem außer Plan insbesondere dann, wenn sich grundlegende Veränderungen abzeichnen, denen mit strukturellem Wandel (in) der Unternehmung zu begegnen ist.

Die möglichen Gründe für Wandel sind vielfältig. Beispielhaft genannt seien
- staatliche Deregulierungsmaßnahmen und veränderte aufsichtsrechtliche Vorgaben;
- die Vergrößerung der relevanten Märkte (Internationalisierung);
- die Reform des nationalen Wirtschaftssystems;
- technologische Neuerungen;
- Veränderungen in den Wertvorstellungen der Abnehmer;
- Produkt- und Prozeßinnovationen der Wettbewerber.

In hochgradig regulierten Märkten, wie etwa im Bereich der Telekommunikation, des Postwesens oder auch des Schienenverkehrs, müssen die Unternehmen auf (international vereinbarte) Deregulierungsmaßnahmen vorbereitet sein, die ihren angestammten Marktanteil und ihre monopolistische Position in Frage stellen, weil sie ausländische Konkurrenz und Nischenanbieter zulassen (Stöckl 1995). Von solchen Veränderungen ist nicht zuletzt auch der weit verzweigte Bereich der Zulieferer unter Umständen nachteilig betroffen. Auf der anderen Seite eröffnen sich Möglichkeiten für Unternehmen, die bisher keinen Zugang zu diesem Markt besaßen und um so erfolgreicher sind, je besser und schneller sie auf diese Entwicklungen reagieren können.

Zu einer Vergrößerung der relevanten Märkte tragen in vielen Branchen weiter verbesserte und kostengünstigere Transportsysteme und Kommunikationsmöglichkeiten bei, durch die sich die ökonomisch relevante Entfernung maßgeblich reduziert. Abrupter noch ist der Wandel, der sich durch die Aufhebung von Handelsbeschränkungen ergibt. So führt der Beitritt eines Staates zu einer Wirtschafts- oder Zollunionen, wie etwa Spaniens zur EU, umgehend zu einer Vergrößerung des relevanten Wirtschaftsraums, wodurch sich nicht nur neue Konkurrenz, sondern auch eine erhebliche Vergrößerung des Absatzmarktes ergeben können. Im Marketing ergibt sich für das einzelne Unternehmen hieraus ein Perspektivenwechsel von der begrenzt lokalen zu einer globaleren Sicht (Trevor 1991). Vom Personal sind fürderhin mehr Bereitschaft zu Innovation im Denken und Handeln anstelle perfekter Administration nach tradierten Mustern gefordert (Echevarría/del Val Núñez 1995).

Fundamental ist der Wandel, der von Unternehmungen verlangt wird, die einer Änderung des Wirtschaftssystems ausgesetzt sind, wie er sich seit dem Ende der achtziger Jahre z. B. in ehemaligen Ostblockstaaten vollzieht. So mußten vormals sozialistische Betriebe der DDR erkennen, daß in dem neuen Umfeld kurzfristig nicht nur ganze Märkte zusammenbrachen und viele Techniken und Fähigkeiten des Personals ihren Wert verloren, sondern auch gänzlich neue Zielvorgaben für das Unternehmen zu definieren und in den Managementprozeß einzubeziehen waren (Albach 1995).

In einigen Branchen ist ein grundlegender Wandel in der Einstellung der Kunden zu den Unternehmen zu beobachten. So ist z. B. auf dem Markt für Finanz- und Bankdienstleistungen, auf dem zunehmend auch Non- und Nearbanks zur Erhöhung der Wettbewerbsintensität beitragen, aufgrund eines verbesserten Informationsstandes und erweiterten Angebotes das Qualitäts- und Preisbewußtsein der Nachfrager gestiegen; ihre schon sprichwörtlich gewordene Bankloyalität ist erodiert und einer nüchternen Offenheit für kurzfristige und auf Einzelgeschäfte beschränkte Mehrfachbankverbindungen gewichen. In der Folge sehen sich die traditionell auf diesem Markt agierenden Kreditinstitute gezwungen, die Perspektiven ihrer Geschäftsfelder neu zu bewerten. Konstitutive Maßnahmen, wie z. B. Fusionen, neue Kooperationen oder auch die Ausgliederung von Geschäftsbereichen oder Konzernteilen, sind in vielen Fällen die Folge.

Die Bedeutung technologischer Neuerungen für den Unternehmenswandel ist offensichtlich, wenn hierdurch die Lebenszyklen ihrer eigenen Produkte rapide verkürzt werden. So führen die Entwicklungen im Bereich der Mikroelektronik in kurzen Abständen dazu, daß alte Produkte ihren Wert verlieren oder sich neue Anwendungen ergeben. Sie verlangen hohe Anpassungsgeschwindigkeiten der Unternehmen. Aber auch der verstärkte Einsatz der immer leistungsfähigeren neuen Technologien als Inputfaktor im Produktionsprozeß verändert das Aussehen des Unternehmens, weil er zu neuen optimalen Faktorkombinationen und Verschiebungen der Vorteilhaftigkeit von Geschäftsfeldern führen kann.

Ein dynamisches Umfeld, zumal wenn es von strukturellen Veränderungen gekennzeichnet ist, stellt eine große Herausforderung an das Management dar. In einem Unternehmen, das sich im Wandel befindet, werden Entscheidungen nötig, die unter großer Unsicherheit getroffen werden müssen, weil sie von grundlegender Bedeutung sind, das Beschreiben neuer Wege verlangen und über längere Sicht keineswegs konstante Erfolgsbeiträge erwarten lassen.

Dabei ist jede einzelne Maßnahme im Hinblick auf ihren Beitrag zur Realisierung der Unternehmensziele zu beurteilen. Hierzu ist ein Bewertungssystem zu verwenden, das in einer dynamischen Perspektive der möglicherweise unstetigen Entwicklung der Erfolgsbeiträge und dem besonderen Risiko in geeigneter Weise Rechnung trägt und überdies für Steuerungszwecke auf Ebene strategischer Geschäftsfelder wie der Gesamtunternehmung gleichermaßen geeignet ist.

2. Steigerung des Shareholder Value als Managementaufgabe

Während nach der "traditionellen" Führungsphilosophie und auch heute noch in der Praxis der Führung insbesondere kontinentaleuropäischer Unternehmen der Eindruck entsteht, das Management bestimme letztlich, was für das Unternehmen erstrebenswert und damit gut oder schlecht ist, setzt sich zunehmend eine marktorientierte Betrachtung durch (Bühner/Tushce 1997). Danach bestimmt sich der Wert einer Unternehmung und jeder einzelnen Maßnahme danach, was am Markt für Eigentümerrechte an diesem Unternehmen gezahlt wird. Der Wert des Unternehmens, genauer: seiner Anteile, wird zum "Maß aller Dinge" (Rappaport 1986, Copeland/Koller/Murrin 1993, Bühner 1994, Drukarczyk 1997)

Die Durchsetzung des Shareholder-Value-Konzeptes folgt dem anglo-amerikanischen Beispiel (Baden 1996) und wird durch die Liberalisierung der Kapitalmärkte und zunehmende Effizienz auf dem Markt für Unternehmenskontrolle begünstigt. Hinzu kommen die Unzufriedenheit mit der rein qualitativen Bewertung strategischer Maßnahmen, deren Erfolgswirkung sich eben nur zu einem geringen Teil in der aktuellen Periode erfassen läßt, und die zunehmende Bedeutung der Erkenntnisse aus der neoklassischen Kapitalmarkttheorie, die auch im deutschsprachigen Raum eine (Neu-)Ausrichtung auf das Wohl der Investoren forcieren (Wagner 1997). Dabei ist die neuerliche Shareholder-Value-Orientierung durchaus auch als Gegenreaktion zu verstehen auf die Entwicklung unkontrollierter Entscheidungsspielräume und überhöhter Verhandlungs-, Steuerungs- und Überwachungskosten in Strukturen, die überwiegend von Nicht-Eigentümern bestimmt werden (Bühner/Tuschke 1997).

Das Shareholder-Value-Konzept soll hier als eine Managementkonzeption verstanden werden, nach der alle Entscheidungen im Unternehmen darauf ausgerichtet sind, den Wert des Unternehmens für die Anteilseigner auf lange Sicht nachhaltig zu steigern. Dieses bedeutet eine Abkehr von einem Verständnis von Unternehmenserfolg, der ausschließlich an der Größe oder am Wachstum festgemacht wird oder an einfachen periodenbezogenen Gewinn- oder Renditegrößen gemessen wird. Vielmehr geht es um die auf das Eigenkapital bezogenen dynamische Betrachtung der Entwicklung von Zahlungsüberschüssen unter Unsicherheit.

Aus dieser Definition ergeben sich in normativer, theoretisch konzeptioneller und praktischer Perspektive drei grundsätzlich separat abzuhandelnde Fragestellungen (Schierenbeck 1997, S. 5). So ist aus der normativen Sicht zunächst und grundsätzlich zu klären, ob der Shareholder Value als alleiniges Erfolgskriterium für die Unternehmensführung herangezogen werden soll (Wagner 1997). Die eher skeptische Aufnahme des Shareholder-Value-Begriffes durch die deutsche Öffentlichkeit ist wohl in erster Linie auf die Befürchtung zurückzuführen, die rigorose Ausrichtung von Unternehmensstrategien an den Zielsetzungen der Anteilseigner müsse fast zwangsläufig zu Lasten der übrigen Anspruchsgruppen (Stakeholder) gehen, zu denen neben den Mitarbeitern und Management auch die Kunden, Lieferanten, Gläubiger und der Staat in seinen verschiedenen Funktionen zählen.

Tatsächlich werden nach dem reinen Shareholder-Value-Ansatz die Ansprüche der Shareholder in den Vordergrund gestellt; die Berücksichtigung der Interessen der übrigen Anspruchsgruppen, die im übrigen über sehr unterschiedliche Möglichkeiten verfügen, ihre Interessen durchzusetzen, ist nicht Wert per se, sondern stellt eine Nebenbedingung für die Steigerung des Shareholder-Value dar. Je nach Kooperationsbereitschaft und Bedrohungspotential empfiehlt sich ein differenzierter Umgang - insbesondere mit den Mitarbeitern und dem Management, um mögliche Nachteile aus der "Agency-Beziehung" (u. v. a. Jensen/Meckling 1978; Elschen 1991) zu minimieren.

Bevor auf Ebene der einzelnen Unternehmung aus praktischer Sicht der Frage nachgegangen werden kann, durch welche Maßnahmen konkret und in welchem Umfang eine Steigerung des Unternehmenswertes zu erreichen ist, ist aus theoretisch konzeptioneller Sicht zu klären, wie eine adäquate Messung des Unternehmenswertes erfolgen kann und von welchen Größen er bestimmt wird.

Exkurs: Zum Neuigkeitscharakter des Shareholder-Value-Konzepts

Präsentationen neuer Managementkonzepte ziehen regelmäßig die nicht immer ganz unberechtigte Kritik nach sich, es handle sich dabei um kein eigenständiges Gedankengut, sondern lediglich um altbekannte Elemente in modischer Verpackung. Dieser

Vorwurf konnte dem Shareholder-Value-Ansatz gleichfalls nicht erspart bleiben (u. a. Mirrow 1991, S. 243) und ist insoweit auch berechtigt, als der Leitgedanke bereits seit längerem in der Bewertungspraxis Verwendung findet, beispielsweise anläßlich von Unternehmenskäufen und -zusammenschlüssen.

Ein fundamental neues Element besteht jedoch in der Ausweitung des Anwendungsbereiches auf die (laufende) Planung und Erfolgsbeurteilung von Geschäftsstrategien und Restrukturierungsmaßnahmen (Rappaport 1986). Die Institutionalisierung eines solchen wertorientierten Managements auf sämtlichen Unternehmensebenen kann den Vorrang einer langfristig orientierten Suche nach nachhaltigen Wettbewerbsvorteilen in einem dynamischen Umfeld vor einem Streben nach kurzfristigen Gewinnen (d. h. dann i. d. R. Kostensenkung vor Investitionen) festschreiben.

3. Theoretisch konzeptionelle Perspektive: Die Abbildung des Shareholder Value

3.1. Investitionstheoretische Grundlagen der Shareholder-Value-Ansätze

Zur Bewertung des Shareholder Value des Unternehmens insgesamt als auch zur Bewertung einzelner Maßnahmen im Hinblick auf ihren Beitrag zum Unternehmenswert kann auf Verfahren der Investitionsrechnung zurückgegriffen werden, die in der deutschen Literatur seit längerem bekannt sind. Hier sind insbesondere die dynamischen Verfahren der Kapitalwertmethode und der Internen-Zinsfuß-Methode zu nennen (Perridon/Steiner 1997, S. 58). Beide greifen auf die **Ein- und Auszahlungen** zurück, die durch die Investition oder unternehmerische Maßnahme **über die Zeit** t=0 bis t=T provoziert werden.

Zur Berücksichtigung des **Risikos** der Maßnahme liegt es nahe, den wertrelevanten Nutzungszeitraum zu verkürzen oder alternativ Abschläge auf die periodischen Rückflüsse vorzunehmen, wodurch die erwarteten unsicheren Zahlungen in eine Reihe fiktiver sicherheitsäquivalenter Zahlungen transformiert werden (Ballwieser 1993). Im allgemeinen präferiert ist schließlich die dritte Möglichkeit der Risikoadjustierung, die über eine Anpassung des Kapitalkostensatzes erfolgt.

3.2. Alternative Verfahren des Shareholder-Value-Ansatzes im Überblick

Wenn sich auch das Grundprinzip des Shareholder-Value-Ansatzes – die Bewertung der zukünftigen finanziellen Überschüsse eines Unternehmens unter besonderer Berücksichtigung der Faktoren Zeit und Risiko – wie ein roter Faden durch sämtliche Abhandlungen zu diesem Thema zieht, bleibt doch festzuhalten, daß die vorgeschlagenen quantitativen Analyseinstrumente zum Teil erheblich voneinander abweichen.

3.2.1. Der Cash-Flow-ROI-Ansatz

Nach der Internen-Zinsfuß-Methode ist eine unternehmerische Maßnahme vorteilhaft, wenn die interne Rendite des investierten Kapitals den Kapitalkostensatz übersteigt. An dieser Methode orientiert sich ein Shareholder-Value-Ansatz, der insbesondere von der Boston Consulting Group propagiert wird (Lehmann 1992; Lewis 1994) und als Cash-Flow-ROI-Ansatz bekannt ist.

Wie gezeigt werden kann, gewährleistet die Einführung der wertrelevanten Faktoren Kapitalintensität, Cash Flow und Nutzungsdauer eine erhebliche Verbesserung der Aussagekraft gegenüber traditionellen einperiodigen Performancemaßen, wie ROI und ROE (Lewis/Lehmann 1992, S. 5). Dies sollte jedoch nicht über gravierende Schwachstellen des CFROI-Modells hinwegtäuschen. So gelten die bekannten Nachteile der Internen-Zinsfuß-Methode für Zecke der dynamischen Investitionsrechnung analog für den CFROI. Hervorzuheben sind die Inkonsistenz des Modells bei mehrfachem Vorzeichenwechsel im Zahlungsstrom sowie die fehlende Darstellbarkeit unterschiedlicher Zinsstrukturkurven.

Weitere Kritik bezieht sich auf Merkmale des CFROI in der praktischen Anwendung. So werden die Überschüsse nicht mehr für jede Periode einzeln bestimmt, sondern aus **einem** (in der Regel dem ersten) Jahresabschluß abgeleitet und über die Perioden des Planungszeitraums als konstant unterstellt (Lewis/Lehmann 1992, S. 11). Der Nachteil dieser unrealistischen Annahme gleichbleibender Periodenüberschüsse wiegt besonders schwer für Unternehmen, deren Entwicklung insgesamt wie auch einzelner Teileinheiten sich angesichts veränderter Umweltbedingungen eben nicht schlicht fortschreiben lassen. Daneben wird in der Anwendung die Projektlaufzeit über den Quotienten aus historischen Anschaffungskosten und jährlichem Abschreibungsbetrag geschätzt. Da die bilanzielle Nutzungsdauer nur in Ausnahmefällen der tatsächlichen entspricht, erscheint das Verfahren entgegen anders lautenden Beteuerungen (Lewis/Lehmann 1992) kaum geeignet, Verzerrungen, die z. B. aus unterschiedlicher Abschreibungspolitik resultieren können, auszuschalten.

Aufgrund der beschriebenen konzeptionellen Mängel und gestützt auf empirische Untersuchungen wird der CFROI gelegentlich auch den "klassischen Lenkungskriterien" zugeordnet (Siegert 1995, S. 585).

3.2.2. Das Economic-Value-Added-Konzept

Als Alternative zum CFROI-Ansatz wird u. a. von Stern/Stewart ein Konzept vorgeschlagen, das auf den Economic Value Added als Zielgröße abstellt (Stewart 1990, Stewart 1991). Hierbei handelt es sich um eine periodische Residualeinkommensgröße, die sich als Überschuß des bereinigten operativen Gewinns vor Zinsen nach Abzug der Opportunitätskosten der Kapitalgeber ergibt. Dabei ist das Ergebnis soweit möglich um bilanzpolitische Maßnahmen und nicht zahlungswirksame Positionen bereinigt, so daß sich eine Cash-Flow-ähnliche Größe ergibt; ein separater Ausweis von Investitionsein- und -auszahlungen erübrigt sich.

Damit weicht der Ansatz (zunächst) von der kapitaltheoretischen Betrachtung der Zahlungsgrößen ab. Statt direkt auf Basis der Zahlungen zwischen Anteilseignern und Unternehmen erfolgt die Bewertung indirekt auf der Ebene von Aufwendungen und Erträgen in der Auseinandersetzung des Unternehmens mit den übrigen Kontraktpartnern. Zur Wertanalyse werden – um keinen zusätzlichen Rechnungskreis neben den bereits vorhandenen aufzubauen – bewußt Buchwertgrößen verwandt, die in bereinigter Form aus dem Rechnungswesen zu entnehmen sind.

Auch wenn sich das EVA-Konzept auf Größen des periodisierten Rechnungswesens stützt, ist es zur Beurteilung und Steuerung unternehmerischen Handelns im Sinne der Marktwertmaximierung unter bestimmten Bedingungen geeignet. Mit Hilfe des Lükke-Theorems (Lücke 1955) läßt sich zeigen, daß die Erreichung des Ziels, den Kapitalwert der Zahlungssalden zu maximieren, mit Hilfe einer Periodenerfolgsrechnung kontrolliert werden kann, wenn wie hier im EVA-Konzept der um kalkulatorische Zinsen auf das eingesetzte Kapital verminderte Gewinn als Erfolgsmaßstab gilt (Hachmeister 1995, S. 150). Verzerrte Steuerungsimpulse ergeben sich in dem Maße, wie die notwendigen Bedingungen nicht erfüllt sind.

Auf die grundsätzliche Problematik der Verwendung von Zahlen des externen Rechnungswesens für andere als die ihnen zugedachten Zwecke wird in der Literatur immer wieder hingewiesen. Insoweit auf Buchwerte statt auf Marktwerte Bezug genommen wird, betrifft diese Kritik auch das EVA-Konzept.

Insgesamt ergibt sich eine Überlegenheit des EVA gegenüber traditionellen buchhalterischen Kennzahlen, die auch in empirischen Untersuchungen zur Korrelation alternativer Performancemaße mit Börsenkursen bestätigt wurde. Die Vorziehenswürdigkeit gegenüber Discounted-Cash-Flow-Verfahren steht gleichwohl weiterhin in Frage.

3.2.3. Varianten des Discounted-Cash-Flow-Ansatzes

Eine Anwendung der Kapitalwertmethode, nach der eine unternehmerische Maßnahme vorteilhaft ist, wenn die Summe der mit den Kapitalkosten auf den Entscheidungsstichtag diskontierten Zahlungen positiv ist, stellen die Discounted-Cash-Flow-Verfahren dar (Hachmeister 1995, Richter 1997).

In der Literatur und auch in der Praxis wird der DCF-Ansatz häufig im Sinne eines abgeschlossenen theoretischen Modells verwendet und anderen Verfahren, wie insbesondere der in Deutschland verbreiteten Ertragswertmethode, gegenübergestellt (Serfling/Pape 1996, Schmidt 1995). Tatsächlich stehen jedoch mit dem **Weighted-Average-Cost-of-Capital-**, dem **Total-Cash-Flow-**, dem **Adjusted-Present-Value-** und dem **Flow-To-Equity-Ansatz** zumindest vier eigenständige DCF-Varianten zur Verfügung, die hinsichtlich der Zielgröße, der Cash-Flow-Definition sowie der rechnerischen Erfassung des Tax-Shields der Fremdfinanzierung divergieren. Weitere (mögliche) Modifikationen innerhalb dieser Ansätze betreffen die Einbeziehung von Erweiterungsinvestitionen und Annahmen über die Besteuerung.

Gemeinsam ist den drei erstgenannten Verfahren die Vorgehensweise nach dem sogenannten Entity-Approach (auch Brutto-Methode oder Gesamtkapitalkostenverfahren): In einem ersten Schritt werden für die Peridoden t des Bewertungszeitraums die Cash Flows $CF_{GK,t}$ aus dem operativen Geschäft vor Zinsen und nach Steuern (und Investitionen) für eine Verteilung an Fremd- und Eigenkapitalgeber zur Verfügung stehen, ermittelt und mit den Gesamtkapitalkosten $k_{GK,t}$ des Unternehmens diskontiert. In einem weiteren Schritt wird der Wert des Fremdkapitals FK subtrahiert, um schließlich zum gesuchten Wert des Eigenkapitals zu gelangen.

$$SV = \sum_{t=1}^{n} \frac{CF_{GK,t}}{\left(1 + k_{GK,t}\right)^t} - FK$$

Unterschiede bestehen hingegen in der Erfassung der diskriminierenden Wirkung einer ertragsabhängigen Steuer mit Abzugsfähigkeit von Zins-, nicht aber von Dividendenzahlungen (Steuereffekt der Finanzierung). Im TCF-Ansatz schlägt sich dies in einer Erhöhung der Cash-Flow-Größe um die Steuerersparnis und im APV-Ansatz in einem separat ermittelten Barwert des Tax-Shields nieder. Im WACC-Konzept, nach dem sich der Kapitalkostensatz mit Rücksicht auf die Anteile von Fremd- und Eigenkapital als gewichtetes Mittel aus Fremdkapitalkosten $k_{FK,t}$ und Eigenkapitalkosten $k_{EK,t}$ ergeben, wird der Steuereffekt über eine Korrektur der Fremdkapitalkosten um den effektiven Steuersatz s_t erfaßt, vereinfacht gemäß

$$k_{WACC,t} = k_{EK,t} \cdot \frac{EK_t}{EK_t + FK_t} + k_{FK,t} \cdot (1 - s_t) \cdot \frac{FK_t}{EK_t + FK_t}$$

Variieren die Steuersätze oder die Kapitalstruktur, was für Unternehmen im Wandel eher die Regel als die Ausnahme ist, erweist sich der APV-Ansatz im Vergleich zu dem im anglo-amerikanischen Raum vorherrschenden WACC-Ansatz, der eine periodische Anpassung des durchschnittlichen Kapitalkostensatzes erfordert, als deutlich anpassungsfähiger und als im besonderen geeignet, die Auswirkungen der Finanzierung auf den Unternehmensgesamtwert aufzuzeigen (Drukarczyk/Richter 1995).

Im Unterschied zu den drei vorgenannten DCF-Ansätzen folgt der FTE-Ansatz (auch Netto-Methode, Equity-Approach) einem grundlegend anderen Prinzip. Die Periodenüberschüsse werden nur so weit berücksichtigt, als sie den Anteilseignern zustehen (Cash Flow **nach** Zinsen) und mit den Eigenkapitalkosten diskontiert, um auf diese Weise direkt zum Wert des Eigenkapitals zu gelangen.

Auch die vom Institut der Wirtschaftsprüfer (IdW 1983) empfohlene und in Deutschland für die Unternehmensbewertung sehr verbreitete **Ertragswertmethode** läßt sich prinzipiell hier einordnen. Ihre methodische Eigenständigkeit gewinnt sie erst durch die Bestimmung von Diskontierungssätzen aus individuellen Opportunitäten (im Gegensatz zu marktdeduzierten Kostensätzen) sowie durch die Verwendung einer modifizierten Aufwands- und Ertragsrechnung als Ersatz für eine theoretisch richtige zahlungsstromorientierte Betrachtungsweise. Diese Eigenarten der Bewertungspraxis in Deutschland stehen jedoch in keinem fundamentalen Widerspruch mit den genannten DCF-Ansätzen. Beispielsweise läßt sich der individuelle Opportunitätskostensatz ohne konzeptionelle Schwierigkeiten zur Bestimmung der Gesamtkapitalkosten in die WACC-Formel integrieren.

3.3. Zur Bestimmung der Zahlungsüberschüsse und des Kapitalkostensatzes

Die gesuchte Überschußgröße ist grundsätzlich als Zahlungsstrom zwischen Kapitalgebern und Unternehmung zu erfassen und nur ersatzweise als Zahlungsstrom zwischen Unternehmen und Unternehmensumwelt anzunähern (Schmidt 1995, S. 1095; Serfling/Pape 1996, S. 58). Aus Sicht der Anteilseigner "ist für die Beurteilung des Investitionsobjektes 'Unternehmen' nur der Saldo zwischen den zukünftigen Entnahmen aus dem und den zukünftigen Einlagen in das Unternehmen von Bedeutung, da ... (ihnen) nur aus diesem zukünftigen Nettoentnahmestrom Nutzenpotentiale erwachsen" (Schmidt 1995, S. 1095; ähnlich Elschen 1991, S. 217).

Im Equity-Approach wird die Verwendung von Überschüssen aus der Geschäftstätigkeit (Zahlungsstrom zwischen Unternehmen und Umwelt) in der Praxis damit begründet, daß die notwendigen Informationen über die zukünftige Ausschüttungspolitik der Unternehmung i. d. R. nicht vorliegen. Aber auch dann sei eine solche Rechnung aus Plausibilitätsgründen angezeigt, um die Fähigkeit der Unternehmung zu überprüfen, die Ausschüttungen auch tatsächlich zu generieren. Tatsächlich kommen beide Verfahren zum selben Ergebnis, wenn – was gelegentlich nicht zu unrecht als realitätsfremd und deswegen unbefriedigende Umgehung eines zentralen Problems verurteilt wird (Schmidt 1995, Kümmel 1995) – unterstellt werden kann, daß die Überschüsse vollständig ausgeschüttet werden oder thesaurierte Beträge eine Rendite in Höhe des Kalkulationszinssatzes erbringen. Unter diesen Bedingungen kann als wertbestimmende Größe der Cash Flow nach Zinsen verwandt werden, wie er sich als Überschuß aus der Unternehmenstätigkeit nach Auszahlungen für notwendige Investitionen und nach Finanzierungsmaßnahmen ergibt und für die Ausschüttung oder zur Erhöhung der Liquidität zur Verfügung steht. Analog ist für den Cash Flow vor Zinsen im Entity-Approach zu argumentieren.

Für die Wertsteuerung der Unternehmung bzw. einzelner Maßnahmen sind im Idealfall die jährlichen Cash Flows über die Gesamtlebensdauer bzw. -wirkdauer T (mit möglicherweise T=∞) zu planen. Weil aber mit zunehmendem Abstand zum Planungszeitpunkt die Unsicherheit über die Höhe der zukünftigen Zahlungen wächst, empfiehlt sich für größere T eine Unterteilung des Bewertungszeitraums in einen Detailplanungszeitraum t=0 bis t=n, in dem für jede Periode einzeln der zuzurechnende Überschuß noch relativ gesichert genannt werden kann, und einen Abschnitt t=n+1 bis t=T, in dem vereinfachend pauschale Annahmen über die Entwicklung der Cash Flows getroffen werden.

Die Planung der Cash Flows geschieht unter Unsicherheit, auch wenn die Werte schließlich als Punktschätzer angegeben werden. Häufig werden - etwa auf Basis von Simulationen - für die periodischen Cash Flows zusätzlich mögliche Bandbreiten geschätzt. Dabei wird in der Regel entweder eine Gleichverteilung zwischen "relevanten" Minimal- und Maximalwerten oder eine Normalverteilung um den wahrscheinlichsten oder mittleren Wert unterstellt. Diese Unsicherheit bzgl. der wertrelevanten Rückflüsse stellt das Risiko der Investition dar, das bei der Bewertung zu berücksichtigen ist (Perridon/Steiner 1995, S. 97). Es wird bevorzugt über die Anpassung des Kalkulationszinssatzes erfaßt, der damit aus einer Zeitprämie als Opportunität für die entgangene Rendite aus risikolosen Alternativanlagen, beispielsweise in Bundesanleihen, und einer Risikoprämie besteht.

Zur Bestimmung der Risikoprämie wird in den DCF-Verfahren (auch im EVA-Approach) im allgemeinen das Capital Asset Pricing Model (CAPM) verwandt, weswegen der Rückgriff auf diese Modell gelegentlich auch als wesentliches Merkmal der DCF-Verfahren gesehen wird. Nach dem CAPM ergibt sich die Risikoprämie in Abhängigkeit vom Preis, der am Markt für die Übernahme von Risiko gezahlt wird, und vom systematischen Risiko der Investition, dem sog. Beta-Faktor β_I. Dieses entspricht dem Quotienten aus den Schätzwerten für die Kovarianz $cov_{I,M}$ der Rendite des Investments mit der Marktrendite und der Varianz σ_M^2 der Marktrendite (Perridon/Steiner 1997, S. 263). Unter Einbeziehung des risikolosen Zinssatzes R_F ergeben sich die Eigenkapitalkosten:

$$k_{EK,I} = R_F + \frac{E(R_M) - R_F}{\sigma_M^2} \cdot cov_{I,M} = R_F + \left[E(R_M) - R_F \right] \cdot \beta_I$$

Für börsennotierte Unternehmen läßt sich der Beta-Faktor mit Hilfe von Renditereihen, berechnet aus Kursveränderungen und Ausschüttungen, ableiten. Der Markt wird dabei durch einen Marktindex, etwa einem umfassenden Aktienindex, repräsentiert. Schwierigkeiten ergeben sich bei Unternehmen und Investitionen, die nicht an der Börse notiert sind. Hier liegen keine Börsenrenditereihen vor, aus denen Beta-Faktoren zu bestimmen wären. Hier ließe sich nach der Analogie-Methode der unbekannte Beta-Faktor durch den Beta-Faktor vergleichbarer Unternehmen oder Investitionen schätzen; oder aber es wird ein Beta-Wert (Accounting-Beta) über Buchrenditen ermittelt. Nach einer sehr pragmatischen Vorgehensweise schließlich wird das relative Risiko mit Hilfe von Risikoprofilen und Scoring-Techniken geschätzt (vgl. auch Kapitel 4).

Die Ermittlung von Risikoprämien mit Hilfe des CAPM ist nicht unumstritten. Zum einen wird die Eignung des CAPM als Bewertungsmodell in Frage gestellt. Zum anderen wird auf Probleme bei der Schätzung eines gesicherten Beta-Faktors - auch bei börsennotierten Unternehmen - verwiesen. Problematisch ist aber auch die Schätzung der Marktrendite $E(R_M)$, selbst wenn stellvertretend eine durchschnittliche Aktienrendite verwandt wird. Diese weist - auch im langjährigen Mittel - erhebliche Schwankungen auf, die wesentlich vom jeweiligen Beobachtungszeitraum abhängen, und ist darum als Prognosegrundlage nicht unumstritten.

4. Shareholder Value einzelner Geschäftseinheiten

Von einem Steuerungskonzept, das insbesondere in Zeiten des Umbruchs zum Einsatz kommen soll, ist zu verlangen, daß es nicht nur auf der Ebene der Gesamtunternehmung, sondern auch zur Bewertung und Steuerung einzelner Unternehmensteile und Strategien eingesetzt werden kann. Unabhängig davon, wie weit der Gegenstand der Steuerung heruntergebrochen wird, muß gewährleistet sein, daß sich die Wertbeiträge der untersten Einheiten jeweils zum Wert der nächsthöheren Einheit ergänzen und schließlich in der Summe dem Wert der Gesamtunternehmung entsprechen. Das ist mit den DCF-Ansätzen im Prinzip möglich, setzt aber voraus, daß ein Informationsstand gegeben ist, nach dem die jeweiligen Erfolgsfaktoren, Ergebnisbeiträge und Risiken exakt zugerechnet werden können. Dieses gestaltet sich um so schwieriger, je stärker die Verflechtungen und Verbundwirkungen zwischen den Steuerungseinheiten sind.

Besonders deutlich wird das Problem bei der Bestimmung der spezifischen Kapitalkosten, die den Unterschieden hinsichtlich der Risiken der einzelnen Unternehmensbereiche und Maßnahmen Rechnung zu tragen haben. Dabei ist zu berücksichtigen, daß sich die Einzelrisiken nicht zum Gesamtrisiko der Unternehmung addieren. So tragen möglicherweise Einheiten mit gleichem Einzelrisiko in unterschiedlichem Maße zum Gesamtrisiko der Unternehmung bei. Theoretisch relevant ist damit ausschließlich der systematische Risikobeitrag einer Einheit, wie er sich im Gesamtzusammenhang der Unternehmung (gar des unternehmensübergreifenden Marktes) darstellt. In der Praxis werden sich die Kovarianzen der unsicheren Renditen der Einheiten zur Ableitung der spezifischen Beta-Faktoren nicht oder nicht mit vertretbarem Aufwand bestimmen lassen. Um die unterschiedlichen Risikobeiträge dennoch im Bewertungsansatz zu berücksichtigen, bietet es sich an, auf das Erfahrungswissen der Geschäftsleitung zurückzugreifen. Zwar ist ein gewisser Mangel an Objektivität bei diesen Methoden nicht zu leugnen, jedoch ermöglichen sie – anders als die Extrapolation von Vergangenheitsdaten – eine Einbeziehung sämtlicher (auch zukunftsgerichteter) Informationen.

Als sinnvoll hat sich in der Praxis ein Verfahren nach dem Risikoklassenkonzept erwiesen, das nachfolgend in den Grundzügen an einem Beispiel zu beschreiben ist. Gegeben seien n strategische Geschäftseinheiten eines Unternehmens, das auf Unternehmensebene mit einem risikoadjustierten Kapitalkostensatz k_U kalkuliert. Zur Unterscheidung der Risikobeiträge der einzelnen Geschäftseinheiten stehen m Risikoklassen zur Verfügung, die mit gleichen, aber im vorhinein nicht festgelegten Abständen auf einer Intervallskala um den Nullpunkt positioniert sind. In den Klassen RK_{min} und RK_{max} befinden sich die Einheiten mit dem geringsten bzw. größten Risiko.

Die Zuordnung der einzelnen Einheiten zu diesen Risikoklassen kann nun nach dem Expertenurteil der Geschäftsleitung erfolgen. Auf dieser Grundlage und unter der Maßgabe, daß die Summe der mit spezifischen Kostensätzen (R_F+RP_I) einzeln abgezinsten Cash-Flows der Teileinheiten I dem mit dem k_U diskontierten Gesamt-Cash-Flow entspricht, ergibt sich ein Gleichungssystem, aus dem sich die risikoklassenspezifischen Risikoprämien RP_I und damit die Kalkulationszinssätze der Geschäftseinheiten ableiten lassen:

$$RP_I = NP + \left[RK_I - (RK_{min} + RK_{max}) \right] / 2 \cdot \Delta RP$$

$$...$$

$$RP_n = NP + \left[RK_n - (RK_{min} + RK_{max}) \right] / 2 \cdot \Delta RP$$

Der Risikoprämienabstand ΔRP zwischen den Risikoklassen ist gleich, aber in der Höhe abhängig von der Verteilung der Geschäftseinheiten über die Risikoklassen. Bei der "Nullprämie" NP handelt es sich um den Risikozuschlag der mittleren (im Falle eines geraden m der fiktiven) Risikoklasse, der im übrigen nicht mit dem Risikoaufschlag der Gesamtunternehmung übereinstimmen muß.

5. Zusammenfassung

Klassische periodenbezogene Performancemaße erweisen sich für die Steuerung von Unternehmen, die sich in einem dynamischen Umfeld und im Umbruch befinden, als unzulänglich, insoweit sie (ausschließlich) auf Daten des externen Rechnungswesens basieren und zukünftige unsichere Erfolgsbeiträge nicht berücksichtigen können.

Abhilfe verspricht das Shareholder-Value-Konzept. Es stellt einen Bewertungs- und Steuerungsansatz dar, nach dem alle Entscheidungen im Unternehmen darauf ausgerichtet sind, den Wert des Unternehmens für die Anteilseigner auf lange Sicht nachhaltig zu steigern. Dies impliziert eine auf das Eigenkapital bezogene dynamische Betrachtung der Entwicklung von Zahlungsüberschüssen unter Unsicherheit.

Zur konkreten Umsetzung des Shareholder-Value-Ansatzes, die im Grunde nach dem Muster seit längerem bekannter dynamischer Investitionsrechenverfahren funktioniert, finden vor allem CFROI-, EVA- und DCF-Konzepte Beachtung. Eine Auswahl aus diesen sollte schließlich mit Rücksicht auf die unternehmensspezifischen Bedingungen erfolgen, wenngleich im allgemeinen sich die DCF-Varianten als vorziehenswürdig erweisen, die nach dem Entity- oder nach dem Equity-Approach konzipiert sein können. Sie lassen sich sowohl zur Bewertung und Steuerung der Gesamtunternehmung als auch einzelner Teileinheiten und Strategien verwenden, soweit das Informationssystem im einzelnen eine exakte Zuordnung der Erfolgsfaktoren, Ergebnisbeiträge und Risiken ermöglicht.

Literatur:

Albach, H. (1995), The Management of Transition in East German Firms, in: Management of Structural Change. Contributions to Modern Management, Wiesbaden 1995, S. 53-83

Baden, K. (1996), Zum Wohl der Aktionäre. Erst machte Shareholder Value in Amerika Furore, jetzt reagieren endlich auch deutsche Topmanager auf die Forderungen ihrer Eigentümer, in: manager magazin 1996, Heft 4, S. 146-157

Ballwieser, W. (1993), Methoden der Unternehmensbewertung, in: Gebhardt, G., Gerke, G, Steiner, M. (Hrsg.), Handbuch des Finanzmanagements, München 1993, S. 151-176

Bühner, R., Tuschke, T. (1997), Zur Kritik am Shareholder Value - eine ökonomische Analyse -, in: Betriebswirtschaftliche Forschung und Praxis, 1997, S. 499-516.

Bühner, R. (1994), Unternehmerische Führung mit Shareholder Value, in: Bühner, R. (Hrsg.), Der Shareholder-Value-Report. Erfahrungen, Ergebnisse, Entwicklungen, Landsberg/Lech 1994, s. 9-75

Copeland, T., Koller, T., Murrin, J. (1993), Unternehmenswert. Methoden und Strategien für eine wertorientierte Unternehmensführung, Frankfurt am Main 1993

Drukarczyk, J. (1997), Wertorientierte Unternehmenssteuerung, in: Zeitschrift für Bankrecht und Bankwirtschaft, 1997, S. 217-226

Drukarczyk, J., Richter, F. (1995), Unternehmensgesamtwert, anteilseignerorientierte Finanzentscheidungen und APV-Ansatz, in: Die Betriebswirtschaft, 1995, S. 559-580.

Echevarría, S. G., del Val Núñez, M. T. (1995), The Human Resource Manager in Spain. His Contribution to Develop the Spanish Management, in: Management of Structural Change. Contributions to Modern Management, Wiesbaden 1995, S. 11-33.

Elschen, R. (1991), Shareholder Value und Agency-Theorie - Anreiz und Kontrollsysteme für Zielsetzungen der Anteilseigner, in: Betriebswirtschaftliche Forschung und Praxis, 1991, S. 209-221

Hachmeister, D. (1995), Der Discounted Cash Flow als Maß der Unternehmenswertsteigerung, Frankfurt am Main 1995

IdW Institut der Wirtschaftsprüfer in Deutschland e. V. (1983), Stellungnahme HFA 2/1983: Grundzüge der Durchführung von Unternehmensbewertungen, in: Die Wirtschaftsprüfung, 1983, S. 468-479

Jensen, M. C., Meckling, W. H. (1976), Theory of the Firm: Managerial Behavior, Agency Costs and Ownership Structure, in: Journal of Financial Economics, 1976, S. 305-360

Kümmel, A. T. (1994), Bewertung von Kreditinstituten nach dem Shareholder Value Ansatz: unter besonderer Berücksichtigung des Zinsänderungsrisikos, Ludwigsburg / Berlin 1994

Lehmann, S. (1992), Evaluation der Methoden zur Rentabilitätsmessung und Bewertung börsennotierter Aktiengesellschaften auf Basis empirischer Befunde in Deutschland, Wiesbaden 1992

332

Lewis, T. G. (1994), Steigerung des Unternehmenswertes. Total Value Management, Landsberg/Lech 1994

Lewis, T.G., Lehmann, S. (1992), Überlegene Investitionsentscheidungen durch CFROI, in: Betriebswirtschaftliche Forschung und Praxis, 1992, S. 1-13

Lücke, W. (1955), Investitionsrechnung auf der Grundlage von Ausgaben oder Kosten?, in: Zeitschrift für handelswissenschaftliche Forschung (neue Folge), 1955, S. 310-324

Mirrow, M. (1991), Shareholder Value als Zielgröße der Unternehmensführung (Meinungsspiegel), in: Betriebswirtschaftliche Forschung und Praxis, 1991, S. 241-253.

Perridon, L., Steiner, M. (1997), Finanzwirtschaft der Unternehmung, München 1997

Rappaport, A. (1986), Creating Shareholder Value, New York/London 1986

Richter, F. (1997), DCF-Methoden und Unternehmensbewertung: Analyse der systematischen Abweichungen der Bewertungsergebnisse, in: Zeitschrift für Bankrecht und Bankwirtschaft, 1997, S. 227-237

Schierenbeck, H. (1997), Ertragsorientiertes Bankmanagement im Visier des Shareholder Value-Konzepts, in: Basler Bankenvereinigung (Hrsg.), Shareholder Value-Konzepte in Banken, Bern/Stuttgart/Wien, S. 3-48.

Schmidt, J. (1995), Die Discounted Cash-flow-Methohde - nur eine kleine Abwandlung der Etragswertmethode?, in: Zeitschrift für betriebswirtschaftliche Forschung 1995, S. 1088-1118

Serfling, K., Pape, U. (1996), Strategische Unternehmensbewertung und Discounted Cash Flow-Methohde, in: Wirtschaftsstudium 1996, S. 57-64

Siegert, T. (1995), Shareholder Value als Lenkungsinstrument, in: Zeitschrift für betriebswirtschaftliche Forschung 1995, S. 580-607

Stewart, G. B. (1990), The Quest for Value. A Guide for Senior Managers, New York 1990

Stewart, G. B. (1991), The Quest for Value. The EVA^{TM} Management Guide, New York 1991

Stöckl, E. G. (1995), A United Europe: The Shock of Deregulation, in: Management of Structural Change. Contributions to Modern Management, Wiesbaden 1995, S. 1-9.

Trevor, M. (Hrsg., 1991), International Business and the Management of Change, Aldershot/GB 1991.

Wagner, F. W. (1997), Shareholder Value: Eine neue Runde im Konflikt zwischen Kapitalmarkt und Unternehmensinteresse, in: Betriebswirtschaftliche Forschung und Praxis, 1997, S. 473-498.

Originäre und derivative Finanzinnovationen als Instrumente zum Management von Zinsrisiken

Jens Jokisch

Summary:

Original and derivative finance innovations are the subject of this article. Examples of original finance innovations are Euro-Commercial-Papers and Euro-Note-Facilities. Examples of derivative finance innovations are Interest Futures and Interest Forwards. The management of interest rate risks by means of original and derivative finance innovations is described in detail.

1. Problemstellung

In den vergangenen Jahren ist es durch die Entwicklung von Finanzinnovationen zu einer Veränderung im Finanzierungsverhalten von Unternehmen höchster Bonität gekommen. Während sich solche Unternehmen früher vornehmlich mit Internationalen Industrieanleihen vom so bezeichneten Euro-Kapitalmarkt (die Formulierung Euro-Kapitalmarkt wird seit den fünfziger Jahren verwendet, wenn eine Währung außerhalb ihres Domizillandes in Europa, Amerika oder Asien an internationalen Finanzplätzen gehandelt wird und sollte nicht mit der Bezeichnung für die künftige europäische Währung Euro verwechselt werden) und/oder mit Schuldscheindarlehn vom nationalen deutschen Kapitalmarkt langfristig finanziert haben und damit die klassische Erscheinungsform der **zinsfixierten** Finanzmittelaufnahme präferierten, ist heute zunehmend zu beobachten, daß diese Unternehmen einen nennenswerten Anteil ihrer Finanzmittel über die originären Finanzinnovationen Euro Commercial Papers und Euro Note Facilities zu **zinsvariablen** Konditionen beschaffen und sich somit zu im Regelfall niedrigen kurzfristigen Finanzmarktkonditionen finanzieren und die daraus resultierenden **Zinsrisiken** durch derivative Finanzinnovationen wie Zins Futures, Forward Rate Agreements und Zinsoptionen zu managen versuchen.

Der Begriff der Finanzinnovation ist in der Literatur nicht eindeutig definiert. Grundsätzlich ist laut Duden unter einer Innovation eine "neue, fortschrittliche Lösung eines (technischen) Problems bei Produkten oder Verfahren" zu verstehen. Innovationen wirken sich dann eindeutig erlöserhöhend und/oder kostensenkend aus. Ein derartig technisch bzw. leistungswirtschaftlich orientierter Innovationsbegriff kann auch auf finanzwirtschaftliche Fragestellungen angewendet werden. Wenn man unter einer Finanzinnovation einen auf den Geld-, Kredit- und Kapitalmärkten erst in jüngerer Zeit gehandelten Finanztitel oder eine neue Finanzdienstleistung versteht, dann bleiben aber entscheidende Abgrenzungsfragen offen (Hielscher 1989, S. 69 f.). Es ist *erstens* unklar, wie lange Innovationen als innovativ bezeichnet werden können (Zeitbezug), zweitens ob auf einem Teilmarkt neu angebotene Instrumente als innovativ angesehen werden können, wenn sie auf anderen Teilmärkten seit Jahren gehandelt werden (Marktbezug) und *drittens* wie ausgeprägt sich das Merkmal der Innovation vom Merkmal des klassischen (etablierten) Instruments unterscheiden muß (Merkmalsbezug). Es kann hier ohne weiteren Beleg festgestellt werden, daß es sich bei vielen als Finanzinnovationen bezeichneten Finanzprodukten lediglich um eine geringfügige Modifikation der Ausstattungsmerkmale längst bekannter Produkte handelt und daß der Name Finanzinnovation somit oft irreführend verwendet wird.

Eine den Namen verdienende Finanzinnovation muß zu einer Veränderung im finanzwirtschaftlichen Verhalten führen. Solche das Finanzierungs- und Anlegerverhalten verändernde Finanzinnovationen können originäre oder derivative Finanzprodukte sein. Mit originären Finanzinnovationen werden Finanzmittel zu variablen Zinsen beschafft, wird also eine mit Zinsrisiken behaftete Unternehmensfinanzierung betrieben. Demgegenüber können mit den derivativen Finanztiteln die aus den originären Finanztiteln resultierenden Risiken (hier Zinsrisiken) gehandelt, d.h. übernommen oder abgegeben werden, ohne die Rechte aus den Finanztiteln selbst zu handeln. Allgemein ausgedrückt wird also durch Finanzderivate das Risiko eines Finanztitels losgelöst vom Finanztitel selbst gehandelt. Im folgenden sollen innovative originäre und derivative Instrumente der Geld-, Kredit- und Kapitalmärkte hinsichtlich ihrer Eignung zum Management von Zinsrisiken untersucht werden. Es wird aufgezeigt, daß die originären innovativen Instrumente mit Derivaten kombiniert werden müssen, um die erwünschte finanzierungskostensenkende und finanzierungskostenbegrenzende Wirkung zu erzielen.

2. Das Management von Zinsrisiken mit den klassischen Instrumenten und den originären Finanzinnovationen Euro Commercial Papers und Euro Note Facilities aus entscheidungs- und zinstheoretischer Sicht

2.1. Der klassische Ansatz

Als klassische Ausprägung des Zinsrisikomanagements sind fristenkongruente Investitionsfinanzierungen mit fixierten Zinssätzen anzusehen. Es ist das Ziel der sich mit diesen Produkten finanzierenden Unternehmen, das Zinsrisiko auszuschalten. Diese Konstruktion hat auch heute noch ein großes Handelsvolumen am Markt für langfristige Finanzmittel. Solche Finanzierungen können aber bei der üblicherweise herrschenden Fristigkeitsstruktur der Zinssätze (term structure of interest rates) nur zu ca. 2% bis 2,5% über den Geldmarktkonditionen liegenden

Zinssätzen getätigt werden, d.h. sie sind bei normalen Zinssituationen zunächst teurer als zinsflexible Finanzierungen. Es liegt im Ermessen des Finanzmanagements, ob es die Wahrscheinlichkeitsverteilung der Finanzierungskosten unabhängig von Zinsänderungen machen will und dafür ex ante höhere Finanzierungskosten zu tragen bereit ist oder ob es unter Inkaufnahme von Zinsrisiken die Finanzierungskosten auf Basis von Geldmarktsätzen gegenüber einer fristenkongruenten Zinsfixierung senken will.

Die Fristigkeitsstruktur der Zinsen stellt eine Beziehung zwischen den Zinssätzen auf dem Geldmarkt und dem Kapitalmarkt her. Sie beschreibt den Zusammenhang zwischen der Fristigkeit der Finanzmittelüberlassung und der Zinshöhe für die verschiedenen Fristigkeiten. Nach der **Liquiditätspräferenzhypothese** haben die Finanzmittelanleger eine Vorliebe für kurzfristige Geldanlagen und sind zu längerfristigen Engagements nur bereit, wenn ihnen dafür ein höherer Zinssatz geboten wird. Die Finanzmittelaufnehmer haben ihrerseits eine Liquiditätsvorliebe und sind bereit, für langfristige Kapitalaufnahmen höhere Zinsen als für kurzfristige Geldaufnahmen zu zahlen, weil kurzfristige Finanzmittelaufnahmen ein höheres Prolongationsrisiko als langfristige Engagements haben und daher das Halten höher dimensionierter Liquiditätsreserven erfordern, die ihrerseits nur niedrig verzinslich angelegt werden können. Langfristige Kapitalaufnahmen sollten aber fristenkongruent in hochrentierliche Vermögenswerte investiert werden, bei denen der Geldumwandlungsprozeß erst langfristig beendet wird. Aus diesem Grunde liegen bei normaler Fristigkeitsstruktur der Zinssätze die Zinsen für kürzerfristige Transaktionen auf den Finanzmärkten sowohl innerhalb des Geldmarktes als auch zwischen Geld- und Kapitalmarkt unter den Konditionen für längerfristige Transaktionen. Die Abhängigkeit des risikozuschlagfreien Zinsniveaus von der Fristigkeit der Finanzmittelüberlassung kann gewöhnlich durch eine **konkave Zinsfunktion** beschrieben werden (Jokisch 1989, Sp. 1255).

Nach der **Erwartungshypothese** der Zinssätze wird der langfristige Zinssatz als geometrisches Mittel der erwarteten kurzfristigen Zinssätze aufgefaßt (Süchting 1991, S. 349). **Inverse** Zinsfunktionen können als Erwartung der Mehrheit der Marktteilnehmer auf künftig sinkende Zinssätze interpretiert werden. **Konkave Zinsfunktionen** enthalten aber auch eine Erwartung der Mehrheit der Marktteilnehmer über künftige (kurzfristige) Zinsen. Es könnte argumentiert werden, daß aus der Steigung der konkaven Zinsfunktion eine implizierte Zinserhöhungserwartung abzulesen ist. Je steiler die konkave Zinsfunktion, desto höher ist die von den Marktteilnehmern erwartete Zinssteigerung. Bei Kenntnis zweier Punkte auf der Zinsfunktion (z.B. der Zinssatz für Ein Jahres Aufnahmen sei 5% und der für Zwei Jahres Aufnahmen sei 6%) kann gefragt werden, wie stark der Zinssatz für Ein Jahres Aufnahmen in einem Jahren steigen darf, daß eine heute getätigte Ein Jahres Aufnahme mit anschließender Ein Jahres Revolvierung zum dann geltenden Ein Jahres Zinssatz ökonomisch äquivalent einer heute getätigten Zwei-Jahres-Aufnahme ist. Dieser in einem Jahr geltende Ein Jahres Zinssatz kann bei gegebener Zinsfunktion als ein Gleichgewichtszinssatz angesehen werden und wird als implizierter Zinsterminsatz (hier 7,07%) bezeichnet. Dieser Zinssatz wird dann als Erwartung der Mehrheit der Marktteilnehmer für den in einem Jahren geltenden Ein Jahres Geldmarktsatz interpretiert.

2.2. Finanzierung und Zinsrisikomanagement mit originären Innovationen

Die Entstehung von innovativen Finanzprodukten ist vor dem Hintergrund der Deregulierung und Globalisierung der Finanzmärkte sowie der Tendenz zur Securitization zu sehen. Der umfassende Abbau der den Handel mit Finanzprodukten regelnden Bestimmungen (Deregulierung) und die verschiedene internationale Finanzmärkte nutzende internationale operative Geschäftstätigkeit der großen Industrieunternehmen und der internationalen Anleger (Globalisierung) haben eine Unterlegung der Finanzmittelüberlassung durch verbriefte Wertpapiere (Securitization) und daraus folgend einen Handel dieser Wertpapiere auf Sekundärmärkten nach sich gezogen und wegen der besseren Liquidisierbarkeit dieser Finanztitel zu sinkenden Transaktionskosten und damit zu einer Effizienzsteigerung der Finanzmärkte für beide Marktseiten, also für Finanzmittelanleger und - aufnehmer, geführt (Hielscher 1989, S. 66 ff.).

Große international tätige Unternehmungen, die durch ein gutes (Markowitz-) Investitionsportfolio, durch eine gute Kapital- und Kostenstruktur und damit durch ein geringes finanzwirtschaftliches Gesamtrisiko gekennzeichnet sind, können sich die Übernahme von Zinsrisiken mit der daraus folgenden begründeten Erwartung auf niedrigere Finanzierungskosten ohne Bonitätsverluste leisten und finanzieren daher schon seit Jahrzehnten erhebliche Teile ihres Kapitalfonds mit zinsflexiblen Finanzmitteln. Die Finanzinnovation der fünfziger Jahre, der klassische revolvierende Kredit vom internationalen Finanzmarkt (**Euro-Kredit**) zum Libor-Zinssatz (dem in London/Luxemburg unter Banken gehandelten Angebotssatz für kurzfristige Finanzmittel) zuzüglich eines bonitätsabhängigen Spreads, der für erste Adressen mittlerweile nur noch 30 Basispunkte (0,3% p.a.) beträgt, hat neben den zinsfixierten Instrumenten eine bedeutende Marktstellung erlangt. Da auch der klassische Euro-Kredit mittelfristig (bis fünf Jahre) zugesagt wird, entfällt das für kurzfristige Finanzierungen typische Prolongationsrisiko und die Finanzmittelaufnehmer tragen nur das Zinsrisiko.

Unternehmen höchster Bonität sehen sich aber heute in der Lage, das Prolongationsrisiko zu tragen und versuchen erfolgreich, dafür den die Finanzierungskosten bestimmenden Spread fühlbar zu verringern. Die seit einigen Jahren gehandelten **Euro Commercial Papers** sind kurzfristige Wertpapiere mit hohem Nominalwert (Stückelung nicht unter DM 250.000), die unter Vermittlung von Banken an nur kurzfristig anlegende kommerzielle Marktpartner verkauft werden, die ihrerseits ihre Anlage schon vor Fälligkeit unter Inkaufnahme geringer Kursrisiken auf einem ergiebigen Sekundärmarkt wieder auflösen können. Von diesem neuen Instrument profitieren beide Marktseiten. Die Finanzmittelaufnehmer zahlen nur noch 5 Basispunkte Spread auf den Libor-Geldmarktsatz und haben damit die

Marge gegenüber dem klassischen Eurokredit (Libor plus 30 Basispunkte) auf ein Sechstel verringert. Die Anleger bekommen nun bei hoher Flexibilität hinsichtlich der Auflösung der Anlage einen über dem Geldmarktsatz liegenden Zinssatz, während sie früher ihre Finanzmittel nur bei Banken zum niedrigeren Libid-Satz anlegen konnten oder unter Inkaufnahme von geringer Flexibilität ins Industrie-Clearing gehen mußten. Das Prolongationsrisiko des finanzierenden Unternehmens erster Bonität wird als verschwindend gering angesehen, da weltbekannte Unternehmen immer Käufer für marktgerecht ausgestattete Commercial Papers finden werden und folglich eine Prolongation der Finanzmittelaufnahme zu niedrigen Finanzierungskosten fast immer möglich erscheint.

Als Finanzinnovation, die eine Ausschaltung dieses geringen Prolongationsrisiko ermöglicht, kann die seit einigen Jahren gehandelte **Euro Note Facility** angesehen werden. Bei diesem Finanzierungsinstrument garantiert eine als Lead Manager fungierende Bank einer Industrieunternehmung für mittel- bis langfristige Zeiträume eine bis zu mehreren hundert Millionen DM (oder US-$) reichende Finanzierungslinie, wobei der Lead Manager und die zum Konsortium gehörenden anderen Banken die Wertpapiere (Notes) der Industrieadresse ins eigene Anlageportfolio übernehmen, wenn zu einem Ausgabe- bzw. Revolvierungszeitpunkt der Notes die Nachfrage nach kurzfristigen Wertpapieren dieser Unternehmung nicht für eine volle Plazierung ausreicht. Zusätzlich kann die Industrieunternehmung zu den Drei oder Sechs Monats Revolvierungsterminen über das Ausmaß der Inanspruchnahme der Linie entscheiden. Dies ist als eine dem Kontokorrentkredit nicht unähnliche Flexibilitätseigenschaft der Euro Note Facility anzusehen. Für diese Garantie berechnet der Lead Manager eine aus fixen und variablen Komponenten bestehende Bereitstellungsgebühr, die die Kosten der Euro Note Facility gegenüber dem Euro Commercial Paper zwar um 10 Basispunkte bei voller Ausnutzung der Linie verteuern, die aber auch bei nur fünfzigprozentiger Ausnutzung der Linie noch zu einer Verbilligung der Finanzierung gegenüber dem klassischen Euro-Kredit führt.

Beim Einsatz von originären Finanzinnovationen werden also Finanzmittel mittel- bis langfristig zu variablen Zinsen auf Basis z.B. der Drei oder Sechs Monats Libor Sätze aufgenommen, d.h. die Unternehmen gehen unter Inkaufnahme bzw. Ausschaltung des Prolongationsrisikos bewußt ins Zinsrisiko. Solange es während des Zeitraums der Finanzmittelaufnahme bei konkaver Zinsfunktion nicht zu einem fühlbaren Anstieg des Zinsniveaus kommt, sind auf kurzfristigen Zinssätzen basierende Finanzierungen billiger als die klassischen fristenkongruenten Fixierungen des Zinssatzes. Es besteht aber die Möglichkeit von Zinssteigerungen während der Laufzeit, die über den implizierten Zinsterminsatz hinausgehen. Dieses mit den originären Finanzinnovationen zwingend einhergehende Zinsrisiko soll mit den derivativen Finanzinnovationen in tragbaren Grenzen gehalten werden. Dem liegt die finanzwirtschaftliche Erkenntnis zugrunde, daß die Übernahme unvermeidlicher, d.h. richtig selektierter Risiken durch den Markt mit höheren Prämien, hier also mit niedrigeren Finanzierungskosten, abgegolten wird.

Die künftigen Zinssätze bestimmen immer dann die künftigen Finanzierungskosten, wenn die mittel- und langfristigen Finanzmittel nicht mit für die Laufzeit fixierten Zinssätzen aufgenommen wurden. In der finanzwirtschaftlichen Theorie gilt es aber als unmöglich, künftige Zinssätze erfolgversprechend vorherzusagen. Dies wird mit der **Markteffizienzhypothese** und der **Random walk Hypothese** begründet. Auf effizienten Finanzmärkten enthalten die aktuellen Konditionen (hier Zinsen) alle verfügbaren Informationen über die konditionenbestimmenden Faktoren. Die aktuellen Zinskonditionen können also als Erwartungswert (bester Schätzwert) künftiger Zinsen aufgefaßt werden, d.h. die Wahrscheinlichkeit einer Abweichung ist in beide Richtungen gleich. Neue konditionenbestimmende Informationen über die Determinanten der Zinsen ergeben sich ex ante gesehen zufällig, d.h. die künftigen Zinssätze befinden sich auf einem Zufallspfad (sie sind at Random walk). Nur wer bessere Informationen als die Mehrheit der Marktteilnehmer hat, kann mit auf Zinsprognosen basierenden Finanzierungen erfolgreich sein.

Die künftigen Zinssätze können als Zufallsvariable aufgefaßt werden, die mit bestimmten Wahrscheinlichkeiten bestimmte Ausprägungen annehmen. Es existiert eine Wahrscheinlichkeitsverteilung der künftigen Zinssätze und aus entscheidungstheoretischer Sicht werden Zinsrisiken durch die Wahrscheinlichkeitsverteilung der Finanzierungskosten beschrieben. Einer mittel- bis längerfristigen Finanzierungsentscheidung kann dann nicht ein eindeutiges Ergebnis der Finanzierungskosten zugeordnet werden, sondern die Finanzierungskosten hängen von der künftigen Entwicklung der Referenzzinssätze zu den Revolvierungszeitpunkten ab. Es ist möglich, daß die Zinssätze und damit die Finanzierungskosten noch weiter fallen (umgangssprachlich wird dies als **Chance** bezeichnet), es ist aber auch denkbar, daß zu späteren Revolvierungszeitpunkten (stark) steigende Zinssätze und damit Finanzierungskosten zu erheblichen Liquiditätsbelastungen während der Revolvierungsperioden führen und die Finanzierungskosten über das bei fristenkongruenter Fixierung angefallene Niveau ansteigen lassen (umgangssprachlich wird nur dieser Fall als **Risiko** bezeichnet).

Aus entscheidungstheoretischer Sicht handelt es sich bei dem auch in der wissenschaftlich fundierten Literatur gebräuchlichen Begriff des **Zinsänderungsrisikos** um einen Pleonasmus; die Möglichkeit einer **Zinsänderung** und damit einer Änderung der Finanzierungskosten ist als das Zinsrisiko anzusehen. Damit ist auch die umgangssprachliche Differenzierung in Chancen und Risiken überflüssig, da es sich um verschiedene Ausprägungen derselben Zufallsvariablen handelt. Die Bezeichnung einer Zinserhöhung als Risiko und einer Zinssenkung als Chance für Finanzmittelaufnehmer führt nur zu einer völlig überflüssigen terminologischen Differenzierung für den gleichen Sachverhalt: der Variation einer Zufallsvariablen.

Eine Entscheidung, der kein determiniertes Ergebnis, sondern nur eine Wahrscheinlichkeitsverteilung der Ergebnisse zugeordnet werden kann, wird als **Ent-**

scheidung unter Unsicherheit oder synonym als **Entscheidung unter Risiko** bezeichnet (Schneeweiß 1967, S. 27 ff.). Das Risiko einer Entscheidung wird dabei nicht definiert, sondern durch die möglichen Auswirkungen, also die gesamte Wahrscheinlichkeitsverteilung der finanzwirtschaftlichen Ergebnisse beschrieben (Karten 1972, S. 158 ff.). Die Entscheidungssituation kann in einer Entscheidungsmatrix abgebildet werden und das Risiko der Entscheidungsalternativen wird durch die Ermittlung verschiedener Streuungsmaße gemessen (Franke/Hax 1990, S. 183 ff.). Als Management von Zinsrisiken kann in diesem Sinne die zielorientierte Auswahl einer bestimmten aus der Vielahl der **möglichen** Wahrscheinlichkeitsveteilungen der Finanzierungskosten verstanden werden.

3. Zur Bedeutung derivativer Finanzinnovationen (Zins Futures, Zins Forwards und Zinsoptionen) für das Management von Zinsrisiken

3.1. Zum Begriff von Future, Forward und Option

Die innovativen Finanzderivate zum Management von Zinsrisiken können zunächst in Future-Geschäfte, Forward-Geschäfte und Options-Geschäfte eingeteilt werden. Mit diesen Finanzderivaten kann zwar Zinsrisikomanagement, nicht aber Finanzierung betrieben werden, d.h. es können mit Finanzderivaten (einige) unerwünschte Ausprägungen der Wahrscheinlichkeitsverteilung der Finanzierungskosten vermieden werden, während über die Beschaffung von Finanzmitteln separat zu entscheiden ist. Gemeinsam ist den drei Geschäften, daß zwischen dem Zeitpunkt des Vertragsabschlusses und dem Erfüllungszeitpunkt eine standardisierte oder individuell vereinbarte Frist liegt. Insoweit können diese drei Geschäfte als Termingeschäfte bezeichnet werden, weil sie nicht zur sofortigen Erfüllung abgeschlossen werden. Zum Zeitpunkt des Vertragsabschlusses erfolgt die Fixierung der Bedingungen, d.h. der Preis des Handelsobjektes wird festgelegt. Die Unternehmen können sich damit unabhängig von zwischenzeitlichen Konditionenänderungen machen. Futures und Forwards sind **unbedingte Termingeschäfte**, d.h. beide Marktseiten sind unabhängig von den künftigen Konditionen zur Erfüllung verpflichtet. Demgegenüber handelt es sich bei einem Optionsgeschäft um ein **bedingtes (asymmetrisches)** Geschäft, d.h. eine Marktseite (der Käufer der Option) hat das Recht, nicht aber die Pflicht zur Vertragsabwicklung, während die als Stillhalter bezeichnete andere Marktseite (der Verkäufer der Option) auf Wunsch des Käufers die Vereinbarung erfüllen muß (Franke 1990, S. 43 ff., Büschgen 1993, S. 261 ff.).

Während Futures an Terminbörsen gehandelt werden und daher wegen des Zwanges zur Erreichung eines großen Handelsvolumens notwendigerweise standardisiert sein müssen, können Forwards im so bezeichneten OTC (Over the counter) Handel durch individuelle, in der Praxis aber ebenfalls (wenn auch geringer) standardisierte Vereinbarungen mit den Banken besser an die betrieblichen Erfordernisse (hinsichtlich Betrag und Zeitraum) angepaßt werden. Als weiterer

Unterschied zwischen Futures und Forwards kann festgestellt werden, daß Futures grundsätzlich auf Differenzherauszahlung (d.h. die Handelsobjekte werden nicht ausgetauscht, sondern es kommt nur zu Ausgleichszahlungen hinsichtlich des Preises dieser Objekte) gehandelt werden, während es bei Forwards oft zu einer tatsächlichen Lieferung kommt.

3.2. Zur Eignung von Zins Futures und von Zins Forwards zum Management von Zinsrisiken

Zins Future Geschäfte können erst seit 1988 an der Londoner (Liffe) und seit 1991 an der Deutschen (DTB) Terminbörse getätigt werden. Das größte Handelsvolumen hat der **Bund Future**. Es gibt vier standardisierte Erfüllungstermine im März, Juni, September und Dezember, wobei derzeit jeweils auf die nächsten zwei Termine gehandelt wird. Daneben gibt es noch einen Future Markt für die (fünfjährige) Bundesobligation, während der Future Handel auf Basis einer dreißigjährigen Bundesanleihe wegen fehlender Marktliquidität eingestellt wurde. Beim Bund Future werden mit einem Kontrakt DM 250.000 einer fiktiven Bundesanleihe mit einer (festen) Nominalverzinsung von 6% (jährlich nachschüssig zahlbar) und einer Restlaufzeit von 8,5 bis 10 Jahren gehandelt. Dieser Kontrakt kann je nach Zinserwartung und abzusichernder Position gekauft und verkauft werden. Entsprechend dem Zusammenhang zwischen Effektivzins und gehandeltem Kurs muß der Kurs eines Bund Future Kontraktes mit einer Nominalverzinsung von 6% bei einer Marktrendite von zehnjährigen Staatsanleihen von 5,5% über pari liegen. Der Kurszettel der Süddeutschen Zeitung weist für den 10.7.97 einen Kurs in Höhe von 102,74 für die Septemberfälligkeit aus.

Von Banken wird für den Handel mit Bund Future Kontrakten folgendermaßen geworben: Wenn ein Unternehmen eine Finanzmittelaufnahme zu variablen Zinsen gegen einen erwarteten oder befürchteten Anstieg des Zinsniveaus absichern möchte, dann müßte es Bund Future Kontrakte verkaufen. Dabei sollten der Revolvierungszeitpunkt der originären und der Erfüllungszeitpunkt der derivativen Position möglichst nahe beieinander liegen. Zum nächsten Revolvierungszeitpunkt der Finanzmittel hätte es dann zwar höhere Zinszahlungen für die originäre Position (Kredit) zu leisten. Diese Mehrausgaben werden aber durch eine Einnahme aus der Ausgleichserfüllung des derivativen (Future) Geschäftes (teil-) kompensiert. Bei steigenden Zinsen fällt der Kurs der im Umlauf befindlichen Anleihen mit fester Verzinsung. Folglich muß auch der Kurs des Bund Future fallen und das Unternehmen kann zum nächsten Erfüllungstermin den bereits verkauften Bund Future billiger einkaufen bzw. erhält die Differenz zwischen dem Verkaufspreis von 102,74 (vom 10.7.97) und dem niedrigeren Einkaufspreis vom September-Erfüllungstermin herausgezahlt. Das Bund Future Geschäft wird also im Regelfall nicht durch Lieferung bzw. Abnahme von DM 250.000 Nominalwert einer Bundesanleihe erfüllt, sondern durch die Differenzzahlung des Marktwertes zum Vertragszeitpunkt im Vergleich zum Marktwert des Erfüllungstermins. Die höheren Finanzierungskosten werden also durch die Gewinne aus dem Bund Future Geschäft kompensiert. Die Kompensation ergibt sich auch bei einer Zinssenkung. Zum nächsten Revolvierungstermin würden dann niedrigere Finanzierungskosten anfallen, die durch zu leistende Ausgleichszahlungen bei der Erfüllung des Bund Future Geschäfts wieder ausgeglichen werden, da es infolge der Zinssenkung zu Kurssteigerungen beim Bund Future kommt und das Unternehmen die bereits billiger verkauften Future Kontrakte nun teurer eindecken muß. Insofern sind die Zinsrisiken aus der originären Position immer durch die Zinsrisiken aus der derivativen Position kompensiert. Dieser Effekt wird in der Praktikerterminologie als **Hedging,** also als Eingrenzung von (Zins-) Risiken bezeichnet. Entsprechend der auf Paul Einzig zurückgehenden Terminologie handelt es sich hier aber um **Covering,** da die derivative Position die Veränderung der **Finanzierungsausgaben** kompensieren soll. Wenn dagegen der Marktwert eines Rentenportfolios gegen befürchtete (temporäre) Kursabschwächungen durch Verkauf von Zins Futures abgesichert werden soll, dann könnte man von Hedging sprechen, da dann die Sicherungsmaßnahme gegen einen **Vermögenswert** und nicht gegen laufende Zahlungen (Cash flows) erfolgt.

Auch durch **Zins Forward Geschäfte** läßt sich ein vergleichbarer Effekt der Immunisierung der Finanzierungskosten gegenüber Zinsänderungen erzielen. Bei diesen als **Forward Rate Agreements** (FRAs) bezeichneten innovativen Finanzderivaten handelt es sich um Kontrakte zwischen Unternehmen und Banken über die Fixierung von Zinssätzen für erst in der Zukunft (nach Vorlaufzeiten) beginnende Zeiträume. Es kommt dabei zur Zinszahlung für vereinbarte Kapitalbeträge, ohne daß diese Kapitalbeträge von der Bank dem Unternehmen zur Verfügung gestellt werden müssen. Die Vorlaufperiode kann bis zu 18 Monate, die Gesamtlaufzeit eines solchen Zins Forwards bis zu 24 Monate betragen. Über diesen Zeitraum hinaus ist der Markt nicht mehr liquide. Das größte Marktvolumen ist jedoch bei Gesamtlaufzeiten von 12 Monaten zu beobachten. Außer über die Gesamtlaufzeit mit der Vorlauf- und der Zinsperiode (die Formulierung 3 x 9 bedeutet 3 Monate Vorlaufzeit und 9 Monate Zinsperiode) einigen sich die Kontraktparteien über den der Zinszahlung zugrunde liegenden Kapitalbetrag und die jeweilige Währung (bis zu mehreren 100 Millionen DM), den FRA-Zinssatz und den Referenzzinssatz (z.B. Sechs Monats Libor) sowie über die Zeitpunkte, an denen der Forward Zinssatz zur Bestimmung des Herauszahlungsbetrages mit dem Referenzzinssatz verglichen wird.

Von Banken wird folgendermaßen für den Kauf von Forward Rate Agreements geworben: Durch den Kauf eines FRAs können jetzt oder künftig aufzunehmende zinsvariable Kredite gegen das Risiko steigender Zinsen abgesichert werden. Zu den Referenzzeitpunkten wird der im FRA vereinbarte Zinssatz (z.B. 6%) mit dem Referenzzinssatz verglichen. Bei zwischenzeitlichen Zinssteigerungen des Referenzzinssatzes (z.B. 7% Libor), die zu höheren Finanzierungskosten bei der originären Kreditposition führen, bekommt der Käufer die Differenz zwischen FRA Zinssatz und Referenzzinssatz herausgezahlt. Dagegen muß der Käufer des FRAs bei eingetretenen Zinssenkungen (z.B. 5% Libor) die entsprechende Differenz bei der derivativen Position herauszahlen, hat aber auch niedrigere Finanzierungskosten. Insofern ist der beim Zins Future skizzierte Risikoeingrenzungs-Effekt auch beim Zins Forward gegeben. Damit ist die Wahrscheinlichkeitsverteilung der Finanzierungskosten sicherer gemacht worden, ohne daß Zinszahlungen in der Höhe einer fristenkongruenten Zinsfixierung auf dem originären Finanzmarkt zu leisten sind.

Für eine **Beurteilung** der Zins Future und Forward Geschäfte ist darauf hinzuweisen, daß sowohl Zins Futures als auch Zins Forwards die Wahrscheinlichkeitsverteilung der Finanzierungskosten stabilisieren können. Unabhängig von der tatsächlichen Zinsentwicklung können die auf niedrigen Geldmarktkonditionen basierenden Finanzierungskosten ex ante fixiert werden. Die Unternehmung wird nicht mit höheren Zinssätzen belastet, profitiert aber auch nicht von sinkenden Zinssätzen. Das auf den Derivatmärkten mögliche hohe Handelsvolumen kann tendenziell zu geringen Transaktionskosten für die Sicherung eines niedrigen Zinsniveaus bei der originären Position (Kredit) führen. Der Einsatz dieser Finanzderivate ist für die Unternehmung aber nur dann risikolos, wenn die originären Positionen (Finanzmittelaufnahmen zu variablen Zinsen) auch wirklich existieren. Durch Zins Futures und Zins Forwards werden also die aus langfristigen Rentenwerten (underlying) resultierenden Zins- und Kursrisiken gehandelt, ohne daß man die Rentenwerte selbst handeln muß. Der Handel mit Zins Futures und Zins Forwards ohne Existenz der originären Positionen ist damit letzten Endes eine Zins- und (Renten-) Kursspekulation und damit mit erheblichen finanziellen Risiken verbunden. Bereits geringe Zinsänderungen können bei langfristigen Rententiteln (die durch die Derivate nachgebildet werden) große Kursänderungen auslösen.

Ein Problem könnte aber im Zeithorizont des Zinsrisikomanagements gesehen werden. Bund Future Kontrakte sind praktisch nur bis zur nächsten oder übernächsten Drei Monats Fälligkeit erhältlich und auch Forward Rate Agreements sind nicht über zwei Jahre hinaus handelbar. Für spätere Erfüllungszeitpunkte besteht keine ausreichende Marktliquidität. Insofern werden die Zinsen zunächst nur für sehr kurze (Bund Future) bzw. mittelfristige Zeiträume (FRA) festgeschrieben. Die Kontrakte für die späteren Revolvierungstermine können erst dann getätigt werden, wenn der Derivatmarkt die entsprechende Liquidität, also das Marktvolumen auf der Angebots- und der Nachfrageseite aufweist und sind natürlich nur zu den dann geltenden Zins- und Kurskonstellation möglich. Entsprechend dem Grundgedanken einer revolvierenden Sicherung können jedoch die zu Beginn einer Sicherungsperiode geltenden Konditionen fixiert werden, wenn die Revolvierung der derivativen Position konsistent, also ohne Unterbrechungen weitergeführt wird (Lipfert 1979, S. 106 ff. und Jokisch 1987, S. 73 ff.).

3.3. Zur Eignung von Zinsoptionen zum Management von Zinsrisiken

Eine **Zinsoption** ist ein Kontrakt, durch den der Käufer der Option gegen Zahlung einer Optionsprämie an den Verkäufer der Option (Stillhalter) von diesem das Recht, nicht aber die Pflicht erwirbt, für eine bestimmte Zeitspanne nicht mehr als einen fixierten Zinssatz (Basis- oder Strike-Preis) zu zahlen (Call oder Kaufoption für Aufnahmen) oder nicht weniger als den Basispreis zu erhalten (Put oder Verkaufsoption für Anlagen). Das Zinsrisiko einer zinsflexiblen Finanzmittelaufnahme wird also auch hier unabhängig von den Finanzmitteln gehandelt und kann durch den Kauf einer Call Option nach oben begrenzt werden, ohne daß die positiven Auswirkungen möglicher Zinssenkungen ausgeschlossen werden. Solche Zinsoptionen werden als Caps bezeichnet (Perridon/Steiner 1995, S. 307 ff.). Ein **Cap** ist demnach ein Kontrakt über eine Zinsobergrenze für einen (separat gehandelten) Kapitalbetrag, der aber im Capvertrag der Höhe nach (erhältlich sind Referenzbeträge bis über 100 Millionen DM) fixiert werden muß. Wenn ein Unternehmen eine Fünf Jahres Finanzmittelaufnahme auf Basis des Sechs Monats Libor (derzeit: 4,5% + Spread) durchführen möchte, dann könnte es das Zinsrisiko durch einen Cap in Höhe von z.B. 6,5% (Basispreis) begrenzen. Ein solcher langfristiger Capvertrag besteht theoretisch aus zehn einzelnen Capverträgen, die sich auf die Revolvierungszeitpunkte der Finanzmittelaufnahme beziehen. Die Optionen können jeweils zu den vereinbarten Erfüllungsterminen ausgeübt werden. Insofern handelt es sich bei Zinsoptionen wie üblicherweise auch bei Devisenoptionen um european style options, während Aktienoptionen grundsätzlich **american style options** sind und damit während der gesamten Laufzeit des Optionsvertrages ausgeübt werden können.

Sollte der im Capvertrag definierte Referenzzinssatz (z.B. Sechs Monats Libor) den fixierten Zinssatz (Basispreis) zu den festgelegten Revolvierungszeitpunkten der originären Position übersteigen, dann erhält der Optionskäufer vom Stillhalter (Optionsverkäufer) die Zinsdifferenz ausgezahlt. Wenn der Referenzzinssatz unter dem vereinbarten Basispreis liegt, dann wird die Option nicht ausgeübt und die **Finanzierungskosten** für den entsprechenden Revolvierungszeitraum ergeben sich aus **Libor + Spread + annualisierter Prämie**. Insofern profitieren die sich gegen Zinsrisiken sichernden Unternehmen bei Zinsoptionen - anders als bei Zins Futures und bei Zins Forwards - von sinkenden Zinsen. Die Wahrscheinlichkeitsverteilung der Finanzierungskosten ist nur "nach oben" sicherer gemacht worden, während die erwünschten Zinsrisiken "nach unten" als finanzierungskostensenkende Möglichkeit offen gelassen werden.

Inhalt des Managements der Zinsrisiken ist also die Bestimmung der tragbaren und der nicht tragbaren, folglich zu sichernden möglichen Auswirkungen von Zinsänderungen auf die Finanzierungskosten. Im Rahmen von Optionskontrakten liegt das Entscheidungsproblem in der Festlegung des Basispreises, also der Zinsobergrenze. Mit der Festlegung des Basispreises erfolgt uno actu die Fixierung der Sicherungskosten. Je höher der Basispreis ist, desto niedriger liegt bei Call-Zinsoptionen die ex ante zu zahlende Prämie, weil die Wahrscheinlichkeit der Ausübung der Option immer geringer wird. Die Option (bzw. der Basispreis) ist dann **out of the money**. Umgekehrt gilt für Call-Zinsoptionen, daß bei niedriger angesetztem Basispreis die Optionsprämie steigt, weil die Wahrscheinlichkeit der Ausübung größer wird. Bei Zinsoptionen ist der Basispreis **at the money,** der dem implizierten Zinsterminsatz der gegebenen horizontalen Zinsstruktur entspricht. Die Absicherung erfolgt also gegen größere Zinssteigerungen, als sie von der aktuell geltenden Zinsstrukturkurve reflektiert werden. Bei einem vereinbarten Basispreis unterhalb des implizierten Zinsterminsatzes ist die Call-Zinsoption **in the money.**

Die zu zahlende Optionsprämie kann gedanklich in zwei Elemente aufgespalten werden, in den **inneren Wert** (intrinsic value) und in den **Zeitwert** (extrinsic value) der Option (Hielscher 1990, S. 71 ff.). Der so bezeichnete **innere Wert** der Option entspricht ihrem Wert bei fiktiver sofortiger Ausübung der Option. Er ergibt sich aus der für den Optionskäufer (Finanzmittelaufnehmer) positiven (vorteilhaften) Differenz zwischen dem Basispreis und dem implizierten Zinsterminsatz der Optionslaufzeit. Daraus folgt, daß nur **in the money** Optionen einen inneren Wert haben, während die Optionsprämie von **at the money** und **out of the money** Optionen nicht durch einen inneren Wert, sondern nur durch den Zeitwert der Option bestimmt wird. Der dann die Höhe der Optionsprämie ausschließlich bestimmende Zeitwert kann für unterschiedliche Basispreise durch eine Wahrscheinlichkeitsverteilung der Inanspruchnahme des Stillhalters durch den Optionskäufer beschrieben werden. Bei in the money Optionen ist der hier so bezeichnete innere Wert der Option zusätzlich zum Zeitwert zu zahlen.

Der intrinsic value (innere Wert) ergibt sich allein daraus, daß im Optionsvertrag ein Basispreis gewählt wird, der bei Call-Zinsoptionen unterhalb der Markterwartungen liegt, wie sie sich im implizierten Zinsterminsatz ausdrücken. Für diese "Besserstellung" gegenüber einer möglichen fristenkongruenten Zinsfixierung ist selbstverständlich eine Prämie (abgezinste "Besserstellung") zu zahlen, die aber unabhängig vom eigentlichen Inhalt der Optionsprämie ist, die dafür entrichtet wird, daß man durch die Ausübung der Option gegen mögliche (befürchtete) Zinssteigerungen über den implizierten Zinsterminsatz hinaus gesichert ist und durch ein Verfallenlassen der Option von möglichen (erhofften) Zinssenkungen profitieren kann. Während sonst in der Betriebswirtschaftslehre (z.B. bei der Bewertung der Unternehmung als Ganzes) der ökonomische (investitionstheoretisch fundierte) Wert des Handelsobjektes als **innerer Wert** bezeichnet wird, gibt es in der Terminologie der Optionspreistheorie von diesem Grundsatz eine Abweichung. Als der eigentliche **ökonomische** Wert der Option ist **der** Bestandteil der Optionsprämie anzusehen, der durch den extrinsic value (Zeitwert) bestimmt wird.

Die Unsicherheit über die Optionsausübung ist bei at the money Optionen am größten. Je weiter die Option out of the money (in the money) ist, desto geringer (größer) ist die Wahrscheinlichkeit der Inanspruchnahme des Stillhalters. Somit sind Sicherungsmaßnahmen für den Stillhalter bei at the money Optionen am teuersten, weil bereits geringe Konditionenänderungen zu einer Erfüllung des Optionsgeschäftes führen können, und damit wird dann der Zeitwert der Optionsprämie am höchsten sein. Bei out of the money Optionen werden Sicherungen für den Stillhalter immer unwichtiger (entbehrlicher) und bei in the money Optionen immer wichtiger und damit billiger, da sie über Futures bzw. Forwards getätigt werden können. Folglich ergibt sich um den at the money Basispreis eine glokkenförmige Verteilung des Zeitwertes der Optionsprämie. **Deep in the money** Optionen haben zwar eine hohe, durch den inneren Wert bestimmte Prämienhöhe, aber nur einen geringen Zeitwert, während die Prämie von **far out of the money** Optionen nur durch das geringe Niveau des Zeitwertes bestimmt wird. Insofern sind starke Zinssteigerungen neutralisierende **out of the money** Zinsoptionen als billig anzusehen, während zu niedrig angesetzte Basispreise bei Call-Zinsoptionen gerade wegen der durchaus noch tragbaren Zinsrisiken als relativ teuer bezeichnet werden können.

Um die im Vergleich zu Zins Futures und Zins Forwards höheren Kosten der Zinsoptionen zu reduzieren, kann erwogen werden, gegen den Kauf einer **out of the money** Call Option einen betragskongruenten Verkauf einer **out of the money** Put Option zu tätigen. Bei einer solchen Put Option handelt es sich um einen **Floor**, den Finanzmittelanleger gegen erwartete/befürchtete Zinssenkungen bei ihren kurzfristigen Anlagen kaufen. Sie sichern sich damit unter Zahlung einer Optionsprämie Mindestzinsen für ihre Anlage, wenn der Referenzzinssatz unter den vereinbarten Basispreis sinkt. Das die Zinsrisiken von Finanzmittelaufnahmen begrenzende Unternehmen müßte also die Put Zinsoption verkaufen, also als Stillhalter fungieren und damit das Risiko übernehmen, bei starken Zinssenkungen an den Käufer des Floors Ausgleichszahlungen leisten zu müssen. Diese möglichen Ausgleichszahlungen in die Put Option würden aber durch niedrige Zinskosten bei der originären Finanzmittelaufnahme kompensiert werden und die gekaufte Call-Zinsoption könnte man verfallen lassen. Umgekehrt würde das Unternehmen bei starken Zinssteigerungen die Call Option ausnutzen, während die Käufer der Put Zinsoption diese verfallen lassen würden, da sie für die originären Anlage-Positionen höhere Zinsen bekommen. Eine solche Konstruktion des **Kaufs** einer Call Zinsoption und des **Verkaufs** einer Put Zinsoption wird als **Collar** bezeichnet und reduziert das Zinsrisiko durch die Wahl der Basispreise auf eine tragbare Bandbreite der Finanzierungskosten. Sowohl sehr ungünstige, als auch sehr günstige Zinskonditionen werden vermieden und die Prämieneinnahmen aus dem Verkauf der Put Zinsoption verringern die Prämienausgaben der gekauften Call-Zinsoption. Auch wenn man durch diese Kombination verschiedener Finanzinnovationen bei Zinsoptionen nicht wie bei Devisenoptionen zu so bezeichneten **Zero Cost Optionen** kommt, so kann doch festgestellt werden, daß eine solche Übernahme tragbarer Zinsrisiken unter Ausschluß als untragbar angesehener Zinsrisiken die Finanzierungskosten gegenüber den klassischen Maßnahmen des Zinsrisikomanagements durch Zinsfixierungen über die gesamte Laufzeit der Finanzmittelaufnahme reduzieren kann.

Es kann angesichts des großen Marktvolumens und der Bonität der Marktpartner kein Zweifel daran bestehen, daß der wohl erwogene Einsatz von Zinsoptionen durchaus als sinnvoll anzusehen ist. Im Gegensatz zu Zins Futures und Zins Forward können Zinsoptionen auch für längere (5 bis 10 Jahre) Zeiträume erworben bzw. verkauft werden und sichern daher ein aktuell als besonders günstig angesehenes Zinsniveau gegen im langfristigen Bereich immer existente große Zinsrisiken. Aus diesem Grunde können Zinsoptionen für große Beträge in Kombination mit originären Instrumenten der Finanzmittelaufnahme als sinnvolles Derivat der Finanzmittelmärkte angesehen werden.

4. Zusammenfassende Beurteilung des Einsatzes originärer und derivativer Finanzinnovationen

Damit ist dargelegt, daß der kombinierte Einsatz originärer und derivativer Finanztitel grundsätzlich als eine gegenüber traditionellen Festzinsinstrumenten die Finanzierungskosten senkende und die Zinsrisiken begrenzende Maßnahme anzusehen ist. Die skizzierten kompensatorischen Wirkungen der Futures und Forwards und die einseitig die Wahrscheinlichkeitsverteilung "verbessernden" Wirkungen der Optionen treten aber nur dann ein, wenn die Derivate kongruent mit originären Finanztiteln eingesetzt werden. Die hier nicht diskutierten Überlegungen zur kongruenten Abstimmung der Höhe der einzusetzenden Derivatkontrakte mit den zu sichernden originären Positionen werden in der Literatur als Problem zur Ermittlung der **Hedge-Ratio** (Steiner/Meyer 1993, S.735 ff.) behandelt. Es fällt auf, daß alle von Banken (als den am Handel mit Derivaten verdienenden Institutionen) genannten Anwendungsbeispiele immer von solchen "Hedging"-Überlegungen ausgehen, obwohl angesichts des großen Marktvolumens der Finanzderivate nicht übersehen werden kann, daß diese Instrumente auch (oder sogar überwiegend?) "offen", also ohne die originären Titel, eingesetzt werden.

Dann handelt es sich aber eindeutig um Zinsspekulationen, als deren Ergebnis sich große Gewinne, aber auch Verluste ergeben können. Unter einer (Zins-) Spekulation ist die "durch die realen Gegebenheiten unzureichend begründete (feste) Erwartung, daß bestimmte Ereignisse ... eintreten werden" (Wörterbuch der deutschen Gegenwartssprache 1976, S. 3484) zu verstehen. Künftige Zinssätze können wie alle anderen künftigen Finanzkonditionen nicht verläßlich, also durch die realen Gegebenheiten begründet, vorausgesagt werden. Selbst die Richtung der Zinsänderung ist nicht gesichert vorhersagbar, sonst wäre es nach dem Zusammenhang zwischen Zins- und Kursrisiko möglich, risikolos Geld zu verdienen. Es unterliegt daher keinem Zweifel, daß die beschönigend als **Trading** bezeichneten (Zins-) Spekulationen bei Banken und Nicht-Banken zu beträchtlichen Schieflagen führen können.

Letzten Endes werden die Unternehmen von den Banken auch bei sinnvoller (kongruenter) Anwendung der Finanzinnovationen zu einer begrenzten Zinsspekulation aufgefordert. Mit den Derivaten kann man sich jeweils nur gegen Zinssteigerungen absichern, die über das in der gegebenen Zinsstruktur reflektierte

Ausmaß hinaus eintreten. Insofern müssen die dem Einsatz der Derivate zugrundeliegenden Zinsprognosen besser als die Prognosen der Mehrheit der Marktteilnehmer sein, wie sie im implizierten Zinsterminsatz zum Ausdruck kommen. Nach der Markteffizienzhypothese und der Random walk Hypothese gibt es jedoch keine Experten, die solche Zinsvorhersagen auf Dauer erfolgreich machen können, sondern Experten erkennt man daran, daß sie sich solcher Vorhersagen enthalten und ausgehend von den allen Marktteilnehmern bekannen aktuellen Konditionen lediglich eine Wahrscheinlichkeitsverteilung der Zinssätze aufstellen.

Grundsätzlich kann das Ziel eines Managements von Zinsrisiken auch die Zinsspekulation sein, also die Wahl einer "unsicheren" Wahrscheinlichkeitsverteilung der finanziellen Ergebnisse. Angesichts der großen leistungswirtschaftlichen und finanzwirtschaftlichen Risiken streben jedoch seriös geführte, d.h. die finanzwirtschaftlichen Erkenntnisse berücksichtigende Unternehmen eine Verbesserung der Risikosituation an. Während eine Immunisierung der Finanzierungskosten gegenüber Zinsrisiken bei den klassischen Finanzierungsinstrumenten nur unter Inkaufnahme höherer Finanzierungskosten möglich ist, kann die Übernahme von begrenzten Zinsrisiken sich finanzierungskostensenkend auswirken, wenn die Zinsrisiken durch Zins Futures, Zins Forwards und Zinsoptionen reduziert werden.

Literatur:

Büschgen, H. E.(1993), Internationales Finanzmanagement, 2. Aufl., Frankfurt 1993

Einzig, P. (1975), A Dynamic Theory of Foreign Exchange, 2. Aufl., London 1975

Franke, G., Hax, H. (1990), Finanzwirtschaft des Unternehmens und Kapitalmarkt, 2.Aufl., Berlin 1990

Franke, G. (1990), Grundlagen der Options- und Futures-Kontrakte, in: Göppl, H.W., Bühler, R., v.Rosen (Hrsg.), Optionen und Futures, Frankfurt 1990, S. 43-63

Hielscher, U. (1989), Nationale und internationale Rentenmärkte, in: Jokisch, J., Raettig, L., Ringle, G. (Hrsg.), Finanz-, Bank- und Kooperationsmanagement, Frankfurt 1989, S. 65-80

Hielscher, U. (1990), Investmentanalyse, München 1990.

Jokisch, J. (1987), Betriebswirtschaftliche Währungsrisikopolitik und Internationales Finanzmanagement, Stuttgart 1987.

Jokisch, J. (1989), Länderrisiken und Zinsniveau, in: K. Marcharzina, M. Welge (Hrsg.), Handwörterbuch Export und Internationale Unternehmung (HWInt), Stuttgart 1989, Sp. 1255-1268.

Karten, W. (1972), Die Unsicherheit des Risikobegriffs, in: P. Braess, D. Farny R. Schmidt (Hrsg.), Praxis und Theorie der Versicherungsbetriebslehre, Karlsruhe 1972, S. 147-169.

Lipfert, H. (1979), Kursrisiko-Politik bei unsicheren Devisen-Cash-flows innerhalb des Terminmarkt-Zeithorizonts, in: Schriften zur Unternehmensführung, Bd. 26 (1979), S. 95-125.

Perridon, L., Steiner, M. (1995), Finanzwirtschaft der Unternehmung, 8. Aufl., München 1995.

Schneeweiß, H. (1967), Entscheidungen bei Risiko, Berlin 1967.

Steiner, M., Meyer, F. (1993), Hedging mit Financial Futures, in: G. Gebhardt, W. Gerke und M. Steiner (Hrsg.),.Handbuch des Finanzmanagements, München 1993, S. 721-749.

Süchting, J. (1995), Finanzmanagement, 6. Aufl., Wiesbaden 1995.

Wörterbuch der deutschen Gegenwartssprache (1976), Bd. 5, Berlin 1976.

Siebter Teil

Change Management
und
Management Information Systems

Benchmarking, Innovation and Reengineering: Should we Pull the Plug on the Internet or Make it Serve us Better?

Urs E. Gattiker

Zusammenfassung:

Benchmarking, Reengineering und Innovation müssen in angemessener Weise durch geeignete Kommunikations- und Informationssysteme und das Internet gestützt werden. Auf dem Hintergrund der Globalisierung werden die relevanten Trends im Kommunikations- und Informationsbereich herausgearbeitet. Angemessene Unternehmensstrategien als Antwort auf diese Trends werden dargestellt. Die Bedeutung des Human Resource Management wird betont.

1. Introduction

Seldom a day passes without hearing about the Internet in the news. In a previous chapter (Gattiker/Kelley/Janz 1996) published in an earlier book of this series (Global Management, 1996), we discussed how the Internet might influence marketing efforts while privacy concerns must be managed carefully. In this chapter, the focus is on how new information technologies, as well as the Internet, might relate to benchmarking and reengineering efforts by the firm. Digital communications and transport allow firms to take better advantage of digitally-rendered products by reducing warehousing and distribution costs (e.g., commissions and margins paid to retailers and wholesalers). A survey in Japan in 1996 suggested that 30% of newspapers would be distributed digitally by the year 2000 (Nihon Keizai Shimbun, June 6, 1996). While one might look at such findings with some scepticism, they indicate that the market for such products and services is growing and may become substantial by the year 2000. Digitally-rendered products can also be offered as a supplement to the traditional form. For instance, newspapers in digital form may be the best way to provide timely information at low cost to individuals on-the-road or living abroad. Various newspapers have entered this market providing this service for a fee (e.g., Wall Street Journal; cumbersome to use) while others do it for 'free' asking only for voluntary contributions (e.g., TAZ, Berlin; easy to navigate with a quick response). Pointcast in conjunction with Globe & Mail (Canadian national newspaper) is offering a news service for free, funded by advertisers, which allows one to customise the type of news and with what frequency one wishes to receive the news (Windows 95 required, http://www.pointcast.com, Canadian version for international news recommended). Nevertheless, digitally-rendered products (e.g., music or reading a newspaper on the Web) may still be less convenient for customers than products purchased through the more traditional retail channels (e.g., daily delivery of a newspaper). As this chapter will show, CIS and the Internet will continue to affect retailing, customer services and manufacturing.

How do the above issues relate to reengineering, benchmarking and innovation? To start with, it raises issues and questions about which tools are needed to make the necessary organisational changes and adjustments to take better advantage of new technologies. The physical technology being used, is obvious - computers, software, Internet access, and so on. The other essential part of successful reengineering depends upon individual and organisational requirements, including how the technology is managed. The Internet offers new opportunities in delivering products in a variety of ways and using a number of strategies effectively; however, success is achieved when firms innovate and take advantage of new opportunities. Benchmarking allows the organisation to set out specific targets against which its efforts will be measured (e.g., increased profits, reduced costs). Finally, to succeed, the organisation needs to balance stakeholder demands while harnessing its human resources by getting them involved in the process and allowing employees to take charge. Downsizing, reorganizing and rightsizing without employee involvement, will affect the potential success of reengineering efforts. These issues are addressed further, below.

2. Organisational Change, Innovation and Reengineering

The reader might ask what reengineering really means. Numerous definitions of reengineering are offered by various researchers and practitioners. However, as Table 1 suggests, reengineering is nothing more nor less than organisational change, transition, and innovation. The definitions outlined in Table 1 indicate that reengineering efforts produce changes in organisational processes and output-related activities. Looking at industry applications, however, one of the primary thrusts of such efforts is lowering costs (e.g., production) while improving product quality. The latter should reduce warranty work, while increasing sales due to better values for customers.

Based on Table 1 and the above, reengineering may entail many things including organisational change and efforts to reduce strategic transaction costs (i.e., costs incurred for the production of a product and/or service). For people familiar with the literature dealing with organisational change and development, as well as its application in practice, reengineering offers little more than being a newer term and possibly being more "sexy." Organisational change and development and reengineering, as well as post-engineering, are processes which have been used in

---

Organizational change is the alteration and transformation of the firm, as well as its goals, to survive better in a never-changing environment (e.g., competition, governmental policy, innovation and consumer needs).

Organization transition represents a major change in organizational strategy, structure or processes, while helping the firm to reposition itself in the marketplace or environment and revitalizing a declining organization.

Innovation is a departure from the state of the art and usually encompasses technological innovations concerning technology and administrative practices. Administrative innovations tend to facilitate the adoption of technological innovations more readily than the reverse.

Reengineering embraces organizational change and transitions, as well as innovation, in order to use capital and human resources more effectively, thereby positively influencing long-term growth and profitability of the firm.

Table 1: Definitions of Organizational Change, Innovation and
Reengineering

various forms under similar or different labels for a long time. For instance, Kieser (1987) described how Catholic monasteries were organising and changing their structure during Medieval Times. Similarly to organisational change and development, reengineering requires the studying of processes, structures and management/production/service approaches in order to refine them, resulting in better allocating of scarce resources (e.g., capital and labour). Thus, the reengineering hype is a welcome tool for consultants and organisations trying to realign their resources hoping to make better use of it in an ever more competitive environment.

In practice, however, reengineering has been primarily used to reduce costs and often results in massive layoffs, at least in North America, where workers are less protected than in Europe (e.g., Germany). In the context here, some of the opportunities and challenges with reengineering are outlined, focussing in particular on the Internet and new telecommunication technologies. In addition to cutting costs, technology can be used to reengineer production, distribution, marketing and coordination of tasks. Additionally, as Table 1 suggests, reengineering also means getting more out of a firm's human resources, thereby requiring the appreciation of the human dimension of reengineering. Some of these issues will be discussed below in greater detail.

2.1. Satisfying Critical Stakeholders

Reengineering (as outlined in Table 1) assists firms in better allocating scarce resources. The risks inherent in any investment, demands an appropriate return for investors in comparison to other choices and options offered to them for their capital. In contrast, employees insist on the highest possible wages for their labour. March and Simon (1958) called this balancing act of divergent interests the "satisfying of stakeholder needs." If these are met, stakeholders will continue to contribute to the organisation in the form of capital and labour. Today's business climate whereby service has become of paramount importance for a business to succeed in the marketplace, suggests that customers or clients are another important stakeholder group which must be satisfied to assure survival of the firm. Customers demand good service, better quality and lower prices for products and/or services purchased, before they are willing to part with their hard-earned money.

Demands by these three stakeholders upon the organisation, however, do not necessarily go hand-in-hand. Greater return on investment or equity may put pressure on wages, as well as exact higher prices for products/services sold. Accordingly, new computer-mediated communication and information systems (CIS) are used by the organisation to help balance these divergent demands as successfully as possible.

The conflicting triangle (as shown in Figure 1) can be applied to any type of organisation, including the government, whereby taxpayers take over as investors (e.g., when purchasing government debentures such as bonds) as well as clients/users of the services provided (e.g., receiving an old age pension or using the country's infrastructure). Today's pressure for lower taxes and elimination of government debt (i.e., especially its continuing growth) and the increasing burden of retirement payments for an aging population in some countries, does not make the balancing act outlined in Figure 1 easy for private or public organisations.

In this chapter, the spotlight is on how CIS supports the efforts of organisations to better balance the conflicting triangle, for instance, by taking advantage of digitally-rendered products to reduce labour, infrastructure and other costs. Accordingly, new developments in the CIS domain permit the firm to reengineer various processes and other systems by using such means as telework and downsizing or outsourcing certain activities (e.g., subcontracting). All these efforts are undertaken to help the organisation balance the conflicting triangle; i.e., producing better products at lower costs; paying higher dividends to investors at a lower risk for needed equity; providing employees with attractive salary packages, a safe work environment and job security.

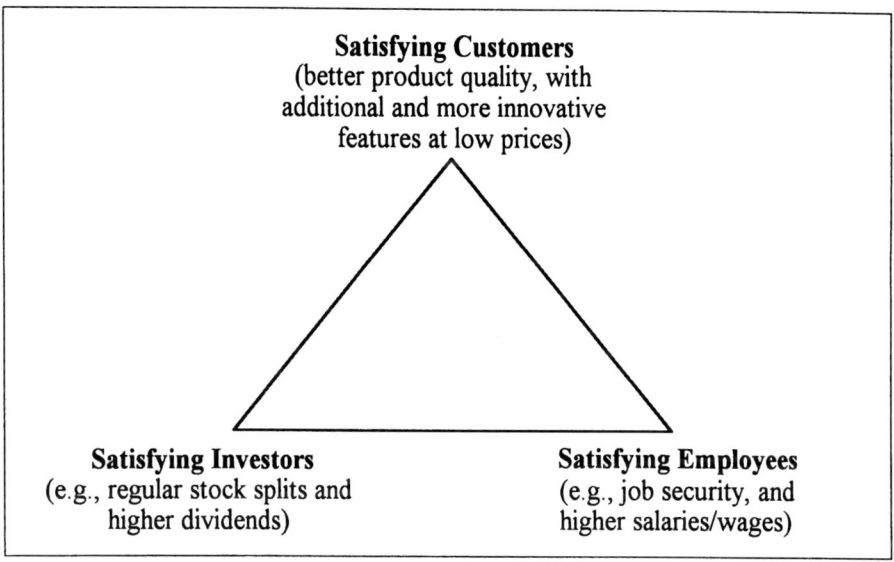

Fig. 1: The Conflicting Triangle

2.2. Benchmarking and Computer-Mediated Communication and Information Systems (CIS)

As Table 2 suggests, benchmarking is not much different from setting organisational objectives which are comprehensive and measurable. Thus, time needed and money required to do the task, quality and quantity of output necessary to do well, must be carefully defined. As described in our previous article in Volume 2 (Gattiker et al. 1996, e.g., Tables 1 - 3), once the firm has set strategic goals, the latter must be put into specific descriptions as to what is expected of the input, transformation or production and output, using the Internet or CIS (e.g., product quality and sales).

With the help of the framework in Table 2 and the information/facts provided through a benchmarking process, the organisation can then proceed to identify a comprehensive set of input and output measures that describe performance using new technology. Various periods may be used to develop data points to find "best practices" which influence refinement of the firm's strategy and its implementation. In turn, the firm is able to support its organisational change and reengineering efforts while success of such efforts can again be compared, using benchmarking. Once an organisation has established what it intends to accomplish with reengineering efforts, benchmarking is used for closely examining the output measures (objectives) which reflect the firm's efficiency and effectiveness. Benchmarking helps the organisation to overcome resistance to change and subsequently, permits it to pursue efforts for further improving performance (cf. Table 2).

Benchmarking provides:

(1) a useful framework for organizational introspection;

(2) support for the development of a fact-based philosophy of decision making and continuous improvement;

(3) help with identifying a comprehensive set of input and output measures that describe performance in the new media domain or for any business area;

(4) support with establishing commonly agreed upon definitions of terms to allow valid and reliable comparisons across organizations and departments/profit centres;

(5) backing for developing a comprehensive database spanning various periods (e.g., quarters and years) permitting meaningful comparisons with industry average;

(6) help for searching and subsequent implementation of "best practices";

(7) guidance for the development of strategy and its implementation by furnishing relevant points of reference (e.g., point (5) above);

(8) support for organizational change and reengineering efforts, while its success can also be compared using benchmarking.

Table 2: What Benchmarking can do for Reengineering/Organizational Change Efforts

Where and how do CIS and the Internet come in? Once benchmarking efforts have produced the blueprint for what should be accomplished with reengineering over a six-month period (or whatever period one chooses, depending upon the gravity of change), a hard look must be taken at CIS and the Internet to determine how these technologies can be used to facilitate reengineering. Often organisations embark on reengineering efforts without taking technology into careful consideration. Since technology is constantly changing, effective use of technology, CIS, and the Internet in particular, is no small feat. Accordingly, if human resources for software maintenance are scarce in Germany, such work can be effectively performed in Bangalore, India instead of Germany (cf. Table 3 and also Section 3.1.). These issues will be addressed below.

Telework can be defined as work performed with the help of computer-mediated communication and information systems (CIS). Accordingly, it does not imply that the employee has a constant online connection with his or her main office but, it may simply mean that one uses computer technology for performing tasks, while being geographically in a different location than the head office.

Generally, literature has identified three forms of telework which are:

A) **Isolated telework** whereby the employee performs tasks at home, tend to be low-skilled jobs and is comparable to homework done in the past, which was paid as piecework (e.g., data entry).

- **long-term employment** extends the same benefits to the employee doing isolated telework (e.g., training and career development) as is offered to his/her counterparts at the main office, at least in principle and on paper; difficulties of social interaction, visibility and measurement of performance do remain and, therefore, may hinder career advancement.

- **contract-type employment** is the employee doing isolated telework as sub-contractor, and may not accrue seniority benefits (e.g., during an economic downturn), nor receive fringe benefits (e.g., vacation and sick days). This method represents outsourcing of certain duties to reduce costs, improve productivity while acquiring the human resources necessary for heavy business periods.

B) **Satellite offices and plants** are used to locate parts of the firm nearby where workers live (e.g., San Bernardino County, East of Los Angeles) to reduce commuting and where property prices, rent and living expenses are lower than in the downtown or metropolitan area of a large city (e.g., Zurich). In some instances, satellite offices may be in other countries to take advantage of economic and political environments (e.g., low labour costs) compared to the head office.

C) **Partial telework** is a situation whereby the individual may spend one or two days during a week at the office, while working at the home office the rest of the time (e.g., executive doing administrative chores at home every Friday). Some countries allow a tax deduction for a home office, if substantial working time is spent at home.

Recent developments suggest two additional types of telework as defined and outlined below:

D) Mobile Computing is an approach using telework in its various forms as described above for reducing staff at the main office, whereby employees work in the field and/or at home most of the time; in turn, fewer clerical support staff, custodians and less need for expensive office buildings and furniture materialize for the firm. For instance, regular offices may no longer be assigned to individuals; such employees are expected to spend more time at the customer's location (e.g., service and/or sales representatives).

E) Virtual offices/stores/malls and outsourcing are used with the help of new media, CIS, to reduce costs (e.g., labour and investment), while focussing on the organization's strengths (or core competencies). For instance, a publisher may outsource various parts of the publishing process by using other firms (e.g., to print) and/or freelancers (e.g., technical editor to put a journal on the Web). Here any of the forms of telework described in A through C above, may occur in some form or another including mobile computing. Finally, the virtual office and outsourcing may be done using individuals and/or organizations/subsidiaries to do certain parts of the work (see also Table 4). The virtual office/store/mall may be realized, whereby a firm sells its products/services or does its administrative tasks without a customer ever visiting its physical premises because they either do not exist or tasks are performed from various locations such as home offices.

Note: The above definitions benefited from work by Dürrenberger/Jaeger/Bieri/ Dahinden (1995).

Table 3: Various Possible Forms of Telework and Mobile Computing

2.3. Telework and Mobile Computing

Once the firm has developed the appropriate benchmarks for its reengineering efforts it needs to consider how CIS may be used to help achieve benchmarking-based objectives for change, as quickly and smoothly as possible. New CIS and the Internet may offer the firm the opportunity to restructure work processes and production. For instance, the organisation may distribute and coordinate various tasks differently while, hopefully, reducing transaction costs. Telework has been heralded as the wonder drug since the late 1960s but is still rarely used, although increasingly applied, to make better use of CIS. Table 3 profiles the definitions for isolated telework, satellite plants and offices, as well as partial telework.

Dürrenberger et al. (1995) succinctly outlined the difficulties and advantages of telework in their article. Isolated telework helps the firm to reduce its costs (e.g., office space). Doing isolated telework under a contract, results in the employee having less interaction with peers and not gaining privileges through accumulation of tenure (e.g., higher wages and severance pay in case of layoffs). In addition, contracts of a specific duration, or for particular projects, can be signed between the firm and the worker (e.g., Gattiker 1990, Chap 6). In turn, due to a business downturn, a firm may be able to reduce staff without having to pay a severance package by simply not renewing such contracts at the end of the term.

Satellite offices and plants offer the firm an opportunity to reduce various costs while improving productivity. For instance, Citibank transferred its credit card processing operations from New York to South Dakota where three types of savings were realised. First, lower real estate costs for the office facilities meant savings for the firm; second, wages paid to workers are lower in South Dakota, in part, due to lower living costs; and third, poaching from other firms for highly qualified employees is less likely thereby reducing labour costs (e.g., wages and turnover). Similarly, Credit Swiss formed a satellite office in a mountainous region of Switzerland to attract highly qualified labourers who, otherwise might have been forced to leave the region due to a lack of employment opportunities (Dürrenberger et al. 1995). Needless to say, the bank also realised savings due to lower real estate and labour costs, compared to the costs it would have had to pay in or around Zurich. Additionally, this allowed the bank to retain human capital (i.e., qualified employees) longer, since poaching workers by another employer in that area was less likely than in Zurich. Less drastic examples are firms which locate within 100 kilometres of a major city to realise similar savings (e.g., Hamburg and Berlin).

In the above cases, satellite offices and branch plants are primarily used to better manage the conflicting triangle (see Figure 1) by reducing strategic transaction costs (i.e., costs incurred for the production of a product and service) (cf. Gattiker/Willoughby 1997). Moreover, in contrast to isolated or partial telework (cf. Table 3), satellite offices reduce social isolation for the employee, while they increase the control and supervising possibilities for managers (e.g., Soares 1992). Unless output can be measured satisfactorily, isolated telework always entails the possibility of one party being short-changed. For instance, research indicates that women feel isolated telework is attractive, but only if children are not staying at home (e.g., spend time at day-care, school and after-school care) during working hours (Hartman/Stoner/Arora 1991; Olson/Primps 1984). In turn, this offers the uninterrupted time required to concentrate and produce higher output, possibly more so than at an office with fellow workers, interfering phone calls, questions and chatter.

While much attention has focussed on isolated telework (see Table 3 A), few firms offer their workers the opportunity for such employment as managers tend to be worried about difficulties for supervising, while employees may feel isolated. From a career development perspective, the employee may also suffer from the 'out-of-sight, out-of-mind' syndrome, whereby future promotional opportunities pass one by simply, because people tend to forget those one rarely sees, even if they are high performers. Some firms offer partial telework, for instance, by permitting some employees and also managers to stay home one day (often Fridays) to catch up on their administrative backlog. Satellite office and plants as well as virtual offices/stores and outsourcing, however, are on the rise everywhere, in part due to the Internet. Mobile computing (see D in Table 3) may be realised by not assigning a specific office space to sales representatives, but rather providing them with a filing cabinet on wheels, asking them to work wherever they find space. The assumption here is that such employees are supposed to be "on the road" making sales, instead of in the office. Such strategies to make better use of CIS, help save administrative expenses and reap other benefits (e.g., productivity and higher quality of output), if they are used carefully, taking into consideration the pros and cons when deciding to take any of the routes outlined in Table 3.

3. Reengineering the Organisation to Make Better Use of Computer-Mediated Communication and Information Systems (CIS)

The above sections illustrate how benchmarking can be used to set targets for reengineering efforts, while the fit and support of CIS technology must be predetermined, before embarking on reengineering. Additionally, telework in its various forms (as outlined in Table 3) usually requires administrative and technology-related innovations, while changes and transitions to reach the objectives set out in the benchmarking process, must be carefully considered and recorded. In this section, the primary interest is to discuss how reengineered processes and activities, using new CIS, can be applied for outsourcing and manufacturing a product or service, and how Internet developments may require transition and change by the firm to secure revenue growth and high quality jobs for employees.

While it may be an old product in newer clothing, reengineering efforts are increasingly supported by CIS technology in hopes of achieving the objectives set out by benchmarking (e.g., reduce costs). Accordingly, while technology itself is without an inherent value, its application represents a value system (Gattiker 1992, p. 297; 1994, p. 255). In the context here, the challenges faced by management (as illustrated in Figure 1), forces the organisation to use CIS most effectively to balance the interests of stakeholders. Outsourcing and downsizing are intricately linked to each other in many ways but, unfortunately, too much emphasis has been put on these, giving reengineering a worse reputation than it deserves. In other words, misapplication of a tool can cause results requiring damage control. Instead, firms should also carefully consider reengineering their distribution, customer service and sales marketing. Most importantly, the firm's employees are at the core of any reengineering and benchmarking efforts. Without their commitment, efforts and thoughtful participation, the firm's attempts may be futile, as the sections below will illustrate.

(1) The firm needs to decide if it wishes to outsource a particular part of the production process (machinery) or a component of a product/service (e.g., fuel system for a car), in order to reduce transaction costs (e.g., labour, parts, machinery, etc.).

(2) Outsourcing may occur in various forms such as:
  (a) contracting out to another firm (i.e., a legal entity) to produce a product/service,
  (b) hiring labour to produce the product/service under a contract-type agreement (e.g., six months, as is often done in the construction industry),
  (c) hire some employees for casual part-time work.

(3) Outsourcing can occur on-site (renting or leasing space, as done by component suppliers for the Swatch/Mercedes car produced in Lothringen/ France) or off-site.

(4) Based on the above, the organization has to assess and determine benchmarks for how the use of CIS can be beneficial in better managing the conflicting triangle in Figure 1 (see also Table 3) through a combination of:
  (a) telework
  (b) satellite offices and plants
  (c) partial telework
  (d) mobile computing
  (e) virtual office/store/mall/firm and outsourcing
  (f) any combination of a-e

(5) Outsourcing may also occur by firms using various means and services to reach customers and distribute information/products via the Internet (cf. Sections 3.1.2.; 3.2.1. and 3.3.).

(6) Unions may resist the above developments as much as possible using various means (e.g., strike, work slow-downs) or trying to change legislation (e.g., unions in the U.S. are attempting to change the Labour Code to organise workers employed part-time, under contract or other means).

(7) Finally, the above steps will affect and possibly result in changes such as product and process innovation, production, sales and distribution management and customer services (see also Table 5, Section 3.3.).

Note: The above list is far from complete and can be expanded upon. However, it points out some of the strategic alignments which are necessary to take advantage of CIS. In turn, reengineering and benchmarking can be applied to achieve the objectives set out by the firm. Benchmarks and specific targets for CIS must be set out at the beginning, and regular and thorough assessment will help the change process along.

Table 4: Outsourcing and CIS: Challenges and Opportunities

3.1. Outsourcing and CIS

Generally, outsourcing is understood to represent a situation whereby the firm contracts with another legal entity for some of the products and/or services which it then uses to produce its own products and services. An example would be a car manufacturer such as Daimler Benz and General Motors both using Magna to produce various car components for their automobiles. To be considered a success, outsourcing should result in cost-savings, as compared to doing the tasks in-house, while maintaining, if not exceeding, quality standards met when produced in-house. As Table 4 and the sections below illustrate, however, various forms of outsourcing have evolved, all providing new opportunities and challenges for firms. These developments are affected by and influence reengineering, as well as benchmarking efforts, which will be outlined in more detail in the sections below. As Table 4 suggests, various forms of outsourcing can be used but in order to manage the challenges and opportunities successfully, a strategy needs to be in place and certain issues must be considering before an extensive process is put into motion.

3.1.1. Firm and Individual Contracting

Firms everywhere use outsourcing to focus more on their core competencies. For instance, while most universities and larger firms in Germany or Denmark offer an employee/student cafeteria, the facility is usually run by another firm which has been subcontracted for a certain period. If the benchmarks for the quality/price relationship are being met, the contract can be extended and/or renewed; if the benchmarks are not being met, it is opened again for competitive tenders toward the end of the contract period. A publisher may provide the capital for a product (e.g., a magazine or book) while graphical design, typesetting, printing and binding, as well as distribution, may all be outsourced. Sometimes internal divisions or profit centres may submit competitive bids for in-house jobs and depending upon the price/quality relationship, in-house divisions may get some of these jobs, but many go out-of-house.

The classical form of individual contracting, of course, is the employment contract whereby the individual provides the firm with human capital and time for a salary/wage in return. Other well-known forms are the freelance workers (freie(r) Mitarbeiter/In), such as freelance journalists or reporters, who are hired to do particular projects (e.g., provide a news segment for a news show). Construction of private houses (single-unit dwellings) in Canada is often accomplished by hiring a contractor who, in turn, subcontracts the majority of the job to other small firms which may have one or two employees. Furthermore, the subcontracting firm may, in turn, go out and hire one or more employees for doing a specific contract. Employment or subcontracting ceases once the contract has been completed.

Another approach is to hire casual part-time and contract workers who do not accrue seniority rights and are less likely to be promoted than other workers (Gattiker 1990, Chap. 6). Some organisations such as the Toronto-Dominion Bank in Canada (since summer of 1996) extend employee benefits to their casual part-time workers. For Toronto-Dominion Bank, this meant that people who routinely work an average of 15 hours per week received access to group life insurance, short and long term disability insurance, as well as a range of optional benefits (Canada NewsWire, June 24, 1996). By hiring part-time employees, the bank is able to provide better service (e.g., during peak times by having more tellers), while avoiding overtime or other charges, if regular full-time employees were to work more hours (e.g., for extending banking hours to evenings and weekends). Also the bank's back office operations can continue during weekends without incurring overtime charges by using casual part-time workers. While such approaches may run into problems in Germany, recent revisions to laws allow stores to remain open till 20:00 hours during the week and 16:00 hours on Saturdays, which represents an improvement for consumers (e.g., previously 18:30 and 13:00 hours). Sick leave provisions are also being changed by many employers to reflect the possibility of paying 80% of the employees' wages when they are absent from work due to illness. Further changes in Germany's restrictive labour laws are likely, thereby making it easier for employers to increase flexibility (e.g., due to extended shop hours) while using various employment contracts (e.g., contract-type employment or part-time work) to reduce labour costs and overtime pay, in particular. In turn, this will likely help German organisations to improve customer service.

Table 5 outlines some of the issues the firm must consider when using various labour contracts, outsourcing and CIS to reduce costs, while improving quality of the products/services it offers to clients. Such strategies require greater coordination of efforts and data management to keep all operations running smoothly. Naturally, this does not come without any costs, either. CIS has increased the opportunities for outsourcing, primarily, because information and data can be transferred easily between various units in different locations as discussed below.

3.1.2. CIS and the Removal of Geographical Borders for Production

Usually industries tend to gather in certain geographical locations. For instance, in the garment industry, purchasing and production may occur within a few blocks of each other (e.g., New York or Los Angeles). However, haute-couture and designing for the mass clothing market may occur somewhere in Europe, while the manufacturing of the garment is done somewhere in Asia. Consequently, CIS offers the firm the opportunity to perform high value-added versus labour-intensive tasks in different geographical locations, thereby taking advantage of various factors (e.g., highly-skilled employees versus an abundance of cheap low-skilled labour).

Increased outsourcing through freelance, telework and casual part-time employment may improve performance through reductions in wages and fringe benefit costs, as well as having the quality of products improved; nonetheless, such benefits do not come without such costs as:

(1) Coordination of various sub-contracts and workers requires additional personnel (e.g., administration, quality control and processing of time-sheets submitted by part-time workers and approved by their supervisors).

(2) Supervision of people working freelance or for a sub-contractor is more difficult than one's own employees working in-house.

(3) Using CIS (see Table 3) with or without the combination of outsourcing requires careful scheduling of tasks, coordination of delivery and quality control to meet time schedules.

(4) Verbal and non-verbal communication signals used by people to decode material when communicating with others may be more difficult when parties are in different locations; while e-mail, video phone and other means help, communication is not as easy as if the other party were just down the hall.

(5) Creating group-cohesiveness and d'esprit de corps with employees/job partners being located around the globe or a few kilometres away can be a challenge and takes effort (e.g., time and resources).

Note: Whenever a firm decides to use either telework and/or outsourcing, the issues outlined here should be discussed before decisions are made and implemented. This will help to reduce misunderstandings and surprises later on.

Table 5: Outsourcing and Benchmarking: Some Things to Think About

Citibank Germany uses data-communication links to send billing information about its clients to Denmark (recently also to The Netherlands), where after printing and stuffing the information in an envelope, it is then mailed directly to the German customer of Citibank. The savings for Citibank were so large that the German Post Office perceived this as a threat to its first class mail monopoly and, took Citibank to court. The last word has not been spoken. Similarly, with the help of Web pages incorporating a list of and explanations to Frequently-Asked-Questions (FAQ), customer support can be facilitated, whereby the information can be accessed 24 hours a day, every day of the week. Search engines allowing the client to search for key words on the Web site, make finding the information needed relatively easy (e.g., design drawings or installation hints for re-sellers). In turn, such technology helps the firm to reduce its customer relations staff. Specific questions submitted by customers via e-mail, will usually be answered by customer service representatives within 24 hours. Unfortunately, having such technology available does not mean the firm is ready to make effective use of it. My own experience with airlines has shown that providing them with feedback or questions about products and services does not mean one receives answers. Similarly, the five largest Canadian banks failed miserably in a test conducted for feedback of information on their Internet activities (Carrol/Broadhead 1996).

As much as one can send digitally-rendered data (e.g., designs of a coat) via the Internet to the manufacturer, retailing in its classical form (i.e., shopper visits store and conducts a purchase), is experiencing a growing threat from the Internet. For instance, Levis offers its customers in the U.S., jeans at a small surcharge, whereby personal measures are taken and within about a fortnight the customer can pick up the customised jeans at the store. Here Levis offers its clients a customised product resulting in better fitting jeans while, more importantly, enabling the firm to manufacture the product on demand. Accordingly, the firm is saving finance and warehousing charges for stockpiling the product in the warehouse or the store. Instead, on-demand production is helping Levis to lower costs, while providing clients with a better fitting pair of jeans.

3.2. Downsizing and Rightsizing

Both of the two above terms have been used by managers and researchers alike. In both instances, reengineering and benchmarking may be used to determine if the changes were a success. In the above section, we outlined how reengineering in combination with CIS can be used to outsource certain production and service functions. For instance, in North America, Xerox and many other small companies, are offering firms to do their copying and printing of documents for a fee. In turn, clients no longer do their own copying and printing, and therefore, do not need to pay for leasing such machines. Such business has been growing rapidly, due to the cost savings for clients. Nevertheless, organisational changes and possible job losses will materialise from shifting in-house jobs to out-of-house contractors which will be discussed below.

The Internet and new telecommunication media have been used to downsize, in particular, to lay off workers. For instance, AT&T has reduced the number of telephone operators from 60,000 during regulatory times to 15,000 in late 1996, due to voice recognition (e.g., customer provides name and other information about party one needs a telephone number for, and computer dispenses information) and consolidation (Peres 1996). Interactive voice response is able to handle 70 to 80 percent of all customer requests on the spot. By 1999, many U.S. phone companies, with the help of interactive computer systems, will be able to have 80 percent of all customer calls automated, compared to 50 percent in 1996, while 70 percent of all repairs (e.g., problem with phone service such as not getting a dial-tone) will be completed before the customer hangs up, compared to the current less than one percent (Peres 1996).

In other instances, highly-skilled employees may be replaced with low-skilled ones. For instance, Fidelity Investments replaced an experienced U.S. $100,000-a-year stockbroker with recent college graduates as phone representatives, who made about U.S. $30,000 (Davis 1996). The latter were backed up with an expert system, also saving the firm labour costs.

As suggested previously (see also Tables 4 and 5), while outsourcing may help in reducing labour costs, administrative and necessary information needed to keep on top of things can also increase costs. Temporary workers may come and go making it harder to create a culture conducive to the firm and its part-time and contract workers (Gattiker 1990, Chap. 4 & 5). When General Motors' workers in Canada went on strike during October 96, the major reason was outsourcing. Jobs performed by General Motors in-house which were paying more than Can. $21 per hour with fringe benefits, were threatened to be outsourced, resulting in an hourly wage of about Can. $15 or less, including fringe benefits. Obviously, labour costs are one major reason why car manufacturers are trying to outsource some jobs. Component suppliers may have acquired economies of scale and know how to affect the bottom line positively, resulting in cost reductions for the manufacturer and likely, in a more price competitive product for the consumer. Here CIS may be used to coordinate logistics and transportation to assure the just-in-time delivery from suppliers to the car manufacturer's plant.

The above illustrates that downsizing or rightsizing has often resulted in using CIS to reduce labour and costs. In turn, companies try to focus on their core competencies, while support operations are outsourced (contracted out) to low-bid firms or else, core workers (i.e., "permanent" part-time and full-time) are supplemented by temporary/casual employees to cut down on employment and reduce the number of higher paid professionals.

3.3. Reengineering of Distribution, Customer Service and Sales Marketing: The Internet Opportunity

In sections 3.1. and 3.2., I discussed how production costs can be reduced by using CIS to transfer and exchange data and information between various firms and units of the organisation, thereby allowing firms to take advantage of locational factors (e.g., lower labour and real estate costs, as well as attractive local tax laws). Fortunately, downsizing and rightsizing is only one small part of reengineering. The major focus should be on improving, with the help of CIS and the Internet. Accordingly, new opportunities have and continue to emerge for innovative approaches, while the involvement of workers in reengineering and benchmarking is the key to long-term revenue growth and reductions in service transaction costs for products (e.g., distribution). This will be discussed in greater detail in this section.

3.3.1. Television, Radio, Newspapers and Music/Film Entertainment

The Internet is not making a halt in front of your factory's doors, nor does it bypass television (TV) and others in the entertainment industries, without having some impact. For instance, a TV station in North Carolina (URL http://www.wral-tv.com) started its Web site in January 1996. The site is visited extensively during lunch hour and in the afternoon for obtaining news, weather, sports and updates. In turn, the TV station uses its Web site to inform visitors about upcoming shows and program content during the evening. Eight out of 100 news staff help with this venture, primarily seen as a tool to attract viewers for the TV station's programs during prime-time (evening hours) (Harris 1996). Others have argued that radio stations might be the biggest beneficiaries of the Internet by taking advantage of visual images for the audio experience (Davis 1996).

Radio stations, with the help of the Internet, can also reach listeners well beyond their geographical area as defined for advertising dollars. Consequently, listeners from far away places could make up a substantial percentage of a particular show or newscast's total audience. Some radio and TV stations are still reluctant to use this new medium to their advantage. When stereo was first available for radio broadcasting, stations were also reluctant to invest in this new technology, however, when advertisers such as Proctor & Gamble started to look for stations which were able to broadcast their spots in stereo, radio stations quickly adopted the technology. Similarly with the Internet, in a few years major advertisers will expect TV and radio stations to offer them a spot/icon on their Web page as part of their total advertising contract with a station. Being pro-active and testing the waters now, is probably wiser than waiting to catch up to the competition later on.

3.3.2. Automobile and Furniture Sales

Until recently the Internet has not been an important tool for purchasing an automobile, but things are changing rapidly. For instance, any consumer from around the world can call up repair incidents and maintenance costs per annum for a car one intends to purchase from consumer associations and federal government agencies (e.g., Canada and U.S.). The firm's Web site may provide one with video clips and a message from a spokesperson for the company (e.g., a famous race car driver). Moreover, a search engine on the site facilitates locating important information (e.g., Volvo North America), while visual aids provide the person with a better idea about the aesthetics, looks and other features of one's favourite car.

Once the customer has acquired all the information needed and decided which car he or she wants to purchase, one can proceed to use the Internet to find the best price. For instance, using Edmund's auto page, the individual can fill out a form called Auto-by-Tel and submit the car type, specifications and options which he or she would like to buy. Participating dealers get the information and call the client with a firm offer. Dealers save commissions paid to sales representatives, as well as inventory and advertising costs. By the latter part of 1996 and a year after making its debut, Auto-By-Tel had facilitated the sale of more than 80,000 cars (Lerner 1996).

Auto-by-Tel intends to expand to Europe by 1997/1998 which will substantially affect the distribution and sales in that market, as it already has in the U.S. and Canada. Even if such Internet supported sales only impact less than 5 percent of total sales, dealers and manufacturers will feel the impact. Consumers using CIS and the Internet will be better informed about how high-ticket items such as car and household appliances rate in product tests (e.g., crash statistics). While comparative advertising is not possible in Germany, its permission in Austria will enable consumers to find such information using the Internet. Moreover, it will be easier for consumers to get competitive bids for cars and other high ticket items (e.g., home furnishings) by gathering information, facts and other pertinent data by surfing the Web.

Italian interior design firms are offering their ware directly to German retail customers at a substantial discount with the help of advertisements in major newspapers. This can now be done via the Internet. Moreover, with the appropriate software, three-dimensional graphics either on the firm's Web page or the client's computer, allows the client to visualise how new furniture may look in one's apartment. Again, technology supports the consumer to make a wiser, better informed decision, and will likely end up being more satisfied with the product or service chosen. Moreover, any customer reluctance is easily overcome by the few hundred to thousands of dollars one saves by purchasing a car or major home furnishings using the Internet.

3.3.3. Insurance, Extended Warranty Purchases and Banking

Once the customer has decided to purchase a car from a particular dealer, car insurance needs to be secured before the car can be registered. Swissline [a division of Winterthur Versicherung (insurance)] offers various products including price quotes via the Internet. Savings (e.g., no insurance broker costs) are supposedly passed on to clients. While Swissline takes customer data online and subsequently prepares an offer, which is still mailed using "snail" mail. In contrast, Auto-by-Tel offers the user to submit an information sheet to a car insurer, whose response with a definite quote is provided online within a maximum two days (including weekends!).

The individual might also want to protect the high-ticket item (i.e., car) by purchasing an extended warranty. Auto-by-Tel offers the purchase of an extended warranty online, through Warranty Gold, again saving the consumer several hundred dollars over a 2-8 year contract, depending on the car, as opposed to buying the extended warranty through a car dealer. The individual might also need a loan to finance the car and the developments in banking suggest that arranging a loan via the Internet will soon be quite common while, most importantly, resulting in savings for the customer.

In Germany, banking institutions are under pressure to reduce costs and offering clients longer service hours. One way to accomplish this goal is with telephone banking, but recent data indicate that in 1996, most of these ventures were still not profitable (e.g., Bank 24). A recent survey reported the cost of an average payment transaction on the Internet to cost about 13 cents or less (U.S.). Using the bank's own software to do personal computer banking costs about 26 cents per transaction, while the same transaction costs about U.S.$1.08 at the bank branch (Graham 1996, p. 1). In this scenario, the individual might use the Internet to negotiate an advantageous car loan with a bank.

The above cost structure explains why banks will continue to make more extensive use of CIS technology to improve service while cutting costs as much as possible. There is now a group of banks (e.g., Sparda Bank Hamburg) which offers Internet banking to its clientele from anywhere in the world. Security is assured by providing each client with a personalised chip which encrypts his or her communication and enables the bank's computer to verify the client. Here CIS technology is used to reduce monthly account charges for the client. Moreover, similar developments have been undertaken by some investment firms in North America, whereby transactions are being initiated and executed with the help of CIS, again reducing costs for the client and reducing processing and handling charges for the investment firm.

3.3.4. Retail Shopping

If we take the above example further, the individual might require a change of clothing to fit his or her new car, and again, the Internet might be used for part of or the entire transaction. In conjunction with changing trade laws, the sale of clothing may change drastically within the next decade. For instance, in Germany, jeans cost at least 100 German Marks a pair. The new free-trade agreement with Turkey enables a firm to offer its clients that their personal measurements, taken at a store or distribution centre in Germany, are digitally transferred to Turkey, where the jeans are manufactured. The jeans are then shipped to Europe and the customer may be able to pick them up within a fortnight.

This "jeans" example can be easily altered, whereby the client is given the opportunity to enter his or her personal measures on the Internet (e.g., the virtual mall at http://www.Kelb.com), pay by credit card and receive the jeans by mail or pick them up at a local distribution centre after a fortnight. A total satisfaction guarantee, permitting the customer to return the jeans if they are defect or do not meet his or her expectations, a service offered by all mail-order houses in North America, is also available on the Internet and will remove any apprehension the person might have about spending money this way. Circumventing the retailer may save the customer 40 to 60% of the retail price paid today in any store in Germany. Such substantial savings are made possible, in part, by eliminating the retailer, reducing warehousing costs (i.e., produce on demand only) while taking advantage of cheaper labour and other costs in Turkey. Accordingly, people's fears will be overcome by such savings and convenience (order online from home, 24 hours a day, every day).

3.4. Innovation and Computer-Mediated Communication and Information Systems (CIS): How Can a Firm Use its People Better?

If the changes and suggestions described above are to be realised in an organisation, human resources must be managed more effectively and carefully than is often done. Today, consulting firms and reengineering gurus are changing their tune and pointing out to their clients that simply cutting staff, instead of reorganising the way people work in different functions and departments is not necessarily resulting in "quantum leaps" in performance (White 1996). To boost growth and foster innovation and to bring new ideas to fruition by having them realised in new products succeeding in the marketplace, the human dimension must be appreciated. Human resources are critical to the success of the organisation when striving to change and transform itself to better satisfy critical stakeholders' demands (cf. Figure 1).

Accordingly, people need to work smarter and become more effective to help the organisation realise its objectives and meeting benchmarking targets (cf. Gattiker 1990). Commitment by employees can only be assured if their needs are being met, including job security and wages. Layoffs, overwork and regular upheaval stemming from continuous and substantial changes, will not foster an environment where employees feel that someone cares about them, and values their ideas and output. Instead, morale may suffer, and in turn, organisational change efforts and innovation may be jeopardised unnecessarily.

3.4.1. End-User Focus

Innovation often results in administrative and technological change for employees and customers. While firms have always put an emphasis on customer issues, the employees and end users of new technology or systems are sometimes not consulted enough. For instance, research indicates that users should be involved in the analysis and the planning phase of change or transition (cf. Table 1). Accordingly, training needs can be identified early, and resistance to change can be reduced considerably (e.g., Gattiker/Kelley/Paulson/Bhatnagar 1997). Gattiker et. al. (1997) reported that end-user involvement and support, as well as training, are all important factors which will facilitate change and subsequent effective use of new technology.

To make benchmarking and reengineering efforts a success, employees and end users must be involved from the start. Otherwise, strategic behaviour may permit workers to meet goals while they know that these have little meaning, if not being detrimental, to the firm's efforts in fostering continuous revenue growth. Finally, restructuring and changes are implemented more smoothly and successfully if affected employees understand the rationale for doing so. They can better accept, maybe even support these efforts, because they will benefit from them.

3.4.2. Innovation and Employee/Union Issues

End-user focus also requires that employees can see the benefits of reengineering efforts in the technology and/or innovation domain. For instance, Gattiker/Kelley/ Paulson (1997) report that non-union members and managers, in contrast to union members, appear to be concerned primarily about wages, benefits and job security as well as how changes affect their skill levels, training and job safety. Union members feel that the function of their union assisting them to cope with change and innovation is to assure that the job becomes more interesting thereafter.

In conjunction with CIS and the Internet, a more extensive use of such technology will likely result in substantial reengineering efforts, which should result in change in administration and production. To make this a success, however, employee needs must be addressed to avoid resistance and possible productivity losses while having to absorb unnecessary costs (directly or indirectly) due to grievances. In turn, this requires long-term planning and farsightedness, to reduce frequent and unnecessary change which causes workers to worry unnecessarily. Also, a long-term outlook enables the firm to take advantage of fluctuations in employment and attrition. In turn, severance packages and fear about job security can be avoided, while potential revenue growth might even allow for additional workers.

3.4.3. Reengineering and People

As the above sections indicate, successful reengineering of processes and tasks within the firm, as well as in the customers' domain, requires careful benchmarking and the involvement of end users, i.e., employees and clients (see also Figure 1) to make it a success. Another consideration is that innovation and organisational change does not proceed without hiccups and mishaps. Consequently, the perfect Internet presence does not exist, but becoming part of and taking advantage of the Internet, even with the less-than-perfect solution is advantageous to the firm. In the process, the learning organisation is becoming a reality by enabling both employees and customers to actively participate in the venture by contributing ideas and participating in the further development of the technology.

End user, employee and customer involvement is far more likely to remove any possible resistance by: (1) helping participants to acquire and learn about the new technology; (2) preventing rumours from spreading due to lack of understanding or not having the facts, (3) helping the reengineering efforts along, and finally, (4) getting everybody involved in the effort to achieve, if not exceed, benchmarking targets. This approach is more likely to help everybody get a better grip on technology while helping to accept the change and technology, which in turn, affects the firm's bottom line.

4. Summary and Conclusion

This chapter is meant to highlight the opportunities and challenges for consumers, organisations and governments who use, or are being affected by, reengineering efforts involving CIS technology and the Internet, and to outline how these matters may develop within the next decade. As the previous sections have illustrated, new technologies provide organisations with the opportunity and challenge to innovate and transform themselves to take advantage of environmental changes by adjusting both administrative processes and procedures for CIS technology in an innovative manner.

4.1. Practical Implications

While reengineering may be an old product in newer clothing, reengineering efforts are often supported with CIS to achieve the objectives set out by management. However, not all is rosy on the home front. Some have argued that the residue of botched reengineering simply means that firms have taken a good concept and overdid it in the process. Some firms have replaced clerical and support personnel as much as possible but, in turn, much of the secretarial work and chores may now be done by an individual who draws an executive salary. For instance, local area networks require service personnel and specialists to assure smooth work and support for all personnel. Some organisations, however, have not provided such service personnel, or job duties and strategies are unclear. In turn, highly paid professionals try to maintain their own computers and small local area networks (link four to five offices) and spend unnecessary hours on jobs which they are neither fully qualified for, nor paid to do (e.g., set up new computers or do regular tape backups and maintenance jobs themselves) (see also Table 3). In turn, reengineering may result in a situation whereby some labour costs have been saved through laying off lower-level employees, while highly paid professionals are now wasting valuable time doing the work previously done by lower-level employees, instead of accomplishing tasks they are more qualified to do.

In other instances, reengineering and downsizing led to developments where mid- and lower-level management was laid off first, due to lack of union contracts protecting such workers. Unfortunately, in case of subsequent growth or needs for such personnel, it is difficult to grow and develop such talent in-house for middle management and executive positions, since many potential candidates were let go earlier, or simply fired, to cut costs to the bone. The above simply indicates that any good thing can be overdone to meet short-term budgetary constraints and goals, while forgetting to accommodate long-term objectives outlined in the strategic plan.

Nevertheless (as suggested in Tables 1 and 2), reengineering and benchmarking can be used to achieve change and transitional objectives, as well as innovation, in the administrative and technology domain to better balance the conflicting triangle in Figure 1. If the issues outlined in Tables 3 and 4 are carefully addressed, before reengineering efforts are put into motion, long-term growth and survival are more likely to be realised for the benefit of all stakeholders. While outsourcing and telework may be a viable strategy, they do not come without some costs (both social and economic) for the organisation, as Table 5 advocates.

People between the ages of 20 and 50 will increasingly use the Internet and CIS to meet their needs. Accordingly, the percentage of people using the Internet to obtain services and products as well as information and entertainment, is on the rise. Moreover, the use of e-mail increased from 67% in 1990 to 98% in 1991, in Fortune 500 companies. In 1993, estimates suggested that approximately 75% of all U.S. corporations used e-mail. Industry data also suggest that by the end of 1998, approximately 25% of households in Canada, U.S. and Germany will have Internet access, while probably another 25% have access from school and/or work. Since the end of 1997 in most industrialised countries, school children, as well as high school and university students, have had access to the Internet at their educational institution. Some have already taken advantage of this technology for years. Consequently, the market segment for Internet applications for consumers is growing. This will also positively influence and enhance Internet literacy of workers who might have used the technology before during their schooling and education or from home during their spare time.

The above indicates also that workers will be Internet literate. In turn, much change for organizations will come through **extranets** (e.g., computer networks between firm and dealers, and/or suppliers) and their vast impact with electronic commerce, permitting firms to do business with other firms around the world using computer networks. While in 1997 the hype and media attention was focussing on retail sales and the Internet, 1998 is showing us a shift toward business-to-business sales and transactions. Here CIS technology is having an ever great impact upon organisations and requires reengineering and benchmarking to stay ahead of the competition.

This challenge must be met by organisations worldwide by offering their services, products, and information on the Internet 24 hours a day, seven days a week. Changes will continue while reengineering efforts and benchmarking will become a regular task. Additionally, the firm has the challenge to manage these efforts either pro-actively or reactively. The latter are similar to fighting fires and usually take a lot of effort while lost market shares may be hard to recover, if ever. It is hoped that the information provided herein will further facilitate the success of these important tasks within organisations.

4.2. Policy, Social and Research Implications or Should we Pull the Plug on the Internet?

The social implications of the changes described above (making more extensive use of CIS and the Internet, in particular) will be well beyond job losses as touched on in Section 3.2. What it will also do is to tear down national borders while facilitating international trade on a larger scale. While the World Trade Organisation (WTO) has not been known to succeed much in liberalising trade since its inception in 1994 - policy initiatives to liberalise world financial services, telecommunications and maritime markets collapsed since the majority of the 125-member nations gave in to domestic interests - the increasing use of the Internet will put pressure on such efforts. Only international agreements will enable countries to partake in the mushrooming growth of business transactions on the Internet, while benefiting by collecting taxes. Without such agreements, tax losses will mushroom to gigantic proportions. To illustrate, producing and shipping a printed brochure using traditional mailing channels is likely to include some tax benefits for the government (e.g., value-added tax [VAT] or customs duties). In contrast, an electronic and digitally-rendered brochure to the client's computer may have been designed and produced in country A, while being put remotely onto a computer server in country B, by employees in country A. In turn, producing the product in country A while "exporting" it in country B avoids taxation if the bill is sent and paid for by a firm in country C under current laws. Similarly, a computer game produced in country A, may be sold digitally from a server in country B to clients in country C (e.g., purchasing a software upgrade in the U.S. using file-transfer-protocol, avoiding Canadian VAT).

Additional change is expected from electronic currency managed by private organisations (e.g., Digicash), which is largely outside the control of federal reserve banks. In a December 1996 press release, the Bank of International Settlements in Basle pointed out that reserve banks will lose a large portion of their lucrative coin and currency production business, simply, because the need and use of such payment tenders will decrease, while the use of electronic cash will increase substantially by the year 2000 and beyond.

Unfortunately, more extensive data are lacking to provide us with information about these developments, as far as consumer behaviour, ethics and firms' strate-

The Centre for Technology and Innovation Management (TIM-Research) at the University of Aalborg and the Corporate Technology and Environmental Management Group at the Aarhus School of Business have been collaborating on various Internet projects since 1995.

Current projects include:
− Assessing end-user behaviours on the Internet
− E-commerce, in Particular:
  - Acceptance and resistance
  - Privacy and security management
  - Corporate strategy and benchmarking
  - Marketing and customer loyalty
  - Change management and implementation
− Malicious software (malware) and communication/data exchange
− Reengineering and benchmarking.

A survey is currently being prepared to gauge the needs of business and private users with respect to the issues addressed in this article. If you are interested in participating in this survey or wish to receive more information about past project findings or references for this article, please contact the author at:

Telephone: +45 9635 8990
Fax: +45 9815 3030
E-mail: Internet_Research_Prgram@bigfoot.com

Please check out our Web Site at:
                    Http://www.TIM-research.com

Table 6: Internet Research and Collaboration

gies are concerned. More information is needed and as Table 6 suggests, small steps are being undertaken to increase our understanding of these developments while marshalling our resources to take advantage of them.

4.3. Conclusion

For all that we already know, there is still much more remaining to be explored and synthesized. If we want to guide future research and policy for the information highway, we must meet the challenges regarding the social effects of the increasing use of CIS and the Internet for education, marketing, communication and social activities by firms, consumers and investors.

With CIS and the Internet, the following should be carefully taken into consideration when deciding to undertake organizational changes and transformations to innovate and take better advantage of technology, both in administrative and product/service areas:

- The printing press allowed one person to reach many.
- The telephone allowed one to reach one other.
- The Internet allows many to reach many!

Moreover, the Internet is cheaper and faster for communicating with clients, co-workers, and friends than it is to mail a letter/brochure (e.g., design, production, packaging and shipping), by using direct mailing and/or telephoning a person (i.e. often phone tagging requires several attempts till the parties finally talk to each other directly, instead of to their answering machines).

Internet literacy and skill requires users to discriminate, and therefore, become effective when searching for information. In turn, this will make things more difficult for parties wanting to reach customers through the Internet in order to sell products and/or services. Similar to today's TV viewers tuning out commercials, Internet users might begin to do the same when bombarded with advertising. Accordingly, with the help of the EU's Privacy Directive going into force by October 98, e-mail spamming (i.e. direct marketing to people who did not request information nor are they current customers) will become difficult not only from an ethical but also legal point-of-view.

Table 7: Change and the Internet

Many consulting firms may scramble to remodel their reengineering vehicles with such new candidates as "knowledge management," enterprise software to better link workers together, as well as intranet technology and growth "strategy." Nevertheless, most firms will continue with their efforts to improve their management of reengineering projects, thereby fostering innovation and revenue growth so vital for the survival of the company, and thus, providing job security for employees. This paper represents an outline of the issues which should be addressed before, and during, reengineering with a particular focus on CIS and Internet-related concerns.

As Table 7 indicates, new CIS technology, in combination with the Internet, provides us with new opportunities to communicate better with critical stakeholders while, hopefully, doing our jobs better than before. Its efficiency, as well as being relatively inexpensive, may also be the Internet's Achilles heel, since it may result in too great a volume of information, whereby important data transmitted might sometimes be overlooked or missed in the flood of information one receives regularly.

Bibliography:

Canada NewsWire (1996), TD Bank extends benefits package to casual part-time employees, in: NewsPage, June 24, 1996

Carroll, J., & Broadhead, R. (1996), On-Line banking, in: Globe & Mail, October 22, 1996

Davis, J. (1996), Technology and jobs: Forging a new social contract?, in: The CPSR Newsletter, Vol. 14, No. 1, pp. 1-2, 8-10

Davis, T. (1996), Squeezing money from the Internet, in: Broadcaster, September, 1996, pp. 14-19

Dürrenberger, G., Jaeger, C., Bieri, L. & Dahinden, U. (1995), Telework and vocational contact, in: Technology Studies, 2, pp. 104-131

Gattiker, U. E. (1990), Technology Management in Organizations. Newbury Park, CA 1990

Gattiker, U. E. (1992), Where do we go from here? Directions for future research and managers, in: U. E. Gattiker (ed.), Studies in technological innovation and human resources (Vol. 3), Technology-mediated communication, Berlin, New York, pp. 289-311

Gattiker, U. E. (1994), Where do we go from here? Directions for future research and managers, in: U. E. Gattiker (ed.), Studies in technological innovation and human resources (Vol. 4), Women and technology, Berlin, New York, pp. 245-286

Gattiker, U. E., Kelley, H. (1997), Predicting the success of end-user training in management education, in: Information Systems Research (currently being revised)

Gattiker, U., Willoughby, K. (1997), Interorganizational alliances and profitability: A study of the biotechnology industry, in: Aarhus School of Business, Working Paper Series

Gattiker, U. E., Kelley, H., Janz, L. (1996), The Information Highway: Opportunities and Challenges for Organizations, in: R. Berndt (Ed.): Global management, Berlin, New York, pp. 417-453

Gattiker, U. E., Kelley, H., Paulson, D., Bhatnagar, D. (1997), User information satisfaction: A comparison of three countries, in: Aarhus School of Business, Working Paper Series

Graham, G. (1996), Rise of Internet threatens traditional banks' market, in: Financial Times, August 12, 1996, pp.1

Harris, J. (1996), On line with WRAL-TV, in: Communicator, September, 1996, pp. 29, 31,32, 34

Hartman, R. I., Stoner, C. R., Arora, R. (1991), An investigation of selected variables affecting telecommuting productivity and satisfaction, in: Journal of Business and Psychology, Vol. 6, pp. 207-

Kieser, A. (1987), From asceticism to administration of wealth. Medieval monasteries and the pitfalls of rationalization, in: Organization Studies, pp. 8, 103-123

Lerner, P. (1996), Attention shoppers. Finally, some good news about buying a car, in: Automobile, October, 1996, pp. 122

March, J. G., & Simon, H. A. (1958), Organizations, New York

378

Nihon Keizai Shimbun (1996), Electronic newspaper will gain in popularity, in: NewsPage, June 28, 1996

Olson, M. H., Primps, S. B. (1984), Working at home with computers: Work and non-work issues, in: Journal of Social Issues, Vol. 40, No. 3, pp. 97-112

Peres, K. (1996), Restructuring telecommunications, in: The CPSR Newsletter, 14 Vol. 1, pp. 5-7

Soares, A. S. (1992), Telework and communication in data processing centres in Brazil, in: U. E. Gattiker (ed.), Studies in technological innovation and human resources (Vol. 3) - Technology-mediated communication, Berlin, New York, pp. 117- 145

White, J. B. (1996), Management guru re-engineers message in: Globe & Mail, November 26, 1996, pp. B11

Decision Support Systems for Strategic Management – What Will DSS Systems Do to Help Senior Managers with Strategic Management Tasks?

William K. Holstein

Zusammenfassung:

Gegenstand des Artikels ist eine kritische Auseinandersetzung mit Entscheidungs-Unterstützungs-Systemen. Die Hauptfrage ist, in welchem Maße diese Systeme für das Strategische Management geeignet sind. Die Entwicklung der Informationssysteme wird aufgezeigt. Die Nutzenpotentiale der Entscheidungs-Unterstützung-Systeme werden herausgearbeitet.

1. Introduction

More than a decade ago, a large multi-national consumer products company had just completed the largest acquisition ever achieved by purchasing a large American food products company for $3.5 billion in cash. The Chairman of the acquiring company was asked what contribution to the acquisition was made by the several hundred MIS people in the company's headquarters organization. His physical reaction was a wrinkled brow and a puzzled look. He said: None, of course. In the five days that we analyzed the acquisition and concluded the negotiations, I got more information from a five-year-old article in Fortune magazine than I got from our MIS staff and their systems. What could they have done to help? All of the information that our MIS people manage is about us, not the company that we were acquiring or its strategic value to us.

That was a long time ago. Has the situation changed? Do computer and information systems people have a lot to contribute to corporate strategy? The answer is a qualified „yes." A few companies have decision support systems for senior managers that do contribute to strategy. Such systems include explicit, external, strategic information on markets, competitors and the environment. But in the vast majority of companies, real strategic information still comes from magazines and newspapers, conversations with suppliers, consultants and others who know what is going on.

In this paper we trace some of the reasons that information systems still do not do a good job at supporting strategic decision-making. We also suggest some of the elements that must be included in future systems to make them more useable for strategic tasks. Before we begin, we take a short tangential excursion to consider just what **strategic** means. To us, whose interest is more on information systems to support strategy than on strategy per se, the word strategic means an act of great value or importance to an organization (Anthony/Dearden/Bedford 1984, S. 14). The term **strategic planning** has an organization-wide implication. It refers to the development of statements of policy, strategies and goals. More important, these statements, goals, etc. must be communicated so that various parts of the organization function as a **unified whole** to attain them. If an information system is to assist with strategic tasks, it must deal with these acts of great value to the organization and it must help the organization to act as the unified whole. This is a tall order. It is therefore not surprising that truly strategic information systems are in their infancy at best.

Before we leave this discussion of definitions, let us note one important point. The definition of what is strategic **is changing**, and the changes are being brought about largely by information systems. As an example, contemporary decision support systems allow:
- the measurement of variables previously unmeasured or uncontrolled,
- the integration of the efforts of several different groups across functions, and
- for decisions to be made quickly in response to changes in the external environment.

If the decisions supported by such systems are viewed solely as decisions that control inventory better, or reduce manufacturing cycle time, or manage sales calls better, the systems that support those decisions might be considered as operational systems. However, if the sum of those seemingly operational decisions **change the nature** of the business, for example by allowing the company to compete on the basis of time, or superior quality, or superior service, then the systems that support such decisions are, in our view, truly strategic systems.

2. The Evolution of Information Systems

The use of computers and information systems for business and government has progressed through three eras. Each new era has signaled a significant shift in the focus of computer applications, from the automation of clerical applications, to computer support of business operations, to contemporary systems that extract information and knowledge from raw data and support high-level decision-making.

2.1. Era I – The "Accounting" Era

During the early 1950s, computer technology began to be used to automate clerical functions such as payroll and general ledger accounting. The computer was
used as an electronic clerk to replace the humans who processed the data manually. The benefits of these systems were greater accuracy, faster processing and,
in many instances, lower cost. Era I systems focused on highly structured, well-
understood problems, and dealt entirely with historical data. Since these systems
mostly automated tasks handled by the accounting staff, this era could be called
the Accounting Era.

Era I systems are as relevant today as they were in the 1950s. They typically
constitute the "bread and butter" systems of the organization that are critical for
its functioning. Without the invoicing system, for example, the business will come
to a halt. Further, the data captured in these accounting systems contain important
information for management. Unfortunately, however, Era I systems are often
designed with a narrow focus on the needs of accounting and financial functions,
resulting in a common problem faced by many organizations – the **data gap**
problem. That is, there are gaps in the Era I databases when it comes to using that
data to supply information for management. A simple example will illustrate the
point. This example deals with a problem of some concern to marketing managers
in consumer packaged goods companies that sell through supermarkets, drug-
stores and other retail stores – the effectiveness of their expenditures on trade
promotions to get their products on the shelves. The accounting system will
surely contain data on the dates when promotional incentives were paid to the
stores. What is needed for management information, and what is typically not
found in such systems, is data on the dates when the promotion was **actually run
in the stores**. The latter set of dates is needed to correlate expenditures with the
sales for the period when the promotion ran. Without the second set of dates, the
sales impact of promotions must be evaluated manually. Such problems are not
easy to fix since the data is usually handled in old, mainframe (legacy) systems
whose structure is not easily changed. The best approach is to look beyond the
needs of the accounting function when designing Era I systems to avoid the data
gap problem.

„Information" in many companies and government agencies has not moved much
beyond what we call „data" – bits and pieces of facts and detail that are almost
always historical. The overwhelming majority of installed **information systems**,
and the target of most investments in information technology, are what might
more accurately be called **data processing systems** – systems that store, shuffle,
process, sort, re-organize, filter, sift, and then retrieve and dispense data, not information

A key characteristic of "information" that is missing from "data" is some sense of "knowledge" communicated or received concerning some fact or circumstance. Data is the fact or circumstance; information is the knowledge gleaned from the data. Hence, data has to be **converted** into information for use by management. But, without the right data, there is no foundation for information. Referring back to the previous example, the dates on which the promotions ran and the sales on those dates are data; the information is derived by processing that data to determine the effectiveness (increase in sales or margin) that can be attributed directly to the promotion.

2.2. Era II – The "Operations" Era

Advances in computer technology in the mid-1960s made on-line systems a reality and brought about the second era. The focus shifted from accounting to operations. Applications such as inventory control and on-line order entry were put in place during this period. Other applications that took advantage of the new technology were on-line systems for airline reservations, banking operations, and retail store credit card services. Since the purpose of all of these systems is to support the operations of the firm, Era II has been labeled the Operations Era. For example, inventory control systems did not just process the transactions pertaining to goods received from suppliers, but also generated information on "when" and "how much" to reorder.

Era II systems not only automated clerical tasks but also generated additional benefits such as up-to-date information for better customer service, and better utilization of assets (e.g. working capital tied up in inventory).

Management participation in the development of computerized systems increased during Era II because these systems often had significant impact on the organization's operations. Yet the focus of most Era II systems, like that of Era I, was on paperwork processing tasks that were previously handled manually. While there were some improvements in the effectiveness of the organization's functioning (due to such things as inventory control and production planning models being embedded in computer systems), the main benefit was improved efficiency – doing faster and cheaper what had historically been done with people and paper.

2.3. Era III – The "Information Support" Era

The third era, which began in the mid-1970s, was triggered not by technological advances, but by the frustration of managers in companies such as Coca-Cola, Nabisco and others in the consumer packaged goods industry. They found that their information systems were **data-rich** but **information-poor**. This era has been labeled the Information Support Era to signify the shift in emphasis to applications that are solely concerned with providing information to help managers do their jobs better. A significant benefit of Era III systems is an increase in **mana-**

gerial productivity – the ability of managers to better analyze, plan, and control their operations. The focus of these systems is on organizational effectiveness rather than efficiency, and they perforce require a high level of management participation in their development and implementation.

The initial Era III applications were called Decision Support Systems (DSS) to emphasize the fact that these systems aim to **support,** not replace, management in making decisions. The next wave of applications that appeared in the early 1980s were called Executive Information Systems (EIS) to highlight the focus on supporting **executives,** or top management. Their information needs are, by the nature of their function and responsibility, very different from those of their subordinates. Subsequently, the distinctions between EIS and DSS began to blur and both academic researchers and practitioners began to use a more general term, Management Support Systems (MSS) to embrace all levels of management.

Another distinctive application emerged in the mid-1980s for supporting a decision-making process that involves a **group** of people – appropriately named Group Decision Support Systems (GDSS). The latest Era III applications, called Expert Systems, draw from advances made in artificial intelligence to glean the knowledge of experts for filtering out routine decisions from the ones that need special attention. Expert systems are also being employed to sift through mountains of data to extract knowledge of value to decision-makers.

Almost ten years ago, Peter Drucker (1988, S. 45) asserted that the typical large business of the future will be "knowledge-based" and "composed largely of specialists who direct and discipline their own performance through organized feedback from colleagues, customers, and headquarters".

Thus, managers are not the only decision-makers; not the only people who need information support. This also ties in with the contemporary management imperative of empowering all employees. All **knowledge-workers**, not just managers, will require information to make better decisions. It is therefore entirely appropriate to call Era III the Information Support Era. We use the **Decision Support Systems** (or DSS) label in a broad sense for **all applications that provide information support**. In the following sections we concentrate on DSS broadly defined, not just strategic DSS. We then return to the question of strategic content.

3. Efficiency vs. Effectiveness

At the beginning of our discussion of Era III systems, we noted that the focus of these systems is on organizational effectiveness rather than efficiency. The distinction between **efficiency** and **effectiveness** is quite important for understanding the basic thrust of Era III systems and how these systems differ from those in earlier eras. In simple terms:

- Effectiveness – Doing the right thing.
- Efficiency – Doing it right.

Efficiency is a straightforward, easy-to-measure concept, since it deals with an input/output ratio. Improved efficiency entails reducing the input required for one unit of output, or increasing the output generated from one unit of input. Effectiveness, on the other hand, deals with the objective of the whole operation and the impact of the end-result on the organization. Thus, an operation could be very efficient and yet most ineffective – such as producing in a very efficient manner a high-quality, low-cost product that does not sell. Keen and Scott Morton observe that efficiency is performing a given task as well as possible in relation to some predefined performance criterion. Effectiveness involves identifying what should be done and ensuring that the chosen criterion is the relevant one (Keen/Morton 1978, p. 7).

The distinguishing feature of Era III systems is that they deal **both** with effectiveness and efficiency, whereas earlier-era systems tended to focus solely on efficiency. To use a marketing example, Era III systems help to answer effectiveness questions such as those listed below, sorted in order of strategic importance from more strategic to operational, or less strategic. As noted in the introduction, however, many times the **results** of what appear to be operational decisions may, in fact, be strategic for the enterprise.

- Are we marketing the right products?
- Is our sales effort targeted at the right customers?
- Are we using the correct pricing and discounting policies?
- Are we getting product to the customers in the right manner?
- Are salespeople calling on customers at the right frequency?

4. Decision Support Systems Defined

Our definition of a DSS is derived from one proposed by John Little (1979, p. 11) of MIT: a coordinated collection of data, **systems, tools, and techniques** along with requisite software and hardware, by which an organization gathers and **interprets** relevant information from the business and **environment** and turns it into a **basis for action**.

Note the bold-faced words – they are crucial to understand Decision Support Systems. Not just data, but **systems, tools and techniques** as well. Not just gathering, but interpreting and sorting out the **relevant** from the irrelevant as well. Not just internal information from the business, but information from the (external) **environment** as well. And, most important, a focus on the information which can become the **basis** for action.

In the context of this paper, the relevant question is how can a system help management to focus on the information which can become the **basis for strategic action** or action at the strategy level that will unify the organization around clearly-enunciated goals.

How can one judge whether a specific information system is an example of a strategic information system? One clue is whether the system makes the strategy feasible. If you cannot execute the strategy without the system, the system is, by our definition, strategic.

As an example, consider the case of Mrs. Fields Cookies, Inc., a multi-national retail chain with several hundred outlets. They have a highly integrated store management system that connects each store with headquarters and allows for frequent contact with each store manager. The system uses expert system models to provide detailed decision support to store managers (Applegate/McFarton/McKenney 1996, S. 279-291).

The system offers such good guidance at the local level that it enables the company to hire relatively young, relatively unsophisticated, untrained and inexpensive people to be store managers. Despite a relatively high turnover of store managers, the company is able to maintain high levels of customer service and product quality, and higher prices and higher margins than the competition. The system clearly makes this strategy possible. It is clearly a strategic information system by our definition.

5. Actionable Information

As noted in our definition of a Decision Support System, actionable information is information that can become the **basis for action**. What are the defining characteristics of **strategic** actionable information? First and foremost, actionable information has to be **timely**. Returning to John Little (1970, p. 5): Quick. Quick. Quick. If you can answer people's questions right away, you will affect their thinking. If you cannot, they will make their decision without you and go on to something else. This is particularly important if the system is trying to support senior level executives, most of who have little patience for slow systems that do not work **exactly** the way they want.

If strategic actionable information has to be timely for it to be useful, how **complete and accurate** does it have to be? There is an issue of cost here – more complete, more accurate and more timely data will obviously cost more. Here we stumble on a trade-off. If information is timely, but incomplete, is it still useful? If information is timely, complete, but inaccurate, is it useful? How incomplete, or how inaccurate can the information be and still be useful? This is obviously a question that cannot have a simple answer in all contexts, but we can enunciate some generalities. Completeness, in the way scientists might use the term, is not relevant for business decisions. The focus has to be on what managers **absolutely** need to know versus that which would be merely nice to know. The same argument can be extended to accuracy. Real three-decimal place accuracy is needed for earlier-era accounting systems, but it is not needed for strategic decision-making. In the former case, numerical accuracy is absolutely essential because of the nature of the task. While a penny discrepancy in your bank balance really doesn't mean anything, you wouldn't tolerate it – you demand exact balances, exact payment of invoices, exact computation of money owed to you. "Close" doesn't count in Era I systems.

In a strategic system, accuracy need only be good enough to make an **informed decision**. In other words, only **operational accuracy** is needed rather than numerical accuracy. In our experience, the higher the executive in the organization, the more strategic the issue at hand, the **less important** is accuracy and cost. Rough estimates are better than nothing. The cost of external data on markets and competitors, if it is deemed useful, will not be considered a problem. Actionable information has to incorporate estimates and **data about the future** in most instances. Strategic management can be said to involve **managing the future**. Hence, external, future-oriented data is an important component of actionable information.

Finally, the subjective judgments of managers, based on their experience and intuition, are an important source for getting estimates of things that are currently difficult to measure or that cannot be measured in the time available (Little 1970, p.5). Competitive intelligence on market share provided by salespeople is a good example of judgmental data. Systems can help in this area with sensitivity analysis (or "what-if" analysis) to determine what impact softness in the data inputs might have on the final decision.

From a historical perspective, the notion of using judgments as a substitute for hard data and incorporating them in computer-based systems was a prime distinguishing feature of DSS systems as they emerged in the early 1970s. Until then, the only soft data that was in common use was demand forecasts used for production planning and inventory control.

6. DSS vs. MIS

Earlier, we discussed information system **applications** in the context of the three eras. We begin this section with the labels used for the information system *function* in the three eras. In Era I, the function was called **Electronic Data Processing**, or EDP. Essentially, the computer was used only for the processing of data. When the computer evolution moved into Era II, the EDP label was replaced by

MIS, or **Management Information Systems**, to reflect the expanded focus of these systems. The scope of the systems went beyond data processing and provided information for management.

In Era III, **Decision Support** became the focus of new computer applications. Most organizations have, however, not moved much beyond Era II. Appropriately, the MIS label for the information systems function is prevalent today in organizations the world over. Why then a new label for Era III? Because MIS systems, for the most part, produce piles of printouts with lots of data, but not much information to manage the business. This data overload was particularly frustrating in the MIS reports for the marketing and sales functions in many companies. The DSS label, coined by researchers at MIT in addressing this problem, is self-descriptive – a system that provides information to support managerial decision-making (Gorry/Morton 1971, p. 55-70).

Why are traditional MIS systems data-rich but information-poor (and therefore not of much strategic value)? From a management perspective, three factors underlie this problem:
- MIS systems are usually limited to hard data from internal sources since they deal, for the most part, with accounting and operations applications.
- MIS staffs tend to be technically-oriented and wedded to the standard system development life cycle method.
- MIS systems are not flexible enough to respond to the changing needs of management.

7. Hard vs. Soft Data

Hard data represents the results of measuring quantifiable variables. It is usually historical, or based on past events or activities. Things that have already happened are, of course, more readily and easily measured than those which have not. In contrast, only **soft data** can be collected for qualitative variables (even if they deal with past events). For example, the impact of a TV commercial on viewers cannot be easily quantified and measured, even though it is a past event. Of course, every piece of data that involves the future is soft.

Accounting data is usually considered to be hard – but is it? Without question, your social security number or your hourly or monthly salary is hard data. The materials and labor cost of a product is, by and large, hard data. But what happens when overhead is added to get the "fully loaded" cost of the product? The overhead rate is anything but hard data – it is a subjective number based on management **judgment.** That judgment includes a myriad of sub-judgments about what should be included and what should be left out; how much of some costs should be covered by overhead allocations; and even what the costs to be allocated actually are, or the methodology to be used to calculate them.

For example, it is not uncommon to encounter situations where senior management issues explicit instructions to "not burden the new product with MIS overhead costs" – in other words, not to allocate any corporate MIS costs to the new product. Of course this makes the new product look more profitable. In this circumstance, hard cost data is, indeed, quite soft.

It is an obvious oversimplification but, in essence, we can say that hard data is the least interesting data in a decision support system – largely because it is usually old, often already well known and well-understood, and internal, and therefore unrelated to current management problems. The far more interesting and powerful data is soft data, but it is also the most difficult to obtain and process.

While hard data from internal sources is sufficient for some management purposes, it is of limited value for others, for example in marketing. Marketing managers have to contend with customers, an uncontrollable factor, and competitors that are not only uncontrollable, but also hostile (in the sense that they will react to decisions made by the firm and attempt to thwart the achievement of the firm's objectives). A means has to be found for handling these external entities whose data is intrinsically soft.

A similar situation arises in the case of systems to support the human resources function, where the data that matters is soft. A telling example is a DSS to support the career development and succession planning process. The basic data required for this DSS pertains to the identification of "high-potential" employees who can progress up the ladder and assume greater responsibilities. This is an extremely soft concept whose quantification and measurement requires considerable ingenuity. The only hard data in that system is the employee's date of birth and a few other demographic characteristics, the history of his/her education and professional experiences. Unfortunately, most of these have very little to do with "high-potential."

8. Systems Analysis and Design Methodology Problems

The standard system development life cycle methodology works well for Era I and Era II applications.(Remember, many of these systems are still in use, and will still be developed in the future. Our numbering of eras does not imply that earlier eras are done and finished.) The methodology works because these applications are **structured,** i.e. what is needed from the system can be specified up front, whether it be a system for invoicing, airline reservations, or for inventory control. Once the requirements are specified, the data to be captured is also well defined. The system can be designed, programmed and installed in a sequential process, with no backtracking to the initial task of specifying requirements.

A fundamental problem with this methodology for the development of Era III systems arises because the information requirements to support management decision-making are ill defined and difficult to describe – "fuzzy" at best. In turn, it is difficult to specify the data needed to drive the system. One manager's "absolutely essential" data might be considered by another to be nothing more than "extraneous noise."

A different methodology is therefore needed for developing DSS systems. Instead of a sequential approach, the method is **iterative:** build a prototype or test version of the system first so users can test-drive it; then expand and refine the system based on their feedback. The whole system evolves incrementally. The user plays a much more significant role in an Era III system since the sole purpose of the system is to support the user. If the system is *not* used, it is *useless*. Indeed, the user should be the driver and owner of the system. Quite different from earlier-era systems, the IS staff play a **supportive role** in making the DSS system a reality, not a central, independent one.

9. Flexibility

DSS systems also have to be **flexible** to meet the changing information needs of management. Traditional MIS systems did not require such flexibility because the information requirements for accounting and operations applications, once defined, are not subject to much change. Thus, MIS systems tended to last a long time, and therefore can justify large development expenses.

Most MIS systems have been developed and implemented by MIS (technical) professionals, working independently from end users of the system. The systems run on mainframe or minicomputers using COBOL or some other language that processes masses of data efficiently. The output is primarily a hard copy report in a predefined, fixed format, using the full capacity of large-format computer paper. Since managers' information needs are not static, it is not hard to see why these reports are not useful for strategic management tasks. Further, programming languages such as COBOL work well where the program (code) is written, debugged, and then "put to bed" in a production system that will last for years. They are cumbersome to work with in a dynamic environment where the system has to be responsive to constantly changing user needs and demands.

MIS reports, since they are difficult to change, tend to include all the data for all users for all time so that, in theory at least, any user should be able to find whatever he or she wants. That is the underlying cause of the **data overload problem** in traditional MIS systems.

A simple solution to the data overload problem is a *screen-oriented system* where users view a report or graph on a screen, with an option to print a hard copy if

	Traditional Systems MIS	Information Support Systems DSS
Requirements	Well-Defined	Fuzzy
Function	Process Masses of Data	Support Management Taks
Emphasis	Mechanical Efficiency	Organizational Effectiveness
Data Used	Limited to Internal, Hard Data	Includes External, Soft Data
System Design	Specified Up Front	Evolves through Actual Use
Type of System	Rigid Hard Copy-Oriented Fixed Format	Flexible Screen-Oriented Menu Driven Easy-to Acess Database Graphics
Computer Environment	Mainframe Computers COBOL and other procedural languages	Personal Computers 4 GL Tools
Implementation	Full-Scale at Birt	Prototype at Birth Expands on Basisi of User Feedback
User	Recipient of Agreed-upon Product	Driver/Owner of the System
Role of MIS Staff	Dominant	Suportive

Fig. 1: Comparison of MIS and DSS

desired. The size of the computer monitor screen acts as a brake on the tendency to put too many rows and columns on the screen. Smaller displays of data, by definition, reduce the data overload problem, but begs the question: **if not all data, which data?** A short answer is: not data, but the **relevant information** to address the problem at hand. Users should be able to get:
- What they want,
- When they want it,
- How they want it.

The What? is the key to the system. It requires conversion of data, or raw numbers, into relevant information to support decision-making. The flexibility required in a DSS necessitates a menu-driven and interactive system. Graphics capability is practically mandatory for the process of converting data into information. Such flexible systems are easier to develop in the PC (networked) environment with low-cost 4GL (fourth generation language) tools than in the mainframe environment. Figure 1 summarizes this discussion of the differences between traditional MIS systems and DSS systems for information support.

10. Potential Benefits of Decision Support Systems

One of the most significant benefits derived from Decision Support Systems is that managers can make better use of more data. As information has become more important to managers, they have gone in search of more data. But, to reiterate a point made earlier, more data is not enlightening unless it is made **actionable** – this is what a well-designed DSS delivers. One CEO stated: the system provides me with an improved ability to ask the right questions, and know the wrong answers (Rockart/Treacy 1982, p. 86).

Here is a summary of the ways in which a DSS can increase managerial productivity:
- Spot problems (opportunities).
- Trace problems to the root causes.
- Examine more alternatives to solve problems.
- Better analysis of decision problems.
- New insights into the business.
- Better use of data resources.

11. Technology, Software and End-users

Stephen S. Roach, Senior Economist at Morgan Stanley, a large US investment bank, made a dramatic statement early in this decade: Technology has been part of the problem, but it can also be part of the solution. It has to deliver in this decade, or the whole information age is a sham.

Era III systems have been made possible by significant changes in the underlying computer and information technology, most notably the advent of the personal computer and networking and telecommunications. Companies can now create large, complex and powerful information systems because of dramatic advances in computer technology and increasingly clear standards among the various computer vendors. Thus the technology that supports information systems in now robust enough to move information systems toward a new role in the organization – to truly support strategy and be a real **enterprise intelligence system**. All three words in this version of EIS are significant: a system dealing with the **whole enterprise**, not just one or a few of its parts, providing not data, but real synthesized information that might be described as **intelligence,** or having significant knowledge content. This description has a managerial, not a computer systems focus. The technology is not the only answer – we need users (senior managers who do strategy) who can lead the development of more powerful, more useful systems. As we approach the millennium, we are confident that such managers will be available and that strategic systems as we know them today will be just a pale shadow of the real power and decision support to come.

Bibliography:

Anthony, R. N., Dearden, J., Bedford, N. M. (1984), Management Control Systems, Homewood, Ill. 1984

Applegate, L.M., McFarlan, F.W., McKenney, J.L. (1996), Corporate Information Systems Management Text and Cases, 4th ed., Chicago, Ill. 1996

Drucker, P.F. (1988), The Coming of the New Organization, in: Harvard Business Review, January/February 1988, S. 45-53

Gorry, G.A., Morton, M. S.S. (1971), A Framework for Management Information Systems, in: Sloan Management Reviev, Vol. 13, No. 1 (Fall 1971), S. 55-70

Keen, P., Morton, M.S.S. (1978), Decision Support Systems, An Organizational Perspective, Reading (Mass.) 1978

Little, J.D.C. (1970), Modells and Managers, The Concept of a Decision Calculus, in: Management Science, Vol. 16, No. 8 (April 1970), S. 466-485

Little, J.D.C. (1979), Decision Support Systems for Marketing Managers, in: Journal of Marketing, Vol. 43, Summer 1979, S. 9-26

Rockart, J., Treacy, M. (1982), The CEO Goes On-Line, in: Harvard Business Review, January/February 1982, S. 82-88

Acknowledgement:

The author acknowledges the important contributions of two colleagues to this work. Much of the structure and many of the ideas in this paper were developed with Prof. Lakshmi Mohan of the University at Albany in the process of writing a co-authored textbook, Decision Support Systems: An Applications Approach. Prof. Jakov Crnkovic of the College of St. Rose contributed many of the ideas on systems development methodology.

Achter Teil

**Change Management
und
Human Resources Management**

Managing Organizational Changes and the Role of Human Resources Management

Randall S. Schuler
Susan E. Jackson

Zusammenfassung:

Führungskräfte und deren Mitarbeiter müssen akzeptieren, daß der Wandel im Umfeld von Unternehmen notwendig ist und einen kontinuierlichen Prozeß darstellt. Es ist erforderlich, alle Einflußfaktoren zu erkennen und den Prozeß des Wandels so gut wie möglich zu verstehen. Im Bereich des Human Resource Management können dann spezielle Maßnahmen gefunden werden. Für verschiedene Beispiele des organisatorischen Wandels werden die Konsequenzen im Bereich des Human Resource Management aufgezeigt.

1. Introduction

> People always ask, „Is the change over? Can we stop now?" You've got to tell them, „No, it's just begun." They must come to understand that it is never ending. Leaders must create an atmosphere where people understand that change is a continuing process, not an event.
>
> Jack Welch, CEO,
> General Electric Company

Through the 21st century, companies such as General Electric, ABB, Unilever, and Roche will need to respond to many events associated with **changes** in the global environment. Because many of these changes involve people and will affect people, they have major implications for managing human resources and they raise significant issues for the stakeholders of human resources. To address these implications effectively, organizations need to understand the changes themselves an understand the **process of change**. As Jack Welch suggests in the quote introducing this article, managers must accept and get their employees to accept the idea that change is both necessary and a continuous process. The environmental forces necessitating organizational change are certainly likely to vary over time and across different businesses, but the process of change will be constant. Once the environmental forces are known and the process of change understood, the company can act on the human resource implications by developing specific HR actions.

Changes in Enviroment Factors	Organizational Changes	Implications for Managing Human Resources	HR Planning Activities
– Domestic and International Competition – Work Force Characteristics – Economic Conditions – Organizational Conditions	– Downsizing and Layoff – Work Force Diversity – Mergers and Alliances	– Behaviors – Competencies – Assignment – Motivation	– Identify Key Business Issues and Objectives – Determine HR Supply and Demand – Develop HR Objectives – Design HR and Implement HR Actions – Monitor Results, Evaluate, Revise

Fig. 1: Major Organizational Changes and their Implications for Managing Human Resources

This article looks at three examples of organizational changes that have major implications for managing human resources and that are likely to remain into the 21st century: (a) the continued activities of companies to delayer, downsize, and layoff employees; (b) increased diversity in the workforce; and (c) the continued number of mergers and alliances such as Upjohn, Pharmacia, and Novartis. This article also describes the process of change and the role of HR professionals in that process. Because addressing these three organizational changes requires that future human resource requirements be anticipated and fulfilled, the chapter then discusses systematic HR planning tools and techniques. The relationships between these changes and activities are shown in Figure 1.

Managing organizational changes takes time in part because realigning human resource capabilities with new organizational conditions takes time. Furthermore, the process of change itself takes time: because organizations are complex systems with multiple interdependencies, bringing about change involves collaboration and partnerships between line managers, HR professionals, and all employees. Possible activities of these three groups are shown in Figure 2. Ideally, this

Line Managers	HR Professionals	Employees
Be aware of the implications of managing human resources from organizational changes like downsizing and diversitiy! Work with employees to become comfortable with change! Make the decisions on which employees need to be outplaced! Describe their business plans and human resource needs!	Identify the implications of business changes on the targets of HR! Help establish policies and procedures for down-sizings and diversity! Facilitate change! Identify supply of human resources to help match needs of line managers! Develop HR programs relevant for each target of HR action!	Participate in training programs to prepare for downsizing and layoffs! Enhance skills and abilities for flexibility and change! Respond to empowerment programs and actively participate in team work! Learn to work with diversity in organizations! Anticipate being asked to change behaviors, assignments, competencies, and motivation!

Fig. 2: Partnership in Managing Organizational Changes and Human Resource Management

collaboration occurs during all phases of change, beginning with an understanding of the nature of the organizational changes and continuing through human resource management, especially human resource planning.

The phrase „organizational changes and human resource management" refers to the activities and processes related to aligning, redesigning, and repositioning an organization's human resources to map onto the realities and objectives of the business. We illustrate the activities and processes involved in organizational changes and HR planning with three examples. First we begin by describing a framework for analyzing the human resource implications of organizational changes.

Organizational Changes Targets of HR Actions	Downsizing and Layoffs	Work Force Diversity	Mergers and Alliances
Employee Assignment - Right Numbers? - Right Place?	- Provide Outplacement! - Early Retirement!	- Make sure work force diversity is represented throughout the firm!	- Reduce - duplication, - outplacement!
Employee Competencies - Now Available? - Needed?	- Select those to stay on basis of performance!	- Train about dimensions of diversity! - Institutionalize new learning!	- Select those to stay on basis of performance!
Employee Behaviors - Now Rewarded? - Needed?	- Define the behaviours needed for succes in the new smaller firm!	- Change corporate culture! - Change top management style and assumptions!	- Communicate behaviours to new employees!
Employee Motivation - Productivity! - Retention! - Attraction!	- Help survivors stay focused! - Ensure fairness in process!	- Motivate diverse employees to work together in teams!	- Ensure fairness in process! - Ensure high motivation for those who stay!

Fig. 3: Framework for Analyzing the Implications of Organizational Changes for Managing Human Resources

2. Framework for Analysis

Figure 3 depicts a framework we can use to understand the possible implications of major organizational changes on managing human resources. The three major changes shown in Figure 3 are: (a) downsizings and layoffs; (b) work force diversity; and (c) mergers and alliances. These are just a few of the major organizational changes resulting from the environmental forces of the 21st century. Their implications for managing human resources are described more thoroughly in this article using the framework in Figure 3.

Targets of HR Actions. Human resource management in organizations has four primary targets. Because we use a multiple stakeholder model of human resource management, social and legal aspects are respected as are employee concerns for health and safety when analyzing the targets. In using this framework, the analysis of the targets serves to help us detail the implications for managing human resources and develop HR action plans to address those implications. This framework is used in our discussion of the three major organizational changes and so is further explained by example.

Employee assignments. The key questions here are: (a) do we have the right number of people? and (b) are they in the right place? For companies that are downsizing, they typically have too many people. Companies that are merging often have too many people and many need to be reassigned to different jobs in the new organization.

Employee competencies. The key questions here are: (a) what knowledge, skills and abilities do the employees now have? and (b) what knowledges, skills and abilities are needed? If an organization is changing its products or technologies, the employees may not have the necessary knowledge, skills, and abilities to perform adequately.

Employee behaviors. The key questions here are: (a) what behaviors do the employees now use in the company? and b) what behaviors are needed from the employees? If the firm is adapting a competitive strategy of quality improvement and customer focus, the behaviors of the employees may need to change substantially. Now they may need to be friendly with customers, answer detailed questions, and solve problems with the customers.

Employee motivation. The key questions here are: (a) how productive are the employees; (b) how can we increase the retention rates of those we need to keep; and (c) how can we become more attractive to the best and the "brightest?" If a company merges with another, duplication is likely to result. For the person remaining, the resulting job is bigger yet the firm needs to motivate this person to perform this larger job at a salary that may be only slightly greater than the previous smaller one.

As we go through the rest of this chapter, we use this framework to analyze the implications of managing human resources from the major organizational changes.

3. Managing Downsizing and Layoffs

In their quest for efficiency. survival, global competitiveness, and profitability, many firms are also going through another form of organizational change: they are restructuring, reengineering, and delayering their operations. Almost without exception, this means lost jobs and layoffs, and feelings of job insecurity (Nocera 1996; Byrne 1994). These feelings of insecurity are likely to continue into the 21st century, particularly in larger organizations. Fortunately, many firms recognize that restructuring, downsizing, and layoffs significantly affect the lives of employees (Uchitelle/Kleinfield 1996).

3.1. Analysis for HR Actions

Using the framework in Figure 3, how would you analyze the implications on human resource management of downsizing and layoffs? Let's look at the targets of HR action. It appears as if employee assignments are a key target: the company no longer has the right number of employees. HR actions here could be provision of outplacement services and early retirement opportunities. Employee motivation may be another key target: the remaining employees, "the survivors", may need help to stay focused on performing well. Let's look at this in detail.

3.2. The Survivors' Side of Downsizing and Layoffs

The employees who remain in the company - the survivors - are also affected by layoffs (Stamps 1996; Stuart 1992; Faltermayer 1996). Facing the threat of job loss and seeing others lose *their jobs* can be a traumatic and bitter experience (Caudron 1996; Knowdell/Branstead/Moravec 1994; Stamps 1996). It appears, however, that the **process** by which jobs are eliminated can make a difference. In summarizing the effect of job loss resulting from an acquisition, one study concluded that loss of attachment, lack of information, and a perception of "apparent managerial capriciousness" as the basis for decisions about who will be terminated, cause anxiety and an obsession with personal survival (Leana/Feldman 1989). The negative cycle of reactions may not be inevitable. If survivors feel that the process used to decide who to let go was fair, their productivity and the quality of their job performance may not suffer as much. The same study found that „it was apparently not the terminations *per se* that created ... bitterness but the manner in which the terminations were handled. Those who remained ... expressed feelings of disgust and anger that their friends and colleagues were fired ... [and] felt guilty that they were not the ones who were let go because they believed their coworkers performed at least as well or better than they did" (Schweiger/Ivancevich/Power 1986). Thus, in developing human resource policies, procedures, and practices for effective downsizing and layoffs, even the needs of survivors require attention.

3.3. Managerial Responsibilities during Downsizing

As with any major organizational change, the steps of diagnosing the current situation and developing a careful plan to implement change are essential. But even the best plan is little guarantee that chaos will not break out. The process of carrying out change is not just about strategies and plans; it is also about relationships between the people in a company and it is about personal character. Perhaps the greatest challenge to managers is maintaining employee morale while the actions of the company seem to say, „You are not valuable." A manager who had the challenge of maintaining the morale and performance of employees until the closing of more than six General Motors auto plants offers the following tips for how to be effective in such situations:

- **Communicate.** Give notice as far in advance as possible - certainly before workers read it in the paper. Be thorough and repetitious, because they may not be able to absorb everything the first time.
- **Be visible.** Take personal responsibility for guiding people through the change. Don't just have an „open door" policy; wander around outside your office.

- **Be honest.** False hope isn't helpful for anyone. Be blunt about the plant closing, even if you don't know the exact date.

- **Be positive.** Reward top performers and implement worker ideas for improvements. Also, encourage plant tours by schoolchildren and customers. They imply that workers are worth showing off.

- **Demand more.** Remind workers that improving skills will help the plant today and make them more marketable later.

- **Keep the plant looking good.** Clean it, paint it. Don't let the equipment deteriorate. Morale is iffy enough already.

Craig B. Parr, Manger, General Motors (Treece 1992, pp. 58-59).

3.4. Alternatives to Layoffs

Regardless of the cause, the loss of a job can be traumatic for employees. Providing outplacement services and severance pay may help to reduce this trauma (Moser Illes 1996; Flynn 1995; o.V. 1994). But given the evidence that downsizing may not always lead to better productivity anyway, some companies seek alternatives to layoffs (o.V. 1996; Koretz 1995; Presley Noble 1994; Rose 1994).

Job Sharing. Rather than terminating those with less seniority or poor performance, some companies have initiated job-sharing programs. Job sharing involves reducing an individual employee's workweek and pay. This helps the company cut labor costs and may actually lead to higher overall productivity because each employee is working more concentrated hours. One apparent cost-related disadvantage is that expenses per employee may increase because benefits costs are usually a function of the number of employees, not the number of hours worked or amount of pay. On the other hand, cost savings are realized by reduced severance pay, unemployment insurance, outplacement and employee assistance expenses, and so on.

Early Retirement. Age-based mandatory retirement is illegal for most employees because it is considered a form of unfair discrimination in the United States. This means employers cannot rely on attrition due to forced retirement as a planned form of downsizing. Early retirement programs, however, can attempt to create voluntary attrition. The key to a successful early retirement program is understanding the needs of targeted employees and providing incentives that meet those needs. Incentives may include pension payments before and after age sixty-two, when Social Security payments start, and company-paid health and life insurance. Alternatively, a company may maintain its current retirement program but lower the qualifying age in order to increase the pool of potential retirees. This, of course, is expensive and accounts for some of the „restructuring charges" companies take when they downsize. Giving employees severance pay, essentially bonus pay for leaving, also adds to the expenses.

4. Workforce Diversity

The publication in 1987 of the U.S. Department of Labor monograph **Workforce 2000** created a widespread awareness in the United States of the need for business to develop competence in managing a workforce filled with diversity of many types. One chart from Workforce 2000 dramatically shows that the **entry-level** workforce in the year 2000 will be much more diverse than the 1985 workforce in general. This, of course, is true today for all firms operating globally. After reading and digesting Workforce 2000, many managers realized that successful companies would react to diversity as the important business issue it is by implementing proactive, strategic human resource planning. Today, this view is very widely shared (Foster 1988).

4.1. Analysis of HR Actions

Using the framework in Figure 3, how would you analyze the implications on human resource management of work force diversity? As you see in Figure 3, there are some suggestions under each of the four targets of HR action: employee assignment, employee competencies, employee behaviors, and employee motivation. As you read over the discussion on work force diversity, develop and extend the entries made in Figure 3.

4.2. The Importance of Managing Diversity

Surveys of business leaders confirm the perception that interest in managing diversity successfully is widespread. For example, in one study of 645 firms, 74 percent of the respondents were concerned about increased diversity, and of these, about one-third felt that diversity affected their corporate strategy. Why are companies so concerned? The two primary reasons cited were a belief that supervisors did not know how to motivate their diverse work groups, and uncertainty about how to handle the challenge of communicating with employees whose cultural backgrounds result in differing assumptions, values, and even language skills (o.V. 1990; Caudron 1995).

As the term **managing diversity** implies, the organizational interventions that fall within the realm of this label focus on ensuring that the variety of talents and perspectives that already exist within an organization are well utilized.

Organizations that attack the diversity issue with full force do so because they believe that taking action is a strategic imperative (Anfuso 1995; Flynn 1995). For most organizations, simply knowing the facts about workforce diversity - which are now parading as headlines in our daily newspapers - does not stimulate major changes in management practices. The facts are most significant when they are considered in the context of the changing business environment: increased emphasis on the highly interpersonal task of providing quality service, globalization of markets and businesses, and the increasing use of work teams are all making diversity management a high priority. These changes are bringing more and more people from diverse backgrounds into contact with each another, and, at the same time, mean that businesses are becoming more reliant on person-to-person contact as a way to get things done. Add to these trends the changing demographics of both consumers and the workforce, and the stage is set for diversity to emerge as a strategic business issue.

4.3. Dimensions of Diversity

Many companies understand and value many dimensions of diversity, including gender, ethnicity, culture, age, functional areas of expertise, religion, lifestyle, and so on. By considering just three aspects of diversity, you may begin to understand the bigger picture.

Gender Diversity. In the late 1950s in the United States, when many of the CEOs of the 1990s were entering the labor force as young professionals, they were almost exclusively men. Back then, men were receiving 95 percent of the MBA degrees. As these men are finishing their careers, forty years later, the picture is dramatically different. In 1990, women received approximately 31 percent of the MBA degrees awarded, as well as 39 percent of the law degrees, 13 percent of the engineering degrees, and half of all undergraduate degrees (Butruille 1990).

Today, females are better educated than ever before, and more are choosing to be in the active labor force. Furthermore, gender-based segregation within U.S. organizations is gradually decreasing, although in 1990, women held fewer than 0.5

percent of the top jobs in major corporations (Fierman 1990, pp. 40-62; Brett/Reilly 1992; Fagenson 1993).

Maximizing the productivity of women is essential to achieving competitiveness. This often requires attacking the artifical barrier of a male-dominated corporate culture. As the CEO of Avon Products has noted: Cultural discrepancies can come out in little ways. We used to have a lot of white male traditions at Avon. We bought season tickets to sporting events, and we called the annual management outing President's Golf Day. Our first two women officers complained ... We realized these activities were no longer appropriate. They were too male-oriented and unwittingly made others feel like outsiders (Edwards 1991).

According to one survey, 60 percent of women executives in large firms feel that their organization's male-dominated corporate culture is an obstacle to the success - that is, productivity - of women (o.V. 1990). These women may be underestimating the problem. In a poll of 241 Fortune 1000 CEOs, nearly 80 percent of the respondents said women face barriers that keep them from reaching the top. And of those who admitted that barriers exist, 81 percent identified stereotypes and preconceptions as problems women face (Edwards 1991).

Cultural and Ethnic Diversity. After gender diversity, cultural and ethnic diversity is the second most frequently noted change in the workforce. Cultures have consequences that are easily experienced but more difficult to describe. For many people, the concept of culture conjures up images of the exotic customs, religions, foods, clothing, and lifestyles that make foreign travel - as well as trips into the ethnic enclaves in our local cities - both stimulating and enjoyable. These aspects of a foreign culture can be experienced without ever engaging in conversation with someone from that culture.

The deeper consequences of culture - such as values and ways of interpreting the world - cannot be handled merely by changing menus and policies. And it is these deeper consequences that organizations are struggling with today. When people with different habits and world views come together in the workplace, misunderstandings and conflicts inevitably occur as a result of dissimilar expectations and norms. Employees who behave according to the cultural adage that „the squeaky wheel gets the grease" may be viewed as offensive and undesirable teammates by employees who were taught that „the nail that sticks out gets hammered down." Employees behaving according to the latter adage may be viewed as ineffective by those following the former.

Several circumstances seem to account for employers' current recognition that cultural diversity requires active management: (1) Although the proportion of African Americans in the United States has remained stable, their employment patterns have changed considerably during the affirmative action era, with substantial integration occurring for clerical, technical, and skilled crafts jobs (o.V.

1991). Also, although often overlooked, educational levels of African Americans have risen during this time, providing another stimulant for workplace integration; (2) Although the number of immigrants entering this country each year is relatively small, over the years, the number of employees with strong ties to another national culture grows owing to the continuing effect of nationality on second- and third-generation citizens (Fugita/O'Brien 1991); (3) The variety of the immigrant population has itself increased, as Asians and Latins from dozens of countries join European immigrants; and (4) Insightful business leaders recognize that they can use their multicultural domestic workforce as an educational resource and training ground for learning some of the tough lessons associated with conducting business internationally.

Age Diversity. In developed areas such as the United States and Europe, the median population age has been increasing. Along with this comes the bulging ranks of „older" employees trying to climb the corporate ladder, which creates havoc for traditional, hierarchical organizations. Such organizations are structured to accommodate large cohorts of entry-level employees and smaller cohorts of employees at more advanced career stages. These organizations tend to segregate employees by age. Organizational elders supervise the cohorts who will soon replace them, who in turn supervise their own replacements.

But these old hierarchies are a dying breed. As layers of hierarchy are removed, previously segregated generations of employees find themselves working together and even rotating jobs among themselves. Often, the result of all these forces is an unfamiliar reversal of roles. As one restaurant manager put it, giving orders to older workers „is sort of like telling your grandma to clean the table". If younger generations find this uncomfortable, so do older generations. As one working retiree explained: „For 30 years I was a supervisor, and then one night I step out of one role and into another ... When you're being supervised by someone younger, you see a lot of things that aren't going to work, but you have to bite your tongue" (Hirsch 1990).

The combination of changes in the age distribution of employees and new, flatter organizational structures means that three generations of workers can find themselves working side by side. Even if employees from these generations were all born and raised in the United States, they will differ in their values and attitudes about work, their physical and mental functioning, and the everyday concerns that reflect their stages in the life cycle. Of course, within each generation, gender and cultural variety also abound, yielding a workforce that reflects the complete palette of human potential (Elder 1975; Rhodes 1983; o.V. 1986).

4.4. Diversity Managers

Businesses are taking the diversity issue very seriously - so seriously, in fact, that many large corporations have followed Digital Equipment Corporation's early lead, which was to create a new job with the title „manager of valuing differences." For example, Honeywell Incorporated has a director of workforce diversity, and Avon Products has a director of multicultural planning and design (Anfuso 1995; Flynn 1995). What do the people with such titles do? Fundamentally, their jobs are about creating change in organizations. Long term, their goals include changing corporate cultures. Short term, their goals include changing the behaviors of individuals and ensuring that all employees fulfill their potential.

To achieve these goals, managers of diversity engage their organizations in many types of activities designed to create change. For example, Hewlett-Packard Company conducts training sessions for managers to teach them about different cultures and ethnic groups and about their own gender biases and training needs (Nelson-Horchler 1988). Procter and Gamble has implemented „valuing diversity" programs throughout the company. A mentor program designed to retain black and female managers was developed at one plant, and one-day workshops on diversity were given to all new employees (Copeland 1988). Equitable Life Assurance encourages minority group members to form support groups that periodically meet with the CEO to discuss problems in the company pertaining to them. At Avon, women have made significant inroads into management, however, more remains to be done. To help improve the progress of women and minority group members, the company uses councils that represent various groups, each having a senior manager present at meetings. These councils inform and advise top management (Copeland 1988).

Breaking the Glass Ceiling. The **glass ceiling** is a barrier that although hard to see, nevertheless prevents women and people of color from gaining access to promotions. Until recently, the dominant approach has been to focus on helping nonmajority individuals develop a „winning style" to succeed in a „white man's" world. This has worked to some extent, but it is not enough. The more long-term approach to helping break the glass ceiling, and the one that might determine whether businesses will survive in the future, is to ensure that the workplace has no artificial barriers to performance in day-to-day activities or to advancement. That way, everyone can offer their individual talents to a company, rather than suppress them to conform to deep-rooted prejudices.

Until companies change their culture to become truly merit based, a short-term practical approach is for women and people of color to be aware of the kinds of behavior management prefers and to respond to those preferences. Some believe that „[to] be successful in upper management, women must constantly monitor their behavior, making sure they are neither too masculine nor too feminine" (Morrison/White/Van Velsnor 1987). Some women in upper management have achieved success by altering their behavior to what is desirable to the male management hierarchy already in place. Nevertheless, simply expecting everyone to change themselves to „fit" into the existing culture of upper management is not the long-term solution. The long-term objective is to increase an organization's effectiveness by improving management practices. Changing organizational norms, policies, and structures that inhibit full utilization of the workforce is the goal (Jackson 1993; Goodchilds 1991; Fernandez 1991).

Because organizations have so little experience in changing their culture to fit a more diverse workforce, it is too soon to say what approaches to change are the most effective. Nevertheless, we can examine some of the many strategies companies are experimenting with (Cox 1993).

Several activities focus on increasing awareness of discriminatory attitudes and practices. For example, managers can be trained to work and manage in a diverse workforce, and everyone can be educated about how our reliance on stereotypes is often counterproductive. Managers and supervisors can work with their employees to identify ways in which traditional performance-ranking and performance-rating systems can be improved so that they do not perpetuate disadvantage. Task forces can be formed to plan new programs and make recommendations for change based on problems discovered in the workplace. These task forces could also review and monitor such programs on a continuing basis.

Other programs can be implemented that will benefit a diverse workforce by helping everyone reach their potential. For example career planning can be used to ensure that everyone has the opportunity to gain experience, knowledge, and exposure as well as to provide career guidance. Mentorship programs can be encouraged as a means of giving everyone access to advice from the upper ranks. Companies can address the need to balance work and family by offering more generous adoption- and pregnancy-related leaves of absence and flexible hours (some even provide on-site child care, flexible projects, and opportunities to work at home) (Myers 1990; Powell 1990; Hall 1989; Ehrlich 1989; Schwartz 1989).

Companies that have taken action to remove the glass ceiling are already seeing results. For example, Merck reports that about 25 percent of its middle managers were women in 1990, versus approximately 10 percent in 1980, and the Prudential Insurance Company of America had 50 percent women managers in 1990 versus 30 percent in 1980.

These are just a few of the interventions that can chip away at the glass ceiling in organizations. In the best companies, such activities fit within a larger strategic plan focused on improving organizational effectiveness. These companies tend to follow several basic principles

4.5. Basic Principles

Many options and choices must be made when introducing initiatives for working through diversity. Fundamental to any of them is that it can be a major change for many companies. There are a few basic principle that can guide change processes related to initiatives for managing diversity: (1) develop a comprehensive understanding of the many types of diversity in the organization and decide which to address; (2) stay close to the customers; (3) anticipate possible problems and be prepared to deal with them; and (4) institutionalize new learning. Although these principles could easily apply to any organizational change efforts, they are particularly relevant to attend to when considering new initiatives for managing diversity (Fernandez 1991; Fyock 1990; Loden/Rosener 1991; Morrison 1992).

5. Mergers and Alliances

Upjohn-Pharmacia represents a major trend in business today: alliances between companies. Even big companies with vast resources need to form alliances. Upjohn and Pharmacia thought that an alliance, a joint venture, that pools their unique strengths, made sense. Ciba-Geigy and Sandoz thought the same.

In other cases companies are joining to form a new, single company. The Chemical Bank and the Chase Manhattan Bank in New York City merged their operations into one: in this case the new bank is called Chase. It was decided to use this name, even though Chase Manhattan was the smaller bank, because of its greater worldwide name recognition. Although the merger of these two banks was really an acquisition by Chemical of Chase, in many respects the new company represents a merger of the two companies, their cultures, the businesses and their ways of managing human resources.

Analysis for HR Actions. Using the framework in Figure 3, how would you analyze the implications of human resource management of mergers and alliances?

Employee assignments. Especially in mergers, the challenge is often to reduce duplication. There are literally two people for each job after a merger. If the merger is between companies of different sizes, the larger one can often call the shots in deciding who stays. This is especially true if the larger firm actually buys or acquires the smaller firm. This situation is often called a takeover. In this situation it is not surprising if the human resource practices of the new firm are those of the dominant, acquiring firm.

Employee competencies. More typically, the two firms agree that keeping the „best people" is the most business-like thing to do when the merger takes place. So the two firms go through a rather extensive process to determine what competencies are needed in the new company and what competencies the employees of both companies have. Once these matches are determined, the result still leaves some going out. Some offers of job outplacement and severance are often made to ease the career transition of otherwise very good people.

Employee behaviors. If two firms are merging and remaining in their same business, new employee behaviors may not be necessary for many employees. If one of them has been more successful and better at getting the needed employee behaviors, however, the employees who remain from the other company may need to adopt the behavior of the other firm. Use of the human resource practices of the more successful firm will aid all the employees in adopting and maintaining the needed behaviors.

Employee motivation. For those employees who stay, an essential human resource challenge is motivating them to perform at even higher levels. The process of merging usually eliminates position duplication, for example, two human resource managers, but it increases the amount of work and responsibility. While compensation for this new, larger position may increase, it will not be equal to the salaries of the two former positions. So the remaining employees will need to be motivated with other things besides money. The thrill of the new job is certainly one way. The chance to have the job and the security it brings is often another key way.

In summary, there are substantial HR implications resulting from a merger or alliance and as with all major organizational changes, the challenge rests with top management. Let's look at the special implications of organizational changes on top management leadership with frequent reference to Charles Bingham at the Fores Products Company of Weyerhaeuser Company.

6. Top Management Leadership and the Process of Change

It is now widely recognized that for change to occur in organizations, leaders must get others to change **and** they themselves must also change (Kotter 1995; Goodstein/Burke 1991; Tichy 1982; Hamel/Prahalad 1994; Huey 1994). All the changes we have described thus far - downsizings and layoffs, managing diversity, and mergers and alliances - start at the very top and cascade down. Jack Welch at GE is an excellent example. He is what current leaders need to be, or what companies need to search for in their selection of a new leader: one who Figures new leader behaviors.

New Leadership Behaviors. Like Jack Welch, CEOs and all other managers must change before other employees will. Managers have to move from the command-and-control style to empowering, visioning, cooperating, and supporting. They must also change the way they behave with respect to suppliers and customers outside the organization, the environment, social and ethical issues of business and society, and the strategy and direction of the organization.

These changes in leadership are seen as vital to many companies today, but they are not likely to occur unless systematic strategies are in place to help managers make them. Companies like Novartis, McDonald's, General Electric, Levi Strauss, ABB, Federal Express, and Roche are systematically linking specific on-the-job experiences and training and development programs to the new behavioral competencies required in the new organizational forms. Some companies are even establishing leadership institutes.

Leadership Institutes. In the late 1980s, Weyerhaeuser's Forest Products Company (FPC) established its own leadership institute to help its managers change their behaviors. This was during the time when the firm was repositioning strategically from a functionally organized company to a divisional one with strategic business units, just like GE. Within FPC, Chief Executive Charles W. Bingham, his executive team, and the director of strategic education, Horace Parker, concluded that a major strategic repositioning called for upgrading the firm's human capabilities through executive development:

How the organization was sold on the worth of an executive development program is an important lesson. The trump card used in closing the deal was to involve the executives at various levels of the organization in the planning stages. During those stages, they came to see, as did the executive team, that an intensive development program such as the Leadership Institute was not an expensive frill but a prerequisite for survival. The Leadership Institute, top management was convinced, would be a powerful catalyst that could accelerate the normal process of change-of everything from a corporate culture to how a salesperson deals with customers (Bolt 1989).

Working with others in human resource management and with the top management team, FPC created a leadership institute where managers could come to discuss the new strategy and its implications for them. In addition, the institute offered training to help managers acquire needed skills, knowledge, and leadership styles. A success, this institute grew into a total quality company program. By 1994, the entire Weyerhaeuser Company used the institute grew into a total quality company program. By 1994, the entire Weyerhaeuser Company used the institute to help managers learn new leadership behaviors. The new leadership behaviors identified as critical for total quality management flow directly from what leadership means to the company:

We are committed to leadership behavior that empowers people to fully contribute to company goals. This means that

– Leadership behavior and standards are well defined and understood throughout the organization and are linked with company values.
– The criteria for selecting leaders include demonstrated commitment to company values and leadership skills.
– Leaders set clear goals and expectations and inspire other to meet them.
– Development is provided for existing and current leaders.
– Leaders seek and use feedback to improve their leadership skills.
– A key measure of leadership success is the development of others.

Management Development on-the-Job. When systematically developed and coordinated by the HR department, education and job experiences can go a long way toward helping managers change themselves and, in the process, change their organizations.

The Weyerhaeuser Company went from a centralized structure to a decentralized structure; then later to a decentralized structure coordinated through shared vision, values, and leadership philosophy. At the same time, it has moved from a maker of undifferentiated commodity products to one of customer-focused, total quality products. Continuous management development helps ensure that all these changes last and continue to filter down in the company. Frequent meetings between top managers are one type of activity facilitating on-the-job development. Working as a team develops, shares, and coordinates efforts to help each individual manager learn more about the company as a whole. A deeper understanding of the business puts each manager in a better position to lead in ways that are consistent with the several separate businesses, yet coordinated to reflect the functions of these businesses as part of one larger company.

7. The Role of the Human Resource Department in Organizational Change

From hiring and firing to training and performance management, every HR activity influences human resources and, thus, the success or failure of most efforts for organizational change and competition (Howard 1994). Keeping HR systems aligned with business strategies, such as the changes at Weyerhaeuser for total quality and customer focus, will be a major HR challenge going into the 21st century. Weyerhaeuser's organizational change provides specific illustration of how the HR department can facilitate strategic business goals. In general, however, the HR department can:
- Help formulate the firm's strategic business principles and strategies,
- Identify an HR mission or culture consistent with the business needs,
- Identify the key strategic HR imperatives that result from the business principles and strategies,
- Develop and implement HR initiatives and activities consistent with the HR culture.

7.1. The HR Department at Weyerhaeuser

The human resource department changed dramatically as part of the retrenchment strategy. While the human resource department had been fulfilled in very traditional ways in the past, Bingham and the vice president of Human Resources designed more creative and innovative methods to better serve the HR department.

Rather than providing the traditional services of recruitment, selection, compensation, training and development, and employee relations centrally, the HRM function was decentralized. An HR adviser was assigned to each business unit. This adviser worked within the business so he or she could better understand the products and markets of the business and, therefore, better assess its human resource needs. The adviser would involve the team members in the business in all elements of the HRM process. For example, the teams assumed responsibility for hiring their own people based on the assessed needs of their business. What had once been a top-down approach to human resource management was transformed into an integrated, team-based process.

7.2. Reducing Resistance to Change

An HR department can be very helpful in reducing resistance to change. Often individuals resist change for reasons such as:
- More work,
- Concerns about ability to perform,
- Loss of control,
- Excess of uncertainty,
- Threats to power and influence,
- Resource limitations,
- Habit,
- New social relationships,
- New boss (Fisher 1995; Stewart 1994).

The HR department can reduce these reasons by:
- Generating excitement about the „new way",
- Lowering perception of personal risk,
- Communicating potential rewards,
- Involving employees in planning and implementation,
- Training the employees.

These can be done more effectively, however, with the active partnership and involvement of the line managers.

7.3. Partnership Between HR and Line Managers

Line managers play a critical role in managing change. They contribute by providing answers to questions such as:
(1) What are the implications of the business strategy on the four human resource targets of action (implications will vary, of course, by the degree of change in the business strategy)?
(2) What types of key behaviors/skills are currently rewarded?
(3) What types of key behaviors/skills not presently available are needed?
(4) What action steps are you taking to ensure these behaviors/skills are available?

(5) What types of key behaviors/skill presently available are no longer used/ needed?

(6) What action steps are you taking to ensure that there is a minimum of redundant skills? Retraining? Transfer? Promotion? Termination?

(7) What action steps are you taking to ensure you get the key employee behaviors?

(8) What are the right numbers of employees really needed to ensure success? What plans are in place to deal with excess numbers? What shortages?

(9) How much more productive will employees need to be to ensure success? Can reductions in absenteeism and turnover be helpful here? Do new people need to be attracted?

(10) What specific objectives do you have for each of the points 1-9?

(11) Who is responsible for meeting these objectives?

(12) What measures of success vis-a-vis the objectives are you using?

(13) What constraints exist in moving ahead?

(14) What do you need from the HR department to help you be successful?

8. Summary

Change is everywhere, and as the 21st century approaches and unfolds, it becomes more pervasive and intense. Consequently, the organizations that are learning to deal with major change associated with the key business issues of today are positioning themselves quite nicely for the future. This article highlighted some of the key issues that companies are working on today, including: (a) downsizing and layoffs; (b) managing diversity; and (c) mergers and alliances. Each of these issues involves organizations and their people in major organizational change efforts. Successful organizational change, in turn, requires effective human resource planning. When major business issues are involved, the cycle of anticipating change, planning and carrying out change, and evaluating and readjusting becomes continuous. Change becomes the constant in managing human resources effectively.

Downsizing and layoffs may result when companies manage for efficiency. Organizations are likely to continue in their efforts to become more competitive and efficient because of the worldwide onslaught of intense competition. As they do so, they are likely to find that some approaches are more effective than others. Effective approaches help companies to become more competitive while also attempting to minimize the negative side effects by respecting the rights of individuals to fairness and due process. Here, again, we see the importance of considering the needs of the employee as a key stakeholder in programs to manage human resources.

Managing diversity is another people-related business issue that is likely to remain a challenge well into the 21st century. Just as the workforce is becoming more diverse, so the need for organizations to maximize the skills and abilities of all employees is becoming even more critical if organizations are to be globally competitive. This means that major organizationwide changes must be put in place to ensure that all employees are given a fair chance for training and advancement and that ideas as well as people move throughout the organization. And just as diversity is an expansive phenomenon, so are the human resource activities that can be put in place to support organizationwide initiatives to manage diversity effectively.

Mergers and alliances are also a key business concern with many implications for managing human resources. Common to all these major issues are the necessary involvement of top management, the necessary involvement of the HR department, and the necessary use of human resource planning. Without the leadership and support, and even change, of top management, these three major issues are not likely to be effectively managed. As Charles Bingham and his team at FPC realized, before they could expect the rest of the company to embrace total quality management, they had to change first. So change they did, and then the rest of the organization followed. The HR department helped the organization determine the content of the needed changes (e.g., what skills the employees needed), and the process of change (e.g., who should change first and how fast the changes should be made). Like any effort that affects the entire company, the changes required a great deal of business and human resource planning.

Human resource planning is critical for organizations engaged in organizationwide change efforts. This is because these programs involve many resources and require the change-modification-alignment of many HR policies and practices. Selecting, designing, and implementing the appropriate policies and practices requires a great deal of information, wise judgement, and managerial skills. A quick review of downsizing indicates just how much planning is required to do an effective job when laying off large numbers of employees while at the same time making conditions favorable for those who stay.

Proceeding through the tried-and-true steps and phases of human resource planning can help ensure that most of the bases are covered and that everything and everyone are in nearly the right place at nearly the right time.

Bibliography:

Anfuso, D. (1995), Diversity Keeps Newspaper Up With the Times, in: Personnel Journal, July 1995, pp. 30-41

Bolt, J. (1989), Executive Development, New York 1989

Brett, J. M., Reilly, A. H. (1992), All the Right Stuff: A Comparison of Female and Male Managers Career Progression, in: Journal of Applied Psychology, Vol. 77 (1992), pp. 251-260

Butruille, S. G. (1990), Corporate Caretaking, in: Training and Development Journal, April 1990, pp. 49-55

Byrne, J. A. (1994), The Pain of Downsizing, in: Business Week, May 9, 1994, pp. 60-69

Cameron, K. S., Freeman, S. J., Mishra, A. K. (1991), Best Practices in White Collar Downsizing: Managing Contradictions, in: Academy of Management Executive Vol. 5 (1991), No. 3, pp. 57-73

Cascio, W. F. (1993), Downsizing: What Do We Know? What Have We Learned?", in: Academy of Management Executive Vol. 7 (1993), No. 1, pp. 95-104

Caudron, S. (1995), Sexual Politics, in: Personnel Journal, May 1995, pp. 50-61

Caudron, S. (1996), Teach Downsizing Survivors How to Thrive, in: Personnel Journal, January 1996, pp. 38-48

Copeland, L. (1988), Valuing Diversity, Part 2: Pioneers and Champions of Change, in: Personnel, July 1988, p. 48

Cox, T., Jr. (1993), Cultural Diversity in Organizations: Theory, Research, and Practice, San Francisco 1993, pp. 216-218

Edwards, A. (1991), Special Report: Cultural Diversity in Today's Corporation, in: Working Woman, January 1991, p. 60

Ehrlich, E. (1989), The Mommy Track, in: Business Week, March 20, 1989

Elder, G. H., Jr. (1975), Age Differentiation and the Life Course, in: Annual Review of Sociology, Vol. 1, (1975), pp. 165-190

Faltermayer, E. (1996), Is This Layoff Necessary? in: Fortune, June 1, 1996, pp. 71-86

Fernandez, J. P. (1991), Managing a Diverse Workforce: Regaining the Competitive Edge, Lexington 1991

Fierman, J. (1990), Why Women Still Don't Hit the Top, in: Fortune, July 30, 1990, pp. 40-62

Fisher, A. B. (1995), Making Change Stick, in: Fortune, April 17, 1995, pp. 121-127

Flynn, G. (1994), Use of Outplacement Services, in: Bulletin to Management, February 10, 1994, pp. 44-45

Flynn, G. (1995), Do You Have the Right Approach to Diversity, in: Personnel Journal, October 1995, pp. 68-75

Flynn, G. (1995), Does Your Severance Plan Make the Cut? in: Personnel Journal, August 1995, pp. 32-40

Foster, B. P. (1988), Workforce Diversity and Business, in: Training and Development Journal, April 1988, p. 59

Fragenson, A., ed. (1993), Women in Management, Vol. 4, in: Women and Work, Newbury Park, 1993

Fugita, S. S., O'Brien, D. (1991), Japanese American Ethnicity: The Persistence of the Community, in: University of Washington Press, 1991

Fyock, C. D. (1990), America's Workforce Is Coming of Age, Lexington 1990

Goodchilds, J. D., ed. (1991), Psychological Perspectives on Human Diversity in America: Master Lectures, Washington 1991

Goodstein, L. D., Burke, W. W. (1991), Creating Successful Organization Change, in: Organizational Dynamics, Spring 1991, pp. 5-12

Hall, D. T. (1989), Moving Beyond the Mommy Track: An Organization Change Approach, in: Personnel, December 1989, pp. 23-29

Hamel, G., Prahalad, C. K. (1994), Competing for the Future, Boston 1994

Hirsch, J. S. (1990), Older Workers Chafe under Young Managers, in: Wall Street Journal, February 26, 1990

Howard, A., ed. (1994), Diagnosis for Organizational Change: Methods and Models, New York 1994

Huey, J. (1994), The New Post-Heroic Leadership, in: Fortune, February 21, 1994, pp. 42-50

Jackson, S. E., ed., (1993), Diversity in the Workplace: Human Resource Initiatives, New York 1993

Knowdell, L., Branstead, E., Moravec, M. (1994), From Downsizing to Recovery-Strategic Transition Options for Organizations and Individuals, Palo Alto, 1994

Koretz, G. (1995), America's Trade Ace in the Hole, in: Business Week, February 20, 1995, p. 26

Kotter, J. P. (1995), Leading Change: Why Transformation Efforts Fail, in: Harvard Business Review, March-April 1995, pp. 59-67

Leana, C. R., Feldman, D. C. (1989), When Mergers Force Layoffs: Some Lessons about Managing the Human Resource Problems, in: Human Resource Planning, Vol. 12 (1989), No. 2, pp. 123-140

Loden, M., Rosener, J. B. (1991), Workforce America! Managing Employee Diversity as a Vital Resource, Homewood 1991

Morrison, A. M. (1992), The New Leaders: Guidelines on Leadership Diversity in America, San Francisco 1992

Morrison, A., White, R. P., Van Velsnor, E. (1987), Executive Women: Substance Plus Style, in: Psychology Today, August 1987, pp. 18-21, 24-26

Moser Illes, L. (1996), Site Shutdown: One HR Leader Tells Her Story, in: Personnel Journal, March 1996, pp. 95-107

Myers, K. (1990), Cracking the Glass Ceiling, in: Information Week, August 27, 1990, pp. 38-41

Nelson-Horchler, J. (1988), Demographics Deliver a Warning, in: Industry Week, April 18, 1988, p. 58

Nocera, J. (1996), Living With Layoffs, in: Fortune April 1, 1996, pp. 69-108

o. V. (1982), Managing Change Strategically: The Technical, Political, and Cultural Keys, in: Organizational Dynamics, Autumn 1982, pp. 59-80

o. V. (1986), Work Attitudes: Study Reveals Generation Gap, in: Bulletin to Management, October 2, 1986, p. 326

o.V. (1990), Welcome to the Woman-Friendly Company Where Talent Is Valued and Rewarded, in: Business Week, August 6, 1990, pp. 48-50

o. V. (1991), Race in the Workplace: Is Affirmative Action Working? in: Business Week, July 8, 1991, pp. 50-63

o.V. (1995), Staff Cuts Scrutinized, in Bulletin to Management, November 9, 1995, p. 360

o.V. (1996), Severance Practices, in: Bulletin to Management, January 11, 1996, pp. 12-13

Powell, G. N. (1990), Upgrading Management Opportunities for Women, in: HR Magazine, November 1990, pp. 67-70

Presley Noble, B. (1994), Questioning Productivity Beliefs, in: New York Times, July 10, 1994, F21

Rhodes, S. R. (1983), Age-Related Differences in Work Attitudes and Behavior: A Review and Conceptual Analysis, in: Psychological Bulletin Vol. 93, (1983), pp. 328-367

Rose, F. (1994), Job-Cutting Medicine Fails to Remedy Productivity Ills at Many Companies, in: Wall Street Journal, June 7, 1994, A5

Schwartz, F. N. (1989), Management Women and the New Facts of Life, in Harvard Business Review, January-February 1989, pp. 65-76

Schweiger, D. M., Ivancevich, J. M., Power, F. R. (1986), Executive Actions for Managing Human Resources Before and After Acquisition, in: Academy of Management Executive, Vol. 1 (1986), No. 2, pp. 127-138

Stamps, D. (1996), Corporate Anorexia, in: Training, February 1996, pp. 24-30

Stewart (1994), Rate Your Readiness to Change, in: Fortune, February 7, 1994, pp. 106-110

Stuart, P. (1992), New Internal Jobs Found for Displaces Employees in: Personnel Journal, August 1992, pp. 50-56

Treece, J. B. (1992), Doing It Right, Till the Last Whistle, in: Business Week, April 6, 1992, pp. 58-59

Uchitelle, L., Kleinfield, N. R. (1996), On the Battlefields of Business, Millions of Casualties, in: New York Times, March 3, 1996, p. 26

Welch, J. F. (1993), A Master Class in Radical Change, in: Fortune December 13, 1993, p. 83

Sachverzeichnis

Acquisition of Loral 191 ff.

Andragogik 80 ff.

Anreiz-Beitrags-Theorie 282 f.

Bedarfsmanager 280

Benchmarking 351 ff.

Beschaffungsmarketing, strategisches 277 ff.

Beschaffungsmarketingprozeß 283 ff.

Beschaffungsmarktforschung 292 ff.

Bevölkerungsdynamik 5

Brand Associations 246 f.

Brand Knowledge 242 ff.

Business Process Reengineering 79

Business Relationships 59 f.

Business School 90 ff.

Cash-Flow-ROI-Ansatz 324

Category-Management 212 ff.

CD-ROMs 264 ff.

Change Managament 23 ff., 77 f., 352 ff.,

    and the Internet 351 ff., 375 f.

    and the Learning Organization 41 ff.

    and the Role of Human Resources Management 395 ff.

    im Marketing 197 ff.

    in der Management Andragogik 77 ff.

    in the US Defense Industry 191 ff.

    strategisches 19 ff., 379 ff.

    und Corporate Strategy 117 ff.

    und Finance Management 317 ff.

    und Human Resources Management 393 ff.

    und Management Education 75 ff.

    und Management Information Systems 349 ff.

    und Marketing 197 ff.

und Operations Management 301 ff.

Unternehmensführung im 78 f.

China, German Strategy in 173 ff.

Content Agenda 66 ff.

Contract Personnel Acquisition 148 ff.

Core Company 142 f.

Corporate Identity 239 ff.

Decision Support Systems 379 ff.

Discounted-Cash-Flow-Ansatz 325 ff.

Distributionspolitik 209 ff.

Downsizing 365 f., 399 ff.

Economic-Value-Added-Konzept 324 f.

Efficient Consumer Response 215 ff.

Efficient Product Introductions 217 f.

Efficient Promotions 217

Efficient Replenishment 217

Efficient Store Assortments 215 ff.

Euro Commercial Papers 336 f.

Euro Note Facility 337

Event-Marketing 232 ff.

Evolution 12 f.

Executive Development 80 ff.

Fachpromotor 311

Fallstudie, genetisch wachsende 92 f.

Fernsehen, digitales 263 f.

Finanzinnovationen 333 ff.

Globalisierung 20 ff.

Globalisierung, Prozeß der 20 f.

Globalisierungsprobleme 6

GSBA 92 ff.

Handelstrends 201 ff.

Hyperwettbewerb 6 ff.

Information Pyramid 163 f.

Information Systems, Evolution of 380 ff.

Informationsmanager 280

International Branding Strategies 239 ff.

Internet 351 ff.

Kiosksysteme 266 f.

Ko-Evolution 14 ff.

Koalitionstheorie 281 f.

Kommunikationsbedingungen, derzeitige 226 ff.

Konsumentenverhalten, Trends beim 201

Kostenreduktion 27 f.

Leadership 10 ff.

Learning Organization 43 ff., 167 f.

Lerntransfer, lateraler 92 ff.

Leverage-Effect 157 ff.

Lieferantenmanager 280

Lieferantenverhandlung 291 f.

Machtpromotor 311

Machtverteilung in der Welt 6

Management-Andragogik 80 ff.

Mapping Activity System 33 ff.

Markenmanagement 199 ff., 223 ff., 239 ff.

Markenmanagement, kooperative Systeme 211 ff.

Markenpolitik 206

Markenwert 200 f., 242 ff.

Marketing-Kommunikation 206 ff.

Marktanalyse, strategische 29 ff.

Master of Business Administration 86 ff.

    - Typen 87

Medien, interaktive 261 ff.

Mehrstufige Märkte 199 ff.
Mobile Computing 358 ff.

Neue Medien 261 ff.

Online-Medien 267 ff.
Organisationsentwicklung 309
Organizations, Virtualizing 139 ff.
Outsource Procurement 155
Outsourcing 361 f.

Partnering Relationships 59 ff.
Partnering, Principles of 60 ff.
Prämarketing 231 f.
Preispolitik 208 f.
Procurement Processes 149 ff.
Produzentenseite, Trends 203 f.
Programmsponsoring 234 f.
Prozeßforschung 304
Prozeßpromotor 310
Pull-Strategie 200
Purchasing 139 ff.
Push-Strategie 199 f.

Reengineering 351 ff.
Reminder-Werbung 235 f.
Retailing, virtuelles 218
Rightsizing 365 f.
Russian Management Education 101 ff.

Shareholder-Value 319 ff.
Shareholder-Value-Ansätze 323 ff.
Shopping, Convenience 118 f.
Sonderwerbeformen 235
Strukturwandel 319 ff.

Tandem-Werbung 235 f.

Teams, corss-funktionale 303 ff.

Telework 358 ff.

Total Quality Management 78

Trust 62

Unternehmensentwicklung 308 f.

Unternehmensleitbild, Wandel von 119 ff.

Unternehmensziele 119 ff.

Value in exchange 29 ff.

Vvalue in use 29 ff.

Value of happiness 29 ff.

Wertschöpfung 27 f., 35

Wettbewerb, Arenen des 8 ff.

Wettbewerb, Spielregeln des 3 ff.

Zeitalter, interaktives 261 ff.

Zins Forwards 340 ff.

Zins Futures 340 ff.

Zinsoption 342 f.

Zinsrisiken, Management von 333 ff.

Herausforderungen an das Management

Herausgegeben von R. Berndt

Band 4

Business Reengineering

Effizientes Neugestalten von Geschäftsprozessen

1997. XVI, 277 S. 80 Abb., 11 Tab. Geb. **DM 98,-**; öS 715,40; sFr 89,50 ISBN 3-540-62546-1

In diesem Buch wird von führenden Fachvertretern aus Europa und den USA zur Frage Stellung genommen, in welcher Weise krisenhaften Situationen von Unternehmen, beispielsweise in der Rezession, begegnet werden kann.

Band 3

Global Management

Mit einem Geleitwort von **Dr. Lothar Späth,**
Vorsitzender der Geschäftsführung der Jenoptik, Jena

1996. XIX, 509 S. 125 Abb., 8 Tab. Geb. **DM 98,-**; öS 715,40; sFr 89,50 ISBN 3-540-60903-2

Dieses Buch zeigt, wie ein Global Management in allen betrieblichen Bereichen vom strategischen Management über das Marketing-, Operations-, Finance-Management bis hin zum Controlling und Human Resources Management realisiert werden kann.

Band 2

Total Quality Management als Erfolgsstrategie

1995. XV, 300 S. 85 Abb. Geb. **DM 108,-**; öS 788,40; sFr 98,50 ISBN 3-540-58952-X

Führende Fachvertreter aus Europa und den USA machen deutlich, in welcher Weise ein Total Quality Management in allen betrieblichen Bereichen (von der Führung über das Strategische Management bis hin zum Marketing-, Operations-, Finance-, Human-Resources-Management) durchgesetzt werden kann.

Band 1

Management-Qualität contra Rezession und Krise

1994. XV, 304 S. 60 Abb., 1 Tab. Geb. **DM 108,-**; öS 788,40; sFr 98,50 ISBN 3-540-57566-9

In Krisensituationen ist Management-Qualität im doppelten Sinn zu entwickeln: Zur Sicherung der Existenz eines Unternehmens sind besondere Qualitäten seiner Manager (seiner Führungskräfte) als auch ausgefeilte Management-Techniken notwendig. Zu nennen sind hier Frühwarnsysteme, angemessene strategische und operative Ansätze des Marketing der Produktion der Finanzierung und der Personalentwicklung. Einen wesentlichen Beitrag zur Entwicklung dieser erhöhten Anforderungen an die Management-Qualität leistet dieses Buch.

■■■■■■■■■■■

Springer

Preisänderungen vorbehalten

Springer-Verlag, Postfach 31 13 40, D-10643 Berlin, Fax 0 30 / 827 87 - 3 01 / 4 48 e-mail: orders@springer.de   rbw.BA.64072/2.SF

R. Berndt, C. Fantapié Altobelli, M. Sander

Internationale Marketing-Politik

1997. XXI, 442 S. 227 Abb. Brosch. **DM 59,80**; öS 436,60; sFr 54,50 ISBN 3-540-63322-7

Dieses Buch bietet sowohl Studierenden als auch Praktikern eine fundierte und ausführliche Darstellung internationaler Marketing-Politik. Für die internationalen Basisstrategien „Standardisierung" und „Differenzierung" werden die Einsatzmöglichkeiten aller Marketing-Instrumente im Detail erörtert.

Vollständigkeit, klare Gliederung und Verständlichkeit zeichnen dieses dreiteilige **Standardwerk** aus. Theoretisch fundiert und zugleich praxisorientiert wendet es sich an alle, die sich mit Fragen und Aufgaben auf dem Gebiet des Marketing auseinandersetzen.

R. Berndt

Marketing 1
Käuferverhalten, Marktforschung und Marketing-Prognosen

3., vollst. überarb. Aufl. 1996. XV, 378 S. 176 Abb., 6 Tab. Brosch. **DM 39,80**; öS 290,60; sFr 37,- ISBN 3-540-60812-5

Band 1 liefert die absatzwirtschaftlichen Verhaltens- und Informationsgrundlagen.

Marketing 2
Marketing-Politik

3. Aufl. 1995. XIX, 594 S. 295 Abb. Brosch. **DM 49,80**; öS 363,60; sFr 46,- ISBN 3-540-60182-1

Das Kernstück des Gesamtwerkes ist Band 2. Hier werden die Teilbereiche der Marketing-Politik umfassend und entscheidungsorientiert dargestellt. Dabei sind neue Komunikationsinstrumente wie Product-Placement und Sponsoring aufgenommen.

Marketing 3
Marketing-Management

2. Aufl. 1995. XVI, 253 S. 100 Abb. Brosch. **DM 29,80**; öS 217,60; sFr 27,50 ISBN 3-540-58748-9

Im letzten Band werden Marketing-Planung, -Organisation und -Führung dargestellt. Das methodische Instrumentarium wird durchweg anhand von Beispielen erörtert.

 Springer

Preisänderungen vorbehalten

Springer-Verlag, Postfach 31 13 40, D-10643 Berlin, Fax 0 30 / 827 87 - 3 01 / 4 48 e-mail: orders@springer.de   rbw.BA.64072/1.SF